Cross-Border Enforcement of Claims in the EU

EUROPEAN MONOGRAPHS

Editor-in-chief Professor David O'Keeffe

In this series *European Monographs* this book *Cross-Border Enforcement of Claims in the EU* is the sixty-fifth title. *The titles published in this series are listed at the end of this volume.*

Kluwer Law International

Cross-Border Enforcement of Claims in the EU

History, Present Time and Future

Mikael Berglund

Wolters Kluwer
Law & Business
Norstedts Juridik
a Wolters Kluwer Company

Published by:
Kluwer Law International
PO Box 316
2400 AH Alphen aan den Rijn
The Netherlands
Website: www.kluwerlaw.com

Sold and distributed in North, Central and South America by:
Aspen Publishers, Inc.
7201 McKinney Circle
Frederick, MD 21704
United States of America
Email: customer.care@aspenpubl.com

Sold and distributed in all other countries by:
Turpin Distribution Services Ltd.
Stratton Business Park
Pegasus Drive, Biggleswade
Bedfordshire SG18 8TQ
United Kingdom
Email: kluwerlaw@turpin-distribution.com

Sold and distributed in the Nordic countries by:
Norstedts Juridik AB
Kundservice
SE-106 47 Stockholm, Sweden
www.nj.se
Email: kundservice@nj.se
Tel. +46 (8) 690 91 90
Fax. +46 (8) 690 91 91

Printed on acid-free paper.

ISBN: 978-90-411-2861-4 (Kluwer Law International)
ISBN: 978-91-39-01434-8 (Norstedts Juridik)

Printed in Great Britain.

Table of Contents

Preface **xiii**

Abbreviations **xv**

Table of Annexes **xxi**

Chapter 1
Introduction **1**

1.1 The Problems Motivating the Choice of the Subject 1
1.1.1 Subject 4
1.1.1.1 Interests, Principles and Their Balance 6
1.1.1.1.1 Privacy versus Efficiency 9
1.1.1.1.2 Non-discrimination 10
1.1.1.1.3 Proportionality 11
1.1.1.1.4 Territoriality 12
1.1.1.1.5 Universality 14
1.1.1.1.6 Mutuality 15
1.1.1.1.7 Legal Integration in the Internal Common Market 17
1.1.1.2 History and Legal Developments 17
1.1.1.3 Enforcement and Recovery Agents 18
1.1.1.4 Public International Law 20
1.1.1.5 Scope of Application of EC Law and Conventions 22
1.1.1.6 Procedures in EC Law and Conventions 25
1.1.1.7 Harmonization of Civil Execution Laws 29
1.1.1.8 Examples of the Subject 30

1.1.1.8.1 Cross-Border Enforcement of Contractual Claims 30
1.1.1.8.2 Cross-Border Recovery of Tax Claims 31
1.2 Delimitations 31
1.3 Purpose 34
1.4 Method 35
1.4.1 Legal Method 35
1.4.2 Treatment of the Sources of Law 38
1.5 Previous Research 39
1.6 Terminology 39

Chapter 2
History and Legal Developments **43**

2.1 Roman Law 43
2.1.1 Civil Execution Law 43
2.1.2 Tax Collection 49
2.1.3 Insolvency 49
2.2 Middle Ages 52
2.2.1 Civil Execution Law 55
2.2.2 Tax Collection 57
2.2.3 Composition 58
2.2.4 Insolvency 58
2.3 Period of 1500-1806 60
2.3.1 Civil Execution Law 62
2.3.2 Tax Collection 65
2.4 Period of 1807 to Our Age 65
2.4.1 National Procedural Laws 65
2.4.2 The Way to Conventions and EC Law 66
2.5 EC Law and Conventions on Contractual Claims 69
2.5.1 Brussels I Regulation 71
2.5.2 European Enforcement Order for Uncontested Claims 72
2.5.3 European Order for Payment Procedure 73
2.5.4 European Small Claims Procedure 74
2.5.5 Nordic Convention on Recognition and the Enforcement of Judgments in Civil Matters 74
2.5.6 New York Convention on Foreign Arbitral Awards 75
2.6 EC Law and Conventions on Tax Claims 75
2.6.1 Recovery Directive 77
2.6.2 Council of Europe and OECD Convention on Mutual Administrative Assistance in Tax Matters 78
2.6.3 Nordic Agreement on Assistance in Tax Matters 79
2.7 EC Law and Conventions on Insolvency 80
2.8 Conclusions 81
2.9 Differing Features of Cooperation in EC Law 82
2.9.1 Brussels I Regulation 82

2.9.2 Recovery Directive 82
2.9.3 Conclusions 82
2.10 Works in Progress and Present Development Trends 83
2.10.1 European Union 83
2.10.2 Hague Conference on Private International Law 84
2.10.3 Nordic Council of Ministers 85
2.10.4 International Institute for the Unification of Private Law 85
2.10.5 L'Union Internationale des Huissiers de Justice et Officiers Judiciaires 86
2.10.6 United Nations 88
2.10.7 Intra-European Organization of Tax Administrations 88
2.10.8 Conclusions 88

Chapter 3
Enforcement and Recovery Agents **91**

3.1 History of Enforcement and Recovery Agents 91
3.1.1 Roman Empire 91
3.1.2 Belgium, France and the Netherlands 92
3.1.3 United Kingdom 94
3.1.3.1 England and Wales 94
3.1.3.2 Scotland 96
3.1.4 Germany 96
3.1.5 Nordic States 98
3.1.5.1 Denmark 98
3.1.5.2 Iceland 100
3.1.5.3 Norway 101
3.1.5.4 Sweden 102
3.1.5.5 Finland 104
3.1.6 Conclusions 105
3.2 Civil Enforcement Law Area of Today 106
3.2.1 National Enforcement Agents 106
3.2.2 Competent Authorities 110
3.2.3 Conclusions 110
3.2.3.1 European Common Educational and Training Standard for the Right to Exercise the Profession of an Enforcement Agent 112
3.2.3.2 Recognition of the Profession of an Enforcement Agent in Other European States 113
3.2.3.3 Euroex, a European Cooperation Body between States in the Civil Execution Law Area 115
3.3 Tax Recovery Law Area of Today 118
3.3.1 National Recovery Agents 118
3.3.2 Competent Authorities 119
3.3.3 Recovery Committee 120

Chapter 4
Public International Law **121**

4.1 Foreign State's Immunity against Civil Execution 121
4.1.1 European State Immunity Convention 121
4.1.2 Vienna Conventions on Diplomatic and Consular Relations 122
4.2 Enforcement Outside the Scope of Conventions 123
4.2.1 Civil Law Claims 123
4.2.2 Public Law Claims 125
4.3 European Convention on Human Rights 126
4.3.1 Civil Execution Law 128
4.3.2 Tax Penalties 134

Chapter 5
Scope of Application of EC Law and Conventions **135**

5.1 Territorial Scope 135
5.1.1 EC Law 135
5.1.2 Conventions Related to the Enforcement of Contractual Claims 137
5.1.3 Conventions Related to the Recovery of Tax Claims 138
5.1.4 Conventions on Insolvency 139
5.2 Scope of Claims 139
5.2.1 Contractual Claims 139
5.2.1.1 EC Law 139
5.2.1.1.1 Brussels I Regulation 139
5.2.1.1.2 Other Regulations Related to Contractual Claims 145
5.2.1.2 Conventions 146
5.2.1.2.1 Nordic Convention on Recognition and the Enforcement of Judgments in Civil Matters 146
5.2.1.2.2 New York Convention on Foreign Arbitral Awards 147
5.2.2 Tax Claims 147
5.2.2.1 Recovery Directive 147
5.2.2.2 Conventions 153
5.3 Relationship between EC Law and Conventions 155
5.3.1 Relationship between Different Parts of EC Law 155
5.3.1.1 Contractual Claims 157
5.3.1.1.1 Brussels I Regulation 157
5.3.1.1.2 Conventions 158
5.3.1.2 Tax Claims 159
5.3.1.2.1 Recovery Directive 159
5.3.1.2.2 Conventions 164
5.3.1.3 Service of Judicial Documents 165

5.4 Limitation to Persons: Creditors, Debtors and Co-debtors – Affected by Claims 166
5.4.1 Creditors 166
5.4.2 Debtors and Co-debtors 167
5.4.2.1 Contractual Claims 168
5.4.2.2 Tax Claims 168
5.4.2.2.1 Debtors 169
5.4.2.2.2 Co-debtors 170
5.4.3 Disqualification Orders against an Individual for Carrying on a Non-serious, or Illegal, Business Activity 173

Chapter 6
Procedures in EC Law and Conventions **175**

6.1 Recognition and Enforceability 175
6.1.1 Parallel Enforcement Proceedings in Several States and Actual Enforcement 177
6.1.1.1 Contractual Claims 178
6.1.1.1.1 EC Law 178
6.1.1.1.1.1 Brussels I Regulation 178
6.1.1.1.1.2 European Enforcement Order for Uncontested Claims 186
6.1.1.1.1.3 European Order for Payment Procedure 187
6.1.1.1.1.4 European Small Claims Procedure 187
6.1.1.1.2 Conventions 188
6.1.1.1.2.1 Nordic Convention on Recognition and the Enforcement of Judgments in Civil Matters 188
6.1.1.1.2.2 New York Convention on Foreign Arbitral Awards 189
6.1.1.2 Periods of Limitation 189
6.1.1.3 Enforcement of a Contested Claim and Appeals 190
6.1.1.3.1 EC Law 190
6.1.1.3.2 Conventions 191
6.1.1.4 Costs and Repayment 191
6.1.2 Tax Claims 192
6.1.2.1 Recovery Directive 192
6.1.2.1.1 Grounds of Refusal 193
6.1.2.1.2 Interim Measures 193
6.1.2.2 Conventions 194
6.1.2.2.1 Grounds of Refusal 194

6.1.2.2.2 Interim Measures 195
6.1.2.3 Periods of Limitation 195
6.1.2.4 Enforcement of a Contested Claim and Appeals 197
6.1.2.4.1 Recovery Directive 197
6.1.2.4.2 Conventions 197
6.1.2.5 Costs and Repayment 198
6.1.3 Conclusions 201
6.1.3.1 Recognition and Enforceability 201
6.1.3.1.1 Brussels I Regulation 201
6.1.3.2 Interim Measures 203
6.1.3.2.1 Recovery Directive 205
6.1.3.3 Grounds of Non-recognition or Grounds of Refusal 206
6.1.3.3.1 Service of Legal Documents 206
6.1.3.3.2 Exhaustion of National Means of Recovery 207
6.1.3.3.3 Debt Thresholds 208
6.1.3.3.4 Public Policy 208
6.1.3.4 Periods of Limitation 209
6.1.3.5 Enforcement of a Contested Claim and Appeals 211
6.1.3.6 Costs and Repayment 212
6.2 Referral Provisions to National Laws 213
6.2.1 Contractual Claims 215
6.2.1.1 EC Law 215
6.2.1.1.1 Brussels I Regulation 215
6.2.1.1.2 Other Regulations Related to Contractual Claims 216
6.2.1.2 Conventions 216
6.2.1.3 Priority Rights 216
6.2.2 Tax Claims 218
6.2.2.1 Recovery Directive 218
6.2.2.1.1 Recovery Measures 218
6.2.2.1.1.1 Insolvency Proceeding 218
6.2.2.1.1.2 Retention of a Tax Credit 221
6.2.2.1.1.3 Set-Off of a Tax Claim 222
6.2.2.1.2 Precautionary Measures 223
6.2.2.2 Conventions 223
6.2.2.3 Priority Rights 224
6.2.3 Conclusions 224
6.3 Access to Information for Enforcement Purposes in the International Context 227
6.3.1 Contractual Claims 227
6.3.2 Tax Claims 229
6.3.2.1 Recovery Directive 230
6.3.2.2 Conventions 232

6.3.3 Conclusions 234
6.3.3.1 Contractual Claims 235
6.3.3.1.1 European Assets Declaration 236
6.3.3.1.2 European Garnishee's Declaration 238
6.3.3.1.3 Other Proposals 239
6.3.3.1.4 Evaluation 240
6.3.3.2 Tax Claims 242
6.3.3.2.1 Use of Exchanged Information Based on the Recovery Directive after a Decision on Collective Insolvency Proceeding 242
6.3.3.2.2 New Communication Obligation in the Implementing Recovery Directive in Case of a Refund of a Tax Credit 243
6.3.3.2.3 Tax Law Area 243
6.3.3.2.4 Implementing Recovery Directive 244
6.3.3.2.5 Evaluation 245
6.4 International Insolvency 245
6.4.1 Insolvency Regulation 245
6.4.2 Conventions 250
6.4.3 Transnational Judicial Cooperation in Insolvency Management 251

Chapter 7
Harmonization of Civil Execution Laws **255**

7.1 EC Law, International Principles and Recommendations 255
7.2 Differences in National Enforcement Procedures 261
7.2.1 Attachment of the Earnings of the Debtor 263
7.2.2 Time-Limits 266
7.2.3 Access to Information for Enforcement Purposes in the National Context 269
7.2.3.1 Access to Information before a Title of Execution 269
7.2.3.2 Access to Information after a Title of Execution 269
7.2.3.3 Different Techniques of Access to Information 271
7.2.3.4 Public Law Sector 274
7.2.3.5 Improved Access to Information for Enforcement Purposes 275
7.3 Uncitral Facultative Model Law on Enforcement Law 279

Chapter 8
Bibliography **281**

8.1 Legal Historical Material Until 2001 281
8.1.1 Belgium 281
8.1.2 Denmark 281

8.1.3 Finland 281
8.1.4 France 282
8.1.5 Germany 282
8.1.6 Iceland 282
8.1.7 Italy and Roman law 282
8.1.8 Luxemburg 283
8.1.9 Netherlands 283
8.1.10 Norway 283
8.1.11 Sweden 283
8.1.12 Switzerland 284
8.1.13 United Kingdom 284
8.1.14 European Community Law 284
8.2 European Community Law and Conventions 285
8.2.1 Contractual Claims 285
8.2.2 Tax Claims 286
8.2.3 Insolvency 289
8.2.4 Other European Community Law and Conventions 290
8.3 National Laws and Other Sources 295
8.3.1 Belgium 295
8.3.2 Denmark 296
8.3.3 Finland 296
8.3.4 Luxemburg 297
8.3.5 Norway 297
8.3.6 Sweden 297
8.3.6.1 Legislation and Decrees 297
8.3.6.2 Travaux Préparatoires 298
8.3.6.3 Others 298
8.3.7 United Kingdom 299
8.3.8 United States of America 299
8.4 Literature 300
8.5 Table of Court Cases 318
8.5.1 European Court of Human Rights (ECHR) 319
8.5.2 European Court of Justice (ECJ) 323
8.6 Websites 335

Annexes **337**
Index **359**

Preface

This book is dedicated to the readers in and outside of Europe, who are interested in the subject of *Cross-Border Enforcement of Claims in the EU: History, Present Time and Future*.[1] It has been a pleasure to write this book which hopefully will provide some useful information and guidance.

I would like to thank all persons, not least my colleagues, who have given me inspiration in my work.

In particular, I wish to express my gratitude and appreciation to professor Gunnar Karnell, at the Stockholm School of Economics, for his constructive and stimulating discussions with me. I am grateful to the Stockholm School of Economics which has given me the opportunity to make the legal research resulting in this book.

I also want to express my appreciation to professor Michael Bogdan, at the University of Lund, professor Georges de Leval, professor Patrick Wautelet, and professor Frédéric Georges, at the University of Liège, as well as to professor Konstantinos Kerameus, at the University of Athens, for inspiration of great importance. In addition, a special thanks goes to professor Amparo Grau, at the Complutense University in Madrid, for our fruitful discussions.

I am grateful to my family, my wife Ingela, my son Gustav, and my daughter Sofia, who all of them have supported me throughout my work.

Mikael Berglund
Stockholm 24 September 2008

---

1. This book is essentially based on the manuscript of a legal thesis on the same subject which was put forward by Mikael Berglund at a public academic disputation for a Doctor of Laws degree at the Stockholm School of Economics on 19 Sep. 2008.

Abbreviations

The following abbreviations are used for European community law, conventions, and common expressions, which are used with certain frequency in the text.

Action plan of the Council and the Commission	Action plan of the Council and the Commission on how best to implement the provisions of the Treaty of Amsterdam on an area of freedom, security and justice of 3 December 1998
ALI	American Law Institute
ALI-UNIDROIT Principles of Transnational Civil Procedure	Principles of Transnational Civil Procedure adopted by the American Law Institute (ALI) in May 2004 and by the International Institute for the Unification of Private Law (UNIDROIT) in April 2004
Art.	Article
Bankruptcy convention between France and Monaco	La Convention relative à la faillite et à la liquidation judiciaire entre la France et la principauté de Monaco du 13 Septembre 1950
Benelux convention on the mutual assistance for the recovery of tax claims	La Convention entre la Belgique, le Grand-Duché de Luxembourg et les Pays-Bas, relative à l'assistance réciproque en matière de recouvrement de créances fiscales du 5 September 1952
Brussels convention	Convention on jurisdiction and the enforcement of judgments in civil and commercial matters, done at Brussels on 27 September 1968

Brussels I regulation	Council regulation (44/2001/EC) on jurisdiction and the recognition and enforcement of judgments in civil and commercial matters
CEPEJ	European Commission for the Efficiency of Justice
Confiscation Framework Decision	Council Framework Decision 2006/783/JHA of 6 October 2006 on the application of the principle of mutual recognition to confiscation orders
Council of Europe and OECD convention on mutual administrative assistance in tax matters	Convention on mutual administrative assistance in tax matters, done at Strasbourg on 25 January 1988, Council of Europe and OECD
Council of Europe's recommendation on archiving of electronic documents in the legal sector	Council of Europe's recommendation on archiving of electronic documents in the legal sector, Rec (2003) 15, of 9 September 2003
Council of Europe's recommendation on enforcement	Council of Europe's recommendation on enforcement, Rec (2003) 17, of 9 September 2003
Council of Europe's recommendation on the interoperability of information systems in the justice sector	Council of Europe's recommendation on the interoperability of information systems in the justice sector, Rec (2003) 14, of 9 September 2003
Council's programme of measures for implementation of the principle of mutual recognition	Council draft programme (2001/C 12/01) of measures for implementation of the principle of mutual recognition of decisions in civil and commercial matters
Data protection Directive	Directive 46/95/EC of the European Parliament and of the Council of 24 October 1995 on the protection of individuals with regard to the processing of personal data and on the free movement of such data
Ds	Departementsserien (Series of Swedish Ministries)
EBR	European Business Register
EC	European Communities
ECHR	European Court of Human Rights

ECJ	European Court of Justice, Court of Justice of the EC
EC Treaty	Treaty establishing the European community
ETS	European Treaty Series
Eulis	European Land Information Service
EUR	International currency code for Euro/European currency unit
European Convention on Human Rights	Convention for the protection of human rights and fundamental freedoms, Council of Europe, done at Rome on 4 November 1950, as amended by protocol No. 11
European Enforcement Order for uncontested claims	Regulation (805/2004/EC) of the European Parliament and of the Council of 21 April 2004 creating a European Enforcement Order for uncontested claims
European Judicial Network in civil and commercial matters	Council decision (2001/470/EC) of 28 May 2001 establishing a European Judicial Network in civil and commercial matters
European Order for payment procedure	Regulation (1896/2006/EC) of the European Parliament and of the Council of 12 December 2006 creating a European order for payment procedure
European Small Claims Procedure	Regulation (EC) No 861/2007 of the European Parliament and of the Council of 11 July establishing a European Small Claims Procedure
European State immunity convention	European convention on State immunity, done at Basle on 16 May 1972
European Union	EU
Financial penalties Framework Decision	Council Framework Decision 2005/214/JHA of 24 February 2005 on the application of the principle of mutual recognition to financial penalties
ICJ	International Court of Justice
Implementing agreement to the Nordic agreement on assistance in tax matters	Agreement according to article 20 of the agreement between the Nordic countries for mutual administrative assistance in tax matters of 7 December 1989, as amended on its entry into force on 1 January 1998

Implementing recovery directive	Commission Directive (2002/94/EC) of 9 December 2002 laying down detailed rules for implementing certain provisions of Council Directive 76/308/EEC on mutual assistance for the recovery of claims relating to certain levies, duties, taxes and other measures
Insolvency regulation	Council regulation (EC)/No 1346/2000 of 29 May 2000 on insolvency proceedings
IOTA	Intra-European Organisation of Tax Administrations
Late payment's directive	Directive 2000/35/EC of the European Parliament and of the Council of 29 June 2000 on combating late payment in commercial transactions
LNTS	League of Nations Treaty Series
Moscow Resolution	Resolution No. 3 of the 24th Conference of European Justice Ministers in Moscow in October 2001 on the 'General approach and the means of achieving effective enforcement of judicial decisions'
New Lugano convention	Convention on jurisdiction and the recognition and enforcement of judgments in civil and commercial matters, done at Lugano on 30 October 2007
New service of legal documents' regulation	Regulation (EC) No 1393/2007 of the European Parliament and of the Council of 13 November 2007 on the service in the Member States of judicial and extrajudicial documents in civil or commercial matters (service of documents)
New social security regulation	Regulation (883/2004/EC) of the European Parliament and of the Council of 29 April 2004 on the coordination of social security systems
New York convention on foreign arbitral awards	Convention on the recognition and enforcement of foreign arbitral awards, done at New York on 10 June 1958
Nordic agreement on assistance in tax matters	Agreement between the Nordic countries for mutual administrative assistance in tax matters, done at Copenhagen on 7 December 1989
Nordic bankruptcy convention	Convention between Denmark, Finland, Iceland, Norway and Sweden regarding bankruptcy of 7 November 1933, as amended in 1977 and 1982

Nordic convention on recognition and the enforcement of judgments in civil matters	Convention between Sweden, Denmark, Finland, Iceland and Norway on recognition and the enforcement of judgments in civil matters, done at Copenhagen on 11 October 1977
OJ	Official Journal of the European Communities
OECD	Organization for Economic Co-operation and Development
Old Lugano convention	Convention on jurisdiction and the enforcement of judgments in civil and commercial matters, done at Lugano on 16 September 1988
Old service of legal documents' regulation	Council regulation 1348/2000/EC of 29 May 2000 on the service in the Member States of judicial and extrajudicial documents in civil or commercial matters
Old social security regulation	Council regulation 1408/71/EEC of 14 June 1971 on the application of social security schemes to employed persons and their families moving within the Community
para.	Paragraph
Prop.	Regeringens proposition (proposal from the Swedish Government to the Parliament concerning a new act, travaux préparatoires to legislation)
Proposal for a Council regulation on jurisdiction, applicable law, recognition and enforcement of decisions and cooperation in matters relating to maintenance obligations	Commission of the European communities' proposal for a Council regulation on jurisdiction, applicable law, recognition and enforcement of decisions and cooperation in matters relating to maintenance obligations, COM (2005) 649 final
Recovery directive	Council Directive 2008/55/EC of 26 May 2008 on mutual assistance for the recovery of claims relating to certain levies, duties, taxes and other measures (Codified version)
Rome convention on the law applicable to contractual obligations	Convention on the law applicable to contractual obligations, opened for signature in Rome on 19 June 1980
s.	Section
SE	Societas Europaea
SEK	International currency code for Swedish currency, krona

SvJT	Svensk Juristtidning (Swedish Law Journal)
Tampere conclusions	Presidency conclusions of the European council 15 and 16 October 1999 in Tampere
TEE	Titre Exécutoire Européen
Treaty of Lisbon	Treaty of Lisbon amending the Treaty on European Union and the Treaty establishing the European Community, signed at Lisbon, 13 December 2007
UIHJ	L'Union Internationale des Huissiers de Justice et Officiers Judiciaires
UN	United Nations
Uncitral	United Nations Commission on International Trade Law
UNIDROIT	International Institute for the Unification of Private Law
UNTS	United Nations Treaty Series
VAT	Value Added Tax
Vienna convention on consular relations	Vienna convention on consular relations, done at Vienna on 24 April 1963
Vienna convention on diplomatic relations	Vienna convention on diplomatic relations, done at Vienna on 18 April 1961
Vienna Convention on the Law of Treaties	Convention on the law of treaties, done at Vienna on 23 May 1969

Table of Annexes

The order of an annex here is determined by its first appearance in the text.

Annex 1 Overview of some subjects in the Recovery directive and in the Implementing recovery directive

Annex 2 Details on the entry into force and on certain reservations in relation to the States which are parties to the Convention on the recognition and enforcement of foreign arbitral awards of 10 June 1958

Annex 3 Agreement between the Nordic countries for mutual administrative assistance in tax matters of 7 December 1989, translation

Annex 4 Details on the entry into force in relation to the States which are parties to the Convention on jurisdiction and the enforcement of judgments in civil and commercial matters of 27 September 1968

Annex 5 Details on the entry into force in relation to the States which are parties to the Convention on jurisdiction and the enforcement of judgments in civil and commercial matters of 16 September 1988

Annex 6 Details on the entry into force and on certain reservations in relation to the States which are parties to the Convention on mutual administrative assistance in tax matters of 25 January 1988

Annex 7 Convention between Denmark, Finland, Iceland, Norway and Sweden regarding bankruptcy of 7 November 1933, as amended in 1977 and 1982, translated extracts

Annex 8 Draft of a Nordic agreement on the exchange of information in recovery matters, translation of pp. 25-30 in the report Nordiskt samarbete om indrivningsfrågor (Nordic co-operation in recovery matters) to the Nordic Council of Ministers

Annex 9 Details on the entry into force in relation to the States which are parties to the European convention on State immunity of 16 May 1972

Annex 10 National authorities designated by the Member States of the European Union in accordance to article 256 of the EC Treaty for the verification of the authenticity of decisions of the Council or of the Commission

Chapter 1

Introduction

1.1 THE PROBLEMS MOTIVATING THE CHOICE OF THE SUBJECT

The study is dedicated to the need for extensive systematic information, and the problems, related to the subject. The title chosen for this work is mainly dedicated to some problems in the legal areas of the civil execution/enforcement of contractual claims for money and the recovery of tax claims, after the establishment of a title of execution.[1] It relates to developments until 24 September 2008. The word enforcement needs here often to be used to cover also recovery. This use indicates that the creditor's application for enforcement measures only constitutes one of his possible legal initiatives, which may be classified as a recovery measure in relation to his claim.[2]

The indicated problems in the fields of concern will here be briefly described. Legal actions against a debtor related to the areas of the enforcement and recovery of claims, after the establishment of a title of execution, are often described as some of the possible final steps in the all-over legal chain available to a creditor in order to secure the payment of his claims.[3] As the strength of this legal chain is not stronger than its weakest parts, this indicates that to the extent that one part of it is not efficiently strong; the total result of this chain will be undermined. This statement may be true in a lot of different legal areas, but it is certainly also well aimed to

1. Compare the Latin word *executio*, which may, depending on the circumstances, *i.a.* be translated into: the action of carrying out performance; the enforcement (of a law), the administration (of a province), the development, discussion (of a subject), and an action taken to obtain satisfaction (for a wrong), *see* Oxford Latin Dictionary, p. 655.
2. *See* 1.6 about the use of the term enforcement compared to the use of the term recovery.
3. Compare Kerameus, Enforcement in the International Context, Recueil des cours, collected courses of the Hague Academy of International Law, 1997, Tome 264 de la collection, p. 406, who describes enforcement as being 'the end of the law'.

illustrate the importance of efficiency in the legal areas related to the enforcement of contractual claims and the recovery of tax claims and their important contributions to an all-over well-functioning legal system. Consequently, without sufficient efficiency in the legal areas of enforcement and recovery, both in the national and international contexts, the creditor becomes lost. This incisive conclusion indicates that the value of an enforceable title of execution against a debtor may, both in the private law area and in the public law area, in practice be diminished to the extent that national laws, European Community (EC) law and conventions, do not provide enough sufficiently efficient solutions for the benefit of creditors at the moment of enforcement and recovery, based on their titles of execution.

A well developed legal framework for the enforcement and recovery of claims, in their quality of ordinary and provisional titles of execution, means, both in the national and international context, increased efficiency for the benefit of the creditors, but also supports a higher degree of respect for court judgments and decisions by authorities in society. Consequently, States that do not provide such a sufficient level of efficiency for enforcement and recovery purposes of titles of execution, judgments rendered by their own courts, or decisions handed down by their administrative bodies, correspondingly diminish the efficiency of justice, the actual value of such titles. The lack of such efficiency results in that the value of these titles of execution to the creditors are reduced only into some beautiful pictures that they could put on their walls, while the debtor despite of these titles actually still may continue undisturbed to dispose over and move his assets.

The problems of cross-border enforcement in the region which is of interest here, that of the European laws, may also be described in the following way. The complexity due to the differences between the national enforcement systems and the lack of sufficiently efficient legal cooperation between Member States in matters having cross-border implications hinder the free movement of judgments, goods, persons and services within the Internal Common Market. The efficiency decreases for the creditors in their recovery of debts abroad and encourage bad faith debtors to channel their funds into Member States where they may be easily concealed. This results in that the effects of the free movement of judgments within Europe is severely impaired; creditors may not consider it worth while to try to enforce their claims in other Member States, but instead write them off.[4] This scenario requires, at an early stage, a private creditor, before entering into a contractual agreement, respectively a public creditor/organ, which takes a decision of taxation, both in the national and international context, to reflect *i.a.* on preventive security arrangements, the possible use of precautionary measures to secure their claims, how to obtain an enforceable title of execution and how to enforce and recover these claims in the event of non-payment by the debtor.

Even if it may be argued that a lack of efficiency after the establishment of a title of execution constitutes a main problem in the legal area of the enforcement of

4. *See* about a similar opinion, EC Study JAI/02/03/2002, A, II, 1.

claims,[5] both in the national and international context, also other relevant counter or interplaying interests and principles established in the legal objectives of EC law and other parts of public international law have to be considered in this balance between different interests and principles,[6] *e.g.* the interest of privacy of the debtor and the principle of proportionality. It may also be argued that the legal objective of the general State interest of a more efficient enforcement of claims in society does not only include the creditor's interest of efficiency, balanced against the debtor's interest of dignity and privacy, but also the debtor's interest of efficiency, because a too slow, inefficient and in time unpredictable enforcement proceeding may also be harmful to the interest of legal clarity of the debtor.

The task to establish this justified balance between these conflicting interests of the debtor and the creditor, in the work of enforcing judgments and recovering claims, is in each Member State of the European Union (EU) entrusted not to the creditors, or to the debtors, but instead to the national professionals, the regulated enforcement agents of the enforcement and recovery organs. These professionals may work either as civil servants in the administration, or as free professionals, or in courts, as officers of an enforcement court in the civil enforcement law area, and as recovery agents in the tax recovery law area.[7] The intervention of these professionals in enforcement and recovery matters often has the positive effect for the debtor that the pressure of payment from the creditors stops or decreases, when the contacts with the creditors instead become organized and the payments of the debtor as a consequence also become structured and limited by the *beneficium* of the debtor. A positive effect of this intervention for the creditors is that they may make a more realistic estimation of what amount of payments they may expect to receive, or not. All these reflections have motivated and determined the choice of the subject of this work.

Readers should be aware that, when here a reference is first made in any of the parts of this work to a part of EC law, a convention, or a part of public international law, no more information than its name and the date upon which it was decided will be given. When such a reference is made it is often completed by an indication in brackets of the following use of an abbreviated form of use of wordings for a part of EC law, or for a convention, *e.g.* the Regulation 44/2001/EC of 22 December 2000 on jurisdiction and the recognition and enforcement of judgments in civil and commercial matters (Brussels I regulation).[8] Readers, who would like to have

---

5. *See* about a similar opinion, de Leval, Subject of the proceedings, The execution of court decisions in civil cases, p. 52, where he concludes that: 'Basically, the main problem associated with execution is that of making it effective.' and de Leval, Civil Procedure in Europe 1, Une harmonisation des procédures d'exécution dans l'Union européenne est-elle concevable?, p. 595, where he *i.a.* argues that: 'La libre circulation des jugements est illusoire si le titre ne se concrétise pas avec la même efficacité dans les États membres.'
6. *See*, about a discussion on the balance between different interests and principles, Verbeke, Execution Officers as a Balance Wheel in Insolvency Cases.
7. The regulated European enforcement and recovery agents and their international bodies of cooperation are treated in the context of 2.10.5, 3.2.1-3, and 3.3.1-2.
8. *See* <http://eur-lex.europa.eu/LexUriServ/LexUriServ.do?uri=CELEX:32001R0044:EN:HTML>.

more detailed information about such European law and conventions, *e.g.* about the number of a published regulation in the Official Journal of the EU (OJ), or about a number of a convention published in some of the international Treaty Series, may consult the bibliography.

Readers should also be aware, when reference at the first time is made in any of the parts of this work to a ruling of the European Court of Human Rights (ECHR), or to a ruling of the European Court of Justice (ECJ) of the EC, that no more information than about the parties involved and the date of the decision is given. These rulings are treated as briefly as possible in the main text, supplemented by more extensive details in the corresponding footnotes. Also, brief summaries of these rulings appear in the bibliography. Some parts of EC law and conventions, which are treated as parts of the subject, are found in Annexes.

1.1.1 Subject

The subject exposes the balance between and limits of some legal interests as well as principles and their impact related to the private and public creditors and the debtor, in the work of regulated European enforcement agents, and departure from the legal historical developments resulting in the present legal solutions.

From a strictly legally scientific point of view the subject may be seen to be about matters, after the establishment of a title of execution, having cross-border implications in relation to a comparison between the legal areas of the civil execution of contractual claims and the recovery of tax claims in EC law and multilateral conventions valid in Europe, as regards their opposed, or differing, or similar, solutions. This is compared to the legal objectives expressed in such European law and conventions, public international law, and in other international principles and recommendations accepted by States which are valid in the EC. This part of the subject is in particular influenced by EC law, but also to some extent by multilateral conventions and public international law, which interplay with national laws and determine the conditions to be fulfilled before the actual enforcement of the claim can take place in another European State.

Of equal scientific interest, as a part of the subject, may be perceived the need and interest of a possible harmonization in Europe of certain selected parts in differing national civil execution laws, and in national laws on access to information for enforcement purposes, in relation to matters having cross-border implications. This is compared to the legal objectives expressed in EC law and in other international principles and recommendations accepted by States which are valid in the EC.

Some, but not all of the provisions related to the subject treated, may be classified as administrative or procedural law. Public international law constitutes a source of law of a general aim and application to the issues of cross-border enforcement and recovery outside the scope of EC law and of conventions, *e.g.* in relation to the territorial limits of enforcement and recovery, and in relation to a foreign State's immunity against civil execution measures. Another part of public international law of the same broad aim and application of incidence related to the subject is the Convention for the protection of human rights and fundamental freedoms of the Council of Europe of 4 November 1950, as amended by protocol No. 11 (European Convention on Human Rights) and the legal usage of the ECHR related to matters of enforcement and recovery.

Influences by the ever-growing importance of EC law explain why the text is mainly focused on such law, compared to conventions. Conventions are treated to the extent they still are in force and when their solutions are of a comparative interest. The EC law treated concerns provisions, which influence national procedural law in the enforcement and recovery areas, such as in the Brussels I regulation,[9] and in the Recovery directive,[10] but also other provisions in such law that interplay with them.

The provisions of enforcement and recovery in EC law and in multilateral conventions are, with one important exception,[11] part of such European law and conventions, which also regulate legal issues outside the enforcement area.[12] The fact that the Recovery directive to a greater extent includes recovery provisions compared to the enforcement provisions of the Brussels I regulation is mainly explained by their different features of cooperation.[13] The multilateral conventions on both the enforcement of contractual claims and on the recovery of tax claims are to a varying degree in force in European States, some of them also being applicable in relation to a lot of European States outside of the EC and non-European States. Examples are the New York convention on foreign arbitral awards and the

9. *See e.g.* Arts 38-52 of the Brussels I regulation which treat procedural law related to exequatur proceedings in enforcement matters.
10. The ECJ has, in its decision in the joint cases of *Greece v. Tsapalos and Diamantakos* of 1 Jul. 2004, considered the provisions of the Recovery directive to be procedural law. The cases concerned customs claims, which arose in one Member State, Italy, under an instrument issued by that State before the directive entered into force in the other Member State, Greece, where the requested authority was situated. This decision is also further treated in the context of 5.2.2.1. *See* for further details about the Recovery directive footnote 11.
11. *See* Council Directive 2008/55/EC of 26 May 2008 on mutual assistance for the recovery of claims relating to certain levies, duties, taxes and other measures (Codified version) and Annex I to the directive, (Recovery directive), <http://eur-lex.europa.eu/LexUriServ/LexUriServ.do?uri=OJ:L:2008:150:0028:01:EN:HTML>, and the thereto connected Commission Directive 2002/94/EC of 9 Dec. 2002 laying down detailed rules for implementing certain provisions of Council Directive 76/308/EEC on mutual assistance for the recovery of claims relating to certain levies, duties, taxes and other measures (Implementing recovery directive), <http://eur-lex.europa.eu/LexUriServ/LexUriServ.do?uri=CELEX:32002L0094:EN:HTML>. *Also see* the overview in annex 1 regarding the Recovery directive and the Implementing recovery directive.
12. Compare the Brussels I regulation (<http://eur-lex.europa.eu/LexUriServ/LexUriServ.do?uri=CELEX:32001R0044:EN:HTML>), and the New York convention on foreign arbitral awards (<www.uncitral.org/pdf/english/texts/arbitration/NY-conv/XXII_1_e.pdf>), to the Recovery directive and the Implementing recovery directive. *Also see*, for details on the entry into force and on certain reservations in relation to the States, which are parties to the New York convention on foreign arbitral awards, annex 2.
13. *See* 2.9 for further comment on some different features of cooperation in the cross-border area of contractual claims compared to the corresponding area of the recovery of tax claims in EC law and multilateral conventions.

Convention on mutual administrative assistance in tax matters of 25 January 1988 Convention on mutual administrative assistance in tax matters). Indirectly, this means, that the text also, partially, assumes a broader multilateral approach than only the EC States.

More information about the parts of the total framework of the subject is provided in the following subsections. The order of treatment of this information is governed by what is initially, and then gradually, motivated for a treatment and understanding of the parts of the subject and their interplay.

1.1.1.1 Interests, Principles and Their Balance

Legal enforcement and recovery matters frequently involve a lot of legal interests and principles, both in the national and international context, which counter or interplay. The existence and balance between these interests and principles vary, as will be demonstrated in the further context of this work, as a consequence of that the legal objectives in EC law, conventions, and other parts of public international law vary correspondingly. These interests and principles have often been, more or less, explicitly weighted against each other, or have been given different priorities to each other, in relation to the different objectives that have been established in EC law, conventions, and public international law.

Sometimes the principles of public international law have to be taken into account at the application and interpretation in national law of EC law and conventions.[14] This may *e.g.* be the case to the extent that an application, either of a part of EC law, or of a convention, would in national law be contrary to and violate an important principle in the European Convention on Human Rights.

Hence, to be treated here are certain interests and principles, which are based on the legal objectives of the legal framework of EC law and public international law. Also treated are some interests and principles, which are based on the legal objectives in established political decisions, aimed to govern the direction of future law reforms, either from the EU, or from other international organizations, including recommendations and principles, accepted by States. Among political decisions, which include important legal objectives for the development of future law reforms, both in the national and international context, there are the Presidency conclusions of the European Council 15 and 16 October 1999 in Tampere (Tampere conclusions), where the European Council called for a further reduction in intermediate measures needed for enforcement of foreign judgments accompanied by the setting of minimum standards on specific aspects of civil procedural law,[15]

14. *See* 1.4.1 about some principles on the interpretation of public international law.
15. *See* B, VI. The conclusions also emphasized the need to obtain greater convergence in civil law, including to prepare new procedural legislation in cross-border cases, in particular on these elements which are instrumental to smooth judicial cooperation and to enhance access to law, *e.g.* provisional measures and orders for money payments. As regards substantive law, an overall study was requested on the need to approximate the legislation of Member States in civil matters in order to eliminate obstacles to the good functioning of civil proceedings, B, VII.

as well as the Council draft programme of measures for implementation of the principle of mutual recognition of decisions in civil and commercial matters of 15 January 2001 (Council's programme of measures for implementation of the principle of mutual recognition), based on the Tampere conclusions, with the aim to abolish all procedures needed for the enforceability of judgments in civil and commercial matters and to introduce effective measures to improve the enforcement of judgments. This programme provides for a series of measures aiming at strengthening the effects in the requested State of judgments given in the State of origin and by these means promote a more effective cooperation between the Member States of the EU.[16]

The programme mentioned has been reaffirmed in the Hague Programme of the European Council in March 2005 (Hague Programme of the European Council), which emphasizes the importance of facilitating civil law procedure across borders and the mutual recognition of decisions.[17] It was a logical step

---

The conclusions followed after the first initiative in this field in the Commission's communication to the Council and the European Parliament 'Towards greater efficiency in obtaining and enforcing judgments in the European Union', OJ 1998 C 33/03. In this communication the Commission underlined that the swift and effective enforcement of judicial decisions is regarded as a *sine qua non* for the efficient administration of justice. The Treaty of Lisbon amending the Treaty on European Union and the Treaty establishing the European Community, signed at Lisbon, 13 December 2007, (Treaty of Lisbon), which in the area of judicial cooperation in civil matters emphasizes the principle of mutual recognition of judgments and decisions in extrajudicial cases, includes in such cooperation the adoption of measures for approximation of the laws and regulations of the Member States, *see* Art. 65.

16. The Council's programme includes proposals on measures directly affecting mutual recognition in areas already covered by the existing instruments, limiting the reasons which can be given for challenging recognition, or enforcement of a foreign judgment, establishing provisional enforcement despite the possibility of appeal, establishing protective measures at European level, improving attachment measures concerning banks and the abolition of any checks on the foreign judgment by courts in the requested State, *see* programme's II, A. It further includes proposals on measures ancillary to mutual recognition, minimum standards for certain aspects of civil procedure and on efficiency of measures providing for improved enforcement of decisions and on improving judicial cooperation on civil matters in general, *see* Part II, section B of the programme. *Also see* about measures ancillary to mutual recognition, 2. Efficiency of measures providing for improved enforcement of decisions compared to Part III, section E. Ancillary measures of the programme.

17. *See* Part I and Part III, section 3.4 about the judicial cooperation in civil matters. Section 3.4.1 of the programme reads: 'Civil law, including family law, concerns citizens in their everyday lives. The European Council therefore attaches great importance to the continued development of judicial cooperation in civil matters and full completion of the programme of mutual recognition adopted in 2000. The main policy objective in this area is that borders between countries in Europe should no longer constitute an obstacle to the settlement of civil law matters or to the bringing of court proceedings and the enforcement of decisions in civil matters.' Section 3.4.2 of the same programme *i.a.* reads: 'Mutual recognition of decisions is an effective means of protecting citizens' rights and securing the enforcement of such rights across European borders. Continued implementation of the programme of measures on mutual recognition must therefore be a main priority in the coming years to ensure its completion by 2011. Work concerning the following projects should be actively pursued: . . . a European Payment Order . . . and concerning small claims. . . . The effectiveness of existing instruments on mutual recognition

of development following the Action plan of the Council and the Commission on how best to implement the provisions of the Treaty of Amsterdam on an area of freedom, security and justice of 3 December 1998 (Action plan of the Council and the Commission), which in the area of judicial cooperation in civil matters emphasized availability of speedy and fair proceedings and effective enforcement procedures.[18] This was followed by: the Resolution No. 3 of the 24th Conference of European Justice Ministers in Moscow in October 2001 on the'General approach and the means of achieving effective enforcement of judicial decisions' (Moscow Resolution),[19] the Council of Europe's recommendation on enforcement of

---

should be increased by standardising procedures and documents and developing minimum standards for aspects of procedural law, such as the service of judicial and extra-judicial documents, the commencement of proceedings, enforcement of judgments and transparency of costs.'

18. *See* Part I, C, section 16 and part II, B, II, section 39.

19. The Moscow Resolution acknowledges the need to improve the enforcement of judicial decisions, and states *i.a.* the following: 'Recognising the importance of ensuring the effectiveness not only of criminal sanctions but also of judicial decisions in civil, commercial, administrative and social matters; Bearing in mind the requirements of the European Convention on Human Rights and, in particular, the recognition by the European Court of Human Rights that the enforcement of court decisions, in particular within a reasonable time, has to be regarded as an integral part of the right to a fair trial for the purpose of Art. 6; Recalling Resolution No. 1 on "Delivering justice in the 21st century", adopted at their 23rd Conference in London in Jun. 2000 and welcoming the decision of the Committee of Ministers to prepare an appropriate legal instrument or legal instruments aimed at promoting efficiency of justice throughout Europe, and encouraging their rapid completion; Recalling also the results achieved within the intergovernmental cooperation, as well as the multilateral and bilateral legal cooperation activities carried out by the Council of Europe and its member States, and convinced of the need for these results to be properly followed up by means of legislative or other practical measures aiming at improving the enforcement of court decisions;... Noting the importance of promoting international cooperation to ensure the effectiveness of foreign judicial decisions; Recognising that without an appropriate enforcement procedure, court decisions will be rendered inoperative and illusory both for the State and individuals; Aware that economic activity, in particular trade and industry, is likewise dependent on confidence in an effective enforcement system; Underlining the essential role played by bailiffs (or any other enforcement agent) and the need for their work to be carried out, according to the law, fairly, impartially, efficiently and transparently; Bearing in mind the principles of cost-effectiveness and proportionality when carrying out the enforcement process; Agree that the proper, effective and efficient enforcement of court decisions is of capital importance for States in order to create, reinforce and develop a strong and respected judicial system; Recognise that enforcement procedures have to comply with the requirements of the European Convention on Human Rights; Decide to promote efficiency of justice through greater mutual cooperation amongst States, with a view to improving the functioning of their judicial system by means of appropriate mechanisms; Invite the Committee of Ministers to instruct the European Committee on Legal Co-operation (CDCJ) to identify common standards and principles at a European level for the enforcement of court decisions. To this end, particular attention has to be paid to: I. enforcement procedures, in particular (a) role of the parties (e.g. creditors, debtors, third parties); (b) assets (e.g. sales of assets, distribution, attachment, exempted assets) and other types of safeguards and guarantees; (c) procedures (e.g. settlements, access to court and review, the role of the judges, proportionality); (d) costs (e.g. interests, court fees, costs of enforcement, fees of bailiffs); (e) special cases (e.g. family cases, labour disputes, landlord and tenant, enforcement of injunctions, transfrontier cases); and II,

9 September 2003 (Council of Europe's recommendation on enforcement), and the Principles of Transnational Civil Procedure adopted by the American Law Institute (ALI) in May 2004 and by the International Institute for the Unification of Private Law (UNIDROIT) in April 2004 (ALI-UNIDROIT Principles of Transnational Civil Procedure).[20]

1.1.1.1.1 Privacy versus Efficiency

The interest of private and public creditors is mainly focused on an efficient treatment in the enforcement, or recovery, of their claims in the assets of the debtor, while the interest of the debtor is mainly focused on how to be protected from too far-reaching enforcement, or recovery, measures. Some of the most important and frequent examples of conflicting, or competing, interests, in the areas of enforcement and recovery of claims are on the one hand the demand from society for the legal protection of the debtor's private integrity, *e.g.* taking into account humanity and immunity against too far-reaching enforcement measures, privacy, and on the other hand the demand from society of an efficient treatment in the recovery of the creditor's claim, efficiency. This interest of efficiency may be expressed in many different ways. Examples are effective preventive measures to make it more difficult for the debtor to over indebt himself, measures that make the debtor pay voluntarily instead of being exposed to the actual enforcement and recovery measures, the actual enforcement and recovery of payments, or related to other assets, and time saving enforcement and recovery procedures.

Important examples of EC law and conventions, related to such interests, are the Brussels I regulation, which is more balanced in favour of the interest of protecting the debtor,[21] the Recovery directive, which is more balanced in favour of the interest of efficiency of the creditor,[22] and the Council of Europe and OECD convention on mutual administrative assistance in tax matters, which represents a

---

bailiffs (or any other enforcement agents), in particular (a) recruitment and education; (b) role, competence and powers; (c) cooperation with the parties and other legal professionals (including settlements); (d) use of new information technology and means to reduce costs; (e) control of judges of the acts of bailiffs; (f) professional codes of conduct (including duties, liability and disciplinary measures).'

20. *See*, about the text of the ALI-UNIDROIT Principles and the accompanying commentary adopted by the ALI and by the UNIDROIT, Unif. L. Rev. 2004-4.
21. *See* Preamble, about the provisions to simplify the formalities with a view to rapid and simple recognition and enforcement of judgments from Member States, which are essential (2), the principle of proportionality (4), the procedure for making enforceable in one Member State a judgment, by virtue of the principle of mutual trust (17) and the respect for the rights of the defense by making an appeal in adversarial procedure against the declaration of enforceability (18).
22. *See* Preamble of the directive which emphasizes the interests, to meet the threat to the financial interests of the Community and the Member States and to the internal market posed by the development of fraud, to safeguard these interests in order to protect better competitiveness and fiscal neutrality of the internal market (3) and to permit more efficient and effective recovery of claims by treating the instrument permitting enforcement of the claim in principle as an instrument of the Member State in which the requested authority is situated (9).

more combined balance of private integrity and efficiency.[23] The debtor's right of privacy, the creditor's right to enforce a claim efficiently, and the creditor's right of peaceful enjoyment of his possessions are all guaranteed by the European Convention on Human Rights.[24] The Council of Europe's recommendation on enforcement emphasizes some guiding principles concerning enforcement in enforcement procedures such as efficiency, legal certainty, predictability and the establishment of a proper balance between the interests of the claimant and the defendant, bearing in mind, in particular Articles 6 and 8 of the European Convention on Human Rights.[25]

The ALI-UNIDROIT Principles of Transnational Civil Procedure also emphasize the interest of efficient enforcement procedures.[26] The public interest, *i.e.* the State interest, does not only stand equal to the role of a public creditor, but is also focused on how to satisfy and to uphold other general interests of a more impartial nature in relation to both the private creditors and the debtor. Examples are an equal treatment according to the law in the same kind of matters, protection from any discrimination on grounds of nationality, fast, efficient and predictable enforcement proceedings and the maintenance of certain State interests based on public international law, such as sovereignty and territoriality.

1.1.1.1.2 Non-discrimination

The EC principle of non-discrimination on grounds of nationality in the Treaty establishing the EC (EC Treaty)[27] means that private and public creditors and debtors of Member States of the EU must not be discriminated on grounds of nationality. A case where the ECJ has paid attention to this principle is *Lease Plan Luxembourg SA v. Belgian State*, where it was established that the application of more advantageous conditions for the calculation of interest in internal situations, compared to cross-border situations, constitutes discrimination.[28] Another example of a case, which constitutes discrimination, is *Mund & Fester v. Hatrex Internationaal Transport*, where a provision in German law on the conditions for

23. *See* Preamble and compare Explanatory report on the Convention on Mutual Administrative Assistance in Tax Matters, p. 50.
24. *See* Art. 8, 1 in relation to the interest of privacy, Art. 6, 1 in relation to the interest of efficiency, and Art. 1 of the Protocol No. 1 to the convention in relation to the creditor's right of peaceful enjoyment of his possessions.
25. *See* s. III.
26. *See* s. 29. ('Procedures should be available for speedy and effective enforcement of judgments, including money awards, costs, injunctions, and provisional measures.')
27. *See* Art. 12 of the Treaty establishing the EC, consolidated version of 24 Dec. 2002, which corresponds to the previous Art. 7 of the EC Treaty. The corresponding provision in the Treaty of Lisbon is Art. 16 d.
28. *See* the decision of the ECJ in *Lease Plan Luxembourg SA v. Belgian State* of 7 May 1998, where the ECJ concludes, in relation to Art. 9, 1 and 2, e of the Sixth VAT-Directive, that the application of more advantageous conditions for the calculation of interest in internal situations, compared to cross-border situations, constitutes discrimination. *See* paras 38 and 39 of the ruling.

granting a seizure order were differentiated depending on whether the forthcoming judgment was to be enforced in the Member State of jurisdiction or in another Member State.[29] The same principle as in the EC Treaty is also found in the European Convention on Human Rights.[30] The importance of this principle will be further demonstrated in the context of this work.[31]

1.1.1.1.3 Proportionality

A principle, which is closely related to the European Convention on Human Rights, and which is inherent to enforcement, is proportionality. It applies to the establishment of a balanced equilibrium between the competing rights, including the right of peaceful enjoyment of possessions, and interests of the parties, and means *i.a.* that enforcement measures should be efficient, but not unnecessarily infringe upon the debtor and third parties, *i.e.* disproportionate or vexatious measures should not be admitted.[32] The Moscow Resolution emphasizes that the enforcement procedures have to comply with the European Convention on Human Rights and it also emphasizes the principles of cost-effectiveness and proportionality when carrying out the enforcement process.[33] This Resolution was followed by the Council of Europe's recommendation on enforcement, which states that the attempts to carry out the enforcement process should be proportionate to the claim,

---

29. *See* the decision of the ECJ in *Mund & Fester v. Hatrex Internationaal Transport* of 10 Feb. 1994, which concerns the acquired rights by subrogation as the result of a transfer of a debt to claimed damages, caused by damaged goods. To ensure that this debt was recovered, Mund & Fester lodged an application for a seizure order to a German court against the assets in Germany of Hatrex Internationaal Transport, an international carrier, having its registered seat in the Netherlands. The ECJ ruled that Art. 7 of the EC Treaty, read in conjunction with Art. 220 of the Brussels convention, precludes a national provision of civil procedure which, in the case of a judgment to be enforced within the national territory, authorizes seizure only on the ground that it is probable that enforcement will otherwise be made impossible, or substantially more difficult, but, in the case of a judgment to be enforced in another Member State, authorizes seizure simply on the ground that enforcement is to take place abroad.
30. *See* Art. 14.
31. *See* 5.2.2.1, 6.1.3.1.1 and 6.2.1.3.
32. *See* Bernitz, Sverige och Europarätten, p. 41, who states that the principle of proportionality mainly has its background in German law and in legal usage on the application of the European Convention on Human Rights and in particular the first article of the First Additional Protocol to the convention, warranting each person the right to an undisturbed enjoyment of his property and ownership, and Leach, p. 163, who states that the concept of proportionality is also a fundamental constituent element of other Convention rights, such as the prohibition of discrimination (Art. 14), the right of peaceful enjoyment of possessions (Art. 1 of Protocol No. 1) and freedom of movement. *Also see* Att klaga till Europadomstolen, pp. 58-59, Danelius, pp. 49-50, Verbeke, Execution Officers as a Balance Wheel in Insolvency Cases, pp. 7-15, on the opposed rights of the debtor related to humanity and privacy and the creditor related to an efficient recovery and on the balancing of the conflict of these interests, and about the same opinion, EC Study JAI/02/03/2002, A, I, 4, on making more efficient the enforcement of judicial decisions within the EU, Transparency of a Debtors assets, Attachment of bank accounts, Provisional Enforcement and Protective Measures.
33. *See* 1.1.1.1.

the anticipated proceeds to be recovered as well as the interests of the defendant.[34] The ALI-UNIDROIT Principles of Transnational Civil Procedure also emphasize the principle of proportionality in relation to provisional and protective measures, and the principle of efficiency balanced against the principle of protecting the debtor related to immediate enforceability of judgments.[35] The principle of proportionality is also mentioned in the Insolvency regulation.[36]

1.1.1.1.4 Territoriality

The concept of public international law emerged in Europe in the period after the Peace of Westphalia in 1648 which concluded the Thirty Years War.[37] States are, based on their sovereignty in such law, even if they, like Monaco, San Marino and the Vatican State, have relatively few inhabitants and a small territorial surface, able to conclude conventions and to exercise their own jurisdiction in enforcement matters on their territory. The Lateran Treaty between the Holy See and Italy of 1929 refers, regarding the enforcement of judgments issued by the courts of the Vatican State, to the provisions in public international law. However, the Treaty also stipulates, that such judgments will have complete legal effectiveness in Italy concerning all civil effects.[38] The sovereignty of States, according to public international law related to their authority on the territory, has resulted in the

34. *See* III, 4.
35. *See* section 8 ('8.1 The court may grant provisional relief when necessary to prevent the ability to grant effective relief by the final judgment or to maintain or otherwise regulate the status quo. Provisional measures are governed by the principle of proportionality. 8.2 A court may order provisional relief without notice only upon urgent necessity and preponderance of conditions of fairness. The applicant must fully disclose facts and legal issues of which the court properly should be aware. A person against whom ex parte relief is directed must have the opportunity at the earliest practicable time to respond concerning the appropriateness of the relief. 8.3 An applicant for provisional relief should ordinarily be liable for compensation of a person against whom the relief is issued if the court thereafter determines that the relief should not have been granted. In appropriate circumstances, the court must require the applicant for provisional relief to post a bond or formally to assume a duty of compensation.'). *Also see* section 26 ('26.1 The final judgment of the first-instance court ordinarily should be immediately enforceable. 26.2 The first-instance court or the appellate court, on its own motion or motion of a party, may in the interest of justice stay enforcement of the judgment pending appeal. 26.3 Security may be required from the appellant as a condition of granting a stay or from the respondent as a condition of denying a stay.').
36. *See* Preamble (6).
37. *See* Akehurst, p. 9.
38. *See* Art. 23 of Trattato fra la Santa Sede e L'Italia, Inter Sanctam Sedem et Italiae Regnum, Acta Apostolicae Sedis – Commentarium Officiale, N. 6, Annus XXI – Vol. XXI, 7 Iunii 1929, which reads: 'Per l'esecuzione nel Regno delle sentenze emanate dai tribunali della Città del Vaticano si applicheranno le norme del diritto internazionale. Avranno invece senz'altro piena efficacia giuridica, anche a tutti gli effetti civili, in Italia le sentenze ed i provvedimenti emanati da autorità ecclesiastiche ed ufficialmente comunicati alle autorità civili, circa persone ecclesiastiche o religiose e concernenti materie spirituali o disciplinari.'

principle of territoriality in such law, which limits the use of the State powers to its own territory, in the absence of permission from another State.[39] The actual exercise of acts in civil execution law matters and acts in tax recovery law matters of one State in the territory of another State, such as the actual attachment of assets by regulated enforcement agents from one State in the territory of another State, without the permission of that State, would therefore constitute a violation against public international law. The convention on the law of treaties of 23 May 1969 (Vienna Convention on the Law of Treaties) stipulates that unless a different intention appears from the treaty or is otherwise established, a treaty is binding upon each party in respect of its entire territory.[40] The territorial scope in public international law is, however, sometimes modified and limited by specific provisions on territorial scope in EC law and in conventions.[41]

According to general principles in public international law, only the State where the assets of the debtor are located can authorize, normally only after applications for exequatur and enforcement have been brought in that State, any measures of authority based on an original foreign judgment or decision.[42] Consequently, this competence demands in the first place the existence of a valid foreign enforceable title in the territory of enforcement, which may be based on EC law, or a convention. If, in addition, the debtor holds assets on the territory, this

---

39. *See*, about more detailed comments on the State territory and its limits under public international law, Oppenheim, pp. 563-670. *Also see*, about the territorial authority of States, as an aspect of sovereignty in public international law, Oppenheim, pp. 382-390. He concludes, *i.b.*, p. 386, that a State is not allowed to exercise an act of administration or jurisdiction on foreign territory without permission. He also states, *i.b.*, p. 458, that: 'As all persons and things within the territory of a state fall under its territorial authority, each state normally has jurisdiction – legislative, curial, and executive – over them.' He continues, *i.b.*, p. 462, about jurisdiction over citizens abroad, that: 'International law does not prevent a state from exercising jurisdiction, within its own territory, over its nationals traveling or residing abroad, since they remain under its personal authority. Accordingly, it may legislate with regard to their conduct when abroad, levy taxes in respect of their assets or earnings abroad, or legislate in respect of their foreign property. In all such cases, however, the state's power to enforce its laws depends upon its national being in, or returning to, its territory or having there property against which they can be enforced.' *Also see* Akehurst, p. 109, who concludes that even if the word jurisdiction in public international law can have a lot of different meanings it sometimes means territory, but most often it refers to powers exercised by a State over persons, property, or events. He also points out, *i.b.*, that the term powers may refer to a number of situations, including the powers of physical interference exercised by the executive, such as the arrest of persons, seizure of property, *i.e.* the enforcement jurisdiction.
40. *See* Art. 29.
41. This is further developed in the context of 5.1.1 (EC law), 5.1.2 (Conventions related to the enforcement of contractual claims), 5.1.3 (Conventions related to the recovery of tax claims), and 5.1.4 (Conventions on insolvency).
42. *See* Kennett, The Enforcement of Judgments in Europe, p. 247, who concludes that: '... States have the exclusive right to undertake acts of sovereign authority such as forced execution within their own territory, and conversely any attempt to do this by a foreign State would be an infringement of that sovereignty.'

gives raise to a competence in the area of civil execution law, which could be exercised by the national regulated enforcement agents.[43]

However, there also exist exceptions when the recognition and enforcement of foreign titles of execution, a judgment, or a decision of sequestration, in civil law matters are possible outside the scope of conventions and when an application of the principle of territoriality is excluded.[44] The development of the principle of mutuality in the EU also means that the principle of territoriality will become of diminishing importance in the relations between the Member States of the EU.[45] The principle of territoriality in public international law will remain of interest between States when there exist no EC law or convention.

1.1.1.1.5 Universality

The principle of universality is applied in relation to some few provisions in the area of international enforcement and recovery proceedings, such as about automatic recognition and enforcement. This means that the principle, in the quality of its more extensive use as implemented in the area of international insolvency proceedings,[46] is not presently applicable in the area of international enforcement and recovery proceedings.

Consequently, this principle of universality, as developed and more extensively used in the international insolvency area, has not yet been frequently implemented in EC law, or in any conventions, in the area of enforcement and recovery

43. *See*, about some information on the territorial competence in civil execution law matters in certain European States, Krings, Synthèse, Le droit des saisies dans les États membres de l'Union européenne, Civil Procedure in Europe 1, Seizure and Overindebtness in the European Union, p. 26, and compare to: p. 159 (Belgium), p. 203 (Denmark), p. 289 (France), pp. 358-359 (Greece), pp. 453-456 (Luxemburg), and pp. 572-573 (Sweden). *Also see*, about this Swedish competence, Berglund, Svensk internationell exekutions- och obeståndsrätt, pp. 55-59, and for more extensive comments on the same issue, Bogdan, Om svensk exekutionsbehörighet, SvJT 1981, pp. 401-426.
44. *See* 4.2.1 for further details about some European States which are, subject to certain conditions, but without the support of any convention, prepared to recognize and enforce a foreign judgment. Also, they give effect to private rights acquired under the legislation of foreign States without such support, such as in the transnational judicial cooperation, based on Common Law, between the United Kingdom and the Commonwealth countries and some other States. *Also see i.b.* about international comity, Comity of nations, where some States, when asked to honour a judgment of a foreign country, give effect to rights acquired under the legislation of foreign States.
45. *See* 1.1.1.1.6.
46. *See* Council regulation 1346/2000/EC of 29 May 2000 on insolvency proceedings (Insolvency regulation), where bankruptcy orders are recognized and enforced in other States, Arts 16, 17 and 25, and end of Preamble (11), which mentions main insolvency proceedings with a universal scope, and where the trustee in bankruptcy is empowered to collect the assets of the debtor located abroad, Art. 18, 1. *Also see* Directive 2001/17/EC of the European Parliament and of the Council of 19 Mar. 2001 on the reorganization and winding-up of insurance undertakings, Preamble (10), and Directive 2001/24/EC of the European Parliament and of the Council of 4 Apr. 2001 on the reorganization and winding-up of credit institutions, Preamble (16), which mention both the principles of unity and universality.

proceedings. This may be explained by that the objectives and needs in insolvency and enforcement proceedings are not identical, even if one similar feature exists, the realization of the assets of the debtor in the interest of the creditor. Still other important objectives and structures of insolvency are different from enforcement and recovery. These different objectives in the insolvency area are *e.g.* the interest of all creditors, through the intermediary of a trustee in bankruptcy, appointed by a court, to stop the debtor to continue harmful, or illegal, business activities and by means of a litigation proceeding try to recapture assets to the bankruptcy estate. This has also resulted in different proceedings and requirements in the insolvency proceedings, as compared to the enforcement and recovery proceedings, such as in applications for decisions in court. Also, priority rights and distribution schemes may vary in comparison between these two areas.

It has been said that the aims of both the enforcement and insolvency proceedings to collect and satisfy the creditor's claims by access to the assets of the debtor should make it seem conceivable, at least in principle, to replace the territoriality paradigm with the principle of universality in the enforcement area.[47] However, for the mentioned reasons, such a suggested general shift of principles would be inappropriate, due to the different needs in the respective proceedings and their partially different objectives. A more general and extensive application of the principle of universality, as in the area of international insolvency, should therefore be excluded in the area of international enforcement and recovery proceedings, but a more limited application and development of this principle may be possible also in such proceedings.

1.1.1.1.6 Mutuality

The EC law principle of mutuality is applied at different, more or less developed levels, also in the area of mutual recognition and enforcement. This is based on the different objectives as evidenced in EC law. A further development of this principle could, no doubt, be foreseen to meet the objectives of the Tampere conclusions and of the Council's programme of measures for implementation of the principle of mutual recognition. This programme was reaffirmed in the Hague Programme of the European Council, which emphasizes the importance of facilitating civil law procedure across borders and the mutual recognition of decisions, and was a logical step of development following the Action plan of the Council and the Commission.[48]

The EC principle of mutuality, which is more, or less, evidently reflected in such law, has, in many legal areas, been developed into a more far-reaching and demanding principle of cooperation than the more traditional principle of mutuality, which has often previously been applied between the Member States of the EU in their cooperation based on conventions. More advanced expressions of an application of the EC principle of mutuality have been developed and implemented

47. *See* EC Study JAI/02/03/2002, A, I, 3.
48. *See* 1.1.1.1.

in many areas of EC law. Examples are: the Recovery directive,[49] the Regulation 805/2004/EC of the European Parliament and of the Council of 21 April 2004 creating a European Enforcement Order for uncontested claims (European Enforcement Order for uncontested claims),[50] the Regulation 1896/2006/EC of the European Parliament and of the Council of 12 December 2006 creating a European order for payment procedure (European Order for payment procedure),[51] the Regulation (EC) No. 861/2007 of the European Parliament and of the Council of 11 July establishing a European Small Claims Procedure (European Small Claims Procedure),[52] and in the criminal law area.[53]

This trend in EC law to strengthen mutuality is therefore of great importance for the further development of possible progress of improvements in many legal areas of the EU, but it also leads to that the principle of territoriality will become of a diminishing importance in the relations between the Member States of the Union.[54] A well developed system of mutual recognition of titles of execution, judgments and decisions, between the Member States of the Union, based on the EC principle of mutuality, requires that Member States should not oppose such titles from other Member States despite differences in substantial law and in procedural law, and consequently also demands a high degree of mutual trust and respect for the national laws of Member States.

Hence, the EC principle of mutuality has developed into a leading principle in many areas of EC law, not only evident in provisions on recognition, but also in other parts of such European law. Mutuality is, both in EC law and outside such

49. *See* Art. 8, 1 of the directive which stipulates that the instrument permitting enforcement of the claim shall be directly recognized and automatically treated as an instrument permitting enforcement of a claim of the Member State in which the requested authority is situated; compare Preamble (9) of the same directive.
50. *See* <http://eur-lex.europa.eu/LexUriServ/LexUriServ.do?uri=CELEX:32004R0805:EN:HTML>.
51. *See* <http://eur-lex.europa.eu/LexUriServ/LexUriServ.do?uri=OJ:L:2006:399:0001:01:EN:HTML>.
52. *See* <http://eur-lex.europa.eu/LexUriServ/LexUriServ.do?uri=OJ:L:2007:199:0001:01:EN:HTML>.
53. *See* Programme of measures to implement the principle of mutual recognition of decisions in criminal matters of 15 Jan. 2001. *Also see* Council Framework Decision 2005/214/JHA of 24 Feb. 2005 on the application of the principle of mutual recognition to financial penalties (Financial penalties Framework Decision), Council Framework Decision 2006/783/JHA of 6 Oct. 2006 on the application of the principle of mutual recognition to confiscation orders (Confiscation Framework Decision), and the Treaty of Lisbon, which in the area of judicial cooperation in criminal matters emphasizes the principle of mutual recognition of judgments and judicial decisions and includes in such cooperation the approximation of certain laws and regulations of the Member States, *see* Art. 61, 3.
54. *See* about the same opinion, EC Study JAI/02/03/2002, A, I, 3. *Also see* Léger, p. 47, who concludes, with references to examples of EC regulations that: 'Ces textes tendent au rapprochement des législations, expriment, conformément à l'objectif de création d'un espace judiciaire européen, un abandon certain du principe de la territorialité au profit d'un ordre juridique procédural élargi, et sont fondés sur le principe de la reconnaissance mutuelle des décisions judiciares.'

European law, including the areas of enforcement and recovery of claims, balanced against and limited by some other important, sometimes conflicting, or competing, interests, *e.g.* privacy and efficiency. These conflicting interests are often expressed as provisions relating to grounds of non-recognition, or grounds of refusal of enforcement.

1.1.1.1.7 Legal Integration in the Internal Common Market

The interest of increased legal integration in EC law to support a free competition towards the developments of an Internal Common Market is often based on the legislative basis and competence of the EC legislator of Articles 65 and 95 of the EC Treaty for a possible harmonization of national civil execution laws. This supports and adds strength to other interests in such European law, *e.g.* efficiency and mutuality.

1.1.1.2 History and Legal Developments

It is necessary, before entering into a treatment of the present legal solutions in the fields of the subject, to provide a European legal historical exposé to cover the legal developments from the period of Roman law up to our age. This exposé comments on some common legal and other influences, ideas, and events in society, which have called for changes, and their impact, illustrated by examples, on the developments of the subject into its present stage of solutions. This also includes comments on the development of the balance between the interests of the debtor and the interests of the creditor. Here the ambition has been to provide a treatment of the historical development in the perspective of the history of ideas and principles, rather than in detail to follow the historical development of a legal institute in different national laws of European States.[55] This has, however, not meant refraining from illustrative examples from various States taken from the European history.

Both the general historical development trends, in order to place the subject in its historical environment, and that of the subject of the study during the same periods, have been integrated and illustrated. A reason to treat historical information, as a knowledge forming part of the subject, is that it corresponds to a need of a sufficient background for an understanding of the developments resulting in the present legal solutions. Another reason is that such information is of value to the legislator in his work on future law reforms. As this information has not been told before at such a detailed level in relation to the subject it aims at giving both a more complete background and an overview.

The periods treated cover, in turn, Roman law, the Middle Ages, the period of 1500-1806, where 1806 is the year of the enactment of the French Code de

55. *See* Strömholm, Användning av utländskt material i juridiska monografier. Några anteckningar och förslag, SvJT 1971, p. 256, who also generally argues in favour of describing historical developments in the perspective of the history of ideas rather then in detail following the development of a legal institute in legislation and in legal usage.

Procédure Civile, and the period of 1807 to our age.[56] This latter period includes a brief comment on three development trends that could be identified after 1807 to our age. One shows to what extent historical common European influences have affected and developed national laws during the nineteenth and twentieth centuries in the procedural law area, including enforcement and insolvency laws. Two others are the development of conventions and EC law. This is followed by a study in more details about related EC law and conventions on contractual claims, tax claims, and insolvency. In some parts of the exposé facts and examples from the history of the Nordic States have been used to illustrate the historical development. The reason why the text about the Nordic States is more extensive, as compared to the texts related to other European States, is that relatively less has been published about the Nordic States in an international context. Because of the close relationship and interaction between legislative and organization issues some information on such issues are also included in the part of the legal historical exposé and of the more recent development and vice versa in the following part related to the history of enforcement and recovery agents.[57] Consequently, these parts have to some extent to be considered together.

There exist some differing features of cooperation in EC law and in conventions in comparison between the area related to the enforcement of contractual claims and the area related to the recovery of tax claims. As these two areas are systematically compared in the study it is motivated to treat these differing features, which, sometimes, make these two areas of cooperation comparable, or not. This is to some extent illustrated by references made to the Brussels I regulation and the Recovery directive, but the same kind of differences are normally also found in conventions in the same areas of law.

The initiatives of the EU, and other international organizations, have resulted in a lot of works in progress related to the areas of enforcement and recovery, and are likely to result in further future developments in this area. It is therefore necessary to direct an outlook towards some works in progress and some present development trends as a background to the discussion of possible future reforms.

1.1.1.3 Enforcement and Recovery Agents

This part concerns regulated European enforcement and recovery agents, who were, or are, authorized by the States to carry out the actual enforcement of private claims, including contractual claims, and the actual recovery of taxes. It is necessary, before entering into a treatment of the enforcement and recovery agents of today, to first provide some brief historical remarks in relation to the professionals, who were in charge of the civil law procedure for the execution of private

56. Compare Hesslén, Asset transparency – finding information – measures to make enforcement more effective, Globalization of law in an area of universal justice. 'Is the creation of a World Area of Justice a utopic vision?', pp. 23-27, who makes a distinction between the historical periods of ancient times, the Middle Ages, and the modern eras of 1500-1800 and 1800-1914.
57. *See* 3.1.

claims and for the procedure of collection and recovery of taxes. Remarks are made in relation to the period of the Roman Empire, and to the history of some differing modern enforcement agents in certain European States. The first States treated are Belgium, France and the Netherlands, then followed by the United Kingdom, Germany and the Nordic States.

A reason to make historical remarks on the developments of these professionals, and their activities, is to provide a sufficient background for an understanding of the still remaining differences in comparison between European modern enforcement agents, differences of essence which often go back to, at least, the period of the Middle Ages. Readers, who would like to have more extensive details on this subject, may consult the indicated literature under the respective European States. The reason why also here the text about the Nordic States is more extensive, as compared to the texts related to these other European States, is that relatively less has been published about the Nordic States in an international context.

A reason to treat these regulated agents of today, including their international bodies of cooperation, is that they have the task, in their independent work of enforcing judgments and recovering claims in enforcement procedures to establish a justified balance between the conflicting interests of the debtor and the creditor, *e.g.* between privacy and efficiency. This is based on their exercise of public powers when they apply provisions in EC law, the European Convention on Human Rights,[58] other conventions and national laws.

Consequently, these agents form part of the subject of this treatment for constituting the meeting place for the creditor and the debtor, in various places in the Member States of the EU, where the agents typically act upon an application for the actual enforcement of a claim from the creditor. Another reason to treat enforcement and recovery agents of today is the close relationship and interaction, also in practice, between legislative and organization issues which motivates information on enforcement agents for the benefit of the creditor and the debtor to facilitate the understanding of the sometimes differing national European functions of the enforcement agents in the cross-border perspective. Yet another reason to treat enforcement agents is the interest of making progress by a harmonization of the conditions of the profession of enforcement agents in the European context, for the benefit of the creditors and debtors, which demands an increased knowledge and motivates an extensive treatment related to these professionals.

The non-equal national standards have an impact on the level of quality of the work of the enforcement agents. If it would become possible to agree on common European standards for educational and training requirements for the right to exercise the profession of an enforcement agent it would also give raise to the

58. *See* 4.3, where examples, with further references, are given about provisions in the European Convention on Human Rights, which also have an impact on the work of enforcement agents, *e.g.* the execution of a court judgment within a reasonable time. *Also see* section III of the Council of Europe's recommendation on enforcement, which takes several principles derived from the European Convention on Human Rights into account, about the relevant interests and their balance in the enforcement procedures.

issue if it would become possible for an enforcement agent, who would meet such possible educational and training standards, to be recognized as being able to exercise his profession in other European States. The conditions, which have to be fulfilled, and some arguments in relation to these possible issues of future development therefore merit a treatment. Also, the idea of the possible creation of a Euroex, a European cooperation body between States in the civil execution law area, merits a treatment.

Presently, the work of enforcement of foreign contractual claims is dealt with by a variety of national regulated professional enforcement agents, with the task to enforce claims in the civil law area. This work may also relate to the granted applications for the recognition and enforcement of foreign titles of execution, which have been filed by private creditors to courts or to enforcement agents, which have been designated to perform the national functions of competent authorities based on provisions in EC law and conventions.

The work of actual recovery of tax claims, based on international cooperation of mutual assistance, is dealt with by officials in various national public administrations. The work of forwarding and receiving matters of such international cooperation between them is mainly organized through the national functions of competent authorities in these administrations. A EC committee, the Recovery Committee, also deals with submitted matters of application related to the Recovery directive. Seminars related to the cooperation under the Recovery directive have, on several occasions, been arranged for officials of the competent authorities of Member States by the Commission together with Member States under the Fiscalis programme, in order to promote an efficient, effective and extensive cooperation between the Member States.[59]

1.1.1.4 Public International Law

This part treats some issues related to principles of public international law concerning the enforcement and the recovery of claims, which are of particular importance to the private and public creditors, the debtor and the enforcement agents. EC law and conventions related to the enforcement of contractual claims

59. *See* Decision 2235/2002/EC of the European Parliament and of the Council of 3 Dec. 2002 adopting a Community programme to improve the operation of taxation systems in the internal market (Fiscalis programme 2003-2007). The programme is intended to promote an efficient, effective and extensive cooperation between Member States and includes *i.a.* exchanges of officials and seminars in the tax area, but has also financed exchanges and seminars in the area of administrative cooperation related to the Recovery directive. The Fiscalis programme has helped finance three seminars on mutual assistance for recovery related to the Recovery directive during 2003-2005, *see* the Report from the Commission to the Council and the European Parliament on the use of the provisions on mutual assistance for the recovery of claims relating to certain levies, duties, taxes and other measures, COM (2006) 43 final, p. 10. A new Fiscalis programme has been established for 2008-2013, *see* Decision No. 1482/2007/EC of the European Parliament and of the Council of 11 Dec. 2007 establishing a Community programme to improve the operation of taxation systems in the internal market (Fiscalis 2013) and repealing Decision No. 2235/2002/EC.

and the recovery of tax claims will not be treated here. The issues treated are parts of public international law of importance both in the national and international context in relation to the civil enforcement and tax recovery law areas. They relate to a foreign State's immunity against civil execution, the enforcement of civil and public claims outside the scope of conventions and the applicability of the European Convention on Human Rights.

Three conventions are of predominant importance in relation to a foreign State's immunity against the civil execution through enforcement measures. These conventions, which are treated, are the European State immunity convention, the Vienna convention on diplomatic relations and the Vienna convention on consular relations.

Provisions in a convention on the recognition and the enforceability of foreign titles of execution, judgments and decisions, are in principle required in most European States to create an international treaty obligation for the enforcement of such titles in the cross-border context. The establishment of such a treaty obligation constitutes public international law and prevails over the otherwise applicable principle of territoriality in such law. This has the effect of making such foreign titles enforceable by means of forced execution in another State.[60] However, some European States are, subject to certain conditions, but without the support of any convention, prepared to recognize and enforce a foreign judgment, *i.e.* outside the scope of conventions. This is penetrated both in relation to civil law claims and public law claims.

The European Convention on Human Rights is important for several parts of this work because of the many rights guaranteed by this convention. The main relevant rights are the debtor's right of privacy and the creditor's right to enforce a claim efficiently,[61] the right of non-discrimination of the creditor and the debtor on grounds of nationality,[62] and the creditor's right of peaceful enjoyment of his possessions, *e.g.* his claim in the quality of a title of execution.[63] The convention treats the interests of the creditor and the debtor in a balanced, proportionate way.[64] A prohibition of imprisonment for debts related only to the inability to fulfil a contractual obligation has also been entered into the same convention,[65] and, as a result, it has strengthened the interest of the debtor about integrity. The Council of

60. *See* 1.1.1.1.4 for further comments on the principle of sovereignty in public international law and about the principle of territoriality in such law and its diminishing importance in relation to some parts of EC law and conventions.
61. *See* 1.1.1.1.1.
62. *See* 1.1.1.1.2.
63. *See* 1.1.1.1.1. *Also see*, about further comments on the right of peaceful enjoyment of one's possessions, Danelius, pp. 453-484, and Leach, pp. 353-363. *Also see*, Leroy, L'efficacité des procédures judiciaires au sein de l'union Européenne et les garanties des droits de la defense, Transparence patrimoniale, L'efficacité de la justice civile en Europe, pp. 307-309, and Att klaga till Europadomstolen, pp. 211-220.
64. *See* 1.1.1.1 and 1.1.1.1.3.
65. *See* Art. 1 of Protocol No. 4 to the Convention.

Europe's recommendation on enforcement explicitly refers to the European Convention on Human Rights.

1.1.1.5 Scope of Application of EC Law and Conventions

This part relates to the scope of application of EC law and conventions of interest for the enforcement of contractual claims and the recovery of tax claims. Issues treated are the scope of application of EC law and conventions, including their territorial scope and their scope of claims, as well as the relationship between such European law and conventions. The definition and limitation to persons, creditors, debtors and co-debtors, affected by claims, who fall under, or outside, the scope of application of such EC law and conventions, are, as well, treated. A specific category of debtors treated, in this context, are individuals affected by disqualification orders against them for carrying on a non-serious, or illegal, business activity, *e.g.* by not honouring contractual obligations and paying taxes.

The territorial scope in EC law and in conventions in the enforcement, recovery and insolvency areas is of interest to the creditor, the debtor, and the enforcement agents. It determines the limits of territories, to be included or excluded, where assets are located, and subsequently may, or may not, be made available and realized for the purposes of enforcement, recovery and insolvency. This explains why attention is paid to the territorial scope in EC law and in multilateral conventions and their sometimes differing territorial scopes. Public international law constitutes the logic point of departure on how to define the scope of territories of States.[66] To the extent that issues of territorial scope are not treated and modified by specific provisions on territorial scope in EC law, *e.g.* by Article 299 of the EC Treaty, or in conventions, it is thus governed by public international law.

The territorial scope in public international law is, however, sometimes modified by specific provisions of territorial scope in conventions. So may States extend the application of the European Convention on Human rights and the right of individual petition to any of their territories for whose internal relations they are responsible.[67] This latter situation is also of a particular interest for a creditor when such European law gives him the possibility instead to apply a convention with such a greater scope.[68] The relevant provisions in EC law and in conventions related to the enforcement of contractual claims, the recovery of tax claims, and insolvency are treated.

The scope of contractual claims is presently more complete in comparison to tax claims in EC law and conventions. An additional dimension to be aware of,

66. *See* 1.1.1.1.4 about further comments on territoriality in public international law in relation to the enforcement of claims.
67. *See* Art. 56, 1. To do so, the Secretary-General of the Council of Europe must be notified, either on ratification of the Convention or at any later time. The Convention shall then be applied in such territories, according to Art. 56, 3, with due regard to local requirements.
68. This is further developed in the context of 5.3.1.1.1 about the Brussels I regulation and conventions related to contractual claims and 5.3.1.2.1 about the Recovery directive and conventions related to the recovery of tax claims.

which may change the scenario, is that a claim, which once was classified as of a civil nature by the national legislator, after a law reform instead has become reclassified by this legislator to be of a public law nature, and vice versa. Such a reclassified claim may either fall within the scope of claims under another part of EC law, respectively conventions, than before this change, or it will not fall under any such European law or conventions.

The scope of claims consists in the categories of principal claims, ancillary claims, sanctions, and enforceable costs, in their quality of national titles of execution, judgments, other titles of execution and decisions, in EC law or in conventions. The scope is of interest to both the creditors and the debtors because it determines if a national claim is enforceable, or not. Also, the differences, in comparison between the scope of claims, in EC law and in conventions, is of interest for a creditor to the extent that such European law gives him the possibility instead to apply conventions of a greater scope of claims. Some comments will also be made on the provisions of repayment of the claims. If a private, or a public, claim would fall outside the scope of EC law and conventions, the remaining chances for a creditor, who would like to have his claim enforced in another State, are governed and limited in accordance with principles in public international law.[69]

The relationship between different parts of EC law, and their relationship to conventions, their inter or counter play, are of importance for both creditors and debtors in matters of enforcement and recovery. Creditors have to identify and are obliged to support their applications for enforcement and recovery of claims in another State by referring to the correct parts of EC law, or to conventions. If they fail to fulfil this obligation their applications risk to be rejected by the competent court or enforcement agent of the requested State.

Also, a public State creditor has to be aware of the possibilities in such European law to instead chose to apply conventions, which may provide more advantageous solutions, *e.g.* in relation to the territorial scope, the scope of claims, and debt thresholds, *i.e.* when no request for mutual assistance related to the recovery of a tax claim may be made if the total amount of the claim is less than that of a specific amount. Furthermore a debtor has to know if there exists a legal basis for applications of enforcement according to EC law, or conventions. If no such legal basis exists there may nevertheless exist some possibilities of making such applications according to principles of public international law.[70]

There exist more, or less, detailed and developed provisions in different parts of EC law about their inter relationship and their relationship to conventions, their inter or counter play, related to their scope of application and entry into

---

69. *See* 1.1.1.1.4 about the principles of sovereignty and territoriality in public international law. *Also* compare 4.2.2 about the possibilities, restrictions and conditions for the enforcement outside the scope of conventions.
70. *See* 4.2 about cross-border enforcement and recovery outside the scope of international conventions and about Comity of nations.

force. Such provisions often determine what EC law should replace, complete, or be of alternative use, compared to other parts of such European law, or compared to a convention, when their scope of application are identical, subject to that this European law or convention have entered into force in relation to the relevant States. These provisions in EC law and conventions related to the enforcement of contractual claims, the recovery of tax claims, and the service of judicial documents, are treated.

At a first glance, it may seem peculiar to pay any attention at all to the definition and limitation to persons, creditors, debtors and co-debtors, affected by claims, which appear to be self-explanatory. Any creditor, who is in the possession of a private contractual claim, *e.g.* an enterprise, or an individual, or the State, should, at the enforcement of such a claim based on EC law and conventions, be treated equally. However, the actual enforcement of contractual claims against the State as a debtor was, at least during the end of the twentieth century, not treated equally, in comparison to private debtors, in some national laws. This was due to the national immunity of the State and its organs, or to other national limitations, in some States in relation to the civil execution within the own legal system.[71] Consequently, there, in relation to the State and its organs, a creditor, a seller of goods or services would need to demand payments in advance, or to demand a security for payments. When no executive measures could be taken against the State, and when the State refused to fulfil its obligations of paying an adjudged debt according to a judgment, for any reasons, this would possibly mean a violation of the European Convention on Human Rights, as happened according to the rulings of the ECHR in the cases of *Burdov v. Russia*, *Timofeyev v. Russia* and *Vasiliopoulou v. Greece*.[72]

Debtors relate to the persons, or legal entities, against whom a payment liability has been established according to law by courts, or by authorities. The reasons here to treat the definition of creditors, debtors, and co-debtors are that there exist some differences in comparison between the national levels and the sometimes more restrictive international level, which apply in the context of cross-border enforcement of a foreign claim in another State. The consequences are that sometimes the creditors' claims are treated less efficient and the debtors and co-debtors are protected to a greater extent in the cross-border context compared to the corresponding situations at the national level.

---

71. *See* Kerameus, Enforcement Against the State and State Entities in a Comparative Perspective, Recht in Europa, Festschrift für Hilmar Fenge, pp. 76-79, who mentions some States, which applied such immunity, *e.g.* the former socialist European States, Greece, Italy and Spain. He also reports about the lengthy payment procedures, which were applied when the State was involved in some European States, such as in England and in France. *Also see*, for further information about the domestic immunity of the State and public entities against enforcement, Kerameus, International encyclopedia of comparative law, volume XVI, Civil procedure, chapter 10, Enforcement proceedings, pp. 32-36.
72. *See* 4.3.1, where more information about these cases is available.

1.1.1.6 Procedures in EC Law and Conventions

This part concerns issues related to the procedures in EC law and conventions of interest for the enforcement of contractual claims and the recovery of tax claims.[73] The issues treated are the recognition and enforceability, the referral provisions to national laws, and access to information for enforcement purposes in the international context. In addition, international insolvency, the Insolvency regulation, some bankruptcy conventions, and the transnational cooperation in insolvency management, are treated.

A lot of different requirements exist in EC law and in conventions for the recognition and the declaration of enforceability of foreign titles of execution, judgments and decisions in the legal areas of contractual claims and tax claims. Besides the requirement that a foreign title of execution should fall under their respective scope of application, territorial scope, scope of claims, and scope in time,[74] there also exist additional requirements and limitations of different kinds and frequency to be aware of, often, but not always, found in the context of the establishment of a decision of recognition and of a declaration of enforceability. The reason here to focus on these additional requirements, which give raise to both possibilities and restrictions, is the important role they ultimately play in determining the limits between the enforceability and the non-enforceability of claims in European law and conventions. Consequently, an early analysis related to these provisions becomes of importance to both the creditors and the debtors; it helps them to assess the possibility of success, or risk of failure, that may be the result of an attempt to enforce and recover a claim in the cross-border context.

Provisions in EC law and conventions regarding recognition and enforceability, and the thereto related grounds of non-recognition and grounds of refusal of enforcement or recovery, which may result in that a foreign title of execution is decided to be non-recognizable, or non-enforceable, will be treated. Comments are also included on some other provisions that constitute obstacles to recovery. The extensive and detailed provisions related to the requirements for filing of correct applications for a declaration of recognition and enforceability related to contractual claims, or for making correct requests for the mutual assistance related to tax

73. This part will include parts from the author's following contributions: 'The recovery of a contested claim, costs and repayments and priority rights' for the Fiscalis seminar 2002 for the mutual assistance of recovery of tax claims in Viterbo, Italy, 29-31 May 2002, 'Costs, repayment and priority rights' for the Fiscalis seminar 2003 for mutual assistance for recovery of tax claims in the area of direct taxation, Alicante, Spain, 10-12 Dec. 2003, 'The enforcement of the judgment, Innovative practices as regards the enforcement of judgments, the Swedish example "at the Conference jointly organised by the European Commission and the Council of Europe" Towards an ideal trial: A few examples of the most successful judicial proceedings in Europe', Brussels, 18-20 Nov. 2004 and 'The abolishment of exequatur proceedings in court and a more efficient cross-border enforcement of court decisions of freezing orders related to the Brussels I regulation', La Chambre Nationale des Avoués près les Courts d'Appel, le 30ème anniveraire de l'entreé en vigueur en 1975 du Nouveau Code de Procédure Civile, Paris le 23 juin 2005.

74. *See* 5.1-3.

claims, under the proceedings of this EC law and conventions, are only commented on to some limited extent. The reason is that, even if these provisions are of a practical importance, they only reflect issues of importance that are treated in other parts of this work. These provisions may relate *e.g.* to an application for a declaration of enforceability according to the Brussels I regulation, or to the filing of an application for the enforcement of a claim under the European Enforcement Order for uncontested claims, or to an application for the request of mutual assistance between the Member States in accordance with the Recovery directive. Readers are here instead referred to consult the relevant parts of this European law and conventions for further details.

The provisions on periods of limitation in law fixes the time within which the private creditor, or the public creditor, must take judicial action to enforce their claims or else be thereafter barred from enforcing them through measures of enforcement or recovery. Sometimes the terms prescription and time-limits are also used as alternative terms to the term periods of limitation when they appear in national law and in conventions. National law provides different kinds and length of periods of limitation. The provisions in EC law and conventions, which impose restrictions in terms of periods of limitation are also treated here because they determine the limits of when a claim ceases to exist and consequently no longer will be subject to measures of enforcement or recovery. Also treated are the possibilities and restrictions of enforcement and recovery of a contested claim, appeals, costs and repayment.

The provisions about appeal appear here because of the important role they play for the legal protection of rights for both private and public creditors and debtors. The right to an effective access to the courts when the enforcement measures taken call for a prompt examination of an applicant's appeal, *e.g.* in relation to a stay of execution, in a fair hearing in a contradictory court proceeding, is also guaranteed by the European Convention on Human Rights.[75] At least three main categories of costs of enforcement, or recovery, of claims related to the cross-border level can be identified. Costs of different kinds related to the proceedings, which have resulted in the establishment of the principal claim, are sometimes included in the basic judgment, or decision in the civil law area, or in the tax area. They may also be established in separate judgments, or decisions, but nevertheless relate to the main claim. These costs may be enforced and recovered in a cross-border context to the extent they fall under the scope of claims of EC law and conventions.[76] Costs may also relate to the proceedings of application initiated by the creditor in order to obtain a formal decision on the recognition and enforcement or recovery based on such law and conventions. Costs may, in addition, relate to the actual proceedings of enforcement, or recovery, of the foreign claim initiated by the creditor in another State. These two latter categories of costs are dealt with.

The provisions in EC law and in multilateral conventions, which treat the relationship to national laws, the referral provisions, related to enforcement and

75. *See* 4.3.1-2.
76. *See* 5.2.

recovery measures, precautionary measures, and priority rights regarding contractual claims and tax claims are treated. These provisions illustrate how and to what extent they interplay with national laws and its impact on creditors and debtors.

Priority rights, which already existed for fiscal claims in the procedure of enforcement under Roman law,[77] may relate to both the attachment of claims and to insolvency proceedings, *e.g.* in bankruptcy. An attachment based on certain claims may, or may not, establish a priority right of payment in favour of creditors in the assets of the debtor at the national level. EC law, and multilateral conventions, do not normally, with some few exceptions in the EC area of social security,[78] explicitly provide for the possibility to grant the same level of priority rights to foreign claims as equivalent to national corresponding ones at the domestic collection, enforcement, or recovery, of claims. The different treatment, or non-treatment, of priority rights regarding contractual claims respectively tax claims in EC law and in multilateral conventions will be treated in the context of the attachment of claims.

Access to information for enforcement and recovery purposes in the cross-border context, when there exist enforceable titles of execution, related to contractual claims respectively tax claims, is treated. This is because of the great importance of such access to increase the efficiency in that context.

Briefly treated are the Insolvency regulation, bankruptcy conventions, including some of their provisions on procedures and priority rights, and the transnational judicial cooperation in insolvency management. The intention behind is only to indicate and illustrate some possible effects and consequences closely related to the legal areas of enforcement and recovery, and the fact that a creditor's enforcement, or his recovery, has become, or may later become, part of an insolvency procedure with cross-border effects through a legal action triggered by other creditors. Another reason is that a creditor sometimes has, before he initiates any legal action in a matter of cross-border recovery, or enforcement, of a claim aiming at the realization of the assets of the debtors and to achieve payments for his claims, reflect upon and compare this to the alternative of taking possible legal action on his own in an insolvency procedure with cross-border effects, including its possible advantages and disadvantages. This all-over prognosis and evaluation of the creditor, when he has to make a decision between these two possible alternatives of legal actions, including their advantages and disadvantages, may be more or less complex depending on the circumstances in a specific matter. The following comparison only treats some advantages and disadvantages.

---

77. *See* 2.1.2.
78. Exceptions exist in the area of reciprocal collection of social security charges within the EC, both Art. 92, 1 of the Old social security regulation and Art. 84, 3 of the New social security regulation stipulate that the collection of the requested State shall be governed by its privileges applicable for the collection of corresponding claims. Art. 84, 3 of this new regulation clearly states that: 'Claims of an institution of one Member State shall in enforcement, bankruptcy or settlement proceedings in another Member State enjoy the same privileges as in the legislation of the latter Member State accords to claims of the same kind.'

Typical advantages, compared with an action of enforcement, or recovery, of a claim, may be that the creditor could, through the intermediary of a trustee in insolvency, appointed by a court, stop the debtor from continuing harmful, or illegal, business activities. Another advantage may, of course, be the possibility to initiate litigation proceedings, through this trustee, to recapture assets to the insolvency estate, with the result that the creditor's possible economic share of a distribution out of the realized assets from the insolvency estate, based on differing national laws applicable *i.a.* in relation to costs and priority rights, be satisfactory to him. Yet another advantage may be that the national wage earner's guarantee for unpaid wages to employees in the business of an insolvent employer may apply and help to finance any possible outstanding wage debts in a business.

The Council Directive (80/987/EEC) of 20 October 1980 on the approximation of the laws of the Member States relating to the protection of employees in the event of the insolvency of their employer, as last amended through Directive 2002/74/EC of the European Parliament and of the Council of 23 September 2002, also means that the Member States have to fulfil their obligations for the protection of employees in the event of the employer's insolvency. There exist several rulings of the ECJ, which deal with the obligations of Member States under this directive, but they are not treated here.

Besides, outside the scope of European law and conventions in insolvency matters, there may also exist opportunities to act for a trustee in bankruptcy, in the interest of all creditors, based on his appointment as a legal representative for the bankruptcy estate in a decision of a court in a Member State of the EU, in some other jurisdictions of European States and territories and in some non-European overseas countries and territories, which not are covered by such European law and conventions.[79] This may, however, only be when these jurisdictions are prepared to cooperate with this trustee as a legal representative of the bankruptcy estate, either when he, in a litigation proceeding, is able to act against civil law transactions made by this estate, which constitute violations against civil laws, or criminal laws, in these jurisdictions, or when he is recognized in States and territories based on the transnational judicial cooperation in insolvency management.[80] If the trustee is successful in this context he may be able to bring back assets from abroad to the bankruptcy estate.

A disadvantage of an insolvency, compared to an action of enforcement, or recovery, of a claim, may, of course, be that a creditor will have to compete with several other creditors and risk to receive less, or nothing, in satisfaction to his

79. An example of a European State, which is not a Member State of the EU, is Switzerland. Consequently Switzerland is not covered by the Insolvency regulation, but Switzerland provides, nevertheless, a possibility to assist foreign bankruptcy proceedings, *see* 6.4.3 for further details. *Also see* 5.1.1 about examples of European territories, which not are covered by the Insolvency regulation, *e.g.* the Channel Islands and the Isle of Man, and *i.b.* about some non-European overseas countries and territories, *e.g.* Aruba, Netherlands Antilles and Cayman Islands.

80. *See* 6.4.3 for further information about this cooperation, which is of interest in relation to Switzerland, but most frequently is practised in the Commonwealth States and territories.

claim when the realized assets from the insolvency estate are distributed according to the rules of priority rights among all the creditors.

1.1.1.7 Harmonization of Civil Execution Laws

The needs and interests of a harmonization of certain chosen differing national measures of civil execution, the provisions for the attachment of the earnings of the debtor, the provisions of time-limits in enforcement procedures, and the provisions on access to information for enforcement purposes will be treated. A reason is that they are the most important national measures for the enforcement of contractual claims and for the recovery of tax claims, being of an equal importance in these two legal areas. Another reason is that the result of the interplay between EC law, conventions and measures of civil execution in national laws, and provisions on access to information for enforcement purposes, determines the total level of efficiency in the cross-border context.[81] Therefore, such differing measures constitute obstacles for the total efficiency of the interplay between them and EC law and conventions, in matters having cross-border implications, to the extent they, in comparison between the Member States of the EU, result in less efficiency.

Also treated are some international principles and recommendations accepted by States for a possible harmonization of national civil execution laws, not only in this cross-border context, but also in the national law context of strengthening efficiency. Consequently, differing national laws of civil execution, and provisions on access to information for enforcement purposes, may risk that the development in the cross-border context becomes impaired and therefore it exists a need to harmonize them. Some examples are given of national enforcement procedures and laws that possibly may be harmonized. Also, the idea of a World Code of Enforcement is treated.

The value of an enforceable title of execution against a debtor may, both in the private law area and in the public law area, in practice be diminished to the extent that sufficient information for enforcement and recovery purposes is not made available to the enforcement organs for the benefit of a creditor at the moment of enforcement and recovery, based on his title of execution, in the assets of the debtor. States, which do not provide a sufficiently high level of access to information for enforcement purposes of judgments to their enforcement organs, correspondingly diminish efficiency of justice, the actual value of judgments rendered by their own courts. This cause the value of the judgment to the private creditor to be reduced, while the debtor despite the judgment could actually still continue undisturbed to dispose over and move his assets. Consequently, there exists a need for efficient access to information, which can be used for enforcement and recovery purposes for private and public claims in order to realize the assets of the debtors and achieve payments for the claims of the creditors. An efficient access

81. *See* 1.1 for more information about the motivation and need for the treatment of the harmonization of civil execution laws.

to information also supports a higher degree of respect for court judgments and decisions by authorities in society, *i.e.* efficiency of justice.

A well developed system of access to information means that the enforcement and recovery of claims, in the quality of ordinary and provisional titles of execution, become more efficient for the benefit of the creditors. Such a system has, however, also to take into account certain limitations in relation to the interests of the debtor, such as data protection, as evident in the Directive 46/95/EC of the European Parliament and of the Council of 24 October 1995 on the protection of individuals with regard to the processing of personal data and on the free movement of such data (Data protection Directive), which establishes a regulatory framework to ensure both a high level of protection for the privacy of individuals in all Member States and the free movement of personal data within the EU.[82]

Another limitation is that information about the assets of the debtor, which is derived and obtained from a criminal procedure in which the debtor has been forced to self-incriminate himself by leaving this information before or during this criminal procedure may not, according to the legal usage of the ECHR,[83] be used in a civil execution law procedure by regulated enforcement agents. Separate considerations will in the following be given access to information for national enforcement and recovery purposes in the civil enforcement law area and in the public law area before and after the establishment of a title of execution, different national techniques of access to information and the needs of improvements.[84]

1.1.1.8 Examples of the Subject

In order to give the readers some guiding ideas about what to expect in relation to certain main parts of the subject, here are two examples related to the cross-border context.

1.1.1.8.1 Cross-Border Enforcement of Contractual Claims

When private creditors, legal entities, *e.g.* an ordinary company or a European company, a *Societas Europaea*,[85] or an individual, obtain a title of execution from

82. *See*, for further comments in relation to this directive, Prevention of organized crime: The registration of legal persons and their directors and the international exchange of information, a comparative legal study in the EU Member States on the possibilities for the improvement of the international exchange of information on legal persons with the purpose of (transnational) organized crime prevention, Final Report of the Follow-Up Study, T.M.C Asser Instituut Commissioned by the Netherlands Ministry of Justice, Dec. 2006, p. 198.
83. *See* 4.3.1, where this is further commented on *i.a.* in the context of the ruling of the ECHR in the case of *Funke v. France*.
84. This part also includes parts from the authors contribution 'Access to information for enforcement and recovery purposes and international cooperation' of 28 May 2003, annexed to the Swedish national report on European transparency of assets to EC Study JAI/02/03/2002.
85. *See* Council regulation 2157/2001/EC of 8 Oct. 2001 on the Statute for a European company (SE).

a court based on a contractual claim, they arrive at the stage of enforcement of the claim. If the debtor then lacks assets for the payment of the claim in the State of origin, *e.g.* France, but possesses assets in other European States, *e.g.* Germany or Sweden, the creditor *i.a.* initially has to find out what is the scope of application of EC law and conventions and what additional requirements and conditions in such European law, or in conventions, have to be fulfilled for the recognition and enforcement of the court judgment in another European State, before he can apply for the actual enforcement of his claim at the enforcement agencies in that other State. Besides, a private creditor has sometimes also to initially consider the conditions and limitations on the enforcement of claims in public international law, and the possibility, or restriction, related to access to information for enforcement and recovery purposes.

1.1.1.8.2 Cross-Border Recovery of Tax Claims

When the public creditor, the tax administration, concludes that the debtor lacks assets for the payment of a tax claim, based on a recoverable tax decision of the tax administration or of a court, in the State of origin, *e.g.* France, but possesses assets in another European State, such as Germany, France may apply for the recovery of the tax claim in Germany. The French tax administration may *e.g.* apply for the recovery of French income and value added taxes (VATs) related to an ordinary French company or to a European company, a *Societas Europaea*, which has a relevant French connection under EC law, in the assets of these companies in Germany, or related to a co-debtor, *e.g.* a managing director of these companies in his assets located in Germany. The public creditor's chances of a successful recovery of national tax claims in other European States are governed by the requirements and conditions in EC law and in conventions in the tax recovery area, and outside that context by public international law.

1.2 DELIMITATIONS

An important reason to delimit the subject only to certain claims, contractual claims and tax claims, has been that they, in economical terms, both in the international, European[86] and national context, constitute the two most important

86. *See* statistics for the years 1996-1999 from the Swedish national tax board on the enforcement of private and public claims with a foreign connection relating to the activities of the enforcement authorities, which make it evident, from a Swedish perspective, that most money in the cross-border recovery context related to public claims is derived from tax claims. These statistics also confirm, from the same perspective, the large number of cases relating to contractual claims under this period dealt with under the relevant multilateral conventions related to private claims in exequatur proceedings by the exclusive competent Swedish court in such proceedings, the court of appeal resident in Stockholm (Svea hovrätt), and thus indirectly the possible impact on the Swedish enforcement authorities. *Also see* Kennett, The Enforcement of Judgments in Europe, pp. 21-22, where she reports that in 1997 about 700 judgments of other contracting

groups of claims. They have substantial effects on both individuals and legal entities in their capacity of creditors and debtors. Another reason to delimit the subject only to the enforcement and recovery of these claims, and mainly to refer to EC law and some multilateral conventions valid in the EC, is the fact that certain parts of such European law and conventions,[87] but not all of them, compared with each other,[88] clearly reflect conflicting or competing interests, *e.g.* the debtor's interest of privacy *versus* the creditor's interest of efficiency in the enforcement

States had been granted an order for exequatur by the Tribunal de Paris, and about 600 such judgments had been granted an order for exequatur in the Netherlands, while in England and Wales 99 applications for registration of judgments under the Brussels and Lugano Conventions were made in 1996. *Also* compare EC Study JLS/C4/2005/03, Report on the Application of Regulation Brussels I in the Member States, p. 16, where it is concluded that the number of cases related to the application of the Brussels I regulation is relatively small, often less than 1%, or even less than 0, 1%, of all civil cases in the Member States. *See i.b.*, pp. 16-24, for further details about statistics related to specific Member States. *Also see* Grau Ruiz, pp. 241-243, on statistics for the years 1995-2001 on the recovery of Spanish tax claims abroad and on the recovery of foreign tax claims in Spain. It is a generally accepted knowledge that the facts, here represented by the Swedish and Spanish statistics, also are of a similar importance in other European States. Statistics for the years 2003-2004 from the Commission of the ECs on the use of the provisions on mutual assistance in the Recovery directive between the Member States of the EU for the recovery of tax claims show that the number of recovery requests received by all Member States amounted in 2003 to 2 797 and in 2004 to 3 735. Total sums recovered by these Member States amounted in 2003 to EUR 5 050 090.55 and in 2004 to EUR 13 857 040.55. Statistics do not necessarily reflect the overall impact of mutual assistance for recovery that Member States afford each other because they do not include the results of any mutual assistance given on the basis of other, non-Community agreements, such as bilateral and multilateral conventions. Figures do not take account of the amounts which debtors pay directly to the applicant State, following notification of a debt or initiation of a recovery procedure by the requested State. Also, figures available concern only amounts already collected by the requested State and fail to take account of possible debt settlement plans agreed or achieved by recovery procedures that are often slow or still under way, *see* Report from the Commission to the Council and the European Parliament on the use of the provisions on mutual assistance for the recovery of claims relating to certain levies, duties, taxes and other measures, COM (2006) 43 final, pp. 6-7 and 9. Statistics for the year 2005 from the Swedish Tax Agency, Belopp i allmänna mål avseende utlandsindrivningen, studie från skatteverket (Study from the Swedish Tax Agency about the amount related to public claims recovered abroad), show that the total sum recovered abroad from all other States by the Swedish enforcement authorities related to public claims amounted to 106 978 874 Swedish crowns (SEK), which equals, at an exchange rate of SEK 9, 15 for EUR 1, approximately EUR 11 691 679.

87. *See* 1.1.1.1.1.

88. *See*, about the Convention on the recognition and enforcement of foreign arbitral awards of 10 Jun. 1958 (New York convention on foreign arbitral awards), (<www.uncitral.org/pdf/english/texts/arbitration/NY-conv/XXII_1_e.pdf>), and for details on the entry into force and on certain reservations in relation to the States, which are parties to this convention, *see* annex 2. *Also see* the Convention between Sweden, Denmark, Finland, Iceland and Norway on recognition and the enforcement of judgments in civil matters of 11 Oct. 1977 (Nordic convention on recognition and the enforcement of judgments in civil matters), and the Agreement between the Nordic countries for mutual administrative assistance in tax matters of 7 Dec. 1989 (Nordic agreement on assistance in tax matters), annex 3. All these conventions lack declarations of interests in Preambles, but this does not mean that they have been unaffected by different interests. The enforcement provisions of these conventions are also of a clearly comparative interest.

and recovery of his claim. Other examples of conflicting, or competing, interests and principles treated in relation to the subject concern proportionality *versus* efficiency, territoriality *versus* mutuality, and non-discrimination *versus* efficiency. These examples do not, however, mean that other possible conflicting, or competing, interests and principles are disregarded.

The European Enforcement Order for uncontested claims, the European Order for payment procedure, and the European Small Claims Procedure, are treated, but to a more limited extent than the Brussels I regulation. A reason is that these first mentioned regulations frequently make references to the provisions of the Brussels I regulation. Another reason is that relatively few matters have been dealt with, so far, between the Member States of the EU according to these three first mentioned regulations. This is despite the great potential of titles of execution, such as uncontested claims in summary procedure, they represent compared to judgments in national statistics.

Consequently, no other private and public claims are treated than contractual claims for money and tax claims, expressed as payment liabilities in their quality of nationally enforceable titles, or being part of the legal basis for a decision of a disqualification order against an individual debtor for carrying on a non-serious, or illegal, business activity.

This means that *e.g.* the following claims are not part of the subject: non-contractual damages, maintenance allowances in family matters, litigation costs in civil matters, claims related to criminal matters, such as fines and confiscation of money, customs duties, social security charges, to the extent the real substance of the related decisions to these latter claims is not taxation. Another reason for not treating matters of the enforcement of fines and the confiscation of money according to EC law is the fast development of such law. This has, however, not meant refraining from making comparisons with solutions in EC law and conventions in criminal law areas and in other law areas, and in relation to works in progress and present development trends, in order to add yet a comparative dimension to the subject.[89] The use of the notion'public law' covers all kind of public claims, tax claims inclusive, in this work.

Provisions, which relate to measures for the enforcement, or the recovery, of a sum of money, are treated, but not the provisions related to the enforcement assistance for the execution of Non-Monetary Orders, *i.e.* of an obligation to do, or not to do, something. Other provisions in such European law and conventions, which are not of importance in the enforcement and recovery contexts, are not dealt with, *e.g.* matters of jurisdiction and court proceedings in litigation matters, such as in the Brussels I regulation. Treated are issues related to the procedure of special civil execution law, not those related to the procedure of general civil execution law in insolvency.[90] International insolvency is nevertheless touched upon, to some limited extent, due to its importance and close relationship to the areas of enforcement and recovery of claims and because

89. *See* 2.10 for further information on works in progress and present development trends.
90. *See* 1.6 about the use of the term insolvency.

international insolvency may be a possible alternative compared to cross-border enforcement.[91] The harmonization of national laws related to matters having cross-border implication only concerns certain measures of civil execution and access to information for enforcement purposes. No use is made of the legal usage of national courts and few national laws are treated by direct reference.

1.3 PURPOSE

The purpose of the subject consists of the following parts. Historical facts are provided to create a sufficient understanding of the legal developments of the subject into its present solutions.

A comparison is made between the present legal solutions in the private and public law areas, in particular with regards to those that can be found in the areas of the cross-border enforcement of contractual claims respectively of the recovery of tax claims, based on their balance of differing interests and principles, and an account is made of an analysis of the opposed, or differing, or similar, solutions. An evaluation is made of the present status of legal solutions against the background of the legal objectives in EC law, other parts of public international law, legal reform objectives established by political decisions for this European law, and legal reform objectives of international recommendations and principles, which have been accepted by States.[92]

Facts of history and present time are provided to create an understanding of the differences of functions and activities in comparison between European modern enforcement agents in the national and cross-border perspectives. Also, facts are provided to create a sufficient background for a discussion about the interest of making progress by a harmonization of the conditions of the profession of enforcement agents in the European context, for the benefit of the creditors and debtors. An analysis and an evaluation are made of the scope of application of EC law and conventions, including their territorial scope and their scope of claims, as well as the relationship between such European law and conventions. The definition and limitation to persons, creditors, debtors and co-debtors, affected by claims, who fall under, or outside, the scope of application of such EC law and conventions, are, as well, analyzed and evaluated. A specific category of debtors, in this context, are individuals affected by disqualification orders against them for carrying on a non-serious, or illegal, business activity, *e.g.* by not honouring contractual obligations and paying taxes.

An analysis and an evaluation are made of certain provisions in procedures in EC law and international conventions related to the recognition and enforceability,

91. *See* 1.1.1.6, where the reasons to treat international insolvency in comparison to the enforcement and recovery of claims are developed in more details.
92. *See* 1.1.1.1 about the legal reform objectives of established political decisions, which are aimed to govern the direction of future reforms in EC law, and about the legal reform objectives of international recommendations and principles, which have been accepted by States.

the referral to national laws, as well as the issue of access to information for enforcement purposes in the international context. An analysis and an evaluation are made of the possibilities of a harmonization of certain parts of the differing civil execution laws, and of the laws on access to information for enforcement purposes, of the Member States of the EU related to matters having cross-border implications. This is made against the background of EC law, the European Convention on Human Rights, the rulings of the ECHR, legal reform objectives established by political decisions in EC law, and legal reform objectives of international recommendations and principles, which have been accepted by States. The idea of the creation of a World Code of Enforcement is also analyzed.

Conclusions are drawn about how to better satisfy the interests and principles under all these international legal objectives by identifying possible issues of improvement. The conclusions are often currently integrated in the text, but are also sometimes found under a separate headline. Consequently, the work expresses preference for certain solutions and possible ways of development.

1.4 METHOD

1.4.1 Legal Method

The work on this study has been carried out according to a method of legal dogmatics of a relatively conventional type adapted to the sources of law. In relation to EC law, a systematic and teleological approach of interpretation is used, as applied by the ECJ and as supported by most legal writers in this field.[93] In this approach the importance of making community law effective by paying attention to its structure and objectives, often also evident in a Preamble, is emphasized. Such objectives vary in EC law and are often a combination of legal interests and principles, *e.g.* privacy, efficiency, non-discrimination, proportionality, the unification of the conflicts of rules, predictability, mutuality, and the further development of the EU's Internal Common Market.[94] The ECJ often applies an autonomous interpretation of EC law, a principle that also frequently has been applied in relation to the Convention on jurisdiction and the enforcement of

93. *See* Due, pp. 71-80, about the methods of interpretation of the ECJ and about the Vienna Convention on the Law of Treaties, Europarättens grunder, pp. 33-37 and 181-182, Chevallier, pp. 21-35, Introduction to the Law of the ECs, pp. 77-82 on the nature of community law, and pp. 275-280 and 282-292 on the application of unwritten law, public international law and fundamental rights by the ECJ and on its role in the process of integration, Kutscher, pp. 5-47, and Nerep, p. 264. *Also see* Pålsson, Brysselkonventionen, Luganokonventionen och Bryssel I-förordningen, pp. 33-45, about the interpretation of the Brussels convention, the Brussels I regulation, and the Old Lugano convention, including the principles and methods of interpretation of the ECJ, and Wahl, pp. 45-79, on the legal integrational aspects of interpretation of the Old Lugano convention and on the method of interpretation of conventions used by the ECJ.
94. *See*, about some of these principles, 1.1.1.1.1-3 and 1.1.1.1.6-7.

judgments in civil and commercial matters of 27 September 1968 (Brussels convention),[95] such as in the case of *Somafer SA v. Saar-Ferngas AG.*[96]

In its practice the ECJ has also paid attention to the principles of the European Convention on Human Rights in a number of decisions, *e.g.* in the cases of *Dieter Krombach v. André Bamberski,*[97] *Roquette Frères SA v. Directeur général de la concurrence, de la consommation et de la repression des fraudes,*[98] and *ASML Netherlands BV v. Semiconductor Industry Services GmbH,*[99] even if this convention and EC law constitute two separate international legal systems, with two independent supreme courts. The EU has not become a party to the convention.[100] Since the ECJ has paid attention in its practice to the principles of this European

95. *See* Pålsson, Brysselkonventionen, Luganokonventionen och Bryssel I-förordningen, about the principle of an autonomous interpretation, other principles and methods of interpretation applied by the ECJ in relation to the Brussels convention, pp. 37-40, compared to the principles of interpretation applied by the ECJ related to acts of EC law, such as the Brussels I regulation, *i.b.*, p. 42.
96. *See* the decision of the ECJ in *Somafer SA v. Saar-Ferngas AG.* of 22 Nov. 1978 which concerns the interpretation of the words 'Branch' and 'Agency' within the meaning of Art. 5, 5 of the Brussels convention. The ECJ concluded that the need to ensure legal certainty and equality of rights and obligations for the parties as regards the power to derogate from the general jurisdiction of Art. 2 requires an independent interpretation, common to all Contracting States, of the concepts in Art. 5, 5 of the Convention. *Also see* 5.2.1.1.1 and 6.1.1.3.1 for more examples of rulings of the ECJ, where an autonomous interpretation of EC law has been applied.
97. *See* the decision of the ECJ in *Dieter Krombach v. André Bamberski* of 28 Mar. 2000, which concerns the enforcement in Germany of a French judgment for the payment of damages to Mr. Bamberski, due to a criminal offence committed by Mr. Krombach. The judgment related to damages was decided by the French court without hearing the defence counsel instructed by Mr. Krombach. The ECJ treated the interpretation of the term public policy in the State in which recognition is sought according to Art. 27, 1 of the Brussels Convention. It concluded that it follows from the foregoing developments in the case-law that recourse to the public-policy clause must be regarded as being possible in exceptional cases where the guarantees laid down in the legislation of the State of origin and in the Convention itself have been insufficient to protect the defendant from a manifest breach of his right to defend himself before the court of origin, the right to a fair hearing, as recognized by the European Convention on Human Rights. *See* paras 25, 37 and 42-45 of the ruling. *Also see* 6.1.1.1.1.1 for further comments on this case.
98. *See* the decision of the ECJ of 22 Oct. 2002 in *Roquette Frères SA v. Directeur général de la concurrence, de la consommation et de la repression des fraudes*, which treats Art. 14 of Regulation No. 17 of the Council of 6 Feb. 1962 related to competition law, where reference is made to the convention, *see* para. 25 of the ruling.
99. *See* the decision of the ECJ of 14 Dec. 2006 in *ASML Netherlands BV v. Semiconductor Industry Services GmbH*, which treats the service of a judgment under the Brussels I regulation, *see* paras 26-28 of the ruling. *Also see* 6.1.1.1.1.1 for further comments on this case.
100. *Also see* about the convention and the EU: Att klaga till Europadomstolen, pp. 25-28, Danelius, pp. 20-21, Introduction to the Law of the ECs, pp. 284-288, Kutscher, p. 28, and Leroy, L'efficacité des procédures judiciaires au sein de l'union Européenne et les garanties des droits de la defense, Transparence patrimoniale, L'efficacité de la justice civile en Europe, pp. 277 and 296. The Treaty of Lisbon, which shall enter into force on 1 Jan. 2009, provided that all the instruments of ratification have been deposited, or, failing that, on the first day of the month following the deposit of the instrument of ratification by the last signatory State to take this step, *see* Final provisions, Art. 6, 2. The Treaty of Lisbon stipulates that the EU shall recognize the rights, freedoms and principles set out in the Charter of fundamental rights,

convention, the rulings of the ECHR must also be respected at the application of EC law.

The emphasis that has been attributed to the objectives and purpose of the European Convention on Human Rights has lead to that the ECHR sometimes applies a so-called dynamic, or evolutive, method of interpretation, meaning that the convention and its articles shall be understood and applied in the meaning they have in the contemporary society.[101] Interpreting the European Convention on Human Rights, the ECHR also takes into account the Vienna Convention on the Law of Treaties and thereby also indirectly other relevant rules of international law.[102] The dynamic method of interpretation applied by the ECHR means that new issues of relevance and importance continuously will have to be considered in the civil execution and tax recovery law areas.

For the interpretation of conventions and other parts of public international law, fundamental principles of interpretation of public international law are taken into account, derived from the statute of the International Court of Justice (ICJ),[103] annexed to the Charter of the United Nations of 26 June 1945, and from the Vienna Convention on the Law of Treaties.[104] Even if the principles on the interpretation of this statute and this convention are only formally addressed and binding in

---

see Art. 6, 1. In addition, it stipulates that the Union shall accede to the European Convention on Human Rights, *see* Art. 6, 2. Also, fundamental rights, as guaranteed by this Convention and as they result from the constitutional traditions common to the Member States, shall constitute general principles of the Union's law, *see* Art. 6, 3. *Also see* 4.3 about the European Convention on Human Rights and some rulings of the ECHR.

101. *See* about the dynamic interpretation and some other methods of interpretation of the convention applied by the ECHR Att klaga till Europadomstolen, pp. 55-59. *Also see*, about examples of principles of interpretation of the convention applied by the ECHR, Danelius, pp. 47-52.

102. *See* Leach, p. 172. *Also see* Att klaga till Europadomstolen, p. 54, about the relationship between the Vienna Convention on the Law of Treaties and the European Convention on Human Rights.

103. *See* Art. 38.

104. The interpretation of conventions involves, besides the wordings of the convention, several other interpretative considerations *e.g.*: good faith, the ordinary meaning, the special meaning, the context, the object and purpose, the subsequent agreements and the subsequent practice, the relevant rules of public international law, the supplementary means, including travaux préparatoires, and the plurilingual texts, *see* Arts 31-33. *Also see*, about an interpretation according to the Vienna Convention on the Law of Treaties, Sinclair, pp.114-154, and Oppenheim, pp. 1268-1283. *Also see*, about that a rule shall be given the interpretation, which best conforms to the purposes of the treaty and that ambiguities shall be resolved in order to give full effectiveness to the treaty, Nerep, p. 264. *Also see*, about that travaux préparatoires should also be taken into consideration, Schwebel, pp. 797-804, where he departures from the Vienna Convention on the Law of Treaties, and develops his views on this question. He finally, *i.b.*, p. 804, concludes 'That practice and that precedent demonstrate that preparatory work is often brought to bear in the interpretation of treaties, by the parties to these treaties and by their interpreters, and this whether the travaux préparatoires confirm or correct an interpretation otherwise arrived at.' Legal usage, literature and official reports, *e.g.* explanatory reports, may also constitute important sources of interpretation.

relation to the ICJ and respectively to the States, they nevertheless provide important guidelines on the principles of interpretation relating to bilateral and multilateral conventions and to other parts of public international law, which is evident from the use of these sources of law by many authors on public international law.[105] Not all States have become parties to the Vienna Convention on the Law of Treaties. The ICJ has nevertheless treated the convention as expressive of customary international law binding upon States parties and non-parties to it alike.[106]

1.4.2 Treatment of the Sources of Law

Almost all parts include a comparison between the civil law enforcement area and the public law recovery area. The comparative approach, which relates to EC law and conventions, has in particular been applied so as to compare the legal solutions in the area of the enforcement of contractual claims with the legal solutions in the area of the recovery of tax claims, which include similar, or different, solutions based on similar, or different objectives/principles. Also, in this context, international principles and recommendations accepted by States, have been taken into account. Use is also made, to some extent, of comparisons with solutions in EC law and conventions in other law areas.

Primary legal sources, such as EC law regulations and directives, and conventions, are used in this work. Also, secondary sources, the legal usage of the ECJ and of the ECHR, the travaux préparatoires to EC law and conventions, and legal doctrine, are used. Primary historical sources have only been used to some limited extent,[107] supplemented by secondary sources of recognized authors in the field.

Only some few national laws are treated in this work by direct reference, when illustrating examples are given about the interplay between EC law and national laws and in relation to the international cooperation outside of the EU, which concerns one or more Member States of this Union. No extensive comparative research of differing national laws is made, but referrals are made to comparative studies conducted by other authors, or international organizations, to the extent that has been motivated to provide readers with information about facts related to the subject.[108]

---

105. *See* Oppenheim, pp. 22-52, who departures from Art. 38 of the statute of the ICJ and comments on the impact of and how to treat the following possible sources of public international law, custom, treaties, general principles of law, decisions of tribunals, writings of authors, equity, international organizations and international comity and morality. *Also see*, on the same subject and on the Vienna Convention on the Law of Treaties, Akehurst, pp. 35-62, Harris, pp. 23-68, Lysén, pp. 26-37, and Sevastik, pp. 62-63 and 85-105.
106. *See* Schwebel, p. 797.
107. *See e.g.* 2.3 about the constitutional doctrines of Montesquieu and 2.3.1 about the Swedish, German and French civil execution legislations.
108. Given the needs of exactitude and to reflect the environment in which the discussions have taken place and to do justice to this some quotations have become extensive.

Most of the text in this book is in English, but when motivated text from several other languages appear, such as in quotations. Also, extensive references are made to sources from several other languages than English.

1.5 PREVIOUS RESEARCH

The extent of previous works of importance in the different areas varies.[109] There exists a large number of works on European legal history, but relatively few of them treat issues related to the subject. Some few works treat European enforcement agents. Several works on public international law also include comments in relation to the subject. Many works include comments on the European Convention on Human Rights, but only a limited number treat this convention in relation to issues of enforcement and recovery. In the area of contractual claims related to EC law and multilateral conventions there exists a large number of works mainly related to the Brussels convention and other conventions. Some of them are also of importance to *e.g.* the Brussels I regulation and certain still valid conventions, but only very few are focused on matters of cross-border enforcement of contractual claims. In the area of cross-border recovery of tax claims there exists a rather limited number of works related to the Recovery directive and multilateral conventions. Relatively few treat the harmonization of national laws related to the civil execution law area.

1.6 TERMINOLOGY

Readers should be aware that certain legal expressions in English, which have a specific meaning in English law, are also used to illustrate legal figures, or notions, from non-English speaking States, even when these legal figures, or notions, do not have an identical legal counterpart in English law. These differences between the national legal systems also mean that English terminology sometimes uses more words to illustrate a legal figure in an enforcement proceeding in comparison to some other languages.[110] Consequently certain expressions in English are

109. One of the aims behind the text is to present the readers extensive systematic information of law, and documentation inclusive, and may perhaps sometimes have been fulfilled to a greater extent in relation to what has been necessary in the performance of this work. Hence, it constitutes a service to the readers.

110. Examples are the Swedish words utmätning and verkställighet, that correspond to the French words saisie and exécution forcée and to the German words Pfändung and Zwangsvollstreckung, and which, depending on the situation, may be translated into the following English words: attachment, distress, execution, garnishment and seizure, *see* Ordlista för exekutionsväsendet på engelska, franska och tyska (Wordlist for the Enforcement Service in English, French and German), pp. 92-93, 154-155 compared to pp. 31 and 49. *Also see* about the meaning and definition of these English words Barron's Law Dictionary, pp.: 33, 139, 167, 202 and 432 and English Law Dictionary, pp.: 22, 98, 115, 134 and 289.

sometimes incorrect in this sense, but instead appropriate to use in a more general sense. Some terms are used in the same sense as defined in the Council of Europe's recommendation on enforcement.[111] In order to facilitate an understanding of in what sense certain terms are used, a brief explanation to some of them is provided here:

Collection, either a demand for voluntary payment by an authority, or a demand of payment subject to recovery measures, including measures of enforcement.

Competent authority, the court, or authority, designated by States to be in charge of matters of international cooperation, exequatur proceedings, or assistance in other matters of multilateral cooperation.[112]

Composition, an agreement between a debtor and creditors to settle a debt immediately by repaying only part of it.[113]

Contractual claim, a private claim based on an enforceable title, which could be derived from a contractual relation.

Creditor, one to whom money is owed by the debtor, or one to whom an obligation exists.[114]

Debtor, one who has the obligation of paying a debt, or one who owes a debt.[115]

Enforcement, the carrying into effect of judicial decisions, as well as of other judicial, or non-judicial enforceable titles of execution, in compliance with the law, which compels the defendant to do, to refrain from doing, or to pay what has been adjudged. Enforcement could also mean that by virtue of the judicial decision, the condemned party may be forced to respect the judgment, either directly, or indirectly, with, or without the imposition of a fine, *i.e.* by the forced performance.[116] The term execution,[117] used in the context of the execution of a claim, is normally used, in this work, in the same sense as the term enforcement in the corresponding situation. An application for enforcement measures constitutes one of several possible legal initiatives of recovery in the total recovery process. The word enforcement is therefore normally, but not always, used in a more narrow sense than the word recovery. Provisions of enforcement are frequent in EC law and in conventions, which relate to contractual claims.

Enforcement agent, a person authorized by the State to carry out the civil execution law procedure irrespective of whether that person is employed by the State or not.[118]

---

111. *See* Council of Europe's recommendation on enforcement, section I. Definitions.
112. Competent authorities are treated in the context of 3.2.2 and 3.3.2.
113. *See* English Law Dictionary, p. 61.
114. *See* Barron's Law Dictionary, p. 109.
115. Ibid., p. 118.
116. *See* Manual for the collection of a sum of money abroad, p. 19.
117. Compare 1.1 about the origin of the word execution.
118. *See* 3.2.1 for further details, where the national regulated enforcement agents are treated, the liberal professionals, the civil servants in the administration, and the enforcement officers of the courts.

Exequatur proceeding, a proceeding applied to a creditors' claim in order to obtain a formal declaration from a court, or from an authority, that a foreign judgment is enforceable.

Insolvency proceedings, such general civil execution procedures, as fall under the scope of application of the Council regulation 1346/2000/EC of 29 May 2000 on insolvency proceedings,[119] corresponding to *e.g.* bankruptcy and winding up.

Periods of limitation fix the time within which parties must take judicial action to enforce rights or else to be thereafter barred from enforcing them,[120] through measures of recovery or enforcement. The term periods of limitation sometimes also corresponds to the terms prescription and time-limits.[121]

Recovery, all legal initiatives of a private creditor, or a public creditor,[122] when acting from the establishment of a title of execution to the end of the total recovery process, which may or may not, depending on the position of national law, include *e.g.* a demand of voluntary payment, an agreement on an instalment plan, an application for enforcement measures, and an application for bankruptcy. The expression recovery is therefore normally used in a wider sense than the expression enforcement. Provisions of recovery are frequent in EC law and in conventions, which relate to tax claims.

Recovery agent, a person authorized by the State to carry out the recovery of public claims, including tax claims.[123]

Tax claim, any claim derived from an enforceable tax decision from a tax authority, or from a court.

Title of execution, a judgment from a court, or a decision from any other part of the administration of a State, which are enforceable according to its legislation, and which gives a creditor the right to apply to a regulated enforcement agent, or to a regulated recovery agent, for measures of enforcement, or recovery, against a debtor for the satisfaction of the creditor's claim.

119. Mainly corresponding to the insolvency proceedings referred to in Art. 2, a in Annex A to this regulation.
120. *See* Barron's Law Dictionary, p. 454.
121. Compare Explanatory report on the Convention on Mutual Administrative Assistance in Tax Matters, p. 38, which explains, under the headline time-limits in connection to Art. 14 of this convention, that: 'What is envisaged hereunder is the rule of law according to which the debtor can be relieved from enforcement by lapse of time.'
122. Compare International Tax Glossary regarding the expression recovery of tax from the tax administration's point of view, p. 218.
123. *See* 3.3.1 for further details, where the national regulated recovery agents in the administration are treated.

Chapter 2
History and Legal Developments

2.1 ROMAN LAW

The Roman civil and procedural laws were, compared to the Roman penal and civil execution laws, highly developed. These procedural laws were characterized by a free examination of evidence, a verbal proceeding before the judge, in which both parties had the opportunity to pronounce themselves, *audiatur et altera pars, i.e.* according to the contradictory principle. Also, the principle of immediateness, *i.e.* only that which had been subject to the actual proceeding constituted a basis for the decision and the principle of a public court proceeding.[1]

2.1.1 Civil Execution Law

In the Roman procedure, such as developed in the legal action system, the determination of what was right was the only task of the judge, and the Roman *actio* was mainly directed at its achievement. The hereby determined obligations imposed on the parties corresponded to a special right for the plaintiff, which was derived from the judgment, but had to be sought and handled in a special separate legal enforcement procedure. This separate procedure could be carried through after the authorization of the enforcement of the judgment from the organs, which were in charge of the administration of justice, and when needed also by their assistance. Such an authorization was normally given to the applicant, without any further proceedings, by the relevant high official, in Rome by the *Praetor*, in a *duci jubere*, an order for the imprisonment, or for the execution/putting to death,[2] in a case of the

1. *See* Kaser/Knütel, pp. 364 and 395.
2. Compare the Latin expression *aliquem duci iubere*, Norstedts latinsk-svenska ordbok, p. 281, which means in Swedish ge order om någons fängslande eller avrättning, and in English give an

personal execution for a claim, and in an order for the *missio in bona* in case of the real execution for a claim.

The Old Roman law only recognized, as a main rule, the personal execution for a claim. The real execution for a civil claim, through which performance was sought in the property of the debtor, was only recognized in this law in exceptional cases.[3] It was first later, even if the possibility of the personal execution for a claim still remained then, that different new constructions of real civil execution were created. The original severe procedure for the personal execution for a claim in the law of the Twelve Tables, of about 451-450 B.C., granted the creditor, through a specific procedure of legal action and subject to that certain conditions were fulfilled, the right to take the debtor in his possession as a prisoner. If the debtor did not pay his debt within certain time, the creditor had the right to kill him, or sell him into slavery. This specific procedure against the debtor was supported by official announcements, limited to certain deadlines, in order to permit for the relatives and the friends of the debtor to buy him off in due time. The relevant provisions of the law of the Twelve Tables, III, reads as follows:[4]

1. For the payment of a recognized debt of money and for the compliance with a judgment, which has gained legal force, is 30 days a justifiable set term.
2. Afterwards the debtor may be arrested. He shall transfer him to the court.

---

order for someone's execution/putting to death. *Also* compare the Latin word *ducere*, which may, depending on the circumstances, *i.a.* be translated into: to take away into one's possession, to lead off, or away to punishment, and the Latin word *iubere*, which may, depending on the circumstances, *i.a.* be translated into: to order something to be done, or to designate in a command, *see* Oxford Latin Dictionary, pp. 576-577 and 977.

3. *See* Tamm, p. 75, who refers to the exceptional cases mentioned by Gaius as *legis actio per pignoris capionem* as evident from the law of the Twelve Tables, XII (Gaius, Institutiones, IV, 28, which reads (Translation of quotation by Mikael Berglund from Swedish to English): '1. But in law pignoris capio was introduced, *e.g.* through the law of the Twelve Tables against the one, who had bought a sacrificial animal and not paid the purchase-sum, as well as against the one who did not pay the rent for a draught-animal which another one had rented out to get money to a sacrificial meal.'
4. *See* Tamm, p. 73 (Translation of quotation by Mikael Berglund from Swedish to English). Tamm also reports, *i.b.*, that an important element in the law of the Twelve Tables was the rules on execution, which were meant to prevent the most pronounced abuses of the position of the debtor. He concludes that the rules appear today to be severe, but they were meant, and have also originally functioned as a protection for the debtor. He explains that because a Roman citizen could not be the slave of another Roman, he had to be sold outside of Rome (*trans Tiberim*), and also that the provision about the cutting of the debtor into pieces has caused research problems, which have lead to different opinions of interpretation. It is also uncertain to what extent the threatening sanction of killing the debtor actually was carried through, *see* Kaser/Knütel, p. 372, who report as follows: 'Doch ist kein konkreter Fall der Tötung des Schuldners überliefert und auch im Prinzipat nicht bekannt gewesen, so daβ schon *Sextus Caecilius* (bei *Gellius* s.o.) annahm, die Sanktion sei nur deshalb so schrecklich gefaβt, weil und damit es nie zu ihr komme. Eine Möglichkeit, sie abzuwenden, war offenbar schon früh dadurch gegeben, daβ der Haftende sich als *nexus* in die Schuldknechtschaft des Gläubigers begab, um dort die Haftungssumme abzuarbeiten. Im übrigen hat sich im *ius civile* ein von der Personalvollstreckung losgelöster Vorläufer der prätorischen Vermögensvollstreckung entwickelt.' *Also see* Spann, p. 15, who concludes that the poor sources of material means that the question of the actual aim of the provision related to the killing of the debtor remains unanswered.

3. If he does not comply with the judgment and nobody wants to put up a security for him before the court, shall the creditor take him away and bind him with a strap or with foot irons, which may not weigh more than 15 pound, but preferably less.
4. If the debtor wants he shall himself supply his food. In the opposite case shall the one, who has put him into irons, daily, give him one pound of wheat bread.
5. There existed, however, a right under the time to enter into a settlement, but if nothing else was agreed upon the debtors were held imprisoned during 60 days. Under this set term they were brought face to face with the preator on the comitium at three after each other following market days, and one called out how much they had been judged for. On the third market day they then got killed or sold beyond the Tiber.
6. On the third market day they shall cut the debtor into pieces. If they cut too much or too little, they shall not be demanded any responsibility for this.

This execution consequently had the character of personal execution, which was claimed by way of a *legis actio per manus iniectionem* through which the creditor, meanwhile he pronounced a decided formula, laid his hand on the debtor. This formula reads, according to Gaius, Institutiones, IV, as follows:[5]

> 21. One used per manus iniectionem in these cases where this was stipulated in one or another law, *e.g.* regarding the one, who was judged according to the law of the Twelve Tables. This plaintiff's case came about in that way that the plaintiff pronounced: AS YOU ARE JUDGED (or convicted) FOR THE PAYMENT TO ME OF 10.000 SESTERTIER AND AS YOU HAVE NOT PAID, I LAY, FOR THIS REASON, THE HAND ON YOU AS JUDGED FOR 10.000 SESTERTIER and simultaneously he caught hold of another part of his body. And the convicted was not allowed to free himself and to defend him in the matter; but he put up a guarantor (vindex) who represented him in the matter; the one who did not put up a guarantor was by the plaintiff transferred to his house and put into irons.

This law corresponded to the needs of legal provisions in a primitive agricultural society and was characterized by the same kind of severity in the law of execution as that in Athens before the reform of law by Solon[6] in 594 B.C. Solon, who was elected to Arkont, the highest office in Athens, for one year, 594-593 B.C., and during that time was given an absolute position, was appointed an arbitrator, who's

---

5. *See* Tamm, p. 74 (Translation of quotation by Mikael Berglund from Swedish to English).
6. Solon, statesman in Athens in about 600 B.C., one of the seven wise of Greece. Solon introduced in 594 B.C., as an Arkont, a new constitution, which *i.a.* divided the citizens into four classes of wealth with different rights and obligations. He described his ideal State in a number of still partially preserved poems, *see* Norstedts uppslagsbok, p. 1536. It is highly likely that Solon also carried out a complete codification of the legislation in Athens. At least two fundamental phenomenon in the democracy of Athens are possible to trace back to Solon, the equality before the law, isonomía, and the people's tribunal, heliaía, which meant that the judging power ultimately belonged to the sovereign people, *see* Anners, Den europeiska rättens historia, del 1, pp. 35-36.

task was to ward off the crisis that Athens got into due to a catastrophic credit system. Solon corrected the unsatisfactory state of affairs with the so-called discharge, which meant that all debts were written off and in addition a prohibition against the personal execution for a claim was introduced.[7] Through the Roman *lex Poetilia*, about 330 B.C., it was decided that the creditor should not have the right to kill, or sell the negligent debtor, and that the right of the creditor was limited to keep the debtor in custody until he had paid or worked off his debt. The civil execution law of claims in Roman law was fairly primitive under the emperor Augustus,[8] who instituted reforms into the criminal law area and the organization of the police, but left the area of the law of execution of claims untouched.[9]

The defendant debtor was able to be arrested by the authorization from the judge/Magistrate and put into the private custody of the creditor until he had paid or worked off his debt which was the normal procedure until the emperor Zenon prohibited private prisons.[10] The judge was able, subject to certain conditions, either to enforce a natural obligation or an obligation for the payment of a sum of money against the debtor and the debtor was also risking public imprisonment, as told in the following quotation:[11]

> Si l'exécution en nature était possible, le juge y procédait à l'aide de son *officium*, quand le défendeur n'avait pas exécuté dans un délai de deux

7. In a society, which likes Athens, proves to be under a transition from a society based on the family to a society organization based on the idea of a State are the possibilities to mortgage land limited. Land was rather considered to belong to the family than to the individual, but as on the other hand the collective responsibility of the family for the debt of the individual in such agricultural societies was weakened, the result was that the creditor only had one real security of substantial value, *i.e.* the debtor in person. These circumstances have normally demanded an implementation of very severe rules about personal execution in such societies. The main rule was that a debtor, who could not pay his debt, became the slave of the creditor, or according to a milder rule, at the earliest observed in Egyptian law, was forced to work off his debt while he was kept imprisoned by the creditor. This main rule was the one which was applicable in Athens before Solon, *i.e.* the negligent debtor became the slave of the creditor. Yet another factor was the high interest rate on loans due to the prevailing uncertain conditions making the interest level crushingly heavy for the indebted farmer. Consequently a large number of farmers from Athens became slaves of their creditors or were sold as slaves abroad. In this situation Solon was called in to save the society out of the socially catastrophic condition that had been caused to it through a too undeveloped law of execution, which resulted in that he warded off the misery by writing off the burden of the agricultural debts and prohibited the personal execution for claims.
8. Augustus lived between 63 B.C.-14 A.D., and was a Roman emperor between 27 B.C.-14 A.D., *see* Suetonius, p. 68.
9. *See*, about the law of execution of claims in Roman law, some other legal influences by Roman law, including its Hellenistic reception, and the rebirth of Roman law in Italy, Anners, Den europeiska rättens historia, del 1, pp. 35-40, 65-66, 77-80 and 125-139. *Also see*, about the law of execution of claims in Roman law, Hagerup, pp. 2-3, Declareuil, pp. 95-97, and 365, Kaser/Knütel, pp. 37, 159-162, 364, 369, 371-372, 375, 391, and 394-397, Spann, pp. 3-68 (Entwicklung der Vermögenshaftung aus der Personalexekution heraus im Römischen Rechts als Vorbild für die spätere Rechtsentwicklung auf mitteleuropäischem Boden), and Tamm, pp. 73-77.
10. *See* Declareuil, p. 95.
11. *See* Declareuil, p. 365.

> mois, porté ensuite à quatre. Si elle était impossible ou s'il s'agissait d'une somme d'argent, les voies d'exécution étaient: le *pignus ex causa judicati captum*, saisie d'objets appartenant au débiteur, qui, au bout de deux mois, à défaut de paiement, étaient vendus aux enchères jusqu'à concurrence du montant de la créance ou, faute d'enchérisseurs, adjugés en paiement au créancier; ou la *bonorum distractio*, à la requête soit du créancier, soit du débiteur faisant cession de biens. Dans le premier cas, elle pouvait se cumuler avec un emprisonnement qui, depuis Théodose, dut avoir lieu dans une prison publique. La vente en détail par le *curator* n'était plus permise qu'après un délai de deux ans entre présents et quatre entre absents afin de laisser aux créanciers le temps de produire leurs titres. Justinien limita le bénéfiçe de la cession de biens au cas d'insolvabilité par force majeure, à moins d'un privilège impérial.

Later a new construction of real civil execution was created, not in a procedure of special civil execution, but in a procedure with features of modern general civil execution in insolvency for the transfer of the assets of the debtor. This development will here be further treated under the following headline Insolvency. It was first under the reign of emperor Justinianus[12] in the sixth century that rules on immunity from seizure, *beneficium competentiae*, were introduced, *i.e.* that a debtor, who was subject to forced execution, should be entitled to keep what he indispensably needed to support his living. A kind of real execution of forced seizure of the goods of the debtor's estate, *manu militari*, was constructed first under the late period of Roman emperors and became then gradually the ordinary procedure. The use of different interim measures in order to assure the execution of interim decisions by the judge/Magistrate was possible according to Roman law, including sequestration. This is described in the following quotation:[13]

> Il arrivait que le magistrat mît au service de sa juridiction les pouvoirs souverains qu'il tenait de l'*imperium*. Pour garantir, en l'absence d'action, certains situations, parer à des dommages éventuels, assurer l'exécution de décisions interlocutoires, il ordonnait aux parties ou à l'une d'elles de s'engager à cette exécution, à la réparation de ce dommage, au respect de cette situation par contrat verbal: stipulations prétoriennes, tantôt simples (*cautiones*), tantôt garanties par fidéjusseurs (*satisdationes*), auxquelles il contraignait par des menaces de saisie, de refus ou de déliverance d'actions, selon les cas. D'autres fois il autorisait, comme moyens de contrainte, des envois en possession (*missiones in possessionem, in rem, in bona*) de tout ou partie des biens de l'un des plaideurs au profit de l'autre, tantôt comme mesure conservatoire, tantôt en vue de la vente des choses ou du patrimoine saisi, et protégeait la situation ainsi créée par des actions *in factum* ou des interdits.

---

12. Justinianus I lived between 482-565 A.D. and became an East Roman emperor in 527 A.D., *see* Norstedts uppslagsbok, p. 760.
13. *See* Declareuil, p. 97, under the headline L'emploit de l 'imperium' dans la procedure. *Also see* Kaser/Knütel, p. 391.

When the original severe procedure for the personal execution of a claim in Roman law, the law of the Twelve Tables, was changed through the *lex Poetilia*, it meant that the interests of the debtor still remained weak, but his interest of humanity and dignity was improved, while the right of the creditor was limited correspondingly. The advanced development of economy made this primitive form of execution of a claim insufficient, which resulted in the introduction in Roman law of a method of collective enforcement of private claims, a procedure of insolvency. The debtor's interest of humanity and dignity was, in this context, first improved when the severity of this procedure was modified through the introduction in Roman law of the *cessio bonorum*. The debtor's interests of humanity and dignity were further improved when rules on the debtor's immunity from seizure, *beneficium competentiae*, were introduced. The introduction in Roman law of a kind of real execution of forced seizure from the goods of the debtor's estate, *manu militari*, meant that the interest of efficiency of the creditor was better satisfied, but also that the privacy of the *civis romanus* debtor was limited correspondingly.

Several factors contributed to that the law of execution of claims in Roman law did not achieve a level corresponding to the constructive progresses primarily in civil law, but also in penal law. The restraint of a civil procedure, which for long could only lead to a judgment for the payment of a sum of money, the primitive procedure for the execution of a claim against an individual of the agricultural society, and the insufficient development of efficient legal forms of real security in real estate property, were some of them. This position seems, however, ultimately go back on the unwillingness of the Romans to accept the intrusion of the State into the personal sphere of the Roman master, who as a Roman citizen, *civis romanus*, should be protected from forced interference by the State within his own home.

Many of the new legal constructions, which were created under the Hellenistic cultural era, from Alexander the Great to the emperor Augustus, were preserved in Roman law, and were passed on into the European legal tradition. The following reception of Roman law, also including its Hellenistic influences by philosophy and rhetoric, into national laws were to form part of European history under a long period of time. Influences of Roman law remain in our age, *e.g.* some legal systems of States are still classified as Romanic systems, also in the enforcement area.[14]

14. *See* Kerameus, Enforcement in the International Context, Recueil des cours, collected courses of the Hague Academy of International Law, 1997, Tome 264 de la collection, where he treats certain issues in enforcement proceedings of some States as belonging to the Romanic system, *e.g.* about the provisional enforceability of judgments, pp. 240-242, the classification of enforcement and types of monetary enforcement, pp. 254-255, time-limits to enforcement, pp. 258-259, the litigation pertaining to enforcement, pp. 282-285, parties to garnishment, pp. 299-300, and distribution proceedings and relationship among creditors, pp. 307-310; also Kerameus, International encyclopedia of comparative law, volume XVI, Civil procedure, chapter 10, Enforcement proceedings, who treats certain issues in enforcement proceedings of some States as belonging to the Romanic system, *e.g.* about the provisional enforceability of judgments (France and Italy), pp. 21-22, the parties involved in enforcement proceedings (France and Italy), pp. 30-31, and the enforcement against the State (France, Italy, Spain and Colombia), pp. 33-34.

2.1.2 Tax Collection

Different taxes and a variety of customs duties were imposed, collected and recovered in the interest of efficiency by the Roman administration, as told in the following quotation:[15]

> Das antike Zollsystem hat nicht nur die Grenzzölle, *portoria*, sondern auch alle Binnenzölle, vor allem die Export-, Import- und Durchgangszölle zu Wasser und zu Lande, die ausdrücklich unterschieden werden, weiter die Wegegelder, Tor- und Brückenmauten usw., auch die Markt- und Monopolzölle, ja selbst die Gewerbersteuern und die Abgaben bei Kauf und Verkauf (Umsatzsteuer . . . etc.) umfaβt. Sie wurden für Handelswaren aller Art, Tiere und Sklaven, aber auch für Personen erhoben, und nich nur für allemal, sondern, da das römische Reich keine Zolleinheit war, nicht nur an der Reichsgrentze, sondern an jeder weiteren Zollgrenze. Das Zolltarif war nach Warenart, Zeit und Ort verschieden und muβte an jeder Station aushängen'

and

> Die Erhebung indirekter Steuern, wie der Verbrauchssteuern, der Import-, Export-, und Durchgangszölle, der Wege-, Tor- und Brückenmauten, der Markt- und Monopolzölle u. dgl., also aller *vectigalia*, war Staatsmonopol.

During the time of the Roman Principate a shift from indirect to direct taxation took place. Fiscal claims enjoyed priority rights in the procedure of enforcement.[16] The Roman emperors' right to receive contributions from the people was already recognized in Christianity during the first century A.D.[17]

2.1.3 Insolvency

The advanced development of economy made the primitive form of the personal execution of a claim insufficient. A new construction of real civil execution law was therefore created, not in a procedure of special civil execution law, but in a procedure with features of modern general civil execution law in insolvency in three stages, originally called *missio in possessionem*, which meant that the creditor became a part owner to the assets of the debtor. If there existed several creditors, they could all become part owners, but the Praetor then normally appointed a trustee in bankruptcy, *Curator bonorum*, who took care of their common interests

---

15. *See* Langhammer, pp. 117 and 121. *Also see* for more details about taxes and customs duties, collection and recovery of taxes in Roman law *i.b.*, pp. 21, 37, 113-122, and 146-147, and Kaser, pp. 30, 81, 102-103, 182 and 194.
16. *See* Kaser/Knütel, p. 389.
17. The question if the people should pay contributions to the Roman emperor is given in a dialogue with Jesus, which reads: 'They said, "Caesar's." Then he said to them, "Render therefore to Caesar the things that are Caesar's, and to God the things that are God's",' *see* Bible, Matt 22:21.

in relation to the debtor. If the debtor did not fulfill his obligations a *Magister bonorum* was appointed with the task to make an account of the assets and debts of the estate as a preparation for its sale. The final stage was the sale of the estate with its assets and debts to the highest bidder, and subsequently the creditor got his share of the percentage of the total amount of debts, as the buyer had committed himself to pay.

The original precedent in Roman law to the modern institute of bankruptcy was the *missio in bona* and was a kind of real civil execution law at the application of a creditor, normally including all the assets of the debtor.[18] The sale of goods, *vendition bonorum*, had originally serious effects on a debtor, he became subject to a severe form of infamousness called *infamia*. It was, however, decided during the rule of emperor Augustus, that a debtor, who involuntarily became insolvent, and voluntary gave up his estate to bankruptcy, *cessio bonorum*, should escape from both infamousness and the procedure of personal execution. This and the ensuing development is told in the following quotation:[19]

> Mais assez vite, apparut la cession de biens (*bonorum cessio*) qui procura au débiteur, avec le bénéfice de compétence, un moyen d'éviter la prison et l'infamie. D'autre part, après la loi Aebutia, peut-être vers 636, le préteur avait organisé une exécution sur les biens: d'abord pour les cas d'impossibilité d'exécution sur la personne, puis pour chaque fois qu'il plairait au demandeur. Cela devint le mode ordinaire. C'était une vente en masse des biens du débiteur (*bonorum venditio*), calquée sur celle (*bonorum sectio*) que pratiquait déjà l'État à l'égard des siens, comportant publicité par affiches (*proscriptiones*) et vente aux enchères (*auctio*). A la requête de l'un des créanciers, le préteur ordonnait au profit de tous une saisie conservatoire, qu'ils devaient faire publier et suivre de la nomination d'un curateur aux biens; puis faute d'exécution, confirmation de la saisie à fin de vente était accordèe à leur requête. Trente jours après l'affichage annonçant la vente, si le débiteur était vivant, quinze s'il était mort, affichage entraînant l'infamie et l'incapacité d'ester en justice comme défendeur, un décret appelait les créanciers à nommer un liquidateur (*magister bonorum*) qui rédigeât et fît afficher par extraits un cahier des charges et finalement procéder à la vente en bloc du patrimoine saisi au profit de l'enchérisseur offrant le plus fort dividende aux créanciers. Celui-ci (*bonorum emplor*) acquérait la propriété prétorienne sur les choses corporelless et le droit, pour protéger sa possession, à l'un de ces moyens de

18. *See*, about the influences of Roman law for the development of the institute of bankruptcy in the legislations of some European States, Welamson, pp. 7-10. *Also see* Vertragstreue und Erfüllungszwang in der mittelalterlichen Rechtswissenschaft, p. 46, where the alternative uses either of a procedure for the personal execution of a claim or of a procedure of general execution are commented as follows: 'Die Vollstreckung im Formularverfahren konnte entweder eine traditionelle Personalexekution oder seit der Prinzipatszeit in bestimmten Fällen eine Vermögensexekution (*missio in bona*) sein, die eine Art von Konkurs des Schuldners war.'
19. *See* Declareuil, pp. 95-97. *Also see* Tamm, pp. 75-77.

> défense appelés interdits (*interdictum possessorium*). Les actions, existant pour ou contre le débiteur, lui étaient adaptées à titre utile, si celui-ci était vivant, au moyen d'une formule à transposition (*formula rutiliana*) où le nom du débiteur inséré dans l'*intentio* était remplacé par le sien dans la condamnation et, s'il était mort, par une fiction d'hérédité (*formula serviana*). Le débiteur, pour les dettes antérieures à la vente, ne pouvait être de nouveau poursuivi, même après retour à meilleure fortune, que dans la mesure de ses moyens et après le délai d'une année.

The *actio Pauliana* had the character of an action for damages based on criminal conduct and was in principle only available when the debtor had taken legal actions with a verifiable aim to harm his creditors by acting in a fraudulent way against their rights. This *actio*, which strengthened the interest of efficiency of the creditor in insolvency, was applicable on transactions made by the debtor before the moment of the taking of possession of the insolvency estate.[20] The *actio Pauliana*, which was further developed under the Middle Ages in the customary laws of the Italian merchant cities,[21] has, in various ways, influenced the provisions of regaining transactions made by the debtor in the bankruptcy laws of many States.[22] The Latin word *concurcus*[23] and the English word bankruptcy also have a long history.[24]

---

20. *See* Kaser/Knütel, pp. 137-139. *Also see*, about the *actio Pauliana* in Roman law, Fliniaux, pp. 460-461, and Tamm, p. 77.
21. *See* 2.2.4, where this is further treated.
22. *See*, about the influences of *actio Pauliana* in Roman law for the developments of provisions of regaining transactions made by the debtor in the legislations of some European States, *e.g.* in French, German and Italian laws, Welamson, pp. 206-207 and 270-271. *Also see*, about *actio Pauliana* and its modern correspondences in French, English and German legislations, Munch-Petersen Konkurssurrogater, chapters XXIII and XXIV, and, about *actio Pauliana* in Roman law, the development under the Middle Ages and the new Era to 1800 and modern correspondences in Dutch, French, German and Anglo-American laws, Göransson, pp. 47-52 and 63-207. *Also see*, about L'action paulienne in Belgium law, Leroy, L'efficacité des procédures judiciaires au sein de l'union Européenne et les garanties des droits de la defense, Transparence patrimoniale, L'efficacité de la justice civile en Europe, pp. 370-373.
23. The Latin word *concursus* may, depending on the circumstances, *i.a.* be translated into: a gathering of a crowd, assembly, concourse, conjunction (of things), collision, a coincidence, concurrence, combination and joint right, *see* Oxford Latin Dictionary, pp. 392-393.
24. The English word bankruptcy is derived from the Latin wordings *bancus ruptus*, 'broken bench', which is originally explained by the medieval custom in the Italian merchant cities to break the bench of an insolvent changer. The English word bankruptcy has maintained the meaning of bankruptcy in general. The French wording banqueroute now is used only in the sense of bankruptcy fraud. Ordinary bankruptcies in some States instead use terms that are derived from the Latin *fallere, i.e.* defraud, such as in the French faillite, which, however, is less used today as compared to the word liquidation judiciaire, the Italian fallimento and the Danish fallit. The word *concurcus* derives its origin from a famous Spanish work from Salgado de Somoza, 'Labyrinthus creditorum concurrentium' of 1645, where it meant the convergency of creditors. Later, linguistically improper, it has has been used in language about the bankruptcy of the debtor, *see* Welamson, pp. 8-9.

2.2 MIDDLE AGES

During the twelfth century papacy the religious perception of the Roman Catholic Church was transformed into legal reality.[25] This work, which was undertaken and continued by a long line of lawyer-popes, resulted in papal judgments, papal decretals, or formal papal letters embodying legal decisions; a flood of legislation, which was matched by legal codification in Canon law, as evident from the following quotation:[26]

> As the Consistory increasingly became the supreme court of Christendom, the business heard before it became immensely varied, but often maddeningly trivial. Rome had originally been conceived as the court of final appeal: in the course of the twelfth century it took on the role of a court of first instance. With the journeying of Urban II in France and the sudden accessibility of the papal court outside of Italy, business multiplied, and that trend intensified in the course of the next century. The pope became the 'universal ordinary', exercising direct jurisdiction in every corner of Christendom, dispensing judgments which were built into the precedent books and became the basis of law. The roots of this development were religious, based on the traditional Roman interpretation of the commission of Peter. . . . It was the work of the twelfth-century papacy to transform this religious perception into legal reality. The great originator here was Pope Alexander III (1159-81), the first of a long line of lawyer-popes. About a thousand papal decretals, of formal papal letters embodying legal decisions, survive for the twelfth century. An amazing 700 of them are Alexander's, of which more than half concern English matters. . . . The study and practice of canon law had made a huge stride forward with the compilation by the Bolognese monk Gratian of the *Concordia discordantium canonum*, 'the harmony of discordant laws', about the year 1140. This massive collection and systematization of the whole body of canon law to the mid-century brought order and a dialectic method of resolving legal contradictions to a previously chaotic situation. It helped establish canon law as one of the principal fields of intellectual effort and advance over the next century. Gratian's work was the enterprise of a private scholar, as most medieval legal collections were: the papacy had no hand in it. . . . Canon law was papal law, and the growing dominance of law within the Church was a key factor in the establishment of the papacy at the heart of the Church, as the monarch and his courts lay, at the heart of secular legal systems.

Roman law has influenced Canon law, and Canon law has in its turn influenced the general European development of laws, in particular during the Middle Ages.[27]

---

25. *See* Nouveau Petit Larousse illustré, Dictionnaire encyclopédique, p. 166, where the word catholique is explained as follows: 'adj. (du gr. katholikos, universel)'.
26. *See* Duffy, p. 101. *Also see*, about Canon law and its influences, Tamm, pp. 270-276.
27. *See* Strahl, p. 29. *Also see* Anners, Den europeiska rättens historia, del 1, p. 142, who reports that not even Roman law, under the Middle Ages, had such profound effects on the Western European legislations as Canon law.

The legal cultures of Europe have through the centuries been formed by the common point of departure *ius commune, i.e.* Canon law and Roman law.[28] On the strength of its legal system of Canon law, the church enjoyed considerable authority in Europe and Canon law was applied alongside Roman law.

The jurisprudence, which in the eleventh century began to study and treat the Roman *Corpus iuris civilis*, the glossarists,[29] discussed the conflict of interests between the freedom of the debtor to indebt himself and the right of the creditor, based on the contractual obligation, to a compulsory compliance of his claim, and arguments were put forward both in favour of and against such a compliance. Some glossarists, who were in favour of a compulsory compliance, argued with reference to the *opinio communis*, or situation of insolvency of the debtor, or the situation when a compliance by the debtor was easy to achieve, without too much trouble, but they thought, however, that a conflict between these interests was possible in some few situations because the individual freedom of the debtor should hardly not be violated.[30]

Important contributions to the legal science and development in Europe, including the civil execution law area, have also been made by the universities. The foundation of the oldest university in Europe in Bologna in 1088 constituted the beginning of this important development.[31] This was followed later on by the foundation of universities in many other European States, which also are of considerable age. Some few examples are these in: Paris in about 1150, Oxford in 1249, Cambridge in 1280, Praha/Prague in 1348, Kraków in 1364, Uppsala in 1477 and Copenhagen in 1479.[32]

The transition from a barter economy to a monetary economy during the thirteenth and fourteenth centuries gave raise to the appearance of the first bankers in Europe, most of them of an Italian origin, the *mercatores*, merchants who's activities related to all kind of commerce,[33] which naturally meant that they also

28. *See* Modéer, p. 83, who concludes that all of the legal cultures of the European countries have a relationship to the *ius commune*, the learned law, *i.e.* Canon law and Roman law.
29. *See* about the glossarists and their work Anners, Den europeiska rättens historia, del 1, pp. 125-131.
30. *See* Vertragstreue und Erfüllungszwang in der mittelalterlichen Rechtswissenschaft, p. 188, where this is expressed as follows: 'Der Interessenkonflikt zwischen der schuldnerischen Freiheit und der Vertragstreue war im letzten Fall auch denkbar gering, weil die persönliche Freiheit des Schuldners kaum beeinträchtigt werden konnte'. Some other glossarists, who were against a precise compulsory compliance, argued that it was against the debtor's individual freedom and one of them, Dinus, even compared such a compliance to a kind of slavery, *see i.b.*
31. *See* Norstedts uppslagsbok, p. 180. *Also see*, about the important role that Bologna played for the development of a legal science, Tamm, pp. 257-259.
32. *See* Stora Focus, Band 10, p. 212, and Norstedts uppslagsbok, p. 236 (Among the 17 colleagues of the university of Cambridge the oldest is St. Peter's colleague), p. 860 (Copenhagen), p. 896 (The Jagellonian university in Kraków), p. 1210 (The university of Oxford consists of 25 colleagues, is independent from the City, and has two representatives of its own in the Parliament), p. 1295 (Praha/Prague), and pp. 1750 and 1753 (Uppsala).
33. Their commercial monetary activities included: the reception of depositions of money in their hands, *depositum*, nearly always under the terms of an irregular deposit, the banker became owner of the money with a liability to reimburse an equal amount, which lead to the practice of a

included the trade in money into their business.[34] The clients of these merchants came from all classes in the society, the burghers from the cities, and even from the inhabitants in the countryside of Flanders and Hainaut,[35] to the loan tables, 'tables de prêt', which the Lombards had established in all cities of a certain importance.[36] Not only ordinary people were the clients of these merchants, but also the most important and forceful persons, both in the secular and the ecclesiastical worlds, like the popes, the emperors and the kings. Some of these merchants cooperated through their established branches at the Curia with the Holy See and other people from the church, and some of them also enjoyed a privileged position in their relations with the church as *mercatores camerae apostolicae*. The collection of the payments of the tithe and the Peter's pence in the provinces of the church was often entrusted by the Curia to the *mercatores*. These Italian *mercatores* were, given their important disposal, such as by the rapidity they were able to make their movements of funds, besides the Jews and the Order of Knights Templar, the only ones who were able to satisfy the needs of money to these persons. Nearly all monarchs and feudal lords in Christianity were to be found there, and who, for various reasons, such as the burdensome support of wars, or costs of luxury, or departure for a crusade, or a stay in the Holy Land, called for credits of sometimes enormous amounts from these Italian merchants.[37]

During the feudal times of the Middle Ages in Europe, when the nobles and magnates controlled large parts of life in society, sometimes without any stronger interventions by the respective Crowns, the administration and control of justice, including the enforcement and recovery of claims, were left to the Councils of the various rulers, to the Courts in the Provinces and Cities, or to the possible legal initiatives available to the private creditor under the law. This was successively changed when the Crown of the respective States restored an effective central power in society in the private and public law areas.

---

current account, the loans of money, *mutuum*, given under certain conditions among which the most used concept was the reimbursement of capital lended in the market places in Champagne and in Brie, and in the case of non-reimbursement on the due day a stipulation of a damage for the reasons of *damna, interesse* and *expensa*, when this was agreed between the parties, the remittance of funds, which either was made to them for their commercial use, with a stipulation of a division of the loss and the gain, *comodatum*, or which they made on behalf of their own, under the same conditions, to other merchants, and all the activities concerned the change in general, *cambium* or *scambium*, whether it concerned the change of money or the transport of money by use of bills of exchange.

34. *See*, about the activities of the *mercatores*, when they acted as bankers and collectors and about some features of modern composition and bankruptcy, Fliniaux, pp. 436-472.
35. In German called Hennegau, a province in the south of Belgium. Under the Middle Ages a German County, which in 1815 was united with the Netherlands, and in 1830 with Belgium, *see* Norstedts uppslagsbok, p. 611.
36. Such similar permanent establishments also existed in *e.g.* Germany, France and the two Bourgognes.
37. Some few examples are: the German emperor and king of Sicily Frederick II, the kings of England, and in particular Edward III, the counts of Flanders and the French king.

2.2.1 Civil Execution Law

The enforcement of a civil law judgment was in Germanic laws, *e.g.* in Danish, German and Swedish laws, originally entrusted to the winning party alone.[38] It consisted in a non-legally regulated procedure, which completely had the character of private self-help, and therefore was different from the assistance available to the winning plaintiff in Roman law.[39] The means through which the purpose of the execution in Germanic laws was gained was outlawry.[40] It meant that an individual, who had violated the law in the society, lost the peace and protection granted by the society and was in that sense expulsed from it. Consequently the individual became subject to a sanction of a criminal nature, and it was possible to kill the outlaw with impunity and devastate his property. A violation of the law was also possible if it was based on the contumacy of the debtor to pay his debt, when the debt was stipulated in a judgment, and meant a break of the judgment. Outlawry then became the means for the creditor to receive payment for his claim.

The execution of judgments under the medieval Danish Provincial Codes was largely entrusted to the winning party alone.[41] The creditor was, subject to certain conditions, able to practice a method of self-help, or by the use of fines achieve the enforcement of the judgment. The creditor was able to practice a method for the payment of the debt through a declaration of outlawry, with serious consequences for the debtor. This was, however, first possible, in a part of Denmark called Sjælland, after that the creditor had tried to execute his claim in the assets of the debtor by the assistance of the king's Ombudsmand, who then also acted so as to execute both the fines belonging to the applicant creditor and to the king. At this execution the creditor's claim and fines should be covered before the fines of the king. When the debtor in a procedure of outlawry gave up all his assets, it was, however, no longer possible to declare him an outlaw. Another method available to the creditor was that of Nam,[42] which was an action of self-pledge by the creditor in the tangible assets of the debtor. Nam was the means of gaining security, but often required a procedure that involved the people from the Ting, the place where legal matters were dealt with. In the merchant cities it was normally, according to the

---

38. *See*, about the development in the civil execution law area in German law, Spann, pp. 69-104 (Das frühe Mittelalter – Pfandnahme als Zwang zur Leistung), and 105-186 (Zersplitterung des Rechts – Betrachtung des Vollstreckungsrechts ab dem 12. Jahrhundert unter dem Einfluss der Rezeption).
39. Compare 2.1.1 about the procedure in Roman law in relation to the execution of the winning plaintiff's claim.
40. *See* Kottmann, pp. 1-3, and about further details on the legal concept of outlawry and the treatment of the execution of a claim in the Swedish Provincial Codes and City Codes Wrede, pp. 4-13. *Also see* Anners, Den europeiska rättens historia, Några huvudlinjer, del 1, pp. 180 and 182, about the Swedish Provincial Codes, the common Country law of king Magnus Eriksson of 1347, and the common City law, which was enacted a short time after the Country law.
41. *See* Lemann Kristiansen, pp. 105 and 187, and Stemann, pp. 257-261.
42. Nam is an old Danish word, which corresponds to the Swedish word utmätning, *see* Norstedts dansk-svenska ordbok, p. 396. The corresponding words in English are distress or attachment.

medieval Danish City Codes the task of the Byfoged, partially together with the appointed officials of the Council, to recover fines due. An exception was the City Code of Ribe, according to which it was possible to hold the debtor imprisoned until he had paid his debt. Other exceptions were the later City Codes, according to which the debtor could be transferred to the creditor in order to work off his debt, when his assets were found insufficient.

In Sweden the enforcement of a judgment was originally entrusted to the winning party alone and the creditor was then either able to practice a method for the payment of his claim through a declaration of the outlawry of the debtor, or by a method of Nam.[43] Also here, the method of Nam was an action of self-pledge by the creditor in the tangible assets of the debtor, without an intervention of court, and did not mean the annulment of the debt, but was rather a means of gaining security. The legal concept of outlawry is evident from all the Swedish Provincial Codes from the thirteenth and fourteenth centuries, and was of a greater importance in the older ones compared to the younger ones, but did not exist in the contemporary Swedish City Codes. These Provincial Codes did not normally, as opposed to the City Codes, accept the execution of all claims, but only certain claims, and then in a procedure in the presence of the assembled people from the Ting, the place where legal matters were dealt with, or in the presence of the neighbours of the debtor, in the home of the debtor. Even if the introduction of the Swedish common Country law of king Magnus Eriksson of 1347 meant the approval of the execution of all claims and that the procedure was simplified, matters of civil execution law still required court treatment. These matters remained formally within the court system until 1669, when they were transferred to the administrative authorities.[44]

The enforceable document by the consent of the parties, *e.g.* notarial documents, appeared under the Middle Ages, first in the legal systems of the Italian cities and then gradually as an institution of the *ius commune*.[45] The legal foundation was provided by a rule, which required a confession before the judge, but already under the Middle Ages a declaration had the same effect. Later any public document was assimilated. A private document became in fact enforceable when it was recognized by the debtor in court. The profession of the Notary derives its historical origins from both the Roman Empire and the developments under the Middle Ages.[46]

43. Compare 3.1.5.3 about the corresponding Norwegian meaning and use of the word nam.
44. *Also see* 3.1.5.4 where this is further treated.
45. *See*, for further details about the history of enforceable notarial documents, Kerameus, Enforcement in the International Context, Recueil des cours, collected courses of the Hague Academy of International Law, 1997, Tome 264 de la collection, p. 230.
46. The website of the Notaires de France, <www.notaires.fr>, headline L'historique, reads: 'Les origines: Au troisième siècle de notre ère, durant le Bas Empire romain, des fonctionnaires dont le rôle s'apparentait à celui des notaires, authentifiaient déjà des contrats au nom de l'État. La colonisation introduisit l'institution en Gaule, et les "notaires gaulois" rédigeaient des actes, notamment en vue de recenser les terres pour déterminer l'assiette de l'impôt foncier. L'institution disparaîtra avec les invasions barbares et fera sa réapparition au IX° siècle en vertu d'un

2.2.2 Tax Collection

An early example of the restoration of an effective central power to the Crown under the Middle Ages in Europe, with obvious consequences in the tax collection and recovery areas, is England after the Norman Conquest in 1066 by William the Conqueror, who became king of England. He was known as a merciless taxer, assisted by his Norman knight's bailiff, based on a record of feudal holdings directly or indirectly liable to the Crown, including a detailed survey of assets, compiled by him in the so-called Domesday Book, because there was no possibility of appeal against it. The efficiency of these bailiffs is illustrated by the following quotation:[47]

> Above all, William was a merciless taxer. His first act after his coronation was to 'lay on a geld exceeding stiff'. Close-fisted and grasping – a monk complainted that, while the Saxon kings gave their courtiers four meals a day, he gave his only one – he had compiled after 1085, mainly that he might tax his realm more closely, a record of all feudal holdings directly or indirectly liable to the Crown. 'So narrowly did he cause the survey to be made', wrote an English chronicler, 'that there was not one single hide nor rood of land, nor – it is shameful to tell, but he thought it no shame to do – was there an ox, cow or swine that was not set down in the writ'. Using commissioners to hold local enquiries or inquests in every shire and hundred, he had recorded, with meticulous efficiency, the ownership and taxable value of every manor or village under lordship, both at the Conquest and at the time of the survey. This included the number of its hides or ploughlands, of the freemen, villeins, cottars and slaves living on it, of its mills, fish-ponds and plough-teams, the extent of its woodland, meadow and pasture – everything, in short, that was capable of being taxed. Originally drawn up on long parchment rolls stored in the Treasury at Winchester, the survey was copied into two volumes christened by the English 'Domesday', because there was no appeal against it. It was the most remarkable administrative document of the age; there is nothing like it in the contemporary annals of any other country. It enabled

capitulaire de Charlemagne. A l'avènement du royaume de France: Saint Louis, peu avant sa dernière croisade, en 1270, et Philippe le Bel, en 1302, contribuèrent à développer le rôle du notaire. On doit au premier la nomination, au Châtelet, de 60 notaires qui instrumentent au nom du prévôt. On doit au second l'extension de la fonction notariale à l'ensemble des domaines placés sous l'autorité du souverain. De Villers-Cotterêts au siècle des "lumières": Au XVIème siècle, la France est devenue une nation. En 1539, par l'ordonnance de Villers-Cotterêts, François Ier préfigure ce que sera l'organisation de la profession de notaire: les actes devront être rédigés en français, la conservation devra en être assurée et leur existence devra être consignée dans un répertoire. En 1597, Henri IV fait du notaire le détenteur du sceau de l'État. La Révolution et le 19ème siècle: La Révolution n'a pas remis en cause l'institution notariale. Dans la dernière phase du Consulat, Bonaparte, consul à vie, donne au notariat, par la loi du 25 ventôse an XI, un statut dont les fondements et les grands principes n'ont pas été, pour l'essentiel, modifiés depuis.'

47. *See* Bryant, pp. 170-171.

the king to know the landed wealth of his entire realm; 'how it was peopled and with what sort of men,' what their rights were, and how much they were worth. The taxation William imposed fell directly on the rich, but, as the rich could pass it on, even more severely on the poor.

2.2.3 Composition

The customary laws of the Italian merchant cities also provided another way of promoting a settlement, a composition, in a situation of insolvency, between the fugitive debtor and his creditors, the grant of a safe-conduct to the debtor by those who exercised the power in these merchant cities. It was given for a determined period of one month, or two months, or more, and its effects were capable of being more, or less, extensive. They normally concerned the security of persons and assets, but were sometimes limited to the security of a person, but their goal were, nevertheless, to facilitate a composition between the debtor and the creditors. A composition could either mean an agreement by the consent of the creditors with the debtor to repay a part of the debt, or the grant from the creditors of an extension of the period of repayment to the debtor of his debt. The compositions between the creditors and the debtor concerning in particular the repayment of a part of the debt required initially the approval of all creditors, but later only the consent of a majority of the creditors. This development of the concept of a composition with one's creditors, which established its essential characteristics under this period, is illustrated in the following quotation:[48]

> Pendant longtemps de tels accords, surtous en ce qui concerne la remise d'une fraction de la dette, exigèrent le consentement de tous les créanciers (Statut de Pistoie de 1296). Mais on finit par admettre que la majorité des créanciers aurait assez de force pour imposer sa volonté à la minorité. Ce jour là, on peut dire que l'institution du concordat était définitivement établie avec ses caractères essentiels (Statut réformé de Padoue de 1420).

2.2.4 Insolvency

In the regulations of the Italian merchant cities a new construction, based on the Roman law concept of *venditio bonorum*,[49] was further developed as customary law in the fourteenth century, from which the origins of modern bankruptcy may be traced. A typical fact, which was attributed great importance in this customary law, was the run away of the debtor, which was assumed to be a sufficient external sign of the suspension of payments, which was not necessary to be proven in other ways. The principal effect of insolvency, according to this customary law, was the

48. *See* Fliniaux, pp. 465-466.
49. *See* 2.1.3.

withdrawal of the debtor, which meant that the debtor lost the right to decrease his assets, and that he could not dispose of them to the detriment of the creditors.

The concept in Roman law of the *actio Pauliana*[50] was also further developed in this customary law. The invalidity, which according to this Roman law, was only applicable to transactions made by the debtor before the moment of the taking of possession of the insolvency estate, was now, in addition, introduced, under the presumption of fraud, for the period after this moment. Bilateral bankruptcy conventions were also concluded during this period. A treaty was concluded between Verona and Trent in 1204 that governed the transfer of a debtor's assets, and Verona and Venice reached an agreement in 1306, which sanctioned the extradition of fugitive debtors.[51]

A financial crisis began in 1298 with the breakdown of the Italian merchant banker of Buonsignori de Sienne, followed in 1300 by the breakdown of the Italian merchant banker of Ricciardi de Lucques, both of them due to purely financial reasons, as opposed to the breakdown in 1302 of the Italian merchant banker of Ammanati de Pistoie, which was caused by political circumstances. This development of financial breakdowns, which continued without interruption during the first part of the fourteenth century lead to the intervention from the Holy See, by the use of different means, in order to organize insolvency proceedings, with features of modern bankruptcy, and to reach settlements between the creditors and the debtors. An example of an intervention from the Holy See in one of these breakdowns of Italian merchant bankers is the so-called Ammanati affair. This affair, which is not a court case, also illustrates the practical application of the principle of universality in the international insolvency area, where the pope[52] acted when the Ammanati bank, resident in the republic of Pistoia in the present Italy, became insolvent.[53]

The bank owned branches and assets located in the whole of Europe at the time, *i.a.* in Spain, England, France and Germany. When the bank became insolvent its owners fled to an unknown location and there were reasons to believe that they would attempt to dispose of the assets, *e.g.* by means of demanding payments from the debtors of the bank. The creditors of the bank were also located in different countries and they tried, as fast as possible to secure the local assets of the bank. It became obvious that such an unstructured proceeding of liquidation was not in the collective interest of the creditors and could be harmful to certain creditors, including the pope in Rome. The pope therefore intervened and made an attempt to organize a proceeding in total harmony with modern considerations of international insolvency. Despite that were the worldly powers of the pope limited to the territory of the papal State. He enjoyed nevertheless in his capacity of the supreme head of the Catholic Church, an authority

50. *See* 2.1.3.
51. *See* Wood, chapter 17 International insolvency treaties, section 17-1.
52. Boniface VIII, Benedetto Caetani, was pope 1294-1303, Bl. Benedict XI, Niccolo Boccasino 1303-1304 and Clement V, Bertrand de Got 1305-1314, *see* Duffy, p. 298.
53. The following summary of the Ammanati affaire from 1302 is based on Fliniaux, pp. 436-472, and Bogdan, Sveriges och EU:s internationella insolvensrätt, pp. 14-15.

which was considerably greater than that, in particular through his powers in relation to the clergy in the different countries. This authority was used by the pope to prohibit all the debtors of the bank to pay their debts to the owners of the bank without the permission from the Holy See and to prohibit the owners to dispose of the assets of the bank. Legal acts contrary to these prohibitions were declared invalid. The owners of the bank were offered guarantees for their personal security, *salvus conductus*, in case they would return and make a settlement with the creditors. All assets from all countries were, according to the plan of the pope, to be gathered through the financial channels of the church into the hands of the Curia, in order to thereafter be distributed in arranged forms among the creditors. The pope gave one or several men of the church, *executores*, the task to follow up the enforcement of the claims belonging to the bank in a fixed region, and the debtors were to be urged to fulfill their obligations, if not they were to be forced *per censuram ecclesiasticam*. It is not evident from the material of the archives if the efforts were successful.

2.3 PERIOD OF 1500-1806

The influences of Canon law decreased in certain European States as a result of the break between the kings of these States and the Pope of the Roman Catholic Church, for various reasons, under the crisis of Christendom in the period of Reformation and Counter Reformation of the church. This was *i.a.* brought about as a consequence of the influences by Luther and Calvin, and meant that a new theological concept was formulated under this period. The economic development in European societies also demanded a corresponding development of national laws,[54] which also included enforcement laws. The foundation of universities in Europe continued, as *e.g.* in: Vilnius in 1579, Tartu/Dorpat in 1632, Turku/Åbo in 1640, and Lund in 1668.[55] The invention of the printing press also contributed to the rapid development of legislation during this period.

The constitutional doctrines of Montesquieu[56] in his work De L'esprit des Lois of 1748, introduced the idea of a separation within the State of legislative, executive and judicial powers as a guarantee against the abuse of powers and to promote a greater freedom for the citizens. This work provided important

54. *See*, about the economic, social and cultural background to the legal development of the period of 1500-1800, Anners, Den europeiska rättens historia, Några huvudlinjer, del 2, pp. 11-19.
55. *See* Norstedts uppslagsbok, pp. 353, 983, 1822 and 1876, and Stora Focus, Band 8, p. 275.
56. Charles Louis de Secondat de La Brède et de Montesquieu (1689-1755), French baron and author, one of the most important representatives of the Age of Enlightenment, who, in connection to Locke and the English form of government, recommended, as a guarantee against the abuse of powers, a division of the powers of the State-legislation, executive powers and the administration of justice-between separate State organs, *see* Norstedts uppslagsbok, p. 1088. Compare Strömholm, Inledning och urval: Om lagarnas anda eller det förhållande som bör råda mellan lagarna och respektive styrelses författning, seder, klimat, religion, handel, etc: vartill

influences into national constitutions and limited correspondingly the royal authority over legislation. Montesquieu expressed the problem of lack of freedom, when the legislative, executive and judicial powers were united under the powers of the same person, or the same group of persons, as told in the following quotation:[57]

> Lorsque dans la même personne ou dans le même corps de magistrature, la puissance législative est réunie à la puissance exécutrice, il n'y a point de liberté; parce qu'on peut craindre que le même monarque ou le même sénat ne fasse des lois tyranniques pour les exécuter tyranniquement. Il n'y a point encore de liberté si la puissance de juger n'est pas séparée de la puissance législative et de l'exécutrice. Si elle était jointe à la puissance législative, le pouvoir sur la vie et la liberté des citoyens serait arbitraire: car le juge serait législateur. Si elle était jointe à la puissance exécutrice, le juge pourrait avoir la force d'un oppresseur. Tout serait perdu si le même homme, ou le même corps des principaux, ou des nobles, ou du peuple, exerçaient ces trois pouvoirs: celui de faire des lois, celui d'exécuter les résolutions publiques, et celui de juger les crimes ou les différends des particuliers.

Montesquieu also further commented on the relationship, interplay and necessary cooperation between the legislative and executive powers, as evident from the following quotation:[58]

> Le corps législatif y étant composé de deux parties, l'une enchaînera l'autre par sa faculté mutuelle d'empêcher. Toutes les deux seront liées par la puissance exécutrice, qui le sera elle-même par la législative. Ces trois puissances devraient former un repos ou une inaction. Mais comme, par le mouvement nécessaire des choses, elles sont contraintes d'aller, elles seront forcées d'aller de concert. La puissance exécutrice ne faisant partie de la législative que par sa faculté d'empêcher, elle ne saurait entrer dans le débat des affaires.

An example of a State, where a separation between the executive and judicial powers was established before the doctrines of Montesquieu, is Sweden, through the Swedish Execution Ordinance of 1669.[59] Examples of States, which still have not separated the executive and judicial powers, are: Denmark, England and Germany.[60] Montesquieu recommended, in his same work, that la contrainte par corps, a personal coercive measure, a special kind of imprisonment of the debtor, which seems to have shared some similar features with the *lex Poetilia* in Roman law[61] and the

---

författaren fogat nya forskningar över de romerska successionslagarna, de franska lagarna och feodallagarna.

57. *See* Montesquieu, De L'esprit des Lois, livre XI, chapitre VI de la constitution d'Angleterre, Tome premier, p. 164.
58. *See* Montesquieu, De L'esprit des Lois, livre XI, chapitre VI de la constitution d'Angleterre, Tome premier, p. 172.
59. *See* 2.2.1, and 3.1.5.4, where this is further treated.
60. *See* 3.1.5.1 about the Danish Fogedret, and 3.2.1 about the English and Wales' systems and 3.1.4 about the German system.
61. Compare 2.1.

imprisonment of the debtor according to the Law of Sweden of 1734,[62] should apply in ordinary civil matters, but he concluded that there were no reasons to observe it in matters of trade, as told in the following quotation:[63]

> Cette loi est très bonne pour les affaires civiles ordinaires; mais nous avons raison de ne point l'observer dans celles du commerce.

The administration and control of matters of enforcement and recovery were gradually strengthened during the period of 1500-1806 by the central powers in society.

2.3.1 Civil Execution Law

Because the procedure in the wordly courts was time consuming and expensive, clerical courts were instead sometimes used in Denmark for the enforcement of debts before the Reformation of the church in Denmark in 1536. The application of the law of the church was faster and also more efficient being combined with a specifically fearful means of enforcement, the threat of excommunication, which in the wordly law corresponded to a declaration of outlawry.[64] Some situations when the creditors were able to turn to the clerical courts were: neglected payments of debt, which were equaled to a break of an agreement or to a break of a contract, or in case of a break of an oath on the willingness of payment, which was not followed by any payment. The use by the church of excommunication in debt matters was, however, controversial because it would lead to that a man's salvation became in danger, not only because he was not willing to pay, but also when he was not able to. King Frederik I stopped this use of the clerical courts through his letter of 1527 on the subject of how debts shall be enforced by the use of the Herredsting.[65] In this letter it was made evident that no one shall be summoned to receive the judgment of the church for debt or other matters that should be treated by the wordly courts of the Herredsting or the Landsting and it was also made clear that these matters for the future belonged to the worldly courts.[66]

Only a minor part of the Swedish legislation was in the sixteenth and seventeenth centuries devoted to the rules of civil execution law, but it was subsequently enlarged during the two following centuries.[67] The Law of Sweden of 1734

62. Compare VIII. Cap. Om qwarstad och bysättning (About sequestration and imprisonment), in the Enforcement Code (Utsökningsbalk), pp. 304-308, included in the Sweriges rikes lag gillad och antagen på riksdagen åhr 1734 (The Law of the Swedish Realm accepted and approven by the Parliament the year 1734). *Also see*, about bysättning, Jacobsson, p. 486.
63. *See* Montesquieu, De L'esprit des Lois, livre XX, chapitre XV de la contrainte par corps, Tome second, p. 18.
64. *See* 2.2.1 for further details about outlawry.
65. Frederik I lived between 1471-1533, *see* Norstedts uppslagsbok, p. 493.
66. *See* Lemann Kristiansen, pp. 190 and 192-193.
67. This has been described as follows: 'In the Royal Statutes, Resolutions and Ordinances concerning the Judicature from 1528 one out of 670 pages was devoted to the rules of enforcement. That page was also part of Gustavus II Adolphus' Court Proceedings from 1615 . . . In

included a civil Enforcement Code, Utsökningsbalk, of 23 pages, which represented nearly six percent out of the total of all the provisions under this Law.[68] An example, among several German States, is the Allgemeines Landrecht für die Preuβischen Staaten of 1792, which included 6 pages of rules on civil execution law, Von Pfändungen, but these provisions only represented less than one percent out of the total of all the provisions under this legislation.[69] The French Code de Procédure Civile of 1806 included 57 pages of rules on civil execution law, or

---

1669 the Execution Ordinance appeared. It was commented on by Claudio Kloot in the Looking-Glass of Swedish Legal Practice. In his book one can find the seeds of several rules of enforcement, which are still valid today. It deals with the creditors request for enforcement and with the exemption from execution of necessary agricultural implements.... The commentary is a volume of 404 pages, 10 of which are devoted to enforcement. The Code of Judicial Procedure from 1734 contained rules on enforcement, which were extracted into an Enforcement Code in 1877, seemingly without any greater changes. It may be noted that in a commentary of 1801 by Jacob Albrecht Flintberg great stress was put on a party's possibility to appeal against enforcement at a court. Carl E. Bachmann's Handbook of Law (1883) deals with both civil law and legal regulations of enforcement and procedure. In terms of volume the balance is now 70 pages of enforcement rules versus 170 pages of rules of procedure. Still the rules of enforcement appear meagre in comparison with those of today', *see* Jacobsson, p. 486. *Also see* about more details and comments on the historical development of the Swedish enforcement legislation: Backman, pp. 404-447 and 465-474, Hallin, pp. 1-12 and 19-44, Hassler, pp. 341-368, Nehrman-Ehrenstråle, pp. 439-466, Schrevelius, pp. 392-431, Sjögren, pp. 1-43, and Sjöholm, pp. 1-4. The attachment of the earnings of the debtor has been possible according to Swedish legislation since at least by the end of the seventeenth century, *see* Fridén, p. 50.

68. Compare this Enforcement Code (Utsökningsbalk), pp. 288-311, included in the Sweriges rikes lag gillad och antagen på riksdagen åhr 1734 (The Law of the Swedish Realm accepted and approven by the Parliament the year 1734), to the total of all provisions in this Law from 1734, pp. 1-416. This Enforcement Code consisted of the following chapters: I. Cap. Om Konungens Befalningshawande, och betiente, som under honom lyda (The king's commander, and the servants, who were obedient to him), pp. 288-291, II. Cap. Huru förfaras skal, då utmätning sökes (How to act when execution is sought), pp. 291-293, Cap. III. Om utmätning å domar (About the execution of judgments), pp. 293-295, IV. Cap. Om utmätning å skuldebref, klara förskrifningar, och goda mäns utslag, (About the execution of a promissory note, clear certificates of debt, and the decision of trustees), pp. 296-299, V. Cap. Huru utmätning skal ske (How execution shall take place), pp. 299-302, VI. Cap. Huru fast gods wärderas skal (How immovable property shall be valued), pp. 302-303, VII. Cap. Om thet, som wid utmätning undantagas bör (About that, which should be excluded from execution), pp. 303-304, VIII. Cap. Om qwarstad och bysättning (About sequestration and imprisonment), pp. 304-308, IX. Cap. Huru ändring i Konungens Befalningshawandes utslag sökas må (How revision of the decision of the king's commander may be sought), pp. 308-311, and X. Cap. Huru then plichta skal, som i twistemål ej mächtar betala thet wite, eller the böter, som honom ålagda äro (How the one, who in civil cases is not capable of paying that penalty, or these fines, which have been imposed on him, shall be obliged), p. 311.

69. Compare Erster Theil, Vierzehnter Titel: Von Erhaltung des Eigenthums und der Rechte, Vierter Abschnitt: Von Pfändungen (§§ 413-465), pp. 605-611, to the total of all provisions in Allgemeines Landrecht für die Preuβischen Staaten von 1792, pp. 3-1400. *See*, for further comments on this legislation, Anners, Den europeiska rättens historia, Några huvudlinjer, del 2, pp. 44-46. *Also see*, about the development in German law, Spann, pp. 173-186 (Die Nürnberger Reformation von 1479 und 1564 als Vorbild einer systematischen Kodifikation des Vollstreckungsrechts für die spätere bayerische Landrechtsentwicklung), and pp. 187-243 (Bayerisches

thereto related matters, which represented nearly 25 percent out of the total of all the provisions under this Code.[70] Even if it is not possible to base a comparison of these three national legislations, all of them valid at the time of the enactment of this French Code, *i.e.* in 1806, only on their respective volumes of rules on civil execution law, still this French legislation appears to have been both more advanced, extensive and developed in details compared to these two other national legislations. Both the Swedish and French legislations included rules about sequestration.[71] The prototype of provisional enforceability is to be found in French law and has existed there since the fourteenth century. It was adopted by the Napoleonic Code de Procédure Civile, one of Les cinq codes, and has spread over to other States, especially to Germany.[72] The Napoleonic cinq codes were not only applied in France, but also in other European States or constituted prototypes of inspiration to legislators in a number of European States.[73]

Landesrecht ab Beginn des 16. Jahrhunderts bis ins 19. Jahrhunderts mit Hinweisen zum gemeinem Recht).

70. Compare Première partie, Livre Premier, Titre V., Des jugements qui ne sont pas définitifs, et leur exécution, pp. 11-12, Livre V., De l'exécution des jugements: Titre VI., Règles générales sur l'exécution forcée des jugements et actes, pp. 125-127, Titre VII., Des saisies-arrêts ou oppositions, pp. 127-132, Titre VIII., Des saisies-exécutions, pp. 132-140, Titre IX., De la saisie des fruits pendants par racine, ou de la saisie-brandon, pp. 141-142, Titre X., De la saisie des rentes constituées sur particuliers, pp. 142-146, Titre XI., De la distribution par contribution, pp. 146-149, Titre XII., De la saisie immobilière, pp. 149-160, Titre XIII., Des incidents sur la poursuite de saisie immobilière, pp. 160-166, Titre XIV., De l'ordre, pp. 167-172, Titre XV., De l'emprisonnement, pp. 172-179, and Titre XVI, Des référés, pp. 179-180, to the total of all provisions in the Code de Procédure Civile from 1806, pp. 5-234, *i.e.* without taking the articles du Code Civil, insérés dans le Code de Procédure, into consideration in this comparative context. *Also see*, for some comments on the saisies mobilières and the saisie immobilière, Traité théorique et pratique de Procédure civile et commerciale en justice de paix et devant les conseils de prud'hommes, Garsonnet et Cézar-Bru, Tome IV, troisième partie, Voies D'Exécution, Volume I, Saisies mobilières – Saisie immobilière, et Tome V, troisième partie, Voies D'Exécution, Volume II, Saisie immobilière Ordre et Contribution.
71. *See* the Swedish Enforcement Code, chapter VIII. about qwarstad/sequestration, pp. 304-307, and the French Code de Procédure Civile, Livre II., Titre VII. Des jugements (Arts 135-137), pp. 38-39, Titre XXV. Procédure devant les tribunaux de commerce (Arts 439-441), pp. 103-104, Livre III. Titre unique. De l'appel, et de L'instruction sur l'appel (Arts 458-461), p. 108, Livre V., Titre VI. Règles générales sur l'exécution forcée des jugements et actes (Art. 548), p. 126. Compare 2.1.1 about measure of sequestration in Roman law.
72. *See* Kerameus, Enforcement in the International Context, Recueil des cours, collected courses of the Hague Academy of International Law, 1997, Tome 264 de la collection, p. 240, compared to Kerameus, International encyclopedia of comparative law, volume XVI, Civil procedure, chapter 10, Enforcement proceedings, p. 21.
73. *See* Modéer, pp. 76-77, who reports that the French laws were not only applied outside France in Belgium, the Netherlands and in the Western parts of Germany, but they constituted also inspiring prototypes for the legislators in a number of other European States, including Sweden, and were implemented in North America in Louisiana and in Quebec, in a number of States in Latin America, and of importance for several States in parts of Africa and Asia. He also concludes that Napoleon succeeded through 'Les cinq codes' to create an optimal French legal culture and in these laws legally unite through a merger a Roman law tradition and a Germanic tradition, which was more common law orientated, *see i.b.*, p. 82. *Also see* Anners,

2.3.2 Tax Collection

During the period of the Danish Provincial Codes, when the economy was primitive, it was only possible to assume debts to a limited extent.[74] Following the introduction of the monetary economy the problems of debts and their recovery increased, but the burghers economical dealings with the public were limited, normally in relation to fines and taxes. Some typical taxes that had to be paid immediately were customs charges or other charges in order to be able to travel into the market place with the goods. This meant that this access demanded payment and therefore the appearance of a debt became excluded. Before the introduction of the autocracy by the Danish king in 1660, when the king received a complete right of taxation, the ordinary expenses of the State were to be covered by the ordinary incomes of the State, such as mainly the incomes from the estates of the Crown, customs and turnover charges.

Direct taxation was only possible at extraordinary occasions, *e.g.* in connection to war, but as the wars were quite frequent from the beginning of the seventeenth century it then rather became a rule than an exception. At extraordinary occasions of direct taxation the king issued a letter of taxation for each County with an indication of the amount and when it was due for payment. The tasks of the Lensmand were then to publish the letter, to undertake the collection and the recovery of the taxes, and finally their payment to the Rentekammeret. In 1628 the land owners from the nobility got the right to impose tax on their farmers, and in 1635 they also got the right to make their payments directly to the County administration, which meant that they then became a part of the tax administration. Shortly afterwards the Landkommissariaterne were established, and they became consequently administered by the land owning nobility, which meant that this nobility disposed over a substantial part of the tax incomes until the introduction of the autocracy by the king.

2.4 PERIOD OF 1807 TO OUR AGE

2.4.1 National Procedural Laws

The sometimes nationally secluded attitude to procedural law during the nineteenth and twentieth centuries have been remarked by several authors, but they have also noted, in relation to the same periods, illustrations to an opposite development trend.[75] Consequently, the common European influences on national laws in the

---

Den europeiska rättens historia, Några huvudlinjer, del 2, pp. 47-49, for some comments on 'Les cinq codes'.

74. *See*, about tax collection before and after the introduction of the autocracy by the Danish king in 1660, Lemann Kristiansen, pp. 105-106.

75. *See* Storme, Rapprochement du Droit Judiciaire de l'Union européenne/Approximation of Judiciary Law in the European Union, the general introductory report, p. 38, where he refers

procedural law area in the nineteenth century, and in more than one half of the twentieth century, seem generally, with some exceptions, to have relatively decreased under these periods.

2.4.2 The Way to Conventions and EC Law

When the different Empires in Europe, after 1800, gradually were replaced by an increasing number of independent European States, the earlier unifying powers of these Empires were broken, and the recognition and execution of foreign judgments became a genuine problem in Europe in the nineteenth century due to the rapid expansion of commerce and the free movement of people, merchandise and capital.[76] Instead, gradually developing under the nineteenth century, but yet more evident under the twentieth century, the establishment of new European States and their increasing interdependency in different areas gave raise to the need to increase the level of mutual cooperation by regulating a large number of legal issues through the conclusion of bilateral and multilateral treaties, conventions and agreements of cooperation. This mutual cooperation related *i.a.* to the areas of: recognition and enforcement of foreign civil law judgments, assistance for the recovery of foreign tax claims, and recognition of foreign bankruptcy decisions.

The conventions related to contractual claims were mainly established to satisfy an increased efficiency in the interest of the private creditors, while the conventions in the public law area were established to satisfy the State interests, mainly in their capacity of public creditors. This legal cross-border cooperation, based on conventions, and on reciprocity arrangements between Common law States, was developed between many European States into extensive treaty networks, which superseded the otherwise applicable principle of territoriality in public international law.[77] The legal cooperation framework of European States on the recognition and enforcement of foreign civil law claims was thus during the last century developed earlier and included more bilateral and multilateral

---

to a position during the nineteenth century, when procedural law was regarded as an area of the law which was of a specifically national character not aimed for a successful export to other States, but also to the opposite example of the translation and incorporation of the German Code of Procedure in Japan in the same century, and to some other opposite examples in the twentieth century and he concludes that the political nature of procedural law no longer justifies any divergences in the legal rules which apply within the EC. *Also see* Storme, Procedural Law and the Reform of Justice: from Regional to Universal Harmonisation, Uniform law review/Revue de droit uniforme 2001-4, Harmonising Transnational Civil Procedure: The ALI/UNIDROIT Principles and Rules/Vers une procédure civile transnationale harmonisée: Les Principes et Règles ALI/UNIDROIT, p. 774, about such opposite examples. *Also see* Lindblom, pp. 793-795, who concludes that the nationally secluded attitude to procedural law, which is common in certain European States, *i.a.* in Sweden, is a completely wrong attitude and he gives several examples which illustrate an opposite development trend.

76. *See* Thomashausen, p. 103.
77. *See* 1.1.1.4.

conventions than the corresponding legal cooperation framework of European States on the recovery of foreign tax claims.

A State, which early concluded bilateral treaties with other States in these areas, is France.[78] An early example of a regional multilateral cooperation is that between the Nordic States. From 1861 and more than a century ahead, this broad Nordic legal mutual cooperation, in the areas of international private and procedural laws, resulted in conventions *i.a.* on the recognition and enforcement of judgments in civil matters, on the recovery of maintenance claims, and on bankruptcy.[79] In the public law areas it resulted in an agreement on the recovery of tax claims, and an agreement for the enforcement of fines, confiscation or compensation for litigation costs, combined with the enactment of laws of a similar content in these States.[80] Yet another example of a regional multilateral cooperation is that between Belgium, the Netherlands and Luxemburg, which resulted in a Treaty on Jurisdiction, Bankruptcy, and the Validity and Enforcement of Judgments, Arbitration Awards and Authentic Instruments, and an agreement on the

78. *See* Walter and Baumgartner, p. 6, who report that: '... France, originally a champion of both révision au fond and recognition treaties, concluded treaties as early as 1760 (with Sardinia; renewed with Italy in 1860), 1828 (with Switzerland; renegotiated in 1869), and 1846 (with the Grand duchy of Baden).'

79. A Nordic convention on recognition and the enforcement of judgments in civil matters of 16 Mar. 1932 was replaced by a new convention in the same area, which entered into force in 1978, but was partially replaced by the Brussels I regulation, *see* 2.5.1, but still remains partially in force between the Nordic States, *see* 2.5.5 about further details on this latter convention. *Also see* the Convention between Denmark, Finland, Iceland, Norway and Sweden regarding the enforcement of maintenance claims, done in Oslo on 22 Mars 1962 (Nordic convention regarding the enforcement of maintenance claims). This convention has been made applicable on the Faeroe Islands through a decree for the application of the Nordic convention regarding the enforcement of maintenance claims, *see* Bekendtgørelse nr. 269 af 28 juni 1963 om inddrivelse af underholdsbidrag i henhold til konvention af 23 marts 1962 mellem Danmark, Finland, Island, Norge og Sverige, som ændret ved bekendtgørelse nr. 156 af 19 marts 2002 and the convention has also been made applicable in Greenland through a decree about the use of the law in Greenland, *see* Bekendtgørelse af Lov om rettens pleje i Grønland nr. 99 af 21 marts 1984, som ændret ved Lov nr. 476 af 12 juni 1996. *Also see* 2.7 about the Nordic bankruptcy convention. For further details about this cooperation in the areas of international private and procedural laws, *see* Arnt Nielsen, International privat- og procesret, pp. 23, Eek, pp. 39-40, and Karlgren, pp. 38-39.

80. *See* 2.6.3 about the Nordic agreement on assistance in tax matters, where it is treated in more details. *Also see* the Nordic agreement on the cooperation concerning the mutual assistance of enforcement of judgments or decisions on fines, confiscation or compensation for litigation costs of 1962. This Nordic agreement of cooperation is based on Art. 7 of a previous agreement of a more general nature, Samarbetsöverenskommelse mellan Danmark, Finland, Island, Norge och Sverige, Helsingfors den 23 mars 1962 (Cooperation agreement between Denmark, Finland, Iceland, Norway and Sweden, done in Helsinki on 23 Mars 1962). This Nordic agreement of cooperation in the penal law area is implemented through similar enacted legislations in the Nordic States, compare Kungl. Maj:ts proposition nr 203 år 1962 (the Swedish travaux préparatoires to the specific Nordic agreement), p. 94. The Swedish counterpart to the Nordic agreement is published in Lag (1963:193) om samarbete med Danmark, Finland, Island och Norge ang. verkställighet av straff, m.m. (Act on the cooperation with Denmark, Finland, Iceland and Norway concerning the enforcement of punishment).

mutual recovery of tax claims.[81] The practice of publishing collections of treaties concluded by certain States, or group of States, began during the second half of the seventeenth century, and constitutes a starting point for the following development of the increase of international treaties, which has resulted in an expansion of public international law beyond all recognition in about the last 140 years.[82]

A remarkable development of common European influences, which began in the second half of the twentieth century, is the gradual development of the ECs and the EU. A mayor development event affecting our subject of interest is the Treaty establishing the European Economic Community, done at Rome on 25 March 1957, by the six founding Member States: Belgium, France, Germany, Italy, Luxemburg and the Netherlands. This was followed by the important enlargement of this community/the EU, at different occasions, by the accession of other new Member States, including altogether: Austria, Bulgaria, Cyprus, Czech Republic, Denmark, Estonia, Finland, Greece, Hungary, Ireland, Latvia, Lithuania, Malta, Poland, Portugal, Romania, Slovakia, Slovenia, Spain, Sweden and the United Kingdom. In 2008, the EU included a total of 27 Member States.[83]

The growing importance of common European influences through EC law has influenced national laws. This European law has also replaced a lot of conventions related to the enforcement of foreign contractual claims and in the insolvency area, and has increased the possibilities for the recovery of foreign tax claims between many Member States of the EU, as compared to the treaty network of these States.[84]

EC law has consequently increased the legal integration of Member States in the cross-border context through indirect harmonization by means of such European law, which either may be balanced in favour of the interest of the creditor of efficiency or in favour of the interest of the debtor of privacy.[85] The common

81. *See* the Treaty between Belgium, the Netherlands and Luxemburg on Jurisdiction, Bankruptcy, and the Validity and Enforcement of Judgments, Arbitration Awards and Authentic Instruments of 24 Nov. 1961, and la Convention entre la Belgique, le Grand-Duché de Luxembourg et les Pays-Bas, relative à l'assistance réciproque en matière de recouvrement de créances fiscales, du 5 Sep. 1952 (Benelux convention on the mutual assistance for the recovery of tax claims).
82. *See* Akehurst, pp. 36-37.
83. *See* Treaty establishing the EC, consolidated version of 24 Dec. 2002, and Treaty between the Kingdom of Belgium, the Czech Republic, the Kingdom of Denmark, the Federal Republic of Germany, the Republic of Estonia, the Hellenic Republic, the Kingdom of Spain, the French Republic, Ireland, the Italian Republic, the Republic of Cyprus, the Republic of Latvia, the Republic of Lithuania, the Grand Duchy of Luxemburg, the Republic of Hungary, the Republic of Malta, the Kingdom of the Netherlands, the Republic of Austria, the Republic of Poland, the Portuguese Republic, the Republic of Slovenia, the Slovak Republic, the Republic of Finland, the Kingdom of Sweden, the United Kingdom of Great Britain and Northern Ireland (Member States of the European Union) and the Republic of Bulgaria and Romania, concerning the accession of the Republic of Bulgaria and Romania to the European Union of 21 Jun. 2005.
84. *See* Art. 69 of the Brussels I regulation, Art. 44 of the Insolvency regulation, and Art. 23 of the Recovery directive compared to Art. 27, 2 of the Council of Europe and OECD convention on mutual administrative assistance in tax matters. *Also see*, for further comments on the relationship between EC law and multilateral conventions, 5.3.1.1 (contractual claims), 5.3.1.2 (tax claims) and 6.4.1 (insolvency).
85. *See* 1.1.1.1.1 for some examples.

European indirect influences on national laws have increased during the last two decades in the areas of enforcement, recovery and insolvency. The significance of the developments, in a shorter time perspective, of the Recovery directive, especially through the amendment in 2001 of this directive, has been more remarkable than the ones related to the Brussels I regulation.[86] This has created more equal means of cross-border recovery of tax claims compared to the existing corresponding means of cross-border enforcement of private claims based on the Brussels I regulation. The European Convention on Human Rights and the Council of Europe's recommendation on enforcement have resulted in increased Common European influences in the enforcement area, and the ALI-UNIDROIT Principles of Transnational Civil Procedure are also aimed at strengthening these influences.

2.5 EC LAW AND CONVENTIONS ON CONTRACTUAL CLAIMS

During the last century the legal cooperation framework of many European States on the recognition and enforcement of foreign civil law claims developed based on a large number of bilateral conventions,[87] and on some important multilateral conventions.[88] This cooperation has, however, since the end of the last century and during the present one increasingly developed as based on EC law. This development may be illustrated by the Brussels I regulation of 2001, which replaced the Brussels convention.[89] The convention was originally negotiated and ratified by the six founding Member States of the EC and came into force on 1 February 1973, and later on in relation to other new Member States.[90] A large number of earlier bilateral and multilateral conventions were superseded by the Brussels convention and the Convention on jurisdiction and the enforcement of judgments in civil and commercial matters of 16 September 1988 (Old Lugano

86. *See* 2.6.1 about the Recovery directive compared to 2.5.1 about the Brussels I regulation.
87. *See* Manual for the collection of a sum of money abroad, pp. 21-30, which illustrates a large number of early and later on concluded bilateral conventions between European States and in relation to other States during the last century. *Also see* Walter and Baumgartner, pp. 5-8, about the activities of concluding recognition treaties by some European States.
88. *See* the New York convention on foreign arbitral awards from 1958, the Brussels convention from 1968, the Nordic convention on recognition and the enforcement of judgments in civil matters from 1977, which replaced a Nordic convention in the same area of 16 Mar. 1932, and the Lugano convention from 1988.
89. *See* Art. 68, 1 of the regulation. *Also see* for details on the entry into force of the convention in relation to the States, which are parties to the convention, annex 4.
90. *See*, for further comments on the background and history of the Brussels convention and on the accession to the convention by new Member States, the Schlosser report, p. 77, the Jenard report, pp. 3-6, the Giuliano/Lagarde report, pp. 4-8, the Evrigenis/Kerameus report, p. 4, and the Allmeida Cruz/Desantes Real/Jenard report, pp. 38-42. *Also see* Arnt Nielsen, International privat- og procesret, p. 24, International Civil Procedure, pp. 201-203, and Pålsson, Brysselkonventionen, Luganokonventionen och Bryssel I-förordningen, pp. 21-22.

convention),[91] and formally later on also by the Brussels I regulation,[92] *i.e.* to the extent their scope of application coincided with the Brussels convention and the Old Lugano convention and the Brussels I regulation.

There also exists a Convention on jurisdiction and the recognition and enforcement of judgments in civil and commercial matters, done at Lugano on 30 October 2007 (New Lugano convention). This convention is of interest in relation to certain States members of the European Free Trade Association, such as Iceland, Norway, and Switzerland, but has not yet entered into force.[93] Another example is the European Enforcement Order for uncontested claims, which originates from the initiative and proposal of the French union of Huissier de Justice in 1993 to create a Titre Exécutoire Européen (TEE) for uncontested claims, mainly based on features close to some national proceedings of injunction to pay.[94]

Another development aimed at facilitating the recognition and enforcement of foreign decisions was the introduction of a registration procedure for the judgments of certain countries, subject to certain common standards and accepting the rule of reciprocity, with origins from the first part of the last century in the United Kingdom.[95] The Hague Conference on Private International Law, which was created in 1893, and is the oldest of all inter-governmental organizations within the legal field,[96] has, under the last century, made important contributions in the field of recognition and enforcement in conventions related to *e.g.* foreign judgments in civil and commercial matters and maintenance obligations.[97] This Hague

91. *See* for details on the entry into force of the convention in relation to the States, which are parties to the convention, annex 5.
92. The bilateral and multilateral conventions, which formally were replaced by the Brussels I regulation, are mentioned in its Art. 69.
93. The Convention will enter into force in respect of Switzerland earliest on 1 Jan. 2010, *see* website de la Confédération suisse, Federal Office of Justice, <www.bj.admin.ch/bj/en/home.html>.
94. A presentation of the proposal of the TEE was made by the French Union de Huissier de Justice at a meeting in Paris during 3 and 4 Jun. 1993 arranged by l'Union Internationale des Huissiers de Justice et Officiers Judiciaires (UIHJ).
95. *See* International Civil Procedure, p. 197, which reports that the judgments from the courts of countries covered by statute, such as the Foreign Judgments Reciprocal Enforcement Act 1933, or which are party to a reciprocal enforcement convention with the UK, may be registered with the English court and enforced as a judgment of the English court and that a number of conventions and statutory regimes are in force, covering most notably fellow members of the EU and EFTA, UK dependent territories and Commonwealth countries, and Thomashausen, p. 103, reporting that this practice was introduced as a formal law in the United Kingdom with the Reciprocal Recognition of Foreign Judgments Act of 1993, and in the United States in the terms of the Uniform Act on Recognition and Reciprocal Application. *Also see* Enforcement of Foreign Judgments Worldwide, pp. 223-225, about the enforcement *in personam, e.g.* based on the payment of a debt, or for damages for breach of contracts, of a foreign judgment in the United Kingdom based on the Administration of Justice Act 1920 in relation to Commonwealth countries and based on the Foreign Judgment (Reciprocal Enforcement) Act 1933 in relation to the following States and territories: Israel, Pakistan, Surinam, Tonga, Guernsey, Jersey and Isle of Man.
96. *See* Arnt Nielsen, International privat- og procesret, p. 23, and Bernasconi, pp. 9-10.
97. *See*, about the extensive work of the Hague Conference on Private International Law, Arnt Nielsen, International privat- og procesret, pp. 23-24, Eek, pp. 36-39, Karlgren, pp. 33-37, and website of the Hague Conference on Private International Law, <www.hcch.net>, headline conventions.

Conference has also provided rich sources for the works of the EU in relation to its directives and regulations.[98]

The Council of Europe has also made important contributions. One example is the European Convention on Human Rights.[99] The application of the Convention is important in matters having cross-border implications related to the interplay between EC law and national laws. Other important examples are its recommendation on enforcement,[100] and works by the European Commission for the Efficiency of Justice (CEPEJ),[101] which also includes the civil execution law area.[102] Yet another important example of interest for future developments in the enforcement area is the ALI-UNIDROIT Principles of Transnational Civil Procedure.[103]

EC law and some multilateral conventions, which directly or indirectly are related to the legal areas of enforcement of contractual claims treated here are the Brussels I regulation, the European Enforcement Order for uncontested claims, the European Order for payment procedure, the Nordic convention on recognition and the enforcement of judgments in civil matters and the New York convention on foreign arbitral awards. The Nordic convention on recognition and the enforcement of judgments in civil matters is still partially applicable between the Nordic States and completes correspondingly the regulation between those that are Members of the EU. The scope of titles of execution of the New York convention on foreign arbitral awards does not coincide with the regulation, even if such awards may be based on contractual claims. Thus this convention, which covers a lot of States on a global basis, completes the regulation in relation to awards based on contractual claims between the States that are Members of the EU.

2.5.1 Brussels I Regulation

The Brussels I regulation, which entered into force on 1 March 2002 and then replaced the Brussels convention and formally a lot of other earlier bilateral and multilateral conventions, regulates directly the exercise of international jurisdiction

---

98. *See* Lortie, pp. 183-190, where he comments on the conventions of the Hague Conference as being sources of inspiration for the works of the EU, and on the work of the Conference for le Développement de la norme et la Mise en œvre de la norme.
99. *See* 4.3 for further details about the Convention and some rulings of the ECHR.
100. *See* 1.1.1.1.
101. *See* Desch, pp. 85-89, about the missions entrusted to the CEPEJ by the Committee of Ministers of the Council of Europe, and the works of the CEPEJ. He describes these missions, *i.b.*, p. 86, as follows: '– promouvoir la mise en œuvre effective des instruments du Conseil de l'Europe en vigueur en matière d'organisation de la justice; – veiller à ce que les politiques publiques en matière judiciaire tiennent compte des usagers de la justice, et notamment des acteurs du système judiciaire; – contribuer à désengorger la Cour européenne des droits de l'homme en offrant aux États des solutions effectives en amont de recours, en prévenant les violations de l'article 6', and he further states that the CEPEJ, within that framework, has decided to evaluate the functions of the legal systems in Europe and to optimize the delays in legal procedures. *Also see* for further information about the CEPEJ, website of the CEPEJ, <www.coe.int/cepej>.
102. *See* Report on European judicial systems, pp. 136-146, about enforcement of court decisions.
103. *See* 1.1.1.1.

by courts of the Member States of the EU and provides a unification and a simplification of the reciprocal recognition and enforcement of judgments. The Brussels I regulation has been adopted on the basis of Article 65 of the EC Treaty.[104] Denmark is not bound by this regulation,[105] but a parallel agreement to the Brussels I regulation between the EC and Denmark of 19 October 2005 exists, and entered into force on 1 July 2007.[106] That the Brussels I regulation has replaced the Brussels convention explains why here more attention is paid to the regulation than to the convention.

The legal usage of the ECJ and literature in relation to the Brussels convention are, however, still of importance for the interpretation of the Brussels I regulation, since the substantial scope of application of the Brussels I regulation is almost identical to the corresponding scope of application of the Brussels convention. There exist several relevant explanatory reports on the Brussels convention.[107] The Old Lugano convention is only treated here to the extent motivated by its validity, mainly in relation to non-Member States of the EU.[108] Some conventions are, however, still of interest in relation to judgments, which have been instituted, or rendered, before the coming into force of the Brussels I regulation and in relation to States which are not covered by the regulation, mainly non-Member States of the EU.[109]

2.5.2 European Enforcement Order for Uncontested Claims

The purpose of the European Enforcement Order for uncontested claims, which entered into force on 21 January 2004 and applies from 21 October 2005,[110] is to permit, by laying down minimum standards, the free circulation of judgments, court settlements and authentic instruments throughout all Member States without any need for intermediate proceedings to be brought in the Member States of enforcement prior to recognition and enforcement.[111] The regulation has been

104. Preamble (3).
105. *See* Preamble (21) and Art. 1, 3.
106. *See* Art. 12, 2 of the Agreement between the EC and the Kingdom of Denmark of 19 Oct. 2005 on jurisdiction and the recognition and enforcement of judgments in civil and commercial matters compared to Information concerning the date of entry into force of the Agreement between the EC and the Kingdom of Denmark on jurisdiction and the recognition and enforcement of judgments in civil and commercial matters, OJ 2007 L 94.
107. *See* the Jenard report, the Schlosser report, the Giuliano/Lagarde report, the Evrigenis/Kerameus report and the Allmeida Cruz/Desantes Real/Jenard report.
108. A relevant explanatory report to the Old Lugano convention is the Jenard/Möller report. *Also see* Wahl for further comments on this convention, and Berglund, Luganokonventionen i ett verkställighetsperspektiv, SvJT 1995, pp. 481-496, about comments in relation to the enforcement of judgments under the Old Lugano convention.
109. *See* 5.3.1.1.1 for further details on the relationship between the Brussels I regulation and some multilateral and bilateral conventions and in particular about the application of the transitional provisions of the regulation in relation to such conventions.
110. *See* Art. 33.
111. *See* Art. 1. *Also see*, for further comments on this regulation, Un titre exécutoire européen, Les Dossiers du Journal des tribunaux 53.

adopted having regard to Article 61, c and Article 67, 5 of the EC Treaty.[112] Denmark is not bound by this regulation.[113]

2.5.3 European Order for Payment Procedure

The European Order for payment procedure, which has entered into force, shall apply from 12 December 2008, with some exceptions,[114] for the collection of uncontested pecuniary claims of a specific amount that has fallen due at the time when an application for a European order for payment is submitted. It constitutes a facultative option. This option is based on certain common minimum levels of community harmonization of standards, introduced for the benefit of a creditor compared to the use of existing ordinary, or summary, procedures available under the law of a Member State.[115] The regulation has been adopted having regard to Article 61, c and Article 65, c of the EC Treaty.[116] Denmark is not bound by this regulation.[117] Examples in national laws of summary procedures are a French injunction de payer, or a German Mahnverfahren, but others, sometimes more or less differing, procedures also exist under the laws of other Member States.[118] However, despite these differences between the existing national models of law, all of them share the following distinctive features that can serve as elements of a definition of a payment procedure, as told in the following quotation:[119]

> Upon application of the claimant, the court or other competent authority takes a decision on the claim at issue *ex parte, i.e.* without any prior possibility for the defendant to participate. This decision is served on the defendant with an instruction to abide the order or to contest the claim within a certain time limit. If the defendant fails to act either way, the payment order acquires enforceability. Only if he lodges a statement of opposition, the case is transferred to ordinary proceedings. Hence, as opposed to normal procedural rules, the burden to initiate adversarial proceedings rests with the addressee of the payment order. This shift of responsibility, referred to in French as '*inversion du contentieux*', combined with the protection of the rights of the defense as

112. *See* the introduction of the Preamble.
113. *See* Preamble (25) and Art. 2, 3.
114. *See* Art. 33.
115. *See* Art. 1.
116. *See* Preamble (2) and its introduction.
117. *See* Preamble (32 and Art. 2, 3.
118. *See* Green paper on a European order for payment procedure and on measures to simplify and speed up small claims litigation, Commission of the ECs, COM (2002) 746 final, part II, section 3.1.1, which provides a summary overview of the different models that exist in the Member States.
119. *See*, about the definition of an order for payment procedure, Commission of the ECs' proposal for a regulation of the European Parliament and of the Council creating a European order for payment procedure, COM (2004) 173 final/3, section 2.1.2.

embodied in the opportunity to prevent an enforceable title from coming into being, constitutes the core characteristic of the payment order procedure.

2.5.4 European Small Claims Procedure

The European Small Claims Procedure, which has entered into force, shall apply from 1 January 2009.[120] It establishes a European procedure for small claims, where the value of the claim does not exceed EUR 2 000, intended to simplify and speed up litigation concerning small claims in cross-border cases, and to reduce costs.[121] The regulation, which eliminates the intermediate proceedings necessary to enable recognition and enforcement in other Member States of judgments given in one Member State in the European Small Claims Procedure,[122] has been adopted having regard to Article 61, c and Article 65, c of the EC Treaty.[123] Denmark is not bound by this regulation.[124]

2.5.5 Nordic Convention on Recognition and the Enforcement of Judgments in Civil Matters

The Nordic convention on recognition and the enforcement of judgments in civil matters, which entered into force on 1 January 1978, and then replaced an earlier convention in the same area,[125] is structured as a framework convention, which refers most issues, *e.g.* the enumeration of titles of execution included under its scope of application, to be determined through similar enacted laws in the Nordic States.[126] This convention is now only partially valid between the Nordic States and in relation to the remaining scope of claims in their quality of titles of

120. *See* Art. 29.
121. *See* Art. 1 compared to Art. 2.
122. *See* Art. 1.
123. *See* Preamble (2) and its introduction.
124. *See* Preamble (38) and Art. 2, 3.
125. *See* 2.4.2.
126. *See* Art. 1 compared to Art. 2, para. 2 of the convention compared to the: Danish enacted Act Lovbekendtgørelse 1986-09-15 nr. 635 om anerkendelse og fuldbyrdelse af nordiske afgørelser om privatretlige krav og om ændring af retsplejeloven, som ændret ved L 1995-03-29 nr. 209 og L 1995-06-14 nr. 389 (Act including the recognition and the enforcement of Nordic judgments in civil matters), Finish enacted Act Lag om erkännande och verkställighet av nordiska domar angående privaträttsligt anspråk 21.7 1977/588 (Act on the recognition and the enforcement of Nordic judgments in civil matters), Norwegian enacted Act Lov om anerkjennelse og fullbyrding av nordiska dommer på privatrettens område av den 10 juni 1977 (Act on the recognition and the enforcement of Nordic judgments in civil matters) and the Swedish Act Lag (1977:595) om erkännande och verkställighet av nordiska domar på privaträttens område (Act on the recognition and the enforcement of Nordic judgments in civil matters). The convention's structure as a framework convention follows the intentions of cooperation in Art. 4 of the Cooperation agreement between Denmark, Finland, Iceland, Norway and Sweden, done in Helsinki on 23 Mar. 1962.

execution not covered by the Brussels I regulation, the Brussels convention and the Old Lugano convention.[127]

2.5.6 New York Convention on Foreign Arbitral Awards

The Geneva Protocol on Arbitration Clauses on 24 September 1923,[128] and the Geneva Convention on the Execution of Foreign Arbitral Awards on 26 September 1927,[129] were both worked out under the auspices of the League of Nations. The New York convention on foreign arbitral awards, which was worked out under the auspices of the United Nations,[130] and deals both with the validity of arbitral agreements and with the execution of arbitral awards, entered into force on 10 June 1958. This convention has thereafter taken effect in relation to a great number of States, on the respective dates when the concerned States have become parties to it,[131] and was aimed to replace the Geneva Protocol and the Geneva convention.

The convention allows each State, which is a party to it, to make certain reservations, the mutual reservation and the commercial reservation,[132] and a lot of States, which are parties to the convention, have made such reservations.[133] The mutual reservation means that a State may limit its obligation to awards rendered in the territory of another contracting State. If this reservation is made, two categories of awards covered as a general rule by the convention are excluded, awards rendered in a State, which is not bound by the New York convention and awards made in the territory of a contracting State, but which are not regarded as national awards in this State. The effect of this reservation may be avoided if the seat of the arbitration is fixed to one of the contracting States. The commercial reservation allows the contracting States to limit their undertaking to disputes arising from legal relations, whether contractual or not, which are regarded as commercial by their national law.

2.6 EC LAW AND CONVENTIONS ON TAX CLAIMS

The legal cooperation framework of European States on the recovery of foreign tax claims was during the last century initially developed based on a rather limited

127. *See* 5.2.1.2, where this is further developed in more details, and about examples of recognized and enforceable titles of execution in the remaining areas of application from the Norwegian and Swedish enacted legislations related to the convention.
128. *See* Protocol on Arbitration Clauses, done at Geneva on 24 Sep. 1923, p. 157. *Also see*, for further comments about this Protocol, David, pp. 143-144.
129. *See* Convention on the Execution of Foreign Arbitral Awards, done at Geneva on 26 Sep. 1927, p. 301. Art. 1 of the convention refers to an arbitral award made in pursuance of an agreement covered by the Geneva Protocol of 1923. *Also see*, for further comments about this Convention, David, pp. 144-145.
130. *See*, for further comments about the history of the Convention, Van den Berg, pp. 6-8.
131. *See* annex 2.
132. *See* Art. I, 3.
133. *See* annex 2.

number of bilateral double tax treaties, which included recovery provisions,[134] as opposed to most other such treaties, which normally at the time did not include such provisions.[135] This cooperation framework was then further developed in some few regionally limited multilateral conventions, the Benelux convention on the mutual assistance for the recovery of tax claims of 5 September 1952, and the Agreement of 9 November 1972 between Sweden, Denmark, Finland, Iceland and Norway on administrative assistance in tax matters. A beginning of developments followed in EC law, starting with an amendment of the Recovery directive in 1979 related to the recovery of VAT.[136] The following step in developments was established by the Council of Europe and OECD convention on mutual administrative assistance in tax matters in 1988.[137]

Since then the developments have been increasingly focused and based on EC law, through the amendments of the Recovery directive in 1992 related to the recovery of certain excise duties,[138] and in 2001 related to the recovery of taxes

134. *See* Berglund, Svensk internationell exekutions- och obeståndsrätt, pp. 95-113, who makes references to some bilateral conventions, double tax treaties with recovery provisions, which Sweden concluded with other States during the last century: Belgium in 1968, amended in 1991, Estonia in 1993, France in 1972, amended in 1991 and gift- and inheritance tax Treaty 1937, amended in 1994, Germany in 1935, amended in 1992, Latvia in 1993, Lithuania in 1993, Luxemburg in 1984, the Netherlands in 1968, amended in 1992 and inheritance tax Treaty 1953 and the United States of America in 1965, amended in 1994. In addition Sweden has concluded such conventions with: India, Art. 28 of the convention between the government of the kingdom of Sweden and the government of the republic of India for the avoidance of double taxation and the prevention of fiscal evasion with respect to taxes on income and on capital from 1997, and Japan, Art. 25A of the convention between Sweden and Japan for the avoidance of double taxation and the prevention of fiscal evasion with respect to taxes on income from 1983, as amended in 1999. *Also see* about Belgian and German bilateral conventions, Grau Ruiz, pp. 107-108. She states that there exist recovery provisions in double tax treaties, which Belgium has concluded with: Denmark, France, Norway, Greece, Finland, Romania, Korea, the Philippines, Thailand and Spain. She further mentions that Germany at one time concluded conventions with Austria and Italy on administrative and legal assistance in fiscal matters and the double tax convention between Germany and Sweden from 1935, which included a recovery provision.

135. Compare for further details on to what extent the large number of tax treaties concluded by European States have included or lacked recovery provisions in such treaties, Tax Treaties concluded by European Countries, International Bureau of Fiscal Documentation.

136. *See* amendment (d) of Art. 2 of directive 76/308/EEC in Council Directive 79/1071/EEC of 6 Dec. 1979 amending Directive 76/308/EEC on mutual assistance for the recovery of claims resulting from operations forming part of the system of financing the European Agricultural Guidance and Guarantee Fund, and of agricultural levies and customs duties.

137. *See* <www.conventions.coe.int/Treaty/en/Treaties/Html/127.htm>. *Also see* annex 6 for details on the entry into force and on reservations against the recovery provisions of the convention in relation to the States, which are parties to it.

138. *See* amendment (e) of Art. 2 of directive 76/308/EEC in Council Directive 92/108/EEC of 14 Dec. 1992 amending Directive 12/92/EEC on the general arrangements for products subject to excise duty and on holding, movement and monitoring of such products and amending Directive 81/92/EEC.

on income and capital and taxes on insurance premiums.[139] The Recovery directive is the most important legal instrument, providing a mutual cooperation for the assistance of recovery of foreign tax claims between the Member States of the EU. The Council of Europe and OECD convention on mutual administrative assistance in tax matters also covers a lot of non-Member States of the EU, which are Member States of the Council of Europe and OECD. The Nordic agreement on assistance in tax matters also covers the Nordic States and territories, which are not members of the EU, *i.e.* Iceland, Norway, Greenland and the Faeroe Islands.

2.6.1 Recovery Directive

The developments in the area of mutual cross-border recovery of taxes between the Member States of the EU in EC law started in 1979 and was initially quite slow, but have on the other hand been of a more remarkable significance thereafter and in particular during recent years. The Recovery directive establishes mutual assistance for the cross-border recovery of certain debts, and it provides for three types of requests: on the exchange of information, on the service of instruments or decisions relating to claims or their recovery, and on the recovery of the claims.[140] The latest amendment of the Recovery directive entered into force at the latest 1 July 2002.[141] The ECJ has in a ruling in the case of *Commission v. Council* made clear that the Council acted correctly in adopting this last directive of amendment on the basis of Articles 93 and 94 of the EC Treaty, because the directive related to fiscal provisions.[142]

There exists an officially approved consolidated version published in the OJ of the present version of the Recovery directive, Council Directive 2008/55/EC of 26 May 2008 on mutual assistance for the recovery of claims relating to certain levies, duties, taxes and other measures (Codified version).[143] The Recovery directive is supplemented, based on provisions in this directive of a procedure

139. *See* Art. 2, g-i compared to Art. 3 of Council Directive 2001/44/EC of 15 Jun. 2001 amending Directive 76/308/EEC on mutual assistance for the recovery of claims resulting from operations forming part of the system of financing the European Agricultural Guidance and Guarantee Fund, and of agricultural levies and customs duties and in respect of VAT and certain excise duties.
140. *See* Arts 4-6.
141. *See* Art. 2 of the Council Directive 2001/44/EC of 15 Jun. 2001 amending Directive 76/308/EEC on mutual assistance for the recovery of claims resulting from operations forming part of the system of financing the European Agricultural Guidance and Guarantee Fund, and of agricultural levies and customs duties and in respect of VAT and certain excise duties.
142. The ECJ has in a decision of 29 Apr. 2004 in *Commission v. Council*, made clear that Directive 2001/44/EC does relate to fiscal provisions within the meaning of Art. 95, 2 of the EC Treaty, with the result that Art. 95 of the Treaty cannot constitute the correct legal basis for the adoption of that directive and concluded that the Council acted correctly in adopting this directive on the basis of Arts 93 and 94 of the Treaty.
143. *See* <http://eur-lex.europa.eu/LexUriServ/LexUriServ.do?uri=OJ:L:2008:150:0028:01:EN:HTML>.

of adoption of implementing certain detailed rules, by implementing provisions in the Implementing recovery directive, which in its turn refer back to the mandate of the Recovery directive.[144] Member States should comply with the Implementing recovery directive by the 30 April 2003, at the latest, and this directive repeals the previous implementing directive.[145] The Implementing recovery directive was adapted in 2004 to the accession of new Member States.[146] Legal usage in relation to the Recovery directive is scarce, and literature only comments on it to a rather limited extent.[147]

2.6.2 Council of Europe and OECD Convention on Mutual Administrative Assistance in Tax Matters

The Council of Europe and OECD convention on mutual administrative assistance in tax matters is the fruit of a joint effort by the Council of Europe and the OECD. The convention was initiated in a Council of Europe Parliamentary Assembly resolution in 1978 and a draft convention was approved by the OECD Fiscal Committee in 1986.[148] The convention provides for the following types of assistance: exchange of information, simultaneous tax examinations and participation in tax examinations carried out in other countries, service of instruments or decisions relating to claims or their recovery, and recovery of claims, and has a broad scope of tax claims.[149] It was opened for signatures by the Member States of the Council of Europe and the Member countries of OECD on 25 January 1988.[150] The convention shares some similar features with the Nordic agreement on assistance in tax matters, *e.g.* related to the scope of cooperation and that of claims.[151]

---

144. *See* Preamble and Art. 1 of the Recovery directive and Art. 1 of the Implementing recovery directive.
145. *See* Preamble (4) and Arts 30 and 32.
146. *See* Commission Directive 2004/79/EC of 4 Mar. 2004 adapting Directive 2002/94/EC, in the field of taxation, by reason of the accession of the Czech Republic, Estonia, Cyprus, Latvia, Lithuania, Hungary, Malta, Poland, Slovenia and Slovakia.
147. *See* Berglund, Svensk internationell exekutions- och obeståndsrätt, pp. 72, 75, 79, 83, 87, 93 and 116, European Tax Law, pp. 693-695, Garcia Prats, p. 62, and Grau Ruiz, pp. 127-128, 131, 170 and 229-234.
148. *See* Council of Europe Parliamentary Assembly recommendation 833 (1978) on cooperation between Council of Europe member States against international tax avoidance and evasion of 24 Apr. 1978, which invited the member States to ensure that the agreement covers assistance in the recovery of tax debts, *i.b.* section 10, b, iii, and OECD, Committee on Fiscal Affairs, approval of the draft OECD Council of Europe multilateral convention on mutual administrative assistance in tax matters, at its 31st Session in Paris on 9-10 Jul. 1986, document CFA/M(86)2, *i.b.*, section III. *Also see* Grau Ruiz, p. 120.
149. *See* Art. 2.
150. *See* Art. 28, 1.
151. Compare Art. 2 of the convention and its annex A and Explanatory report on the Convention on Mutual Administrative Assistance in Tax Matters, pp. 11-13, to Arts 2 and 20, 1 of the agreement. Art. 20, 1 of the Nordic agreement refers the definition of taxes and fees according to Art. 2, 1. h) 2-5 of this agreement to the Implementing agreement to the Nordic agreement

It allows its parties to develop, on common foundations and respecting the basic rights of tax-payers, extensive administrative cooperation covering all compulsory taxes, with the exception of customs duty.

Any State wishing to accede to the convention may tailor the extent of its obligations, by virtue of a detailed system of reservations expressly provided for. A State may also restrict its participation to certain types of mutual assistance or to assistance in connection to certain taxes. A great number of States are consequently invited to become parties to it, but so far, the convention has only entered into force in relation to a rather limited number of States and between them the recovery provisions of the convention only apply to: Azerbaijan, Belgium, and Denmark, including Greenland, Finland, Iceland, Norway, Sweden and the United Kingdom.[152] The explanatory report to the convention is of interest for its interpretation.[153] Literature, which comments on the convention exists only to a rather limited extent.[154]

2.6.3 Nordic Agreement on Assistance in Tax Matters

The Nordic agreement on assistance in tax matters of 7 December 1989, which replaced the earlier agreement in the same area of 9 November 1972, entered into force on 1 May 1991.[155] The agreement includes a provision, which enables the competent authorities of the contracting States to enter into an agreement for the implementation of the Nordic agreement.[156] The present implementing agreement to the Nordic agreement, the Agreement according to Article 20 of the agreement between the Nordic countries for mutual administrative assistance in tax matters of 7 December 1989 (Implementing agreement to the Nordic agreement on assistance in tax matters), which replaced the previous implementing agreement on 19 June 1991, entered into force on the 1 January 1998. The more detailed reason to treat this Nordic agreement is that it is still on some aspects more developed than the Benelux convention on the mutual assistance for the recovery of tax claims, the Recovery directive, and the Council of Europe and OECD convention on mutual

on assistance in tax matters. This implementing agreement includes, in para. 3, A and C-D, detailed enumerations from the contracting parties of the agreement of national motor-vehicle taxes, excise duties, social insurance duties and other public fees.

152. *See* annex 6.

153. *See* Explanatory report on the Convention on Mutual Administrative Assistance in Tax Matters.

154. *See* Berglund, Svensk internationell exekutions- och obeståndsrätt, pp. 72, 75, 78-79, 93 and 114-115, European Tax Law, pp. 690-691, Garcia Prats, p. 62, and Grau Ruiz, pp. 120-124.

155. *See* Art. 24, 1 compared to förordning (1991:171) om avtal mellan de nordiska länderna om handräckning i skatteärenden (Swedish government decree on the entry into force of an agreement between the Nordic States on assistance in tax matters).

156. *See* Art. 20.

administrative assistance in tax matters.[157] Legal usage in relation to the agreement is scarce, and literature only comments on it to a rather limited extent.[158]

2.7 EC LAW AND CONVENTIONS ON INSOLVENCY

An early example of a bilateral convention, which also included bankruptcy matters, after the even earlier examples from Italy during the Middle Ages,[159] is the convention between France and Switzerland of 1869[160] that applied until the end of 1991. The day after it was superseded by the Old Lugano convention,[161] which did not apply to bankruptcy, and then entered into force between France and Switzerland.[162] Many bilateral and some few multilateral conventions related to insolvency, *e.g.* on the recognition and enforcement of foreign bankruptcy decisions, were developed between some European States, mainly during the last century, and these conventions were superseded by the Insolvency regulation from 2000 between the Member States of the EU.[163]

Even if the Convention between Denmark, Finland, Iceland, Norway and Sweden regarding bankruptcy of 7 November 1933, as amended in 1977 and 1982 (Nordic bankruptcy convention)[164] consequently does not apply between Finland and Sweden, the convention still applies between on the one hand Finland and Sweden and on the other hand Denmark and the other contracting Nordic States to the convention, which are non-Member States of the EU,

157. The later developed Council of Europe and OECD convention on mutual administrative assistance in tax matters corresponds mainly with the Nordic agreement, *see* the Swedish travaux préparatoires to the convention, prop. 1989/90:14 om godkännande av Europarådsoch OECD-konventionen om ömsesidig handräckning i skatteärenden, m.m., p. 57. *Also see* Explanatory report on the Convention on Mutual Administrative Assistance in Tax Matters, where the Nordic agreement is mentioned as a reference in the work on the convention, p. 17. *Also see* Grau Ruiz, who confirms the importance of the Nordic agreement as for having provided a basis for the works on the Council of Europe and OECD convention on mutual administrative assistance in tax matters, and on her opinion that the Nordic agreement was more detailed than any other convention at the time (1972), *e.g.* the multilateral Benelux convention on tax matters, and merits to be used as a benchmark for future norms of mutual assistance, pp. 114-117.

158. *See* Berglund, Svensk internationell exekutions- och obeståndsrätt, pp. 72, 75-76, 83, 88, 92 and 111, Garcia Prats, p. 62, and Grau Ruiz, pp. 115-117.

159. *See* 2.2.4.

160. *See* Arts 6-9 of the Convention between the Swiss Confederation and France on jurisdiction and enforcement of judgments in civil matters, signed at Paris on 15 Jun. 1869, which treat bankruptcy matters.

161. *See* Art. 55.

162. *See* annex 5.

163. The conventions, which were superseded by the Insolvency regulation between the Member States of the EU, are listed in Art. 44, 1.

164. Extracts of the convention are translated in annex 7.

i.e. Iceland and Norway.[165] La Convention relative à la faillite et à la liquidation judiciaire entre la France et la principauté de Monaco du 13 Septembre 1950 (Bankruptcy convention between France and Monaco) applies between France and Monaco, which is of interest because Monaco is outside the scope of the EC Treaty,[166] and Monaco is therefore not bound by the Insolvency regulation.

2.8 CONCLUSIONS

The legal historical developments under the treated periods are no doubt complex and multi-layered, involving as they do the historical development of the modern State, with its institutions, and the cross-fertilization of ideas from one State to another across a long period of time. It is, nevertheless, possible to identify some common legal historical influences, ideas, and development trends since the early age of the Roman Empire, including its reception of Hellenistic influences, until our age, and to draw some brief general conclusions in relation to all of these treated periods. During this long period the balance of the creditor's interest of efficiency against the debtor's interests of humanity, dignity and privacy have shifted. From the early age of the Roman Empire this balance was clearly pro creditor, it has ever since gradually until our age moved towards a position, which to a greater extent than before also has taken the interests of the debtor into account, *i.a.* influenced by the principles of the European Convention on Human Rights.[167]

The *ius commune* has had an impact on the subject as well as the constitutional doctrines of Montesquieu. Historical events in society such as an advanced development of economy, or the need to finance costs as a result of the centralization of State powers by increased efficiency in the recovery of public claims, or the appearance of financial crises, or increased legal cooperation between European States such as in the EU, have called for changes. This has sometimes also created common legal European influences resulting in the establishment in law of more developed and detailed rules in the legal areas of the enforcement of private claims, the recovery of public claims, and insolvency.

---

165. *See* 6.4.1, where the relationship between the Insolvency regulation and the Nordic bankruptcy convention is further treated. *Also see* 5.1.4 and 6.4.2 about the Nordic bankruptcy convention, and for further information on the convention, Arnt Nielsen, International privat- og procesret, pp. 289-291, Berglund, Svensk internationell exekutions- och obeståndsrätt, pp. 321-329, Bogdan, Sveriges och EU:s internationella insolvensrätt, pp. 142-153, Bogdan, The Nordic Bankruptcy convention, pp. 701-708, Cross-Border Insolvency Law, International Instruments and Commentary, pp. 32-34 (*Also see* for a complete translation into English of the convention, Annex 19, pp. 761-769), and Wood, chapter 17, International insolvency treaties, section 17-3. A translation of parts of the convention is enclosed in Annex 7.
166. *See* 5.1.1.
167. *See* 4.3 for further information on this convention and some rulings of the ECHR.

2.9 DIFFERING FEATURES OF COOPERATION IN EC LAW

2.9.1 Brussels I Regulation

The Brussels I regulation is an example of a cooperation between the Member States of the EU in the commercial and contractual law areas, which concerns titles of execution established in a contradictory proceeding that emanate from and are based on legal acts between private parties regulated by civil law. This regulation treats to a greater extent other legal issues than enforcement matters, *e.g.* jurisdiction and recognition, and makes available, by reference to national laws, the resources of enforcement measures of the Member States to the private creditors. Other kinds of recovery measures than enforcement measures fall outside the scope of the Brussels I regulation and the private creditor remains therefore directly in control of them.

2.9.2 Recovery Directive

The Recovery directive is an example of a cooperation for the mutual assistance in recovery matters related to certain public claims, *e.g.* tax claims, between the Member States of the EU, which concerns titles of execution that emanate from and are based on the exercise of legal acts of public law of the different organs of the State, in relation to private parties. In this cooperation the Member States both act in their capacity of creditors and recovery/enforcement agents, depending on whether a Member State acts as an applicant creditor State, or as a requested enforcing State. This cooperation sometimes also includes an element of responsibility to represent the other Member State as a creditor in a recovery matter of assistance in a similar way as follows from the requested Member State's tax creditor's role, which then becomes applicable in relation to the recovery of corresponding domestic tax claims. This is, however, subject to certain exceptions. The applicant Member State maintains its role of a tax creditor, but does not directly control the process of recovery regarding a matter in another Member State. Typical measures of recovery besides enforcement measures, which may be at the disposal of a foreign tax creditor in another State are *e.g.* an agreement on an instalment plan, or an application for bankruptcy, before or after a request for recovery.[168]

2.9.3 Conclusions

In the commercial and contractual law areas the cooperation between the Member States laid down in EC law and between States bound by conventions, regarding

168. *See* 6.2.2.1.1 about the possibilities of an agreement on an instalment plan and Art. 9, 2 of the Recovery directive, and 6.2.2.1.1.1 about the possibilities of an application for bankruptcy as a recovery measure by use of Art. 6 of the Recovery directive, and about an application for bankruptcy after a request for recovery, Art. 16, 2 of the Nordic agreement on assistance in tax matters.

the enforcement of contractual claims, mainly aims at and is limited to provide access to the legal national enforcement systems. The private creditor remains in principle directly in control of the process, even if he has chosen to be represented by a lawyer, based on a power of attorney. The Brussels I regulation provides, in comparison with the Recovery directive, a more narrow support to the private creditor, who holds a title of origin from another Member State, than provided by the Recovery directive to the tax creditor, who holds a title of execution from another Member State.

The features of cooperation in the tax recovery area, where requested States act both in their capacities of representing an applicant State as a creditor and as a recovery agent in the recovery proceeding, compared to the corresponding area of enforcement of contractual claims, where the requested States only act in their capacity of enforcement agents in relation to the private creditor, illustrate that the scope of cooperation related to the mutual assistance for the recovery of tax claims is often much wider in comparison to the corresponding scope of cooperation related to the enforcement of contractual claims. This also explains why the Recovery directive provides more detailed provisions related to the cooperation of recovery compared to the provisions during the procedure of declaration for enforcement in the Brussels I regulation.

Another factor of importance, which is reflected into these two legal areas, and also explains some differing solutions in them, is the fundamental differences, which are found in the first phase of the establishment of a title of execution in relation to the nature of the claims. In this phase, the parties in the contractual law area are governed and protected under the principle of contradictory proceeding, while in the tax recovery law area the debtor receives a decision in a non-contradictory proceeding of taxation emanating from the *imperium* of an authority of the State. This difference in the first phase exists, even if there, in a second phase, exists a possibly of appeal against such a decision of taxation. These fundamental differences may also explain why the interests of a possible debtor sometimes are better safeguarded in the cross-border contractual law area than in the corresponding tax recovery law area.

2.10 WORKS IN PROGRESS AND PRESENT DEVELOPMENT TRENDS

2.10.1 European Union

Several studies and proposals, which include matters of interest in the area of enforcement and recovery of claims, are under preparation in the EU, here to be reported on in brief. A proposal for a regulation on European enforcement exists, but has so far not been realized.[169] The Commission of the ECs' proposal for a

169. *See*, about a proposal of a separate regulation on European enforcement, including *i.a.* a European Assets Declaration of the debtor, a European Garnishment Order, a European

Council regulation on jurisdiction, applicable law, recognition and enforcement of decisions and cooperation in matters relating to maintenance obligations (Proposal for a Council regulation on jurisdiction, applicable law, recognition and enforcement of decisions and cooperation in matters relating to maintenance obligations) is of interest because it introduces several new possible solutions of indirect or direct importance in the area of the recovery of maintenance obligations, which are aimed to ensure effectiveness and continuity of recovery in the cross-border context.[170] Examples of such provisions in the proposal are those on the automatic recognition and enforceability of decisions, enforcement, Order for monthly direct payment, Order for temporary freezing of a bank account, enforceability of authentic instruments and agreements, cooperation between central authorities, as representatives for a creditor, for an exchange of information, *i.a.* for the purpose to recover efficiently a maintenance claim, and on access to information.[171] A study has been initiated on improving the efficiency of the enforcement of judgments in the EU related to the attachment of bank accounts.[172] There also exist studies related to the application of the Brussels I regulation and the transparency of Debtors' assets.[173]

2.10.2 Hague Conference on Private International Law

The Hague Conference on Private International Law[174] started a work in 1997 on a convention on jurisdiction and foreign judgments in civil and commercial matters, which included provisions on the recognition and enforcement of judgments.[175] However, this work has, so far, only resulted in the Hague Convention of 30 June 2005 on Choice of Court Agreements.

Garnishee's Order and a European Protective Order, EC Study JAI/02/03/2002, B, V, 5 and C, III, 2 and D, VI, b) compared to E, III, 1-4.

170. *See* Commission of the ECs' proposal for a Council regulation on jurisdiction, applicable law, recognition and enforcement of decisions and cooperation in matters relating to maintenance obligations, COM (2005) 649 final.

171. *See* Arts: 25 (Enforceability), 26 (Provisional enforcement), 27-33 (Enforcement; Enforcement proceedings, Documents, Legal aid, Security, bond or deposit, Legalisation or other similar formality, No review as to the substance of a decision, Refusal or suspension of enforcement), 34 (Order for monthly direct payment), 35 (Order for temporary freezing of a bank account), 37 (Enforceability of authentic instruments and agreements), 38 (Enforcement of authentic instruments and agreements), 41b) (Cooperation in specific cases between central authorities, as representatives for a creditor, for the exchange of information for the purpose to recover efficiently a maintenance claim) and 44 (Access to information).

172. *See* Green paper on improving the efficiency of the enforcement of judgments in the European Union: the attachment of bank accounts, COM (2006) 618 final.

173. *See* EC Study JLS/C4/2005/03, Report on the Application of Regulation Brussels I in the Member States and Green paper Effective enforcement of judgments in the European Union: Transparency of Debtors' assets, Commission of the ECs, COM (2008) 128 final.

174. *See* 2.5 about the history of this Conference.

175. *See* Arts 7-13 on recognition and enforcement, Preliminary Document No. 8 of Mar. 2003 (corrected) from the preliminary result of the work of the informal working group on the

2.10.3 Nordic Council of Ministers

The Nordic Council of Ministers, which was founded in 1971, is a cooperation organ for the Nordic governments, *i.a.* within the framework of maintaining and further developing the cooperation between the countries in the law area.[176] Within this framework of cooperation we find in the enforcement and recovery areas a draft of a Nordic agreement on the exchange of information in recovery matters, which includes the objective to establish a Nordic agreement on the exchange of information in recovery matters between the Nordic States related to both private and public claims, in the report to the Nordic Council of Ministers on Nordiskt samarbete om indrivningsfrågor (Nordic cooperation in recovery matters) of July 2002.[177] We also find the report SKUNORD, Nordiskt arbetsseminarium i skuldsaneringsfrågor (Nordic working seminar concerning debt relief) to the Nordic Council of Ministers of 2 March 2000, which aimed to analyze the differences of the debt relief legislations from the Nordic States and to make suggestions that would lead to that a debt relief decision would be able to take legal effect within all of the Nordic States.[178] Some conclusions from this report were that there existed a clear need for a Nordic regulation in the sphere of debt relief and that alternative forms for such a Nordic agreement could be either the introduction of new rules into the Nordic bankruptcy convention, through the creation of a new convention, or through the enactment of similar rules in national legislations.

2.10.4 International Institute for the Unification of Private Law

The International Institute for the Unification of Private Law (UNIDROIT) is an independent inter-governmental organization, which was established in 1926.[179] The ALI-UNIDROIT Principles of Transnational Civil Procedure were adopted by the ALI and by the UNIDROIT in 2004.[180] These principles provide some transnational standard principles, which aim at reconciling differences among various

---

judgment project for the attention of the Special Commission of Apr. 2003 on General Affairs and Policy of the Conference. *Also see* for comments on the work of this draft convention, Arnt Nielsen, Forhandlingerne om en global domskonvention, Retsvidenskabeligt Tidsskrift 2002, pp. 66-73, and Bernasconi, pp. 12-13.

176. *See* website of the Nordic Council of Ministers, <www.norden.org>.
177. *See* Nordiskt samarbete om indrivningsfrågor (Nordic cooperation in recovery matters), report to the Nordic Council of Ministers of Jul. 2002. Most texts in the report are not translated into English, but it includes an introduction and summary of the project in English, *see i.b.*, pp. 21-24. The draft of a Nordic agreement on the exchange of information in recovery matters has not been translated in this report, but a translation of this draft agreement into English, corresponding to pp. 25-30 of the report, is enclosed here as annex 8.
178. *See* SKUNORD, Nordiskt arbetsseminarium i skuldsaneringsfrågor (Nordic working seminar concerning debt relief), report to the Nordic Council of Ministers of 2 Mar. 2000. The report includes a summary of the project in English, *see i.b.*, pp. 11-13.
179. *See* website of UNIDROIT, <www.unidroit.org>.
180. *Also see* 1.1.1.1 about these principles.

national rules of civil procedure, taking into account the peculiarities of transnational disputes as compared to purely domestic ones.[181] These Principles are of importance because they may serve as a basis for future initiatives in reforming civil procedure in the member States, including issues of provisional and protective measures, immediate enforceability of judgments and efficiency of enforcement procedures, both in the national and international context.

2.10.5 L'Union Internationale des Huissiers de Justice et Officiers Judiciaires

An international organization for enforcement agents, L'Union Internationale des Huissiers de Justice et Officiers Judiciaires (UIHJ)/the international union of judicial officers, was founded in 1952.[182] In 1949, at the French national congress of officers of court Jean Soulard presented the idea of creating the UIHJ and the first congress of this organization was held in Paris in 1952 in the presence of representatives from Belgium, France, Greece, Italy, Luxemburg, the Netherlands and Switzerland.[183] The UIHJ has since its foundation developed a large commitment in works at international organizations and it is also a Member of the United Nations Economic and Social Council.[184] The UIHJ has nearly 70 members or associated organizations,[185] including some European associations of enforcement agents.[186]

---

181. *Also see*, for further comments on these principles, Uniform Law Review/Revue de droit uniforme 2001-4, Harmonising Transnational Civil Procedure: The ALI/UNIDROIT Principles and Rules/Vers une procédure civile transnationale harmonisée: Les Principes et Règles ALI/UNIDROIT, and Ferrand, pp. 37-49.
182. Information about the European associations of enforcement agents, and the associations of such agents from other continents, which are members of the UIHJ, as well as additional information, is available on the website of the UIHJ, <www.uihj.com>. *Also see*, about the UIHJ, Kennett, Regulation of Civil Enforcement Agents, Regulation of enforcement agents in Europe: a comparative survey, vol. 1 Text, report in the Grotius program 2001, pp. 137-140, and for further information on the history and developments of the UIHJ during the years 1952-2002, 'Si L'Union m'était contée . . . ', and about comments in relation to the foundation of the UIHJ, Lesage, p. 293.
183. *See* Focus on International association of judicial officers, p. 3, and 'Si L'Union m'était contée . . . ', pp. 7-8 and 18-22.
184. *See* Focus on International association of judicial officers, p. 8, and 'Si L'Union m'était contée . . . ', pp. 13 and 15.
185. *See* UIHJ Europe, p. 5.
186. European associations of enforcement agents, which are members of the UIHJ, are the national associations of the: Austrian and German Gerichtvollziehers, Belgian, French and Luxemburgian Huissiers de Justice, Czech Soudni exekutor, Danish Foged, Dutch Gerechtsdeurwaarders, English High court enforcement officers and Enforcement officers, Estonian Kohtutäiturid, Finish Ulosottomiehet, Greek Dikastikos Epimelitis, Hongarian Onallo Birosagi Vegrehajto, Irish Sheriffs and County registrars, Italian Ufficiali Giudiziari, Latvian Zvērinātu tiesu izpildītāju, Lithuanian Antstolių, Polish Komornik Sadowy, Portugese Solicitadores de execuçâo, Scottish Messangers-at-Arms and Sheriff officers, Slovakian Sudni exekutori, Slovenian Izvrsiteljica, Spanish Procuradores, and Swedish Kronofogde.

According to its Statutes, the UIHJ is a non-governmental organization incorporated to promote, coordinate and develop the activity of the judicial officers internationally in order to safeguard, through closer cooperation between the representative professional organizations on a national level, the dignity and independence towards a better service to persons and to the community. Its registered office is located in Paris.[187] The UIHJ represents, according to its Statutes, the spiritual unity and the international institutions of all legal independent and impartial practitioners commissioned with the starting of legal procedures, service of judicial decisions and other enforceable documents by delegation of public authority, of amicable collection of claims and debts, of the implementation of provisional and protective measures, of the drawing up of official statements of facts, auctions, evaluation of property, legal advice, whatever may be the term used to designate them and even if they only perform part of these functions.[188] The objects of the UIHJ are presented in its Statutes.[189]

The UIHJ, which is engaged in the development of international civil enforcement law, supported the initiative to create a TEE for uncontested claims,[190] which provided inspiration for the creation of a European Enforcement Order for uncontested claims.[191] At the Congress of the UIHJ in Washington in 2006 the issue of the creation of a World Code of Enforcement was raised, and the construction of this Code was suggested to rest on the following nine pillars: speed of engagement of measures, effectiveness, transparency, access to patrimonial information,

---

187. *See* Art. 1, ss 1 and 4.
188. *See* Art. 1.2.
189. The objects of the UIHJ are, according to Art. 2, sections a)-i) of its Statutes the following. The representation of the union and of its members with other international organisations and cooperation to their activities. The cooperation with national professional organisations. The study and the improvement of national procedural rights and of international treaties and cooperation in activities that aim at their harmonisation. The spreading and the defence of principles set out in the provisions of Art. 6 of the European convention for the protection of human rights and fundamental freedoms signed in Rome on 4 Nov. 1950. The spreading of ideas, projects and initiatives aimed at the progress, the elevation and promotion of the most appropriate independent status to meet the requirements of the proper functioning of justice in compliance with the rights of all parties concerned. The promotion of international conferences and patronage of professional meetings that reach beyond the purely national framework. The setting up relations; with evolving 'judicial officers' who do not yet have a professional organisation, to assist in their structuring and organisation in view of their affiliation to the union. Also to give them moral assistance and help to improve their training and promote their status; with professional organisations that are not composed of 'judicial officers' in order to cooperate with them in fields of common interest. The creation and organisation of any service or network aiming at maintaining the link between the 'judicial officers' of the various States, namely as far as the trans-border collection of debts and the international forwarding of judicial and extrajudicial documents are concerned. Finally, the implementation of any action aimed at promoting the professional training of 'judicial officers', including, whenever necessary, the one of their staff or trainees.
190. *See* 2.5.
191. *See* 2.5.2.

proportionality of measures, simplification of the rules of procedures, liability of the enforcement agent, ethics and reasonable cost of measures.[192]

2.10.6 United Nations

In 1983 an ad hoc group of experts on international cooperation in tax matters of the United Nations prepared a guideline on tax collection assistance in the cross-border context and this guideline was reviewed in 1987 by the group.[193] In 2002 it was asked to consider if provisions of mutual assistance for the recovery of tax claims should be entered into the United Nations Model Convention on double taxation between developed and developing countries,[194] but, so far, no entry of such provisions into this Model Convention has been realized.[195]

2.10.7 Intra-European Organization of Tax Administrations

The Intra-European Organization of Tax Administrations (IOTA), domiciled in Budapest, was created on 30 October 1996, and 38 tax administrations in the European region are members of this organization. The IOTA shall provide a forum of discussion of practical tax administration issues, to strengthen cooperation, to support their development according to their individual needs and to encourage the adoption of good practice.[196] The works of the IOTA also involve tax recovery matters.[197]

2.10.8 Conclusions

In addition to the *acquis communautaire*, the extensive works in progress and the initiatives of the EU, the works and initiatives of the Council of Europe, and by other international organizations have meant an increased focus on issues, which are either entirely or partially related to the enforcement and recovery law areas.[198]

---

192. *See*, for further details on this issue, Menut.
193. *See* Garcia Prats, pp. 57-58, and Grau Ruiz, pp. 117-118. *Also see* Amissah, pp. 1-27.
194. *See* Grau Ruiz, p. 224.
195. Compare Model Convention on double taxation between developed and developing countries, United Nations, 1979, second version 2001.
196. *See* website of the IOTA, <www.iota-tax.org> and Arts 1-2 of the Charter of the IOTA.
197. Examples of works are a seminar-workshop about Tax Enforcement-Management of Taxpayer Debts for Tax Enforcement Officials held in Budapest 4-7 Jun. 2002, a workshop about Developing an Effective Debt Management Strategy for Senior officials responsible for enforcement and collection strategy held in Budapest 1-3 Sep. 2004 and a workshop about Strategies for Effective Enforced Debt Recovery for Officials involved in debt management and recovery held in Budapest 7-9 Sep. 2005.
198. *Also* compare Isnard, pp. 9-25, about the contributions from the institutions to the construction and development of civil execution law in Europe.

The total of related activities of the EU, the Council of Europe and other international organizations represents a strong development trend, which also clearly proves the importance that these organizations attribute to the needs of making further progress in developments in these law areas. The European States are moving in the direction of a gradual development and birth of a new kind of *ius commune* in the civil execution law area, not only in the cross-border context, but also in the national context, even if its final timetable is unpredictable.[199]

199. Compare, for a more pessimistic view about the prospects of a harmonisation in the area of contractual law, Vogenauer and Weatherill, The European Community's competence for a comprehensive harmonisation of contract law – an empirical analysis, European Law Review, Dec. 2005, pp. 821-837.

Chapter 3
Enforcement and Recovery Agents

3.1 HISTORY OF ENFORCEMENT AND RECOVERY AGENTS

3.1.1 Roman Empire

The responsibility of the *Praetor* was related to the functions of the Magistrates, which meant *e.g.* matters of military command, administration and jurisdiction, including the civil law procedure for the execution of claims.[1] The responsibility for the administration of the Roman Treasury, which included the taxation, the collection and the recovery of taxes, was the most important task of the Roman official *Quaestor*, who, however, also had some other varying tasks, *e.g.*: receiving the money or security for the money due to the treasury through criminal condemnations, the sale of public land, and the sales of booty or pledged security.[2]

---

1. *See* 2.1.1 about civil execution law. *Also see*, about the tasks of the *Praetor*, Lintott, pp. 104-109. He reports as follows: 'the original title of the chief annual magistrates of the Republic is said to have been *praetor*, interpreted by Varro as the man who would give the lead in jurisdiction and the army', 'it seems that this chief function, down to the time of Sulla's reforms of 81 BC, was to be a military commander', 'if consuls at Rome were not confined by routine administration and jurisdiction, this was because they had junior magistrates as their colleagues, who were designated by their own original title, *praetor*', '. . . the urban praetor performed jurisdiction between citizens, the peregrine praetor did so when one party at least was a foreigner' and 'Later the status of the praetor became especially dependent on his function as a judicial magistrate. For Cicero the primary element in this was civil jurisdiction. This was not the actual judgment (judication) of private lawsuits – which was left to *iudices* who were private citizens at the time – but the original assessment of whether the plaintiff's suit could be properly made the subject of a legal action, the determination of the nature of this legal action, and the assignation of a single *iudex* or a panel of *recuperatores* to hear the case', *see i.b.*, pp. 104-108.
2. *See* about the responsibility for the administration of the Roman Treasury of the *Quaestor* and some other of his varying working tasks, Lintott, pp. 18, 133, and 135-137. He reports as

The most well known example in history of tax collectors is, however, probably the Apostle Saint Matthew, who lived in the first century A.D. in the Roman Empire.[3]

3.1.2 Belgium, France and the Netherlands

Here to be treated is the enforcement institution of the Huissier de Justice,[4] an institution which in France originally was known under the name of Hostiarii.[5] The origins of the modern profession of the enforcement agent Huissier de Justice may

---

follows: 'The only true subordinate of a consul in civil administration was his own quaestor.' 'In the late Republic the *quaestores* were junior magistrates, who either supervised the treasury at Rome, the *aerarium Saturni*, or held independent administrative posts in Italy, or – and this was the true of the majority – were assistants to consuls or to pro-magistrates abroad.' 'The title, *quaestor urbanus*, is associated in legal texts with supervision of the aerarium from the late second century B.C. This is likely to have been the chief function of the urban quaestors from the beginning. The consular quaestors, on the other hand, would have been expected to deal with financial and other administrative matters relating to the army when it was away from Rome. According to Tacitus, the number of quaestores was raised to eight "with Italy paying tribute and the taxes of the provinces accruing", whereas a late source, John the Lydian, talks of the creation in 267 of twelve quaestores called *classici*, of which there is no further trace in our sources. We find specific posts in Italy in the late Republic and Principate in addition to the quaestores at the treasury, the consular quaestores, and those assigned to provinces.' 'The quaestors attached to major magistrates were their assistants in all kinds of activity. Those of the consuls seem in effect to have held the post of private secretary or aide-de-camp at home and abroad with particular responsibility for money, including army pay. The same was true of those appointed to serve a magistrate or pro-magistrate abroad, though these quaestors had a wider remit, being deputy to the commander or governor and usually his temporary replacement, if he left his post for any reason. . . . However, their financial concerns were as pre-eminent abroad as they were in the city. The quaestors at the treasury at Rome generally supervised ingoings and outgoings under the direction of the senate and the consuls, but also had a number of special duties. We find them *inter alia* pursuing arrears of taxation (*stipendium*) from priests and, on the other hand, paying back to the taxpayers recompense in proportion to their contributions from the proceeds of Manlius Vulso's triumph. . . . The surviving texts of statutes, in particular, show them receiving the money or security for the money due to the treasury through criminal condemnations and through the sale of public land. They also pay out money due to plaintiffs. Furthermore, booty or pledged security was turned into cash by sales conducted by the quaestors. The *aerarium* was a repository not only of money, but of documents.' *Also see* about the *Quaestor* Kaser, pp. 157-158 and 160-161.

3. *See* Bible, Matt 9:9, which reads: 'As Jesus passed on from there, he saw a man called Matthew sitting at the tax office; and he said to him, "Follow me." And he rose and followed him.'
4. *See* Nouveau Petit Larousse illustré, Dictionnaire encyclopédique, pp. 502-503, where the word huissier is explained as follows: 'Garde de la porte chez un souverain, un haut personnage, pour annoncer, introduire, etc. Celui qui fait le service des séances de certains corps, des assemblées délibérantes, etc. Officier ministériel, chargé de signifier les actes de justice, de mettre à exécution les jugements, etc.: il existe au moins un huissier dans chaque chef-lieu de canton. Huissier audiencier, celui qui est chargé d'assister les magistrats à l'audience. L'Huissier est chargé de la signification des actes ou jugements, de l'exécution de ceux de ces jugements qui ont force exécutoire, et de faire le service intérieur des tribunaux. Dans certains cas, il procède aux ventes publiques de meubles. Les offices d'huissier sont transmissibles vénalement.'
5. *See* Hostiarii, p. 6.

be traced back to the thirteenth century, when the birth of the institution became reality through the signature by the French king Philippe-le-Bel of his ordinance of 1285.[6] It was consequently originally introduced in France, and subsequently in the Netherlands, Gerechtsdeurwaarder, and in other francophone States. The monopoly of service of documents of the Huissier de Justice, and by extension of execution of enforceable instruments, has its origins in the medieval councils that were established in about the thirteenth century.[7]

The councils were the bodies through which the king of France and the various feudal lords conducted business. They had legislative, judicial and executive functions. The model introduced in France was copied by feudal lords in other jurisdictions, and notably by the Duke of Burgundy in the Low Countries. The Huissier was the usher and messenger for the council. He kept order in the council chamber, delivered notices and summoned people to appear before the council. From an early date, therefore the Huissier held a public office, closely affiliated to the ruling institutions of the day. Since there was no clear distinction between administrative, criminal and civil matters, the Huissier had responsibilities in all three areas. A further feature of the French legal system, through which the Huissier has obtained a certain distance from the state bureaucracy, is the venality of public offices. The French State could not afford to employ all the personnel it required and thus sold offices in order to increase its revenues. The attraction of the offices

---

6. *See*, about the Fondements historiques de l'institution of the French Huissier de Justice from the birth of this institution through the signature by the French king Philippe-le-Bel of his ordonance from 1285, and about the following history of Les huissiers au Parlement and of Les sergents du Châtelet until 1789, Guinot, pp. 65-70. *Also see* Hostiarii, which also includes rich historical illustrations from art related to the profession, and for more extensive historical comments in relation to the following subjects: La Chambre nationale des huissiers de justice, un cinquantenaire pour 175 ans d'histoire, La discipline des huissiers, Les sergents, les huissiers de justice et les actes de violence au cours des temps, L'huissier et son costume à travers le temps, Les péripéties d'une institution ou la vénalité des charges de Philippe le Bel à Clemenceau, Les grandes controverses du XIXe siècle, bourse commune, clerc assermenté, cantonnement, La formation des huissiers de justice, Cadet Roussel, huissier et chansonnier, La saisie exécution au XVIIe siècle, and Les huissiers à Paris. *Also see* Lesage, who also includes rich historical illustrations from art related to the Huissier de Justice, and for more extensive comments on L'huissier sous l'Ancien Régime (du XIIIe au XVIIIe siécle) about Les huissiers dans le processus de formation de l'État au moyen âge (XIIIe-XVe siècle), Les huissiers dans la jurisdiction centrale: le Grand Conseil de Malines (vers 1435-1794), Les huissiers dans les instances administrative centrales (du XVe au XVIIIe siècle), Les huissiers dans les jurisdictions provinciales (XIVe-XVIIIe siècle), L'huissier pendant la période française (1794-1815) about Les huissiers dans la période de transition entre l'Ancien Régime et le nouveau régime: le cadre legal, L'organisation des huissiers dans quelques départements belges, and L'huissier à l'époque actuelle (XIXe au XXe siécle) about Les huissiers et le régime de Guillaume 1er (1815-1830), Les huissiers dans la Belgique indépendante (1830-vers 1900) and La modernisation dans un cadre national et international (vers 1900-1967).
7. *See* Kennett, Regulation of Civil Enforcement Agents, Regulation of enforcement agents in Europe: a comparative survey, vol. 1 Text, report in the Grotius program 2001, pp. 34-36. *Also see*, for further information about the historical developments later on in the nineteenth century and thereafter about the Huissier de Justice in Belgium, France and the Netherlands, Kennett, *i.b.*, pp. 36-40.

was the monopoly rents the holder could obtain for the services provided. In the case of the Huissier, a charge could be made for the service of documents and for expenses, a charge that in the case of execution of enforceable instruments would ultimately be meet by the debtor.

From the end of the eighteenth century the position of the Huissier was subject to challenges. Following the French Revolution the institutions of the ancient regime were abolished and a radical restructuring of the legislative, administrative and judicial organization of the State took place. The local organizations of Huissiers were banned, as was the sale of offices. In addition state employees became used for tax collection purposes, and the Huissiers lost their police functions to the apparatus of the criminal law. Nevertheless, the Huissiers currently holding office were retained pending the introduction of a new system.

After several difficult and uncertain years, a new regulation of Huissiers was introduced in 1813. It assured the continuation of many of the original functions of the Huissier in the civil and criminal courts, in terms of the service of documents and execution of judgments. They had lost functions, in particular investigative functions which were passed on to judges and prosecutors, but had also gained new ones, such as the public sale of goods seized, and a greater role in the registration and service of extrajudicial public documents. Organizations of Huissiers were also reintroduced. Membership of a local chamber was obligatory. Chambers were organized at the level of the tribunal de première instance, *i.e.* in each arrondissement. While the chamber was intended to have supportive functions, such as the maintenance of a social fund that could be used to help sick and elderly Huissiers or their families, it also had the duty to play a disciplinary role, and to regulate entry to the profession. The sale of offices was resumed in France in 1816, but not in the other jurisdictions influenced by French law, such as Belgium and the Netherlands.

3.1.3 United Kingdom

The enforcement institutions in England and Wales share a common legal history, whereas the history of enforcement in Scotland is different. Reference is here mainly made to the history of these institutions in England and Wales. The Scottish has been limited to some remarks.

3.1.3.1 England and Wales

The history of the sheriffs' officers, who undertake the execution of judgments from the High Court, may be derived from the profession of a sheriff in his Bailiwick,[8] which already at the time of the Norman Conquest in 1066 was well established in England and Wales, *i.a.* with judicial and executive

8. Compare 6.4.3 about the use of the expression Bailiwick as an area of administration related to Guernsey. *Also* compare 3.1.5.4 about the corresponding use of the expression Fogde Counties, Fogdelän, related to Sweden.

functions, while the history of the profession of bailiffs used by the County Court is of a later date.

The enforcement institutions in England and Wales may well have developed from origins similar to those of the Swedish Kronofogde, but if so their history has taken an entirely different course.[9] Historically the sheriff was a person of great local power and influence. At the time of the Norman Conquest the sheriff was already well established, with judicial and executive functions including the dispensing of justice in the old county courts, maintaining the peace, keeping the local goal, and the collection of tithes and levies. The Norman kings made use of the institution, appointing their own vassals to the shrievalty as a means of control. During the medieval period the sheriff was a sort of agent of the Crown, who might be requested to perform a great variety of duties. As elections to Parliament became gradually more formalized, the sheriff was also responsible for organizing the elections in his shrievalty through meetings in the County court. But whereas the Huissier de Justice at about this time was a servant of the ruler, capable of close supervision, the sheriff had his own local power base and could assert a degree of independence from the ruler. Abuse of his power was hard to control and diminished the utility of the sheriff in the eyes of the Crown. The power of the sheriff was to some extent attenuated because of the nature of the feudal system. Feudal lords at different levels had their own courts. There was thus a proliferation of courts at different levels within the system and local lords took responsibility for dispensing justice. The judicial functions of the sheriff were also greatly affected by the centralization of judicial power in the King's courts. Litigants in increasing numbers turned to the cheaper, fairer justice of the King's courts rather than going to local courts where it seemed that every opportunity was taken to exact fees from them.

Court reforms have eventually ensured that the sheriff no longer performs any judicial functions. An important turning point in the fortunes of the sheriff was the restriction of their term of office in the fourteenth century. A statute of 1340 provided that 'no sheriff shall tarry in his bailiwick over one year'. Other more permanent officials thenceforth enjoyed greater importance. These permanent officials gradually assumed most of the executive functions of the sheriff. Over the course of time new forms of administration and taxation were developed, and new institutions were given responsibility for raising and collecting taxes, such as tax commissioners, or the justices of the peace. The taxes collected by the sheriff were gradually abolished. The main responsibility left to the sheriffs today is the enforcement of civil judgments. Even then their responsibility is limited. When the County Courts were created the enforcement of their judgments was not entrusted to the sheriff. It is only the enforcement of High Court judgments within their county that remains within the competence of the sheriff.

County Courts, in something approaching their modern form, were introduced by legislation in 1846, in the process abolishing the motley collection of other local

9. *See* Kennett, Regulation of Civil Enforcement Agents, Regulation of enforcement agents in Europe: a comparative survey, vol. 1 Text, report in the Grotius program 2001, pp. 43-44.

courts that had continued to exist until then. They were self-financing institutions managed by a registrar. The bailiffs used by the County Courts were themselves managed by an office holder called the high bailiff. They were originally independent agents in the same way that sheriff's officers and private bailiffs are independent business people. In the middle of the twentieth century, however, the County Courts registrar assumed the management functions of the high bailiff. When the County Courts became part of the Court Service, this link between the registrar and the bailiff service led to the creation of a corps of bailiffs who were civil servants.

3.1.3.2 Scotland

The institution of the modern Scottish enforcement agent Messengers-at-Arms may be traced back to a statute of 1510, and other later statutes designated the Messenger to be among these two hundred persons, who were authorized to carry the weapons of the sovereign.[10] The establishment of the institution of the office of the modern Scottish enforcement agent Sheriff Officer is supported by documents from the sixteenth and seventeenth centuries.

3.1.4 Germany

Here to be treated is the enforcement institution of the Gerichtsvollzieher in Germany. There exist some similarities between the German and Austrian institutions of the Gerichtsvollzieher.[11] Some of the features of the modern profession of the German enforcement agent Gerichtsvollzieher may be traced back to, at least, the beginning of the nineteenth century.[12] German law has been influenced to some

10. *See* Walker, pp. 263-264. *See*, for further information about the historical developments related to the Sheriff officer and Messangers-at-Arms in Scotland, Macpherson, pp. 77, 79, 81-99, 101-108. *Also* compare Kennett, Regulation of Civil Enforcement Agents, Regulation of enforcement agents in Europe: a comparative survey, vol. 1 Text, report in the Grotius program 2001, p. 46. *Also see* the website of the Society of Messengers-at-Arms and Sheriff Officers, <www.smaso.org>, under headline Background.
11. In Austria the execution of claims and other measures of execution against a debtor required, in the beginning of the twentieth century court treatment, by the Landesgericht, or by the Bezirksgericht, and the actual attachment was carried out by the Vollstreckungsbeamten, who were employed by the court of execution. *See*, about comments on the law of execution in Austria during this period and about these courts, Das Zivil-Prozessrecht der Kulturstaaten, Band III, Der Zivilprozess Oesterreichs, XVI. Die Zwangsvollstreckung, pp. 495-584, and about the Vollstreckungsbeamten, Munch-Petersen, Den danske Retspleje, Tredje del, Den borgerlige retspleje, andet hovedafsnit: Tvangsfuldbyrdelse og foreløbige retsmidler, p. 8. The present Austrian Gerichtsvollziehers still have their offices at the place of the court.
12. *See* Kennett, Regulation of Civil Enforcement Agents, Regulation of enforcement agents in Europe: a comparative survey, vol. 1 Text, report in the Grotius program 2001, pp. 41-42, and for further comments on the relationship of the working tasks of the Gerichtsvollzieher and the Vollstreckungsgericht in the beginning of the twentieth century, Nußbaum, p. 57. *Also see* for a more extensive and detailed comment on the German history of the enforcement organs

extent by the Huissier de Justice system. As a result of the Peace of Lunéville in 1801, the Rheinland became French territory, and the Huissier system was introduced there. The territory later returned to German control, but French legal institutions were retained. From the Rheinland, the Huissier system was also introduced into Bavaria. In Prussia, by contrast, enforcement agents were low status functionaries acting strictly on the orders of the judge and undertaking general clerical and menial functions in addition to enforcement action.

When a uniform code of civil procedure for the whole of Germany was under discussion, from 1859, initial drafts proposed that the Huissier system should be adopted, at least in relation to the financial and organizational independence of the Huissier from the court structure. It was not intended that the German Gerichtsvollzieher should enjoy the full range of functions undertaken by the Huissier de justice. Later drafts increasingly restricted the independence of the Gerichtsvollzieher and the legislation finally adopted offered a compromise solution. The Gerichtsverfassungsgesetz of 1877, § 155, provided that:

> Die Dienst- und Geschäftverhältnisse der mit den Zustellungen, Ladungen und Vollstreckungen zu betrauenden Beamten werden bei dem Reichsgericht durch den Reichskanzler, bei den Landgerichten durch die Landesjustizverwaltung bestimmt.

A variety of different ways of regulating Gerichtsvollzieher therefore continued in place until 1964. Some States gave claimants a free choice among the Gerichtsvollzieher within the territorial competence of each Amtsgericht. These Gerichtsvollzieher were required to maintain their own offices and to obtain their income from enforcement fees. In other States all Gerichtsvollzieher were employed by the State and acted under the directions of the Amtsgericht. In Prussia a system was introduced in the late nineteenth century whereby claimants had a free choice of Gerichtsvollzieher and each Gerichtsvollzieher was remunerated from their fees, with the advantage of a minimum income guarantee provided by the State. A new system was then adopted where each Gerichtsvollzieher had his own area of territorial competence, and competition was excluded. It is this latter system that has now been adopted throughout Germany. Some traces of the influence of the Huissier model remain, particularly in the fact that the Gerichtsvollzieher

---

Kottmann, about Die Vollstreckungsorgane in den ältesten Zeiten deutscher Gerichtsverfassung bis zum Ausgange des 15. Jahrhunderts, Das Vollstreckungswesen vom Ende des Mittelalters bis zum Beginne des 19. Jahrhunderts (Herrschaft des gemeinen deutschen Prozesses), Das Vollstreckungsorgan nach französischem Rechte; der huissier, Das Eindringen des französischen Huissier-Institutes in deutsche Rechtsgebiete, Die Zeit der deutschen Prozeß – Reform – Bestrebungen. Das Vollstreckungswesen in den verschiedenen deutschen Prozeßgesetzentwürfen des 19. Jahrhunderts bis herauf zur Reichscivilprozeßordnung vom 30. Januar 1877, and Die amtliche und vermögensrechtliche Stellung des Gerichtsvollziehers. *Also see*, as a background information about the development in German law, Spann, pp. 187-243 (Bayerisches Landesrecht ab Beginn des 16. Jahrhunderts bis ins 19. Jahrhundert mit Hinweisen zum gemeinen Recht) and pp. 255-266 (Die Reichsgesetzgebungen von 1877) (Reichszivilprozessordnung und Konkursordnung und das aktuelle Recht).

maintains his own office outside the court. Nevertheless, the Gerichtsvollzieher is well integrated within the court bureaucracy.

3.1.5 Nordic States

Denmark, Iceland and Norway have common historical roots, which explain certain uniformity in legislation and jurisprudence between these States. Sweden and Finland have a long common history and these States show a great conformity both concerning procedural and material rules. In Denmark and Norway enforcement takes place as part of the court procedure. In Sweden and Finland enforcement matters have formally been entrusted to administrative authorities, standing free from courts, since the establishment of the Swedish Execution Ordinance of 1669.[13] This basic difference has led to differences in the regulation of many enforcement matters. The partially common history of the Nordic States[14] has, based on the developments in the past, resulted in the creation of organization enforcement systems for agents, which, more or less, share some similar historical features.

3.1.5.1 Denmark

In the late Middle Ages the title Foged was used for a lot of officials and servants, as well as for the king and for private.[15] The title was *i.a.* used for the royal Ombudsmand, later known as the Lensmand, and his assistant the Herredsfoged.

13. *See* 2.2.1.
14. To serve European readers, who are not familiar with the history of the Nordic States, information, with references, is provided here. Norway and Denmark were united under the same Crown from 1319 to 1537, when Norway became a part of Denmark until 1814, as a result of the Peace in Kiel. The three Nordic States, Denmark, Norway and Sweden were united in a union, from 1389, when the Danish-Norwegian queen Margareta conquered Sweden, and this union lasted, with some interruptions, until 1521. Norway and Sweden were united under the same Crown from 1814 until 1905, when Norway became independent from Sweden. The Faeroe Islands, which were independent until 1035, but afterwards paid taxes to Norway, became a part of Denmark in 1709. Greenland, which was administered by Denmark-Norway after 1721, was also transferred to Denmark in 1814. Iceland, which before the era of the Danish-Norwegian union, belonged to Norway since 1264, was, as well, transferred to Denmark in 1814, and became finally independent from the Danish Crown in 1944. When Finland was separated from Sweden in 1809, as a result of the Peace in Fredrikshamn, it became instead a part of Russia until its independency from Russia in 1918. *See* Stora Focus, Band 5, p. 188, Band 6, p. 36, Band 7, p. 51, and Norstedts uppslagsbok, pp. 455-456, 729, 774, and 1155.
15. *See*, about the history of the Danish system: Lemann Kristiansen, pp. 34-36, 38-41, 45, 50, 57, 96, 107, 186-193, Munch-Petersen, Den danske Retspleje, Tredje del, Den borgerlige retspleje, andet hovedafsnit: Tvangsfuldbyrdelse og foreløbige retsmidler, pp. 4-12, Rump Christensen, pp. 530-533, and Stemann, pp. 256-262. *Also* compare, for further details on the Danish organization of the enforcement of private claims and the enforcement and recovery of public claims, Nordiskt samarbete om indrivningsfrågor (Nordic cooperation in recovery matters), report to the Nordic Council of Ministers of Jul. 2002, pp. 31-34.

The working tasks were generally to safeguard the interests of the king, which meant a lot of different legal and administrative tasks, including the execution of judgments, taxes and fines.

The Herredsfoged, also later known as the Tingfoged, had originally both administrative and judicial tasks, but the task of managing the meetings of the Ting, the judicial court function, and the participation in its judgments, became later his most important activity. In the merchant cities the title used was Byfoged, and he managed the city judicial function Ting/Council on behalf of the Lensmand. In these cities, which belonged to the Fadeburet,[16] *i.e.* where the incomes went directly into the Treasury of the king, the Foged, the representative of the king, acted both to safeguard the interests of the king and the burghers. In the fifteenth and sixteenth centuries the self-government of the cities increased, supported by the king, and the Mayor and the appointed officials of the Council got the right to appoint a citizen as Byfoged.

Before the introduction of the autocracy by the Danish king in 1660 there existed no need for any permanently established specific authorities, which imposed and recovered taxes, and the ordinary system of administration was then used at such occasions, such as the Lensmand from the County administration, or the Rentekammeret, an organ in charge of the finances of the State, or an ad hoc authority.[17] After the introduction of the autocracy when the king received a complete right of taxation, the County organization was changed into an organization of Amts, including a function for the collection of the royal taxes, and the royal claims also received priority in relation to the fulfillment of private claims. As the taxation became more frequent a need appeared for specific organs for the collection and recovery of taxes, and for this purpose a number of oppebørselsbetjente/collection servants were appointed under the Rentekammeret.

Both the taxes and the fines of the king were recoverable without the prior need for a judgment in a so-called action of Udpantning and the right of such an action was afterwards also attributed to other claims, mainly public claims. The system of the Sognefoged[18] in the countryside was introduced in 1791, and the Sognefoged was appointed by the Amtmændene in the Counties. The Sognefoged performed Udpantning and civil execution, depending on the circumstances, after the instructions from the Herredsfoged, and later on following the instructions from the local judge.

At the introduction of the Retsplejeloven in 1917 the tasks of the Herredsfoged were divided between the court, the Head of police, which corresponded to the Sognefoged in the countryside, or the Amtsmand. In the merchant places and in the trading locations it was, however, still possible to obtain the civil execution by the assistance of the Head of police, and in the countryside by the assistance of the

---

16. The Danish word Fadebur corresponds to the Swedish word Förrådskammare, *see* Norstedts dansk-svenska ordbok, p. 118. The corresponding word in English is Storechamber.
17. *Also see* 2.3.2 about tax collection before and after the introduction of the autocracy by the Danish king in 1660.
18. The Danish word sogne corresponds to the Swedish words församling or socken, *see* Norstedts dansk-svenska ordbok, p. 551. The corresponding word in English is parish.

Sognefoged, subject to that the claim was below a specific amount and did not concern real estate property. Simultaneously the office of the Byfoged was abolished and the task of being in charge of the civil execution law was then transferred to the judges of the city court in Copenhagen. The title used by the judge, a Dommerfuldmægtig, or a Retsassessor, when they are in charge of civil execution matters in court, in the Fogedret, is still the king's Foged. The Fogedret is a court, which is formally separated from the common Byret/the City court, and the Fogedret is, as a main rule, in charge of the execution of civil law claims, subject to the exceptions in the public law area.

The title Foged is also used by those officials who are in charge of the recovery of debts to the municipalities and to the State. A large number of public claims are collected and recovered, without the need of a previous judgment from court, on behalf of the municipalities and the State, by administrative authorities and their Foged. After the reform in 1932 until 2005 the collection and recovery of debts to the municipalities and of a number of debts to the State, such as individual income taxes, were managed by the Pantefogderne, who were employed by the municipalities. The Toldfogderne, who acted on behalf of the Customs organization had similar tasks. In addition, a large number of officials, employed in the Customs and Tax regions were in charge of the recovery of taxes, VAT and other charges in relation to corporations. A reform in 2005 meant that a new organization called Skat was established for the recovery by the Pantefogderne of all public claims from the State, the Counties and the municipalities, and the use of the Fogedret was in this context limited to civil law claims, imprisonment, and appeals against the decisions of attachment of the Pantefoged and against administrative fines.

3.1.5.2 Iceland

After the independency from Denmark in 1944, new national enforcement and recovery organizations were established.[19] The enforcement of both private law claims and public law claims are taken care of by the Sýslumaður, which are independent State authorities under the ministry of Justice. Besides these enforcement tasks, the civil servant of the Sýslumaður also have other tasks of an administrative nature, *e.g.* the executive sale, registration issues, and family law-related matters, *i.a.* divorces. Public claims, such as taxes, are determined by the tax authorities, but the recovery of these claims is handled by the Customs authority in Reykjavík. Outside of Reykjavík the recovery of public claims is handled by the civil servant of the Sýslumaður, in his capacity of representing the Customs authority and as a part of the recovery authority of the State, and in these situations he is under the supremacy of the ministry of Finance.

19. *See*, about Iceland, for further details on the organization of the enforcement of private claims and the enforcement and recovery of public claims, Nordiskt samarbete om indrivningsfrågor (Nordic cooperation in recovery matters), report to the Nordic Council of Ministers of Jul. 2002, pp. 36-37.

3.1.5.3 Norway

The institution of the modern Norwegian enforcement agent Lensmann has historical traditions, which, at least, go back to the thirteenth century, but may be older.[20] This institution is, nevertheless, clearly mentioned in a decree for the Faeroe Islands, rettarbot for Færøyane, of 1273, signed by Håkon Magnusson, and was therefore officially approved under the final parts of the reign of the king Magnus Lagabøtar (1260-1280). The Lensmann was appointed by the Syslemann, as his assistant, in the Sysle districts. The three main tasks of the Syslemann, and his assistance the Lensmann, during the thirteenth century, were: the administration of the function of the local justice in connection to the Ting, a place where legal matters normally were dealt with, in the presence of the assembled people and the Lagmann, the judge, the recovery of taxes and the command of the military forces. Other judicial tasks were related to the powers in the police and prosecution areas.

The Syslemann was paid from the actual outfall of his activities, and he received the payments of the minor fines, partially or as a whole, while the king received these larger ones completely. The Syslemann often had great interests in the Land estates in his Sysle district. These activities became prosperous for the nobility, who had been appointed a Syslemann in a district, in the period after 1350. A tendency was then successively developed, which meant that more and more of them began to consider these activities as a source of personal income. They let others perform their duties and they were not domiciled in their district. The king tried to counteract this tendency by appointing other officials, called Fut or sometimes Fogd. In the later part of the Middle Ages there was a change in the payment system for the Syslemann, and the County system, which came via Denmark, following a pattern from Germany, was introduced instead. The king then appointed the County lords, who in their turn appointed the Fut and the Lensmann. The Fut, or the Fogd, was originally, since the fourteenth century the servants of the County lords. The County lords were able to lease out their Counties to a leaseholder, who then took on their duties and received the incomes against the payment of a charge.

After a reform in the 1630th the Fut only became the servant of the king, and he was assisted in his tasks by the Lensmann, who was often appointed by the Fut. When the Danish king introduced the autocracy in 1661 the County organization was changed and Norway became instead divided into superior administrative units called Stiftamt, as compared to the less important administrative units, which were called Amt. Both the Fut and the Lensmann were responsible under the Amtsmann, who appointed the Lensmann. The working tasks of the Lensmann

20. *See*, about the history of the Norwegian system: Hagerup, pp. 3-4 and 9-16, Lemann Kristiansen, p. 37, Nordstoga, pp. 13-145, which also includes rich historical illustrations from art related to the subject, and Wingren, p. 2. *Also* compare, for further details on the Norwegian organization of the enforcement of private claims and the enforcement and recovery of public claims, Nordiskt samarbete om indrivningsfrågor (Nordic cooperation in recovery matters), report to the Nordic Council of Ministers of Jul. 2002, pp. 37-39.

remained unchanged during the period of autocracy between 1661-1814. There were some changes in the working tasks of the Lensmann during the period of 1814-1905, and in 1910 the office of the Fut was abolished, but the office of the Lensmann remained. After this period some additional tasks have been added to the work of the Lensmann, while others remain, or have been transferred to other parts of the administration.

The enforcement of private claims are still dealt with locally by the Lensmann, when he acts as an executor, Namsman,[21] and takes care of the enforcement, tvangsfullbyrdelse, of such claims. Even if his main task still is to be the head of the police force in his district, he also has other important tasks, *i.a.* to act as a Notarius publicus, an Organizer of general elections, a Bidragsfogde, in order to establish and recover maintenance allowances, and a Skifterett, as a part of the court of first instance. In this capacity he draws up estate inventories owing to death and bankruptcy. His previous task as a tax recovery agent was successively abolished during the period of 1948-1974, and was then transferred to other parts of the administration.

3.1.5.4 Sweden

The meaning and use of the word Fogde[22] have changed during the history. It is today normally used in a more narrow sense, often in the context of the enforcement of claims by an enforcement officer, Kronofogde,[23] than in the previous history. The Fogde during the earlier Middle Ages was a royal governing official within a certain area, a County, a City, or another administrative area.[24] The Fogde

21. The Norwegian word nam corresponds to the Swedish word utmätning, *see* Norstedts norsk-svenska ordbok, p. 287. The corresponding words in English are distress or attachment.
22. *See* Svensk ordbok 1, A-M, p. 311, which states that the historical meaning of the Swedish word fogde is a royal official with the task to represent the interests of the Crown in a certain area. *Also* compare Norstedts uppslagsbok, p. 471, which reports that the word fogde comes from the Old Swedish word foghati, or fogate, derived from the Latin word *advocatus*, and was used in older times for royal officials, who administered certain areas in the countryside (fogdelän or fögderi), or in the City participated in its government together with the Magistrat, and Wessén, p. 119, which refers to the Old Swedish word foghadhe, ultimately from the Middle Ages Latin *vocatus*, of the Latin *advocatus*. The Latin word *aduocatus* may, depending on the circumstances, *i.a.* be translated into: one who supports or advices a party to a law-suit, a legal assistant or counsellor, a professional pleader, advocate, counsel, a helper, supporter, assistant, a mediator and a witness, Oxford Latin Dictionary, p. 59. *Also see*, for a more extensive etymological explanation of the word fogde, Ordbok över svenska språket, åttonde bandet, pp. 1042-1047.
23. The first part krono in the Swedish word Kronofogde only expresses a connection to the State, compare the word Kronopark, Svensk ordbok 1, A-M, p. 640.
24. *See*, about the history of the Swedish system: Almquist, p. 14 compared to p. 15, Backman, pp. 404-410, Forsman, pp. 1-2, Hallin, pp. 13-18, Hassler, pp. 341-353, Jacobsson, pp. 486-487, Lemann Kristiansen, pp. 36-37, Munch-Petersen, Den danske Retspleje, Tredje del, Den borgerlige retspleje, andet hovedafsnit: Tvangsfuldbyrdelse og foreløbige retsmidler, p. 7, Nehrman-Ehrenstråle, pp. 441-442, Schrevelius, pp. 387-392, Sjögren, pp. 1-43, Sjöholm, pp. 1-4, and Wrede, pp. 3-13.

Counties, Fogdelän,[25] were governed from the castles or strongholds. The larger Fogdelän were governed by the captains from the high nobility. The minor Counties, called Fataburslän, were governed by the captains from the lesser nobility. In the City the Fogde participated in its government together with the Council/ Magistrat. The participation of the Fogde in judicial matters ceased, however, during the fifteenth century, when in the same time the king began to appoint Mayors for the Councils of the cities.

The original tasks of the Fogde were to receive the interest payments to the Crown, administer the property of the Crown, and to make an account for the collection. Under the period of the Provincial Codes and the City Codes from the thirteenth and fourteenth centuries and the common Country law from the fourteenth century matters of civil execution law required court treatment.[26] It was first through the introduction of the Execution Ordinance of 1669, that the practice, from previous centuries, of making direct use of the king's Fogdar, Commanders and Governors for the forced execution of civil law claims, was formally established. This meant a total break with the system from the old laws, according to which the forced execution of claims and other enforcement measures belonged to the courts. During the fifteenth century the Fogde mainly became a tax collector.

The competence of the Fogde was increasingly diminished during the seventeenth century and the title Fogde became then the appellation for a pronounced specialized official, such as a Kronofogde and a Stadsfogde. Some features of the modern profession of the Swedish enforcement agent Kronofogde may be traced back to this period. In the Royal Statutes, Resolutions and Ordinances concerning the Judicature of 1528 one out of 670 pages was devoted to the rules of enforcement. That page was also part of the king Gustavus II Adolphus' Court Proceedings of 1615, which deals with the duty of a court to initiate enforcement by Governors, County administrations, Mayors and Councils and to make certain that they accomplish the enforcement without regard to the person, or the person's standing. The Law of 1734, included an Enforcement Code, Utsökningsbalk, for civil execution law matters, divided into 10 chapters,[27] which essentially was based on the Execution Ordinance of 1669. The executive authority was the king's Commander, and the servants, who were obedient to him/Konungens Befalningshawande, och betiente, som under honom lyda. The Enforcement Code of 1734 was reformed into an Enforcement Law in 1877, which was replaced first in 1982 by an Enforcement Code, Utsökningsbalk.[28]

25. Compare 3.1.3.1 about the corresponding use of the expression Bailiwick as an area of administration related to England and Wales, and 6.4.3 about the use of the same expression related to Guernsey.
26. *See* 2.2.1.
27. *See* 2.3.1 for further details about this Enforcement Code.
28. *See* Utsökningsbalk (1981:774), and about its official translation from Swedish into English Ds 2002:45 The Swedish Enforcement Code (2001:337).

At the reorganization in 1917 of the collection administration the Landsfiskal became distrainer/bailiff in the countryside. In 1932 it also became possible for a City, which lacked the administrative authority of a Magistrat, to appoint an Överexekutor/Chief Executive Officer, and to employ a Stadsfogde/City Executive Officer. The enforcement functions were organized locally by district until 1965. Until then, in the countryside, the Landsfiskal, had responsibilities as chief of police, public prosecutor and enforcement authority. In the cities the comparable figure was the Stadsfogde, who, however, only had the responsibility for enforcement. Enforcement in this context includes the collection of public and private law debts, but a large part of the work of the Landsfiskal and the Stadsfogde was tax collection. The superior authority in the execution field was the Överexekutor/Chief Executive Officer, which was part of the Länsstyrelse/County administration. This superior authority was competent for taking decisions in disputes in enforcement matters, while the actual enforcement was entrusted to a Kronofogde, a Stadsfogde, or a Landsfiskal. Other qualified tasks of this authority were the executive sale of real estate and eviction.

In 1965 the police, prosecution and civil enforcement functions were centralized, and three new nationalized organizations were created to perform the three different functions: the police authorities, the prosecution authorities, and the enforcement authorities. Although originally administration continued to take place at district level, the enforcement authorities have since been even more centralized. The enforcement authorities became administratively subordinated to the National Tax Board in 1973. The office of the Överexekutor/Chief Executive Officer was abolished in 1982, when the new Enforcement Code came into force, and the executive tasks were then transferred to the enforcement authorities. In 1980 the enforcement authorities became supervisory authorities in bankruptcy.

In 1988 the previous 81 enforcement districts were reformed into 24 enforcement authorities, one in each Län/County, and in 1998 these authorities were decreased to 10, with the National Tax Board as the superior authority. From 1992 the summary proceeding is no longer dealt with by the courts, but instead by the enforcement authorities. Matters of debt relief for individuals are, since 1994, a task of the enforcement authorities. In 2006 the national Tax Agency was reorganized with the result that two separate authorities, one national Tax Agency, and one national Enforcement Authority, the latter with a Rikskronofogde in charge, were established.

3.1.5.5 Finland

Up to 1809, Sweden and Finland were one State. The influences of Sweden persisted even after Finland became a part of Russia.[29] The Russian legal system never made its presence felt in Finland, even though Finland was a part of Russia during

29. *See*, about the history of the Finish system: Forsman, pp. 1-2, 6-10 and 47-60, Koulo, pp. 539-543, and Wrede, pp. 3-15, 19-21 and 24-33. *Also see*, for further details about the proposed organization structure in 1995, Regeringens proposition 106/1995 Lag om ändring av utsökningslagen (Finish government bill regarding the change of the enforcement Act) compared to an

the period of 1809-1918. Consequently Finland kept its previous judicial structure under this Russian period, which meant that the enforcement organization, and the procedure followed in enforcement, were based on the previous Swedish system, and during the twentieth century many similar features existed between Swedish and Finish legislations. The structure and fundamental solutions of the Finish enforcement Act of 1895 were largely founded on the Act by the same name passed in Sweden in 1877. This Finish Act has undergone partial changes several times, *i.a.* in 1973 and in the 1980s. In principle the enforcement Act did not cover the enforcement of taxes. Tax enforcement procedure was regulated by means of statutory provisions only; the most important of these being the 1897 statute concerning the attachment of levies and public fees.

An important change took place in 1961 with the passing of the tax enforcement Act. This meant that the separate tax enforcement organization was abolished, and tax enforcement in its entirety was entrusted to the same organization as the enforcement of civil procedural receivables. In 1996 another reform was made and the administrative organization of enforcement authorities was changed. The new organization was adapted to the local administration reform, and meant that the original organization of the enforcement Act with the Överexekutor/Chief Enforcement Officer – enforcement officer – was dismantled. The office of Chief Enforcement Officer was abolished, and enforcement officers became the only remaining enforcement staff in the enforcement authorities. The 1996 reform meant that the enforcement of both private and public claims was taken care of by the enforcement authorities, normally on the Häradenas exekutionsverk. The distrainer, Häradsfogde, is in charge of the enforcement authority. The ministry of Justice is the supreme authority in the coordination, supervision and administration of enforcement and it also appoints the enforcement officers. The enforcement Act was replaced by an Enforcement Code by the Finish Parliament in 2007.[30]

3.1.6 CONCLUSIONS

The historical remarks reported in relation to the origins and later developments of some few modern European enforcement agents illustrate that the features and

---

evaluation of this reform in Lagutskottets utlåtande 14/1999 till riksdagen angående statsrådets redogörelse om verkställighet av häradsreformen (the opinion of the law committee of the Finish parliament about the statement of the minister on the implementation of the organization reform), and for further details on the Finish organization of the enforcement of private claims and the enforcement and recovery of public claims, Nordiskt samarbete om indrivningsfrågor (Nordic cooperation in recovery matters), report to the Nordic Council of Ministers of Jul. 2002, pp. 34-35.

30. A new Enforcement Code was approved by the Finish Parliament on 31 Jan. 2007 based on the Regeringens proposition 83/2006 till riksdagen med förslag till Utsökningsbalk och lag om verkställighet av skatter och avgifter samt vissa lagar som har samband med dem (Finish Government Bill with a proposal on a new Enforcement Code, and law about the enforcement of taxes and charges and certain laws which have a connection to them). The new Finish Enforcement Code was enacted on 15 Jun. 2007, *see* Utsökningsbalk, Nr. 705 in Finlands författningssamling.

activities of these historical professionals have changed over time as a consequence of a lot of historical influences during different periods. Some activities and features have remained from historical time with these agents into our age, *e.g.* the work of service of legal and extra legal documents in these national systems, which originate from the French Huissier de Justice system, and, in particular, in all the treated national systems, the work of the enforcement of judgments, while some previous other activities have not.

The activities of civil enforcement, tax collection and recovery, police, prosecution and the court functions have during certain historical periods been combined in different ways under the same office in some European States. The exercise of these activities, all of them based on public powers, were later in some European States more clearly separated into different offices, such as in France, while some other European States still combine some of these activities under the same office, *e.g.* England, Germany and the Nordic States. Also, the relationship between the enforcement agents and the courts and the powers in society have shifted during different periods, and resulted in a degree of more, or less, dependency or independency for these agents.

The tasks of enforcing civil law claims and the collection or the recovery of public law claims such as taxes and fines, were originally, in most of the States here treated, entrusted to the same organs and officials. However, as a result of the centralization of the powers in the societies, the direct taxation in the States became more frequent and a need appeared for the establishment of specific organs and officials for an efficient collection and recovery of taxes. Such specific organs were normally not needed in the less centralized systems, which were based on the incomes from the estates of the State/Crown, customs and turnover charges. This development trend is evident from the period of Roman law and also, more, or less, from the following periods, and have in most, but not all European States resulted in the present establishment of different organs with employed officials for the enforcement of civil law claims by enforcement agents, respectively for the recovery of taxes by recovery agents.

3.2 CIVIL ENFORCEMENT LAW AREA OF TODAY

3.2.1 National Enforcement Agents

There exists, *i.a.* based on historical[31] and cultural considerations, a wide range of activities and of organizational structures in national enforcement systems related to the nationally regulated professionals, the enforcement agents in Europe, with the main task to enforce civil law claims,[32] both in the national and international

31. *See* 3.1.
32. *See* Kerameus, Enforcement in the International Context, Recueil des cours, collected courses of the Hague Academy of International Law, 1997, Tome 264 de la collection, pp. 272-279, who treats comparative aspects of carrying out enforcement, and Kerameus, International

context. Only some few examples of enforcement agents are indicated here from a limited number of national systems and the readers are referred to consult a more extensive literature for further detailed information on various activities and about the complexity of the organization structures of enforcement agents in Europe.[33] The enforcement agents in some national enforcement systems are part of, or quite closely linked to, the court systems. Examples are the Danish system of a court officer within the enforcement court, Fogedret, the English and Wales' systems, *e.g.* operated by a Under sheriff/a Sheriff's officer and a County court bailiff, both categories responsible for enforcement out of the courts, but under the responsibility of High court and County court judges and administrators for processing applications for various methods of enforcement, and the German system operated by a Gerichtvollzieher, a court officer, but based outside the court itself, and a Rechtspfleger, within the enforcement court, Amtsgericht. In other national enforcement systems a more independent position from court service in enforcement matters exists and specialized enforcement agents exist, as in Finland and in Sweden. No court involvement exists in these States in enforcement matters prior to an appeal to court against a decision of enforcement from these national enforcement agents. In France le juge d'exécution only intervenes to solve possible difficulties, which can emerge during enforcement.

The relationship of the enforcement agents to other parts of the State administration than courts and the judicial status of the profession also vary and have resulted in different levels of dependency to or independency from this administration. Examples are the French Huissier de Justice, who exercises a liberal profession, but operates based on a license granted by the ministry of justice and the similar position of the liberal profession of the Dutch Gerechtsdeurwaarder, and the Swedish Kronofogde, who is employed as a civil servant by the Kronofogdemyndighet, the Enforcement authority, which is a part of the State administration. In 2004 more than half of the enforcement agents in the member States of the Council of Europe were working in a public institution and the other part of

---

encyclopedia of comparative law, volume XVI, Civil procedure, chapter 10, Enforcement proceedings, p. 9, who makes the comparative remarks that the contemporary world offers a variety of enforcement schemes ranging from adjudication like conceptions to purely administrative methods and that most systems tend to the middle ground, entrusting enforcement to officers of the law who, while not exercising judicial functions, are not properly part of the public administration.

33. The following works include information on national enforcement agents in some European States: Arnt Nielsen, International privat- og procesret, pp. 455-456 (Denmark), Bayo Delgado, Persons involved in the execution of court decisions (Spain), The execution of court decisions in civil cases, pp. 18-22, Bogdan, Något om exekutionsväsendet i England, USA och Belgien, Festskrift till P.O. Bolding, pp. 35-44 (England), pp. 44-45 (USA), pp. 45-48 (Belgium), Civil Procedure in Europe, vol. 1, pp. 92-93 (Germany), pp. 161-162 (Belgium), pp. 202-203 (Denmark), p. 292 (France), p. 422 (Italy), pp. 462-463 (Luxemburg), The execution of court decisions in civil cases, about staff responsible for execution of court decisions in: Albania, Armenia, Austria, Azerbaijan, Belgium, Bulgaria, Croatia, Cyprus, Czech Republic, Denmark, Finland, France, Georgia, Germany, Greece, Hungary, Italy, Japan, Latvia, Lithuania, Luxemburg, Moldova, Norway, Poland, Portugal, Romania, Slovak Republic,

enforcement agents were practising in a liberal profession ruled by public authorities, while in the EU, at the same time, more than half of these professionals were practising in such a liberal profession.[34] Many national European associations of regulated enforcement agents are members of the UIHJ.[35]

Even if a main monopolistic activity of enforcement agents in Europe relates to the enforcement of civil law claims based on titles of execution, other monopolistic activities also exist and vary in comparison, *e.g.* the service of judicial documents.[36] Some enforcement agents in Europe also have, besides the monopolistic activities, which are based on the exercise of public powers, additional facultative activities of a more liberal nature related to other legal matters, *e.g.* debt collecting, statements of fact, Les constats, which can, under certain conditions, serve as proof in judicial proceedings, and to give legal advice.[37] Some other

---

Slovenia, Spain, Sweden, the former Yugoslav Republic of Macedonia, Ukraine and the United Kingdom and Synthesis, pp. 150-261, Guinot (France), Jacobsson (Sweden), pp. 488-490, Kennett, Enforcement of judgments, pp. 336-338 (England, France and Germany), Kennett, The Enforcement of Judgments in Europe, p. 76 (Sweden), pp. 76-79 (France), pp. 79-81 (Spain), pp. 81-83 (Germany), pp. 83-85 (England), Kennett, about the independent enforcement agents in France, Belgium, the Netherlands, Scotland, England and Wales and the civil service enforcement agents in Spain, Germany, Italy, Sweden and Denmark, Regulation of Civil Enforcement Agents, Regulation of enforcement agents in Europe: a comparative survey, vol. 1 Text: Fundamental concepts, historical and cultural considerations, qualifications, training and methods of appointment, range of activities: monopolistic, facultative and prohibited activities, territorial competence: communication, cooperation and competition, form of organization and opportunities for growth, insurance and indemnity arrangements, professional bodies, supervision and discipline and remuneration and other incentives, vol. 2 Legislation and annexes, report in the Grotius program 2001, Koulo (Finland), pp. 541-543, Källström, pp. 696-697 and 702 (France), Macpherson (Scotland), pp. 76-145, and about the Nordic States, Nordiskt samarbete om indrivningsfrågor (Nordic cooperation in recovery matters), report to the Nordic Council of Ministers of Jul. 2002, pp. 31-32 (Denmark), pp. 34-35 (Finland), p. 36 (Iceland), pp. 37-38 (Norway), and pp. 39-40 (Sweden), Statut et fonctions de l'Huissier de Justice en droit compare (Germany, Austria, Belgium, France, Italy, Luxemburg, the Netherlands, Switzerland, canton of Geneva and Canada, Quebec), and Walker (Scotland), pp. 263-269. *Also see*, the information that is available about the European associations of enforcement agents, which are members of the UIHJ, website of the UIHJ, <www.uihj.com>.

34. *See*, about the Status and number of enforcement agents from mainly in 2004, Report on European judicial systems, pp. 136-137. The statistics about the number of enforcement agents from some States may, however, sometimes not be comparable to the statistics from other States, because the working tasks of these enforcement agents in these respective States differ.
35. *See* 2.10.5.
36. *See* Kennett, Regulation of Civil Enforcement Agents, Regulation of enforcement agents in Europe: a comparative survey, vol. 1 Text, report in the Grotius program 2001, pp. 79-85 (France, Belgium, the Netherlands, Scotland, Germany, Spain, Italy, Sweden, Denmark, England and Wales). *Also see*, about how the monopolistic activities of the Swedish enforcement authorities are organized compared to some other European States, Berglund, Hur är kronofogdemyndighetens arbetsuppgifter organiserade i några EU-Stater och i Norge?, Ny juridik, no. 4: 2000, pp. 51-68.
37. *See* Kennett, Regulation of Civil Enforcement Agents, Regulation of enforcement agents in Europe: a comparative survey, vol. 1 Text, report in the Grotius program 2001, pp. 85-90. *Also see* about that the French Huissier de Justice may provide the statements of fact (Les constats) at

activities, which are considered to interfere with the professional activities of enforcement agents are prohibited, *e.g.* a Belgian Huissier de Justice is prohibited to exercise any other profession or a Scottish Sheriff Officer may not be an auctioneer with his own auction room.[38] The different monopolistic and facultative activities of European enforcement agents have influenced their organization in a lot of different ways.

The Council of Europe's recommendation on enforcement provides several important guiding principles for the profession of enforcement agents.[39] In literature, an ideal status for the profession of an enforcement agent has been described as that of an independent status from courts, but acting as the 'arm of the judge' in the establishment of proportionality between the parties as a 'balance wheel' in an efficient recovery procedure.[40] A proposal has also been presented to introduce in Europe, even if the activities of the agent are derived from the public powers of the State, the liberal profession of a Huissier de Justice, or rather a Commissaire à l'exécution, subject to certain criteria.[41] The status of the enforcement agent has also in literature been described as requiring absolute neutrality in relation to the parties of the enforcement procedure and independency in his professional activities, at a level of 'auxiliaire du juge', and that the profession is to be practiced as a civil servant, based on the agent's *imperium*, the public powers attributed to him by the State, in order to make his activities effective.[42] The authorities, which have been entrusted the supervision and the control of enforcement agents vary in different States and may either be a professional body, a judge, a ministry of justice, a prosecutor, or some other authority, or a combination of these bodies.[43]

The legal profession of an enforcement agent requires, no doubt, a solid knowledge of law because it involves advanced legal considerations in the establishment of a justified balance of interests between the parties in a civil execution law procedure in the exercise of public powers through different enforcement measures. This does not only require a solid knowledge about the content of

---

the demand of individuals and give legal advice, Statut et fonctions de l'Huissier de Justice en droit compare, pp. 22 and 24-25.

38. *See*, about these examples, Kennett, Regulation of Civil Enforcement Agents, Regulation of enforcement agents in Europe: a comparative survey, vol. 1 Text, chapter four, report in the Grotius program 2001, p. 93. *Also see i.b.*, p. 92, where she states that the decision as to what functions are compatible with enforcement is made at the level of State policy, and reports that the range of activities permitted to professional enforcements agents is largely defined positively, *i.e.* stating the activities that are permitted, rather than negatively, but concludes that there is a scope of interpretation.
39. *See* s. IV.
40. *See* Verbeke, Execution Officers as a Balance Wheel in Insolvency Cases, pp. 15-18.
41. *See* Verbeke, Quel Huissier de Justice pour l'Europe?, Le droit processuel et le droit de l'exécution, pp. 299-324.
42. *See* Civil Procedure in Europe 1, de Leval, Une harmonisation des procédures d'exécution dans l'Union européenne est-elle concevable?, pp. 622-623.
43. *See*, about the Supervision and control of enforcement agents, Report on European judicial systems, pp. 141-142, and also about the Disciplinary proceedings and sanctions against enforcement agents, *i.b.*, pp. 142-143.

national civil execution law, EC law, conventions, and parts of public international law related to that law area. It also requires a knowledge and understanding of the interplay between this total law area and a lot of other parts of the national and international legal systems. The Council of Europe's recommendation on enforcement also makes clear the importance when recruiting enforcement agents that considerations should in examinations be given to the candidates legal knowledge and training in relevant law and procedure.[44] Even if most of the member States of the Council of Europe require specific initial training, or examination, to enter the profession of enforcement agent,[45] the formal rules of qualifications, training and methods of appointment of enforcement agents vary in Europe.[46]

3.2.2 Competent Authorities

The work in a Member State of the EU related to applications on the recognition and enforcement of titles of executions from other Member States based on the Brussels I regulation is normally performed by the officials of a court or by a so-called competent authority.[47] The officials of the competent authorities, normally courts, of the contracting States to the New York convention on foreign arbitral awards deal with the work related to applications on recognition and the enforcement of an arbitral award.[48] The Nordic States have designated courts, or enforcement authorities, to act as competent authorities in relation to the Nordic convention on recognition and the enforcement of judgments in civil matters. Courts have been designated as competent authority by Denmark, Finland and Norway, while Sweden has designated the enforcement authority.[49]

3.2.3 Conclusions

The national professions of regulated recovery agents for the recovery of tax claims in the EU, the officials of the national administrations, and their national

44. *See* s. IV, 3.
45. *See*, about an overview of specific initial training or examination to enter the profession of enforcement agent in the member States, Report on European judicial systems, p. 140.
46. *See* Kennett, Regulation of Civil Enforcement Agents, Regulation of enforcement agents in Europe: a comparative survey, vol. 1 Text, pp. 53-77, and annex to Chapter 3, Independent enforcement agents in: France and Belgium, the Netherlands, Scotland, England and Wales and civil service enforcement agents in: Spain, Germany, Italy, Sweden and Denmark, report in the Grotius program 2001.
47. *See* Art. 39, 1 and Annex II to the Regulation.
48. *See* Art. V, 2 that only states competent authority, which means that the contracting States to the convention are at liberty to designate a suitable State body to perform this working task. *Also see* Van den Berg, pp. 357 and 382, who only mentions courts in the context of the work of the competent authority, *i.e.* not enforcement agents.
49. *See* 3 § and 5 § in Förordning (1977:1005) om nordisk verkställighet på privaträttens område (Swedish government decree on the Nordic enforcement in civil matters).

organizational structures in the public law area are more similar to each other than the national regulated professions of enforcement agents for the enforcement of contractual claims and their national organizational structures in the private law area. There are vast differences between enforcement agents as to the range of functions they undertake. In the majority of Member States in the EU the activities of the enforcement of civil law judgments and other enforceable civil law decisions and the recovery of tax claims are separated between the categories of enforcement agents and recovery agents. An exception in the EU is Sweden, where both the activities of the enforcement of civil law claims and of public law claims are dealt with by the same professional, a Kronofogde.[50] Another similar exception in Europe, but outside the EU, is Iceland, where the civil servant of the State authority Sýslumaður is in charge of the enforcement of both private and public claims.[51] In the majority of States, where there exist separate categories of enforcement agents and recovery agents, the cooperation and interaction between them vary.

The national systems of organization of enforcement agents, which best seem to be in harmony with the constitutional doctrines of Montesquieu,[52] based on the separation of legislative, executive and judicial authorities, are those in Finland and Sweden of civil enforcement agents. This is because they are, unlike some other systems in *e.g.* Denmark, England and Germany, more clearly separated from the national court systems.[53] Some national systems of organization of enforcement agents in the civil law area apply the liberal profession, while some other such systems instead apply the profession of civil servant, but nevertheless, the activities of these two categories of professions are in both these systems derived from the public powers of the State. It may be argued that there exist both advantages and disadvantages by applying the one or the other of these systems in a State, which falls under the political autonomy of States.[54]

The Council of Europe's recommendation on enforcement, which emphasizes the important balance between the relevant interests in enforcement procedures,[55]

50. *See* 3.1.5.4.
51. *See*, for further details, Nordiskt samarbete om indrivningsfrågor (Nordic cooperation in recovery matters), report to the Nordic Council of Ministers of Jul. 2002, pp. 36-37.
52. *See* 2.3.
53. Compare 3.1.5.1 and 3.2.1.
54. *See* Tarzia, Aussichten für eine Harmonisierung des Zwangsvollstreckungsrechts in der Europäischen Union, pp. 239-240, who concludes in the European context that the question, to whom the order of execution should be addressed, can only be subject to a general clause, because it is the competence of the Member States to decide to engage officials or private professionals for enforcement by execution, and Storme, Procedural Law and the Reform of Justice: from Regional to Universal Harmonisation, Uniform law review/Revue de droit uniforme 2001-4, Harmonising Transnational Civil Procedure: The ALI/UNIDROIT Principles and Rules/Vers une procédure civile transnationale harmonisée: Les Principes et Règles ALI/UNIDROIT, p. 776, who points out: '... it is clear that approximation cannot concern itself with the rules of judicial organisation and competence. These are areas that come *par excellence* under the sovereignty of the State. It is, moreover, obvious that today no State will allow its fundamental rights to be interfered with in this sphere.'
55. *See* s. III, 1 g.

makes clear that States should be free to determine the professional status of enforcement agents,[56] but provides at the same time several important guiding principles of quality levels to meet in the profession of enforcement agents.[57] This may, at least in a longer perspective, lead to a more similar content in national laws in relation to the activities of the profession of enforcement agents in the Member States of the Council of Europe, without affecting their structure of organization.

3.2.3.1 European Common Educational and Training Standard for the Right to Exercise the Profession of an Enforcement Agent

There exist several arguments that would motivate the establishment of a particular high European common educational and training standard for the right to exercise the regulated profession of an enforcement agent in European States. The legal profession of an enforcement agent requires a solid knowledge of law because it involves advanced legal considerations in the establishment of a justified balance of interests between the parties in a civil execution law procedure in the exercise of public powers through different enforcement measures. The Council of Europe's recommendation on enforcement makes clear that considerations should be given to legal knowledge and training in relevant law and procedure in examinations. Better conditions would be created for Member States of the Council of Europe to meet their obligations under the European Convention on Human Rights for the establishment of a justified balance between the interest of privacy of the debtor and the interest of efficiency of the creditor in enforcement matters. Better conditions would also be created in the general State interest of a more efficient and highly qualified enforcement of claims in society, which would correspond to the same interest of both the creditor and the debtor. Better conditions would in addition, in the same interest, be created for States to respond to their obligations under EC law and conventions.

A possible harmonization resulting in common educational and training standard would be of importance in matters having cross-border implications and would in that sense contribute to a better functioning of the Internal Common Market. It is therefore motivated to consider the possibilities of the establishment of European common minimum standards for the right to exercise the profession of an enforcement agent, before a candidate could be approved to exercise the profession and become in charge and control of the related activities.

A continued treatment of the issue of the establishment of such a standard may *i.a.* take into consideration an earlier proposal of 1991, which suggested a law degree from a university and a training period in work and further education in the profession, under the supervision of more experienced colleagues. This proposal of a standard for access to the profession of an enforcement agent in the EU would

56. *See* s. IV, 2.
57. *See* s. IV.

correspond to the Council Directive 89/48/EEC of 21 December 1988 on a general system for the recognition of higher-education and training of at least three years duration, published in 1989. The proposal suggested four years of studies at university and three years of professional education, including an ideal statute for the profession, which required an uninterrupted period of work of three years, which, however, might include one year in another legal profession.[58]

A continued treatment of this issue would also have to be based on a more recent comparative study of the present standards in European States, in order to identify what national requirements there exist. It should then be possible to make a suggestion for sufficiently high European common educational and training standards for the right to exercise the profession of an enforcement agent in European States, which would respond to the needs of European States. Any further development on this issue will, however, first require a political initiative to introduce new EC law.

3.2.3.2 Recognition of the Profession of an Enforcement Agent in Other European States

It may be considered that professionals, who would meet a particular high established European common standard of examinations and merits for the regulated profession of an enforcement agent, should also be able to be recognized to practise their profession in other European States. This should be for similar needs and reasons as already have been established for the profession of lawyers in the EU,[59] but under conditions adapted to the profession of an enforcement agent.[60] This would possibly mean the following. An enforcement agent practising under his home-country professional title and who carries on the same professional activities as an enforcement agent practising under the relevant professional title used in the host State may, *i.a.* give advice on the law of his home State, on EC law, on public international law and on the law of the host State, but shall in any event comply with the rules of procedures applicable in the national bodies of execution and in courts. The integration of an enforcement agent of a home State into the profession in the host State may *i.a.* take place by passing an aptitude test, or after a certain period of professional practice in the host State, supported in the end of that period

58. *See* Statut et fonctions de l'Huissier de Justice en droit compare, pp. 13-15 and 42. Belgium, France, the Netherlands and Luxemburg require a law degree and a period of work (stage) between 1-3 years for an enforcement agent, *i.b.*, 40-41.
59. *See* Council Directive 77/249/EEC of 22 Mar. 1977 to facilitate the effective exercise by lawyers of freedom to provide services, Council Directive 89/48/EEC of 21 Dec. 1988 on a general system for the recognition of higher-education and training of at least three years duration, published in 1989, and Directive 98/5/EC of the European Parliament and of the Council of 16 Feb. 1998 to facilitate practice of the profession of lawyer on a permanent basis in a Member State other than that in which the qualification was obtained.
60. Compare Preamble (3 and 4), Art. 5, 1 and Arts 6 and 7 of Directive 98/5/EC of the European Parliament and of the Council of 16 Feb. 1998 to facilitate practice of the profession of lawyer on a permanent basis in a Member State other than that in which the qualification was obtained.

of a verification from the host State that the enforcement agent possesses professional experience in that State. It seems logical that the rules of the host State should govern the activities performed in that State as concern professional conduct and disciplinary proceedings.

A recognition of the profession of European enforcement agents in other European States would be of interest to both the creditor and the debtor because the services and skills of an enforcement agent from another State would become available to them through his possibility of activities in their State and in other European States. This would be of importance in matter having cross-border implications and would in that sense contribute to a better functioning of the Internal Common Market.

The argument that the profession of an enforcement agent should not be comparable in the sense of recognition in Europe to the profession of a lawyer because a lawyer exercises a liberal profession, whereas an enforcement agent exercises a profession based on public powers, either as a liberal profession or as a civil servant, is not justified and in addition irrelevant because each profession has to be treated on its own merits. Even if the activities of an enforcement agent more frequently than those of a lawyer are based on the exercise of public powers, they include, at least in some European States, also liberal services of different kinds,[61] *e.g.* legal advices provided by a Huissier de Justice in France.[62] Some activities of lawyers are also based on the exercise of public powers, *e.g.* when they have been appointed and act as trustees in bankruptcy. In brief conclusion, any possible differences of activities of the profession of a lawyer or any other law-related profession and an enforcement agent, classified either as liberal or based on public powers, should therefore not be of any importance for the issue of granting recognition to the profession of an enforcement agent in Europe.

Consequently, the profession of an enforcement agent, should in this sense, be treated on its own merits, and the important part in such a determination should therefore be the actual competence of each person in any case of recognition that involves a State. If this would become realized it would mean that a French liberal enforcement agent, a Huissier de Justice, would be able to become qualified and recognized as an equivalent professional to a Swedish civil servant enforcement agent, a Kronofogde, in Sweden, and *vice versa.*

There exist, however, also arguments against the recognition of a citizen of the nationality of one Member State as qualified to exercise the profession of a regulated enforcement agent in other Member States. These relate to the demand in national legislations that such an agent must be of the nationality of the enforcing Member State, and the exclusion in the EC Treaty of activities derived from the

61. *See* 3.2.1 for further information about the monopolistic and additional facultative activities of a more liberal nature of some European enforcement agents.
62. More than 5 million legal consultations were given by the French Huissier de Justice in 1986, *see* Statut et fonctions de l'Huissier de Justice en droit compare, p. 25.

exercise of public powers,[63] such as regulated enforcement agents, if not altered through a decision of the Council.[64]

Further developments would first have to be based on a previous establishment of sufficiently high European common educational and training standards for the right to exercise the profession of an enforcement agent in European States, in order to guarantee some equally high standards, before a more detailed suggestion on provisions for the recognition of the profession in other European States is possible to work out in more details corresponding to the needs of European States and their professionals. The possible establishment of the ideas of European common educational and training standards for the right to exercise the profession of an enforcement agent and the recognition of the profession of an enforcement agent in other European States should not risk to intervene into the autonomous right of States to determine the professional status of enforcement agents in the categories of civil servants or in a liberal profession.[65] Even if there exist several arguments in favour of the establishment of a harmonization based on these ideas of development by a possible initiative to introduce new EC law, this would first have to require some additional comparative studies and analysis, so as finally to be based on a political agreement between the Member States of the EU.

There exists, however, also another possible way of initiating a development in this area. One or several national and European-level professional organizations or associations for a regulated profession can make use of their right to make a reasoned request for specific provisions for the recognition of qualifications on the basis of coordination of minimum training conditions according to the Directive 2005/36/EC of the European Parliament and of the Council of 7 September 2005 on the recognition of professional qualifications.[66] Examples of such European national associations, which would have the right to make such a reasoned request to the Commission, are these which are members of the UIHJ, and this Union as a representative of its European members.[67] The Commission shall then assess the appropriateness of adopting a proposal for the amendment of this directive. Any decision following such initiatives would, however, first, on the initiative of the Commission, have to be based on a decision of the Council to grant an exception from the EC Treaty for regulated enforcement agents.

3.2.3.3 Euroex, a European Cooperation Body between States in the Civil Execution Law Area

The involvement of the professionals in the international cooperation in the area of enforcement of contractual claims as compared to in the corresponding area of recovery of tax claims differ *i.a.* as a result of the different positions of the private

---

63. *See* Art. 45, first part.
64. *See* Art. 45, final part.
65. Compare Council of Europe's recommendation on enforcement, IV, 2.
66. *See* Preamble (29). *Also see*, about some conditions, Preamble (3) and (4), *i.b.*
67. *See* 2.10.5.

and public creditors in these areas of cooperation.[68] The EU has expressed that one of its important priorities for the future development is to achieve a better cooperation between the professionals.[69]

The UIHJ is a global union of cooperation between national associations of the regulated professionals of enforcement agents. The UIHJ also includes a lot of European associations of such professionals. The UIHJ is an organization for cooperation, which has as its objectives to further develop the professional interest of its national member associations of professionals and to support the development of civil execution law. These objectives are expressed in the statutes of the UIHJ *i.a.* to promote the establishment of a liberal profession of a regulated enforcement agent in its member States.[70]

However, there does not exist any formally institutionalized legal cooperation in the EU between the regulated professionals from the various European enforcement organs, such as enforcement officers of a court, civil servants in the administration and liberal professionals, all of them designated by the Member States, based on their public powers in the civil execution law area.[71] Examples of such a formally institutionalized legal cooperation already exist in other legal areas, *e.g.* the regulated cooperation in the tax recovery law area based on the Recovery directive, or in the police area, Europol, and prosecution law area, Eurojust. It has been suggested to introduce some kind of equivalent cooperation for regulated enforcement agents.[72]

The needs and interests that should govern the objectives of a possible formally institutionalized legal cooperation in the EU between European regulated enforcement agents remain to be elaborated and established by the Member States. The objectives of this possible cooperation could therefore be expected to be somewhat different from the objectives of the UIHJ, because they will be governed by a mix of needs and interests identified by the Member States, so as not only to departure from the needs and interests identified by the liberal professionals

---

68. *See* 2.2.
69. *See* 3.4.3 of the Hague Programme of the European Council, about enhancing cooperation between the legal professionals of the Member States of the EU, including bailiffs.
70. *See* 2.10.5 for a more extensive information about the UIHJ and its statutes.
71. *See* 3.2.1.
72. *See* Hesslén, Asset transparency – finding information – measures to make enforcement more effective, Globalisation of law in an area of universal justice/'Is the creation of a World Area of Justice a utopic vision?', publication/work of the congress committee from the XVIII Congress of the UIHJ in Tunis on the 6-9 May 2003, p. 41, where she discusses the possibility to create an information centre, an 'Interex', similar to Interpol, with data accessible to those countries having given their approval, where only bailiffs or their equivalents will have access to third parties and individuals, in order for them to be authorized to proceed with researches and investigations into assets. She further suggests, in order to facilitate the search for debtors and their assets, the establishment of a convention, which enables that data processing of the civil status of all citizens of the EU and other States, including the name, address, personal identification number and social security number, and that information on the content of national legislations, may be exchanged directly between the enforcement authorities of the concerned States.

belonging to the UIHJ. Such a possible cooperation would have to be neutral in the sense that it would have to respect the autonomy of Member States to include the regulated enforcement agents designated by them irrespectively of whether their functions are performed as liberal professionals, enforcement officers of a court, or as civil servants in the administration. In addition such a possible cooperation would cover all Member States of the EU as it would not only be limited to the liberal professionals of enforcement agents.

Several arguments may motivate the establishment of a formally institutionalized legal cooperation in the EU between the various enforcement organs designated by the Member States in the civil execution law area. There is a need and interest in the cross-border context of the private creditor, the debtor, and the enforcement agent, to be able to directly contact and receive information from national Contact points about EC law and national legislations, including their procedures of enforcement. A possible cooperation may be more, or less, formally structured and in different ways, preferably as a European bureau, a network with a coordinating Committee, or any other cooperation body related to this possible European cooperation in the civil execution law area (Euroex) for the benefit of an exchange of such information in the cross-border context.

A Euroex would consist of national Contact points as representatives for the designated organs in each Member State, with the task to provide information, general advice, and service, without being operative in actual enforcement matters. However, it would be able to refer such matters for further advice to the relevant enforcement agents. Information about these national Contact points, including practical details such as their telephone and telefax numbers and e-mail addresses, may also preferably be made available at the website of the European Judicial Network in civil and commercial matters, which is open to the public, and be incorporated as a part of the European Judicial Atlas in Civil Matters in this network.[73]

The European Judicial Network in civil and commercial matters presently promotes access to justice through an information system, which is accessible to the general public and specialists, based on the idea of providing information on national laws and international and community instruments in certain law areas.[74] The Network provides an information exchange system for the national Contact points of the Network and an internet based information system and information sheets for the general public.[75] It includes information on rules and procedures for the enforcement of judgments.[76] The Network does, however, not

73. *See* Council decision 2001/470/EC of 28 May 2001 establishing a European Judicial Network in civil and commercial matters (European Judicial Network in civil and commercial matters) and the website of this network, <http://ec.europa.eu/civiljustice/>.
74. *See* Preamble (6), (10-11), and (14-15) of the European Judicial Network in civil and commercial matters regarding the objectives to provide certain information and Arts 14 and 15 of the same decision regarding the content of information to be provided to the general public and specialists. The tasks and activities of the network are defined in Art. 3 of the same decision.
75. *See* Arts 13, 2, 14 and 15.
76. *See* Art. 14, e compared to Art. 15, e.

provide specific sources of information, which may be directly used to satisfy the need for information in a particular enforcement matter of a private creditor at the national and international levels, in the daily operative work of enforcement agents.

Information gathered by the national Contact points of a Euroex about *e.g.* relevant information to establish contact with the designated professionals in each Member State, national, preferably multilingual, forms of application for enforcement, costs of applications, national descriptions of enforcement laws, including what sources of information for enforcement purposes national professionals have access to in their work,[77] should also be made available at the European Judicial Network in civil and commercial matters.[78]

The establishment of a Euroex would be for the benefit of the citizens, the creditors and the debtors, and the professionals of the EU. It would be of importance in matters having cross-border implications and would in that sense contribute to a better functioning of the Internal Common Market. A Euroex may also in its activities be able to identify difficulties and problems in EC law in the cross-border context, which may be of value in a future reform perspective. It would, in addition, be able to provide information of comparative interest in relation to national legislations, functioning as a resource of reference for other European organizations. A Euroex should also be able to cooperate and exchange views with other bodies of cooperation, such as Europol and Eurojust. Even if a principal distinction would have to be made between the task of a Euroex and that of the UIHJ, they will, nevertheless, clearly share some important similar objectives, which should motivate a close cooperation for exchange of views. Consequently, the possible establishment of a Euroex would contribute to increase the total focus on the development of civil execution law matters in the cross-border context.

3.3 TAX RECOVERY LAW AREA OF TODAY

3.3.1 National Recovery Agents

The national professionals who carry out the actual recovery of such tax claims that are based on the international cooperation of mutual assistance are normally the same officials that are responsible in the national public administration for the

---

77. *See* about a similar idea, but a different approach, EC Study JAI/02/03/2002, B, V, 1, where the elaboration of a manual of European enforcement law systems, including all the sources of information about a person's assets which can be accessed in each Member State and the contact addresses of persons who can obtain access to that information if access is limited, the costs of access and other relevant details, is proposed to be published in the European Judicial Network in civil and commercial matters.

78. Compare Green paper Effective enforcement of judgments in the European Union: Transparency of Debtors' assets, Commission of the ECs, Brussels, COM (2008) 128 final, p. 5, about the similar idea to draw up a Manual of National Enforcement Laws and Practices to be made available on the website of the European Judicial Network in civil and commercial matters.

recovery of national tax claims.[79] They work, depending on the chosen structure of the national administration, at local, regional or central levels of various authorities or ministries.[80] Professionals responsible for the collection of taxes are *e.g.*: the French Huissier du Trésor, the Irish Revenue Sheriff,[81] and within the Nordic States, *i.a.* the Swedish Kronofogde.[82] In these Member States, where there exist separate categories of enforcement agents and recovery agents, the interaction and cooperation between these categories of professionals vary. The national functions of recovery agents in various parts of the public administration are more equal in comparison between the Member States of the EU than the corresponding functions of regulated enforcement agents.

3.3.2 Competent Authorities

The work of cooperation under the Recovery directive in the function of the so-called competent authorities of the Member States, which relates to representing the applicant or requested State in different situations of mutual cooperation, *i.a.* for the recovery of claims, is performed by officials of the State bodies appointed by each Member State, often ministries of Finance or national boards of taxation or other authorities. The Recovery directive applies to a variety of different kind of debts.[83] This means that in many Member States a number of different competent authorities are involved at the application of this directive. Member States are obliged to provide each other with a list of authorities authorized to make, or receive, requests for assistance and to notify other Member States and the Commission of the name and address of the competent authorities for the purpose of

79. *See*, for further information about the nationally responsible public administration for the recovery of national tax claims in Denmark, England and Wales, France, Germany, Italy, the Netherlands, Spain and Sweden, Kennett, Regulation of Civil Enforcement Agents, Regulation of enforcement agents in Europe: a comparative survey, vol. 1 Text, report in the Grotius program 2001, pp. 12-17.
80. *See*, about the responsible organs for the collection of social contributions and the significant variations in the organizational structures of revenue bodies of the administrations in OECD, Tax Administration in OECD and Selected Non-OECD Countries: Comparative Information Series (2006), pp. 14 and 16 compared to Tables 1 and 4.
81. *See* Report on European judicial systems, p. 136. *Also see*, about the French Huissier du Trésor, Källström, p. 704.
82. An important part of volumes of work of the Swedish recovery and enforcement agent Kronofogde is tax recovery, but there also exist other parts of work, such as the recovery of other public claims, the enforcement of civil law judgments and other enforceable civil law decisions, debt relief procedure in relation to individuals, summary procedure and supervision in bankruptcy. *Also see*, about the different working tasks of the Kronofogde, Jacobsson, pp. 484-485 compared to pp. 488-489. *Also see*, about the recovery agents in: Denmark, pp. 31-34, Finland, pp. 35-36, Iceland, pp. 36-37, Norway, pp. 38-39, and Sweden, pp. 39-40, in Nordiskt samarbete om indrivningsfrågor (Nordic cooperation in recovery matters), report to the Nordic Council of Ministers of Jul. 2002.
83. *See* 5.2.2.1.

applying the Recovery directive.[84] Communications between the competent authorities related to the Recovery directive take place through a, in relation to the public, closed database called Circa. However, to the extent this database includes information about national laws it should be possible to also make it available to the public.

The competent authorities of the contracting States, as referred to in both the Council of Europe and OECD convention on mutual administrative assistance in tax matters,[85] and in the Nordic agreement on assistance in tax matters,[86] are similar State bodies, often ministries of Finance, or national boards of taxation, or other fiscal authorities. The structures of international cooperation in the public administration and the bodies of such cooperation in the recovery law area differ in comparison to the corresponding civil execution law area.

3.3.3 Recovery Committee

A Recovery Committee exists according to the Recovery directive, and it consists of representatives of the Member States, with a representative from the Commission as chairman. This Committee adopts its own rules of procedure, and it may examine any matter on the application of the directive raised by any of the representatives of the Committee.[87] Representatives to the Committee from Member States, who deal with the mutual cooperation of the Recovery directive, are often officials from ministries of Finance.

84. *See* Art. 19 Recovery directive and Art. 31 Implementing recovery directive.
85. *See* Art. 3, 1. d. and annex B to the convention. *Also see* for further details on the convention about authorities, website of the Council of Europe, <http://conventions.coe.int>.
86. *See* Art. 3.
87. *See* Arts 20 and 21.

Chapter 4
Public International Law

4.1 FOREIGN STATE'S IMMUNITY AGAINST CIVIL EXECUTION

4.1.1 EUROPEAN STATE IMMUNITY CONVENTION

The European convention on State immunity of 16 May 1972 (European State immunity convention) has entered into force between some few European States.[1] The principles of the convention are, however, also of importance to other European States even if they have not become parties to it. The reason is that the convention forms part of customary international law. The convention makes a clear distinction between the immunity from jurisdiction, which foreign States enjoy in respect of acts performed in the exercise of sovereign authority, *acta jure imperii*, and acts of non-immunity from jurisdiction performed mainly in commercial situations, *acta gestionnis.* A contracting State cannot claim immunity from the jurisdiction of the courts in another contracting State in commercial situations.[2] The contracting States to the convention have obliged themselves to give effect to judgment within the scope of the convention. However, no measures of execution, or preventive measures against the property of a contracting State may be taken in the territory of another contracting State except where and to the extent that this State has expressly consented thereto in writing in a particular case.[3] This convention is treated by a large number of authors.[4]

1. For details on the entry into force of the convention in relation to the States, which are parties to the convention, *see* annex 9.
2. *See* Arts 2-11.
3. *See* Art. 20 compared to Art. 23 of the Convention.
4. *See*, for further comments on this Convention, Badr, pp. 129-131, Civil Procedure in Europe 1, p. 18 compared to p. 147 (Belgium), pp. 278-279 (France), p. 412 (Italy) and p. 567 (Sweden),

4.1.2 Vienna Conventions on Diplomatic and Consular Relations

The Vienna convention on diplomatic relations of 18 April 1961 (Vienna convention on diplomatic relations) and the Vienna convention on consular relations of 24 April 1963 (Vienna convention on consular relations) concern immunities against jurisdiction and civil execution.[5] The premises of the diplomatic mission, their furnishings and other property thereon and the means of transport of the mission shall, according to the Vienna convention on diplomatic relations, be immune from search, requisition, attachment or execution.[6] The private residence of a diplomatic agent shall also enjoy the same inviolability and protection as the premises of the diplomatic mission.[7] The members of the family of a diplomatic agent forming part of its household shall normally also, if they are not nationals of the receiving State, enjoy the same privileges and immunities as the diplomatic agent, *e.g.* in relation to its private residence.[8] The Vienna convention on consular relations stipulates to what extent the Consular premises shall be inviolable, but this does not include any provision of immunity against civil execution measures.[9] Actions, which fall outside the scope of the Consular immunity from jurisdiction, may be subject to a judgment and its subsequent execution in the receiving State.[10] The Vienna convention on diplomatic relations is clearly more far-reaching about immunities against jurisdiction and civil execution than the Vienna convention on consular relations. In these conventions, and the European State immunity convention, a distinction is made, in relation to immunity from jurisdiction and civil

---

Enforcement of Foreign Judgments Worldwide, p. 150 (Belgium), pp. 168-169 (Europe), p. 178 (France), p. 192 (Germany), p. 221 (Switzerland), and pp. 247-250 (United Kingdom), International Execution Against Judgment Debtors, Binder 1 (England and Wales, pp. 54-56), Kerameus, Enforcement Against the State and State Entities in a Comparative Perspective, Recht in Europa, Festschrift für Hilmar Fenge, pp. 83-84, about the enforcement against foreign States and case-law developments, legislative arrangements, and the European State immunity convention, Kerameus, International encyclopedia of comparative law, volume XVI, Civil procedure, chapter 10, Enforcement proceedings, pp. 37-38, de Leval, The execution of court decisions in civil cases, pp. 54-55, Lewis, pp. 11, 29-30, et seq., Théry, Droit de l'exécution: France, Actualités du droit, p. 647, Revue de la Faculté de droit de l'Université de Liège. *Also see*, about comments on the position of seizure and attachment of the property of foreign States before the European State immunity convention, Sucharitkul, pp. 347-350. He concludes, p. 347, that: 'It is only with respect to property used in connection with trading activities of the foreign State concerned that attachment by way of execution is permissible.'

5. *See*, about further comments on these Vienna conventions and their application, Akehurst, pp. 123-127, Berglund, Svensk internationell exekutions- och obeståndsrätt, pp. 60-64, Civil Procedure in Europe 1, p. 200 (Denmark), p. 277 (France), p. 567 (Sweden), de Leval, The execution of court decisions in civil cases, p. 54, Harris, pp. 319-336, and Théry, Droit de l'exécution: France, Actualités du droit, Revue de la Faculté de droit de l'Université de Liège, p. 646. *Also see* for more extensive comments on these conventions Lewis, pp. 125-165.
6. *See* Art. 22, 3.
7. *See* Art. 30, 1.
8. *See* Art. 37, 1.
9. *See* Art. 31.
10. *See* Art. 43.

execution, between acts performed by States in their exercise of sovereign authority and acts performed by them mainly in commercial situations.

4.2 ENFORCEMENT OUTSIDE THE SCOPE OF CONVENTIONS

4.2.1 Civil Law Claims

The principal requirement about the existence of an international treaty obligation for the recognition and enforcement of a foreign title of execution does, however, not exclude the existence of other possibly available options outside the scope of conventions in relation to civil law claims. Some European States are, subject to certain conditions, but without the support of any convention, prepared to recognize and enforce a foreign judgment.[11] They give effect to private rights acquired under the legislation of foreign States also without such support. An example is the transnational judicial cooperation, based on Common Law, between the United

11. *See* Civil Procedure in Europe 3, Recognition and Enforcement of Foreign Judgments Outside the Scope of the Brussels and Lugano Conventions, where those areas of European recognition practice that have not been harmonized by the Brussels and Lugano conventions are treated in sections: Austria, Belgium, Czech Republic, England, Finland, France, Germany, Greece, Hungary, Italy, Luxemburg, the Netherlands, Norway, Poland, Portugal, Spain, Sweden, and Switzerland. *Also see* Walter and Baumgartner, pp. 17-18 and 39-42. They report that there are still European jurisdictions that do not recognize any foreign judgments absent a treaty obligation, *e.g.* the Nordic States, where some other jurisdictions *e.g.* Austria, Belgium, England, Luxemburg, and the Netherlands are prepared to recognize and enforce a foreign judgment outside the scope of conventions, if the conditions in their laws and legal usage are meet. They further report, *i.b.*, p. 40, that: 'Among the countries that do generally recognize foreign judgments, the rules regulating recognition are considerably similar. They all require that the judgment be final, and allow for a review of the rendering country's jurisdiction; the propriety of service; the fairness of the foreign proceedings to the losing party; and for a public policy defense, including allegations that the judgment was obtained by fraud. Moreover, they all contain provisions for dealing with inconsistent proceedings, although the content of these provisions may vary considerably, particularly between England and the Continent.' *Also see*, about the requirements or not for reciprocity from an enforcing State of a foreign judgment in relation to the State, which has issued this foreign judgment, Enforcement of Foreign Judgments, chapter Europe, section 2.3 (Austria, Belarus, Belgium, Cyprus, Czech Republic, Denmark, England and Wales, Finland, France, Germany, Greece, Guernsey, Hungary, Ireland, Italy, Jersey, Luxemburg, the Netherlands, Poland, Portugal, Scotland, Spain, Sweden, and Switzerland). *Also see* Enforcement of Foreign Judgments Worldwide, p. 165 (Europe), where it is reported that in Spain and Germany recognition is subject to the condition that the State of origin will recognize judgments from the State addressed. *Also see*, about requirements for recognition, International Execution Against Judgment Debtors, Binder 1, sections: Austria, pp. 5-7, Belgium, pp. 1-4, Bulgaria, pp. 8-9, Croatia, pp. 5-14, Cyprus, pp. 1-3, Czech Republic, pp. 4-10, and France, pp. 5-17, Binder 2, sections: Germany, pp. 4-18, Gibraltar, pp. 1-26, Greece, pp. 1-18, Hungary, pp. 4-8, Ireland, pp. 8-13, Isle of Man, pp. 2 and 4-8, Italy, pp. 1-9, Jersey, pp. 1-12, Luxemburg, pp. 5-6 and 8-15, Malta, pp. 3-8, and Northern Ireland, pp. 1-21, and Binder 3, sections: Portugal, pp. 1-12, Romania, pp. 1-9, Scotland, pp. 1-21, Slovak Republic, pp. 5-8, Spain, pp. 1-13 and 16-40, and Switzerland, pp. 1-17.

Kingdom and the Commonwealth countries and some other States, which is a cooperation for the reciprocal enforcement of a foreign judgment or a decision of sequestration,[12] based on the payment of a debt, or for damages for breach of contracts, in the United Kingdom. In the United Kingdom, this cooperation is based on the Administration of Justice Act 1920 in relation to the Commonwealth countries as well as on the Foreign Judgment (Reciprocal Enforcement) Act 1933 in relation to *i.a.* the following States and territories: Israel, Pakistan, Surinam, Tonga, Guernsey, Jersey and Isle of Man.[13] A majority of States of the United States of America have also, based on the Uniform Foreign Money-Judgment Recognition Act, issued legislation on the recognition and enforcement of foreign civil money judgments.[14] Also, international comity, Comity of nations,[15]

12. *See* Barron's Law Dictionary, p. 390, where reciprocity is explained as generally a relationship between persons, States, or countries, whereby favours or privileges granted by one are returned by the other.
13. *See* 2.5 and for further details about these Acts, Enforcement of Foreign Judgments, section England and Wales, pp. 3-4, 10-11, and 13-14, Enforcement of Foreign Judgments Worldwide, section United Kingdom, pp. 223-234, and International Execution Against Judgment Debtors, Binder 1, section England and Wales, pp. 1-24, 33, and 41-46. *Also see*, about provisional and protective measures in the United Kingdom, Macpherson, La pratique des mesures conservatoires et provisoires en Angleterre, Pays de Galles et Ecosse, Le droit processuel et le droit de l'exécution, pp. 419-429, and about the English freezing order (previously referred to in literature as a Mareva injunction) in the extra territorial context, Cuniberti, Les mesures conservatoires portant sur des biens situés à l'étranger.
14. *See* Uniform Foreign Money-Judgments Recognition Act, drafted by the national conference of commissioners on uniform State laws and by it approved and recommended for enactment in all the States at its annual conference meeting in its seventy-first year, Monterey, California, 30 Jul. to 4 Aug. 1962, with prefatory note and comments. Approved by the American Bar Association 4 Feb. 1963. *Also see*, for further details about this Act, Enforcement of Foreign Judgments, section the United States, pp. 3-14, and International Execution Against Judgment Debtors, Binder 3, section the United States, pp. 1-47. *Also see* Hesslén, Kan verkställighet ske i USA av svenska domar och beslut ?, SvJT 2006, pp. 771-773, mentioning that presently 30 States have adopted the Uniform Foreign Money-Judgments Recognition Act, and for more detailed information on this Act. *Also see* Bluestone about the Recognition and Enforcement of Foreign Country Money-Judgments in the United States, and Kerameus, Enforcement in the International Context, Recueil des cours, collected courses of the Hague Academy of International Law, 1997, Tome 264 de la collection, p. 234, indicating that whereas initially a second suit had to be brought in a sister-State on the original judgment, under the Uniform Enforcement of Foreign Judgments Act the plaintiff needs only to register the judgment by filing a certified copy in the second State.
15. *See* Oppenheim, p. 50, where international comity, Comity of nations, is explained as follows: 'A factor of a special kind which also influences the growth of international law is the so-called comity (*comitas gentium*, convenance et courtoisie internationale, Staatengunst). In their intercourse with one another states observe not only legally binding rules and such rules as have the character of usages, but also rules of politeness, convenience, and goodwill. Such rules of international conduct are not rules of law, but of comity. Thus, for instance, it was as the result of a rule of comity and not of international law that states used to grant diplomatic envoys exemption from customs duties. In the sphere of the law of war chivalry fulfils the same function. The comity of nations is not a source of international law. But many a rule which formerly was a rule of international comity only is nowadays a rule of international law. The distinction, although clear-cut in logic, is not always observed in practice. English and

may apply where some States, when asked to honour a judgment of a foreign country,[16] give effect to rights acquired under the legislation of foreign States. Consequently, Comity of nations to the extent practiced in other States, normally in Commonwealth States, excludes an application of the principle of territoriality. Comity of nations sometimes requires reciprocity between States. Evidently, comity of nations may be of interest to a creditor who seeks to enforce his claim in another State without being able to support his claim by a formal reference to a convention between States, *i.e.* if there is a lack of a convention or if the claim falls outside the scope of application of an existing convention.

4.2.2 Public Law Claims

It is exceptional that States, in the absence of a treaty obligation, are prepared to recognize and enforce foreign fiscal claims.[17] While the courts in many States, *e.g.* in the United Kingdom and in the United States of America, give effect to private rights acquired under the legislation of foreign States outside the scope of conventions, these courts decline to give full effect to the public law, outside the scope of conventions, as distinguished from private law, of foreign States.[18]

American courts often refer to "international comity" in situations to which there ought to be more properly applied the term "international law". It is probable that many a present rule of international comity will in future become one of international law.' *Also see* Bogdan, Svensk internationell privat- och processrätt, pp. 24-25, who tells that the so-called Dutch school, Huber and others, in the fifteenth and sixteenth centuries argued that international politeness, *comitas gentium*, demanded that the courts, to some extent, should use foreign law, and that this idea has been taken over by the Anglo-American lawyers (the doctrine of comity of nations), who also developed the doctrine of Huber of well acquired rights (vested rights or duly acquired rights). According to this latter doctrine, rights which have been acquired in a State according to its laws, should also be recognized by courts in other States, and he concludes that this is evidently only possible to achieve if the courts are prepared to examine the origin of such rights according to foreign law. *Also see*, about Comity of nations in India, International Execution Against Judgment Debtors, Binder 2, section India, pp. 3-4.

16. *See* Barron's Law Dictionary, p. 79.
17. *See*, about an exception, Enforcement of Foreign Judgments, section India, pp. 3-5, where it is reported that foreign money judgments (including fiscal judgments) from some reciprocating States, *e.g.* from New Zealand, Singapore and the United Kingdom, are enforceable in India, if all relevant provisions in Indian law are meet. *Also see*, about another exception in relation to bankruptcy, Baker, p. 318: 'However, if the taxpayer is declared bankrupt and the trustee in bankruptcy seeks assets abroad, it appears that some foreign courts will grant assistance to the trustee, and English courts may grant similar assistance to a foreign trustee, at least where there are ordinary as well as tax creditors. Similarly, where there is a tax claim against an estate or trust, it appears that English courts permit trustees to transfer assets abroad to meet a tax claim, so long as the trustees would otherwise be personally liable for the debt.'
18. *See* Oppenheim, pp. 488-491. It is reported, *i.b.*, p. 489, that these States in particular refuse, in respect of assets within their jurisdiction, to enforce directly, or indirectly, on behalf of a foreign State its revenue law as well as its penal and confiscatory legislation. It is further reported, *i.b.*, p. 490, that: 'Although in such matters courts often base their refusal to enforce foreign public law upon considerations of public policy, in international law a basis for that widespread

Hence, States generally treat civil law claims more favourably compared to public law claims concerning their recognition and enforcement outside the scope of conventions.

4.3 EUROPEAN CONVENTION ON HUMAN RIGHTS

Many rights are guaranteed by this convention. Rights concerned are the debtor's right of privacy and the creditor's right to enforce a claim efficiently,[19] the right of non-discrimination of the creditor and the debtor on grounds of nationality,[20] and the creditor's right of peaceful enjoyment of his possessions, *e.g.* his claim in the quality of a title of execution.[21] The convention treats the interests of the creditor and the debtor in a balanced, proportionate way.[22] Another right is the prohibition of imprisonment for debts on the only ground of inability to fulfil a contractual obligation.

The effect of the prohibition of imprisonment for debts on the only ground of inability to fulfil a contractual obligation was entered into Article 1 of Protocol No. 4 to the European Convention on Human Rights. This part of the convention came into force in 1968, but it is still subject to a reservation from Monaco. However, some European States still apply civil imprisonment in the civil law area in relation to the debtor, and depending on the circumstances, this practice, according to these national legislations, would constitute a violation of the prohibition in this Protocol to the convention.[23]

---

practice is to be found in the principle of territorial authority, from which it follows that states have no right to perform acts of sovereignty within the territory of other states. For a state's public law to be enforced in another state would in effect involve the performance of acts of sovereignty in foreign states in derogation of their territorial authority.' *Also see* Enforcement of Foreign Judgments Worldwide, section United Kingdom, p. 227, where it is reported, with a reference made to a case outside the scope of conventions, that the English courts do not permit, either directly or indirectly, the enforcement of a foreign judgment for the payment of taxes, or for any fine, or penalty.

19. *See* 1.1.1.1.1.
20. *See* 1.1.1.1.2.
21. *See* 1.1.1.1.1. *Also see*, about further comments on the right of peaceful enjoyment of one's possessions, Danelius, pp. 453-484, and Leach, pp. 353-363. *Also see*, Leroy, L'efficacité des procédures judiciaires au sein de l'union Européenne et les garanties des droits de la defense, Transparence patrimoniale, L'efficacité de la justice civile en Europe, pp. 307-309, and Att klaga till Europadomstolen, pp. 211-220.
22. *See* 1.1.1.1 and 1.1.1.1.3.
23. *See*, about Germany, Greece, Ireland and Turkey, the following quotations from Enforcement of Foreign Judgments, section 17 (b) ii); Germany: 'In practice, civil imprisonment is rare. It may, however, be ordered if the debtor does not have sufficient attachable assets and does not give an affidavit stating all of his assets. In rare cases, civil imprisonment may be ordered as interim relief to prevent the dissipation of the assets of the debtor', Greece: 'civil imprisonment by the tradesman who is liable for a commercial cause as well as for tort, i.e., the tradesman may be put in prison for his commercial debts', Ireland: 'by civil imprisonment as a result of failure to comply with an instalment order', and Turkey: 'civil imprisonment would be considered in

Consequently the prohibition does not include the ground of a public obligation,[24] as evident also in the ruling of the ECHR in the case of *Göktan v. France*, in which it was concluded that the convention was not applicable on imprisonment for failing to pay French customs fines.[25] Many States are still in a position to apply imprisonment in case of failure to pay a public financial penalty as evident in the Financial penalties Framework Decision.[26]

Concerning the law applicable in matters related to the cross-border enforcement of judgments the ECHR decided, both in the ruling in the case of *Pellegrini v. Italy*[27] and in the ruling in the case of *Wagner et J.M.W.L. v. Luxembourg*,[28] that a

certain cases, e.g. default in complying with the commitment, the debtor failing to declare his total assets etc.'. This Greek position also seems to be contrary to the recommendations of Montesquieu, *see* 2.3.

24. *See* Danelius, pp. 497-498, who emphasizes that the prohibition in this article shall apply 'merely' on the ground of inability to fulfil an obligation (in Swedish 'på grund av oförmåga att uppfylla en förpliktelse'), and concludes that if there exist any other relevant circumstance, which indicates the unwillingness to fulfil an obligation or a fraudulent or otherwise criminal purpose the prohibition is not applicable. He further finds that the contractual obligation may mean the payment of money, but also relate to other contractual obligations such as an obligation to deliver goods or render services. He also concludes that public obligations fall outside the scope of application of this article, *e.g.* the concept in French law of 'contrainte par corps', a kind of imprisonment of the debtor due to the negligence to fulfil a public law monetary obligation in relation to the State, which therefore does not violate this article. *Also see*, for further comments on this provision, Law of the European Convention on Human Rights, pp. 558-559, Leach, p. 370, and Leroy, L'efficacité des procédures judiciaires au sein de l'union Européenne et les garanties des droits de la defense, Transparence patrimoniale, L'efficacité de la justice civile en Europe, p. 276.
25. The ECHR concluded in *Göktan v. France* of 2 Jul. 2002, where the applicant complained of being imprisoned for failing to pay French customs fines, in addition to his sentence of imprisonment for drug trafficking, even if the Court was critical of the imprisonment in a default system, as being 'an archaic custodial measure available only to the Treasury', that Art. 1 of Protocol No. 4 to the convention would not to be applicable, on the basis that it prohibits imprisonment for debt solely when the debt arises under a contractual obligation, *see* para. 51 of the ruling.
26. *See* Art. 10 about imprisonment or alternative sanction by way of substitution for non-recovery of the financial penalty, which stipulates that where it is not possible to enforce a decision, either totally or in part, alternative sanctions, including custodial sanctions, may be applied by the executing State if its laws so provide in such cases and the issuing State has allowed for the application of such alternative sanctions in the certificate referred to in Art. 4. The severity of the alternative sanction shall be determined in accordance with the law of the executing State, but shall not exceed any maximum level stated in the certificate transmitted by the issuing State. *Also see*, about an example of a national legislation the Swedish law on the enforcement of fines, 15§ Bötesverkställighetslagen (1979:189), where it is made clear that the transformation punishment related to the unpaid fines shall be decided by the court to imprisonment for at least 14 days and for a maximum of three months.
27. The ECHR ruled in *Pellegrini v. Italy* of 20 Jul. 2001 on a question concerning a divorce judgment that there had been a violation of Art. 6, 1 of the Convention. The ECHR concluded that: 'In these circumstances the Court considers that the Italian courts breached their duty of satisfying themselves, before authorising enforcement of the Roman Rota's judgment, that the applicant had had a fair trial in the proceedings under canon law', *see* para. 47 of the ruling.
28. The ECHR ruled in *Wagner et J.M.W.L. v. Luxembourg* of 28 Jun. 2007, in relation to an adoption judgment from Peru, that there had been a violation of Arts 6, 8 and 14 of the Convention.

Contracting State must ensure that the fundamental rights and freedoms are guaranteed when enforcing a judgment.

4.3.1 Civil Execution Law

Article 6, 1 of this European convention confirms the fundamental right to access to justice through a fair and public treatment of one's case involving civil rights and obligations, within a reasonable time by an independent and impartial court. The ECHR has interpreted this provision to also include the civil execution of a court judgment. Following its rulings in *e.g.* the cases of *Scollo v. Italy*,[29] *Di Pede v. Italy*,[30] *Zappia v. Italy*,[31] the ECHR has, in the case of *Hornsby v. Greece* clearly

29. The ECHR ruled in *Scollo v. Italy* of 28 Sep. 1995, that there had been a violation of Art. 6, 1 and Art. 1 of Protocol No. 1 of the Convention, which related to a procedure for the eviction of a tenant from the apartment of the applicant in Rome, which lasted over 11 years before it was settled. The ECHR concluded in the case that: '... by adopting emergency measures and providing for certain exceptions to their application ..., the Italian legislature was reasonably entitled to consider, having regard to the need to strike a fair balance between the interests of the community and the right of landlords, and of the applicant in particular, that the means chosen were appropriate to achieve the legitimate aim. However, the restriction on Mr Scollo's use of his flat resulting from the competent authorities' failure to apply those provisions was contrary to the requirements of the second paragraph of Article 1 of Protocol No. 1 ... ', *see* para. 40 of the ruling. Also, 'Even if, in the instant case, it is not possible to speak of enforcement proceedings in the strict sense, the Court considers that Article 6 para. 1 ... is applicable, regard being had to the purpose of the proceedings, which was to settle the dispute between the applicant and his tenant.... If an eviction is to be enforced, the interested party must take the initiative, and Mr Scollo did not spare any effort to obtain satisfaction, applying on numerous occasions to the bailiff, who systematically requested police assistance, as is proved by all the reports on his visits to Mr V.'s flat. However, the prefectoral committee and the Prefect never acted on these requests. While not overlooking the practical difficulties raised by the enforcement of a very large number of evictions, the Court considers that the inertia of the competent administrative authorities engages the responsibility of the Italian State under Article 6 para. 1 ... ', *see* para. 44 of the ruling.
30. The ECHR ruled in *Di Pede v. Italy* of 26 Sep. 1996, that there had been a violation of Art. 6, 1 of the Convention, which related to the enforcement proceedings initiated in court on the basis of a judgment about the demolishing of a building erected in breach of the statutory provisions on minimum distances from the boundaries of adjacent properties, the remove of four trees for the same reasons, the restoration of the site to its previous state, and the payment of damages. The ECHR found that: '... the enforcement proceedings must be regarded as the second stage of the proceedings ..., and a period of more than eighteen years, for most of which the authorities dealing with the case bear responsibility, cannot be regarded as reasonable', *see* paras 24 and 32 of the ruling.
31. The ECHR ruled in *Zappia v. Italy* of 26 Sep. 1996, that there had been a violation of Art. 6, 1 of the Convention, which related to the enforcement proceedings initiated for damages for breach of a contract of sale of a flat under construction. The ECHR concluded that: '... a period of more than twenty-three years for proceedings which are still pending and are of no particular complexity cannot be regarded as reasonable', *see* para. 26 of the ruling.

confirmed that the execution of a judgment given by any court must be regarded as an integral part of the 'trial' for the purpose of Article 6, 1 of the European Convention on Human Rights.[32] This has also been reconfirmed in the later case-law of the ECHR, *i.a.* in the case of *Estima Jorge v. Portugal*.[33]

Examples of rulings from the extensive case-law of the ECHR, which *i.a.* deal with the enforcement of a title of execution, a judgment, or a notarial deed, within a 'reasonable time' in accordance to Article 6, 1 of the European Convention on Human Rights, and which illustrate the problem of excessive length of national enforcement procedures at the execution of such titles of execution, or the

---

32. The ECHR ruled in *Hornsby v. Greece* of 19 Mar. 1997 that there had been a violation of Art. 6, 1 of the Convention, which related to the refraining of the enforcing of a judgment for more than five years. The case concerned two British citizens, the spouses Hornsby, who during a long period of time had sought authorization to open a private language school on the island of Rhodes. This was first refused because they were not Greek citizens, but since this reason was found not acceptable in a ruling of the ECJ, a Greek court removed the administrative decisions whereby the authorization was denied. The way towards the grant of permission now seemed to be open, but it did not happen. During several years no measures were taken by the authorities to comply with the judgments of the courts. The ECHR concluded that: '. . . However, that right would be illusory if a Contracting State's domestic legal system allowed a final, binding judicial decision to remain inoperative to the detriment of one part. It would be inconceivable that Article 6 para. 1 (Art. 6-1) should describe in detail procedural guarantees afforded to litigants – proceedings that are fair, public and expeditious – without protecting the implementation of judicial decisions; . . . Execution of a judgment given by any court must therefore be regarded as an integral part of the "trial" for the purposes of Article 6 (Art. 6); . . . By refraining for more than five years from taking the necessary measures to comply with a final, enforceable judicial decision in the present case the Greek authorities deprived the provisions of Article 6 para. 1 of the Convention (Art. 6-1) of all useful effect', *see* paras 40 and 45 of the decision. *Also see*, about further comments on the case of *Hornsby v. Greece*, and on some other cases from the ECHR, and the impact of the European Convention on Human Rights in the civil execution law area, Danelius, pp. 149 and 259-262, Fricero, pp. 6-10, Isnard, pp. 15 and 18-19, Leroy, L'efficacité des procédures judiciaires au sein de l'union Européenne et les garanties des droits de la defense, Transparence patrimoniale, L'efficacité de la justice civile en Europe, p. 307, Yessiou Faltsi, pp. 195-210, and Verbeke, Execution Officers as a Balance Wheel in Insolvency Cases, pp. 8-9.
33. The ECHR ruled in *Estima Jorge v. Portugal* of 21 Apr. 1998 that Art. 6, 1 was applicable to enforcement proceedings related to a notarial deed providing security for a specific debt, and has been infringed. The ECHR draw the following conclusions as evident from paras 11, 33-36, and 40 of the ruling. The existence of Mrs. Estima Jorge's right had already been established by an authority to execute, namely the notarial deed of mortgage. That deed meant that her claim was indisputable, of a fixed amount and immediately enforceable. The proceedings in issue had been brought solely to enable the goods over which execution could be levied to be identified and sold and Mrs. Estima Jorge to be paid out of the proceeds. There had been no dispute over the validity of her claim, its amount or the method of payment. The fact that the Portuguese system of enforcement proceedings were, in a formal sense, judicial, did not alter the true nature of execution, which being a practical, not legal procedure, could be conducted by a court or, as in other legal systems, by administrative authorities. The sole object of the enforcement proceedings, which was initiated in a court in Lisbon and lasted 13 years until Mrs. Estima Jorge obtained a payment, was recovery of the debt.

non-execution thereof, are, including all of the cases just mentioned, the cases of *Silva Pontes v. Portugal*,[34] *Janosevic v. Sweden*[35] and *Matheus v. France*.[36]

These rulings show that the ECHR, based on its information about the respective national system, assesses the reasonableness of the length of proceedings in the light of the particular circumstances of the case, which are assessed as a whole, having regard to the criteria laid down in the Court's case-law, in particular the complexity of the case and the conduct of the applicant and of the relevant authorities. These examples show, in addition, that the ECHR counts the length of time for enforcement, irrespectively of how States have chosen to organize their enforcement activities, *e.g.* as a part of the administration, or as a regulated free profession, or as a part of the court system,[37] from the moment when they first are formally initiated by the applicant creditor until the moment when the creditor obtained a payment.[38]

34. The ECHR ruled in *Silva Pontes v. Portugal* of 23 Mar. 1994, that Art. 6, 1 of the Convention was applicable in relation to damages, which the plaintiffs suffered after an accident and that was determined in an enforcement proceedings, in a total of proceedings, which lasted for more than 11 years. The ECHR concluded that: '... If the national law of a State makes a provision for proceedings consisting in two stages – one when the court rules on the existence of an obligation to pay and another when it fixes the amount owed – it is reasonable to consider that, for the purpose of Article 6 para. 1 ..., a civil right is not "determined" until the amount has been decided. The determination of a right entails deciding not only on the existence of that right, but also on its scope or the manner in which it may be exercised ..., which would evidently include the calculation of the amount due', *see* para. 30 of the ruling.
35. The ECHR ruled in *Janosevic v. Sweden* of 23 Jul. 2002 that Art. 6, 1 was applicable and had been violated in a matter relating to a request for a stay of execution for the enforcement of Swedish taxes and tax penalties because the tax authority failed to act with the urgency required by the circumstances of the case and thereby unduly delayed a court determination of the main issues concerning the imposition of additional taxes and tax surcharges in a situation when the enforcement measures taken against the applicant called for a prompt examination of his appeal, and as a consequence the applicant, in respect of the length of the proceedings, did not have effective access to the courts. *Also* compare in this respect the case of *Janosovic v. Sweden* with the similar case of *Västberga Taxi Aktiebolag and Vulic v. Sweden* of 23 Jul. 2002. *Also see* Att klaga till Europadomstolen, p. 137, which remarks, in relation to the case of *Västberga Taxi Aktiebolag and Vulic v. Sweden*, that enforcement measures were taken against the applicant and therefore called for a prompt examination of this appeal.
36. The ECHR ruled in *Matheus v. France* of 31 Mar. 2005 that Art. 6, 1 was violated because of the non-execution of a judgment, rendered in 1988, for the eviction of a tenant in French Guadeloupe, and in addition that the protection of property in Art. 1 of the Protocol No. 1 to the convention was violated. In the Opinion concordante from the judge M. Costa this was made clear as follows: 'Dans cette affaire, l'inexécution d'un jugement d'expulsion (rendu en 1988 !) a certainment eu pour effet de violer au détriment du requérant l'article 6 § 1 de la Convention et l'article 1 du Premier Protocole.'
37. *See* 3.2.1 about these national enforcement systems which are part of the court system and these others that are not.
38. *Also* compare Desch, p. 88, who concludes that: '... selon la jurisprudence de la Cour européenne des droits de l'homme, le délai de procédure court depuis le moment où les autorités commencent à avoir une responsabilité juridique à l'égard d'un citoyen, jusqu'à l'exécution définitive de la décision finale.'

The creditor's right of peaceful enjoyment of his possessions has, besides in the rulings of the ECHR in the cases of *Scollo v. Italy* and *Matheus v. France,* also been confirmed in the cases of *Burdov v. Russia*[39] and *Timofeyev v. Russia.*[40] Also in *Burdov v. Russia* the ECHR confirmed that a claim can constitute a possession if it is sufficiently established to be enforceable.[41] Consequently, a judgment debt, in the quality of a title of execution, constitutes a possession of the creditor. Another case in which the ECHR found that the creditor's right of peaceful enjoyment of his possessions was violated because it did not meet the requirement of lawfulness is *Viktor Konovalov v. Russia.* In this case the bailiff had disregarded the legal requirements applicable to the procedure for enforcement of the custom's decision and sale of the applicant's property through the failure to inform the applicant about the opening of the proceedings affecting his possessions and to ensure his effective participation.[42]

The continued non-enforcement of a national judgment, despite a previous judgment of the ECHR, where the Convention was violated due to the non-enforcement of the same national judgment, constitutes, as evident in the ruling of the ECHR in the second case of *Wasserman v. Russia*, a violation of the

39. The ECHR ruled in *Burdov v. Russia* of 7 May 2002 that Art. 6, 1 and Art. 1 of the Protocol No. 1 were violated in a matter of the enforcement of an awarded penalty in compensation to Mr. Burdov following the Chernobyl nuclear plant disaster. The ECHR concluded that: 'It is not open to a State authority to cite lack of funds as an excuse for not honouring a judgment debt. Admittedly, a delay in the execution of a judgment may be justified in particular circumstances. But the delay may not be such as to impair the essence of the right protected under Article 6 § 1. . . . In the instant case, the applicant should not have been prevented from benefiting from the success of the litigation, which concerned compensation for damage to his health caused by obligatory participation in an emergency operation, on the ground of alleged financial difficulties experienced by the State. . . . By failing to comply with the judgment of the Shakhty City Court, the national authorities prevented the applicant from receiving the money he could reasonably have expected to receive. – In sum, there has also been a violation of Article 1 of Protocol No. 1', *see* paras 35 and 41-42 of the ruling.
40. The ECHR ruled in *Timofeyev v. Russia* of 23 Oct. 2003 that Art. 6, 1 and Art. 1 of the Protocol No. 1 were violated in a matter of the enforcement of compensation to Mr. Timofeyev from the Russian State for confiscation of property. The judgment of compensation remained unenforced for almost three years. The ECHR concluded that: 'It appears that the delays in the execution were caused by the bailiffs' unlawful actions, numerous adjournments due to interference of supervisory-review authorities, and the obscurity of the judgment. The Court considers that the applicant should not pay the price of these omissions of the State. . . . The Court finds it unacceptable that a judgment debt against the State is not honoured for such a long period of time. . . . By failing to comply with the judgment of the Leninskiy District Court of Orsk the national authorities prevented the applicant from receiving the money he could reasonably have expected to receive. . . . There has accordingly been a violation of Article 1 of Protocol No. 1.', *see* paras 42 and 47-48 of the ruling.
41. *See* para. 40 of the ruling.
42. The ECHR concluded in *Viktor Konovalov v. Russia* of 24 May 2007, where the bailiff enforced a non-disputed custom's fine, through the sale of the property of Mr. Konovalov, a car, without informing him that there had been a violation of Art. 1 of Protocol No. 1 of the Convention. *See*, for further details about the ruling, its paras 45-47.

Convention. Here, in this second case, the ECHR found that it was entitled to review an application by an applicant's complaint about the continued non-enforcement of the same national judgment in his favour following the period after its earlier judgment, also taking into consideration the right to have an effective remedy before a national authority.[43]

When no executive measures could be taken against the State, and when the State refuses to fulfil its obligations according to a judgment, this constitutes a violation of the European Convention on Human Rights, the right to a fair trial according to its Article 6, 1. If there exists a judgment, which has gained legal force, against the State, or any authority, it must be enforced by the responsible public organ, and an authority could not refer to a lack of economic resources, or to budget funds, as a reason for not paying the adjudged debt.[44] Yet other rulings of the ECHR, which treat delays in enforcement matters due to that a judgment debt against the State is not honoured, are, besides the cases of *Burdov v. Russia* and *Timofeyev v. Russia*, the cases of *Vasilopoulou v. Greece*[45] and *Sukhorukov v. Russia*.[46]

The ECHR concluded in the case of *Apostol v. Georgia* that States may not demand that a creditor, when he applies to a national enforcement organ requesting the initiation of enforcement proceedings, based on his judgment against the debtor, should bear the preliminary expenses associated with enforcement measures, without specifying which measures are foreseen and what their costs are.[47]

---

43. The ECHR ruled in *Wasserman v. Russia* of 10 Apr. 2008 that Arts 6,1, 13, and Art. 1 of Protocol No. 1 of the Convention were violated in a matter of the continued non-enforcement of the same national judgment as was subject to the earlier ruling of the ECHR, *Wasserman v. Russia* of 18 Nov. 2004. This earlier judgment concerned the non-enforcement of a judgment debt in the favour of Mr. Wasserman, where Art. 6, 1, and Art. 1 of Protocol No. 1 of the Convention were violated.
44. *See* Danelius, p. 260.
45. The ECHR ruled in *Vasilopoulou v. Greece* of 21 Jun. 2002 that there had been a violation of Art. 6, 1 and Art. 1 of Protocol No. 1 of the Convention, which related to the refusal of the State to fulfil its obligation to pay Mrs. Vasilopoulou, a widow of an appeal-court judge, the additional pension as specified in a judgment. *See* paras 16-18 and 24-25 of the ruling.
46. The ECHR ruled in *Sukhorukov v. Russia* of 31 Jul. 2008 that Arts 6,1, 13, and Art. 1 of Protocol No. 1 of the Convention were violated where the non-enforcement of a judgment against a local welfare authority for a delayed payment of social benefits has lasted for over nine years. The ECHR concluded that: 'The Government attributed most of this delay to the applicant's failure to follow the changing procedure of enforcement. However, the Court reiterates that, where a judgment is against the State, a person may not be expected to bring separate enforcement procedures.... By taking no initiative to comply with the judgment for such a considerable time, the authorities have breached the applicant's rights.' *See* paras 5-8 and 14-20 of the ruling.
47. The ECHR ruled in *Apostol v. Georgia* of 28 Nov. 2006 that there had been a violation of Art. 6, 1 of the Convention, which related to the non-enforcement of a judgment after the applicant had applied to the Ministry of Justice requesting the initiation of enforcement proceedings, based on his judgment against the debtor, and after having been informed by this Ministry that he was to bear the 'preliminary expenses associated with enforcement measures', without specifying which measures were foreseen and what their costs were. The ECHR concluded that: 'The right to a court is not merely a theoretical right to secure recognition of an entitlement by means of a final decision but also includes the legitimate expectation that the decision will be

The ECHR noted in the case of *Platakou v. Greece* that Court bailiffs were responsible for an error in the service of court documents.[48]

Another right, which is guaranteed by the convention is the right to an effective access to the courts in a fair hearing[49] in a contradictory court proceeding, *i.e.* according to the contradictory principle, a principle which was practised in Roman law,[50] when the enforcement measures taken call for a prompt examination, *e.g.* in relation to an applicant's appeal for a stay of execution as in the ruling of the ECHR in the case of *Janosevic v. Sweden.*

Yet another right, which is guaranteed is the creditor's right to access to information for enforcement purposes, which, however, is also subject to some important limitations in relation to the debtor. One limitation relates to the balance between privacy and efficiency.[51] Another limitation may relate to information about the assets of the debtor, which has become available to the enforcement and recovery organs in a procedure of civil execution when this information is derived and obtained from a criminal procedure in which the debtor has been forced to self-incriminate himself by leaving this information before or during this criminal procedure when this would have constituted a violation of Article 6, 1 of the European Convention on Human Rights.[52]

---

executed.... the fact that the obligation to pay the enforcement-related expenses in advance prevented the applicant from having the binding judgment enforced in his favour. In so far as enforcement proceedings constitute an integral part of the trial... the Court considers that the right to a court, along with access to first instance an appeal court for the determination of "civil rights and obligations"..., equally protects the right of access to enforcement proceedings..., that is the right to have enforcement proceedings initiated.... by shifting onto the applicant the responsibility of financially securing the organisation of the enforcement proceedings, the State tried to escape its positive obligation to organise a system for enforcement of judgments that is effective both in law and in practise.... The authorities' stance of holding the applicant responsible for the initiation of enforcement proceedings by requesting him to bear the preliminary expenses, coupled with the disregard for his financial situation, constituted an excessive burden and restricted his right of access to a court to the degree of impairing the very essence of that right', *see* paras 54-56 and 64-65 of the ruling.

48. The ECHR ruled in *Platakou v. Greece* of 11 Jan. 2001 that Art. 6, 1 was violated in a matter concerning proceedings following the expropriation of the property of Mrs. Platakou in relation to an error in the service of court documents by court bailiffs. The ECHR concluded that: 'In the instant case, the Court notes that the applicant was penalised by the decision of the Court of Appeal in its judgment... to declare the application inadmissible owing to an error in service. It considers that the applicant cannot be held responsible for that error since, as the domestic legislation requires court documents to be served by court bailiffs, the arrangements for such service are primarily the latter's responsibility. The Court cannot accept that bailiffs are not acting as public State representatives in the exercise of their duties', *see* para. 39.
49. *See*, about further comments on the right to a fair hearing, Danelius, pp. 134-262, Law of the European Convention on Human Rights, pp. 163-272, Leach, pp. 241-278, and Att klaga till Europadomstolen, pp. 120-126.
50. *See* 2.1.
51. *See* 7.2.3.5, where the conclusions related to the balance between the interest of efficiency of the creditor and the interest of the debtor of privacy, including data protection, are further developed.
52. Compare the ruling of the ECHR in the case of *Funke v. France* of 25 Feb. 1993. Art. 6, 1 was violated because Mr. Funke, who was suspected for a violation of currency regulations, was

4.3.2 Tax Penalties

Even if taxation proceedings do not fall within the scope of civil rights and obligations of this European convention,[53] the ECHR has, nevertheless, in several rulings applied Article 6 of this European Convention on national tax penalties, often by initially determining if these tax penalties were to be classified, under this convention, as being of a criminal nature and secondly if these penalties imposed by decisions from the administrative authorities had been subject to an effective possibility of appeal to an independent and impartial tribunal.[54] Examples of rulings of the ECHR, which deal with Article 6 of the European convention in the context of national tax penalties, are, besides the case of *Janosevic v. Sweden*, the cases of: *Bendenoun v. France*,[55] *A.P., M.P. and T.P. v. Switzerland*,[56] *J.J v. the Netherlands*[57] and *Silvester's Horeca Service v. Belgium*.[58]

---

summoned to be sentenced to a fine and a further penalty until he produced certain documents to the authorities about his assets abroad. The ECHR concluded that: 'The Court notes that the customs secured Mr Funke's conviction in order to obtain certain documents which they believed must exist, although they were not certain of the fact. Being unable, or unwilling to produce them by some other means, they attempted to compel the applicant himself to provide the evidence of offences he had allegedly committed. The special features of customs law . . . cannot justify such an infringement of the right of anyone "charged with a criminal offence", within the autonomous meaning of this expression in Article 6 (Art. 6), to remain silent and not to contribute to incriminating himself', *see* para. 44. *Also see*, for further information about the right to remain silent in a criminal procedure and the right not to incriminate oneself in order to facilitate the work of the prosecutor in such a procedure according to the European Convention on Human Rights and about the legal usage of the ECHR, Danelius, p. 247, Att klaga till Europadomstolen, p. 122, and Leach, pp. 255-256.

53. *See* Leach, p. 245, and Att klaga till Europadomstolen, p. 119. *Also see*, about comments in relation to the European Convention on Human Rights and tax enforcement, Gest, pp. 546-562.
54. *See* Leach, p. 242, who refers to that States are required to exercise diligence to ensure the effective enjoyment of Art. 6 rights.
55. The ECHR ruled in *Bendenoun v. France* of 26 Jan. 1994 that Art. 6, 1 in principle was applicable in a matter relating to French tax penalties, but that there had been no breach of it because there were no infringement of the rights of the defense or the principle of equality of arms.
56. The ECHR ruled in *A.P., M.P. and T.P. v. Switzerland* of 29 Aug. 1997, that Art. 6, 2 was applicable and had been violated due to the imposition of Swiss criminal sanction on heirs for tax evasion by a deceased person because it was contrary to the presumption of innocence to impose criminal sanctions on the living in respect of acts committed by a deceased person.
57. The ECHR ruled in *J.J v. the Netherlands* of 27 Mar. 1998 that Art. 6, 1 was applicable and had been violated in a matter relating to an appeal against Dutch tax penalties, which was declared inadmissible on sole ground that court registration fee not had been paid, because the plaintiff in taxation proceedings in Supreme Court was unable to reply to advisory opinion of advocate-general.
58. The ECHR ruled in *Silvester's Horeca Service v. Belgium* of 4 Mar. 2004 that Art. 6, 1 was applicable and had been violated in a matter relating to an appeal against Belgium tax penalties, because the applicant did not have access to a tribunal in the sense of this article of the convention.

Chapter 5

Scope of Application of EC Law and Conventions

5.1 TERRITORIAL SCOPE

5.1.1 EC Law

Parts of EC law relevant to this study give no information on their territorial scope, *e.g.* the Brussels I regulation, the European Enforcement Order for uncontested claims, the European Order for payment procedure, the European Small Claims Procedure, the Recovery directive, and the Insolvency regulation. This means that instead, their territorial scope becomes governed and determined by the provisions on territoriality in Article 299 of the EC Treaty.[1] The Treaty of Lisbon includes a corresponding provision on territoriality.[2] Besides the rule in the EC Treaty, which enumerates the Member States,[3] there also exist several additional provisions by which certain territories are to be included by, or excluded from, the application of this Treaty. Some of these additional provisions are of a rather complex nature, but it is not needed, in this context, to treat them in all details. The readers are for further details referred to consult the prevalent literature.[4]

The EC Treaty applies to certain territories, which in Europe, or outside of Europe, from a constitutional point of view constitute integrated parts of the territory of a Member State, as the French overseas departments Guadeloupe, French Guayana, Martinique and Réunion, Portuguese Azores and Madeira and the

---

1. *See* Art. 299 (former Art. 227) of the Treaty establishing the EC, consolidated version of 24 Dec. 2002, as amended in 2003.
2. *See* Art. 49, c.
3. *See* Art. 299, 1.
4. Examples are the Introduction to the Law of the ECs, pp. 89-94, and Kommentar zum EU-/EG-Vertrag, pp. 443-474.

Spanish Canary Islands.[5] The EC Treaty also stipulates that it shall apply to the European territories for whose external relations a Member State is responsible.[6] The prevalent opinion in literature is that the EC Treaty, in the context of territories for whose external relations a Member State is responsible, is applicable to Gibraltar, but not to Monaco, San Marino, Vatican City and Andorra.[7] The EC Treaty shall also apply to the Åland Islands, but neither to the Faeroe Islands nor to the sovereign base areas of the United Kingdom of Great Britain and Northern Ireland in Cyprus.[8] The EC Treaty shall only to a limited extent apply to the Channel Islands and the Isle of Man.[9]

The EC Treaty is not applicable to such non-European overseas countries and territories, as are associated through special arrangements set out in part four of the Treaty and which are listed in annex II to the Treaty.[10] These countries and territories are: Greenland, New Caledonia and Dependencies, French Polynesia, French Southern and Antarctic Territories, Wallis and Futuna Islands, Mayotte, Saint Pierre and Miquelon, Aruba, Netherlands Antilles, Anguilla, Cayman Islands, Falkland Islands, South Georgia and the South Sandwich Islands, Montserrat, Pitcairn, Saint Helena and Dependencies, British Antarctic Territory, British Indian Ocean Territory, Turks and Caicos Islands, British Virgin Islands and Bermuda. Nor does the EC Treaty apply to such overseas countries and territories, which have special relations with the United Kingdom of Great Britain and Northern Ireland and which are not included in annex II to the Treaty.[11]

---

5. *See* Art. 299, 2.
6. *See* Art. 299, 4.
7. *See* Introduction to the Law of the European Communities, p. 90, where the following conclusions are reported: 'By virtue of Article 227(4) EC, the Treaty applies to the European territories for whose external relations a Member State is responsible: this now in fact only concerns Gibraltar, which is excluded from the very significant parts of Community law, particularly secondary legislation relating to the common agricultural policy and the harmonization of indirect taxation. Gibraltar is also excluded from the customs territory of the Community. While Monaco is part of the customs territory of the Community. San Marino is now not. They are both, like the Vatican City outside of the scope of the EC Treaty. Andorra is no longer a European territory covered by Article 227(4) EC.' *Also see* Kommentar zum EU-/EG-Vertrag, pp. 454-456, and regarding the Brussels I regulation, Pålsson, Brysselkonventionen, Luganokonventionen och Bryssel I-förordningen, pp. 47-48. *Also see* Moss, p. 139, who states that the colony of Gibraltar is within the concept of 'UK', but is treated as a separate jurisdiction for the purpose of the Insolvency regulation. Art. 13 of the Council Framework Decision 2003/577/JHA of 22 Jul. 2003 on the execution in the European Union of orders freezing property or evidence states that it also shall apply to Gibraltar. *Also* compare European Tax Law, p. 334, about the territorial application of the sixth VAT-directive concerning certain territories of some Member States that are excluded for VAT purposes from the territory of the State.
8. *See* Art. 299, 5 and 6, a and b.
9. *See* Art. 299, 6, c. *Also see* Kommentar zum EU-/EG-Vertrag, p. 456, and Pålsson, Brysselkonventionen, Luganokonventionen och Bryssel I-förordningen, p. 48, who concludes that this should mean that the Brussels I regulation is not applicable on these Islands.
10. *See* Art. 299, 3, para. 1 compared to annex II.
11. *See* Art. 299, 3, para. 2.

The exceptions in Article 299 of the EC Treaty for certain European and non-European territories reflect the positions from the national constitutions of the Member States of the EU and mean that EC law does not apply to these territories. This creates different and unequal conditions of competition between the activities that are carried out in these territories compared to the corresponding activities in other parts of the territories within the Internal Common Market of the EU. Hence, the Brussels I regulation and the Recovery directive do not apply between France and the Channel Islands. Also, the Insolvency regulation is not applicable on Andorra, or on Isle of Man, or on the Netherlands Antilles. Certainly, a possible extension of the territorial scope of Article 299 of the EC Treaty to include also additional territories with relations to the Member States[12] would lead to the establishment of more equal conditions of competition between the activities that are carried out on these territories compared to the activities on other parts of the territories within the Internal Common Market.

5.1.2 Conventions Related to the Enforcement of Contractual Claims

The territorial scope of the Brussels convention is to some extent wider than that of the Brussels I regulation. The Brussels I regulation replaces the Brussels convention, except as regards the territories of States, which fall within the territorial scope of that convention and which are excluded from the regulation pursuant to Article 299 of the EC Treaty.[13] This greater territorial scope of the Brussels convention than the Brussels I regulation is, however, of a limited importance and concerns in particular certain by France and the Netherlands dependent non-European territories.[14]

To the extent that EC law is not exclusively applicable, a Member State of the EU may also make use of the sometimes greater territorial scope of conventions in relation to other Member States and in particular in relation to non-EC States, *e.g.* under the Old Lugano convention and the Nordic convention on recognition and the enforcement of judgments in civil matters. Thus an English private creditor, who holds a French title of execution based on a contractual claim, and a German private creditor, who holds a corresponding Swedish title of execution, may both make use of the Old Lugano convention for the enforcement of these titles of execution on Iceland, in Norway and in Switzerland.

Denmark has stated that, until further decision, the Brussels convention will not apply to the Faeroe Islands or Greenland. Iceland, Norway and Switzerland are

12. *E.g.* countries and territories as evident from Arts 299, 3, para. 1 compared to annex II, Arts 299, 5 and 6, a and b and 299, 6, c of the EC Treaty.
13. *See* Preamble (23) and Art. 68, 1. *Also* compare 5.1.1 for further details on the territorial scope of the Regulation.
14. *See* Jenard/Möller report, points 94-95, regarding comments on the territorial application in relation to France and the Netherlands.

parties to the Old Lugano convention.[15] Denmark has also declared that the Old Lugano convention is not extended to the Faeroe Islands or Greenland. The States, which are parties to the Nordic convention on recognition and the enforcement of judgments in civil matters, are Denmark, Finland, Iceland, Norway and Sweden. The Danish law related to this latter convention stipulates that it does not apply to the Faeroe Islands and Greenland, but may be entered into force in these parts of the State through a royal decree.[16] Such a royal decree has entered into force in relation to the Faeroe Islands.[17] A great number of States are parties to the New York convention on foreign arbitral awards, and it provides a possibility for each party to make a declaration on the territorial scope of that State,[18] of which a lot of States have made use.[19]

5.1.3 Conventions Related to the Recovery of Tax Claims

The States and territories, which are parties to the Council of Europe and OECD convention on mutual administrative assistance in tax matters, and which have not made any reservations against the recovery provisions, are Azerbaijan, Belgium, Denmark, including Greenland, Finland, Iceland, Norway and Sweden.[20] The States and territories, which are parties to the Nordic agreement on assistance in tax matters, are Denmark, Greenland, the Faeroe Islands, Finland, Iceland, Norway, Sweden and the United Kingdom.[21] The Nordic agreement does not, however, apply to Svalbard and Jan Mayen and other Norwegian dependencies outside Europe.[22]

The differing greater territorial scope in conventions in the tax recovery area compared to that of the Recovery directive is of importance because the directive allows a greater measure of mutual assistance, *e.g.* as concerns territories falling under such conventions.[23] This is the case, regarding the differing greater territorial scope of the Council of Europe and OECD convention on mutual administrative assistance in tax matters and the Nordic agreement on assistance in tax matters, in relation to Greenland and the Faeroe Islands, compared to the corresponding scope of the Recovery directive. This means that Finland and Sweden,

15. *See* Annex 5.
16. *See* Lovbekendtgørelse 1986-09-15 nr. 635 om anerkendelse og fuldbyrdelse af nordiske afgørelser om privatretlige krav og om ændring af retsplejeloven, som ændret ved L 1995-03-29 nr. 209 og L 1995-06-14 nr. 389, § 14, (Act including the recognition and the enforcement of nordic judgments in civil matters).
17. *See* Ad Ibkg 1986 nr. 635, (26), (Royal decree), which entered the law into force in relation to the Faeroe Islands from 1 Jan. 1987.
18. *See* Art. X.
19. *See* annex 2.
20. *See* annex 6.
21. *See* Preamble.
22. *See* Art. 23.
23. *See* Art. 23 of the Recovery directive. *Also see* 5.3.1.2.1 for further details about the relationship between the directive and bilateral and multilateral conventions.

which are Members of the EU, can make use of these two conventions in relation to the Danish territories of Greenland and the Faeroe Islands, on which the EC Treaty is not applicable.

5.1.4 Conventions on Insolvency

The Nordic bankruptcy convention[24] applies to the States which are parties to it, Denmark, Finland, Norway, Sweden and Iceland.[25] A bankruptcy convention applies between France and Monaco,[26] which is of interest because Monaco is outside the scope of the EC Treaty.[27] Monaco is therefore not bound by the Insolvency regulation.

5.2 SCOPE OF CLAIMS

There exist a variety of national titles of execution both in the civil law area[28] and in the tax law area, in different States, where they represent the legal basis for applications for enforcement and recovery measures.

5.2.1 Contractual Claims

5.2.1.1 EC Law

5.2.1.1.1 Brussels I Regulation

Contractual and commercial claims clearly fall under the scope of claims in the Brussels I regulation, which applies in civil and commercial matters, whatever the nature of the court or tribunal,[29] and whatever the judgment may be called, as well as the determination of costs or expenses by an officer of the court.[30] The regulation does not extend, in particular, to revenue, customs or administrative

24. *See* 2.7.
25. *See* Art. 1 which only refers the territorial scope of the Convention to the territories of the States.
26. *See* Art. 9 of the Bankruptcy convention between France and Monaco which refers concerning France the territorial scope of the convention to 'territoire métropolitain . . . et aux départements français d'outre-mer'. *See* further 5.1.1 about French overseas departments.
27. *See* 5.1.1.
28. *See* The execution of court decisions in civil cases, about writs of execution for the execution of domestic court decisions in: Albania, Armenia, Austria, Azerbaijan, Belgium, Bulgaria, Croatia, Cyprus, Czech Republic, Denmark, Finland, France, Georgia, Germany, Greece, Hungary, Italy, Japan, Latvia, Lithuania, Luxemburg, Moldova, Norway, Poland, Portugal, Romania, Slovak Republic, Slovenia, Spain, Sweden, the former Yugoslav Republic of Macedonia, Ukraine, the United Kingdom, and Synthesis, pp. 150-262.
29. *See* Art. 1, 1 first sentence.
30. *See* Art. 32.

matters.[31] It does not apply to the status or legal capacity of natural persons, rights in property arising out of a matrimonial relationship, wills and succession, bankruptcy, proceedings relating to the winding-up of insolvent companies or other legal persons, judicial arrangements, compositions and analogous proceedings, social security,[32] and arbitration.[33] The ECJ has, in several cases, dealt with the scope of application of 'civil and commercial matters', also in relation to the exclusion of public law matters, under the Brussels convention. Some of them will be treated here, because they provide guidance in relation to the issue of recognition and enforceability.

Even if a commercial claim in the quality of a court settlement may be enforceable at the national level, it was, however, not so under the Brussels convention, which in this sense is essentially identical to the Brussels I regulation,[34] as evident in the ruling of the ECJ in the case of *Solo Kleinmotoren v. Boch*. The reason in this case was that this settlement was not treated as a judgment given by a court or tribunal. This ruling of the ECJ also indicates that a creditor, who would like to be able to enforce his claim in the cross-border context, will have reasons to let a court decide on its own on the issues between the parties in a judgment, instead of making a court settlement.[35] In the sense of the regulation a court is a State organ, which is independent and operates its proceedings according to the principle of contradiction. The nature of the court is therefore of no importance as long as its rendered judgment falls within the scope of application of the regulation.

The legal usage of the ECJ, which is based on an autonomous interpretation of the Brussels convention,[36] also shows that the decisive factor for the determination of whether a claim should be included, or excluded, under the scope of claims in the regulation is not its formal origin from whatever court or tribunal, but the underlying nature of the original claim. This is evident in the case of *LTU*

31. *See* Art. 1, 1 second sentence.
32. *See* Jenard report, pp. 12-13, which states in relation to the corresponding Art. 1, 3 of the Brussels convention, that social security was excluded because it in some countries was treated as a matter of public law and in others it fell in the borderline area between private law and public law.
33. *See* Art. 2, a-d.
34. Compare Art. 51 of the Convention to Art. 58 of the Regulation.
35. The decision in *Solo Kleinmotoren v. Boch* of 2 Jun. 1994 concerned a court settlement between Mr. Boch and Solo Kleinmotoren after an appeal in a German court against an order issued in Germany on the application of Mr. Boch for the enforcement of a final judgment delivered by a civil court in Italy against Solo Kleinmotoren. The ECJ ruled that Art. 27 of the Brussels convention must be interpreted strictly, which precludes treating a court settlement as a judgment given by a court or tribunal. The ECJ concluded that in order to be a 'judgment' for the purposes of the Convention the decision must emanate from a judicial body of a Contracting State deciding on its own authority on the issues between the parties. The ECJ further stated that this condition is not fulfilled in the case of a settlement, even if it was reached in a court of a Contracting State and brings legal proceedings to an end, and that settlements in court are essentially contractual in that their terms depend first and foremost on the parties' intention. The ECJ made in this context also a reference to the Jenard/Möller report, *see* p. 80. *Also see* paras 17-18 and 20 of the ruling.
36. *See* 1.4.1.

Lufttransportunternehmen GmbH & Co. KG v. Eurocontrol,[37] and in the more recent case of *Sonntag v. Weidmann*.[38] Consequently, in the case of *Sonntag v. Weidmann* the ECJ ruled that non-contractual civil law damages, based on the judgment of a criminal court, were to be included under the scope of application of the Brussels convention. Other possible examples of non-contractual civil law damages, which may fall under the scope of claims in the Brussels I regulation, mirror violations that constitute damages to a limited liability company under corporate law, as when a prohibited distribution of assets has taken place, or when a prohibited loan has been received by the shareholders. This is, however, only to the extent that these transactions should not instead be considered only to fall under criminal law.

An action based on a guarantee contract, entered into in order to satisfy a condition imposed by the State on associations of carriers, as principal debtors, for the payment of customs duties, *i.e.* a private law contractual obligation, between the State and an insurance company, has been included under the Brussels convention, as evident in the case of *Préservatrice foncière TIARD SA v. Staat der Nederlanden*.[39] An action under a right of recourse under national legislation providing for payment of allowances by way of social assistance should, as evident in the case of *Gemeente Steenbergen v. Luc Baten*, be included under the Brussels convention to the extent it is governed by ordinary law in regard to maintenance obligations and not by law, which confers on the public body a prerogative of its

37. The decision of the ECJ in *LTU Lufttransportunternehmen GmbH & Co. KG v. Eurocontrol* of 14 Oct. 1976 deals with the enforcement of a Belgian judgment based on that the defendant should pay certain sums to Eurocontrol imposed by it by way of charges for the use of its equipment and services. The ECJ concluded that a judgment given in an action between a public authority (Eurocontrol) and a person governed by private law (LTU), in which the public authority has acted in the exercise of its powers, is excluded from the area of application of Art. 1 of the Brussels convention. The charges imposed by Eurocontrol were based on the Multilateral agreement related to route charges, done at Brussels on 12 Feb. 1981.
38. The ECJ has in its decision in *Sonntag v. Weidmann* of 21 Apr. 1993, which deals with the enforcement in Germany of damages to an injured party based on the judgment of an Italian criminal court, despite of that the defendant had argued that he acted in his capacity of a civil servant at the occasion of the injury, confirmed that such damages fall under the scope of application of Art. 1 of the Brussels convention.
39. The decision of the ECJ in *Préservatrice foncière TIARD SA v. Staat der Nederlanden* of 15 May 2003 deals with the scope of Article 1 of the Brussels convention in relation to the concept of civil and commercial matter and the concept of customs matters in an action based on a guarantee contract, entered into in order to satisfy a condition imposed by the State on associations of carriers, as principal debtors, under Art. 6 of the TIR convention, for the payment of customs duties, between the State and an insurance company. The ECJ concluded in this ruling that: '. . . first paragraph of Article 1 of the Brussels Convention must be interpreted as meaning that "civil and commercial matters", within the meaning of the first sentence of that provision, covers a claim by which a contracting State seeks to enforce against a person governed by private law a private-law guarantee contract which was concluded in order to enable a third person to supply a guarantee required and defined by that State, in so far as the legal relationship between the creditor and the guarantor, under the guarantee contract, does not entail the exercise by the State of powers going beyond those existing under the rules applicable to relations between private individuals.' *See* para. 36 of the ruling.

own.[40] In *Freistaat Bayern v. Jan Blijdenstein* the ECJ ruled that an action for the recovery brought by a public body subrogated to the rights of the maintenance creditor should be excluded under the Brussels convention.[41]

This means that all claims of a public body, which could be originally derived from the exercise of public powers, irrespectively of from whatever court or tribunal they have been issued, will in their quality of titles of execution fall outside the scope of claims in the Brussels I regulation.[42] Examples of claims, which consequently fall outside the scope of the Brussels I regulation, are a title of execution from the Swedish enforcement authority in summary proceeding in a non-contested matter,[43] or a title of execution from a Swedish district court, when these titles are based on a co-debtor liability against *e.g.* a managing director for a corporate tax liability. These titles of execution may instead be used as instruments permitting the recovery of tax claims against the co-debtors under the Implementing recovery directive.[44]

---

40. In *Gemeente Steenbergen v. Luc Baten* of 14 Nov. 2002 the ECJ treats the scope of application of Art. 1 of the Brussels convention in relation to the concepts of 'civil matters' and 'social security' concerning an action under a right of recourse under national legislation providing for payment of allowances by way of social assistance. The ECJ ruled, in its preliminary ruling, that: 'The first paragraph of Article 1 of the Convention . . . must be interpreted as meaning that the concept of "civil matters" encompasses an action under a right of recourse whereby a public body seeks from a person governed by private law recovery of sums paid by it by way of social assistance to the divorced spouse and child of that person, provided that the basis and the detailed rules relating to the bringing of that action are governed by the rules of the ordinary law in regard to maintenance obligations. Where the action under a right of recourse is founded on provisions by which the legislature conferred on the public body a prerogative of its own, that action cannot be regarded as being brought in "civil matters".' *Also see*, for more details, paras 32-38 of the ruling.
41. *See Freistaat Bayern v. Jan Blijdenstein* of 15 Jan. 2004, where the ECJ deals with Art. 5, 2 of the Brussels convention, a special rule of jurisdiction related to maintenance, concerning the recovery brought by a public body subrogated to the rights of the maintenance creditor. The ECJ concluded, in its preliminary ruling, that: 'Article 5 (2) of the Convention . . . must be interpreted as meaning that it cannot be relied on by a public body which seeks, in an action for recovery, reimbursement of sums paid under public law by way of an education grant to a maintenance creditor, to whose rights it is subrogated against the maintenance debtor.'
42. *See*, for a more extensive treatment and discussion about the meaning of 'civil and commercial matters' and of the exclusion of public law matters from the scope of application of the Brussels I regulation, Bogdan, Uteslutning av offentlig rätt från Bryssel I-förordningens tillämpningsområde, Festskrift till Hans-Heinrich Vogel, pp. 47-59. His interpretation of the position of the ECJ, as concerns the application of the exclusion of a litigation from the meaning of 'civil and commercial matters', is mainly that it is governed by to two factors, any of the parties is a public authority, normally the plaintiff, and its case relates to the exercise of public powers, *see i.b.*, p. 57.
43. The regulation equals the Swedish enforcement authority to a court and consequently recognizes the decision of that authority based on a commercial claim as enforceable, *see* Art. 62. This may be explained by summary proceeding being dealt with in courts in all Member States of the EU except in Sweden, where this proceeding has been transferred from the court system to the enforcement authority. *See*, about the task of the Swedish enforcement authority in summary proceeding compared to some other European States, Berglund, Hur är kronofogdemyndighetens arbetsuppgifter organiserade i några EU-Stater och i Norge ?, p. 61.
44. *See* Art. 13 compared to Art. 4, 2 of the Implementing recovery directive. *Also see* 5.4.2.2.2, in which context co-debtors are treated in more details.

Claims in civil and commercial matters, including contractual claims, based on documents formally drawn up or registered as authentic instruments also fall under the scope of claims in the Brussels convention, which in this sense is identical to the Brussels I regulation,[45] *e.g.* extracts from certain public registers and instruments attested by a notary.[46] This has also been confirmed by the ECJ in the case of *Deutsche Genossenschaftsbank v. S A Brasserie du Pêcheur.*[47] In order to be enforceable under the regulation, authentic instruments have to meet some conditions. They must under the law of the State of origin be established by a public authority or other authority empowered for that purpose by this State, as evident from the ruling of the ECJ in the case of *Unibank A/S v. Christensen.*[48]

---

45. Compare Art. 50 of the Convention to Art. 57 of the Regulation.
46. *See* Schlosser report, para. 226, which explains, in relation to the corresponding Art. 50 of the Brussels convention, that in Scotland, instruments establishing a clearly defined obligation to perform a contract can be entered in a public register and that an extract from that register can then serve as a basis for enforcement in the same way as a court judgment. The Jenard/Möller report, point 72, states that the concept of an authentic instrument is contained in the legislation of Austria and that the conditions of such an instrument are that the authenticity of the instrument should have been established by a public authority, this authenticity should relate to the content of this instrument and not only, for example, the signature, and that the instrument has to be enforceable in itself in the State in which it originates. The report mentions that settlements occurring outside courts, which are known in Danish law and enforceable under that law (udenretlig forlig) do not fall under Art. 50 of the Brussels convention as likewise commercial bills and cheques are not covered by the same provision.
47. The decision of the ECJ in *Deutsche Genossenschaftsbank v. S A Brasserie du Pêcheur* of 2 Jul. 1985 deals with the question whether Brasserie du Pêcheur, in its capacity as an interested third party, was entitled to apply for the setting aside of an order for the enforcement in France of an instrument attested by a German notary. The ECJ ruled that the Brussels convention excludes any such procedure of setting aside to interested third parties, which means that the ECJ confirmed the enforceability of the instrument attested by the German notary under the Convention.
48. The decision of the ECJ in *Unibank A/S v. Christensen* of 17 Jun. 1999 concerns the application of the Danish bank Unibank for three acknowledgments of letters of indebtedness (Gældsbrev), documents that expressly stated that they could be used as a basis for execution to be levied, signed by a Mr. Christensen when he resided in Denmark, to be declared enforceable against him after he had moved to Germany. The ECJ ruled that an acknowledgment of indebtedness enforceable under the law of the State of origin, whose authenticity has not been established by a public authority or other authority empowered for that purpose, does not constitute an authentic instrument within the meaning of Art. 50 of the Brussels convention. The ECJ concluded, since the instruments covered by Art. 50 of the Brussels convention are enforced under exactly the same conditions as judgments, that the authentic nature of such instruments must be established beyond dispute so that the court in the State in which enforcement is sought is in a position to rely on their authenticity. Since instruments drawn up between private parties are not inherently authentic, the involvement of a public authority or any other authority empowered for that purpose by the State of origin was needed in order to endow them with the character of authentic instruments. The ECJ noted, with a reference made to the Jenard/Möller report, *see* p. 80, that the conditions which had to be fulfilled by instruments in order to be regarded as authentic within the meaning of Art. 50 of the Lugano convention were the following three: 'the authenticity of the instrument should have been established by a public authority; this authenticity of the instrument should relate to the content of the instrument and not only, for example, the signature; the instrument has to be enforceable in itself in the State in which it originates'. *See* paras 14-21 of the ruling.

Authentic enforceable instruments of a non-judiciary nature, in francophone jurisdictions called actes authentiques or actes notariés, exist in several Member States of the EU, *e.g.* in Belgium, France, Germany, Greece, Italy, Luxemburg, the Netherlands, Scotland and Spain, and are enforceable under the Brussels I regulation subject to certain requirements.[49] The enforceability, la force exécutoire, of an authentic instrument may be described as follows:

> Lorsque le débiteur n'exécute pas ses obligations pécuniaires, l'acte authentique évite au créancier d'avoir à obtenir un judgement, s'il veut le poursuivre en paiement de sa dette, alors que c'est indispensable pour l'acte sous seing privé. L'acte authentique est exécutoire de plein droit, comme une décision judiciaire.[50]

The profession of the notary, which confers authenticity to the documents it draws up, as warrant of juridical security, and also produces authentic enforceable instruments, derives its historical origins from the Roman Empire and the Middle Ages,[51] and exists in some States in Europe and in the rest of the World with Latin type notarial systems based upon the foundations of Roman-Germanic law. Many of the associations of notaries of these States are members of the Unión Internacional del Notariado Latino, a non-governmental organization legally incorporated in 1950, with its administrative seat in Rome. The members of this Union are professionals in legal matters in exercise of a public office, by delegation of public powers from the State, although their activity is not comprised within the category of public administration.[52]

The Brussels I regulation is completed in EC law by the Recovery directive, the Insolvency regulation, the Council regulation 1408/71/EEC of 14 June 1971 on the application of social security schemes to employed persons and their families moving within the Community (Old social security regulation), and the regulation 883/2004/EC of the European Parliament and of the Council of 29 April 2004 on the coordination of social security systems (New social security regulation), which allow for the cross-border collection of contributions.[53] The ECJ confirmed in its ruling in the case of *Henri Gourdain v. Franz Nadler* that a decision relating to bankruptcy and winding-up shall be excluded from the scope of the Brussels convention.[54] Outside the scope of EC law the Brussels I regulation is completed

---

49. *See* Art. 57 of the Brussels I regulation, and L'efficacité de la justice civile en Europe (de Leval/Georges/Matray), pp. 178-179, and for comments related to the corresponding provision, Art. 50 of the Brussels convention, *see i.b.* pp. 179-180.
50. *See* website of the Notaires de France, <www.notaires.fr>, under headlines L'institution and L'acte authentique.
51. *See* 2.2.1.
52. *See* website of the Unión Internacional del Notariado Latino, <www.uinl.org>.
53. *See* Art. 92 of the Old social security regulation, which allows for the cross-border collection of social security contributions. *Also see* about the same opinion, Eichenhofer, p. 22.
54. *See* the decision of the ECJ in *Henri Gourdain v. Franz Nadler* of 22 Feb. 1979, where the ECJ ruled that a decision such as that of a French civil court ordering the de facto manager of a legal person to pay a certain sum into the assets of a company must be considered as given in the

by the New York convention on foreign arbitral awards, which applies to claims derived from arbitral awards. The ECJ concludes in its ruling in the case of *Marc Rich & Co. AG v. Società Italiana Impianti PA*. that the exclusion in the Brussels convention of arbitration also extends to litigation proceedings before a national court concerning the appointment of an arbitrator, even if the existence or validity of an arbitration agreement is a preliminary issue in that litigation.[55]

5.2.1.1.2 Other Regulations Related to Contractual Claims

The scope of claims of the European Enforcement Order for uncontested claims and the European Order for payment procedure is, with some exceptions, identical to that of the Brussels I regulation.[56] Such an exception is that they shall not extend to the liability of the State for acts and omissions in the exercise of State authority, *acta jure imperii*.[57] Another exception is that the European Order for payment procedure does not apply to claims arising from non-contractual obligations, unless they have been subject to an agreement between the parties or there has been admission of debts, or they relate to liquidated debts arising from joint ownership of property. The provisions in the Brussels I regulation and in the European Enforcement Order for uncontested claims, which stipulate that they shall not apply to the status or legal capacity of natural persons, is not included in the European Order for payment procedure.[58] In summary proceedings concerning orders to pay, the expression court includes, in relation to Sweden, the Swedish enforcement authority.[59]

Where a judgment includes an enforceable decision on the amount of costs related to the court proceedings, including interest rates, it shall be certified as a European Enforcement Order also with regard to the costs unless the debtor has specifically objected to an obligation to bear such costs in the course of the court proceedings, in accordance with the law of the Member State of origin.[60] Interest, contractual penalties, and costs, may also be included at an application for a European order for payment.[61]

---

context of bankruptcy, proceedings relating to the winding-up of insolvent companies or other legal persons or analogous proceedings within the meaning of subpara. 2 of the second paragraph of Art. 1 of the Brussels convention.

55. *See* the decision of the ECJ in *Marc Rich & Co. AG v. Società Italiana Impianti PA*. of 25 Jul. 1991, where the ECJ ruled in relation to Art. 1, 4 of the Brussels convention.
56. *See* Art. 2 of the European Enforcement Order for uncontested claims and Art. 2 of the European Order for payment procedure compared to Art. 1 of the Brussels I regulation. *Also see*, about some comments, in relation to the European Enforcement Order for uncontested claims, on the scope of claims, Un titre exécutoire européen, Les Dossiers du Journal des tribunaux 53, pp. 41-43.
57. *See* Art. 2, 1 in these regulations.
58. *See* Art. 1, 2, a of the Brussels I regulation and Art. 2, 2, a of the European Enforcement Order for uncontested claims compared to Art. 2, 2, a of the European Order for payment procedure.
59. *See* Art. 4, 7.
60. *See* Art. 7.
61. *See* Art. 7, 2, b, where it is stipulated that the application shall state the amount of the claim, including the principal and, where applicable, interest, contractual penalties and costs.

The scope of claims of the European Small Claims Procedure is, with some exceptions, identical to that of the European Enforcement Order for uncontested claims.[62] The European Small Claims Procedure applies to civil and commercial matters, whatever the nature of the court or tribunal, where the value of a claim does not exceed EUR 2 000 at the time when the claim form is received by the court or tribunal with jurisdiction, excluding all interest, expenses and disbursements.[63] The European Small Claims Procedure does not apply to: employment law; tenancies of immovable property, with the exception of actions on monetary claims; or violations of privacy and of rights to personality, including defamation.[64]

5.2.1.2 Conventions

5.2.1.2.1 Nordic Convention on Recognition and the Enforcement of Judgments in Civil Matters

The Nordic convention on recognition and the enforcement of judgments in civil matters is structured as a framework convention, which refers most issues, *e.g.* the enumeration of titles of execution included under its scope of claims, instead to be determined through similar enacted laws in the Nordic States,[65] and it continues to have effect in the remaining areas of claims not covered by the Brussels I regulation. The claims based on certain titles of execution, which do not fall under the scope of the Brussels I regulation or by the, in this respect, identical Brussels convention and the Old Lugano convention, but instead under the scope of this Nordic convention are here illustrated by the Swedish and Norwegian enacted laws related to this Nordic convention.

The Swedish legislation stipulates the following titles of execution as recognized and enforceable, a Finish payment order, an injunction to pay issued by a Norwegian prosecutor, which has been accepted by the defendant, a Danish 'out of court settlement' according to specific provisions in Danish legislation if the settlement has been agreed upon and is enforceable in Denmark and the debtor was domiciled there when it was entered into, promissory notes, which according to Danish or Norwegian laws entitle to enforcement without court proceedings if the promissory notes were signed by the debtor in Denmark or Norway if he was then domiciled there, and a decision of a Finish enforcement authority, by which a buyer or seller has been imposed a payment liability, in connection with the recapture of goods purchased by instalments if the person liable for payment at the time for the recapture was domiciled in Finland.[66]

62. *See* Art. 2 of the European Small Claims Procedure compared to Art. 2 of the European Enforcement Order for uncontested claims.
63. *See* Art. 2, 1.
64. *See* Art. 2, 2, f-h.
65. *See* Art. 1 compared to Art. 2, para. 2.
66. *See* 2§, 2-3, 3§ and 5§, 2-5 of the Swedish enacted Act, published in Lag (1977:595) om erkännande och verkställighet av nordiska domar på privaträttens område (Act on the recognition and the enforcement of Nordic judgments in civil matters). *Also see* Arnt Nielsen,

Titles of execution, which do not fall under the scope of the Old Lugano convention, but instead under the scope of the Norwegian enacted legislation, related to this Nordic convention, and which are recognized and enforceable, in addition to those already referred to in the Swedish corresponding Act, are decisions by a Swedish enforcement authority in a matter of an injunction to pay, which oblige anyone to pay an amount of money or decisions by a Swedish enforcement authority in a matter of ordinary (enforcement) assistance.[67] The Finish and Danish laws related to this Nordic convention are similar to the corresponding Norwegian and Swedish laws.[68]

5.2.1.2.2 New York Convention on Foreign Arbitral Awards

The New York convention on foreign arbitral awards covers claims derived from such awards made in the territory of a State other than the State where the recognition and enforcement of such awards are sought and awards made by arbitrators appointed for each case, but also those made by permanent arbitral bodies to which the parties have submitted.[69]

5.2.2 Tax Claims

5.2.2.1 Recovery Directive

Under the scope of claims of the Recovery directive fall some public claims, the most important of them being tax claims. The scope of tax claims under the

International privat- og procesret, pp. 338-339, Berglund, Svensk internationell exekutions- och obeståndsrätt, pp. 190-191, and Pålsson, Brysselkonventionen, Luganokonventionen och Bryssel I-förordningen, p. 68.

67. *See* 2§ , a-c and 4§ , a-d of the Norwegian enacted Act, published in Lov om anerkjennelse og fullbyrding av nordiska dommer på privatrettens område av den 10 juni 1977 (Act on the recognition and the enforcement of Nordic judgments in civil matters). A Swedish certificate, according to 2§ , c of the Norwegian Act, which is required in Norway for the recognition of the Swedish decision in a matter of an injunction to pay (4§ , d of the Norwegian Act) is issued by the Swedish enforcement authority according to § 6 of a Swedish government decree, published in Förordning (1977:1005) om nordisk verkställighet på privaträttens område (government decree on the Nordic enforcement in civil matters). The certificate is issued on the basis of the authority's decision, on the application of a creditor for an injunction to pay related to uncontested claims by the debtor, in a non-contradictory proceeding according to the Swedish Act, published in Lag (1990:746) om betalningsföreläggande och handräckning (Act on the injunction to pay and assistance).
68. *See* 7§ of the Finish Lag om erkännande och verkställighet av nordiska domar angående privaträttsligt anspråk 21.7 1977/588 (Act on the recognition and the enforcement of Nordic judgments in civil matters) and § 2 of the Danish Lovbekendtgørelse 1986-09-15 nr. 635 om anerkendelse og fuldbyrdelse af nordiske afgørelser om privatretlige krav og om ændring af retsplejeloven, som ændret ved L 1995-03-29 nr. 209 og L 1995-06-14 nr. 389 (Act including the recognition and the enforcement of Nordic judgments in civil matters).
69. *See* Art. I, 1-2 of the Convention.

Recovery directive includes: VAT, certain excise duties on manufactured tobacco, alcohol and alcoholic beverages and mineral oils, taxes on income and capital, and taxes on insurance premiums.[70] In a ruling in the case of *Banca popolare di Cremona v. Italy* the ECJ has stated four essential features of VAT in relation to the common system of VAT.[71] The Recovery directive refers the definitions of taxes on income and capital to such taxes as each Member State has enumerated in another separate directive.[72] In a ruling in the case of *Halliburton Services BV v. Staatssecretaris van Financiën* the ECJ has considered taxes on real estate transfers also to fall within the scope of that other separate directive, to which reference is made by the Recovery directive.[73] The Recovery directive defines taxes on insurance premiums by direct enumeration with referral to such taxes in all Member States, except in Sweden.[74] Tax claims relating to identical, similar or analogues taxes, which supplement or replace the taxes on insurance premiums, also fall under the scope of the Recovery directive.[75]

In two rulings in the cases *Commission v. France* the ECJ has concluded that claims of a taxation nature do not fall under the Old social security regulation.[76]

---

70. *See* Art. 2, e-h.
71. The ECJ decided in *Banca popolare di Cremona v. Italy* of 3 Oct. 2006 that the levy of an Italian regional tax on productive activities, imposta regionale sulle attività produttive, 'IRAP', was not subject to the prohibition in the Sixth VAT-directive for Member States to impose other turnover taxes than VAT. The ECJ concluded that the VAT has the following four essential features: '... the principle of the common system of VAT involves the application to goods and services, up to and including the retail trade stage, of a general tax on consumption exactly proportional to the price of the goods and services, whatever the number of transactions which take place in the production and distribution process before the stage at which tax is charged.... VAT is chargeable on each transaction only after deduction of the amount of VAT borne directly by the costs of the various price components.... taxable persons are authorised to deduct from the VAT for which they are liable the VAT which the goods or services have already borne and that the tax is charged, at each stage, only on the added value and is finally borne by the ultimate consumer', *see* paras 21-22 of the ruling. The ECJ further concluded that, because the Italian IRAP lacked two of these features, and therefore was different from the VAT, it was not qualified as a turnover tax, which was prohibited according to Art. 33, 1 of the Sixth VAT-directive, *see* paras 27 and 38-39 of the ruling.
72. *See* Art. 3 of the Recovery directive compared to Art. 1, 3 of the Council directive 77/799/EEC of 19 Dec. 1977 concerning mutual assistance by the competent authorities of the Member States in the field of direct taxation, with amendments.
73. *See* the decision of the ECJ of 12 Apr. 1994 in *Halliburton Services BV v. Staatssecretaris van Financiën*, where taxes on real estate transfers were considered to fall within the scope of Council Directive 77/799, to which reference is made to by the Recovery directive.
74. *See* Art. 3.
75. *See* end of Art. 3.
76. The ECJ has in one ruling on the 15 Feb. 2001 in *Commission v. France*, made clear that France has not fulfilled its obligations under this regulation, by applying the social debt repayment contribution to the employment income and substitute income of employed and self-employed persons resident in France but working in another Member State who, by virtue of the Old social security regulation, are not subject to French social security legislation. The ECJ has in another ruling on the same day in *Commission v. France*, also made clear that France has not fulfilled its obligations under this regulation, by applying the general social contribution to the employment income and substitute income of employed and self-employed persons resident in France but

Such claims could therefore not be subject to collection under this regulation,[77] but may instead be subject to recovery under the Recovery directive to the extent they fall under the scope of the directive. In addition to the tax claims, the Recovery directive also applies to refunds, interventions and other measures forming part of the system of total or partial financing of the European Agricultural Guidance and Guarantee Fund, including sums to be collected in connection with these actions, levies and other duties provided for under the common organization of the market for the sugar sector, import duties and export duties.[78]

It may be discussed if some additional taxes, or even all remaining taxes, classified as taxes under the laws in all Member States, including such social security contributions or charges as are to be classified as of a taxation nature, should be included, or not, under the scope of the Recovery directive. The idea of including all taxes may, at first sight, seems to be a too radical and unrealistic approach to follow, because some national taxes, which exist in one Member State, do not necessarily exist in another Member State. This complexity is also added to by national law reforms in all Member States, which repeatedly change the scenario. The present structure of the scope of tax claims in the Recovery directive has mainly, but not entirely, been based on a concept of mutuality expressed through an enumeration of taxes that exist in all Member States. An exception are taxes on insurance premiums, which are not enumerated concerning Sweden,[79] but despite that, are recoverable, at the request of another Member State, in Sweden.

It may, however, be possible to achieve a future development in this field, even without first having to establish that any possible new taxes that may be added under the scope of claims of the Recovery directive should have an identical counterpart in each Member State. This would, based on a knowledge of the general construction of national tax systems and their differences, however, first require both an increased level of understanding and mutual trust between Member States, meaning a political acceptance of national differences, and as a consequence the political acceptance of a more advanced application of the EC principle of mutuality, than presently, in this area.

A possible development of an implementation of such a more advanced concept of mutuality in the Recovery directive would also correspond to the general trend of reform efforts to further develop mutuality in EC in the civil law area and in the criminal law area.[80] If this would be politically acceptable, it would require Member States to cooperate, in order to meet the general interest of Member States

who, by virtue of the Old social security regulation, are not subject to French social security legislation. This means that these French claims do not fall under the scope of claims in the Old social security regulation. Art. 84 of the New social security regulation also allows for the cross-border collection of social security contributions.

77. *See* Art. 92 of the Old social security regulation.
78. *See* Art. 2, a-d. Included under these provisions are *e.g.* some claims related to the agricultural sector and import and export duties. *Also see* Leroy, La Transparence patrimoniale, p. 145, regarding such claims.
79. *See* Art. 3.
80. *See* 1.1.1.1.6 about the principle of mutuality in EC law.

of efficiency, in the context of cross-border recovery of taxes, irrespective of their national classifications of origin. It would, as a consequence, lead to that such a possibly reformed future scope of tax claims in the Recovery directive would also include *e.g.* gift and inheritance taxes, motor-vehicle taxes, non-harmonized excise duties, and social security charges, the latter, however, only to the extent they should qualify into the category of taxes.[81] If all taxes would be included it would mean that the provisions of the Recovery directive, which directly, or by indirect reference, enumerate specific taxes, would not be needed. It would also, as a consequence, mean that the provision in the Recovery directive, which refers to tax claims relating to identical, similar or analogues taxes, which supplement or replace the taxes on insurance premiums, would become unnecessary.[82]

An argument against the idea of including all taxes is, however, that it would make the future scope of claims too unpredictable. Another argument against this idea is that a new tax in a Member State, which does not fall under the present scope, may be imposed at such an extraordinary level as comes close to, or risks to, equal what would be considered as a measure of confiscation rather than taxation in other Member States, even if the function of the entire tax system of this Member State is taken into consideration.

It may, however, be that these arguments may be balanced off through alternative solutions. One solution may be to introduce a provision which puts an all-over maximum ceiling for what total level of taxation in a Member State should be acceptable for recovery purposes under the Recovery directive. This is of course subject to that it is now, and will be in future, possible to make a relevant comparison between the Member States in relation to their total levels of taxation, and may therefore be too complex to handle. Another solution may be the introduction of a provision of a ground of refusal of mutual assistance if the requested Member State considers the taxation of the applicant Member State to be contrary to generally acceptable taxation principles. Yet another solution may be to continue to add only such additional taxes that have counterparts in all Member States. It is not possible to suggest an extension of the scope of tax claims and other public claims to such other claims which do not fall under the Recovery directive under the present legal objective of mutuality of this directive, even if it may be argued that it would be consistent with the objective of efficiency of the same directive.

Interest, administrative penalties and fines and costs incidental to the tax claims also fall under the scope of claims of the Recovery directive, with the exclusion of any sanction of a criminal nature as determined by the laws of the requested State.[83]

A requested Member State shall also, after the reception of a request for the recovery of a claim from another Member State, according to the directive, treat the calculation of interest on that claim as a claim of the requested Member State.[84]

---

81. Compare 5.2.2.1 about the conclusions in relation to the rulings in the cases *Commission v. France* of the ECJ related to the Old social security regulation.
82. *See* end of Art. 3.
83. *See* Art. 2, i.
84. *See* Art. 9, 2 compared to Art. 6, 2.

If no such interest in a cross-border situation is charged, or charged at less advantageous conditions than in an internal situation for a claim of the requested Member State, this may constitute a violation of the EC principle of non-discrimination in the EC Treaty.[85] Consequently, all such ancillary claims and sanctions related to the scope of claims falling under Article 2, a-h of the Recovery directive are included under this provision. The part of Article 2, i, which stipulates the exclusion of any sanction of a criminal nature, refers the determination of such a sanction decided in the applicant State to the requested State. The European Convention on Human Rights, and consequently also the rulings of the ECHR, are, according to the ECJ, part of EC law.[86] Even if taxation proceedings do not fall within the scope of civil rights and obligations of this European convention, the ECHR has, nevertheless, in several rulings applied Article 6 of this European convention on national tax penalties.[87]

The application of the provision in the Recovery directive about the exclusion of any sanction of a criminal nature means that a requested Member State first, for the purpose of determining if the decision of the sanction from the applicant Member State is enforceable or not, will have to reclassify this title of execution from that national legal system into its own legal system. This demands a solid knowledge about the content of the legal systems of other Member States. Even if the requested Member States would acquire such qualified knowledge in comparative law, and even if it may be argued that there exist similar categories of titles of execution in the requested Member States, the complexity of this problem remains because no national systems are totally identical. This means that the present wordings of this provision obviously risk to create a legal uncertainty and do not therefore constitute a satisfactory legal solution on which to base a decision on the determination of the enforceability by a requested Member State.

Some other parts of EC law that treat the determination of the enforceability of a title of execution refer this determination of the enforceability instead to the State of origin of the title of execution, so the Brussels I regulation,[88] and the European Enforcement Order for uncontested claims.[89] In order to avoid the legal uncertainty, which occurs when the requested Member States must reclassify a decision of a sanction from an applicant Member State, it would be better to change these wordings of the determination of the requested State into a determination of the applicant State. A reason for such a change is that it would only involve

85. *See* 1.1.1.1.2 about this principle and the ruling of the ECJ in the case of *Lease Plan Luxembourg SA v. Belgian State*.
86. *See* 1.1.1.1 and 1.4.1.
87. *See* 4.3.2.
88. *See* Art. 38.
89. The European Enforcement Order for uncontested claims requires that such enforcement titles to be certified as a European Enforcement Order in the Member State of origin shall be recognized and enforced in the other Member States without the need for a declaration of enforceability, but subject to that the creditor presents a certificate that his enforcement title has, on his prior application, been certified by the court of origin, as a European Enforcement Order, *see* Arts 3 and 6.

considerations about the determination of the enforceability of a decision of a sanction in relation to the legal system of one State, the applicant State, while the present solution involves more complex considerations in relation to more than one legal system, *i.e.* both the legal systems of the applicant and the requested States. Consequently, such a shift of the principal position in a possibly changed solution would mean that the decisions from the applicant State would instead be used as titles of execution, *i.e.* without any need that a requested Member State, according to its own legal system, has to determine if a decision from another Member State is qualified as being of a criminal nature.

Another reason for such a change is that it would better be able to guarantee legal certainty because it would secure a qualified legal proof of enforceability from the State of origin of the claim and of the title of execution, from the applicant State that is best capable of determining the enforceability of this title, and consequently to guarantee the proof of it as a legal basis for any requests of mutual assistance. Such a solution would therefore be less complicated, following the similar principal solutions established in the Brussels I regulation and in the European Enforcement Order for uncontested claims, and would also lead to a higher degree of legal clarity. Such a possibly changed solution would therefore also better meet the objectives of efficiency and mutuality, in the interest of both the creditor and the debtor, in the Recovery directive. It is therefore here suggested that this solution, as an amendment, should be contemplated to be entered into this directive. It would also be possible to delete the word 'requested' in Article 2, i of the Recovery directive and instead replace it by the word 'applicant'.

It seems logical that tax penalties, which normally are recoverable in the Member States, also may become recoverable in the cross-border context according to the Recovery directive. It has been argued, in order to take account of the legal usage of the ECHR, that the present wordings of Article 2, i of the Recovery directive should be replaced by 'penalties and fines imposed by the administrative authorities', with regards to all claims under the scope of claims of this directive. It would, however, be legally insufficient just to amend the present Article 2, i in order to render coherent the interplay between the present wordings 'with the exclusion of any sanction of a criminal nature' and some rulings from the ECHR, because in the determination of any criminal charge against an individual he should be entitled to a contradictory court proceeding. The reason why it would be insufficient is that it is to generally worded and would therefore risk to be interpreted as presently also in a corresponding way in the future.

A future possible inclusion of tax sanctions of a criminal nature may, however, be achieved just by clarifying the legal position of the European Convention on Human Rights by inserting the following positive wordings into the Recovery directive 'and any sanctions of a criminal nature that have been subject to an effective possibility of appeal to an independent and impartial tribunal' after the word 'authorities'. Any possible solution would have to be based on a political agreement of an application of a more advanced concept of mutuality in the Recovery directive.

5.2.2.2 Conventions

The Council of Europe and OECD convention on mutual administrative assistance in tax matters, the Nordic agreement on assistance in tax matters, and the Benelux convention on the mutual assistance for the recovery of tax claims, impose a wider, non-identical scope of claims, compared to the Recovery directive, as they cover also several additional tax claims and other public claims than the directive.[90] Examples of claims with a wider scope of claims in these multilateral conventions, compared to the Recovery directive, are: gift and inheritance taxes, motor-vehicle taxes, certain excise duties, certain social security charges and other public fees.[91] Tax claims relating to identical, similar or analogous taxes, which supplement or replace the original taxes, also fall under the scope of the Council of Europe and OECD convention on mutual administrative assistance in tax matters and the Nordic agreement on assistance in tax matters.[92]

The bilateral Treaty networks of European States, which relate to the recovery of tax claims in relation to States outside the EU, vary.[93] The extent of tax claims

---

90. *See* Art. 2 of the Council of Europe and OECD convention and annex A to the same Convention and Explanatory report on the Convention on Mutual Administrative Assistance in Tax Matters, pp. 11-13. *Also see* Arts 2 and 20, 1 of the Nordic agreement. Art. 20, 1 of the Nordic agreement refers the definition of taxes and fees according to Art. 2, 1. h) 2-5 of this Agreement to the Implementing agreement to the Nordic agreement on assistance in tax matters. This implementing agreement includes, in para. 3, A and C-D, detailed enumerations from the contracting parties of the agreement of national motor-vehicle taxes, excise duties, social insurance duties and other public fees. *Also see* Art. 2 compared to Exposé des motifs to the Benelux convention. Compare the scope of the two conventions and of the agreement to the scope of the Recovery directive based on Arts 2 and 3 of the directive and on Art. 1, 3 of the Council directive 77/799/EEC of 19 Dec. 1977 concerning mutual assistance by the competent authorities of the Member States in the field of direct taxation, directive as last amended in 1994.
91. *See* Art. 2, 1. b. ii. and iii. A. and D-F of the Council of Europe and OECD convention (certain social security charges, gift and inheritance taxes, motor-vehicle taxes and certain excise duties), and Art. 2, 1. h) 1 of the Nordic agreement on assistance in tax matters, which includes gift and inheritance taxes. Arts 2, 1. h) 2-5 and 20, 1 of the Nordic agreement on assistance in tax matters refer the definition of taxes and fees according to Art. 2, 1. h) 2-5 of this Agreement to the Implementing agreement to the Nordic agreement on assistance in tax matters, which in its para. 3, A and C-D, includes detailed enumerations from the contracting parties of the agreement of national motor-vehicle taxes, excise duties, social insurance duties and other public fees. *Also see* Art. 2 of the Benelux convention compared to Exposé des motifs to this convention ('. . . le recouvrement de toutes les créances fiscales de l'État, donc aussi pour les taxes assimilées au timbre, les droits d'enregistrement et de succession, les droits de douane et accise, etc. . . . '), *e.g.* including the road and game taxes.
92. *See* Art. 2, 4 of the Convention and Explanatory report on the Convention on Mutual Administrative Assistance in Tax Matters, p. 13, and Art. 2, 3 of the Agreement.
93. Belgian conventional practice is treated by Grau Ruiz, pp. 107-108, also in relation to double tax treaties with recovery provisions in relation to States outside of the EU. She further concludes, p. 236, *i.b.* that the global trend is that double taxation conventions are increasingly incorporating a specific clause – or at least some mention in their protocols or in clauses of exchange of information – dealing with the assistance for the recovery of tax claims and that there are now over 200 conventions on income tax, which contain such a clause, she refers, *i.b.*, pp. 290-292 and 295-301, to extracts from some bilateral agreements and conventions, which include

falling under the scope of multilateral or bilateral conventions vary and have often been inspired by the OECD Model Tax Convention on Income and on Capital.[94] A new article on the assistance in the collection of taxes was included in the OECD Model Tax Convention on Income and on Capital in 2002,[95] which indicates that the OECD Member countries are likely to take this into consideration in present and future bilateral negotiations between themselves. Even if several OECD Member countries have already included collection clauses in one or more bilateral conventions with other OECD Member States,[96] this may lead to a stronger development trend towards that an increasing number of such negotiated treaties will include articles on the assistance in the collection of taxes based on the concept provided in the OECD Model Tax Convention on Income and on Capital.

Another option for OECD Member countries, which desire to further develop the possibilities of mutual tax recovery, without the exclusion of parallel bilateral efforts, on a multilateral basis is, to become parties to the Council of Europe and OECD convention on mutual administrative assistance in tax matters, which provides a more detailed legal framework than the OECD Model Tax Convention on Income and on Capital.

---

collection/recovery clauses, between some European States and States outside the EU (Philippines-Romania, Israel-Norway, France-Norway, Norway-Senegal, Norway-Venezuela, the Netherlands-Ukraine and France-Algeria). Sweden has concluded three double tax treaties with recovery provisions in relation to States outside the EU. These States are India, Art. 28 of the convention between the government of the kingdom of Sweden and the government of the republic of India for the avoidance of double taxation and the prevention of fiscal evasion with respect to taxes on income and on capital from 1997, Japan, Art. 25A of the convention between Sweden and Japan for the avoidance of double taxation and the prevention of fiscal evasion with respect to taxes on income from 1983, as amended in 1999, and the United States of America, Art. 27 of the convention between the government of Sweden and the government of the United States of America for the avoidance of double taxation and the prevention of fiscal evasion with respect to taxes on income from 1994. In addition the multilateral Nordic agreement on assistance in tax matters still applies between Sweden and other Nordic non-EC States and territories, Greenland, the Faeroe Islands, Iceland and Norway, *see* 3.2.3 about the territorial scope of the agreement. *Also see* Berglund, Svensk internationell exekutions- och obeståndsrätt, pp. 95-110 and 112-113, about some overviews of Tax treaties, including recovery provisions, between Sweden and the following States: United States of America, Belgium, Estonia, France, Latvia, Lithuania, Luxemburg, the Netherlands and Germany, and, pp. 111, 114-116, about an overview of the Nordic agreement on assistance in tax matters, an overview of the Council of Europe and OECD convention on mutual administrative assistance in tax matters and an overview of the Recovery directive.

94. *See* Art. 2 of the Model Tax Convention on Income and on Capital and commentary to this article, *i.b.*, pp. 69-71.
95. *See* Art. 27 in the Model Tax Convention on Income and on Capital, pp. 42-43, and commentary to this article, *i.b.*, pp. 295-303, and the OECD Manual on the Implementation of Assistance in Tax collection, Art. 27 and Commentary of the OECD Model Tax Convention on Income and on Capital. *Also see* Ismer and Sailer, pp. 622-632, Jirousek, pp. 215-224, Garcia Prats, pp. 58-59, 64-65, 68-70, 72-74 and 76-77, and Grau Ruiz, pp. 226-229.
96. At least 19 OECD Member States have already included a more global or limited collection clause in one or more bilateral conventions with other OECD Member States, *see* Grau Ruiz, pp. 239-240.

Some bilateral and multilateral conventions related to the tax recovery area, *e.g.* the Tax treaty between Sweden and Germany,[97] the Tax treaties between Sweden and the Baltic States,[98] and the Implementing agreement to the Nordic agreement on assistance in tax matters,[99] that may alternatively be applied instead of the Recovery directive to the extent these conventions provide a greater measure of assistance as compared to the directive,[100] include possibilities for the recovery of different sanctions, including some which may be classified as being of a criminal nature. Another convention, which clearly excludes the possibility of recovery of sanctions of such nature, is the Benelux convention on the mutual assistance for the recovery of tax claims.[101]

5.3 RELATIONSHIP BETWEEN EC LAW AND CONVENTIONS

5.3.1 Relationship between Different Parts of EC Law

The scope of the Brussels I regulation does not coincide with that of the Recovery directive,[102] which means that no relationship exists between them. Neither do their scopes coincide with those of the Insolvency regulation and the Nordic bankruptcy convention.[103] The Insolvency regulation interacts, however, in the

97. *See* the German version, Anlage, Abschnitt IV, g) to the Abkommen zwischen dem Königreich Schweden und der Bundesrepublik Deutschland zur Vermeidung der Doppelbesteuerung bei den Steuern vom Einkommen und vom Vermögen sowie bei den Erbschaft- und Schenkungsteuern und zur Leistung gegenseitigen Beistand bei den Steuern from 1992, which reads: 'die Steuerzuschläge, Verspätungszuschläge, Säumniszuschläge, Zinsen und Kosten'.
98. *See* Art. 27, 8 of the convention between the Kingdom of Sweden and the Republic of Estonia for the avoidance of double taxation and the prevention of fiscal evasion with respect to taxes on income and on capital from 1993, Art. 27, 8 of the convention between the Kingdom of Sweden and the Republic of Latvia for the avoidance of double taxation and the prevention of fiscal evasion with respect to taxes on income and on capital from 1993, Art. 27, 8 of the convention between the Kingdom of Sweden and the Republic of Lithuania for the avoidance of double taxation and the prevention of fiscal evasion with respect to taxes on income and on capital from 1993, all of them which explicitly mention tax penalties.
99. *See* para. 2, a of the Implementing agreement to the Nordic agreement on assistance in tax matters.
100. *See* Art. 23.
101. *See* Art. 2, § 1, which reads: 'La présente Convention s'applique aux impôts, droits et taxes perçus par l'État à son profit ou au profit des provinces et des communes, en principal, accroissements et additionnels, ainsi qu'aux amendes n'ayant pas un caractère pénal, aux intérêts et aux frais y relatifs.'
102. *See* Art. 1 of the Brussels I regulation and in particular its section 1, which explicitly excludes revenue matters compared to Art. 2, e-h of the Recovery directive. For further comments on the scope of contractual claims and of tax claims, *see* 5.2.1, respectively 5.2.2.
103. *See* Art. 1, 2, b of the Brussels I regulation, which explicitly excludes bankruptcy and certain other insolvency proceedings from its scope of application compared to Arts 1 and 2, a and b of the Insolvency regulation, which treat collective insolvency proceedings and compared to

insolvency proceedings, with the provisions of provisional, including protective, measures, recognition and enforcement of the Brussels I regulation.[104] The European Enforcement Order for uncontested claims does not affect the possibility of seeking recognition and enforcement in accordance with the Brussels I regulation of a judgment, a court settlement or an authentic instrument of an uncontested claim,[105] or the application of the Council regulation 1348/2000/EC of 29 May 2000 on the service in the Member States of judicial and extrajudicial documents in civil or commercial matters (Old service of judicial documents' regulation).[106]

The European Order for payment procedure refers to the Brussels I regulation as to the determination of the domicile of a party in a cross-border case and issues of jurisdiction.[107] The European Order for payment procedure does not affect the application of the Regulation (EC) No. 1393/2007 of the European Parliament and of the Council of 13 November 2007 on the service in the Member States of judicial and extrajudicial documents in civil or commercial matters (service of documents), (New service of legal documents' regulation).[108] The European Small Claims Procedure is available to litigants as an alternative to the procedures existing under the laws of the Member States.[109] Hence, this regulation leaves an option to a party to decide if he would like to make use of it or some other options instead, such as the ordinary national procedure in combination with the Brussels I regulation. The European Small Claims Procedure refers the determination of the domicile of a party in a cross-border case to the Brussels I regulation.[110] The European Small Claims Procedure refers to an application of the Council regulation 1348/2000/EC of 29 May 2000 on the service in the Member States

---

Arts 1 and 10 of the Nordic bankruptcy convention, which treat bankruptcy and a composition in bankruptcy.

104. *See* Art. 25 of the Insolvency regulation, which refers to Arts 31-51 of the Brussels Convention regarding provisional, including protective, measures, the recognition and enforcement of judgments concerning the opening of proceedings, the course and closure of insolvency proceedings and compositions approved by that court, judgments derived directly from the insolvency proceedings and which are closely linked with them, even if they are handed down by another court. This referral to the Brussels Convention, which has been replaced by the Brussels I regulation, contains, however, an important exception: the grounds for rejecting the exequatur or registration, *see* Art. 25, 1. These grounds are not taken from the Brussels Convention, but are established by the Insolvency regulation itself. *Also see* The European Insolvency Regulation: Law and Practice, p. 211, which explains that from the genesis of the Insolvency regulation, it is clear that the desire was to exclude the regime of grounds for non-recognition of the Brussels Convention and subject rejection solely to the regime of the Insolvency regulation itself, which explains why Art. 25, 1 of the Insolvency regulation refers to Arts 31-51 of the Brussels Convention, but excludes Art. 34, 2, which contained the grounds for rejection provided for in Arts 27 and 28 of the Convention itself.
105. *See* Art. 27.
106. *See* Art. 28.
107. *See* Art. 3, 2 (domicile) and Art. 6 (jurisdiction).
108. *See* Art. 27.
109. *See* Art. 1.
110. *See* Art. 3, 2.

of judicial and extrajudicial documents in civil or commercial matters,[111] when the service of documents by postal service attested by an acknowledgement of receipt, including the date of receipt, is not possible.[112]

5.3.1.1 Contractual Claims

5.3.1.1.1 Brussels I Regulation

The relationship between the Brussels I regulation and multilateral and bilateral conventions is dealt by with in a clear and detailed way, without leaving any options, how to treat the different aspects on the relationship between the regulation and conventions. The Brussels I regulation replaces, as between all Member States of the EU, with the exclusion of Denmark,[113] with some exceptions, a lot of enumerated multilateral and bilateral conventions[114] to the extent it coincides with them in terms of date of application and the scope of claims.[115] The Brussels convention has entered into force in relation between Denmark and all other Member States of the EU through the parallel agreement to the Brussels I regulation between the EC and Denmark of 19 October 2005.[116] The Brussels I regulation does not prejudice the application of provisions governing the enforcement of judgments in specific matters, which are contained in community instruments or in national legislation harmonized pursuant to such instruments[117] and does not affect conventions to which Member States are parties and which in relation to particular matters, govern the enforcement of judgments.[118] The Brussels I regulation replaces the Brussels convention, except as regards the territories of these States, which fall under the territorial scope of that convention and which are excluded from this regulation pursuant to Article 299 of the EC Treaty.[119]

111. The New service of legal documents' regulation, which applies from 13 Nov. 2008, with an exception, replaces the Old service of legal documents' regulation. The content of the New service of legal documents' regulation is similar to that of the Old service of legal documents' regulation. *See* 5.3.1.3 for further information about the New service of legal documents' regulation.
112. *See* Art. 13, 2.
113. *See* Preamble (21).
114. *See* Art. 69.
115. *See* 5.2.1.1.1 about the scope of claims in the Brussels I regulation compared to 5.2.1.2.1 about the scope of claims in the Nordic convention on recognition and the enforcement of judgments in civil matters and in the New York convention on foreign arbitral awards.
116. *See* Art. 12 about the entry into force of the Agreement compared to Information concerning the date of entry into force of the Agreement between the EC and the Kingdom of Denmark on jurisdiction and the recognition and enforcement of judgments in civil and commercial matters, OJ 2007 L 94.
117. *See* Art. 67 of the Regulation, which corresponds to Art. 57, 1 of the Brussels convention. *Also see* Evrigenis/Kerameus report, point 101, on this article of the Brussels convention.
118. *See* Art. 71, 1. An example is the International convention relating to the arrest of seagoing ships of 10 May 1952. *Also see*, for some other examples, Pålsson, Brysselkonventionen, Luganokonventionen och Bryssel I-förordningen, pp. 70-75.
119. *See* Preamble (23) and Art. 68, 1. *Also see* 5.1.1 compared to 5.1.2 for further details on the territorial scope of the Brussels I regulation respectively the Brussels convention.

Provisions of exception in the Brussels I regulation are the transitional provisions[120] and the provisions, which allow that the enumerated instruments shall continue to have effect in relation to matters to which the regulation does not apply.[121] In the case of *Bavaria Fluggesellschaft Schwabe & Co. Kg and Germanair Bedarfsluftfahrt GmbH & Co. Kg v. Eurocontrol* the ECJ ruled that the provision in the Brussels convention, which allows such a continuancy in relation to matters to which the convention does not apply, and which is similar to the Brussels I regulation,[122] is applicable in relation to the German-Belgian convention.[123] The main transitional rule of the Brussels I regulation stipulates that it shall apply only to legal proceedings instituted and to documents formally drawn up or registered as authentic instruments after its entry into force.[124] It provides, however, an important exception to the main transitional rule of the regulation by giving it retrospective effect, related to two situations, when the proceedings in the Member State of origin were instituted before the entry into force of the regulation. These two exceptional situations occur if the proceedings in the Member State were instituted after the entry into force of the Brussels convention or the Old Lugano convention both in the Member State of origin and in the Member State addressed, and in all other cases, if jurisdiction was founded upon rules accorded with those provided for either in the regulation or in a convention concluded between the Member State of origin and the Member State addressed, which was in force when the proceedings were instituted.[125] Besides the remaining conventional network, which is still in force, after the entry into force of the Brussels I regulation, there also exists a transnational judicial cooperation, based on Common Law, for the enforcement of a foreign judgment in the United Kingdom in relation to the Commonwealth countries and some other States and territories.[126]

5.3.1.1.2 Conventions

The Old Lugano convention still applies between on the one hand Iceland, Norway and Switzerland and on the other hand these Member States of the EU that are

---

120. *See* Art. 69 compared to Art. 66, 2.
121. *See* Art. 69 compared to Art. 70. *See*, about examples of remaining areas of scope of claims in the Nordic convention on recognition and the enforcement of judgments in civil matters, 5.2.1.2.1.
122. *See* Arts 55 and 56 of the Convention compared to Arts 69 and 70 of the Regulation.
123. *See* the decision of the ECJ in *Bavaria Fluggesellschaft Schwabe & Co. Kg and Germanair Bedarfsluftfahrt GmbH & Co. Kg v. Eurocontrol* of 14 Jul. 1977, which treats Art. 56 of the Brussels convention. The ECJ ruled that the Brussels convention does not prevent a bilateral agreement such as the German-Belgian convention, which is the fifth to be listed in Art. 55, from continuing to have effect in relation to judgments which do not fall under the second paragraph of Art. 1 of the Brussels convention, but to which nevertheless that convention does not apply.
124. *See* Art. 66, 1.
125. *See* Art. 66, 2.
126. *See* 2.5.

parties to the convention.[127] The Nordic convention on recognition and the enforcement of judgments in civil matters, which is structured as a framework convention, and also applies to the Faeroe Islands,[128] refers most issues, *e.g.* the enumeration of titles of execution included under its scope of claims, to be determined instead through similar enacted laws in the Nordic States[129] continues to have effect in the remaining areas of scope of claims not falling under the Brussels I regulation.[130] This Nordic convention does not affect any commitment, which the contracting States have entered into through valid agreements, or may enter into in specific areas.[131]

The scope of claims under the Brussels I regulation excludes arbitration, which means that this regulation and the New York convention on foreign arbitral awards do not coincide.[132] This convention stipulates that its provisions shall not affect the validity of multilateral or bilateral agreements concerning the recognition and enforcement of arbitral awards entered into by the contracting States. Also, the convention stipulates that the Geneva Protocol on Arbitration Clauses of 1923 and the Geneva Convention on the Execution of Foreign Arbitral Awards of 1927 shall cease to have effect between the contracting States on their becoming bound and to the extent that they become bound by the New York convention and that a contracting State shall not be entitled to avail itself of the convention against other contracting States except to the extent that it is itself bound to apply.[133] Hence, the Geneva Protocol and the Geneva Convention still apply between a State, which is bound only by them, and another State, which is bound by both the Geneva Protocol, the Geneva Convention and the New York convention.[134]

5.3.1.2 Tax Claims

5.3.1.2.1 Recovery Directive

The relationship between the Recovery directive and multilateral and bilateral conventions is dealt with both in the Preamble[135] and in Article 23 of the Recovery directive. The relevant part of the Preamble reads:

> This directive should not curtail mutual assistance between particular Member States under bilateral or multilateral agreements or arrangements.

This provision in the Preamble of the Recovery directive does not make any distinction on whether or not such mutual assistance should provide for a minor

127. *See* annex 5.
128. *See* 5.1.2.
129. *See* Art. 1 compared to Art. 2, para. 2.
130. *See* 5.2.1.1.1.
131. *See* Art. 2, para. 2.
132. *See* Art. 1, 2, d of the Regulation compared to Art. I of the Convention.
133. *See* Arts VII and XIV.
134. *See* Berglund, Svensk internationell exekutions- och obeståndsrätt, p. 210.
135. *See* Preamble (15) of the directive.

or a greater measure of mutual assistance. This means that the Recovery directive does not curtail a cooperation on mutual assistance even on a level of minor measure of assistance between particular Member States of the EU under bilateral or multilateral agreements than compared to the directive. The Recovery directive therefore leaves an option for Member States to continue to apply a less far-reaching cooperation under such agreements instead of the directive. It is, however, not likely that an applicant Member State, even if it has the right under the Recovery directive, would continue to apply less advantageous conventions as compared to the directive. Member States have also an option to apply any agreements, or arrangements, which include a greater measure of mutual assistance than the Recovery directive, instead of this directive. No distinction is made in this context in relation to conventions concluded between the Member States and conventions between a Member State and a State outside of the EU. This is evident from Article 23 of the Recovery directive, which states:

> This directive shall not prevent a greater measure of mutual assistance being afforded either now or in the future by particular Member States under any agreements or arrangements, including those for the notification of legal or extra-legal acts.

Some examples when multilateral and bilateral conventions provide a greater measure of mutual assistance compared to the provisions of the Recovery directive are given here. The most important one is when the scope of tax claims in conventions is wider than in the Recovery directive. This is the case with both the Council of Europe and OECD convention on mutual administrative assistance in tax matters and of the Nordic agreement on assistance in tax matters, which also cover some other taxes and public claims.[136] Other practically important examples are debt thresholds, provisions which limit the possibilities of cross-border recovery of tax claims by stipulating that no request for mutual assistance may be made if the total amount of the claim is less than that of a specific amount, *i.e.* the claim has to exceed such an amount to be recovered under the relevant convention.

There exist lower debt thresholds in conventions, compared to the debt threshold of EUR 1 500 of the Implementing recovery directive.[137] One example is given by the Implementing agreement to the Nordic agreement on assistance in tax matters of approximately EUR 270.[138] Other examples are contained in seven Tax treaties concluded between Sweden and other Member States of the EU,[139] where lower debt thresholds apply, in the interval of approximately EUR 765-1 100.

136. *See* 5.2.2.2 for further details on such claims.
137. *See* Art. 25, 2.
138. *See* para. 6 of the Implementing agreement to the Nordic agreement on assistance in tax matters. This provision stipulates a debt threshold, expressed in all the currencies of the respective Nordic States, which corresponds to an amount of 2 500 Swedish crowns (SEK). This equals, at an exchange rate of SEK 9, 15 for EUR 1, to approximately EUR 270.
139. *See* the bilateral treaties concluded between Sweden and: Belgium, Estonia, Germany, France, the Netherlands, Latvia and Lithuania.

At least three other examples of a greater measure of mutual assistance exist in the Nordic agreement on assistance in tax matters than compared to the provisions of the Recovery directive and relate to a wider territorial scope, Greenland and the Faeroe Islands, which, however, is of less importance,[140] the recovery of a contested claim,[141] and the explicit possibility in a matter of mutual recovery to initiate a bankruptcy proceeding.[142] The Council of Europe and OECD convention on mutual administrative assistance in tax matters also provides a greater measure of mutual assistance through a wider territorial scope than the provisions of the Recovery directive in relation to Greenland.[143]

When the measure of mutual assistance of the Recovery directive and the Implementing recovery directive is greater than compared to the measure of mutual assistance in conventions the directives may apply. Some situations, when the provisions of the Recovery directive and the Implementing recovery directive provide a greater measure of mutual assistance compared to conventions, are presented here. One is that the co-debtor liability of the Implementing recovery directive[144] shall apply, where there is no such liability in the Nordic agreement on assistance in tax matters, regarding matters of mutual assistance for the recovery of such tax claims between these Nordic States, which are members of the EU, *i.e.* between Denmark, Finland and Sweden. Other provisions in the Recovery directive and the Implementing recovery directive, which may provide a greater measure of mutual assistance compared to the Council of Europe and OECD convention on mutual administrative assistance in tax matters and the Nordic agreement on assistance in tax matters, are those on priority rights,[145] depending on the national positions, and exchange of information.[146]

The Recovery directive and the Implementing recovery directive shall apply between the Member States, when they have not made use of the options in the

140. Both Greenland and the Faeroe Islands are parties to the agreement, *see* the Preamble of the agreement. The territorial scope is not dealt with in the Recovery directive. The EC Treaty shall, however, according to Art. 299, 3, para. 1 compared to annex II to the Treaty and to Art. 299, 6 a of the Treaty, not apply to Greenland and the Faeroe Islands. Hence, an application of the directive in relation to Greenland and the Faeroe Islands is excluded. *See* for further comments on the territorial scopes 5.1.1 and 5.1.3.
141. *See* Art. 12, 2 b of the Directive compared to Art. 14, 1 of the Agreement.
142. *See* Art. 16, 2 of the Agreement, which has no explicit counterpart in the Directive, even if an application for bankruptcy in some Member States may be requested under Art. 6 of the Directive, *see* 6.2.2.1.1.1.
143. Greenland is a party to the Convention, *see* annex 6. The territorial scope is not dealt with in the Directive. The EC Treaty shall, according to Art. 299, 3, para. 1 compared to annex II to the Treaty, not apply to Greenland. This means that an application of the Directive in relation to Greenland is excluded. *See* 5.1.1 compared to 5.1.3 for further comments on the territorial scope.
144. *See* Art. 13 compared to Art. 4, 2.
145. *See* Art. 10 of the Recovery directive compared to Art. 15 of the Convention and Art. 16, 1 of the Agreement.
146. *See* Arts 4 and 16 of the Recovery directive compared to Arts 3-8 of the Implementing recovery directive and compared to Arts 4-5, 10, 18, 1 c, 20, 3, 21, 2 c and d and 22 of the Convention and Art. 1 b and compared to Art. 4, 1, 10 and 13, 3 of the Agreement.

Preamble and in Article 23 of the Recovery directive by making referral in applications for mutual assistance to conventions. In such situations the directives represent EC law, which takes priority in relation to conventions. This principle is based on judgments of the ECJ.[147] Consequently, Member States shall not be at liberty, in a specific matter of mutual assistance, to simultaneously apply various more advantageous provisions from both the Recovery directive, the Implementing recovery directive and from conventions.

Each instrument is self-contained; having its own characteristics, aims, methods of interpretation and its provisions may be incompatible with other instruments.[148] The Recovery directive also indicates in Article 23, by the use of its wordings 'under any agreements or arrangements' that in such situations the entire agreement or arrangement shall apply in a specific matter of mutual assistance, *i.e.* all their provisions. Hence, Member States, when they have a choice of option in a specific matter of mutual assistance, have to apply either the entire Recovery directive and the thereto related entire Implementing recovery directive or the entire convention.

It has been argued that the legal base of the EU should be extended in the Recovery directive to whenever recovery assistance is possible under the directive and that the Member States shall then not apply conventions to their mutual assistance requests. It has, however, also been argued, in that context, that the Member States can agree bilaterally, or multilaterally, to extend their mutual recovery assistance to other taxes, or tax-related claims, than those falling within the scope of the directive. However, in that case this extended mutuality recovery assistance shall also be governed by the conditions and modalities of the Recovery directive and of the Implementing recovery directive.

Such a possible extension may have the advantage of making more evident and clear what other taxes and tax-related claims do not fall under the scope of the Recovery directive, but instead under the scope of conventions. This information may also be of interest in a possible future reform discussion about the extension of the scope of claims of the directive. Another advantage of such a possible extension would be that the Member States maintain their freedom to further develop their cooperation of mutual assistance for the recovery of tax claims to levels exceeding that of the Recovery directive. A possible disadvantage would, however, be the principal shift of the legal base, from the present flexible solution of relatively more independency for the development of bilateral, or multilateral, agreements between the Member States, to only the principal supremacy of EC law, the Recovery directive. This is on the other hand counter-balanced by a possible option for Member States to maintain and further develop their cooperation to levels exceeding that of the Recovery directive.

147. *See* Bernitz, Sverige och Europarätten, pp. 47-48 and 125-127, and Introduction to the Law of the European Communities, pp. 551-573.

148. Compare in a corresponding situation similar reasons related to the Council of Europe and OECD convention on mutual administrative assistance in tax matters, Explanatory report on the Convention on Mutual Administrative Assistance in Tax Matters, p. 69.

The Recovery directive lacks such transitional provisions as correspond to those in the Council of Europe and OECD convention on mutual administrative assistance in tax matters, which entitles a State to declare that it reserves the right not to provide assistance in respect of any tax claim, which is in existence at the date of entry into force of the convention.[149] Also, the directive lacks such provisions as corresponds to those in the Nordic agreement on assistance in tax matters, which stipulate that after the entry into force of the agreement, its provisions apply to matters which, subsequent to the entry into force of the agreement, have been submitted to the competent authority of the contracting State to which a request has been directed.[150]

The ECJ has, however, decided in its ruling in the joint cases of *Greece v. Tsapalos and Diamantakos*[151] that the Recovery directive shall be interpreted as applicable to claims established under an instrument issued by one Member State before that directive entered into force in another Member State for the reason that the provisions of this directive must be considered to be procedural law and that, according to settled case-law, procedural rules are generally held to apply to all proceedings pending at the time when they enter into force and for reasons of efficiency based on the purpose of the directive. This ruling of the ECJ contributes a retrospective effect to claims in existence in one Member State before the entry into force of the original Recovery directive and its subsequent amendments in other Member States, *e.g.* through the latest amendment of the Recovery directive, which *i.a.* extended the directive to include taxes on income and capital.[152]

This retrospective effect only becomes ultimately governed and limited by the provision on periods of limitation in the directive.[153] It may be argued that, for the indicated reasons by the ECJ in this ruling, a new provision should be entered into the Recovery directive. Such a provision may stipulate that this directive should apply to claims established under an instrument issued by one Member State before that the original directive and its subsequent amendments entered into force in another Member State. Even if the present legal position has been made clear by the ECJ, it may, however, alternatively be argued that a new provision in EC law should instead reflect the opposite position, that the Recovery directive shall apply in relation to new Member States of the EU only to legal proceedings and decisions instituted after the date of accession of such Member States. This is, presently an open question. A third alternative would be to maintain the present legal position based on this legal usage of the ECJ.

---

149. *See* Art. 30, 1 c.
150. *See* Art. 24, 2.
151. *See* 1.1.1 for further details about this ruling.
152. Besides taxes on income and capital, the amendment through the Council Directive 2001/44/EC of 15 Jun. 2001 amending Directive 76/308/EEC on mutual assistance for the recovery of claims resulting from operations forming part of the system of financing the European Agricultural Guidance and Guarantee Fund, and of agricultural levies and customs duties and in respect of VAT and certain excise duties, also included taxes on insurance premiums. *See* 5.2.2.1 for further details on the scope of claims under the Recovery directive.
153. *See* Art. 15.

5.3.1.2.2 Conventions

The Council of Europe and OECD convention on mutual administrative assistance in tax matters explicitly confers priority to EC law, without taking into account whether or not the convention would provide a greater measure of mutual assistance compared to the Recovery directive and the Implementing recovery directive.[154] Therefore, the convention does not allow its application between parties to the convention, which are Member States of the EU, *i.e.* between Denmark, Finland and Sweden. They are between them thus referred to apply the directives instead of the convention. The convention does, however, allow its application between parties to the convention, which do not have the status of Members of the EU, Iceland and Norway and parties to the convention, which also are Members of the EU, Denmark, Finland and Sweden. Consequently, a request may be made under the convention for the recovery of tax claims, which is based on a co-debtor liability,[155] between *e.g.* Finland and Norway, because the Nordic agreement on assistance in tax matters does not include such a co-debtor liability. This example indicates that Greenland, Iceland and Norway may in relation to Denmark, Finland and Sweden and *vice versa*, as parties to the convention, choose to apply the convention in a case of recovery based on a co-debtor liability for the settlement of tax claims.

Other parties to the convention, which do not have the status of Members of the EU, *e.g.* Iceland and Norway, and which therefore are not governed by EC law, are not limited by the convention in relation to other existing or future international agreements.[156] The Explanatory report to the convention also makes clear that, when two or more States are parties to the convention and other instruments, or arrangements, the most effective instrument can be used in any particular situation, and that the application of the convention and of other instruments should be considered independently, States are at liberty to choose whichever instrument they think most appropriate to the particular case, but they may not simultaneously apply more than one instrument to a given case.[157] The Nordic agreement on assistance in tax matters is silent about the relationship to other conventions and apply between the Nordic States: Denmark, including Greenland and the Faeroe Islands, Finland, Iceland, Norway, and Sweden. The Benelux convention on the mutual assistance for the recovery of tax claims does not prejudice an application of other particular conventions.[158]

Some conventions in the criminal law area treat, as opposed to the Recovery directive,[159] the mutual cross-border enforcement of proceeds of fines and

154. *See* Art. 27, 2 of the Convention. *Also see* Explanatory report on the Convention on Mutual Administrative Assistance in Tax Matters, p. 69.
155. *See* Art. 1, 3.
156. *See* Art. 27, 1.
157. *See* Explanatory report on the Convention on Mutual Administrative Assistance in Tax Matters, pp. 68-69.
158. *See* Art. 1.
159. *See* Art. 2, i which excludes any sanction of a criminal nature as determined by the laws of the requested State. *Also see* 5.2.2.1 about the treatment of sanctions in the Recovery directive.

confiscation derived from fiscal crimes. These conventions are the European Convention on the international validity of criminal judgments of 28 May 1970,[160] Council of Europe's Convention on the laundering, search, seizure and confiscation of proceeds from crime of 8 November 1990,[161] and Nordic agreement on the cooperation concerning the mutual assistance of enforcement of judgments or decisions on fines, confiscation or compensation for litigation costs of 1962.[162] To the extent the scope of claims of these conventions does not equal, as at the present, to claims falling under the scope of the Recovery directive, the directive does not curtail the application of these conventions. Examples of such claims in these conventions form decisions of fines issued against an individual, who has violated provisions in tax legislation.

In case the scope of claims is greater than the scope of claims under the Recovery directive the mentioned conventions in the criminal law area may still apply. Both the European Convention on the international validity of criminal judgments and the Council of Europe's Convention on the laundering, search, seizure and confiscation of proceeds from crime include provisions, which provide the possibilities of alternative uses of other international agreements.[163] Such alternative uses should also, in principle, include the Recovery directive, which may be of interest if tax penalties would be included under the future scope of claims under this directive.[164]

5.3.1.3 Service of Judicial Documents

EC law and conventions on the service of judicial documents in the context of cross-border matters of enforcement and recovery are of importance for safeguarding the proper interest of legal protection of rights of the debtor and the creditor before the actual enforcement and recovery take place. The New service of legal documents' regulation, which applies from 13 November 2008, with an exception, replaces the present regulation in the same area.[165] The New service of legal

160. *See* Art. 2, b of the European Convention on the international validity of criminal judgments (reservations against the enforcement of judgments dealing with fiscal crimes have been made by Austria and Spain, but not by the Netherlands and Sweden).
161. *See* Art. 7, 2 a compared to Art. 1 a of the Council of Europe's Convention on the laundering, search, seizure and confiscation of proceeds from crime.
162. *See* the Nordic agreement on the cooperation concerning the mutual assistance of enforcement of judgments or decisions on fines, confiscation or compensation for litigation costs, implemented through similar enacted legislations in the Nordic States. These legislations deal *i.a.* also with the mutual cross-border enforcement of proceeds of fines and confiscation derived from fiscal crimes. *See* about the scope of claims 3 § compared to 1, 4 and 35 §§ of the Swedish Act, published in Lag (1963:193) om samarbete med Danmark, Finland, Island och Norge ang. verkställighet av straff, m.m. (Act on the cooperation with Denmark, Finland, Iceland and Norway concerning the enforcement of punishment).
163. *See* Art. 64 of the European Convention on the international validity of criminal judgments and Art. 39 of the Council of Europe's Convention on the laundering, search, seizure and confiscation of proceeds from crime.
164. *See* 5.2.2.1 about the possible idea of including tax penalties under the Recovery directive.
165. *See* Arts 25-26.

documents' regulation applies in civil and commercial matters, including contractual claims, where a judicial or extrajudicial document has to be transmitted from one Member State to another for service there, except where the address of the person to be served with the document is not known.[166]

This regulation is binding for all Member States, except Denmark,[167] and prevails over the provisions contained in bilateral or multilateral agreements or arrangements having the same scope, concluded by the Member States and in particular the Protocol annexed to the Brussels convention, and the Hague convention on the service abroad of judicial and extrajudicial documents in civil or commercial matters of 15 November 1965 in relations between the Member States which are parties thereto.[168] A parallel agreement to this regulation between the EC and Denmark exists, and entered into force on 1 July 2007.[169] The regulation does not, however, preclude Member States from maintaining or concluding agreements or arrangements to expedite or simplify the transmission of documents, provided that they are compatible with the regulation.[170] This Hague convention and other conventions may still apply between the Member States of the EU.[171]

5.4 LIMITATION TO PERSONS: CREDITORS, DEBTORS AND CO-DEBTORS – AFFECTED BY CLAIMS

5.4.1 Creditors

A difference, in comparison to the public law area, is the possibility in the civil law area of shifting the original right to the claim, by a transfer of it, *e.g.* by a private creditor's sale of a title of execution related to contractual claims. Such a transfer related to public claims is not practised in the public law area, where the public creditor remains the same during the entire proceeding. Another difference, in comparison to the public law area, is that the nationality of the creditor, *e.g.* an Australian corporation, which may hold a title of execution of origin from any jurisdiction of the Member States of the EU, is of no importance for its possibilities

166. *See* Art. 1.
167. *See* Preamble (29).
168. *See* first part of Preamble (23) and Art. 20, 1.
169. *See* Art. 10, 2 of the Agreement between the European Community and the Kingdom of Denmark of 19 Oct. 2005 on the service of judicial and extrajudicial documents in civil or commercial matters compared to Information concerning the date of entry into force of the Agreement between the European Community and the Kingdom of Denmark on the service of judicial and extrajudicial documents in civil or commercial matters.
170. *See* end of Preamble (23) and Art. 20, 2.
171. *See*, for further comments on this Hague convention, Practical Handbook on the Operation of the Hague Service Convention, Spinelli, pp. 41-57, Arnt Nielssen, International privat- og procesret, pp. 362-363, and Berglund, Svensk internationell exekutions- och oeståndsrätt, pp. 272-293. *Also see*, about the service of judicial documents, website of the European Judicial Network in civil and commercial matters, <http://ec.europa.eu/civiljustice>, under headline Service of documents, and, about the service of judicial documents in Europe, Les moyens modernes de transmission des actes judiciares et extrajudiciares en Europe.

of enforcing his contractual claims under EC law, *e.g.* under the Brussels I regulation. Another example is that the New York convention on foreign arbitral awards does not require, contrary to the Geneva Protocol of 1923,[172] that the awards to settle a dispute between parties are subject to the jurisdiction of the contracting States. Consequently, the convention does not attach any importance to the nationality of the litigants and it is applicable as soon as the award has been made in a foreign contracting State. In the public law area, each public creditor remains a creditor, based on its public title of execution, during the entire proceeding, *e.g.* the Member States of the EU, in their capacity of creditors, in relation to the Recovery directive.

5.4.2 Debtors and Co-debtors

As already mentioned, there exist some differences concerning who should be considered to be a debtor. These differences relate to both individuals and legal entities, *e.g.* an ordinary limited liability company or a European company, a *Societas Europaea*, which has a relevant national connection under community law, or to a co-debtor, in comparison between the national level and the sometimes more restrictive international level. These differences result, as will be demonstrated, to some extent, in restrictions at the international level, in the context of cross-border enforcement/recovery of a foreign claim in another State. Who should be considered to be a debtor, or a co-debtor, at the national level is determined by different requirements in national laws. In particular the scope and limits of a co-debtor vary in national laws both in the civil law area,[173] and in the tax area,[174] and may relate to different categories of representatives of legal entities, *e.g.* a managing director, or a member of the board of directors, or the actual non-formal manager. These situations are sometimes also characterized as a breakthrough of the independent responsibility of a limited company, or what happens when piercing the corporate veil.

Creditors normally have to conduct their claims through certain national legal procedures to obtain titles of execution before they can apply for measures of recovery or enforcement against the debtors, or co-debtors, to obtain non-voluntary payments. Once the private or public creditors have arrived at this stage there seldom exist any additional restrictions at the national level, which particularly

172. *See* para. 1.
173. *See* Cross Border Debt Recovery, Belgium, pp. 34-35 and European Corporate Insolvency, Denmark, pp.104-106, France, p. 164, Greece, pp. 296-297, Ireland, pp. 362-366, Italy, pp. 399-400, Luxemburg, pp. 440-443, Netherlands, p. 476, Norway, pp. 515-516, Portugal, pp. 555-556, Sweden, pp. 651-654, Spain, p. 614 and United Kingdom, pp. 804-807. *Also see* Ansvarsgenombrott, England, pp. 79-80, France, p. 81 and Germany, pp. 80-81 and Personligt ansvar vid likvidationsplikt, olovlig vinstutdelning, företrädaransvar, m.m., Sweden, pp. 15-92.
174. *See* European Corporate Insolvency, Greece, p. 296, and the Netherlands, p. 476. *Also see* Personligt ansvar vid likvidationsplikt, olovlig vinstutdelning, företrädaransvar, m.m., Sweden, pp. 97-123.

exclude certain categories, or sub-categories, of debtors, or co-debtors, from the possibilities of enforcement, or recovery. Such restrictions exist, however, to some extent, in EC law and multilateral conventions regarding the enforcement of contractual claims respectively of the recovery of tax claims against co-debtors. The original position of a debtor may be subject to changes, also with effects in the international context, in the civil law area, *e.g.* due to the fulfilment by others of a personal civil law guarantee obligation, and in the public law area, *e.g.* due to a co-debtor liability, a subsidiary liability, or joint liability, for the payment of taxes. The position of the original debtor/s will first be established, and then the position of the co-debtors, their subsidiary, or joint responsibility, *i.e.* co-liability for the settlement of claims, *e.g.* in their capacity of representatives of legal entities.

Another limitation to a debtor affected by claims, including contractual claims and tax claims, is that related to decisions of disqualification orders against an individual debtor for carrying on a non-serious, or illegal, business activity. The cross-border implications of such orders, and their limitations, are not only of interest to the different national authorities, but also to the creditors and the debtors, and are therefore also treated here.

5.4.2.1 Contractual Claims

Debtors and co-debtors, who could be subject to the enforcement of contractual claims, are those against whom there exist enforceable titles of execution, which fall under the scope of application of European law and conventions. The most important example of debtors is the contractual debtor. Another example may be a debtor, who has been determined to be directly liable to a civil sanction for the debts of a legal entity derived from damages caused by him in his capacity of the representative of this legal entity in his mismanagement of contractual matters. A director of a company may incur a joint liability under civil law in relation to contractual matters, *e.g.* for mismanagement, or the infringement of the corporate articles of association, or for violations against provisions in corporate legislation. Another example of a joint liability is that of an insurance company based on a guarantee contract as in the ruling of the ECJ in the case of *Préservatrice foncière TIARD SA v. Staat der Nederlanden.*[175]

5.4.2.2 Tax Claims

Two main categories of debtors, the original tax debtors and the co-debtors for the settlement of tax claims could be identified as subjects to cross-border recovery.[176]

175. *See* 5.2.1.1.1 for more details about this ruling of the ECJ.

176. *See* Garcia Prats, p. 67, who states that, apart from the traditional taxpayer, there are other subjects that also have a legal liability, such as withholders or taxpayer substitutes and in addition other persons may also be called upon to guarantee payment (responsible parties, tax successors *ex lege, intervivos, mortis causa*), such that the tax system recognizes a plurality of persons with potential liability for the payment of tax claims.

Besides the original tax debtors mainly two additional sub-categories of other persons and co-debtors who have become liable for the settlement of tax claims could be identified as subjects to cross-border recovery. One sub-category of co-debtors is represented by those who may risk assuming a co-liability for the settlement of tax claims together with the original tax debtors. The common features of this sub-category are normally that they are considered to be subsidiarily responsible and co-liable for the settlement in their capacity of representatives of legal entities, normally when the principal debtor could not pay for various reasons, *e.g.* due to insolvency.

This liability normally arises as a result of a breakthrough of the responsibility of a legal entity when in its original capacity as a tax debtor it did not pay the due formal original tax claims issued against it. Another sub-category of co-debtors is represented by these who are considered to be jointly responsible and co-liable for the settlement of tax claims because they have not fulfilled their obligation to pay withheld taxes to the public sector. The common features of this sub-category are that they are obliged to act for the settlement of tax claims in their capacity of collectors of withheld taxes on behalf of *e.g.* the State. A liability for the settlement of tax claims may risk to arise when anyone, who is obliged to collect taxes to the public, has withheld taxes, *e.g.* an employer from the salaries of his employees, but has not fulfilled his obligation to pay them to the public treasury.

5.4.2.2.1 Debtors

The original tax debtors, individuals and a variety of legal entities, who could be subject to cross-border recovery are defined and limited by the Implementing recovery directive,[177] Council of Europe and OECD convention on mutual administrative assistance in tax matters,[178] Nordic agreement on assistance in tax matters,[179] and the Benelux convention on the mutual assistance for the recovery of tax claims.[180] The common features of this category of debtors are that they, based on various national laws, originally are subject to taxation and are defined as tax liables, or as taxpayers. This category of cases does not only include the debtor whose tax liability is based on an ordinary decision of taxation, but also the original tax liabilities of two tax subjects and debtors, which are based on decisions of taxation derived from a computation of joint tax liabilities. Examples give the

177. *See* Art. 13 compared to Art. 4, 1.
178. *See* Art. 1, 3, which states that assistance shall be provided whether the person affected is a resident or national in the States concerned. The term 'nationals' is further defined in Art. 3, 1. e., i. and ii. in the convention. Annex C to the convention includes further information regarding the definition of the word 'national' for the purpose of the convention in relation to the Netherlands, the Netherlands Antilles and Aruba. *Also* compare Explanatory report on the Convention on Mutual Administrative Assistance in Tax Matters, pp. 9-10.
179. *See* Art. 4, 1 compared to Art. 1 g.
180. *See* Exposé des motifs to the convention, which states that the taxpayer could be subject to recovery in another contracting State in his assets located there. *Also* compare Art. 3 of the Convention.

decisions, which establish an original tax liability for each one of two spouses, based on a computation of a joint tax liability for income or wealth taxes.

5.4.2.2.2 Co-debtors

The Implementing recovery directive also includes another category of debtor than the original tax debtor, which is not based on an original tax liability, but on a co-debtor liability, a subsidiary liability, or joint liability, limited to *any person* as determined by the applicant State's national legislation for the settlement of tax claims.[181] This means that the scope of different categories of co-debtors of the directive, representatives of legal entities and other obligated persons including employers, who may risk to assume a co-debtor liability for the settlement in case the liability for due collection has been violated, should be determined by the applicant State's national legislation.[182] An example of a joint tax co-liability is illustrated in the ruling of the ECJ in the case of *Commissioners of Customs & Excise v. Federation of Technological Industries and Others.*[183] In this case the ECJ interpreted some community directives in the VAT area and ruled that a taxable person, to whom a supply of goods or services has been made and who knew, or had reasonable grounds to suspect, that some or all of the VAT payable in respect of that supply, or of any previous or subsequent supply, would go unpaid, may be made jointly and severally liable, with the person who is liable, for payment of that tax.

A title of execution based on such a co-debtor liability is therefore in principle possible to use as a legal basis for a request for mutual assistance under the Implementing recovery directive. It may, however, be that such a title of execution, which completely, or in parts, is based on or derived from criminal activities, may be excluded from the use of the Implementing recovery directive to the extent it would be classified as a sanction of a criminal nature according to Article 2, i of the Recovery directive.[184] Any third-party holding assets, as mentioned in the

181. *See* Art. 13 compared to Art. 4, 2.
182. Compare Grau Ruiz, p. 167, where she makes reference to Art. 12, 1 b of directive 77/794/EEC, which is identical to Art. 4, 2 of the Implementing recovery directive. She states that a request for collection and/or precautionary measures may refer directly to the principal debtor or to any other person liable in respect of the claim in accordance with the provisions in force in the Member State where the applicant authority is situated and concludes that the procedure for collection in the requested State may be initiated against the person mentioned in the request irrespective of whether that person is liable under the laws of the latter. She also emphasizes the requirements, in cases of jointly or subsidiary liability, and in the latter case when the principal debtor has been declared insolvent, of the establishment of enforcement orders against such co-debtors.
183. *See* the decision of the ECJ of 11 May 2006 in *Commissioners of Customs & Excise and Attorney General v. Federation of Technological Industries and Others*, which treaties Art. 21, 3 of the Sixth VAT-directive.
184. *See* 5.2.2.1 for more details about the application of Art. 2, i of the Recovery directive and 4.3.2 about the legal usage of the ECHR on the European Convention on Human Rights.

Implementing recovery directive, is not defined as a *person* and could subsequently not be qualified as a co-debtor in the sense of the directive.[185]

A tax co-debtor, or a tax debtor, could, however, have a contractual claim in the quality of a title of execution against any third-party holding assets in a Member State, or in another Member State of the EU. The tax creditor State may in such a situation accept a voluntary transfer of the title of execution to it as a payment of tax debts from the tax co-debtor, or the tax debtor, or initiate a proceeding in order to attach it by means of forced execution. Once this title of execution is in the possession of the tax creditor State and it is made aware of that this third party is established in another Member State of the EU it may apply for the enforcement of the judgment against this party under the Brussels I regulation.

It has been argued that a new part should be entered into Article 2 of the Recovery directive. It should stipulate that the directive shall apply to all claims relating to civil or penal liability claims falling under the scope of claims of this directive, if confirmed by law or by judicial decisions. This idea is, however, unnecessary because this possibility of recovery related to co-debtors and subsidiary responsibilities is already sufficiently clear in Article 13 compared to Article 4 of the Implementing recovery directive in relation to the scope of claims under the Recovery directive. Article 4, 2 of the Implementing recovery directive is sufficiently clear also to cover different kinds of third-party co-debtor liabilities that are based on an original tax liability, irrespective of if the title of execution is issued by a court in administrative, civil and penal proceedings and does therefore not need to be amended. In addition, the wordings 'civil or penal liability claims' in this possible new part is unclear in this context and imply that these claims are of a civil or of a penal nature, and if so would give raise to the issue of the relationship between the Recovery directive and other parts of EC law, *e.g.* the Brussels I regulation and EC penal law. The ECJ made clear in its ruling in the case of *Sonntag v. Weidmann* that a civil liability claim in connection to damages in favour of an individual in a penal proceeding falls under the scope of the Brussels convention.[186] Penal claims are, in EC law, in the cross-border context, treated in the Financial penalties Framework Decision and in the Confiscation Framework Decision.

The Council of Europe and OECD convention on mutual administrative assistance in tax matters states that assistance shall be provided if *the person affected* is a resident, or national, in the States concerned.[187] The personal scope of the expression person affected includes, according to the Explanatory report to the convention and some other sources, the taxpayer, or the other persons involved.[188]

---

185. *See* Art. 13 compared to Art. 4, 3.
186. *See* 5.2.1.1.1 about this ruling.
187. *See* Art. 1, 3.
188. *See* Explanatory report on the Convention on Mutual Administrative Assistance in Tax Matters, p. 9 (17.). *Also see* the Swedish travaux préparatoires to the Convention (prop. 1989/90:14 om godkännande av Europaråds- och OECD-konventionen om ömsesidig handräckning i skatteärenden, m.m), p. 73, which state that the expression person affected also

The personal scope of the convention is thus wider than that of the original tax debtor and could be defined as to include also a co-debtor tax liability. The extent of obligations to recover a co-debtor tax liability of another State may, however, be limited by certain provisions in the convention.[189]

The present Nordic agreement on assistance in tax matters does not, as compared to the earlier agreement in the same area, with the exception for a tax liability in connection to the decedent's estate, stipulate any other co-debtor liability for the settlement of tax claims.[190] This position of the present Nordic agreement on assistance in tax matters is, however, for two reasons of a minor importance. One is that the co-debtor liability for the settlement of tax claims of the Implementing recovery directive may prevail and apply between Denmark, Finland and Sweden. Another is that Greenland, Iceland and Norway in relation to Denmark, Finland and Sweden and *vice versa*, as parties to the Council of Europe and OECD convention on mutual administrative assistance in tax matters, may choose to apply the convention in a case of recovery based on a co-debtor liability for the settlement of tax claims.[191] The Recovery directive and the Implementing recovery directive do not apply in relation to the Faeroe Islands for the reason that the Faeroe Islands have a specific position in the EC Treaty.[192] The Faeroe Islands is not a party to the Council of Europe and OECD convention on mutual administrative assistance in tax matters.

A particular category of a debtor derived from the original tax liable person, who could be subject to cross-border recovery, is the decedent's estate. This category of joint, or subsidiary liability, explicitly exists both in the Council of Europe and OECD convention on mutual administrative assistance in tax matters[193] and in the Nordic agreement on assistance in tax matters.[194] The amount recovered may not, according to the convention and the agreement, exceed the value of assets in the decedent's estate. If the estate has been distributed, recovery against an heir, or other person who have acquired assets owing to the decease of the owner, may not exceed an amount, which corresponds to the equal value of assets received on the date of acquisition. According to the Implementing recovery directive, if the decedent's estate has been distributed, and to the extent a joint, or a subsidiary tax liability for heirs, or assigns in succession cases, have been established in national

---

should include a co-debtor liability for recoverable taxes, and for the same opinion, Berglund, Svensk internationell exekutions- och obeståndsrätt, p. 75.

189. *See e.g.* Arts 1, 19 and 21 and Explanatory report on the Convention on Mutual Administrative Assistance in Tax Matters, pp. 8 (10.), 47-48 and 50-53.

190. A co-debtor liability was included under Art. 3, para. 2, in the earlier agreement in the same area of 9 Nov. 1972. *Also see* on the co-debtor liability under the earlier agreement Bogdan, Några spörsmål avseende indrivning utanför Norden av svenska skattefordringar, p. 413.

191. Compare 5.2.2.2 on the relationship between multilateral conventions.

192. *See* Art. 299, 6 a.

193. *See* Art. 11, 3 and Explanatory report on the Convention on Mutual Administrative Assistance in Tax Matters, pp. 34-36. *Also see* the Swedish travaux préparatoires to the Convention, prop. 1989/90:14 om godkännande av Europaråds- och OECD-konventionen om ömsesidig handräckning i skatteärenden, m.m., p. 74.

194. *See* Art. 15 of the Agreement, which content is similar to the Convention.

laws in connection to the tax liability of the decedent's estate derived from the deceased originally tax liable person, the heirs, or assigns, could be subject to recovery under the co-debtor definition of *any person* in this directive.

5.4.3 Disqualification Orders against an Individual for Carrying on a Non-serious, or Illegal, Business Activity

A disqualification order shares one similar feature and purpose of a bankruptcy decision, that of stopping harmful trading activities. There exists no EC law for the mutual recognition of national disqualification orders against an individual debtor for carrying on a non-serious, or illegal, business activity, as bans on conducting business, or as a prohibition by a court, or other administrative body, to exercise the function of a director of a legal entity for a limited, or unlimited period. The national laws on such orders and their registers, as well as permissions of different kind, which are required to conduct certain business activities, vary between the Member States.[195] Also, the national provisions related to these orders are *i.a.* affected by the structures of the business law, insolvency law and penal law.

Several arguments may motivate the establishment of new EC law for the mutual recognition of the national disqualification orders against an individual for carrying on a non-serious, or illegal, business activity, *e.g.* by not honouring contractual obligations and paying taxes. Lack of such EC law means that different and unequal conditions of competition within the Internal Common Market, related to the serious activities, are maintained in the cross-border context. An individual can continue his non-serious, or illegal, activities directed against the private creditors, enterprises and individuals, and the various public creditors, institutions in society, such as the Treasury, in a Member State, after he has moved from another Member State, where he has previously been prohibited by a disqualification order to stop these activities.

The establishment of such EC law would have to include provisions for an efficient publication, and/or an exchange of information about the disqualification orders between the Member States in order to obtain a sufficiently efficient

195. *See* Prevention of organized crime: The registration of legal persons and their directors and the international exchange of information, a comparative legal study in the EU Member States on the possibilities for the improvement of the international exchange of information on legal persons with the purpose of (transnational) organized crime prevention, Final Report of the Follow-Up Study, T.M.C Asser Instituut Commissioned by the Netherlands Ministry of Justice, Dec. 2006, p. 210, Table 4 Disqualification orders register. This Table shows that in 19 of 26 Member States there exist such registers and their place of location. *Also see* for further details on these registers, the relevant part of the country reports, *i.b.*, pp. 19-187 and for a summary comment on these registers, pp. 194-195. *Also see* Rapport om näringsförbudens efterlevnad, Rapport 2004:2, Ekobrottsmyndigheten (Swedish National Economic Crimes Bureau), pp. 41-42. *Also* compare Tax Administration in OECD and Selected Non-OECD Countries: Comparative Information Series (2006), p. 84, where it is reported that powers are given to some of the surveyed revenue bodies to facilitate tax collection, including *i.a.* closure of business or cancellation of business licenses.

supervision of them. Consequently, such EC law would bring important preventive measures in order to render more equal the conditions of competition within the Internal Common Market. This would strengthen the competiveness of the serious business activities. The establishment of such European law would be of importance in matters having cross-border implications and would in that sense contribute to a better functioning of the Internal Common Market. It would also lead to a more efficient fight against non-serious, or illegal, activities, and hence meet another important objective of the EU.[196]

The Council of Europe, or the OECD, or the Hague Conference on Private International Law, or the Nordic Council of Ministers, may also contemplate to take an initiative to work out a convention for the mutual recognition of these disqualification orders. Still, even if there exist several arguments in favour of the establishment of new EC law for the mutual recognition of these orders, or of a convention, through an intervention by other international organizations, in this area, this has first to be subject to a more profound analysis, *i.a.* related to what national orders should be included, or excluded. In any event, it should be contemplated, as a possible first step, to coordinate the present nationally available information about actually issued orders in specific cases from national registers in a suitable European cooperation platform, *e.g.* by developing the use of the European Business Register (EBR).[197]

196. *See* Communication from the Commission to the Council and the European Parliament on measures to be taken to combat terrorism and other forms of serious crime, in particular to improve exchanges of information, Proposal for a Council decision on the exchange of information and cooperation concerning terrorist offences, COM (2004) 221 final, p. 13, where it is recommended that a European Register of Convictions and Disqualifications be established for individuals and bodies corporate convicted of organized crime or terrorism offences.

197. *See* 7.2.3.1 for further information about the EBR. *Also see* Prevention of organized crime: The registration of legal persons and their directors and the international exchange of information, a comparative legal study in the EU Member States on the possibilities for the improvement of the international exchange of information on legal persons with the purpose of (transnational) organized crime prevention, Final Report of the Follow-Up Study, T.M.C Asser Instituut Commissioned by the Netherlands Ministry of Justice, Dec. 2006, p. 202, about some possible ideas of improvements in the international exchange of information, *e.g.* by making the European Business Register more useful in this context and by harmonizing the function of notary public throughout the Member States of the EU.

Chapter 6

Procedures in EC Law and Conventions

6.1 RECOGNITION AND ENFORCEABILITY

The EC principle of the free movement of judgments, and that a foreign judgment, which has been recognized under the Brussels convention, must have the same effects in the State in which enforcement is sought as it does in the State in which judgment was given, have been established in several rulings of the ECJ, such as in the cases of *Hoffmann v. Krieg*,[1] *Coursier v. Fortis*,[2] and *Mund & Fester v. Hatrex Internationaal Transport*.[3]

---

1. The decision of the ECJ in *Hoffmann v. Krieg* of 4 Feb. 1988 concerns the enforcement in the Netherlands of a judgment of the Amtsgericht in Heidelberg ordering the husband to make monthly maintenance payments to his wife. The ECJ ruled that a foreign judgment, which has been recognized by virtue of Art. 26 of the Brussels convention, as the convention 'seeks to facilitate as far as possible the free movement of judgments, and should be interpreted in this spirit', must have the same effects in the State in which enforcement is sought as it does in the State in which judgment was given. *See* paras 10 and 11 of the ruling.
2. The decision of the ECJ in *Coursier v. Fortis* of 29 Apr. 1999 concerns the enforcement of a French judgment ordering Mr. Coursier to repay to the Luxemburg bank Fortis a loan granted by it to him, after his insolvency in France following this judgment, through the attachment of his salary received from his employer in Luxemburg. The ECJ ruled that the term 'enforceable' in the first paragraph of Art. 31 of the Brussels Convention is to be interpreted as referring solely to the enforceability, in formal terms, of foreign decisions and not to the circumstances in which such decisions may be executed in the State of origin. It concluded that the Brussels Convention is intended to facilitate the free movement of judgments by establishing a simple and rapid procedure in the Contracting State, where enforcement of a foreign decision is applied for, and that the enforcement procedure constitutes an autonomous and complete system. The ECJ further concluded that it is the court of the State in which enforcement is sought, in appeal proceedings brought under Art. 36 of the Brussels Convention, to determine, in accordance with its domestic law, including the rules of private international law, the legal effects of a decision given in the State of origin in relation to a court-supervised liquidation. *See* paras 25 and 33 of the ruling.
3. *See* 1.1.1.1.2 for further details about this ruling.

Provisions, which have become closer than before to an automatic recognition and enforceability of foreign titles of execution, *i.e.* without any, or few, requirements that special procedures, or further formalities, have to be fulfilled, have in recent years been entered into parts of EC law in the private and public law areas, *e.g.* the European Enforcement Order for uncontested claims,[4] the European Order for payment procedure,[5] the European Small Claims Procedure,[6] the New social security regulation,[7] and the Insolvency regulation.[8] Besides there exists a Proposal for a Council regulation on jurisdiction, applicable law, recognition and enforcement of decisions and cooperation in matters relating to maintenance obligations.[9] An earlier example of recognition without any demand for a declaration of enforceability is the Nordic convention regarding the enforcement of maintenance claims of 1962, which only requires an application by the creditor in an *ex parte* proceeding for the actual enforcement of the original title of execution and if necessary, completed with a certificate of its enforceability issued in the contracting State of origin of the title.[10]

---

4. *See* Art. 5.
5. *See* Art. 19.
6. *See* Art. 20.
7. *See* Art. 84, 2 of the New social security regulation, which stipulates that enforceable decisions from one Member State relating to the collection of contributions, interest and any other charges or to the recovery of benefits provided but not due under the legislation of one Member State shall be recognized and enforced at the request of the competent institution in another Member State within the limits and in accordance with the procedures laid down by the legislation and any other procedures applicable to similar decisions of the latter Member State. This article of the regulation only allows one deviation from this equal treatment of foreign and domestic claims, which is that foreign enforceable decisions shall be declared enforceable in the requested Member State only in so far as the legislation and any other procedures of that State so require. The regulation entered into force on 20 May 2004, but shall, according to its Art. 91, apply from the date of entry into force of its Implementing Regulation.
8. *See* Art. 16, 1, which stipulates that any judgment opening insolvency proceedings, handed down by a court which has jurisdiction according to Art. 3 shall be recognized in all the other Member States from the time that it becomes effective in the State of the opening of proceedings. Art. 17, 1 stipulates that the judgment opening the proceedings referred to in Art. 3, 1 (Main insolvency proceedings) shall, with no further formalities, produce the same effects in any other Member State, as under this law of the State of the opening of proceedings, unless the regulation provides otherwise and as long as no proceedings referred to in Art. 3, 2 (Territorial insolvency proceedings) are opened in that other Member State.
9. *See* 2.10.1 about this proposal. The following solutions could be found in this proposal. Art. 21, 1, which stipulates that a judgment given in a Member State shall be recognized in the other Member State without any special procedure being required and Art. 26 states that under no circumstances may a judgment be reviewed as to its substance. Grounds of non-recognition exist in Arts 22-23. A judgment on the exercise of parental responsibility in respect of a child given in one Member State which is enforceable in that Member State and has been served shall be enforced in another Member State when it has been declared enforceable there, according to Art. 28.
10. *See* Art. 1, first paragraph which stipulates that the relevant titles of execution, which are enforceable in one contracting State shall, upon request, be enforced forthwith in any of the other contracting States. The authority, which is to effect recovery, may, according to Art. 3, first paragraph if it appears necessary to do so, request a certificate to the effect that the judgment, decision, ruling or undertaking meets the conditions for enforcement laid down in Art. 1, first paragraph.

The more traditional provisions of recognition and declaration of enforceability, or of declaration of enforceability, of foreign titles of execution that exist in many conventions include special procedures, or further formalities, to be fulfilled, at the application of the creditor to the competent authorities of the requested State, courts or authorities, in a exequatur proceeding. A declaration of enforceability means that a decision from the competent authorities of the requested State, courts or authorities, on the enforceability of foreign titles of execution is obtained, which may be used as a legal basis for the following actual enforcement, or recovery, of the claims originally based on these foreign titles.

Judgments of the ECJ and the decisions of the Council or of the Commission, which impose a pecuniary obligation on persons, other than States, shall, according to the EC Treaty, be enforceable.[11] A creditor, who wants to proceed to the actual enforcement of such EC judgments or decisions, has to prove the authenticity of these titles of execution by their verification by the national authority, which each Member State designates for this purpose and shall make known to the Commission and the ECJ.[12] Another kind of test of international enforceability exists in the Directive 2000/35/EC of the European Parliament and of the Council of 29 June 2000 on combating late payment in commercial transactions (Late payment's directive), which imposes an obligation on the Member States of the EU not to declare a commercial claim enforceable if it could be derived from an agreement between the contracting parties on a date for late payment not accepted in the directive or on a level of interest exceeding what has been accepted in the directive.[13]

The treatment of costs in EC law other than those in the areas of cross-border enforcement of contractual claims and recovery of tax claims are also be found in the Council regulation 1206/2001/EC of 28 May 2001 on cooperation between the courts of the Member States in the taking of evidence in civil or commercial matters (Taking of evidence regulation) and the New service of legal documents' regulation, which both stipulate that Member States normally are required to keep ordinary costs of the cooperation, but shall be reimbursed for more extensive services.[14]

6.1.1 Parallel Enforcement Proceedings in Several States and Actual Enforcement

Simultaneous and parallel enforcement proceedings in several States are, in principle, possible subject to certain requirements. Such requirements may be that the creditor's title of execution is accepted for a parallel use in simultaneous

11. *See* Art. 256 compared to Art. 244.
12. *See* annex 10, which includes the national authorities designated by the Member States of the EU in accordance to Art. 256 (ex. Art. 192) of the EC Treaty for the verification of the authenticity of decisions of the Council or of the Commission.
13. *See* Art. 3, 3.
14. *See* Art. 18, 1-2 of the Taking of evidence regulation and Art. 11, 1-2 of the New service of legal documents' regulation.

enforcement proceedings in several States by the concerned courts and regulated enforcement agents, and that the total enforced amount of the payment liability in those States does not exceed the amount in the title of execution. A creditor, who, in such a situation, would accept to receive a greater enforced amount than corresponding to the amount of the title of execution, would, no doubt, violate the rights of the debtor and then risk to have to pay damages in satisfaction to him.

Afterwards a successful termination of the proceedings related to the recognition and the declaration of enforceability of foreign titles of execution, the proceedings of actual enforcement and recovery of the claims may be initiated by the private creditor in the private law area and by the requested authority in the public law area. The national procedures of applications for actual enforcement measures and recovery measures and thereto connected national procedures of appeals against such decisions are not treated here. The procedures of actual enforcement and recovery fall under the procedural autonomy of States.[15]

Applications for the recognition and enforcement of foreign titles of execution related to contractual claims, are filed by private creditors to the national organs that have been designated to perform the national functions of competent authorities based on provisions in EC law and conventions, often courts or enforcement agents,[16] while the work of actual enforcement of foreign contractual claims is dealt with by a variety of national professionals, regulated enforcement agents, with the task to enforce claims in the civil law area.[17]

The work of cooperation related to the procedures of applications in the area of mutual assistance for the recovery of tax claims, in the function of competent authorities of the Member States, is often performed by officials of ministries of Finance or national boards of taxation.[18] As a matter of form, the applicant State, when sending its request, must show the requested State that it is justified, by facilitating hold of the documents needed to enforce the debt. The request of recovery must be accompanied by an official model or a certified copy of the title permitting enforcement, issued by the applicant authority and any other documents necessary for recovery.

6.1.1.1 Contractual Claims

6.1.1.1.1 EC Law

6.1.1.1.1.1 Brussels I Regulation

A judgment given in one Member State shall, subject to some exceptions of non-recognition, be recognized under the Brussels I regulation in other Member States without any special procedure being required,[19] *i.e. ipso jure*, and may under no

15. *See* 7.1.
16. *See* 3.2.2.
17. *See* 3.2.1.
18. *See* 3.3.2.
19. *See* Art. 33, 1.

circumstances be reviewed as to its substance.[20] A judgment creditor may, in order to make obvious that his foreign judgment is recognized in another Member State of the EU apply for a decision of recognition, which is given in the form of a declaration of enforceability (exequatur) in a proceeding in that State.[21]

Grounds of Non-recognition

The grounds of non-recognition of a judgment in the regulation are found in Articles 34-35. A ground of non-recognition of a judgment, which is to be used but in exceptional situations, is if such recognition is manifestly contrary to public policy in the Member State in which recognition is sought.[22] The ECJ has in its ruling in the case of *Régie nationale des usines Renault SA v. Maxicar SpA and Orazio Formento* treated the public-policy provision under the Brussels convention, concerning intellectual property rights relating to vehicle body parts, and found it non-applicable.[23] In its ruling in the case of *Dieter Krombach v. André Bamberski* the ECJ treated this provision under the convention and found it applicable when the guarantees laid down in the legislation of the State of origin and in the Convention itself were insufficient to protect the defendant from a manifest breach of his right to defend himself before the court of origin, the right to a fair hearing, as recognized by the European Convention on Human Rights.[24]

---

20. *See* Art. 36.
21. *See* Art. 33, 2 compared to Art. 38. *Also see*, about the enforcement of judgments in EC law under Headline Enforcement of judgments – Community law, and about an application to the court in the Member State where enforcement is required for a declaration that the foreign judgment is enforceable (exequatur) under headlines European Judicial Atlas in Civil Matters and Recognizing and Enforcing Judgments, website of the European Judicial Network in civil and commercial matters, <http://ec.europa.eu/civiljustice>.
22. *See* Art. 34, 1. The Brussels convention lacks in comparison to the Brussels I regulation the word manifestly, compare Art. 27, 1 of the Convention to Art. 34, 1 of the Regulation. *Also see* Pålsson, Brysselkonventionen, Luganokonventionen och Bryssel I-förordningen, pp. 250-252, where he provides a detailed analysis of this provision. He concludes that it has the character of being a 'catching-up clause' with its help it is possible, even if to a very limited extent, to refuse recognition on other grounds than these explicitly specified ones. He further concludes that in principle it is up to each Member State to freely determine what should belong to the grounds under its laws in the meaning, which is intended in Art. 34, 1 of the regulation. He also remarks that the determination of the limits of how far public policy could be extended falls under the competence of interpretation of the ECJ. The corresponding provision in the Brussels convention was only aimed to be used but in exceptional situations, and it seems rare that Member States in their legal usage accept public policy as a ground of non-recognition.
23. *See* the decision of the ECJ in *Régie nationale des usines Renault SA v. Maxicar SpA and Orazio Formento* of 11 May 2000, which treats Art. 27, 1 of the Brussels convention. The ECJ ruled that a judgment of a court or tribunal of a Contracting State recognizing the existence of an intellectual property right in body parts for cars, and conferring on the holder of that right protection by enabling him to prevent third parties' trading in another Contracting State from manufacturing, selling, transporting, importing or exporting in that Contracting State such body parts, can not be considered to be contrary to public policy.
24. *See* 1.4.1 for further details about this case.

Another ground for non-recognition of a judgment is when it was given in default of appearance, if the defendant was not served with the document which instituted the proceedings, or with an equivalent document in sufficient time, and in such a way as to enable him to arrange for his defence, unless the defendant failed to commence proceedings to challenge the judgment when it was possible for him to do so.[25] The ECJ ruled in the case of *ASML Netherlands BV v. Semiconductor Industry Services GmbH*, which treats the service of a judgment under Article 34, 2 of the Brussels I regulation, and is similar to Article 27, 2 of the Brussels convention, that the regulation shall be interpreted to mean that it is possible for a defendant to bring proceedings to challenge a default judgment against him only if he was in fact acquainted with its contents, because it was served on him in sufficient time to enable him to arrange for his defence before the courts of the State in which the judgment was given.[26] The ECJ ruled in the case of *Plumex v. Young Sports NV* that the Old service of legal documents' regulation must be interpreted to mean that it does not establish any hierarchy between the method of transmission and service and, consequently, it is possible to serve a document by one or both of those methods. In addition the ECJ ruled in the same case that, in order to determine vis-à-vis the person on whom service is effected the point from which time starts to run for the purposes of a procedural time-limit linked to effective service, reference must be made to the date of the first service validly effected.[27]

There exists an extensive case-law of the ECJ concerning Article 27, 2 of the Brussels convention, which also has been subject to comments in literature.[28] Some examples, among others, from this case-law are the rulings of the ECJ in the cases of: *Peter Klomps v. Karl Michel*,[29] *Leon Emile Gaston Carlos Debaecker*

---

25. *See* Art. 34, 2.
26. *Also see* 1.4.1 about *ASML Netherlands BV v. Semiconductor Industry Services GmbH.* The ECJ ruled that Art. 34, 2 of the Brussels I regulation shall be interpreted to mean: '...that it is "possible" for a defendant to bring proceedings to challenge a default judgment against him only if he was in fact acquainted with its contents, because it was served on him in sufficient time to enable him to arrange for his defence before the courts of the State in which the judgment was given', *see* para. 49 of the ruling.
27. *See* the decision of the ECJ in *Plumex v. Young Sports NV* of 9 Feb. 2006. The ECJ ruled that the Old service of legal documents' regulation must be interpreted to mean that it does not establish any hierarchy between the method of transmission and service under Arts 4 to 11 and under Art. 14 thereof, and consequently, it is possible to serve a judicial document by one or other or both of those methods. The ECJ also ruled that, in order to determine vis-à-vis the person to whom service is effected the point from which time starts to run for the purposes of a procedural time-limit linked to effecting service, reference must be made to the date of the first service validly effected.
28. *See e.g.* Pålsson, Brysselkonventionen, Luganokonventionen och Bryssel I-förordningen, pp. 243-245.
29. *See* the decision of the ECJ in *Peter Klomps v. Karl Michel* of 16 Jun. 1981, which related to Art. 27, 2 of the Brussels convention about the service in sufficient time of the document which instituted the proceedings. The ECJ concluded that: 'The words "The document which instituted the proceedings" cover any document, such as the order for payment (Zahlungsbefehl) in German law, service of which enables the plaintiff, under the law of the State of the court in which the judgment was given to obtain, in default of appropriate action taken by the defendant, a decision capable of being recognized and enforced under the provisions of the convention. A decision such as the enforcement order (Vollstreckungsbefehl) in German law, which is

and Berthe Plouvier v. Cornelis Gerrit Bouwman,[30] and *Isabelle Lancray SA v. Peters und Sickert KG.*[31] A case of the ECJ, which illustrates the consequences when the annexes to the documents served, according to Article 8, 1 of the Old service of legal documents' regulation about the refusal to accept a document, are not translated, is *Ingenieurbüro Michael Weiss und Partner GbR v. Industri- und Handelskammer Berlin and Nicholas Grimshaw & Partners Ltd.*[32] A legally

---

issued after service of the order for payment has been effected and which is enforceable under the convention, is not covered by the words "The document which instituted the proceeding". In order to determine whether the defendant has been enabled to arrange for his defence as required by Art. 27, point 2, the court in which enforcement is sought must take account only of the time, such as that allowed under German law for submitting an objection (Widerspruch) to the order for payment, available to the defendant for the purposes of preventing the issue of a judgment in default which is enforceable under the convention. Art. 27, point 2, remains applicable where the defendant has lodged an objection against the decision given in default and a court of the State in which the judgment was given has held the objection to be inadmissible on the ground that the time for lodging an objection has expired. Even if a court of the State in which the judgment was given has held, in separate adversary proceedings, that service was duly effected Art. 27, point 2, still requires the court in which enforcement is sought to examine whether service was effected in sufficient time to enable the defendant to arrange for his defence. The court in which enforcement is sought may as a general rule confine itself to examining whether the period, reckoned from the date on which service was duly effected, allowed the defendant sufficient time for his defence.'

30. *See* the decision of the ECJ in *Leon Emile Gaston Carlos Debaecker and Berthe Plouvier v. Cornelis Gerrit Bouwman* of 11 Jun. 1985, which related to Art. 27, 2 of the Brussels convention about the service of the document which instituted the proceedings in sufficient time. The ECJ concluded that the requirements, laid down in Art. 27, 2 of the Brussels convention, that service of the document which instituted the proceedings should have been effected in sufficient time is applicable where service was effected within a period prescribed by the court of the State in which the judgment was given or where the defendant resided, exclusively or otherwise, within the jurisdiction of that court or in the same country as that court. The ECJ further concluded that in examining whether service was effected in sufficient time, the court in which enforcement is sought may take account of exceptional circumstances which arose after service was duly effected. The ECJ also stated that the fact that the plaintiff was apprised of the defendant's new address, after service was effected, and the fact that the defendant was responsible for the failure of the duly served document to reach him are matters which the court in which enforcement is sought may take into account in assessing whether service was effected in sufficient time.
31. *See* the decision of the ECJ in *Isabelle Lancray SA v. Peters und Sickert KG* of 3 Jul. 1990, which treats Art. 27, 2 of the Brussels convention. The ECJ concluded that: '. . . Article 27 (2) of the Convention . . . is to be interpreted as meaning that a judgment given in default of appearance may not be recognized where the document instituting the proceedings was not served on the defendant in due form, even though it was served in sufficient time to enable him to arrange for his defence'. The ECJ further concluded that: '. . . Article 27 (2) of the Convention is to be interpreted as meaning that questions concerning the curing of defective service are governed by the law of the State in which judgment was given, including any relevant international agreement.' *See* paras 23 and 31 of the ruling.
32. In *Ingenieurbüro Michael Weiss und Partner GbR v. Industri- und Handelskammer Berlin and Nicholas Grimshaw & Partners Ltd* of 8 May 2008 the ECJ decided, in its preliminary ruling, that Art. 8, 1 of the Old service of legal documents' regulation is to be interpreted as meaning that: '. . . the addressee of a document instituting the proceedings which is to be served does not have the right to refuse to accept that document, provided that it enables the addressee to assert his rights in legal proceedings in the Member State of transmission, where annexes are attached

correct service of decisions, judgments and other judicial documents to the debtor regarding a claim is, no doubt, of importance in order to safeguard the proper interests of legal protection of rights of the debtor and the creditor. Another reason is that it may have the effect of prolonging the period of limitation of the claim and correspondingly have the effect to secure any possibly following actions of enforcement or recovery of the claim against the debtor.

Other grounds of non-recognition of a judgment in the Brussels I regulation relate to whether it is irreconcilable with other judgments, a judgment given in a dispute between the same parties in the Member State in which recognition is sought,[33] or an earlier judgment given in another Member State or in a third State involving the same cause of action and between the same parties provided that the earlier judgment fulfils the conditions necessary for its recognition in the Member State addressed.[34] The ECJ ruled in the case of *Italian Leather SpA v. WECO Polstermöbel GmbH & Co.*, which treats the irreconcilability of the enforcement of two decisions of interim measures under Article 27, 3 of the Brussels convention, a provision that is similar to Article 34, 3 of the Brussels I regulation, that a foreign decision on interim measures ordering an obligor not to carry out certain acts is irreconcilable with a decision on interim measures refusing to grant such an order in a dispute between the same parties in the State where recognition is sought, and that a court of the State in which recognition is sought is then required to refuse to recognize the foreign judgment.[35]

---

to that document consisting of documentary evidence which is not in the language of the Member State addressed or in a language of the Member State of transmission which the addressee understands, but which has a purely evidential function and is not necessary for understanding the subject-matter of the claim and the cause of action. It is for the national court to determine whether the content of the document instituting the proceedings is sufficient to enable the defendant to assert his rights or whether it is necessary for the party instituting the proceedings to remedy the fact that a necessary annex has not been translated.' The ECJ further concluded that: '... "the fact that the addressee of a document served has agreed in a contract concluded with the applicant in the course of his business that correspondence is to be conducted in the language of the Member State of transmission does not give rise to a presumption of knowledge of that language, but is evidence which the court may take into account in determining whether that addressee understands the language of the Member State of transmission". Also, the ECJ concluded that:... "the addressee of a document served may not in any event rely on that provision in order to refuse acceptance of annexes to the document which are not in the language of the Member State addressed or in a language of the Member State of transmission which the addressee understands where the addressee concluded a contract in the course of his business in which he agreed that correspondence was to be conducted in the language of the Member State of transmission and the annexes concern that correspondence and are written in the agreed language".'

33. *See* Art. 34, 3.
34. *See* Art. 34, 4.
35. *See* the decision of the ECJ in *Italian Leather SpA v. WECO Polstermöbel GmbH & Co.* of 6 Jun. 2002 which related to the conditions of use of a brand name under a contract for the exclusive distribution of leather-upholstered furniture. The ECJ established that: '... a foreign decision on interim measures ordering an obligor not to carry out certain acts is irreconcilable with a decision on interim measures refusing to grant such an order in a dispute between the same parties in the State where recognition is sought.' The ECJ further concluded that: '... where a

Yet some other grounds of non-recognition of a judgment may relate to the grounds of jurisdiction.[36] The provisions related to the declaration of the enforceability of a judgment given in another Member State and enforceable in that State in a Member State, and some thereto related issues, are found in Articles 38-56 in the regulation.

Interim Measures

A judgment may, under the Brussels I regulation, relate both to the judgment terminating the proceeding and orders made by a court in a proceeding *inter partes* on interim measures,[37] which in national laws have the purpose to provide the plaintiff a provisional legal protection, often within the narrow sense and with the aim to preserve the actual and legal status quo positions during the time before a final judgment, expressed as provisional and protective measures, or sequestration.[38] The existence and concept of such interim measures differ between the Member States, as evident from the Brussels I regulation, which refers to provisional, including protective, measures as may be available under the law of a State.[39] In some Member States such measures are not available, whereas in other Member States they are, but sometimes under differing conditions.[40] The finality, res judicata, of

court of the State in which recognition is sought finds that a judgment of a court of another Contracting State is irreconcilable with a judgment given by a court of the former State in a dispute between the same parties, it is required to refuse to recognise the foreign judgment.' *See* paras 47 and 52 of the ruling. *Also* compare the decision of the ECJ in the case of *Jozef de Wolf v. Harry Cox BV.* of 30 Nov. 1976, where the ECJ concluded that the provisions of the Brussels convention prevent a party who has obtained a judgment in his favour in a Contracting State, being a judgment for which an order for enforcement under Art. 31 of the convention, which is similar to Art. 38, 1 of the Brussels I regulation, may issue in another Contracting State, from making an application to a court in that other State for a judgment against the other party in the same terms as the judgment delivered in the first State. The ECJ further concluded that the fact that there may be occasions on which, according to national law applicable, the procedure set out in Arts 31 et seq. of the convention may be found to be more expensive than bringing fresh proceedings on the substance of the case does not invalidate these considerations. *See* paras 5-14 of the ruling.

36. *See* Art. 35.
37. *See* Art. 33, 1.
38. *See*, about sequestration as a concept in Roman and French laws, 2.1.1 respectively 2.3.1.
39. *See* Arts 31-32. *Also see*, about interim and precautionary measures Enforcement of Foreign Judgments, section 18. Interim Relief in the report on the EU (the Brussels I regulation), and under headline Interim measures and precautionary measures – Community law, and about such measures in national laws under headline Interim measures and precautionary measures – General Information, and about applications for such measures to the courts in the Member States under headlines European Judicial Atlas in Civil Matters and Recognizing and Enforcing Judgments, website of the European Judicial Network in civil and commercial matters, <http://ec.europa.eu/civiljustice>.
40. *See*, for further details on the construction and function of some national systems about provisional enforceability of judgments, Kerameus, International encyclopedia of comparative law, volume XVI, Civil procedure, chapter 10, Enforcement proceedings, pp. 19-26, and, Kerameus, Enforcement in the International Context, Recueil des cours, collected courses of

a judgment is not a prerequisite for its recognition in other Member States, and, therefore, provisionally enforceable instruments are recognized under the Brussels I regulation.[41] This is confirmed in the ruling of the ECJ in the case of *Louise de Cavel v. Jacques de Cavel*, where the court said that an interim judgment is governed by the scope of application for such a judgment and not by the nature of the principal claim, in determining whether or not such an interim judgment comes within the scope of the Brussels convention.[42]

However, as long as an exequatur proceeding has not been terminated, the enforcement of a foreign judgment is restricted to protective measures which do not allow any realization of the claim.[43] This is also illustrated in the ruling of the ECJ in the case of *P. Cappelloni et F. Aquilini v. J. C. J. Pelkmans*.[44] Consequently, the regulation provides a concept of provisional enforceability which is mainly aimed at securing the creditor's prospects for enforcement proceedings which will be undertaken when, or if, the decision according exequatur has become res judicata. This concept of the regulation is more limited than the scope of provisional enforcement in most Member States where a more extensive enforcement, including the realization of the assets seized is allowed.

Besides the interim decisions, which are aimed at the preservation of the actual and legal status quo positions, there exist national interim decisions, which are aimed at a provisional settlement of the dealings of the parties and, which, subject

---

the Hague Academy of International Law, 1997, Tome 264 de la collection pp. 236-249, for more extensive comments on the same issue. *Also see*, about provisional and protective measures in the United Kingdom, Macpherson, La pratique des mesures conservatoires et provisoires en Angleterre, Pays de Galles et Ecosse, Le droit processuel et le droit de l'exécution, pp. 419-429, and about the English freezing order (previously referred to in literature as a Mareva injunction), Cuniberti, Les mesures conservatoires portant sur des biens situés à l'étranger, No. 67-116. *Also see* Andrews, Provisional and Protective Measures: Towards an Uniform Protective Order in Civil Matters, Uniform Law Review/Revue de droit uniforme 2001-4, Harmonising Transnational Civil Procedure: The ALI/UNIDROIT Principles and Rules/Vers une procédure civile transnationale harmonisée: Les Principes et Règles ALI/UNIDROIT, pp. 931-949.

41. *See* Art. 47, 1-2 compared to Art. 31.
42. *See* the decision of the ECJ in *Louise de Cavel v. Jacques de Cavel* of 6 Mar. 1980, which treats Arts 1 and 24 of the Brussels convention, where the ECJ ruled that the convention is applicable, on the one hand, to the enforcement of an interlocutory order made by a French court in divorce proceedings whereby one of the parties to the proceedings is awarded a monthly maintenance allowance and, on the other hand, to an interim compensation payment, payable monthly, awarded to one of the parties by a French divorce judgment.
43. *See* Art. 47, 3.
44. *See* the decision of the ECJ in *P. Cappelloni et F. Aquilini v. J. C. J. Pelkmans* of 3 Oct. 1985 which concerned Art. 39 of the Brussels convention. The ECJ ruled that a party, who has applied for and obtained authorization for enforcement may, within the period mentioned in Art. 39, proceed directly with protective measures against the property of the party against whom enforcement is sought and is under no obligation to obtain specific authorization until the expiry of the period prescribed in Art. 36 for lodging an appeal and, if such an appeal is lodged, until a decision is given thereon. The ECJ also ruled that a party who has proceeded with the protective measures referred to in Art. 39 is under no obligation to obtain, in respect of those measures, any confirmation required by the national law of the court in question.

to that some conditions are fulfilled, also fall under the scope of application of Article 31 of the Brussels I regulation. The ECJ established in the case of *Van Uden Maritime BV, trading as Van Uden Africa Line v. Kommanditgesellschaft in Firma Deco-Line and Another*, that even if arbitration is excluded under the scope of application of the Brussels convention, provisional measures under Article 24 of this convention were possible in relation to the payment of debts arising under a contract containing an arbitration clause, subject to certain conditions.[45] These conditions were that a measure ordering interim payment of a contractual consideration does not have effect unless, first, repayment to the defendant of the sum awarded is guaranteed if the plaintiff is unsuccessful as regards the substance of his claim and, second, the measure sought relates only to specific assets of the defendant located, or to be located, within the confines of the territorial jurisdiction of the court to which application is made. The same conditions were also repeated in the ruling of the ECJ in the case of *Hans-Hermann Mietz v. Intership Yachting Sneek BV.*[46]

An *actio Pauliana*,[47] is not an action, which serves the same purpose as provisional, including protective, measures under the Brussels convention, and is therefore not equaled to such measures at the application of this convention, according to the ruling of the ECJ in the case of *Mario Reichert, Hans-Heinz Reichert and Ingeborg Kockler v. Dresdner Bank AG.*[48] An order made by a court in a proceeding *ex parte* on provisional and protective measures was not recognized under the Brussels convention by the ECJ in the case of *Denilauler v. Couchet Frères.*[49] Consequently, under the application of Article 24 of this

45. *See* the decision of the ECJ in *Van Uden Africa Line v. Kommanditgesellschaft in Firma Deco-Line and Another* of 17 Nov. 1998, which treats Arts 5, 1 and 24 of the Brussels convention in the context of a dispute between Van Uden Maritime BV, established in the Netherlands, and Kommanditgesellschaft in Firma Deco-Line and Another of Germany, concerning an application for interim relief (in kort geding proceedings).
46. *See* the decision of the ECJ in *Hans-Hermann Mietz v. Intership Yachting Sneek BV.* of 27 Apr. 1999, which *i.a.* treats Art. 24 of the Brussels convention, concerning proceedings before a German court with a view to securing an order in Germany for the enforcement of a judgment delivered in the Netherlands following adversarial interim proceedings (kort geding) based on a contract of construction and the delivery of a motor yacht between Intership Yachting Sneek BV., established in the Netherlands, and Mr. Mietz, domiciled in Germany.
47. Compare, about *actio Pauliana* in Roman law and under the Middle ages, 2.1.3 and 2.2.4.
48. The ECJ ruled in its decision in *Mario P. A. Reichert and others v. Dresdner Bank* of 26 Mar. 1992 that an action provided for by national law, such as the action paulienne in French law, whereby a creditor seeks to obtain the revocation in regard to him of a transfer of rights in rem in immovable property by his debtor in a way which the creditor regards as being in fraud of his rights does not come within the scope of Art. 5, 3, Art. 16, 5 or Art. 24 of the Brussels convention, *see* para. 36 of the ruling. The corresponding articles in the Brussels I regulation are: 5, 3 (a person domiciled in one State may, in another State, be sued in matters relating to tort, delict or quasi-delict, in the courts for the place where the harmful event occurred or may occur), Art. 22, 5 (exclusive jurisdiction in proceedings concerned with the enforcement of judgments), and Art. 31 (provisional, including protective, measures).
49. *See* the decision of the ECJ in *Bernard Denilauler v. SNC Couchet Frères* of 21 May 1980, which concerned a dispute between a creditor, SNC Couchet Frères, and its debtor, Bernard Denilauler, where a French court, at the request of the creditor and without the other party's

convention, such orders are subordinated to the condition of territoriality, *i.e.* only enforceable in the national context of the Member State of origin of the order, but not in the cross-border context under this convention.

6.1.1.1.1.2 European Enforcement Order for Uncontested Claims

A judgment on an uncontested claim delivered in a Member State shall, upon application at any time to the court of origin, be certified as a European Enforcement Order, subject to certain conditions. Examples of such conditions are that the judgment is enforceable in the Member State of origin, was given in the Member State of the debtor's domicile, and the debtor is a consumer.[50] The enforcement titles being certified as a European Enforcement Order[51] in the Member State of origin shall be recognized and enforced in the other Member States, with some exceptions, without any need for a declaration of enforceability and without any possibility of opposing its recognition.[52] Exceptions are the grounds of refusal of enforcement in the regulation, which the debtor is entitled to raise upon application to the competent court in the Member State of enforcement.[53]

It is sufficient that the creditor presents a certificate that his enforcement title has, on his prior application, been certified by the court of origin, as a European Enforcement Order.[54] The creditor is not required to put up any security in another Member State on the ground that he is a foreign national or that he is not domiciled or resident in the Member State of enforcement.[55] The creditor shall only, in an *ex parte* procedure of application for enforcement, be required to provide the competent enforcement authorities of the Member State of enforcement with qualified copies of the judgment and the European Enforcement Order, in order to establish their authenticity, and where necessary a transcription of the

---

having been summoned to appear, made an order, which was declared provisionally enforceable, authorizing the creditor to freeze the account of the debtor at a German bank as a security for a debt, which the creditor under French law was authorized to carry out without prior service of the order on the debtor, whose assets were seized. The ECJ ruled that judicial decisions authorizing provisional or protective measures, which are delivered without the party against which they are directed having been summoned to appear and which are intended to be enforced without prior service do not come within the system of recognition and enforcement provided for by title III of the Brussels convention. *Also see* Schlosser report, para. 184, Kennett, The Enforcement of Judgments in Europe, pp. 145-148, and Pålsson, Interim Relief under the Brussels and Lugano Conventions, pp. 634-636.

50. *See* Art. 6, 1. *Also see*, about some comments, on the conditions of certification, Un titre exécutoire européen, Les Dossiers du Journal des tribunaux 53, pp. 79-88.
51. *See* Art. 3.
52. *See* Art. 5. *Also see* the information available about this regulation under Headline Enforcement of judgments – Community law, website of the European Judicial Network in civil and commercial matters, <http://ec.europa.eu/civiljustice>.
53. *See* Art. 21.
54. *See* Art. 6.
55. *See* Art. 22, 3.

European Enforcement Order certificate or a translation thereof into the official language of the Member State of enforcement.[56]

6.1.1.1.1.3 European Order for Payment Procedure

The regulation applies in cross-border cases, where at least one of the parties is domiciled, or habitually resident, in a Member State other than the Member State of the court seised, at the time when the application for a European order for payment is submitted.[57] The determination of the enforceability of a European order for payment is governed by the law of the Member State of origin.[58] Such an order, which has become enforceable in the Member State of origin, shall, with some exceptions, be recognized and enforced in the other Member States without the need for a declaration of enforceability and without any possibility of opposing its recognition.[59]

Exceptions are the grounds of refusal of enforcement in the regulation, which the defendant is entitled to raise upon application to the court, or tribunal, with jurisdiction in the Member State of enforcement.[60] The creditor, who applies for the enforcement of a judgment under the European Order for payment procedure is not required to put up any security in another Member State on the ground that he is a foreign national, or that he is not domiciled, or resident, in the Member State of enforcement.[61] The competent court in the Member State of enforcement may, however, on the application of the defendant, limit the enforcement proceedings to protective measures, or make enforcement conditional on the provision of such security as it shall determine, or, under exceptional circumstances, stay the enforcement proceedings.[62]

6.1.1.1.1.4 European Small Claims Procedure

The regulation applies in cross-border cases, where at least one of the parties is domiciled, or habitually resident, in a Member State other than the Member State of the court, or tribunal, seised, on the date when the claim form is received by the court, or tribunal, with jurisdiction.[63] A judgment given in a Member State in the European Small Claims Procedure shall be recognized and enforced in another Member State, with some exceptions, without the need for a declaration of enforceability and without any possibility of opposing its recognition.[64]

---

56. *See* Art. 20, 2.
57. *See* Arts 2 and 3.
58. *See* Art. 18.
59. *See* Art. 19.
60. *See* Art. 22.
61. *See* Art. 21, 3.
62. *See* Art. 23.
63. *See* Arts 2 and 3.
64. *See* Art. 20.

Exceptions are the grounds of refusal of enforcement in the regulation, which the person against whom enforcement is sought is entitled to raise upon application to the court, or tribunal, with jurisdiction in the Member State of enforcement.[65] A judgment shall, subject to some exceptions, be enforceable notwithstanding any possibility of appeal and the provision of security shall not be required.[66] These exceptions are when the court, or tribunal, with jurisdiction, or the competent authority in the Member State of enforcement, on the application of the party against whom enforcement is sought limit the enforcement proceedings to protective measures, or make enforcement conditional on the provision of such security as it shall determine, or under exceptional circumstances stay the enforcement proceedings.[67]

6.1.1.1.2 Conventions

6.1.1.1.2.1 Nordic Convention on Recognition and the Enforcement of Judgments in Civil Matters

A judgment, another decision and a settlement in a matter of private law, which have been given, or entered into, in a contacting State shall, according to the Nordic convention on recognition and the enforcement of judgments in civil matters, with some exceptions,[68] be recognized and enforced in another contracting State according to the legislation of that State.[69] The convention constitutes an early example of recognition without any demand of declaration of enforceability in the cooperation of Nordic States.[70] The convention only requires an application from the creditor in an *ex parte* proceeding for the actual enforcement of the original title of execution.

This lack of formalities is explained by the here earlier mentioned close mutual cooperation developed between the Nordic States based on this framework convention, which refers most issues to be determined through similar enacted laws in the Nordic States.[71] Certain titles of execution, which are not covered by the Brussels I regulation, or by the Brussels convention, and the Old Lugano convention, but instead by the Nordic convention are illustrated by the Swedish and Norwegian enacted laws related to this Nordic convention.[72]

65. *See* Art. 22.
66. *See* Art. 15.
67. *See* Art. 23 compared to Art. 15, 2.
68. *See* Art. 2.
69. *See* Art. 1.
70. Another example is the Nordic convention regarding the enforcement of maintenance claims of 1962, *see* 6.1.
71. *See* 2.5.5 and 5.2.1.2.1.
72. *See* 5.2.1.2.1.

6.1.1.1.2.2 New York Convention on Foreign Arbitral Awards

Each contracting State shall, according to the New York convention on foreign arbitral awards, with some exceptions of non-recognition,[73] recognize arbitral awards as binding in accordance with the rules of procedure of the territory where the award is relied upon, basically under the same conditions as imposed on the recognition, or enforcement, of domestic arbitral awards.[74] To obtain the recognition and enforcement of a foreign arbitral award a creditor has to submit a formal application where the recognition and enforcement is sought.[75]

Unlike the Geneva Convention of 1927, the New York Convention of 1958 does not specify that States are bound to recognize an arbitral agreement even if it does provide for arbitration in a foreign country. It is, however, certain that this rule still applies, being implicitly adopted by the Convention. The place where the agreement is made and the place where it is to be carried out would seem to be matters of indifference. As regards the enforcement of arbitral awards, on the contrary States are at liberty to restrict their obligation to the enforcement of awards rendered on the territory of a Contracting State.

6.1.1.2 Periods of Limitation

The periods of limitation, the various ways of extinguishing obligations, and prescription and limitation of actions, of a contractual obligation, which falls under the scope of the Convention on the law applicable to contractual obligations, opened for signature in Rome on 19 June 1980 (Rome convention on the law applicable to contractual obligations),[76] are governed by the law applicable to a contract.[77] The convention confers precedence to EC law,[78] and it does not prejudice the application of international conventions to which a contracting State is, or becomes, a party.[79]

As the Brussels I regulation, the European Enforcement Order for uncontested claims, the European Order for payment procedure, and the European Small Claims Procedure lack provisions on periods of limitation, this convention consequently completes this EC law. This means that the cross-border enforcement of contractual claims, which is based on such European law, becomes governed by the law applicable to contractual obligations according to this convention. Conventions on the recognition and enforcement related to contractual claims, which lack

73. *See* Art. V.
74. *See* Art. III.
75. *See* Art. IV.
76. *See* Art. 1.
77. *See* Art. 10, 1 d compared to Arts 3-6. *Also see* Pålsson, Romkonventionen – tillämplig lag för avtalsförpliktelser, p. 102, where he concludes that the issue of periods of limitation in the convention is clearly related to the law applicable to contractual obligations, and therefore should the opinion that this issue should be considered as of a procedural nature, governed by *lex fori*, be rejected.
78. *See* Art. 20.
79. *See* Art. 21.

provisions on periods of limitation, are also completed by this Rome convention to the extent their scopes coincide and the parties to these conventions are identical.

6.1.1.3 Enforcement of a Contested Claim and Appeals

6.1.1.3.1 EC Law

The enforcement of a contested claim is stayed on an appeal on the application of the party against whom the enforcement is sought if an ordinary appeal has been lodged against the judgment in the Member State of origin. The court may also make enforcement conditional on the provision of such security as it shall determine, according to the Brussels I regulation,[80] which in this sense is similar to the Brussels convention.[81] In the case of *Industrial Diamond Supplies v. Luigi Riva* the ECJ concluded that the expression 'ordinary appeal' shall be determined by an autonomous interpretation of the Brussels convention. Also, it concluded that any appeal which may result in the annulment, or the amendment of the judgment, which is the subject-matter of the procedure for recognition and enforcement under this convention and the lodging of which is bound, in the State in which the judgment was given, to a period which is laid down by the law and starts to run by virtue of the same judgment constitutes an 'ordinary appeal' which has been lodged, or may be lodged, against a foreign judgment.[82]

In the case of the ECJ in *Calzaturificio Brennero sas v. Wendel GmbH Schuhproduktion International* the court ruled that a court with which an appeal has been lodged against a decision authorizing enforcement may make enforcement conditional on the provision of security only when it gives judgment on the appeal.[83] This has the effect that, during the time for an appeal, no measures of enforcement may be taken other than protective measures against the property of the party against whom the enforcement is sought.[84]

A decision on the application for a declaration of enforceability, in a exequatur proceeding, may be appealed against by either party and shall be dealt with in accordance with the rules governing procedure in contradictory matters, according to the Brussels I regulation.[85] In the case of *Société d'Informatique Service Réalisation Organisation v. Ampersand Software BV.* the ECJ ruled, however, concerning the submission of an application of appeal against a decision for the authorization to enforce an enforceable judgment of another Member State under the Brussels convention, that this authorization of the court in the enforcing Member State can not be contested by an appeal, which is limited to the

80. *See* Art. 46. *Also see*, about the enforceability in national laws of a judgment subject to an appeal, Civil Procedure in Europe 2.
81. *See* Art. 38.
82. *See* the decision of the ECJ in *Industrial Diamond Supplies v. Luigi Riva* of 22 Nov. 1977, about the meaning of Arts 30 and 38 under the Brussels convention.
83. *See* the decision of the ECJ in *Calzaturificio Brennero sas v. Wendel GmbH Schuhproduktion International* of 27 Nov. 1984, which treats Art. 38 of the Brussels convention.
84. *See* Art. 47, 3 compared to Art. 43, 5.
85. *See* Art. 43, 1 and 3.

examination of points of law, and that this court does not have jurisdiction to impose a stay of the proceedings.[86]

6.1.1.3.2 Conventions

The Nordic convention on recognition and the enforcement of judgments in civil matters, partially in force, even if it has mainly been replaced by the Brussels I regulation and the Old Lugano convention, states, subject to certain requirements, that the claim should not be enforceable if its contested by whom it concerns.[87] The New York convention on foreign arbitral awards also deals with the situation of a contested claim. It is made clear that the enforcement of an award may be refused, at the request of the party against whom it is invoked, however only if that party furnishes certain proof.[88] Neither the Nordic convention nor this New York convention include any provisions on provisional, including protective, measures, meaning that the possibility to take such measures are governed by national law.

6.1.1.4 Costs and Repayment

None of the Brussels I regulation, the European Enforcement Order for uncontested claims, the European Order for payment procedure, the European Small Claims Procedure, the Nordic convention on recognition and the enforcement of judgments in civil matters and the New York convention on foreign arbitral awards, include any provisions, which specifically govern, or determine, the allocation of costs related to obtain a formal decision on the recognition and enforcement. They do not either contain any provisions which govern and determine the allocation of actual costs of enforcement related to a foreign claim, and they also lack provisions on repayment to the creditor.

Costs related to such formal decisions[89] and the actual costs of enforcement of the foreign claim[90] are instead governed and determined by non-identical national

86. *See* the decision of the ECJ in *Société d'Informatique Service Réalisation Organisation v. Ampersand Software BV.* of 11 Aug. 1995, which treats Arts 36-38 of the Brussels convention, where the ECJ ruled that Arts 37, 2 and 38, first paragraph of the Brussels convention shall be interpreted as meaning that a decision by which a court of a Contracting State, to which an appeal has been submitted against the authorization to enforce an enforceable judgment of a court in another Contracting State, refuses a stay or lifts a stay previously ordered can not be contested by an appeal in cassation or similar form of appeal limited to the examination of points of law. Moreover the ECJ ruled that the court, to which an appeal on a point of law under Art. 37, 2 of the Convention has been submitted, does not have jurisdiction to impose a stay of the proceedings.
87. *See* Art. 2.
88. *See* Art. V.
89. *See* Civil Procedure in Europe 3, chapter IV. Recognition and Enforcement Procedure, section 2. Duration and Costs, Summary, pp. 37-38, Enforcement of Foreign Judgments, section 18. Expenses, Legal Fees and Security for Costs in the report on the EU (the Brussels I regulation), Enforcement of Foreign Judgments Worldwide, p. 167 (the Brussels and Lugano conventions) and Pålsson, Brysselkonventionen, Luganokonventionen och Bryssel I-förordningen, pp. 266-268.
90. *See* Civil Procedure in Europe 1, chapter III. Le contentieux de l'exécution et les procédures de saisie-exécution, section 4. Le statut des intermédiaires obligés: le coût de l'exécution: qui

legislation. Repayments to the creditor are also governed by national legislation. At the recovery of a foreign private claim the foreign creditor himself is in control of the process of recovery, *e.g.* to demand enforcement measures and he holds the responsibility for costs in relation to his legal initiatives. He also directly receives a report on the result and the possibly recovered amount from realized assets related to his initiatives.

6.1.2 Tax Claims

6.1.2.1 Recovery Directive

The instrument permitting enforcement of the claim shall, according to the Recovery directive, be directly recognized and automatically treated as an instrument permitting its enforcement of a claim of the applicant Member State.[91] The requested Member States have, however, an option, where appropriate and in accordance with their national laws, to supplement, or replace, this instrument by an instrument of their own, which authorizes the enforcement of an instrument from other Member States.[92]

Instruments permitting the enforcement of claims are such titles of execution, as Member States in their national administration apply to the scope of claims related to the directive. This normally means in relation to tax claims that titles of execution from tax authorities and administrative courts are most frequent, but titles based on tax claims from other parts of the court system permitting their enforcement are also acceptable.

supporte les frais d'exécution ?, in each of the national reports included regarding: Germany, Belgium, Denmark, Spain, France, Greece, Italy, Luxemburg, the Netherlands, Portugal, United Kingdom/England and Wales, Sweden and *i.b.*, pp. 30-32 (Summary). *Also see* Cross Border Debt Recovery, section 15. Costs in each of the national reports included regarding: Austria, Belgium, Czech republic, Denmark, England and Wales, Estonia, Finland, France, Germany, Greece, Hungary, Ireland, Italy, Latvia, Lithuania, Northern Ireland, Norway, Russia, Spain, Sweden, Switzerland, the Netherland and Ukraine). *Also* compare Enforcement of Foreign Judgments, section 18. Expenses, Legal Fees and Security for Costs in each of the national reports included regarding: Austria, Belgium, Cyprus, Czech republic, Denmark, England and Wales, Finland, France, Germany, Gibraltar, Greece, Guernsey, Hungary, Ireland, Italy, Jersey, Liechtenstein, Luxemburg, the Netherlands, Norway, Poland, Portugal, Romania, Russia, Scotland, Spain, Sweden, Switzerland, Turkey and Ukraine. Compare, in addition, Enforcement of Foreign Judgments Worldwide, regarding Interest and Costs the following pp.: 147-148 (Belgium), 196 (Italy), 212 (Sweden), and 220 (Switzerland) and Kennett, Regulation of enforcement agents in Europe: a comparative survey, vol. 1 Text, appendix B – The costs of enforcement, pp. 261-272 (Belgium, Denmark, England, France, Germany, Italy, the Netherlands, Scotland, Spain and Sweden), report in the Grotius program 2001.

91. *See* Art. 8, 1.
92. *See* Art. 8, 2.

6.1.2.1.1 Grounds of Refusal

The grounds of refusal are found in Articles 4 and 14 of the Recovery directive and in Articles 25-26 of the Implementing recovery directive. A ground of refusal is that a requested Member State is not obliged, under the Recovery directive, to supply information, which would be contrary to the public policy of that State.[93] Another ground of refusal is that a requested Member State is not obliged to recover a tax liability to the extent that the recovery of such a claim would, because of the situation of the debtor, create serious economic or social difficulties in the requested State in so far as the requested State's legislation allows such action for similar national claims.[94] Yet another ground of refusal, according to this directive, is that Member States are not obliged to recover tax claims of other Member States, which are more than five years old.[95]

Another provision, which is addressed to the applicant State and which may create an obstacle to mutual assistance under the directive is that the applicant authority shall have applied appropriate recovery procedures available and that the measures taken will not result in the payment in full of the claim.[96] Hence, it is also possible for an applicant Member State to request the recovery of an amount, which exceeds the amount that will be possible to recover by the applicant State through such procedures, *e.g.* by attachment in the present and forthcoming payments from the institutions of pensions or earnings in the applicant State to the debtor,[97] when these payments, or the attachment of other assets of the debtor in the applicant State, will not be able to result in the payment in full of the claim/s. Another obstacle to recovery, which is addressed to the applicant State, is a provision of a debt threshold of EUR 1 500 in the Implementing recovery directive,[98] which limits the possibilities of cross-border recovery of tax claims by stipulating that no request for mutual assistance may be made if the total amount of the claim is less than this amount.

6.1.2.1.2 Interim Measures

The existence and concept of a decision on interim measures, such as precautionary measures, differ in comparison between the Member States of the EU in relation to tax claims, as is evident from the Recovery directive, which states that the requested authority shall take precautionary measures to ensure recovery of a claim in so far as the laws or regulations in force in the Member States in which it is situated so permit.[99] A decision of precautionary measures from an applicant Member State shall, according to this directive, be directly recognized

93. *See* Art. 4, 3 c.
94. *See* Art. 14 compared to Art. 6.
95. *See* Art. 14, b, first part. *Also see* 6.1.2.3 for further comments on the exceptions to this provision.
96. *See* Art. 7, 2 b.
97. *See* 7.2.1 about national laws on the attachment of the earnings of the debtor.
98. *See* Art. 25, 2.
99. *See* Art. 13.

and automatically treated as an instrument permitting enforcement of a claim of the Member State in which the requested authority is situated.[100] A similar view as in the Recovery directive, that a cooperation between States should be based on titles of execution of precautionary measures permitting enforcement, is evident in the OECD Model Tax Convention on Income and on Capital.[101]

6.1.2.2 Conventions

6.1.2.2.1 Grounds of Refusal

The grounds of refusal and other obstacles to mutual assistance, as also presented in more details below, related to the Council of Europe and OECD convention on mutual administrative assistance in tax matters are found in its Articles 14, 18-19 and 21,[102] and in the partially similar Nordic agreement on assistance in tax matters in its Articles 4, 6, 10, and 14.[103] The convention mentioned requires that the applicant State shall have pursued all means available in its own territory, except where recourse to such means would give rise to disproportionate difficulty.[104]

The Nordic agreement on assistance in tax matters requires that administrative assistance may only be requested if the requested measures could not be taken in the own State without significant difficulties,[105] and the Benelux convention on the mutual assistance for the recovery of tax claims also stipulates requirements in a similar formula.[106] Another obstacle to recovery, which is addressed to the applicant State, is a provision of a debt threshold of approximately EUR 270 in the Implementing agreement to the Nordic agreement on assistance in tax matters,[107]

100. *See* Art. 13 compared to Art. 8.
101. *See* Art. 27, 4.
102. *See* Art. 14, 1 (Time-limits beyond which a tax claim can not be enforced), Art. 18 (Information to be provided by the applicant State, Art. 19 (possibility of declining a request), and Art. 21 (Protection of persons and limits to the obligation to provide assistance).
103. *See* Art. 4, 3 (Assistance may only be requested if the requested measure could not be taken in the own State without significant difficulties, and if the Contracting State presenting the request according to its own legislation could render similar assistance to the State to which the request was directed), Art. 6, 1 (A request for administrative assistance may be refused, if the Contracting State from which the assistance is requested, considers this to be in conflict with its own public interests), Art. 10, 2 (A request for the procurement of information may be refused if business, industry or professional secrets would become disclosed if the request would be honoured), and Art. 14, 2-3 (Time-limits beyond which a tax claim can not be enforced).
104. *See* Art. 19 and Explanatory report on the Convention on Mutual Administrative Assistance in Tax Matters, pp. 47-48.
105. *See* Art. 4, 3.
106. *See* Art. 3, § 3, which requires 'L'autorité compétente du pays requis n'est pas tenue de donner suite à la requisition lorsque l'autorité compétente du pays créancier n'a pas épuisé sur son propre territoire les moyens de recouvrement de sa créance.' *Also* compare Exposé des motifs to the convention.
107. *See* para. 6 of the Implementing agreement to the Nordic agreement on assistance in tax matters, which stipulates a debt threshold, expressed in all the currencies of the respective Nordic States, which corresponds to an amount of 2 500 Swedish crowns (SEK). This equals, at an exchange rate of SEK 9, 15 for EUR 1, to approximately EUR 270.

which limits the possibilities of cross-border recovery of tax claims by stipulating that no request for mutual assistance may be made if the total amount of the claim is less than this amount.

6.1.2.2.2 Interim Measures

Provisions on precautionary measures are included in the Council of Europe and OECD convention on mutual administrative assistance in tax matters, the Nordic agreement on assistance in tax matters and the Benelux convention on the mutual assistance for the recovery of tax claims. The first one stipulates that, at the request of the applicant State, the requested State shall, with a view to the recovery of an amount of tax, take measures of conservancy even if the claim is contested, or is not yet subject of an instrument permitting enforcement.[108] The Explanatory report to the convention makes clear that this provision of the convention enables an applicant State to request another State to take measures of conservancy, even if it is not yet possible to ask for assistance in recovery. It also lays down a condition, which must be complied with in every case, the requirement that the amount of the tax be determined beforehand, if only provisionally, or partially, and also that in any event a request for measures of conservancy cannot be made before the applicant State itself can take such measures.[109]

A provision, similar to the convention, exists in the Nordic agreement on assistance in tax matters,[110] which stipulates that in order to secure the payments of tax claims pursuant to this agreement they shall be governed by the laws or the administrative practices in the contracting State where the security has been demanded and that such a security could also exist if the claim has not been established. The Benelux convention on the mutual assistance for the recovery of tax claims provides the possibility to take precautionary measures at the request of an applicant State to guarantee the enforcement of the sum of a contested claim.[111] The requested authority is, however, pursuant to this convention, not obliged to take precautionary measures according to its legislation if similar measures do not exist in the applicant State.[112]

6.1.2.3 Periods of Limitation

The Recovery directive,[113] the Council of Europe and OECD convention on mutual administrative assistance in tax matters[114] and the Nordic agreement on

108. *See* Art. 12.
109. *See* p. 36.
110. *See* Art. 19, 1.
111. *See* Art. 3.
112. *See* Art. 4, § 1.
113. *See* Art. 15, 1.
114. *See* Art. 14, 1 and Explanatory report on the Convention on Mutual Administrative Assistance in Tax Matters, p. 39. *Also* compare Grau Ruiz, pp. 196-198, where she makes reference to that conventions normally establish that issues concerning the time-limits on a tax claim are to be governed strictly by the laws of the applicant State.

assistance in tax matters[115] are, with one exception, ultimately based on the applicant State's legislation of periods of limitation in matters of cross-border recovery of tax claims in another requested State. Provisions, which take into account steps taken in the recovery of claims by the requested State to the extent they would have had the effect of suspending, or interrupting, or prolonging the periods of limitation in the applicant State's legislation exist both in the Recovery directive and in the Council of Europe and OECD convention on mutual administrative assistance in tax matters.[116]

A transmission of a request between Member States, based on the Recovery directive, is not sufficient to interrupt the period of limitation. Only an action taken in relation to the debtor would be sufficient to achieve such an interruption. The exceptional provision in the Nordic agreement on assistance in tax matters also takes into account such steps by the requested State, without a demand that they should have any counterparts in the applicant State's legislation.[117] The ultimate period of limitation for the purpose of recovery related to the age of a tax claim is governed by non-identical national legislations.

The Recovery directive does not oblige, but entitle, Member States to recover tax claims from other Member States if the *initial* request applies to claims, which are more than five years old, dating from the moment the title of execution is established in the applicant State to the date of the request.[118] Consequently, an initial request for information, or for notification, concerning a claim, which at that time is less than five years old, can stop the deadline of the five years period for a following request of recovery of that claim. An exception to this five years provision is a contested claim, or a title of execution, where the time-limit instead shall be accounted from the moment at which they may no longer be contested in the applicant State.[119]

The Council of Europe and OECD convention on mutual administrative assistance in tax matters stipulates that the requested State will in any case not be obliged to comply with a request of recovery which is submitted after an ultimate period of 15 years from the date of the original instrument permitting

115. *See* Art. 14, 2.
116. *See* Art. 15, 2 of the Directive, Art. 14, 2 of the Convention and Explanatory report on the Convention on Mutual Administrative Assistance in Tax Matters, p. 40. *Also* compare Grau Ruiz, p. 199, where she concludes that the provision of exception to the main rule in Art. 15, *i.e.* in the second section of this article, of the Recovery directive highlights a more restrictive approach of the community legislator, which reflects the idea of a duality in the interruption of the time-limit when establishing equivalence.
117. *See* Art. 14, 3.
118. *See* Art. 14, b, first part. *Also see*, about the meaning of the word 'initial', Presidency note, document 5910/00 of the Council of the European Union of 3 Feb. 2000 on the subject of Mutual assistance for the recovery of claims, which includes the Presidency compromise amending the Commission's proposal. This compromise states that the word 'initial' is added in order to make it clear that the introduction of a request for information could stop the deadline for recovery.
119. *See* Art. 14, b, final part.

enforcement,[120] meaning that the contracting States to the convention are not obliged, but entitled to recover tax claims from other contracting States, which are less than 15 years old. The Nordic agreement on assistance in tax matters refers the determination of the ultimate period of limitation to be governed by the applicant State's legislation.[121]

6.1.2.4 Enforcement of a Contested Claim and Appeals

6.1.2.4.1 Recovery Directive

The Recovery directive provides an option for the recovery of a contested claim from the applicant State to the extent such a claim is recoverable under the legislation of the applicant State and the requested State's legislation allows it.[122] If the recovery of a contested claim is allowed by the requested State, the directive also provides for an extension of the time-limits of recovery, which then is to be accounted from the moment at which the claim no longer may be contested in the applicant State.[123] The requested State may also, on a reasoned request from the applicant State, take precautionary measures to the extent possible in national legislation in order to protect the right of the applicant State.[124] In case the applicant State loses a dispute, the previous request of recovery to the requested State becomes unfounded as far as either part of or the whole substance of the claim or the validity of the instrument issued by the applicant authority are concerned.

The applicant State, which carries the risk for costs incurred in such situations, is then obliged to repay the claimed amount together with any compensation of damages due to the potential debtor if it looses a dispute regarding a contested claim.[125] Damages derived from a request of precautionary measures initiated by an applicant Member State are also, according to the directive, payable by the applicant Member State if it looses a dispute regarding a contested claim.[126] These are no doubt important provisions of legal protection favouring the potential debtor. It compensates him from the economic effects of too far-reaching recovery measures taken in the efforts of efficiency on the initiative of the creditor, the applicant State.

6.1.2.4.2 Conventions

The Council of Europe and OECD convention on mutual administrative assistance in tax matters allows the recovery of a contested claim, however, only subject to an

120. *See* Art. 14, 3 and Explanatory report on the Convention on Mutual Administrative Assistance in Tax Matters, pp. 40-41.
121. *See* Art. 14, 2.
122. *See* Art. 12, 2 b.
123. *See* Art. 14, b, final part.
124. *See* Art. 13.
125. *See* Art. 12, 2 b.
126. *See* Art. 13 compared to Art. 12, 2 b.

agreement between the involved States.[127] The Nordic agreement on assistance in tax matters shares some common features with the Recovery directive, but goes even further than the directive in terms of efficiency.[128] The Nordic agreement is not, as is the case of the directive and of the convention, linked to the national acceptance of the requested State of the recovery of a contested claim.

6.1.2.5 Costs and Repayment

States, which participate in a cooperation based on EC law and conventions in the tax recovery law area, normally commit themselves, at least in ordinary recovery cases, to the principle of making available their own resources of recovery measures to another State in its capacity of a creditor, without having any possibilities of reclaiming such costs triggered by the cooperation from the applicant State. This is the principal case, with some exceptions, according to the Recovery directive, the Council of Europe and OECD convention on mutual administrative assistance in tax matters and in the Nordic agreement on assistance in tax matters.[129]

Exceptions to this principle exist, based on specific provisions of reimbursement of costs. The Recovery directive stipulates that the applicant and requested States may agree on reimbursement arrangements for costs specific to where recovery poses a specific problem and concerns a very large amount in cost, or relates to the fight against organized crime.[130] An example where the applicant and the requested States may agree on reimbursement arrangements for costs is when an applicant State requests another Member State to apply for bankruptcy proceeding under the Recovery directive.[131]

The directive also stipulates, as just mentioned, that the applicant State shall remain liable to the requested State for any costs and any losses incurred as a result of actions held to be unfounded, as far as either the substance of the claim or the validity of the instrument issued by the applicant authority are concerned.[132] Such a situation creates a liability, according to this provision, for the applicant State to reimburse the requested State for any costs and any losses incurred as a result of actions taken by the requested State on the initiative of the applicant State. The applicant State is obliged to communicate with the requested State if the request for recovery, or for precautionary measures, becomes devoid of purpose as a result of payment of the claim, or its cancellation, or for any other reason, and where the

---

127. *See* Art. 11, 2 and Explanatory report on the Convention on Mutual Administrative Assistance in Tax Matters, pp. 33-34.
128. *See* Art. 14, 1 of the Agreement compared to Art. 12 of the Directive.
129. *See* Art. 18, 1 and 2 of the Directive, Art. 26, a of the Convention and Explanatory report on the Convention on Mutual Administrative Assistance in Tax Matters, p. 67, and Art. 22 of the Agreement read e contrario.
130. *See* Art. 18, 3.
131. *See* 6.2.2.1.1.1 for further details on an application for bankruptcy under Art. 6 of the Recovery directive.
132. *See* Art. 18, 4.

amount of the claim which is the subject of the request for recovery, or for precautionary measures, is adjusted for any reason.[133]

The provision of reimbursement in the Recovery directive is linked to the provision in the same directive on the recovery of a contested claim, which, as just mentioned, also obliges the applicant State to repay to the debtor the recovered amount together with any compensation due, in accordance with the requested States legislation, if it looses a dispute regarding a contested claim.[134] If the requested State decides to request reimbursement arrangements it shall, according to the Implementing recovery directive, notify the applicant State in writing of the reasons for its view that recovery of the claim poses a specific problem, entails very high costs, or relates to the fight against organized crime.[135] Agreements on such reimbursement arrangements shall, according to the same directive, be decided by an official appointed and duly authorized to make such agreements by each Member State.[136]

The Council of Europe and OECD convention on mutual administrative assistance in tax matters provides an obligation for the applicant State to bear extraordinary costs incurred in providing assistance.[137] The Nordic agreement on assistance in tax matters only stipulates an obligation for the applicant State to bear costs incurred in matters of assistance in certain defined situations. This is the case only for costs in certain litigation proceedings or in bankruptcy proceedings in the other contracting State which have been caused by a matter of assistance initiated by the applicant State.[138] Such proceedings related to a matter of assistance may not, according to this agreement, be initiated by the applicant State before the requested State has given its express consent thereto.[139]

The provision of the Nordic agreement on assistance in tax matters related to matters of litigation or bankruptcy proceedings in another State has no explicit counterpart neither in the Recovery directive nor in the Council of Europe and OECD convention on mutual administrative assistance in tax matters. The Explanatory report to the Council of Europe and OECD convention on mutual administrative assistance in tax matters concludes that the applicant State would under its own law be obliged to refund to the taxpayer any amount of tax wrongly collected, together with interest and related charges in cases where the taxpayer's appeal is subsequently upheld.[140]

---

133. *See* Art. 18.1-2 of the Implementing recovery directive.
134. *See* Art. 12, 2 b compared to Art. 18, 4.
135. *See* Art. 28, 1.
136. *See* Art. 27.
137. *See* Art. 26, b. of the convention and Explanatory report on the Convention on Mutual Administrative Assistance in Tax Matters, pp. 67-68.
138. *See* Art. 22 of the agreement. Para. 3, E, 8 of the Implementing agreement to the Nordic agreement on assistance in tax matters, which stipulates, in relation to Art. 22 of the agreement, that litigation and bankruptcy costs shall first be deducted by the recovering authority from the recovered amount.
139. *See* Art. 16, 2.
140. *See* Explanatory report on the Convention on Mutual Administrative Assistance in Tax Matters, p. 33.

The recovered amount of a tax claim is, contrary to the case in some parts of EC law and multilateral conventions in the criminal law area,[141] to the extent that the above mentioned exceptions would not apply, paid by the requested State, in its currency, to the applicant State.[142] Payments by the requested State are, according to the Implementing recovery directive, calculated as based on the applicable rate of exchange, the latest selling rate recorded on the most representative exchange market, or markets, of the applicant State, on the date when the request for recovery was made by the applicant State.[143]

The Nordic implementing agreement on assistance in tax matters stipulates, as opposed to the Implementing recovery directive, that the applicable rate of exchange shall instead be determined by the requested State into its currency as soon as the request has been received and that payments to the applicant State may be made in the currency of the applicant State.[144] The Benelux convention on the mutual assistance for the recovery of tax claims stipulates that the competent authorities shall reach common agreements on the issues of transfer of recovered money and reimbursement of non-recoverable costs.[145] The requested State, which transfers payments, acts in this situation as a tax-collecting agent on behalf of the applicant State. The applicant State normally also receives a report from the requested State on what recovery measures have been taken, and their result in terms of paid amount, or non-payment of the tax claim.

---

141. The enforced proceeds of fines and confiscation on the initiative of the applicant State are kept by the requested State, in the absence of specific agreements between the involved States if that is possible, according to Art. 47 of the European Convention on the international validity of criminal judgments of 28 May 1970, Art. 5, 5 a of the United Nations Convention against illicit traffic in narcotic drugs and psychotropic substances of 20 Dec. 1988, and Art. 15 of the Council of Europe's Convention on the laundering, search, seizure and confiscation of proceeds from crime of 8 Nov. 1990. *Also see* Explanatory report on the Convention on Laundering, Search, Seizure and Confiscation of Proceeds from Crime, p. 32. *Also see* Art. 13 of the Financial penalties Framework Decision. Both the United Nations convention, *see* Art. 5, 5 b, ii and the European Council's convention, *see* end of Art. 15, allow contrary to the European Convention, the involved States to reach an agreement on profit-sharing of the enforced amount, which may result in a repayment from the requested State of part of the enforced proceeds to the applicant State. The Confiscation Framework Decision also allows, according to its Art. 16, profit-sharing of the enforced amount. The Nordic agreement on the cooperation concerning the mutual assistance of enforcement of judgments or decisions on fines, confiscation or compensation for litigation costs, implemented through similar enacted legislations in the Nordic States, is silent regarding the issue of repayment between the involved States. The enforced amounts according to the Nordic agreement are, however, repaid between the States.
142. *See* Art. 9, 1 of the Recovery directive compared to Art. 19 of the Implementing recovery directive and Art. 18 of the Nordic agreement on assistance in tax matters.
143. *See* Art. 14, 2.
144. *See* para. 7.
145. *See* Art. 7 compared to Exposé des motifs to the Convention.

6.1.3 Conclusions

6.1.3.1 Recognition and Enforceability

The provisions of mutual recognition in both the Brussels I regulation and in the Recovery directive are aimed at providing a developed and high degree of efficiency in the cross-border context. However, a mandatory provision for the declaration of the enforceability, in an exequatur proceeding, exists in the regulation. It decreases the level of efficiency in the cross-border context even if it is aimed at safeguarding other interests, *e.g.* privacy, proportionality and legal certainty.

An optional provision for the declaration of enforceability exists in the directive, which, however, is balanced off against other provisions in the same directive. These provisions take into account the interest of privacy and proportionality, *e.g.* the provisions on the liability of Member States to pay damages and cost to the extent that the recovery of a claim is established to have been unfounded. These different solutions, which are found in the regulation and in the directive, may at least partially be explained by some fundamental differences in these respective law areas.[146]

6.1.3.1.1 Brussels I Regulation

The establishment of a better developed system of mutuality in the Brussels I regulation between the Member States of the EU is required for the enforcement of the titles of execution of a private creditor of origin from one Member State in another Member State by the abolishment of the exequatur proceeding in order to provide the private creditor a more immediate equal and efficient access to justice when he applies for the enforcement of his title of execution.

This better developed system of mutuality should be based on the EC principles of mutuality and mean that Member States should not oppose titles of execution from other Member States, despite differences in substantial law and in procedural law. This would contribute to better promote the free movement of judgments between the Member States of the EU. The EC principle of mutuality is in different areas developed towards the abolishment of intermediate measures and other obstacles, which are contrary to this principle, *e.g.* the provisions of exequatur proceeding.

The principle of equal treatment indicates that a private creditor of one Member State, who holds a nationally enforceable title of execution from that State, should not be unequally treated, so as to be subject to special provisions of exequatur proceeding, which are not applicable to a creditor of the enforcing Member State, who holds a national title of execution from that State.

146. *See* 2.9.

The European Enforcement Order for uncontested claims, the European Order for payment procedure, and the European Small Claims Procedure are examples in EC in the contractual law area, where provisions of exequatur proceeding have been abolished and an *ex parte* proceeding for enforcement has been introduced together with provisions of grounds of refusal of enforcement and other guarantees. Consequently, a development of these community principles would in the case of the Brussels I regulation require the abolishment of provisions of exequatur proceeding related to titles of execution from one Member State of the EU in other Member States,[147] and the introduction of an *ex parte* proceeding for applications of enforcement of such titles of execution, together with provisions of grounds of refusal of enforcement and other sufficient guarantees.

An example of such a guarantee could be the posting of security by the creditor, decided upon by the regulated enforcement agent, related to enforcement proceedings of opposed claims, in order to create efficiency in the interest of the creditor, but also in the interest of protection of the debtor. This amount for security should be fixed at a level, which should be sufficient for the payment of any possible damages in compensation to the debtor, according to the legislation of the enforcing State. Such a development should be able to result in that creditors, who are able to present a nationally enforceable judgment from one Member State under the Brussels I regulation, would come into the same national position as a national creditor in another enforcing Member State, which would guarantee a more equal treatment of creditors and debtors in the European judicial area.

Such an idea of development would also correspond to the legal objectives related to the Tampere conclusions, the Council's programme of measures for implementation of the principle of mutual recognition, the Hague Programme of the European Council, the Action plan of the Council and the Commission, the Moscow Resolution, the Council of Europe's recommendation on enforcement, and the ALI-UNIDROIT Principles of Transnational Civil Procedure.[148]

As a practical matter of service to a private creditor it should be contemplated to introduce a possibility for him to file an application for enforcement under the Brussels I regulation, by the use of a multilingual officially approved form, to the competent authorities of enforcement in the Member State of origin of the title of execution, instead of filing it directly to the corresponding authorities of actual enforcement in another Member State. The Member State of origin should then be obliged to transfer the application to the competent body of actual enforcement in the other Member State. Such a service is already available to a private creditor under the Convention between the Member States of the European Communities on the simplification of procedures for the recovery of maintenance payments, done at Rome on 6 November 1990, even though it has not yet entered into

147. The regulation already provides the possibility of an automatic recognition through its Art. 33, but not for automatic enforceability.
148. *See* 1.1.1.1, 1.1.1.1.1, and 1.1.1.1.3.

force,[149] and under the Nordic convention regarding the enforcement of maintenance claims of 1962.[150]

The Proposal for a Council regulation on jurisdiction, applicable law, recognition and enforcement of decisions and cooperation in matters relating to maintenance obligations[151] also includes a similar provision of service to a private maintenance creditor.[152] It remains to be discussed to what extent and proportion private creditors, respectively the Member States, should pay for the services made available under such a possible service obligation under the Brussels I regulation, *i.e.* what possible fees creditors should pay, or not pay, to their national regulated enforcement agents. As an alternative to the abolishment in the Brussels I regulation of the provisions of exequatur proceeding it has also been discussed to evolve the existing system through making other changes in the regulation.[153]

6.1.3.2 Interim Measures

Both the Brussels I regulation and the Recovery directive include provisions on interim measures. The regulation requires for its application the establishment of a title of execution in a proceeding *inter partes* on interim measures to be applicable, while this requirement has no counterpart in the directive. This lack in the Recovery directive is, however, balanced off by other provisions in the same directive, which take the interest of privacy and proportionality into account, *e.g.* the provisions on the liability of Member States to pay damages and cost, to the extent the precautionary measures taken were unfounded. It may be possible to introduce some principal ideas of solutions from the Recovery directive into the works of reforming the provisions of interim measures in the Brussels I regulation. However, several other considerations have also to be taken into account, discussed and be subject to a more profound analysis, in this law area, which concern a two party relationship governed by civil law.

An idea, to further discuss, is the introduction of a requirement for the assumed private creditor of posting security at a sufficiently high level to compensate his private counter-party if he finally looses the dispute. The aim of such an idea would be to obtain an order on interim measures in an *ex parte* proceeding, which is recognized and enforceable in other Member States, to achieve an

149. *See* Art. 5, 1. The convention has not entered into force, even though it has been signed by some States: Belgium, Denmark, Germany, Greece, Ireland, Italy, Luxemburg, the Netherlands, Portugal and the United Kingdom. *Also see* Leroy on the convention, La Transparence patrimoniale, pp. 144-145.
150. *See* Art. 2, second paragraph, as amended in 2000.
151. *See* 2.10.1 for further information about this proposal.
152. *See* Art. 42, 1.
153. *See* EC Study JLS/C4/2005/03, Report on the Application of Regulation Brussels I in the Member States, p. 357-359, where several possible changes are discussed, *e.g.* a further reduction of the grounds for non-recognition, a further simplification of the exequatur proceeding in the first instance, an introduction of a written procedure in the second instance, and that the certificate provided for in Arts 53-56 of the regulation shall have binding legal force.

efficient subsequent enforcement of that order and at the same time secure the interest of the assumed debtor.[154] Other ideas and considerations may be found in the context of the idea of cross-border attachment of the debtor's financial holdings on accounts administered by garnishees, banks and other financial institutions. This is an issue, which has been treated in literature,[155] and also been subject to a proposal of introducing a European Garnishment Order for Bank Accounts and the similar Proposal for a Council regulation on jurisdiction, applicable law, recognition and enforcement of decisions and cooperation in matters relating to maintenance obligations.[156]

The debtor's freedom of transferring money from his bank accounts in one Member State to bank accounts in other Member States is a right of free movement of capital and payments based on the EC Treaty.[157] The debtor is therefore at liberty to transfer his money, several times per day if he would like, between his bank accounts in the Member States of the EU. His exercise of this legitimate liberty may, however, be harmful to his creditors to the extent they do not dispose of any effective interim measures, which are recognized and enforceable in other Member States in the cross-border context corresponding to such transfer of money. In brief conclusion, to reform and make more efficient the enforcement of interim measures, the provisions of provisional and precautionary measures, under the Brussels I regulation, have to be properly balanced against the sometimes differing interests of *e.g.* the creditor, the debtor, the financial institutions and the society. As this requires a more profound and extensive analysis it is only possible to here raise some ideas for a further discussion, without drawing any final conclusions.

---

154. *See*, for a similar idea of development, EC Study JLS/C4/2005/03, Report on the Application of Regulation Brussels I in the Member States, p. 363, where it is suggested that Art. 31 of the regulation should be supplemented by the following provisions: '(2) In the case of an order for interim measures the court shall make the enforcement of the order dependent on the providing of a bank guarantee (on conditions to be specified by the court) for repayment or damages due whenever the applicant should be finally unsuccessful in the proceedings for the substance of the matter. In order to avoid unusual hardship, however, the court may grant the applicant an exception. (3) The court vested with jurisdiction for, and seized by either party with the substance of the matter has power to discharge, to modify or to adapt to its own legal system any provisional measure granted by a court of another Member State.'
155. *See* EC Study JAI/02/03/2002, C, II and III compared to E, III, 2, Jeuland, Les garanties de la saisie européenne de créances bancaires, Le droit processuel et le droit de l'exécution, pp. 395-406, Kennett, The Enforcement of Judgments in Europe, pp. 250-285, Kerameus, Enforcement proceedings, p. 77, about a bank as garnishee, de Leval, Subject of the proceedings, The execution of court decisions in civil cases, p. 53 and appendix II, pp. 78-81, and de Leval and Georges, La saisie-arrêt bancaire dans l'union européenne, L'efficacité de la justice civile en Europe, pp. 185-204.
156. *See* 2.10.1 about the Green paper on improving the efficiency of the enforcement of judgments in the European Union: the attachment of bank accounts compared to EC Study JAI/02/03/2002, E, III, 2. *Also see* 2.10.1 about the Proposal for a Council regulation on jurisdiction, applicable law, recognition and enforcement of decisions and cooperation in matters relating to maintenance obligations.
157. *See* Art. 56 EC Treaty.

6.1.3.2.1 Recovery Directive

It has been discussed to introduce in the Recovery directive a similar concept of precautionary measures as in the Council of Europe and OECD convention on mutual administrative assistance in tax matters, related to the wordings in the convention, which permits precautionary measures for a claim that is not yet subject of an instrument permitting enforcement,[158] in order to increase the efficiency of the provision of precautionary measures in this directive.[159] A fair balance between the interest of efficiency and the interest of the debtor's protection is, however, already secured by reference in the provision of precautionary measures in the Recovery directive to other articles in the same directive.

The reference made in the provision of precautionary measures in the Recovery directive to the referral provision of the same directive to national laws,[160] guarantees that the original decision of precautionary measures of the applicant Member State is based on a balanced judicial control of the interest of efficiency and the interest of the debtor's protection in a legal proceeding that meets the legal requirements, in a typical *periculum in mora* situation, in that State. The efficiency in the requested Member State concerning the enforcement of the decision of precautionary measures from the applicant Member State is also secured by provisions of direct recognition and automatic enforceability in the directive.[161] In the event an applicant Member State looses a dispute regarding a contested claim, the interest of the debtor's protection is secured by a provision of damages in the directive.[162]

An introduction into the Recovery directive as a legal basis for precautionary measures under this directive of this specific concept of precautionary measures from the convention, would not be acceptable for several reasons. Even though it may be argued that an introduction of such a concept would contribute to an increased efficiency of precautionary measures, a more important argument against such a solution is that a claim, which is not yet subject to an instrument permitting enforcement, lacks sufficient enforceable legal basis. It does not qualify for the category of national enforceable titles of execution of precautionary measures. Another argument against such a solution is that the interest of the debtor's protection would not be satisfied and consequently the present fair balance established in the Recovery directive between the interest of efficiency and the interest of the debtor's protection would be altered negatively in relation to the latter interest.

Consequently, to introduce into the Recovery directive the solution from the convention would lead to a more limited reference from the provision of precautionary measures in the directive than only to parts of the referral provision to

158. *See* Art. 12.
159. *See* Art. 13.
160. *See* Art. 6.
161. *See* Art. 13 compared to Art. 8.
162. *See* Art. 13 compared to Art. 12, 2 b.

national laws of the same directive.[163] It would also alter the present fair balance established between the interest of efficiency and the interest of the debtor's protection and would be contrary to the legal objectives of the directive, presently secured by references in the provision of precautionary measures in the directive to other articles in it.

A cooperation between Member States based on titles of execution of precautionary measures permitting enforcement, as in the Recovery directive, the Benelux convention on the mutual assistance for the recovery of tax claims and the OECD Model Tax Convention on Income and on Capital, is also better aimed to meet the interest of reciprocity between Member States than a cooperation, as in the Council of Europe and OECD convention on mutual administrative assistance in tax matters and in the Nordic agreement on assistance in tax matters, which is based on claims, not yet subject to enforcement.

The present wordings of the provision of precautionary measures in the Recovery directive satisfy, in an all-over evaluation, a fair balance between the interest of efficiency and the interest of the debtor's protection and also meet the interest of reciprocity between Member States. It therefore seems preferable that the wordings of the directive should remain unchanged.

6.1.3.3 Grounds of Non-recognition or Grounds of Refusal

The grounds of non-recognition, or grounds of refusal, or other obstacles in the cross-border context related to the enforcement of contractual claims and the recovery of tax claims differ. This is a result of the differing features of cooperation in these areas.[164] Given this background, the conclusions related to some of these provisions in EC law and conventions are treated here.

6.1.3.3.1 Service of Legal Documents

An incorrect service of legal documents in the area of the enforcement of contractual claims may constitute a ground of non-recognition, as evident from some rulings of the ECJ, or a ground of refusal of enforcement. Even if provisions on the service of documents are included in the Recovery directive,[165] the Council of Europe and OECD convention on mutual administrative assistance in tax matters[166] and the Nordic agreement on assistance in tax matters,[167] in many States the possibility of recovery of taxes does not depend on whether or not the documents have actually reached the taxpayer and recovery can take place even when it

163. *See* Art. 6, 2.
164. *See* 2.9.
165. *See* Art. 5 of the Recovery directive compared to Arts 9-11 of the Implementing recovery directive.
166. *See* Art. 17. Some contracting States, *e.g.* the United States of America, have made reservations against the provision of service of documents, *see* annex 6. *Also* compare Explanatory report on the Convention on Mutual Administrative Assistance in Tax Matters, pp. 43-45.
167. *See* Arts 1 a and 9.

is not certain that the notice to pay or the final demand has reached him.[168] An explanation to the differing solutions in these two legal areas are the fundamental differences, which are found in the first phase of the establishment of a title of execution in relation to the nature of the claims.[169] Consequently, as a result of these fundamental differences, an incorrect service of legal documents is given a greater weight in favour of protecting the possible debtor in the contractual law area than in the tax recovery area.

6.1.3.3.2 Exhaustion of National Means of Recovery

The mutual assistance for the recovery of taxes between States requires that the applicant State first should make certain efforts to recover the tax debts before it is entitled to forward a request for the recovery of the debts to another State. To what extent the applicant State first should have to make such efforts differs. This formal requirement in this tax recovery area has no counterpart in the corresponding area of the cross-border enforcement of contractual claims. Many private creditors are, however, anyway likely to try their best to exhaust every nationally available possibility before they are prepared to assume the extra costs associated with possible cross-border enforcement actions. The Recovery directive does not impose the same high level of restrictions as the conventions, because the directive allows an applicant State to forward a request for recovery without first exhausting all, or almost all, means of national recovery measures in the applicant State when normal appropriate national recovery measures have been taken and they could not be expected to result in the payment in full of the claims.

An applicant Member State, which forwards a request for mutual assistance contrary to the requirements in this provision of the directive risks, if the requested Member State does not turn it down as contrary to the directive, that the following actions can be declared invalid and trigger damages towards the taxpayer concerned. If the assets of the debtor, according to the requirements under the directive, could be expected to be insufficient to cover the total amount of the tax debt, a request for recovery may be forwarded to another Member State for the amount of the debt, which exceeds what is likely to be covered by the debtor's assets in the applicant State, *e.g.* through a continuing attachment in earnings or pensions.

The solution in Article 7, 2 b of the directive provides more flexibility to the applicant State than the conventions. The tax creditors have, for the same reasons as the private creditors, the same interest to make their best efforts to first exhaust every nationally available possibilities of recovery before they request the mutual assistance of another State. It may therefore be contemplated, as an alternative to the present solution in the Recovery directive, to abolish this requirement, and

168. *See* Explanatory report on the Convention on Mutual Administrative Assistance in Tax Matters, p. 44 (161.).
169. *See* 2.9 for further comments on these fundamental differences.

instead stipulate there that an applicant State, which has not exhausted these possibilities, should bear the costs of recovery of the requested State.

6.1.3.3.3 Debt Thresholds

None of the treated parts of EC law and conventions related to the area of the enforcement of contractual claims include any formal debt thresholds, which limit the amount to be enforced on behalf of the private creditor in relation to the debtor. In contrast to this area, such formal debt thresholds frequently exist in the corresponding mutual assistance tax recovery area. The concept of debt thresholds in the tax recovery area may be explained by the desire in cooperating States, both in their capacity of creditors and enforcement agents, to minimize their costs of treatment for requests related to more insignificant amounts in their administrations and instead be able to allocate the resources available for this cooperation to more substantial amounts.

This desire is of a particular importance to the requested enforcing State, which normally holds the costs of recovery in a matter of mutual assistance, in its recovery work on behalf of the applicant State. Consequently, if these debt thresholds would be abolished it would cause the risk that a requested State would have to carry more costs than corresponding to the recovered amount of the claim on behalf of the applicant State. Even if such formal debt thresholds risk to diminish the credibility of recovery efficiency in relation to the debtor in the cross-border context and correspondingly undermine its preventive effect in case of non-payment of taxes, these debt thresholds do not exclude the recovery of tax claims from the debtor, which are below such debt thresholds, in the national context. The solutions in these two legal areas clearly reflect their different features of cooperation between States.[170]

6.1.3.3.4 Public Policy

Provisions of public policy exist, although if not frequently, in the treated law areas, *e.g.* as a basis for non-recognition in the Brussels I regulation,[171] and as a basis for refusal of exchange of information for recovery purposes in the Recovery directive. It may be argued that a possibly even more developed principle of mutuality in EC law may cause provisions of public policy to become unnecessary. On the contrary it may be argued that several rulings of the ECJ, where references are made to the European Convention on Human Rights, indicate that such

170. *See* 2.9 about differing features of cooperation in EC law.

171. *Also see* EC Study JLS/C4/2005/03, Report on the Application of Regulation Brussels I in the Member States, pp. 241-252, where the public policy provision of the Brussels I regulation, Art. 34, 1, is discussed. The study concludes, p. 250, that the application of substantive public policy has been proved to be a rare exception under Art. 34, 1, but, nevertheless, it can not be excluded that a substantive policy exception will still be needed in unavoidable and extreme situations.

provisions, which respond to the requirements of this convention, are important to maintain in EC law. Another factor, which motivates a maintenance of provisions of public policy, is that the national legislations of the Member States will under a predictable time be likely to remain different and only to some extent be harmonized through EC law. It is therefore recommended to maintain such provisions as a ground of refusal of enforcement and of appeal against a decision of enforcement by a regulated enforcement agent.

6.1.3.4 Periods of Limitation

The periods of limitation related to the enforcement of contractual claims in the context of cross-border enforcement of such claims, in relation to the Brussels I regulation, the European Enforcement Order for uncontested claims, and the European Order for payment procedure, are governed by the law applicable to contractual obligations according to the Rome convention on the law applicable to contractual obligations, under the condition that the scope of application of this European law and the convention coincides and the concerned States are identical.

The Rome convention, which completes EC law, is based on the idea that the periods of limitation should be governed by the law of the State of the establishment of the claim. This corresponds in the Recovery directive to the same idea, where reference is made to the applicant State's legislation, *i.e.* to the of the State of the establishment of the claim. Consequently, both the Brussels I regulation and the Recovery directive depart from the same principal position in this context, the law of the State of the establishment of the original obligation, of a civil law nature, respectively of a public law nature.

The exception in the Nordic agreement on assistance in tax matters, where the procedural steps of suspension, interruption, or prolongation of the periods of limitation established by the requested State are to be taken into account, without a demand that they should have any counterparts in the applicant State's material legislation, means that such steps should, even if they would not have been legally possible in the applicant State, have this effect in the applicant State in relation to the debtor. This exception in the Nordic agreement has no counterpart in the Recovery directive, the Council of Europe and OECD convention on mutual administrative assistance in tax matters and in this EC civil law area, where these provisions are instead ultimately governed by the law of the State of the original obligation, not by reference to steps taken according to the procedural law of the requested/enforcing State.

It has been suggested to enter a similar solution as in this exceptional provision of the Nordic agreement into the Recovery directive, supported by the argument that it would be more suitable to base this solution of the directive on the requested enforcing State's legislation,[172] instead of on that of the applicant State. An argument against such a solution is that it seems to be more logical to let the provisions

172. Compare Art. 6 of the Recovery directive.

of suspending, interrupting, or prolonging the periods of limitation of a tax claim only to be ultimately governed by the law of the State of the establishment of the original tax obligation, because of the close relationship to the law of the establishment of the original claim. Another argument against entering a similar solution into the Recovery directive is that the interest of protecting the debtor's position in this context would reasonably require that such a provision would only give effect to the procedural steps of suspension, interruption, or prolongation taken that are predictable to him based on that they exist in both the applicant and the requested Member States.

The suggested change would therefore risk to be counter-productive. As a possible alternative to the present wordings of Article 15, 2 of the Recovery directive it may, however, be contemplated, while maintaining the principle position of the applicant State's legislation, to make a minor clarification, resulting in the following wordings for this provision:

> Steps taken in the recovery of claims by the requested State in pursuance of a request for assistance, which have the effect of suspending, interrupting, or prolonging, the period of limitation according to the laws in force in the requested State, shall have the same effect in the applicant State. However, this shall apply only if suspension, interruption, or prolongation, is provided for by the laws in force in the applicant State. If suspension, interruption, or prolongation, is not provided for by the laws in force in the requested State, it is the laws in force in the applicant State that govern whether or not the steps taken in the requested State shall have such effect in the applicant State. The requested State shall inform the applicant State, without delay, about such steps taken.

The Recovery directive does not oblige, but entitle, Member States to recover tax claims from other Member States, which are more than five years old. The decision on the use of this more far-reaching recovery option is thus entirely left to the requested Member State. This means that a requested Member State could freely choose to apply any longer period of limitation than the five years period up to the limit of the ultimate period of limitation of the applicant State's legislation, even if the recovery of a claim often becomes more difficult by age. This may be of interest *e.g.* when a matter of the recovery of such old claims concerns a large amount or relates to the fight against organized crime, and when the applicant State may have to assume a responsibility for the costs of the requested State.[173]

It may, however, be that a requested State at such a decision would, in the interest of equal treatment at the recovery of foreign and domestic tax claims in the requested State, be influenced to apply a possibly shorter ultimate time-limit than the one of the applicant State if it exceeds five years, as *e.g.* would have been applicable in a corresponding situation related to the national legislation of periods of limitation of the requested State. From this option of the requested State may

173. Compare Art. 18, 4.

ensue that the requests of an applicant State for the recovery of such old claims will result in different and unequal treatments of these claims in other requested States.

6.1.3.5 Enforcement of a Contested Claim and Appeals

The enforcement of an unfounded, previously contested contractual claim, is not specifically dealt with, as in the Recovery directive, in terms of repayment to the debtor of the enforced amount and compensation for incurred damages. The Brussels I regulation is, in the context of the enforcement of a contested contractual claim, more balanced in favour of the interest of privacy of the debtor than that of the interest of efficiency of the private creditor. The recovery of a contested tax claim under the Recovery directive is, compared to this corresponding situation under the Brussels I regulation, more balanced in favour of the interest of efficiency of the creditor, the applicant State, than the interest of privacy of the debtor. These different solutions are to some extent, but not entirely, explained by the different needs of international cooperation which these respective parts of EC law represent and intend to satisfy.

A decision, which has established a contractual claim in the quality of an enforceable title, could normally be appealed against to a court. The same is also valid for a following decision on the enforcement of such a claim. In addition the decisions in exequatur proceedings on applications from private creditors are open to appeal. This is the case regarding such decisions that are based on parts of EC law and multilateral conventions regarding the enforcement of contractual claims in order to obtain a formal decision from competent authorities, courts, to declare the enforceability of a foreign enforceable title in another State.

This possibility of appeal in accordance with the rules governing procedure in contradictory matters, which lacks in the Recovery directive and certain multilateral conventions in the tax recovery area, exist in parts of EC law and multilateral conventions regarding the enforcement of contractual claims, such as in the Brussels I regulation.[174] Various solutions, but all of them of a more restrictive character than in the tax recovery area, regarding the enforcement of a claim, which has been subject to an appeal, are found in parts of EC law and multilateral conventions regarding the enforcement of contractual claims in the private law area.

A decision, which has established a tax claim, could normally be contested. The same is also valid for a following decision for the recovery of such a claim. The decisions of granting mutual assistance by the competent authorities for the recovery of taxes, according to parts of EC law and some multilateral conventions, are, however, not contestable. This is the case in relation to the Recovery directive, the Council of Europe and OECD convention on mutual administrative assistance in tax matters and the Nordic agreement on assistance in tax matters. This lack of possibilities of appeal against the decisions of the competent authorities has no

174. *See* Arts 43 and 44.

counterpart in some parts of EC law and multilateral conventions regarding the enforcement of contractual claims valid in Europe.

When one compares the possibility to appeal against a decision of the competent authorities under the Brussels I regulation, governed by a procedure in contradictory matters, to the lack of such a possibility under the Recovery directive, it becomes clear that the directive is more balanced in favour of the interest of efficiency of the creditor, the applicant State, than that of the interest of privacy of the debtor. It also becomes clear that the Brussels I regulation in this sense is more balanced in favour of the interest of privacy of the debtor than that of the interest of efficiency of the private creditor.

The solutions are to some extent, but not entirely, explained by the different kind of needs of international cooperation that the respective parts of EC law intend to satisfy. The main conclusion is that the solutions express and reflect different chosen positions on the balance of interests, and that they lead to a non-equal treatment between tax claims and contractual claims in EC law. In parts of EC law and multilateral conventions in the tax area, the recovery of a contested claim is possible, but has been treated and solved in different ways. Some, but not all, double tax treaties concluded on a bilateral basis require for the mutual assistance for the recovery of a tax claim that it first has become final, *i.e.* is not subject to a contest.

6.1.3.6 Costs and Repayment

Regarding costs, different solutions in EC law and conventions are established in the private law area related to the enforcement of contractual claims compared to the tax recovery law area. In the tax recovery law area, except in exceptional situations, the requested State normally holds both the costs related to obtain a formal decision on the recognition, when needed, and the actual costs of recovery of the claim. In the corresponding private enforcement law area none of these categories of costs is dealt with, which means that the ultimate allocation of these costs are instead governed by non-identical national laws. The Council of Europe's recommendation on enforcement[175] may, however, contribute to create a more similar treatment of costs of enforcement in national laws of the Member States.

The requested State also acts as a tax-collecting agent on behalf of the applicant State for the transfer of repayments from the debtor or from proceeds related to his realized assets. The private creditor receives, on the other hand, any possible corresponding repayments directly from the enforcement organ. This difference between the international cooperation in the public law area compared to the civil law area is explained by the differing features of these respective cooperations.[176]

175. *See* section III, para. 5 of this recommendation which stipulates: '. . . the necessary costs of enforcement should be ultimately born by the defendant notwithstanding the possibility of other parties who abuse the process to bear costs'.

176. *See* 2.9.

6.2 REFERRAL PROVISIONS TO NATIONAL LAWS

Many multilateral conventions, but not all, include, for efficiency reasons, referral provisions to national enforcement and recovery laws. Examples of conventions, which do not include referral provisions to national enforcement legislation are la Convention pour l'Unification de certaines Règles relatives au Transport Aérien International of 12 October 1929 and the European Convention on International Commercial Arbitration of 21 April 1961. An earlier more frequently used technique of legal cooperation between States, which is based on an agreement to enact laws of a similar content, when consequently no referral provisions to national law is needed, may be illustrated by some remaining parts of the legal cooperation between the Nordic States.[177]

EC law and multilateral conventions related to contractual claims and tax claims, which include referral provisions to national law, do not normally define neither what kind of actual measures of enforcement and recovery, and precautionary measures, States should provide, nor the substance of their content for matters of cross-border enforcement and recovery of claims. Such European law and conventions refer instead, as a main rule, the issues of what actual measures of enforcement and recovery, or precautionary measures, should be permitted to the national law of the enforcing State, only subject to some few exceptions. Exceptions, when considerations related to the national law of the applicant State also are involved, are certain referral provisions to recovery measures, which also include bankruptcy under the definition of such measures, and certain referral provisions to precautionary measures.

The main rule, which refers to the enforcing State's legislation is also applicable in the context of other parts of the international cooperation related to enforcement issues in the civil law area in *e.g.* the following conventions: the International convention relating to the arrest of seagoing ships of 10 May 1952,[178] the Convention on the Contract for the International Carriage of Goods by Road of 19 May 1956,[179] the Convention on Third Party Liability in the Field of Nuclear Energy of 29 July 1960,[180] the Multilateral agreement related to route charges of 12 February 1981,[181] and the Hague Convention of 30 June 2005 on Choice of Court Agreements.[182]

---

177. *See* 2.5.5 about the Nordic convention on recognition and the enforcement of judgments in civil matters and 2.4.2 about the Nordic agreement on the cooperation concerning the mutual assistance of enforcement of judgments or decisions on fines, confiscation or compensation for litigation costs.
178. *See* Art. 6.
179. *See* Art. 31, 3.
180. *See* Art. 13 d.
181. *See* Art. 17.
182. *See* Arts 8 and 9 of the convention, which include provisions on the recognition and enforcement, and thereto related limitations, of a judgment given by a contracting State designated in a choice of court agreement.

Similar referral provisions to national enforcement laws have also been entered into some other parts of EC law and in multilateral conventions outside the areas of contractual claims and tax claims, *e.g.* in the Insolvency regulation,[183] the Late payment's directive,[184] in some multilateral conventions and in EC law in the criminal law area,[185] and in the social security area; the Old social security regulation and the New social security regulation.[186] Referral provisions to national enforcement laws are also included in the EC Treaty, related to the enforcement of the judgments of the ECJ and of the decisions of the Council or of the Commission.[187] The respect for the execution of the judgments of the

183. *See* Art. 18, 3.
184. *See* Preamble (15).
185. The proceeds of fines and confiscation are enforced based on the requested State's legislation, *see* Art. 10, 1 of the European Convention on the international validity of criminal judgments of 28 May 1970, Art. 5, 4 c of the United Nations Convention against illicit traffic in narcotic drugs and psychotropic substances of 20 Dec. 1988, and Art. 14, 1 of the Council of Europe's Convention on the laundering, search, seizure and confiscation of proceeds from crime of 8 Nov. 1990. *Also see* Explanatory report on the Convention on Laundering, Search, Seizure and Confiscation of Proceeds from Crime, pp. 29-30. *Also see* Art. 6 of the Financial penalties Framework Decision, and Art. 12 of the Confiscation Framework Decision. The Nordic agreement on the cooperation concerning the mutual assistance of enforcement of judgments, or decisions on fines, confiscation, or compensation for litigation costs, implemented through similar enacted legislations in the Nordic States, has resulted in that enforcement should be governed by the requested State's legislation. This is evident in para. 2 of the Swedish counterpart to the Nordic agreement, published in Lag (1963:193) om samarbete med Danmark, Finland, Island och Norge ang. verkställighet av straff, m.m. (Act on the cooperation with Denmark, Finland, Iceland and Norway concerning the enforcement of punishment).
186. *See* Art. 92, 1 of the Old social security regulation which clearly refers the content of the procedure for reciprocal collection to the procedural autonomy of the legislation of the requested State for the collection of the foreign contributions. This means that the answer to the question what voluntary measures, or measures of enforcement, or measures of recovery, which are available for a reciprocal collection of the foreign contributions under the notion of collection in the regulation is exclusively referred to the legislation of the requested State. This may lead to different results of application of the regulation in the Member States of the EU depending on what measures they allow under the notion collection in their legislations. Art. 84 of the New social security regulation allows for the reciprocal collection of social security contributions and for the recovery of benefits provided and makes in a similar way as in Art. 92 of the Old social security regulation where reference is made to the content of the procedure for collection and for the recovery to the procedural autonomy of the legislation of the requested State for the collection or for the recovery of the foreign contributions respectively benefits. The New social security regulation entered into force on 20 May 2004, but shall, according to its Art. 91, apply from the date of entry into force of its Implementing Regulation. Arts 70-81 in the Commission of the ECs' proposal for a regulation of the European Parliament and of the Council laying down the procedure for implementing Regulation (EC) No. 883/2004 on the coordination of social security systems, COM (2006) 16 final, include provisions for the recovery of benefits paid in excess, recovery of provisional payments, compensation and assistance with recovery.
187. *See* Art. 256 compared to Art. 244.

ECHR is ensured by the European Convention on Human Rights as well as the control of this execution which is directly placed under the responsibility of the Committee of Ministers.[188]

6.2.1 Contractual Claims

6.2.1.1 EC Law

6.2.1.1.1 Brussels I Regulation

The Brussels I regulation confers the exclusive jurisdiction in proceedings concerned with the enforcement of judgments, regardless of domicile, to the courts of the Member States in which the judgments have been, or will be, enforced.[189] Hence, the actual enforcement of a contractual claim is not governed by the regulation, but instead, as a consequence of this, directly by national enforcement laws. The Brussels I regulation also addresses enforcement in the context of recognition of foreign judgments by referring to national legislation, when making provisional and protective measures available to the applicant before and after the declaration of enforceability,[190] regarding provisional enforcement and the stay of enforcement measures when an appeal against the judgment in the State of origin has been lodged,[191] related to the procedure of application for provisional, including protective, measures,[192] and to what extent the enforcement of penalties is allowed.[193] An *actio Pauliana*[194] is, however, an action, which falls outside the application of the Brussels convention, according to the rulings of the ECJ in the case of *Mario P. A. Reichert and others v. Dresdner Bank*[195] and in the case of *Mario Reichert, Hans-Heinz Reichert and Ingeborg Kockler v. Dresdner Bank AG.*[196]

---

188. *See* Art. 46, 1-2. *Also see* Leach, pp. 101-112, for further comments on the supervision of the enforcement of judgments: the role of the Committee of Ministers.
189. *See* Art. 22, 5.
190. *See* Art. 47.
191. *See* Art. 46.
192. *See* Art. 31.
193. *See* Art. 49.
194. Compare, about *actio Pauliana* in Roman law and under the Middle ages, 2.1.3 and 2.2.4.
195. The ECJ ruled in its decision in *Mario P. A. Reichert and others v. Dresdner Bank* of 10 Jan. 1990, where a donation of immovable property by Mr. and Mrs. Reichert to their son Mario Reichert was challenged by Dresdner Bank, a creditor of Mr. and Mrs. Reichert, in a French court on the basis of French law under which creditors may challenge in their own name transactions entered into by debtors in fraud of their rights by a procedure known as an action paulienne, that such an action does not come within the scope of Art. 16, 1 of the Brussels convention. *See* paras 11-12 and 14-15 of the ruling. Art. 16, 1 of the Brussels convention is essentially identical to Art. 22, 1 of the Brussels I regulation.
196. *See* 6.1.1.1.1.1 for further details on this case.

6.2.1.1.2 *Other Regulations Related to Contractual Claims*

The European Enforcement Order for uncontested claims states that the enforcement procedures shall be governed by the law of the Member State of enforcement and that a judgment certified as a European Enforcement Order shall be enforced under the same conditions as a judgment handed down in the Member State of enforcement.[197] The European order for payment procedure stipulates that the enforcement procedures shall be governed by the law of the Member State of enforcement and that a European order for payment which has become enforceable shall be enforced under the same conditions as an enforceable decision in the Member State of enforcement.[198] The European Small Claims Procedure states that the enforcement procedures shall be governed by the law of the Member State of enforcement and any judgment given in this procedure shall be enforced under the same conditions as a judgment given in the Member State of enforcement.[199] Consequently, these regulations refer all issues related to the actual enforcement procedures in the Member States to be governed by the law of the Member State of enforcement.[200] Also, this may lead to an application of other national grounds of refusal of enforcement than those covered by the regulations.

6.2.1.2 Conventions

Referral provisions to national law regarding measures of enforcement related to contractual claims are present in the Nordic convention on recognition and the enforcement of judgments in civil matters and in the New York convention on foreign arbitral awards.[201]

6.2.1.3 Priority Rights

None of the Brussels I regulation, the European Enforcement Order for uncontested claims, the European order for payment procedure, the European Small Claims Procedure, the Nordic convention on recognition and the enforcement of judgments in civil matters, or the New York convention on foreign arbitral awards, include any provisions which specifically deal with priority rights. Foreign creditors, who are able to present nationally enforceable foreign judgments under these regulations, or any of these conventions, will, as a result of the referral provisions to national enforcement laws, come into the same national position by the treatment of priority rights of their original foreign claims as the corresponding claims

197. *See* Art. 20, 1.
198. *See* Art. 21, 1.
199. *See* Art. 21, 1.
200. *See*, about the same opinion, Un titre exécutoire européen, Les Dossiers du Journal des tribunaux 53, pp. 192-194.
201. *See* Art. 1 of the Nordic convention on recognition and the enforcement of judgments in civil matters and Art. III of the New York convention on foreign arbitral awards.

of a national creditor. Such an equal treatment is also consistent with the principles in EC law of the non-discrimination on grounds of nationality of *e.g.* creditors and of mutuality between cooperating Member States.[202] Hence, priority rights, their scope and limits, for such foreign claims and identical national claims based on national enforceable titles of execution are to be treated equally, *i.e.* governed and determined by non-identical national laws.

The national treatments of priority rights, or non-priority rights, at the attachment of claims differ. These differences are, however, due to some modifications, sometimes not as significant as the first impression may indicate, in comparison between the two different main systems of distribution of assets in the EU which apply at the attachment of claims, the 'first in time first in right' principle and the 'group' principle.[203] The 'first in time first in right' principle, according to which the first creditor gets priority over other competing creditors, means that the money raised from the assets attached is made available to the first in time of attachment creditor related to his claim and later creditors will receive remaining funds depending on the moment at which their claims were attached. The 'group'

---

202. *See*, for further comments about these principles, 1.1.1.1.2 (Non-discrimination) and 1.1.1.1.6 (Mutuality).

203. *See* EC Study JAI/02/03/2002, C. The attachment of bank accounts, c) the occurrence of multiple garnishments, pp. 12-14. Even if national jurisdictions allow several attachments of the same asset, *e.g.* an account, before the transfer of the money seized to the first creditor takes place, the distribution of assets is effected differently, either by an application of the system of the 'first in time first in right' principle, or by the system of the 'group' principle. The differences of application of these principles become, however, less significant because of some modifications. The 'first in time first in right' principle is sometimes modified by different approaches to the relevant moment of the application of priority, *i.b.*, pp. 17-18. Convergences between the systems also exist, *e.g.* related to preferential treatment of creditors for the garnishment of earnings and to specially privileged maintenance creditors, *i.b.*, p. 18. The divergence between the two systems is more important if assets of merchants are targeted. The priority of competing creditors, including banks, which have security in relation to accounts are, however, largely recognized. Banks may, in addition, operate a set-off for preferential claims against the debtor. Divergences in the 'group' system relate to the period after seizure, while additional creditors may join the distribution proceedings. Creditors who join the proceedings in time are treated equally with the creditor who initiated the proceedings, while creditors who did not join the proceedings in time only can attach the remaining assets of the debtor, *i.b.*, pp. 18-20. *Also see* the following works: Civil Procedure in Europe 1, chapter IV. Aspect collectif du recouvrement, section 1. La qualité du premier saississant, confère-t-elle, de manière directe ou indirecte, le droit d'obtenir un traitement préférentiel ?, in each of the national reports included regarding: Germany, Belgium, Denmark, Spain, France, Greece, Italy, Luxemburg, the Netherlands, Portugal, Sweden and *i.b.*, pp. 41-42 (Summary), The execution of court decisions in civil cases, Synthesis on The execution of court decisions in civil cases, about the existence of a 'hierarchy' applicable to the debtor's attachable assets, measures to preserve rights and the distribution of assets in: Albania, Armenia, Austria, Azerbaijan, Belgium, Bulgaria, Croatia, Cyprus, Czech Republic, Denmark, Finland, France, Georgia, Germany, Greece, Hungary, Italy, Japan, Latvia, Lithuania, Luxemburg, Moldova, Norway, Poland, Portugal, Romania, Slovak Republic, Slovenia, Spain, Sweden, the former Yugoslav Republic of Macedonia, Ukraine and the United Kingdom, pp. 151-264, Källström, pp. 707-708 (France), and Kennett, The Enforcement of judgments in Europe, pp. 259-261 (priorities) compared to pp. 93-94 (distribution of proceeds).

principle applies to national systems, which do not confer any priority right at the attachment of claims on the first creditor, and therefore also includes a scheme for the distribution of the proceeds among the competing creditors.

6.2.2 Tax Claims

Referral provisions to national law regarding measures of recovery related to tax claims have been entered into the Recovery directive and conventions, often without explaining in any details what kind of such measures that are to be included. These referral provisions to national law related to precautionary measures are not identical. The provisions are completed in different ways by national laws, which include, to the extent that they are available under such laws, differing measures that are defined as recovery measures[204] and precautionary measures.

6.2.2.1 Recovery Directive

6.2.2.1.1 Recovery Measures

The referral provision to national law regarding measures of recovery related to tax claims, to be found in the Recovery directive,[205] is treated here. This referral provision relates to national recovery measures, which vary, and include, or not; bankruptcy, a retention of a tax credit and a set-off of a tax claim. These measures will be discussed here. In addition, a requested Member State may, in relation to recovery measures taken, where its legislation so permits, and after consultations with the applicant Member State, allow the debtor time to pay, or authorize payment by instalment.[206]

6.2.2.1.1.1 Insolvency Proceeding

An applicant Member State may, as a recovery measure under the referral provision of the Recovery directive, request another Member State to file an application for bankruptcy based on foreign tax claims, to the extent that is possible in the requested State. Requested Member States, which classify a bankruptcy proceeding as a recovery measure are: Austria, Cyprus, Denmark, Estonia, Finland, Germany, Greece, Ireland, Latvia, Malta, the Netherlands, Sweden and

204. *See* Tax Administration in OECD and Selected Non-OECD Countries: Comparative Information Series, p. 84 compared to Table 19 about the powers to enforce tax debt collections, where it is reported that revenue bodies in most surveyed countries have traditional powers to enforce tax debt collection: (1) to grant taxpayer further times to pay; (2) to make payment arrangements; (3) to collect from third parties that have liabilities to taxpayers; (4) to seize taxpayer's asset; (5) to offset taxpayer's liabilities to his/her credits; and (6) to initiate bankruptcy, and that there also exist additional powers in some of the surveyed countries.
205. *See* Art. 6.
206. *See* Art. 9, 2.

the United Kingdom.[207] Member States, which do not are: Belgium, France, Hungary, Italy, Luxemburg, Poland, Slovenia and Spain. Consequently, these latter States have no obligations, under this referral provision of the directive, to assist an applicant Member State by filing an application for bankruptcy based on foreign tax claims.

An example is here given to illustrate the interplay between national legislation and the Recovery directive. It relates to one requested Member State of the EU, Sweden, which classifies bankruptcy as a recovery measure according to national law and under the directive, when the tax administration of another Member State, France, acts in order to get paid for French income tax debts and the debtor/co-debtor has moved to Sweden and transferred his assets to others in Sweden and in other Member States of the EU.[208] The French administration holds information, which indicates all this. The French administration therefore forwards requests for information through the Common Custom Network/Common Services Interface (CCN/CSI) network system[209] to the States mentioned. The Swedish administration confirms that the debtor is domiciled in Sweden, but does not formally seem to hold any assets there. The French administration is, however, convinced that there exist assets in Sweden and in other Member States of the EU.

The French administration therefore asks the Swedish administration for advice on what specific conditions would have to be fulfilled before a formal French request is made to the Swedish administration to file an application for bankruptcy by use of the referral provision of the Recovery directive to the local court. An additional question is also asked about the costs and priority rights in bankruptcy. The aim of a possible forthcoming application for a bankruptcy proceeding, to the extent such a proceeding is at all available for corresponding claims in Sweden, the requested State, as a recovery measure, initiated by the French administration by use of the referral provision of the Recovery directive, would be twofold. It would be to get a bankruptcy decision in court, which would put a trustee in bankruptcy in place, and create a possibility of trying to regain assets previously belonging to the debtor, and it would establish a possibility to stop the debtor from continuing his harmful activities to the French State creditor and related criminal fraud activities in the EU.

The answer from the Swedish administration to the French administration would include the following facts. An application for bankruptcy is, as a recovery measure, available to the Swedish Tax agency,[210] meaning that a Swedish

207. *See* Meddelanden för exekutionsväsendet, MEX 2006:9, notis 9, Ansökan om konkurs i annan EU-stat för svenska skattefordringar (Information to the Enforcement Service, MEX 2006:9, notice 9, Application for bankruptcy in another State of the EU based on Swedish tax claims), which was based on the answers from the Member States (answers were not available from: Lithuania, Portugal and Slovakia) after the Fiscalis seminar 2004 on mutual assistance of recovery of taxes in Brugge, Belgium, 17-19 Nov. 2004.
208. This section includes parts from the author's contribution 'The interaction of cross-border tax recovery and the Insolvency regulation' for the Fiscalis seminar 2004 on mutual assistance of recovery of taxes in Brugge, Belgium, 17-19 Nov. 2004.
209. *See* Arts 2 and 21-23 of the Implementing recovery directive.
210. *See* 6 § lagen (2007:324) om Skatteverkets hantering av vissa borgenärsuppgifter.

application for bankruptcy is included under the referral provision of the Recovery directive. Before filing an application for bankruptcy to court the Swedish Tax agency has to be able to prove the insolvency of the debtor. An attachment without result against the debtor by the Swedish enforcement authority is a sufficient proof in order to establish the fact of insolvency to the court according to the Swedish bankruptcy Act.[211] The Swedish Tax agency may, based on such an attachment without result, apply for a decision of bankruptcy from the court.

The costs of application for the bankruptcy proceeding and the costs of the bankruptcy estate could be expected to amount to a minimum of approximately EUR 546 in a non-complex matter,[212] which if not covered by assets realized by the trustee of the estate, has to be paid by the French administration, because they are to be classified as extraordinary costs as defined under the Recovery directive.[213] In case the bankruptcy estate lacks assets, or they are of a limited importance, the trustee in bankruptcy may ask the concerned creditor if he is willing to put up guarantees for the payment of costs for the treatment of assets of the estate.

A Swedish court decision based on where the centre of a debtor's main interests are situated,[214] *e.g.* the permanent domicile of the debtor in Sweden, answers to the definition of a main proceeding in the Insolvency regulation, which produces legal effects in all Member States of the EU,[215] except in Denmark.[216] Such a court decision would, however, also produce legal effects in Denmark, Norway and Iceland based on the Nordic bankruptcy convention.[217] Priority rights in bankruptcy are determined, according to the Insolvency regulation, by the law of the State of the opening of proceedings.[218] This means that each Member State is entitled to determine whether or not priority rights should be attributed to the foreign claim in bankruptcy law, *i.e.* in this case by Swedish law.

French income taxes will not be attributed any priority rights in bankruptcy as the corresponding Swedish taxes, which have not been subject to seizure, lack priority rights in bankruptcy, and private creditors are normally not attributed any priority rights in a Swedish bankruptcy, except when they hold a mortgage in a company's assets.[219] Once the bankruptcy in Sweden has been established,

211. Unless otherwise shown, a debtor is deemed, according to 2 kapitlet, 8 § konkurslagen (1987:672) (Swedish bankruptcy Act), to be insolvent when, in the event of enforcement under Chapter 4 of the enforcement code, within six months before the bankruptcy petition, it transpired that he did not have assets for full payment of the claim executed. There also exists other ways of proving the insolvency of the debtor according to the Swedish bankruptcy Act.
212. 5 000 Swedish crowns (SEK) equals, at an exchange rate of SEK 9,15 for EUR 1, to approximately EUR 546.
213. *See* Art. 18.
214. *See* Art. 3, 1.
215. Bankruptcy orders are recognized and enforced in other States, *see* Arts 16, 17 and 25.
216. *See* Preamble (33) of the regulation.
217. *See* Art. 1 of the convention, which is still partially in force between Denmark, Finland, Norway, Sweden and Iceland, *i.e.* to the extent the Insolvency regulation should not apply instead, Art. 44, 1, j of the regulation.
218. *See* Art. 4, 2, i.
219. *See* Förmånsrättslagen (1970:979), (Swedish Act on priority rights).

at the application of the Swedish Tax agency, it is the initiative and task of the trustee in bankruptcy to publish the forthcoming court decision in other Member States and to inform the creditors about it, according to the Insolvency regulation.[220] The administrations of all Member States concerned may then, as any creditor, besides tax claims, also lodge any other public claims, and claim that they allege preference,[221] to the trustee in bankruptcy.

An alternative possibility for a Member State to obtain a decision of bankruptcy in another Member State, based on foreign tax claims, if it would either not like to make use of the Recovery directive, or would be unable to make use of this directive in another Member State, for insolvency purposes as a recovery measure, is a direct application for bankruptcy to a court in the other Member State under the Insolvency regulation. A sufficient proof of the debtor's insolvency delivered by the applicant State at a direct application for bankruptcy proceedings to a Swedish court under the Insolvency regulation would be an attachment without result by the Swedish enforcement authority based on a previous request for the recovery of taxes from the French administration. Communications would initially take place between the Swedish court and the French administration and later on between this administration and the Swedish trustee in bankruptcy. The French administration could choose, but is not obliged, to be represented by a local lawyer.

6.2.2.1.1.2 Retention of a Tax Credit

The idea of introducing a measure of the retention of a tax credit to be classified as a 'recovery' measure under the referral provision of the Recovery directive, in view of compensation of tax debts and tax credits in different Member States, has been discussed to support an increased efficiency of this directive. The complexity of this discussion becomes evident due to the fact that any possible solution has to take into account the interests of efficiency and protection of the debtor, as well as legal control. Also, a direct set-off between tax debts in one Member State against a refund of a tax credit in another Member State is not possible, because the parties, the Member States, are not identical. The retention idea may be questionable for several reasons.

One reason is that the internal classification of the concept of the retention of a tax credit by the laws of many Member States is unlikely to be consistent with the existing concept of recovery measures. Another reason is that the interim nature of the retention of a tax credit would rather seem to require national precautionary measures related to the payment of a refunded amount than national recovery measures. Precautionary measures would, in the interest of protecting the debtor, also mean that legal control through a court proceeding would be needed. Yet another reason is that an introduction of the idea of the retention of a tax credit to be classified as a 'recovery' measure in the Recovery directive, would still, due to the fact that a direct set-off of tax debts and tax credits between Member States is not possible, have to require that the Member States forward requests of recovery

220. *See* Arts 21 and 40.
221. *See* Art. 39 and 41.

for such 'recovery' measures to each other in order to create a legal basis for them under the directive.

Consequently, for all these reasons, the idea of the retention of a tax credit to be classified as a 'recovery' measure in the Recovery directive would not be attractive. It would not increase the efficiency of the Recovery directive. A possible alternative solution related to the idea of the retention of a tax credit is that of a preventive measure of an initial communication possibility for the Member State of the tax debt, then matched with a corresponding communication obligation of the Member State of the tax credit. This issue is further treated in the context of another part of this work.[222]

6.2.2.1.1.3 Set-Off of a Tax Claim

Some conditions for a set-off by a Member State creditor of its tax claims against the assets of the debtor in a requested Member State are here briefly commented on because a Member State creditor would normally, like any other creditor, preferably first like to make such a set-off, instead of having to apply for the seizure of the assets of the debtor for his claims. As just mentioned a direct set-off between tax debts from one Member State against a refund of a tax credit from another Member State is not possible, because the parties are not identical.[223] An indirect such set-off based on a bilateral or multilateral convention, or on EC law, *e.g.* on the referral provision of the Recovery directive, may, however, be possible to the extent a requested Member State, following a request for recovery of tax debts from an applicant Member State, is able to make a set-off for a foreign tax claim against the assets of the debtor in the requested State, *e.g.* against a refund of a tax credit, by treating it as a similar domestic claim under its national legislation.

The permissibility and limits of another kind of set-off and its interplay between the national systems of Member States and EC law are illustrated by the ruling of the ECJ in the case *Bent Jensen and Korn- og Foderstofkompagniet A/S v. Landbrugsministeriet*. Here the ECJ made clear that Member States, subject to certain conditions, are not precluded from requiring a national intervention agency to effect set-off with debts payable to the State, such as VAT-claims, in the case of beneficiary of compensatory payments, related to Council regulation 1765/92 establishing a support system for producers of certain arable crops, against debts payable to a Member State.[224]

222. *See* 6.3.3.2.4.
223. *See* 6.2.2.1.1.2.
224. In its decision on the 19 May 1998 in *Bent Jensen and Korn- og Foderstofkompagniet A/S v. Landbrugsministeriet* (Danish State), the ECJ made clear the conditions for set-off of amounts paid under community law, related to Council regulation 1765/92 establishing a support system for producers of certain arable crops, against debts payable to a Member State, in the case of VAT debts. The conclusions of the ECJ can be summarized as follows. Community law does not preclude a Member State from effecting set-off between an amount due to a beneficiary of aid payable under community legislation and an outstanding debt to that Member State. The situation would be different only if that practice were to interfere with the proper functioning of the common organization of the agricultural markets. In that regard,

6.2.2.1.2 Precautionary Measures

The provision of precautionary measures in the Recovery directive interacts with the referral provision of the same directive.[225] Such measures, to the extent they are permitted in the Member States, are completed by national laws, which include differing measures defined as precautionary measures. A requested Member State may, according to the Recovery directive, on a reasoned request from an applicant Member State, take precautionary measures to the extent it is possible in the national legislation of the requested Member State.[226]

What requirements a request from an applicant Member State has to meet in order to be classified as reasoned in this sense of the Recovery directive is determined by the references given in the same directive in between different articles.[227] The referral provision of the directive indicates that a claim by an applicant Member State has to be based on an instrument permitting its enforcement, *i.e.* on a decision of precautionary measures from the applicant Member State and that the enforcement of such a decision shall be treated equivalently to the enforcement of corresponding decisions of the requested Member State.

6.2.2.2 Conventions

Referral provisions to national law regarding measures of recovery related to the recovery of tax claims are included in the Council of Europe and OECD convention on mutual administrative assistance in tax matters, the Nordic agreement on assistance in tax matters and the Benelux convention on the mutual assistance for the recovery of tax claims,[228] without explanation in any details about what such

the capacity in which the Member State grants compensation payments under the regulation, the fact that the rules of that Member State on set-off require, for set-off to be available, reciprocity of debts as between debtor and creditor, the practice generally followed by the Member State regarding set-off and the legal basis of the debt to the State involved in the set-off are of no importance. This is so, provided that the national authorities ensure that the effectiveness of community law is not in any way undermined and that the economic operators enjoy equal treatment. Subject to these conditions, Art. 15, 3 of this regulation, according to which compensatory payments are to be transferred to the beneficiaries in their entirety, must be interpreted as not precluding Member States from requiring a national intervention agency to effect set-off with debts payable to the State in the case of a beneficiary of compensatory payments. Moreover, subject to the same conditions, Art. 10, 1 of the regulation, according to which compensatory payments are to be made between 16 Oct. and 31 Dec. following the next harvest, must be interpreted to mean that payment of compensatory payments may be deferred until it has been verified whether the State has any claim against the beneficiary thereof for which set-off may be available, provided that the payment is made no later than 31 Dec. of the year in question.

225. *See* Art. 13 compared to Art. 6.
226. *See* Art. 13.
227. *See* Art. 13 compared to other articles, *e.g.* Art. 6.
228. *See* Art. 11, 1 of the Convention and Explanatory report on the Convention on Mutual Administrative Assistance in Tax Matters, p. 32, Art. 14, 1 of the Nordic agreement and Art. 4, § 1 of the Benelux convention on the mutual assistance for the recovery of tax claims.

measures shall include. These provisions are completed by national laws, which define such measures. Referral provisions to national law regarding precautionary measures are present in the Council of Europe and OECD convention on mutual administrative assistance in tax matters,[229] the Nordic agreement on assistance in tax matters,[230] and the Benelux convention on the mutual assistance for the recovery of tax claims.[231] The Nordic agreement on assistance in tax matters also stipulates that the applicant State may initiate certain litigation proceedings, or bankruptcy proceedings, in the other contracting State, when a matter of assistance for recovery has been initiated by the applicant State; however, not before the requested State has given its express consent.[232] This Nordic provision has no explicit counterpart neither in the Recovery directive nor in the Council of Europe and OECD convention on mutual administrative assistance in tax matters.

6.2.2.3 Priority Rights

The Recovery directive differs from multilateral conventions in the tax recovery area as the requested Member State has an option, but is not obliged, to choose to apply national provisions on priority rights at the recovery of foreign taxes.[233] Originally, the European Commission made a proposal to the European Parliament, suggesting that claims, which where to be recovered should benefit from identical priority rights as the corresponding claims of the requested State.[234] This was, however, during the following process modified into the present status. The Recovery directive leaves the decision to use this option entirely to the requested Member State. Some even more restrictive approaches than the one in the Recovery directive are applicable in the Council of Europe and OECD convention on mutual administrative assistance in tax matters, the Nordic agreement on assistance in tax matters and the Benelux convention on the mutual assistance for the recovery of tax claims.[235] They stipulate, without leaving any other options to the parties of the conventions, or agreement, that priority rights applicable to the recovery of national taxes do not apply to foreign taxes.

6.2.3 Conclusions

Most, but not all conventions include referral provisions to national enforcement or recovery laws. However, the essential principles laid down in most referral

229. *See* Art. 12 compared to Art. 11, 1.
230. *See* Art. 19, 1.
231. *See* Art. 4, § 1.
232. *See* Art. 16, 2. *Also see*, about the costs of such proceedings, Art. 22.
233. *See* Art. 10.
234. *See* Commission's communication, COM (1999) 183 final.
235. *See* Art. 15 of the Council of Europe and OECD convention and Explanatory report on the Convention on Mutual Administrative Assistance in Tax Matters, pp. 41-42, Art. 16, 1 of the Nordic agreement and Art. 5 of the Benelux convention.

provisions in EC law and in conventions to national law in these two law areas, although they sometimes are stated in different wordings, could be summarized and expressed as follows. A demand that measures of enforcement for foreign private and public claims and measures of collection and recovery for public claims and the treatment thereof, and precautionary measures for such claims, should be governed by the law of the enforcing State. Also, they should be treated equally to any corresponding measures which would have been taken in relation to similar claims of the enforcing State.

In this way interplay is created between EC law, conventions, and national laws. Presently the content of enforcement, recovery, and precautionary measures related to contractual claims and tax claims in matters of cross-border cooperation in these areas becomes, under the national definitions of such measures, supplemented and governed by non-identical national laws. This may lead to a non-equal treatment of the claims at the application of the different non-harmonized national laws and result in a more, or less, inefficient enforcement, or recovery, of a claim in relation to the creditors and debtors. Matters of cross-border enforcement and recovery of claims of private and public creditors may therefore be treated more, or less, efficient in other States, even if they are treated equal to internal claims of the enforcing State, compared to the corresponding measures which would have been available to the creditors in the State of origin of the claims.

Consequently, debtors may for the same reasons, in such situations, be more, or less, protected against enforcement and recovery measures in other States compared to if such corresponding measures would instead have been taken against them in the State of origin of the claims. This non-equal treatment may be changed to the extent EC, international principles and recommendations introduce a harmonization of national enforcement laws.[236]

The referral provisions in EC law and in conventions, which create an interplay with the national laws in the areas of enforcement, recovery, and precautionary measures regarding the actual content of these measures, should be maintained because they constitute a necessary link with these national laws. Such provisions will still be needed, under a predictable future, even if in the future the EC law, or other parts of international law, may indirectly, or gradually, further harmonize such national measures.

None of the treated parts of EC law and multilateral conventions related to the enforcement of contractual claims includes any provisions which specifically deal with priority rights in the context of cross-border enforcement of claims. This means that the issues of privileged, or non-privileged, treatment at the enforcement of foreign contractual claims, which are recognized and judged enforceable in other enforcing States based on such European law or conventions and identical national claims, are treated equally, *i.e.* governed and determined by non-identical national laws of the enforcing States.

236. *See* 7 about harmonization of civil execution laws.

The Recovery directive refers the decision of the option to apply national provisions, or not, of priority rights in the recovery of tax claims of an applicant Member State of the EU entirely to the requested Member State. This option in the Recovery directive is unique in the sense that it has no counterpart in other parts of EC law, or in multilateral conventions, related to the enforcement and recovery in the contractual law area nor in the tax law area. The existence of this option pierces the otherwise negative position in public international law, *i.e.* would it not have existed, to confer any advantages without positive support in such law to foreign tax claims.[237]

This option also indicates that the provision of direct recognition and automatic treatment as an instrument permitting enforcement of foreign tax claims under the Recovery directive,[238] would not, as opposed to what would be the fact in the civil law area, have been sufficient to create an effect of an equal treatment of priority rights for foreign and national tax claims.[239] A more far-reaching solution of privileged treatment than this option exists, however, in EC law in the area of reciprocal collection of social security charges.[240]

Hence, a Member State has an option, under the Recovery directive, to confer priority rights, or non-priority rights, to foreign tax claims at their domestic recovery, without taking into consideration their level of priority, or non-priority, according to the foreign State's law. A reason to confer the same level of priority rights, or non-priority rights, as in the national law of the requested State would be to achieve the advantage of promoting an equal treatment at the recovery of tax claims at the national level, irrespective of whether actually they are of foreign or domestic origins.

However, a requested Member State, which would contemplate to use the option to confer national priority rights to the tax claims of an applicant Member State would likely demand, as a precondition for such a grant to the applicant Member State, an equal treatment of its own tax claims in corresponding situations there. An applicant State, which applies non-priority rights at the recovery of its own tax claims, would, however, not be able to fulfil such a precondition. The reason is that it would not likely be in a national position to treat foreign tax claims there at the domestic recovery in a more preferential way.

The application by the Member States of the option related to priority rights in the Recovery directive risks to produce various non-equal results of treatment, *i.e.* of privileged, or non-privileged, treatment of the claim, and to make a request for the recovery in this sense unpredictable.[241] An alternative solution may, in order to

---

237. *See* 1.1.1.1.4 and 4.2.2.
238. *See* Art. 8.
239. Compare 6.4.1 about similar arguments in relation to the right of the tax authorities to lodge claims in the insolvency proceedings of another Member State of the EU under Art. 39 of the Insolvency regulation and allege preference.
240. *See* 1.1.1.6.
241. *See* Grau Ruiz, p. 203, who contributes a similar criticism in relation to Art. 10 of the Recovery directive. She states that it fails to answer the question of when the same priority rights as for national taxes can be granted and that this wide discretion to the various administrations of the Member States may give rise to considerable differences in the way that claims are recovered under the same mutual assistance procedure.

establish a more predictable and equal treatment of priority rights, or non-priority rights, for claims of other Member States, be, as in the Commission's original proposal, and in EC law in the area of reciprocal collection of social security charges, to apply the law of the requested State. Such an alternative solution would, however, first have to be based on a political agreement of an application of a more advanced concept of mutuality in the Recovery directive.

A possible other circumstance to be aware of in this context is that the treatment of priority rights of a claim may differ before and after a possible insolvency proceeding.[242]

6.3 ACCESS TO INFORMATION FOR ENFORCEMENT PURPOSES IN THE INTERNATIONAL CONTEXT

6.3.1 CONTRACTUAL CLAIMS

There exists no sufficiently efficient multilateral instrument in force in the civil law area in the EU, which provides possibilities for an international exchange of information related to contractual claims in enforcement matters by means of communication between the regulated enforcement agents in the Member States of the EU for the benefit of the contractual and commercial creditor. There exist, however, some ideas and proposals for a solution on this issue, *i.a.* the draft proposal on an 'International legal instrument on the mutual cooperation between European enforcement authorities in the European Union for the exchange of information for enforcement purposes related to private and public claims' (a Euro- Information Assistance System for the exchange of information regarding the enforcement of claims) by Berglund of 1999[243] and the report Nordic cooperation in recovery matters to the Nordic Council of Ministers, including a proposed Nordic agreement on the exchange of information in recovery matters.[244] There also exist two more

242. Compare 6.4.1-2, where priority rights in international insolvency proceedings, under the Insolvency regulation, the Nordic bankruptcy convention, and the Bankruptcy convention between France and Monaco, are treated in more details.

243. This idea was originally proposed in 1997 by Berglund in a presentation 'Mutual co-operation for the exchange of information for enforcement purposes related to private and public claims or is a euro-enforcement information assistance system for the exchange of the information needed ?' at the seminar in Helsinki 17-18 Mar. 1997 about 'Possibilities for European enforcement' held by the Finnish Ministry of Justice.

244. At least two proposals, which cover the options of both the public and civil law areas, of an international exchange of information for enforcement/recovery purposes between regulated enforcement agents of the concerned States, related to the Member States of the EU and the Nordic States have been presented, but are not yet realized, *see* Berglund, draft proposal on an 'International legal instrument on the mutual cooperation between European enforcement authorities in the European Union for the exchange of information for enforcement purposes related to private and public claims (a Euro-Information Assistance System for the exchange of information regarding the enforcement of claims)', La Transparence patrimoniale, annex, pp. 217-237. According to Art. 1, 2 of this draft proposal a request for an exchange of

recent proposals on how to improve access to national information for cross-border enforcement purposes, the European Asset Declaration,[245] and the European Garnishee's Declaration.[246]

The Convention between the Member States of the European Communities on the simplification of procedures for the recovery of maintenance payments, done at Rome on 6 November 1990, includes provisions for the exchange of information for enforcement purposes, even though it has not yet entered into force.[247]

---

information shall be treated as a domestic case and may concern: (a) the state of the affairs of the debtor, *e.g.* the debts and assets of the debtor, including a complete investigation pertaining to enforcement of debts according to national law; (b) the contents of domestic law on enforcement of debts and insolvency, and the States shall also, when needed provide general information on how the enforcement of debts is organized and carried out domestically. In addition, States shall, according to Art. 1, 3 of this draft proposal, give each other assistance regardless of if the debtor, the individual or legal entity concerned, has its domicile in or is a citizen of one or several of the States bound by this legal instrument. In this legal instrument 'debtor' means all individual persons and legal entities that have a duty to pay private and public claims according to domestic law in one or several of the States bound by this legal instrument. *Also see* 2.10.3 about the report Nordic cooperation in recovery matters to the Nordic Council of Ministers, and *see* annex 8 about a translation into English of the proposed Nordic agreement on the exchange of information in recovery matters from pp. 25-30 of this report, and about the scope of application Art. 2-4. The two proposals follow a similar concept and treat *i.a.* applicability, definitions, request for information, protection of persons, limitations on the duty to assist for enforcement, secrecy and final provisions. The proposal related to the Nordic States can, in some senses, be considered as a further developed and more advanced proposal compared to the proposal related to the Member States of the EU.

245. The proposal of establishing a European Assets Declaration is intended to achieve that debtors would be obliged to disclose their assets throughout the European Judicial area ('cross-border' disclosure). The declaration would be made on a standard form available in all Community languages. The minimum standards would be set for the Declarations conditions, content and related sanctions in order to encourage uniformity across Member States and, as a result, creditors would have equal access to information about assets within the European Judicial Area, while debtors within the internal market would receive equal protection. In addition, the present practice of information shopping within the European Judicial Area would be reduced, *see* for further details EC Study JAI/02/03/2002, B, V, 5 and E, III, 1.

246. A European Garnishee's Declaration has been proposed to oblige third-party debtors to give information on the assets seized on the basis of a proposed European Garnishment Order for Bank Accounts, *see* EC Study JAI/02/03/2002, E, III, 3. *Also* compare Green paper Effective enforcement of judgments in the European Union: Transparency of Debtors' assets, Commission of the ECs, COM (2008) 128 final about a discussion on what measures could help to ensure that the creditor obtains reliable information on the debtor's assets within a reasonable period of time.

247. The convention has not entered into force, *see* 6.1.3.1.1 for further information. Art. 3, 2 of the convention *i.a.* reads: 'On receipt of the application mentioned in Article 5 the Central Authority in the State addressed shall take or cause to be taken without delay all appropriate and useful measures to: (I) seek out and locate the debtor or his assets: (II) obtain, where appropriate, relevant information from Government Departments or agencies in relation to the debtor: . . . '. Applications to the central authorities made by the maintenance creditor, or body which has the right to represent him, shall, according to Article 5, 3. of the convention, *i.a.* contain '(III) the name, date of birth, nationality and description of the debtor and all other relevant information regarding his identity or whereabouts or the location of his assets: . . . '. Services rendered by the central authorities under the convention are, according to Art. 2, 2 of the convention, free of charge. *Also see* Leroy on the convention, La Transparence patrimoniale, pp. 144-145.

The Proposal for a Council regulation on jurisdiction, applicable law, recognition and enforcement of decisions and cooperation in matters relating to maintenance obligations[248] also includes some rather advanced provisions, *i.a.* on a cooperation between central authorities, as representatives for a creditor, for an exchange of information for the purpose to recover efficiently a maintenance claim, on the access to information and on the notification of information to the debtor.[249]

6.3.2 Tax Claims

Besides the Recovery directive and some multilateral conventions in the tax recovery area, which are dealt with here, there also exist provisions of exchange of information both in the multilateral tax law area[250] and in the social security law area.[251] One of the earliest multilateral conventions, which, however, only treated the limits of use of information for recovery purpose included in documents for the recovery of a claim between the contracting States in the cross-border tax recovery area, is the Benelux convention on the mutual assistance for the recovery of tax claims.[252] More detailed and developed provisions for the exchange of

248. *See* 2.10.1 for further information about this proposal.

249. *See* Art. 41a and b (Cooperation in specific cases between central authorities for the collection and exchange of information on the situation of the creditor and the debtor and to provide information and assistance to creditors involved in proceedings on their territory, the representation by central authorities, at the request of a creditor, for the exchange of information for the purpose to recover efficiently a maintenance claim), Art. 42 (Working method), Art. 44 (Access to information), Art. 45 (Transmission of information), Art. 46 (Use of information) and Art. 47 (Information to the debtor).

250. *See* Art. 26 of the OECD Model Tax Convention and comments to this article, Model Tax Convention on Income and on Capital, pp. 287-294. Art. 26 of the OECD Model Tax Convention interplays, however, also with Art. 27 on the assistance in the collection of taxes of the same Convention. The OECD Model Tax Convention has influenced a lot of bilateral tax treaties, compare for further details on to what extent the large number of tax treaties concluded by European States include provisions for the exchange of information for the purpose of taxation in such treaties, Tax Treaties concluded by European Countries, International Bureau of Fiscal Documentation. *Also see* International mutual assistance through exchange of information, Cahiers de droit fiscal international, XLIV Congrès International de Droit Financier et Fiscal, Stockholm 1990, volume LXXVb, deuxième sujet, International Fiscal Association (I.F.A.), general report and national reports for: Germany, Austria, Belgium, Brazil, Canada, Denmark, Spain, United States, Finland, France, Hong Kong, Israel, Luxemburg, Norway, the Netherlands, Peru, Portugal, United Kingdom, Sweden and Switzerland regarding international mutual assistance. *Also see* Leroy, L'efficacité de la justice civile en Europe, p. 330, on the mutual assistance in community law for the exchange of information between tax administrations and La Transparence patrimoniale, pp. 145-147, on the exchange of information for value added and income tax purposes in community law.

251. *See* Art. 84, 1-3 of the Old social security regulation and Art. 76, 1-3 of the New social security regulation, which entered into force on 20 May 2004, but shall, according to its Art. 91, apply from the date of entry into force of its Implementing Regulation.

252. *See* Art. 6. The Exposé des motifs to the convention prohibits the use of transmitted information from the requesting State in documents to the requested State for any other purpose than for recovery.

information for recovery purposes between the authorities of the concerned States are included in EC law and some multilateral conventions relating to the recovery of tax claims, the Recovery directive, the Implementing recovery directive and the Council of Europe and OECD convention on mutual administrative assistance in tax matters. The provisions for the exchange of information in the Nordic agreement on assistance in tax matters are also treated here.

6.3.2.1 Recovery Directive

The Recovery directive stipulates that, at the request of the applicant Member State, the requested Member State shall provide any information, which could be useful to the applicant authority in the recovery of its claim and the requested authority shall, in order to obtain this information, make use of the powers provided under the laws, regulations, or administrative provisions, *applying to the recovery of similar claims* arising in the Member State where the authority is situated.[253] The Recovery directive consequently requires that a request for information shall be treated as if a similar claim of recovery existed in the requested State, although such a recoverable claim against a debtor, based on a title of execution from another Member State, has not yet been subject to recognition in the requested State, which means that there exists no formal debtor in this sense in the requested State.

An implementation of this construction of a 'fictitious' debtor in the legislation of requested States, which equals this kind of debtor to domestic debtors in the work of enforcement organs based on the existence of enforceable titles of execution in terms of access to information for recovery purposes, is needed to secure a corresponding access to information for recovery purposes as apply to similar domestic claims. Requested Member States, which fail to implement this construction into national laws, have not fulfilled their obligations to implement the Recovery directive properly because they will not be able to supply information to the applicant States at a level of access, which corresponds to the level of access for a domestically enforceable title of execution.

They will consequently not be able to supply information, or possibly only at a considerably more limited level.[254] The result of this provision, is, however, if properly implemented into national laws, that some Member States under their national laws are able to provide information, including information on the debtor's bank account, and consequently obliged to supply it to other Member States, while some other Member States, which are not able to provide this information for similar domestic recovery purposes under their national laws, are explicitly

253. *See* Art. 4, 1. *Also see* Art. 5, 2 of the Implementing recovery directive, which confirms the same principal position.
254. The different levels of access to information for enforcement purposes before and after the existence of an enforceable title of execution are treated in the context of 7.2.3.1-2.

exempted from the obligation to supply this kind of information to other requesting Member States.[255]

Even if there may exist different possible examples of such exemptions, or grounds of refusal, based on national laws from several other Member States, one example of a Member State, which is exempted from an obligation of supplying information to other Member States because it is not able to provide it under its national law, due to bank secrecy, is Luxemburg.[256] The legislation of Luxemburg consequently indicates that it is first at the actual moment of a recovery procedure, *e.g.* following a request for the mutual assistance for the recovery of a tax claim from another Member State, that strongly indicates a probable result of recovery, that the tax authorities of Luxemburg are able to and have to fulfil an obligation to supply information in relation to the debtor's assets in bank accounts, under Luxemburg law. This leads to the conclusion that Luxemburg is exempted from any obligation of supplying such information that is protected by national bank secrecy law with reference to this provision of exemption in Article 4 of the Recovery directive.

A request, or several requests in parallel,[257] for information from an applicant State, under the Recovery directive, shall indicate some basic facts in relation to the person concerned,[258] and may relate to the debtor, the co-debtor, and any third-party holding assets belonging to the debtor and the co-debtor,[259] but may sometimes not oblige a requested State to supply information[260] and shall in case of refusal be notified to the applicant State with a statement of the reasons of refusal.[261] Information sent to the requested authority under the Recovery directive may only be further communicated by that authority to the person mentioned in the request, persons and authorities responsible for the recovery of the

255. *See* Art. 4, 3 a.
256. *See* Arts 1 and 4 in Règlement grand-ducal du 24 mars 1989 précisant le secret bancaire en matière fiscale et délimitant le droit d'investigation des administrations fiscales, Mémorial (OJ) 1989, pp. 181-182. This position in the Luxemburg legislation is often expressed as follows, or with similar wordings: En l'état actuel du droit luxembourgeois, il n'est pas permis aux autorités fiscales de demander aux établissements financiers des renseignements sur l'existence de comptes ouverts au nom d'une personne déterminée et l'établissement financier n'est tenu de fournir ces informations que dans le cadre et à l'issue d'une procedure de saisie-arrêt. Un créancier n'aura donc recours à cette procédure qu'en cas de forte probabilité que sa mise en æuvre conduira à un résultat acceptable.
257. *See* Art. 3 of the Implementing recovery directive.
258. *See* Art. 4, 2 (the name, address and any other relevant information relating to the identification to which the applicant authority normally has access and the nature and amount of the claim in respect of which the request is made). *Also see* Art. 3 of the Implementing recovery directive about the content of the application for the request for information.
259. *See* Art. 4 of the Implementing recovery directive. *Also see* 5.4.2.2.2 about co-debtors.
260. *See* Art. 4, 3 (the requested authority is not obliged to supply information: (a) which it would not be able to obtain for the purpose of recovering similar claims arising in the Member State in which it is situated, (b) which would disclose any commercial, industrial, or professional, secrets, or (c) the disclosure of which would be liable to pre-justice the security of or be contrary to the public policy of the State).
261. *See* Art. 4, 4 of the Recovery directive and Art. 7 of the Implementing recovery directive.

claims, and solely for that purpose, and the judicial authorities dealing with matters concerning the recovery of the claims.[262] When the requested authority has fulfilled its obligation to transmit information, as applying to the recovery of similar claims arising in the Member State where the authority is situated, to the applicant State, this leads to that the use of this information by the applicant authority becomes limited for recovery purposes in relation to the information obtained in connection to each claim in its request for information, which falls under the scope of claims in the Recovery directive,[263] both in the national and international context.

Consequently, the use of information related to the assets of the debtor received by the applicant authority from the requested authority, after a request for information from an applicant authority based on claims of VAT against a corporate debtor, is limited for recovery purposes related to such claims of the applicant State. The applicant State may, besides a domestic use of the information for recovery purposes, also use it to determine if a possibly later forwarded application for the recovery of its claim to another requested Member State would be likely to result in payments in the assets of the debtor or not. It is thus prohibited to use such information for the purpose of recovery of claims, which fall outside of the scope of claims in the Recovery directive, *e.g.* related to other public law claims and civil law claims. Besides provisions related to communications, including their time-limits, between Member States[264] there also exist provisions for the exchange of information for recovery purposes related to the Recovery directive by the support of an intranet-system, the CCN/CSI-network system, for the transmission 'by electronic means' of information.[265]

6.3.2.2 Conventions

The Council of Europe and OECD convention on mutual administrative assistance in tax matters stipulates that the parties to it shall exchange any information, besides for taxation purposes and prosecution purposes, that is foresee ably relevant to the recovery and enforcement of tax claims. Information, which is unlikely to be relevant to this purpose shall not be exchanged under the convention.[266] At the request of the applicant State, the requested State shall provide the applicant State with any information, which concerns particular persons, or transactions, either available in the tax files, or, if not, after having taken all relevant measures to provide the applicant State with the information requested.[267] A request for

262. *See* Art. 16.
263. *See* 5.2.2.1.
264. *See* Arts 5-6, 8 and 24 of the Implementing recovery directive.
265. *See* Arts 2 and 21-23 of the Implementing recovery directive.
266. *See* Art. 4 and Explanatory report on the Convention on Mutual Administrative Assistance in Tax Matters, p. 19.
267. *See* Art. 5 and Explanatory report on the Convention on Mutual Administrative Assistance in Tax Matters, pp. 21-22.

information from an applicant State, shall indicate, where appropriate, some basic facts in relation to the person concerned.[268] It may be refused by a requested State based on certain grounds of refusal[269] and shall in case of refusal be communicated to the applicant State with a statement of the reasons of refusal.[270]

Any information obtained by a party to the convention shall be treated as secret in the same manner as information obtained under the domestic laws of that party, or under the conditions of secrecy applying in the supplying party, if such conditions are more restrictive,[271] but may be disclosed to the persons, or authorities, involved in the recovery and enforcement of taxes; however, only limited to the use for such purposes.[272] This means, with one exception,[273] that it is prohibited to use information for recovery purposes obtained under the scope of tax claims in the convention[274] for the purpose of recovery of claims which fall outside of this scope of application, *e.g.* related to other public law claims and civil law claims.

The scope of exchange of information available, besides for taxation purposes, for recovery purposes under the Nordic agreement on assistance in tax matters[275] is

---

268. *See* Art. 18, 1. a-c and 2. (the authority, or agency, which initiated the request made by the competent authority, the name, address and any other particulars assisting in the identification of the person in respect of whom the request is made and the form in which the applicant State wishes the information to be supplied in order to meet its needs. The applicant State is also obliged to forward any other information relevant to the request, which comes to its knowledge). *Also see* Explanatory report on the Convention on Mutual Administrative Assistance in Tax Matters, pp. 46-47.
269. *See* Art. 21, 2. and in particular c. and d. (to supply information, which is not obtainable under its own laws, or its administrative practice, or under the laws of the applicant State, or its administrative practice, and to supply information, which would disclose any trade, business, industrial, commercial or professional secret, or trade process, or information the disclosure of which would be contrary to public policy, or to its essential interests.). *Also see* Explanatory report on the Convention on Mutual Administrative Assistance in Tax Matters, pp. 51-53.
270. *See* Art. 20, 2 and Explanatory report on the Convention on Mutual Administrative Assistance in Tax Matters, p. 49.
271. *See* Art. 22, 1 and Explanatory report on the Convention on Mutual Administrative Assistance in Tax Matters, p. 54.
272. *See* Art. 22, 2 and Explanatory report on the Convention on Mutual Administrative Assistance in Tax Matters, pp. 54-56.
273. *See* Art. 22, 4, which stipulates that, under certain conditions, the parties to the convention can agree that received information also may be used for other purposes by a party to the convention, which has received information, and in addition be transmitted, by this latter party to a third party to the convention. *Also see* Explanatory report on the Convention on Mutual Administrative Assistance in Tax Matters, pp. 57-58.
274. *See* 5.2.2.2.
275. *See* Art. 1 b, which stipulates that the contracting States have undertaken to assist each other in tax matters pursuant to this agreement with respect to investigations in tax matters, such as the procurement of tax returns, or other information, and the exchange of information without special request, or upon a request in a specific matter, Art. 4, 1 stipulates that a contracting State is obliged to provide such assistance, Art. 10 refers this obligation to be procured in conformity with national legislation, while Art. 13, 3 allows that information, which results from an investigation in a tax matter according to Art. 13, 1, may be used by officials who handle collection, or recovery of taxes.

unclear, but in any event of a somewhat limited importance, because the Nordic States, which are parties to the Nordic agreement and that also are Member States of the EU are entitled to make an alternative use of the Recovery directive and its provisions of exchange of information for recovery purposes.[276] This is subject to that the request is based on a claim, which falls under the scope of claims in the directive.[277] Also, the Nordic States, except the Faeroe Islands, which are parties to both the Nordic agreement and to the Council of Europe and OECD convention on mutual administrative assistance in tax matters,[278] but are not Member States of the EU, could make alternative use of the convention and its provisions of exchange of information for recovery purposes, subject to that the request is based on a claim, which falls under the scope of claims in the convention.[279]

6.3.3 Conclusions

There exists no sufficiently efficient EC law, or multilateral convention, in force in the civil enforcement law area of the EU, where we find the contractual claims, which enable a private creditor, who holds a title of execution from one Member State, to benefit, through the assistance by regulated enforcement agents, from an international exchange of information about the debtor's assets in another Member State. A private creditor's possibilities to obtain such assistance for information in the international context, such as information to be used for enforcement purposes of his civil law claim in another State, is therefore outside the scope of EC law and most multilateral conventions and thus entirely governed and limited by access to non-identical national laws.[280]

Parts of EC law and multilateral conventions in force in the public law area provide for an international exchange of information, the Recovery directive being the most important one, because it covers the tax recovery area at a rather detailed level and provides possibilities for recovery agents of the concerned States to exchange information for recovery purposes between the Member States of the EU. The exchange of information based on the Recovery directive and the Implementing recovery directive, where we find the tax claims in EC law, is also supported by an intranet-system, the CCN/CSI-network system, for the transmission 'by electronic means' of information in matters of assistance. EC law and multilateral conventions in the tax recovery law area provide access to a developed exchange system for information for the purpose of recovery of taxes, but such a system does not exist in the civil enforcement law area for the purpose of enforcing private claims, including contractual claims.

276. *See* 5.3.1.2.1.
277. *See* 5.2.2.1.
278. *See* 5.1.3.
279. *See* 5.3.1.2.2 compared to 5.2.2.2.
280. National laws on access to information for enforcement purposes in enforcement proceedings are treated in the context of 7.2.3.

6.3.3.1 Contractual Claims

This part initially treats the conclusions based on an analysis of the advantages and disadvantages of the European Asset Declaration and some other proposals and ideas. The establishment of a minimum level of harmonization of national laws for access to information for enforcement purposes and of a sufficiently efficient solution for access to information for enforcement purposes in the cross-border context in the civil enforcement law area are required in order to meet the objectives of the Council's draft programme of measures in seeking to make more efficient the enforcement in the requested State of judgments delivered in another Member State and to enable the precise identification of a debtor's assets in the territory of the Member States for implementing the principle of mutual recognition.[281] This is based on the Tampere conclusions, which also have been reaffirmed in the Hague Programme of the European Council.[282]

In addition, several authors emphasize the importance, and confirm the need, for access to information for enforcement purposes based on various aspects, particularly in the civil enforcement law area and sometimes also including the twofold objectives to increase access to national information and to establish a multilateral cooperation system between States for the exchange of nationally available information.[283]

281. *See* Council draft programme C 12/01/2001/EC of measures for implementation of the principle of mutual recognition of decisions in civil and commercial matters, II, section B. Measures ancillary to mutual recognition, 2. Efficiency of measures providing for improved enforcement of decisions compared to III, section E. Ancillary measures.

282. *See* III, 2.1 of the Hague Programme of the European Council about improving the exchange of information and III, 3.4.1 of the same Programme about facilitating civil law procedures across borders.

283. *See* Berglund, Les recherches et l'accès aux informations des agents chargés de l'exécution, Le droit processuel et le droit de l'exécution, pp. 288-290, regarding the twofold objectives of creating a European system for the exchange of information and of harmonization of national provisions of access to information. In order to make this work advance he proposes that harmonization of national provisions should begin with the identification of common principles, 'minimum standards', which *e.g.* may concern bank accounts and corporate registers, Bertaux, Les dérives de l'exécution forcée: vers un régime d'exécution privé, Le droit processuel et le droit de l'exécution, pp. 279 and 283, states that enforcement measures do not become effective mainly due to the impossibility to obtain the address of the debtor, identify and locate his assets and to receive information about his employer. He further concludes that if such access to information would be given to the regulated enforcement agents it should also contribute to suppress the use of obscure private recovery agencies, Hesslén, Asset transparency – finding information – measures to make enforcement more effective, Globalisation of law in an area of universal justice/'Is the creation of a World Area of Justice a utopic vision?', pp. 28-30, she states that there still exists a great variety in an international context in terms of access to information for enforcement purposes. She further mentions, *i.b.*, p. 31, that there often exist problems at an international level to achieve information from other States, *i.a.* due to different organization structures in other States and language obstacles and proposes, *i.b.*, p. 41, a data base on the civil status on all citizens of the EU for these Member States, which will become parties to an international cooperation. In addition, she emphasizes the importance of an international exchange directly between the professionals of the Member States

6.3.3.1.1 European Assets Declaration

The idea of an introduction in EC law of a European Assets Declaration,[284] which would require the debtor to declare his assets on the initiative of a private creditor, in an affidavit, or other corresponding official document, to the enforcement agents, or in court in a matter of enforcement is to encourage uniformity across Member States. This is intended to result in that creditors would have equal access to information about assets, while debtors would receive equal protection. This idea comes close to the concept of a general disclosure of information in insolvency proceedings, *e.g.* in a bankruptcy. The objectives of insolvency and enforcement proceedings are, however, not identical, even if one similar feature exists, the realization of the assets of the debtor in the interest of the creditor. Still other important objectives and structures of insolvency are different from those of enforcement and recovery.[285]

Therefore, the principle of universality, as implemented in the area of general civil execution, in bankruptcy and in the area of international insolvency

---

and she also promotes the idea of setting up an international center, an 'Interex', as an analogue to Interpol, to support the international exchange of information between professionals of the concerned States. *Also see* Jeuland, Les garanties de la saisie européenne de creances bancaires, Le droit processuel et le droit de l'exécution, p. 404, on the need of obtaining information about assets in bank accounts, and Kennett, Aperçus comparatifs des différents modes d'exécution forcée des obligations pécuniaires dans l'Union Européenne, Le droit processuel et le droit de l'exécution, p. 264, where she suggests, based on the care of making judgments effective, that access to confidential information about the debtor (address, employment and assets) should be justified and be provided by the State, and maybe by financial institutions, to the enforcement agents, not to the creditors. *Also see* Leroy, L'efficacité des procédures judiciaires au sein de l'union Européenne et les garanties des droits de la defense, Transparence patrimoniale, L'efficacité de la justice civile en Europe, p. 379, where he argues in favour of an international cooperation for the exchange of information for enforcement purposes. *Also see* de Leval, Subject of the proceedings, The execution of court decisions in civil cases, pp. 48 and 51-52, on some guiding principles on securing information and some suggestions on how to increase the effectiveness of the law of execution in the EU. He concludes that, if such suggestions are implemented in all Member States, and ... 'supplemented by the requirement to repatriate attached assets ... it would not only increase the effectiveness of procedures in each country but also make transfers of assets between countries to enable the debtor to avoid attachment ineffective'. *Also see* Verbeke, Quel Huissier de Justice pour l'Europe ?, Le droit processuel et le droit de l'exécution, pp. 309-313, on the balance for enforcement purposes between the creditor's right to access to information and the debtor's right of privacy and Verbeke, Execution Officers as a Balance Wheel in Insolvency Cases, pp. 16-17, where he argues in favour of an extensive access, by various means, to information on the debtor's assets to execution officers, however taking into account the privacy of the debtor. The execution officers should, in order to effectuate an efficient recovery, have '... a general and unlimited power of inquiry and examination of the patrimony and income of the debtor, giving him the power, without court authorization but under the condition that the debtor can at any time oppose any abusive action of the execution officer before the court ... '. He also suggests that the proposed system should be applied internationally, eventually leading to cooperation and exchange of information between execution officers of different countries.

284. *See* 6.3.1.

285. *See* 1.1.1.1.5.

proceedings does not seem to be suitable to be introduced for the search for information for enforcement purposes in the area of special execution, the enforcement area, in a European Assets Declaration. The concept of a general disclosure of information in a European Assets Declaration also risks to include more sources of information related to the assets of the debtor in the Member States than needed for the purpose of enforcing the claim of a creditor in the debtors' assets and may consequently, from the perspective of the debtor, be disproportionate in relation to his interest of privacy. On the other hand, it satisfies the right of a creditor to obtain all information in the European judicial area related to the debtors' assets in order to make a choice between them in a matter of enforcement.[286]

There exist States in which only the enforcement agent determines what measures of enforcement to undertake, but also States where the creditor has an almost completely free choice as to the method of enforcement to be adopted.[287] The actual choice of the assets suitable for seizure should, however, not, for reasons of efficiency and privacy, be entrusted to the creditor, even if he may express his preference of choice, but instead to the regulated enforcement agents. The reason is that these agents have the task to establish a justified and proportionate balance in terms of access to information for enforcement purposes, in the enforcement proceeding, between conflicting interests, *i.e.* to make use of no more, or less, information than needed.

It may be argued that States, which allow an intervention by the creditor in the enforcement process by giving him a right to issue instructions to the enforcement organs, the regulated enforcement agents, about the actual choice of assets suitable for seizure, may risk that these agents violate the principle of proportionality of the European Convention on Human Rights in their activities in a non-proportional and harmful way in relation to the debtor. Such a violation may occur if they, following the instructions of indicated information from the creditor about the assets of the debtor, *e.g.* would decide to seizure a property of real estate of the debtor for a small claim, without having first acquired alternative information, which used, might instead have produced a more proportionate and less harmful measure of enforcement in relation to the debtor, such as the attachment of his earnings from his employer.

---

286. *See*, about the same opinion, EC Study JAI/02/03/2002, B, III, 1.
287. *See* Kennett, The Enforcement of Judgments in Europe, pp. 89-90, who makes a distinction between jurisdictions in which one enforcement agent can undertake any of the measures of enforcement provided by the law (*e.g.* in Sweden and in France, where in this latter State the creditor will normally leave the choice to be exercised by the French Huissier de Justice) and those where different agents have different responsibilities (*e.g.* in England and Germany, where the creditor has an almost completely free choice as to the method of enforcement to be adopted). She further finds that where the choice of methods of enforcement is concentrated in the hands of one enforcement agent, and in particular an agent with good access to information about the debtor, a level of flexibility and speed of action becomes available which enhances the likelihood of effective enforcement and that traditional structures for enforcement which rely on the compartmentalizing of responsibilities and cooperation and control by the creditor look rather clumsy in comparison.

The approach of the European Assets Declaration of a general disclosure of information from the debtor in a declaration about his assets in the European judicial area risks, anyway, even to the extent it would be possible to argue that a justified balance between the conflicting interests of the debtor and the creditor is possible to establish, to be contrary to the interest of efficiency of the creditor for several reasons. The declaration only covers information from the debtor, not access to information from independent sources of information of a reliable and official status. The debtor may also, despite a threat of sanctions, refuse to declare his assets, or provide insufficient, or incorrect, information in his declaration. If the debtor disappears, a declaration becomes impossible.[288] If, in addition, the debtor repeatedly changes his domicile from one Member State to other Member States, the creditor risks having to apply for a European Assets Declaration correspondingly, *i.e.* in several Member States, before such a declaration can be obtained.

A demand from a private creditor of a European Assets Declaration seems only possible if it forms part of an application for enforcement measures, based on his title of execution. Otherwise no enforcement matter is established as the necessary legal basis for the declaration.[289] If the private creditor receives useful information from the debtor from his European Assets Declaration, he would still have to make an application for the enforcement of his claim, based on his title of execution, in one or several other requested Member States in parallel, where the assets of the debtor have been indicated by the debtor. The enforcement agents of these requested States would, based on the applications, also have to review and evaluate the indicated information from the creditor in relation to other possible sources of information available about the debtors' assets as an integrated part of the actual enforcement proceeding. This is motivated in order to establish a justified balance in that proceeding between the interest of efficiency of the private creditor and the interest of privacy of the debtor and may, or may not, result in the attachment of assets indicated by the private creditor. Consequently, the possible advantages of a European Assets Declaration are, in an over all evaluation, not of sufficient importance to counter-balance its disadvantages to both the private creditor and the debtor.

6.3.3.1.2 European Garnishee's Declaration

A European Garnishee's Declaration has been proposed to oblige third-party debtors to give information on the assets seized.[290] A better solution would be, when the enforcement organs have received an application for the enforcement of a

288. *See*, about a similar opinion, EC Study JAI/02/03/2002, B, III, 1, regarding the conclusion that the main problem with the debtor's declaration lies in the fact that the declaration must be given personally.
289. *See* EC Study JAI/02/03/2002, B, V, 5, which stipulates as a prerequisite for obtaining a declaration that the creditor must present an enforceable judgment and suggest that the declaration should be taken at the beginning of the enforcement proceeding.
290. *See* 6.3.1.

judgment and before the actual seizure takes place, in order to deal with differences in national laws,[291] to oblige any third-party debtor, including any financial institution, in national laws to provide, at the request of the enforcement organs, to render information on the debtors' assets to these organs.[292] This would also enable the enforcement organs to make a choice between all assets held by this third-party, before their actual decision about seizure.

6.3.3.1.3 Other Proposals

The proposal of 1999 about an 'International legal instrument on the mutual cooperation between European enforcement authorities in the European Union for the exchange of information for enforcement purposes related to private and public claims' and the similar idea in the proposed Nordic agreement on the exchange of information in recovery matters in the report Nordic cooperation in recovery matters to the Nordic Council of Ministers,[293] are based on the idea of a cooperation between national professionals, the regulated enforcement agents, for the exchange of information for enforcement purposes also for the benefit of the private creditor. They relate to the existence of a title of execution in any of the concerned States and their equal treatment in this context, and may be further elaborated into an alternative solution adapted to the civil enforcement law area.

A similar idea as in these proposals has been included in the Proposal for a Council regulation on jurisdiction, applicable law, recognition and enforcement of decisions and cooperation in matters relating to maintenance obligations[294] to facilitate the recovery of maintenance claims through a cooperation between national central authorities for the exchange of information for recovery purposes for the benefit of the maintenance creditors. For social reasons, States have often established more favourable legal solutions to help the maintenance creditors to receive their money from the maintenance debtor than exist in other legal areas, *e.g.* these of contractual and commercial claims.

Examples of such more favourable solutions are a privileged level of priority rights at the attachment of the debtor's earnings,[295] or by advance payments of maintenance contributions from the State, which afterwards are recovered by the State from the debtor. This degree of engagement by the States in relation to the maintenance creditors, and the subsequent interest of an efficient recovery both of the maintenance claims for the benefit of the maintenance creditor and of the advance payments of maintenance contributions of the States from the debtor, may explain a need of cooperation between States for the cross-border recovery

291. *See* 7.2.3.2, where differences in national laws about access to information for enforcement purposes from third-party debtors are treated.
292. *See* 7.2.3.5 about the idea of improved access to information for enforcement purposes in national laws.
293. *See* 6.3.1.
294. *See* 6.3.1.
295. *See* 7.2.1.

of these claims, compared to the needs of other creditors, *e.g.* the creditors in the areas of contractual and commercial claims, where States, so far, have not developed any similar solutions.

Another alternative model of cooperation, which has been discussed, is that of the Taking of evidence regulation. The model of this regulation is, however, not suitable, because it builds on a cooperation between courts in the Member States, whereas most Member States have organized their enforcement activities differently outside the court systems.[296]

6.3.3.1.4 Evaluation

It is possible to develop a solution for the exchange of information for enforcement purposes, which is adapted to private claims in the cross-border context of the civil enforcement law area, such as for contractual and commercial claims, between the Member States of the EU. There exist alternative proposals and ideas for a solution about how to create an improved access to information for enforcement purposes in this context. The idea of creating an improved access to information for enforcement purposes through a cooperation in the cross-border context, which creates an optional right for a creditor, who holds a title of execution, to make use of an exchange of information adopted to contractual and commercial claims, between the regulated enforcement agents of the Member States of the EU seems, however, according to an all-over conclusion, to be the most attractive one. This is for the benefit of a higher degree of service and of efficiency of the private creditor at the enforcement of his title of execution and for a proportionate treatment of exchanged information and privacy in relation to the debtor.[297] This idea would also be able to promote a better functioning of the Common Internal Market.

The ideas in the proposal of 1999 about an 'International legal instrument on the mutual cooperation between European enforcement authorities in the European Union for the exchange of information for enforcement purposes related to private and public claims', in the proposed Nordic agreement on the exchange of information in recovery matters in the report Nordic cooperation in recovery matters to the Nordic Council of Ministers, and in the Proposal for a Council regulation on jurisdiction, applicable law, recognition and enforcement of decisions and cooperation in matters relating to maintenance obligations, therefore seem to be

296. *See*, about a similar opinion, EC Study JAI/02/03/2002, B, V, 7. *Also see* 3.2.1 about structures of organization of national regulated enforcement agents. Kennett, The Enforcement of Judgments in Europe, pp. 122-123, states that the judicial assistance model could be seen as the logical approach for those States in which the court directs enforcement, or is intimately involved in the enforcement process, but concludes that it is difficult to see how courts that do not normally become involved in such information gathering could be used efficiently in the transfrontier context.

297. *See* 6.3.3.1.1 about the importance that a disclosure of information from the perspective of the debtor does not become disproportionate in relation to his interest of privacy compared to 7.2.3.5 about the balance between the interest of efficiency of the creditor and the interest of privacy of the debtor.

best suitable as a base of discussion for a further development into a possible solution.

In such a discussion it may be contemplated that the creditor should have the right to file an application, related to a specific matter, in the Member State of origin of his title of execution, for a following exchange of information for enforcement purposes with another Member State. The Proposal for a Council regulation on jurisdiction, applicable law, recognition and enforcement of decisions and cooperation in matters relating to maintenance obligations and some conventions already include a similar concept of service to a private creditor related to applications for enforcement. A request for information, following the application of the private creditor, should, for reasons of efficiency and integrity, be transmitted electronically in a closed communication system between the Member States.

This solution of cooperation will, as any other alternative, give raise to the question of how to finance the increased costs for the needed work. It remains to be discussed to what extent and proportion private creditors, respectively the Member States, should pay for the services made available under such a possible cooperation, and what possible fees creditors should pay, or not pay, to their national regulated enforcement agents when they want to make use of their services in relation to this available option in a matter for the exchange of information for enforcement purposes. It also remains to be discussed how such a possible cooperation, which would include work in the Member States for communications between the national designated competent authorities, or Contact points, or/and the national regulated enforcement agents, and the private creditors, should best be structured.

These ideas also conform with the objectives of the Council's draft programme. It is also recommended that these issues be further analyzed in connection to the idea of the possible establishment of a European cooperation body between States in the civil execution law area, a Euroex, intended to be of help to the creditors and debtors, who would like to seek the assistance of the enforcement agents in another Member State of the EU,[298] and to the idea of a more developed use of the European Judicial Network in civil and commercial matters.

The establishment of a sufficiently efficient solution for access to information for enforcement purposes in the cross-border civil enforcement law area would also have to take into consideration a sufficiently harmonized level of access to information for enforcement purposes to regulated enforcement agents in national laws[299] in order to guarantee at least some kind of mutually equal acceptable level of exchange of information, which may be used for the benefit of cross-border

298. *See* 3.2.3.3 for further information about the possible idea of the establishment of a Euroex, and of a more developed use of the European Judicial Network in civil and commercial matters.

299. *See* 7.2.3.2, where the important task of the regulated enforcement agent in this context is emphasized and developed. *Also see i.b.*, where an idea of improved access to information for enforcement purposes is developed in more details.

enforcement of a private creditor's claim within the EU.[300] This means that any attempt to improve efficiency by access to information for enforcement purposes in the cross-border context would also have to consider the establishment of a sufficiently high level of access to national information.

6.3.3.2 Tax Claims

The Recovery directive and the Implementing recovery directive provide possibilities of an efficient exchange of information for recovery purposes related to tax claims, but may, subject to certain conditions, be improved. Even if Article 4, 3 a of the Recovery directive in some Member States mean that they are exempted from an obligation to supply information, such as is protected by national bank secrecy,[301] it is, however, not possible to suggest a removal of this provision in the directive, even if it may be argued that such a suggestion would be consistent with the interest of increased efficiency in the mutual assistance cooperation of exchange of information for recovery purposes. Such a suggestion would have to be based on a political agreement about an application of a more advanced concept of mutuality in the Recovery directive.

6.3.3.2.1 Use of Exchanged Information Based on the Recovery Directive after a Decision on Collective Insolvency Proceeding

Even if the Recovery directive and the Implementing recovery directive cover an exchange of information for recovery purposes at a rather detailed level, it may be argued that the use of exchanged information received through this cooperation may be further improved in support of the objective of efficiency of the Recovery directive also after a decision on collective insolvency proceedings under the Insolvency regulation.[302] If a person mentioned in a request for assistance on the exchange of information under the Recovery directive is affected by such a

---

300. *See* EC Study JAI/02/03/2002, B, IV, 1, which concludes that there is no doubt that cross-border recovery of judgments is impaired by the differences between the national legal systems of access to information and that the creditors in Europe are not treated equally. *Also see* Kennett, The Enforcement of Judgments in Europe, pp. 123-125, where she suggests that exchanges of information between regulated professionals may be hampered by lack of transparency of the sources of information available to enforcement agents in other Member States and uncertainty about the quality of information and that any steps towards exchanges of information would be of limited usefulness unless they are supported by European rules providing minimum standards in relation to the nature and quality of information that should be provided domestically to the designated competent authorities and Tarzia, Vers un concept européene du droit de l'exécution ?, Le droit processuel et le droit de l'exécution, p. 165, emphasizing the importance of efficient access to national information as an unconditional requirement for an international cooperation.

301. *See* 6.3.2.1.

302. *See* about the definition of collective insolvency proceedings, Art. 2, a compared to Art. 1, 1 and annex A and definition of liquidator, Art. 2, b compared to annex C of the regulation.

decision under the Insolvency regulation, information received from a requested State in such a matter before such an insolvency proceeding is not allowed to be handed over by the applicant State to a liquidator, such as a trustee and an official receiver in bankruptcy.

It may be contemplated that such information should also be allowed to be handed over by the applicant State to be used by liquidators in such proceedings of the applicant State for the purpose of better satisfying the payments of both private and public claims in the insolvency proceeding. Any such possible change of the Recovery directive would also indirectly contribute to strengthen the efficiency of national insolvency law and of the Insolvency regulation. Any change in this respect would, however, have to be based on a political agreement of an application of a more advanced concept of mutuality in the Recovery directive.

6.3.3.2.2 New Communication Obligation in the Implementing Recovery Directive in Case of a Refund of a Tax Credit

The idea of introducing a measure of the retention of a tax credit to be classified as a 'recovery' measure under Article 6 of the Recovery directive has, for various reasons, been considered not to be attractive.[303] Some other possible alternative solutions related to the idea of the retention of a tax credit and to the idea of a preventive measure of a communication obligation therefore merits to be further discussed and evaluated. Alternative solutions could be to introduce a preventive measure in the tax law area in the Implementing recovery directive, as an initial communication possibility for the Member State of the tax debt, then matched with a corresponding communication obligation of another Member State related to a tax credit of the debtor from the first Member State.

6.3.3.2.3 Tax Law Area

To render efficiency would mean that a Member State of the EU, before a refund of a tax credit becomes due for payment, shall first, at the time when an application for a tax credit refund has been received, without prior request, be obliged to inform other Member States that this forthcoming payment will take place within a certain period of time. All other Member States, in their capacity of tax creditors, or only the Member State of the debtor's domicile, may then be possible addresses for this information. The Member States, which have recoverable tax debts against the concerned legal entity, or the individual, entitled to a refund, must then, prior to that time, make a request for recovery under the Recovery directive. Otherwise the refund of the tax credit shall take place.

This would require that a Member State, which has identified tax credits of debtors of other Member States, would as soon as these credits have been established, without prior request, communicate this information to other Member States. The reason is to enable them to make a request for recovery of their tax

303. *See* 6.2.2.1.1.2.

debts under the Recovery directive before a refund of a tax credit becomes due for payment in the Member State of the tax credit and that the requested Member State, following the request of recovery, would attach the tax refund. The decision about the attachment would be open to appeal, and the judicial control would be secured. This solution may, except in the VAT-area, also be of principal interest to contemplate in other areas of scope of claims in the Recovery directive, *e.g.* for income taxes.

The proposed system may, however, be unrealistic to implement, if only as a separate solution in the tax law area, and for two reasons. A Member State would still be required to refund the tax credit without delay, which means that a possible obligation to communicate would have to be efficient, for time reasons, to produce cross-border recovery results before the time of the refund of the tax credit. Besides, the retention of a refund of a tax credit in the tax law area is normally only possible for national tax control reasons, not for the purpose of promoting a more efficient tax recovery.

A similar proposal would be to introduce a preventive measure as a communication obligation, which would also be extended to the time after the payment of a tax credit has become due, but then secured by an obligation of retention of the refund of the tax credit. This would, however, be a less attractive solution in terms of efficiency, because it would require precautionary measures based on a foreign tax debt to stop the payment, in the interest of protecting the debtor, and would therefore involve legal control in a court proceeding. This other solution therefore also appears to be unrealistic, because the duration of such a court proceeding would probably exceed the possible time for retention.

6.3.3.2.4 Implementing Recovery Directive

Yet, another proposal could be to extend the use of the existing possibility to communicate under the Implementing recovery directive for the benefit of a Member State of a tax debtor, who may be expected to receive a refund of a tax credit in another Member State. This extended communication for the Member State of the tax debt should be an obligation for all Member States to inform, without prior request, all other Member States of the date of a forthcoming refund of a tax credit, based on information received before this date. Consequently, this would enable the applicant Member State to forward a request of recovery to the requested Member State for the attachment of the tax refund. Such cooperation between Member States would, no doubt, demand an efficient use of the intranet-system for the exchange of information for recovery purposes related to the Recovery directive, the CCN/CSI-network system, for the transmission of information. It would maybe also demand further developed technical solutions.

As an alternative idea to transferring this information between the Member States it may be contemplated that this information is made available in a common closed database of tax debts at Community level, where a check quickly can be made by the Member States, so that the compliant taxpayers can get their refunds without delay. An alternative proposal may be to impose an obligation also in relation to other taxes than VAT, as in the Council directive 2008/9/EC of 12 February 2008 laying down detailed rules for the refund of VAT, provided for in Directive 2006/112/EC, to taxable persons not established in the Member State of refund but established in another Member State, requiring that an application for a refund be submitted to the Member State of the establishment of the taxpayer.[304] Such a proposal would have the advantage to enable a Member State, which has non-paid tax debts in relation to a tax debtor, to forward an application for the recovery of the tax refund under the Recovery directive to another Member State.

6.3.3.2.5 Evaluation

Even if possible alternative proposals exist, an all-over evaluation of their advantages and disadvantages leads to that the idea of an introduction of a preventive measure in the Implementing recovery directive of a communication obligation for Member States is best aimed to meet the objective of efficiency of the directive, but it would also than the other proposals better take into account the interest of the debtor's protection. This concerns taxes falling under the scope of claims of the Recovery directive, except VAT.

The management of this preferable proposal applied to a cooperation between Member States would, in order to become efficient *i.a.* demand an efficient use of the CCN/CSI-network system for the transmission of information and maybe, in addition, some other further developed technical solutions. This is to be able to meet the deadline for the request of recovery of a tax debt after an application for a tax credit refund has been received, but before the moment of this refund. It may be contemplated to impose a similar idea, as in the VAT-area, also in other areas of scope of claims in the Recovery directive, which would require that an application for a refund shall be submitted to the Member State of the establishment of the taxpayer. It is, however, not possible to suggest such a cooperation under the present legal objective of mutuality of the Implementing recovery directive, even if it may be argued that this would be consistent with the objective of efficiency of this directive.

6.4 INTERNATIONAL INSOLVENCY

6.4.1 Insolvency Regulation

The Insolvency regulation[305] shall apply only to collective insolvency proceedings, such as bankruptcy, corporate reconstructions and compulsory winding-up by

---

304. *See* Art. 15, which requires that the refund application shall be submitted to the Member State of establishment. *Also see* Art. 25, which stipulates that the Member State of refund shall take into account as a decrease of the amount of the refund any correction where a separate declaration is submitted in the form of recovery. The Directive shall apply to refund applications submitted after 31 Dec. 2009, *see* Art. 28.

305. *Also see* the information available about this regulation under Headline Bankruptcy – Community law, website of the European Judicial Network in civil and commercial matters, <http://ec.europa.eu/civiljustice>.

the court,[306] opened after the entry into force of the regulation on 31 May 2002.[307] It is binding for all Member States of the EU, except Denmark,[308] and it replaces a lot of enumerated multilateral and bilateral conventions in the insolvency area, including the Nordic bankruptcy convention, between the Member States bound by the regulation.[309] Consequently, the Nordic bankruptcy convention does not apply between Finland and Sweden, which instead are bound by the Insolvency regulation, but it applies between on the one hand Finland and Sweden and on the other hand Denmark and the other contracting Nordic States to the convention, which are non-Member States of the EU, *i.e.* Iceland and Norway.[310] The regulation does not exclude an application of the Bankruptcy convention between France and Monaco.

The Insolvency regulation excludes from its scope insolvency proceedings concerning insurance undertakings, credit institutions, investment undertakings, holding funds, or securities for third parties, and collective investment undertakings.[311] These excluded areas are instead governed by the Directive 2001/17/EC of the European Parliament and of the Council of 19 March 2001 on the reorganization and winding-up of insurance undertakings and the Directive 2001/24/EC of the European Parliament and of the Council of 4 April 2001 on the reorganization and winding-up of credit institutions.[312] The scope of the Insolvency regulation, and that of the Nordic bankruptcy convention, do not coincide with those of the Brussels I regulation and of the Recovery directive. The Insolvency regulation interacts, however, in the insolvency proceedings, with the provisions of provisional, including protective, measures, recognition and enforcement in the Brussels I regulation.[313]

The substance of the regulation is identical to the text of the convention on insolvency proceedings, which was opened for signature in Brussels on 23 November 1995, but this convention failed to entry into force because it was not signed by the United Kingdom. Therefore literature, besides that related to the Insolvency regulation,[314] which also relates to this convention,[315] including the

306. *See* Art. 2 a and Annex A about the collective insolvency proceedings of each Member State that are included under the Regulation compared to Art. 1, 1.
307. *See* Arts 43 and 47.
308. *See* Preamble (33) of the Regulation, which stipulates that Denmark is not bound by it nor subject to its application.
309. *See* Art. 44, 1.
310. *See* Art. 44, 1, j of the Regulation, which relates to the Nordic bankruptcy convention, does not prevent a continued application of the convention between on the one hand Finland and Sweden and on the other hand Denmark and the other contracting Nordic States to the convention, which are non-Member States of the EU. *See* 2.1.7 for further information on the Convention.
311. *See* Preamble (9) and Art. 1, 2.
312. *See*, about an extensive commentary on these Directives, EU Banking and Insurance Insolvency.
313. *See* 5.3.1.
314. *See e.g.* Cross-Border Insolvency Law, International Instruments and Commentary, pp. 38-44, The EC Regulation on insolvency proceedings: A Commentary and Annotated Guide, The European Insolvency Regulation: Law and Practice, and Mellqvist, EU:s insolvensförordning, m.m., En kommentar.
315. *See e.g.:* Arnt Nielsen, International privat- og procesret, pp. 291-304, Berglund, Svensk internationell exekutions- och obeståndsrätt, pp. 330-334, Bogdan, Sveriges och

Virgós-Schmit Report on the Convention on Insolvency proceedings,[316] may be of interest for the interpretation of the regulation.

When the Insolvency regulation, after a decision in a main collective insolvency proceeding,[317] *e.g.* a court decision in bankruptcy, takes legal effect in the Member States[318] it will, as in most national laws,[319] hinder any further activities by individual creditors to enforce and recover their claims. Any further actions are instead to be dealt with, in the collective interest of all creditors, by the appointed liquidator in insolvency proceedings,[320] *e.g.* a trustee in bankruptcy. The referral provisions in the Insolvency regulation to national laws result in that a main insolvency proceeding, which has been opened in one Member State does not, in the cross-border insolvency context, become entirely, but largely, governed by the legislation of that State.[321] Depending on in what Member State such a proceeding is opened various non-identical European insolvency laws will apply.[322]

EU:s internationella insolvensrätt, pp. 154-190, and Mellqvist, Gränsöverskridande konkurshantering – EU:s konvention om insolvensförfaranden, Ny Juridik 4/96, pp. 7-44.

316. *See* Report on the Convention on Insolvency proceedings.
317. *See* Art. 3, 1 and 2, a compared to Art. 1, 1 and annex A.
318. *See* Art. 17, 1.
319. *See* Kerameus, International encyclopedia of comparative law, volume XVI, Civil procedure, chapter 10, Enforcement proceedings, p. 41, who makes the comparative remarks that: 'Almost everywhere the opening of bankruptcy or insolvency proceedings brings about the stay of individual enforcement. This statement is in principle undisputed since collective and individual enforcement are incompatible with each other for reasons connected to the nature of proceedings and the methods of distribution. To allow both to run concurrently would only cause confusion and introduce the anarchy of individual pressures within a regime of collective and egalitarian treatment. However, character and scope of the stay vary among the different legal systems.'
320. *See* Art. 2, b compared to annex C.
321. *See* Art. 4, which refers to the legislation of the State of opening of proceedings as the applicable law to insolvency proceedings and their effects, except when otherwise provided in the regulation. Exceptions exist *e.g.* in Arts 5-15 (third parties rights *in rem*, set-off, reservation of title, contracts relating to immovable property, payment systems and financial markets, contracts of employment, effects on rights subject to registration, community patents and trade marks, detrimental acts, protection of third-party purchasers and effects of insolvency proceedings on lawsuits pending). Art. 18, 3 stipulates that the liquidator, in exercising his powers, shall comply with the law of the State within the territory of which he intends to take action, in particular with procedures for the realization of assets.
322. *See* Cross Border Debt Recovery, section 17, which includes information on liquidation and bankruptcy proceedings in the following States: Austria, Belgium, Czech Republic, England and Wales, Estonia, Finland, France, Germany, Greece, Hungary, Ireland, Italy, Latvia, Lithuania, Northern Ireland, Norway, Poland, Portugal, Russia, Spain, Sweden, Switzerland, the Netherlands and Ukraine. European Corporate Insolvency includes information on insolvency law in the following States: Belgium, Denmark, France, Germany, Greece, Ireland, Italy, Luxemburg, the Netherlands, Norway, Portugal, Spain, Sweden, Switzerland and the United Kingdom. Insolvenzen in Europa includes information on insolvency law in the following States: Austria, Belgium, Denmark, Germany, England and Wales, France, Greece, Ireland, Italy, Luxemburg, the Netherlands, Norway, Portugal, Sweden and Spain. *Also see*, about the different structure of insolvency law in some European States, Principles of European Insolvency law.

Consequently, the Insolvency regulation reflects the principle of universality in many aspects of insolvency proceedings.[323] Some rulings of the ECJ, which treat the Insolvency regulation, relate to the case of *Staubitz-Schreiber*.[324] and the case of *Eurofood IFSC Ltd*.[325]

The Insolvency regulation stipulates that the issue of preferential, or non-preferential, treatment of claims in bankruptcy shall be determined by the law of the State of the opening of proceedings.[326] This referral to the opening of proceedings means that each Member State is entitled to determine whether, or not, priority rights should be attributed to a foreign claim in national insolvency law, as in bankruptcy law. This could result in that priority rights are attributed to foreign claims in the State of opening of a proceeding of bankruptcy, even if such rights would not have been attributed to them in pre-existing cross-border enforcement, or recovery matters in the same State.[327]

In the interest of equal treatment of domestic and foreign claims in bankruptcy proceedings it is, however, unlikely that foreign claims would receive more beneficial treatments than corresponding domestic claims in such proceedings. The national treatment of priority rights, or non-priority rights, in insolvency proceedings differ.[328] Any creditor, including the tax authorities and social security

---

323. *Also see* 1.1.1.1.5.
324. In its decision in *Staubitz-Schreiber* of 17 Jan. 2006, the ECJ ruled that Art. 3, 1 of the Insolvency regulation must be interpreted to mean that the court of the Member State within the territory of which the centre of the debtor's main interest is situated at the time when the debtor lodges the request to open insolvency proceedings retains jurisdiction to open those proceedings if the debtor moves the centre of his main interests to the territory of another Member State after lodging the request but before the proceedings are opened.
325. The ECJ has in its decision in *Eurofood IFSC Ltd* of 2 May 2006, treated matters of competent jurisdiction, based on its interpretation of Arts 3, 1, and 16, 1, and 26 of the Insolvency regulation, in some particular circumstances, for the bankruptcy of a subsidiary company situated on Ireland, whereas the parent company was found in Italy.
326. *See* Art. 4, 2, i.
327. Compare 6.2.1.3 about contractual claims, and 6.2.2.3 about tax claims.
328. The following works include information on priority rights in insolvency law: Cross Border Debt Recovery; Finland, p. 122, Greece, p. 192, Italy, pp. 240-241, Lithuania, pp. 288-289, Russia, pp. 351-352 and Sweden, p. 386, European Corporate Insolvency; Belgium, pp. 46-47, Denmark, pp. 96-97, France, pp. 159-160, Germany, 185-186, 213-215, 227-228, Ireland, pp. 331-332, 342-344, 355-357, Luxemburg, pp. 417-418, the Netherlands, pp. 471-472, Norway, p. 491, Portugal, p. 531, Spain, pp. 604, 608-611, Sweden, pp. 623-626, Switzerland, p. 662 and United Kingdom, pp. 740-742, International Execution Against Judgment Debtors, Binder 1, section England and Wales; p. 65, Practitioner's Guide to Cross-Border Insolvencies; England, p. 3, France, pp. 27-30, Germany, pp. 36-38, Greece, pp. 9-10, Ireland, pp. 29-30, Norway, pp. 34-35, and Switzerland, pp. 29-30, and Källström, p. 708 (France). *Also see* Wood, chapter 1, General principles of insolvency, sections 1-14, 1-15, 1-36, 1-44, 1-47, 1-51 and 1-52, where he describes, based on a comparative survey of some selected foreign States, the ladder of payment related to priorities in the bankruptcy hierarchy, which usually comprises at least six main ranks, or steps, as follows: 1. Super-priority creditors (secured creditors, creditors with a set-off, title finance creditors, owners wrongfully deprived of their property, creditors with a direct action and creditors with right of rescission), 2. Priority creditors (expenses of the insolvency proceedings, taxes, employee remuneration and others),

authorities have, according to the Insolvency regulation, the right to lodge claims in the insolvency proceedings of another Member State in writing and should then state whether these authorities allege preference.[329]

An insolvency proceeding may be initiated at the application of a private creditor and of a public creditor. A public creditor, a Member State, may obtain a decision of bankruptcy in an insolvency proceeding in another Member State, based on foreign tax claims, by a direct application for bankruptcy to a court in the other Member State under the Insolvency regulation. This is a possible alternative, which may be of interest if the way of opening a bankruptcy in the other Member State as a recovery measure is not available under the Recovery directive.[330] The

---

3. Pari passu creditors (generally the unsecured creditors of the bankrupt), 4. Deferred creditors (post-insolvency interest, creditors without an *escritura publica* and consequently subordinated creditors), 5. Equity shareholders (shareholders of a company whose claims are generally recoverable only after the dissolution of the company) and 6. Expropriated creditors (late claimants, foreign revenue and penalties, foreign currency creditors and tort claimants).

329. *See* Arts 39 and 41. *Also see*, about Art. 39, The European Insolvency Regulation: Law and Practice, pp. 150-151, where the following comments are made: 'Article 39 makes it very clear that the claims indicated therein cannot be excluded from the proceedings on the grounds that the creditor is foreign, is established in another Member State, or is governed by (another Member State's) public law', and the following comments after the headline Public Law claims: 'Although Article 39 expressly recognises the "right to lodge" claims of these creditors, it is undeniable that they cannot be discriminated against with regard to their participation and payment; this would go directly against the *ratio* of the rule. This is particularly important in the case of tax and social security claims. The right to lodge these claims and participate in insolvency proceedings opened in another Member State derives from the Insolvency regulation itself. However, it falls to the *lex fori concursus* to determine the position of those claims in the *ranking* of claims. Here the question is whether a State can privilege the claims of its own authorities but treat the equivalent claims of the authorities of other Member States as ordinary claims. On this point, the Directives on reorganization and winding-up of credit institutions and insurance undertakings establish a principle of equal treatment for claims of Member States' public authorities: these claims shall be treated in the same way and accorded the same ranking as claims of an equivalent nature lodge able by public authorities of the Member State of the opening (see Article 16 Directive on credit institutions, and more clearly Article 16 of the Directive on insurance undertakings). Given the step taken by these two directives, a strong argument can be made in favour of extending this solution to the Insolvency Regulation. It would seem contrary to the coherence of the Community law system to allow any other solution in the context of this Regulation: there is no obligation to give any special status to public claims, but once a national legislator decides to privilege the claims of its public authorities, the principle of equal treatment of equivalent claims applies and a similar rank should also be accorded to the claims lodged by the public authorities of other Member States. The same argument can be made in favour of admitting claims of Member States' public authorities other than tax or social security authorities.' *Also see*, about Art. 39, The EC Regulation on insolvency proceedings: A Commentary and Annotated Guide, p. 230, section 8.275, where it is concluded that: 'There is a considerable advance in Article 39 in that the tax and social security authorities of other member states are expressly entitled to lodge claims; therefore the principle, which can be found in the law of most states, that foreign tax laws will not be enforced does not apply to the lodging of claims by creditors in proceedings to which the Regulation applies.... It is considered that as a result of the specific inclusion of tax and security authorities of other member states the Article 26 public policy exception cannot be used to block such claims.'

330. *See* 6.2.2.1.1.1.

supervision of the management of the insolvency estate in most Member States of the EU is, with some few exceptions, *e.g.* in Finland and Sweden, carried out under a more, or less, active participation by the courts.[331]

6.4.2 CONVENTIONS

A main collective insolvency proceeding in a Member State, *e.g.* a court decision in bankruptcy, under the Insolvency regulation, may, besides in other Member States, also have the advantage of taking legal effect in other non-Member States of the EU based on multilateral and bilateral conventions to which a Member State is a party. An example is that a decision in a main collective insolvency proceeding in a bankruptcy in Finland, or in Sweden, under the Insolvency regulation, besides in other Member States, also has the advantage of taking legal effect in Denmark, Iceland and Norway under the Nordic bankruptcy convention.[332] Another example is that a main collective insolvency proceeding in France, *e.g.* a bankruptcy, under the Insolvency regulation, besides in other Member States, may also have the advantage of taking legal effect in Monaco under the Bankruptcy convention between France and Monaco.[333]

The Nordic bankruptcy convention stipulates as a main rule that the right of creditors to be granted preferential treatment shall be governed by the *lex concursus*.[334] An application of the main rule of priority rights in the Nordic bankruptcy convention results in the same conclusions and for the same reasons as already developed regarding the Insolvency regulation. The Nordic bankruptcy convention includes, however, important exceptions to this main rule. One exception is that the existence of preferential rights against particular assets, and the question of priority as between such mortgages, pledges, or other rights *in rem* attaching to particular property shall be determined by the law of the country in which the property is situated when the bankruptcy is opened.[335] Another exception in the convention deals with the treatment of general preferential rights, which *i.a.* include taxes, other public dues and the treatment of a lessor and states that they should be determined by the law of the State to which such taxes and dues are payable respectively by the law of the State in which the premises of the lessor are situated.[336] An application of the rule of exception of general preferential right for tax claims in the Nordic bankruptcy convention means that the assets in each

331. *See*, for further details, Berglund, Hur är kronofogdemyndighetens arbetsuppgifter organiserade i några EU-stater och i Norge ?, Ny juridik, No. 4: 2000, p. 62.
332. *See* 5.1.4 for further information about the territorial scope of this convention.
333. *See* Art. 3, first part, which reads: 'Les effets de la faillite ou de la liquidation judiciaire, déclarée, dans l'un des deux pays, par le Tribunal compétent aux termes de l'article précédent, s'étendront au territoire de l'autre pays.' *Also see* 5.1.4 for further information about the territorial scope of this convention.
334. *See* Art. 1, para. 2 of the Convention, Annex 7.
335. *See* Art. 7, para. 1, Annex 7.
336. *See* Art. 7, para. 2, Annex 7.

Nordic State have to be treated as special sub-estates for such priority rights purposes, *i.e.* by a State by State basis, in the bankruptcy estate subject to a specific procedure of calculation.[337]

The non-recognition of priority rights regarding tax claims from one Nordic State in another Nordic State, as in the Nordic bankruptcy convention, is also evident in the Council of Europe and OECD convention on mutual administrative assistance in tax matters and in the Nordic agreement on assistance in tax matters, even if the Convention and the Agreement provide for the mutual assistance of recovery of tax claims.[338] The Bankruptcy convention between France and Monaco stipulates that the law of the State, in which a court has opened a bankruptcy, shall apply to priority rights.[339]

6.4.3 Transnational Judicial Cooperation in Insolvency Management

The legislation of Switzerland provides for the possibility to assist foreign bankruptcy proceedings by organizing ancillary proceedings in Switzerland aiming at the handing over of the assets of the debtor to the administrator of the main proceedings.[340] This is of a particular interest in relation to France after the end of 1991, when a previous bilateral convention between France and Switzerland, including bankruptcy matters, was superseded by the Old Lugano convention, which then entered into force between France and Switzerland.[341]

In relationship between England and other non-EC States, some but not all of them belonging to the Commonwealth, parallel provisions in laws for transnational judicial cooperation in insolvency management and even parallel judge-made-law for cooperation between the courts in bankruptcy[342] remain applicable in relation

337. *See* Art. 7, para. 3 of the Convention, Annex 7. *Also see* Bogdan, The Nordic Bankruptcy convention, p. 705, for an example of how this complex formula may be illustrated.
338. Compare 6.2.2.3.
339. *See* Art. 5, which reads: 'La production et la vérification des créances nées du failli ou du débiteur admis au bénéfice de la liquidation judiciaire seront régies par la loi du Tribunal qui aura déclare la faillite ou la liquidation judiciaire. De même, il sera procédé à la liquidation des biens et droits dépendant de la faillite ou de la liquidation judiciaire en application de ladite loi.'
340. *See* for further conditions Schlosser, Recent Developments in Transit-border Insolvency, pp. 15-19, who also indicates that not only the administrator or the liquidator of the foreign main proceedings has standing to make a petition for ancillary proceedings but also the creditor, which has the advantage that the administrator can make arrangements with such a creditor so that the creditor proceeds abroad at his own risks, but on the chance to be remunerated in the case of success. *Also see* European Corporate Insolvency, pp. 719-722, and Insolvenzen in Europa, pp. 248-249.
341. *See* 2.7.
342. *See* Schlosser, Recent Developments in Transit-border Insolvency, pp. 8-12, who reports that England provides two devices for transnational cooperation in bankruptcy matters, an ancillary winding-up of companies, where the administrator of the ancillary winding-up proceeding must transfer all the assets uncovered or, at least, the proceeds thereof to the administrator of the main proceedings abroad, subject only to the costs of the ancillary proceeding

to the Insolvency regulation. This cooperation may sometimes also lead to that the tax claims related to the taxpayer, who has been declared bankrupt, may be paid.[343] The English tradition is also, to some extent, reflected in the bankruptcy law of the United States of America, which provides both for ancillary winding-up or administration on the one side and for individual assistance of foreign insolvency proceedings on the other side.[344]

An increased development of the transnational judicial cooperation in insolvency management between the Member States of the United Nations could also be expected based on a reception into national laws of the United Nations Commission on International Trade Law (Uncitral) facultative Model Law on Cross-Border Insolvency of 30 May 1997,[345] which to a large extent has been inspired by and based on the Common law tradition. This Model Law serves to the States a law as a model and a source of inspiration concerning the creation of national legislation in cross-border insolvency matters. The purpose of this Model Law is to provide effective mechanisms for dealing with cases of cross-border insolvency so as to promote the objectives of cooperation between the courts and other competent authorities of a State and foreign States involved in cases of cross-border insolvency, greater legal certainty for trade and investment, fair and efficient administration of cross-border insolvencies that protect the interests of all creditors and other interested persons, including the debtor, protection and maximization of the value of the debtor's assets and facilitation of the rescue

---

and the amount necessary to pay 'preferential creditors' and judge-made-law, where the judge can give to the ancillary winding-up a tailor-made structure in view of the main proceedings. Cross-Border Insolvency, A guide to Recognition and Enforcement, p. 101, states that: English insolvency orders are deemed to have universal effect. English legislation states as a general principle that the English courts with insolvency jurisdiction have an obligation to assist their counterparts in any other part of the United Kingdom and in any 'relevant country or territory'. The majority of these countries are either Commonwealth countries or have comparable provisions to English legislation being: Anguilla, Australia, Bailiwick of Guernsey (including Alderney and Sark), Bermuda, Botswana, Brunei, Canada, Cayman Islands, Falkland Islands, Gibraltar, Hong Kong, Malaysia, Montserrat, New Zealand, Republic of Ireland, Republic of South Africa, St Helena, the Bahamas, Turks and Caicos Islands, Tuvalu and Virgin Islands. *Also see i.b.*, pp. 99-100, about the position under general law in England and Wales concerning cross-border insolvency. Insolvenzen in Europa, p. 66, also comments on the Anerkennung ausländerischer Insolvenzverfahren in England and Wales.

343. *See* 4.2.2 for further comments.

344. *See* for further conditions Schlosser, Recent Developments in Transit-border Insolvency, pp. 12-15, who also remarks that unlike the British model the American law does not make the assistance of the American court dependant on a request of a foreign court.

345. *See* for further comments on this Model Law, the enclosed Guide to enactment of the Uncitral Model Law on Cross-Border Insolvency. *Also see* Cross-border Insolvency, A Commentary on the UNCITRAL Model Law, including comments in relation to: British Virgin Islands, Canada, England, Japan, Mexico, Poland, Romania, Serbia and Montenegro, South Africa and the United States of America, Cross-Border Insolvency, A guide to Recognition and Enforcement, Glosband and Proctor, pp. 1-30, Friman, pp. 736-755, and Schlosser, Recent Developments in Transit-border Insolvency, pp. 26-29.

of financially troubled businesses, thereby protecting investment and preserving employment.[346]

This Model Law of Uncitral provides *i.a.* provisions on access of foreign representatives and creditors to courts, recognition of foreign proceeding and relief, including interim protective measures, cooperation with foreign courts and foreign representatives and current proceedings.[347] The national provisions adopted by the Member States of the EU, based on this Model law, are not applicable between them, because these national provisions are instead governed by the Insolvency regulation.[348] Since the adoption of the Model Law of Uncitral by the United Nations in 1997, laws based thereon have been adopted in several States.[349]

Both the transnational judicial cooperation in insolvency management between States, where some but not all of them belong to the Commonwealth, and the cooperation, which could be expected between Member States of the United Nations, based on the Uncitral Model Law, share the features of a more informal cooperation, which sometimes are evident between common law States,[350] rather than that traditional cooperation between civil law States based on formal conventions.

346. *See* Preamble.
347. *See* Chapters II-V of the Model Law.
348. *Also* compare Art. 44, 1 of the Insolvency regulation.
349. These States are: Colombia, Eritrea, Japan, Mexico, New Zealand, Poland, Romania, Montenegro, Serbia, South Africa, Great Britain, British Virgin Islands, overseas territory of the United Kingdom of Great Britain and Northern Ireland, and the United States of America. *See* website of Uncitral, <www.uncitral.org>, headline Uncitral Texts and Status, Insolvency and Uncitral Model Law on Cross-Border Insolvency. *Also see* about the implementing legislation in Great Britain: Act of Sederunt (Sheriff Court Bankruptcy Rules 1996) Amendment (UNCITRAL Model Law on Cross-Border Insolvency) 2006, Scottish Statutory Instrument 2006, No. 197, Act of Sederunt (Rules of the Court of Session Amendment No. 2) (UNCITRAL Model Law on Cross-Border Insolvency) 2006, Scottish Statutory Instrument 2006, No. 199, Act of Sederunt (Sheriff Court Company Insolvency Rules 1986) Amendment (UNCITRAL Model Law on Cross-Border Insolvency) 2006, Scottish Statutory Instrument 2006, No. 200, and The Cross-Border Insolvency Regulations 2006, Statutory Instrument 2006, No. 1030.
350. *See* Schlosser, Recent Developments in Transit-border Insolvency, p. 27, who states that: 'The fact that many details of cooperation are specifically addressed in the Model Law itself reveals that it was primarily drafted in view of lawyers of common law countries who expect many details to be addressed in Statute Law and complementary Rules.' He summarizes, *i.b.*, p 29, that: 'The enactment of the Model Law would certainly give a new dimension to judicial cooperation in cross-border insolvency proceedings and, even more, in the general context of judicial cross-border cooperation. It is however to be apprehended that civil law countries remain reluctant because the jurisdictional law approach is approved substantive law approach, of the draft convention is foreign to their legal tradition.'

Chapter 7
Harmonization of Civil Execution Laws

7.1 EC LAW, INTERNATIONAL PRINCIPLES AND RECOMMENDATIONS

It is evident, in a European historical development perspective, that differences between national procedural laws or their levels of European harmonization, *e.g.* in the enforcement law area, have been governed either by the common European influences that have affected national laws and resulted in a legal integration of European societies or by separate national influences in laws. Consequently, such influences have varied under different periods of history, from an earlier historical position, which included several features of common European legal integration, then under a period of development in national laws, which included more of separate national influences, and then again followed, by a period of more of common influences of European legal integration.[1]

Differences in national laws are often explained by different traditions and cultures, but should not primarily be seen as a problem, and it may sometimes be motivated to maintain them in view of the all-over function of a specific legal

1. *See* 2.1-4 about some common legal and other European influences that have been of importance for a common legal integration of European societies from the period of Roman law to the period of 1807 to our age, related to the legal areas of enforcement, recovery and insolvency. *Also see* Lindblom, p. 798, who remarks that the concept of national law is a relatively new invention, and that in the rear view of centuries and millenniums one distinguishes relatively few, fairly complete, specific national legal systems, and he also mentions the great importance of *ius commune* in the field of procedural law in Europe during several centuries. He concludes, in addition, that one common procedural law or almost identical national systems may be an utopia, but a development towards a significant equality of procedural law is not an unrealistic vision in a historical and a comparative perspective.

system of a Member State of the EU. On the other hand, there may exist such national differences, which are inconsistent with the established legal objectives in EC law, or other international principles, or recommendations, accepted by States, *e.g.* in the interests of equal treatment and efficiency, which nevertheless motivate a harmonization of national laws. Differences in national laws may in that context also have the indirect advantage of providing rich sources of examples, out of which the EC legislator could be inspired in its future reform efforts.

A proposal on the Approximation of Judiciary Law in the EU was raised in a report related to the constant problem of disparate national rules of procedural law, including civil execution law, by a group of European experts in 1994.[2] This report, Rapprochement du Droit Judiciaire de l'Union européenne/Approximation of Judiciary Law in the European Union, sometimes also referred to in literature as the 'Storme' report, after the name of the editor of the report Marcel Storme, produced a series of proposals of approximation to be implemented as a community directive, instead of the initial format contemplated in the group of the compilation of a complete Code of civil procedure in Europe.

The report includes proposals for approximation in the enforcement area about when a judgment shall become enforceable, the stay of execution, an order for the preservation of assets, titles of execution from the State of origin, which shall be recognized in the requested State after it has been declared enforceable, grounds of objections of the debtor to the execution of a judgment, the disclosure of the assets of the debtor, assets exempt from seizure and sale, procedures for the sale of every kind of assets seized, capable of being entrusted to market operators and the indexation of the debt during the period of execution.[3] The discussion of approximation has, after this report, been continued on numerous occasions,[4] but the goal of the working group in its report to obtain a more profound European approximation of procedural law, including rules on civil execution, has still not been realized. Despite the proposal in its report, there exists no EC procedural law, which imposes direct rules for the harmonization of the differing national enforcement laws of the Member States of the EU.[5]

2. Marcel Storme wrote the introduction to the report Rapprochement du Droit Judiciaire de l'Union européenne/Approximation of Judiciary Law in the European Union, pp. 37-70, and the rest of this report was elaborated with the unanimous agreement of the whole group, which consisted by the following persons: A. Pessoa Vaz, M. Storme, J. Normand, J.A. Jolowicz, E. Smith, P. Meyknecht, G. Tarzia, H. Prütting, C. de Miguel, G. de Leval and K. Kerameus, *i.b.*, p. 63. C. de Miguel and G. de Leval had a special responsibility in the report for the aspects on the execution of judgments or orders for the payment of money.
3. *See* Arts 12.1-12.5 in Rapprochement du Droit Judiciaire de l'Union européenne/Approximation of Judiciary Law in the European Union, pp. 209-211.
4. *See e.g.* Tarzia, Aussichten für eine Harmonisierung des Zwangsvollstreckungsrechts in der Europäischen Union, who discusses the prospects of a harmonized European law of enforcement, through EC law, in relation to the title of execution, the attachable assets, the expansion of executing in claims and other rights (*e.g.* to new finance instruments like 'swaps' or 'futures'), the enforcement procedure (adjusting claims to losses produced by inflation and the sanction astreinte, a penalty fee to be paid to the creditor in case of missing cooperation).
5. *See*, about a comparative research of some national systems of enforcement legislations, EC Study JAI/02/03/2002, E, II, which shows that differences exist, but divergences should not be

A possible harmonization of national enforcement laws in the Member States of the EU will, no doubt, require time,[6] and the development of a more advanced application than before by the EC legislator of the EC principle of mutuality.[7] This principle of mutuality, which is of general importance in EC law, has already gradually, on a sectorial basis, resulted in the implementation of measures of harmonization in national procedural laws, including enforcement laws,[8] of the Member States of the EU. Consequently, the Member States have been increasingly affected by this principle in EC law, and in addition by the interest of efficiency, balanced through the principle of proportionality, against the interest of privacy in such European law.[9]

Beside the development in EC law in the cross-border context, this European law has also contributed some other influences of harmonization into the national civil execution law area.[10] Apart from specific legislative measures, another factor of harmonization is the case-law of the ECJ, which has influenced procedural rules by requiring the modification of national rules of procedure that may stand in the way of providing effective remedies for breaches of EC law. This community principle of effectiveness influences all stages of the judicial process, including civil execution law.

The projects of reforms of the EU anticipate a possible continuation of development leading to a further degree of harmonization in the future.[11] The increasing globalization of economic activities constitutes an important factor, which also leads to an indirect effect of harmonization with an impact in various areas within the Internal Common Market. The Member States of the EU have received such influences of harmonization, which originally come from various other States in the World outside of the EU. An example is the Uncitral Model Law on Cross-Border Insolvency, which includes influences of Common law.[12] The ALI-UNIDROIT

---

overstated and that all the relevant Member States provide similar devices in this field, which is suggested to be aligned by a community instrument.

6. *See* for a reflection and discussion on the approximation of rules of enforcement, de Leval, Une harmonisation des procédures d'exécution dans l'Union européenne est-elle concevable ?, Civil Procedure in Europe 1, p. 625, where he concludes that the territorial and multidisciplinary character of enforcement law do not permit to foresee, in short- or mid-terms, a unification or harmonization of that law, because it still remains very secluded.
7. The EC principle of mutuality is treated in the context of 1.1.1.1.6.
8. *See* 1.2 about examples of provisions of procedural law in EC law in the enforcement and recovery areas. *Also see* 2.4.2 and 2.5-6 about influences of indirect harmonization derived from the developments in the cross-border context.
9. The interests of privacy and efficiency are treated in the context of 1.1.1.1.1, and the principle of proportionality is treated in 1.1.1.1.3.
10. *See* Schöberl, pp. 73-82, about the impact of this development in Austria. She makes the following remarks. An effect of harmonization may be observed within the framework of European procedural law when European deeds are handled at the national level, EC law also provides influences in some legal areas of independent national competence outside this framework, and the ECJ is of importance for the interpretation of national law, *see i.b.*, pp. 75-80.
11. *See* 2.10.1.
12. *See* 6.4.3 for further information about the Uncitral Model Law on Cross-Border Insolvency.

Principles of Transnational Civil Procedure give another example, which also includes influences of harmonization from various States outside of the EU.[13]

The legislative basis and competence of the EC legislator for a possible harmonization of national civil execution laws are *i.a.* determined by Articles 65 and 95 of the EC Treaty. Article 65 of the EC Treaty stipulates a possibility for a harmonization of national laws in relation to measures in the field of judicial cooperation in civil matters having cross-border implications. Such measures shall *i.a.* improve and simplify the recognition and enforcement of decisions in civil and commercial cases and eliminate obstacles to the good functioning of civil proceedings, if necessary by promoting the compatibility of the rules on civil procedure in the Member States. The article has been interpreted by the Commission of the ECs as not being strictly limited to matters having cross-border implications, but also to be to some extent applicable on internal matters, whereas the Member States have argued that it only gives a competence to legislate in cases having cross-border implications.[14] Article 95 of the EC Treaty stipulates a possibility to adopt the measures for the approximation of the provisions laid down by law, regulation, or administrative action in Member States which have as their object the establishment and functioning of the Internal Common Market.

A harmonization of national civil execution laws would be of importance because parts of EC law, *e.g.* the Brussels I regulation, and the Recovery directive, interplay, through referral provisions to national laws,[15] with national civil execution laws. Consequently, the total result of efficiency in matters having cross-border implications is determined by this interplay. It may be argued that the differences, in comparison between the civil execution laws of the Member States of the EU, sometimes lead to an unequal treatment in the enforcement of a claim having cross-border implications for both a creditor and a debtor, and therefore also constitute obstacles for a well functioning Internal Common Market.[16]

---

13. *See* 1.1.1.1.1 about these Principles. *Also see* Hazard, Fundamentals of Civil Procedure, Uniform Law Review/Revue de droit uniforme 2001-4, Harmonising Transnational Civil Procedure: The ALI/UNIDROIT Principles and Rules/Vers une procédure civile transnationale harmonisée: Les Principes et Règles ALI/UNIDROIT, p. 753, who reports that the work on these Principles: '...has required careful examination of and reflection upon the specific systems of various legal traditions, most generally those of the civil law and of the common law, but also major variations within these two "families". In an immediate sense, the Reporters and the advisers have been searching for compromises between the solutions that have evolved in the various systems. However, in a larger sense, we have been searching for fundamental similarities, *i.e.*, the mechanisms which, in one formulation or another, respond to basic necessities that must be accommodated in any modern procedural system.'
14. *See* Lenzing, p. 200, where she, on the interpretation of Art. 65 of the EC treaty, concludes: 'L'interprétation de la Commission sur cet article est qu'il ne s'agit pas de limiter un instrument à des cas transfrontaliers: cela peut s'appliquer au-delà des frontières. En revanche, les États membres ne partagent malheureusement pas le même point de vue; ils estiment que ce traité ne donne à la Communauté la compétence de légiférer que pour des cas transfrontaliers.'
15. *See* 6.2.1.1.1 about the Brussels I regulation and 6.2.2.1 about the Recovery directive.
16. Compare EC Study JAI/02/03/2002, A, II, 1, where it is argued that in the Internal Market, the differences between the national enforcement systems hinder the free movement of goods, persons and services, cross-border transactions must be secured by well-operating procedural

A harmonization through EC law of the national civil execution laws is not only motivated to promote a more equal and efficient treatment in the cross-border context,[17] but also required in the interest of further developing mutuality and efficiency in the same context to meet the legal objectives of the EU. Such important objectives are *i.a.* those of the Council's programme of measures for implementing the principle of mutual recognition in seeking to make more efficient the enforcement, in the requested Member State, of judgments delivered in another Member State, based on the Tampere conclusions.[18]

The national procedural autonomy of the civil execution laws of the Member States of the EU has, so far, mainly related to matters of national concern, even if EC law provides a degree of harmonization. Examples of harmonization in EC law with effects in the cross-border enforcement and recovery areas are the European Enforcement Order for uncontested claims, the European Order for payment procedure and the provision of direct recognition and enforceability in the Recovery directive.[19]

The efficiency of EC law is secured by that regulations are 'directly applicable' as part of the national legal system, whereas directives require implementation by the Member States, but within strict time-limits. Under the case-law of the ECJ, if a directive is adopted to provide a particular right, and the directive remains unimplemented by a Member State, a person affected by the failure to implement may be able to rely on the directive directly in the national court, or may have a remedy against the State for breach of EC law. An example from the extensive case-law of the ECJ where a Member State had failed to implement a directive and had to compensate the persons concerned is the ruling of the ECJ in the case of *Andrea Francovich and Danila Bonifaci and others v. Italian Republic*.[20]

The development of a possible harmonization of national civil execution laws is not only affected by EC law, but also by the European Convention on Human Rights. Such a harmonization is, in addition, motivated in the interest of States to implement the legal objectives accepted by them in the Council of Europe's recommendation on enforcement, which followed the Moscow Resolution, and in

---

laws, including enforcement and as a result the free movement of judgments within Europe is severely impaired, creditors do not enforce their claims, but write them off.

17. *See* the Commission communication to the Council and the European Parliament 'towards greater efficiency in obtaining and enforcing judgments in the European Union', section 42, where it is concluded that: 'A prompt and efficient system for enforcing court judgments is vital for justice to be accessible. A free circulation of court judgments would be illusory if enforcement instruments were not equally effective in all the Member States.'
18. *See* 1.1.1.1 about this programme and for further details about the following developments.
19. *See* Art. 8, 1.
20. *See* the decision of the ECJ in *Andrea Francovich and Danila Bonifaci and others v. Italian Republic* of 19 Nov. 1991, where the Italian State had failed to implement the Council Directive (80/987/EEC) of 20 Oct. 1980 on the approximation of the laws of the Member States relating to the protection of employees in the event of the insolvency of their employer. The ECJ ruled that a Member State is required to make good loss and damages caused to individuals by failure to transpose this directive.

the ALI-UNIDROIT Principles of Transnational Civil Procedure,[21] and maybe, in future, in a possible, not yet realized, World Code of Enforcement.[22]

During a predictable future, the procedural autonomy of European States in national civil execution laws seems mainly to remain a matter of national concern, even if EC law, which *i.a.* applies in the cross-border context, has resulted and may gradually result in some further sectorial degrees of harmonization of such national laws. The European Convention on Human Rights, the Council of Europe's initiatives, recommendations, its work by the CEPEJ, and the ALI-UNIDROIT Principles of Transnational Civil Procedure may, however, strengthen this development trend, both in the cross-border and national context, and result in further degrees of harmonization of these laws. The rulings of the ECHR contribute to stimulate a harmonization of national civil execution laws. This effect of harmonization is also indirectly strengthened through the reception of the European Convention on Human Rights in EC law.[23] There will, nevertheless, exist a need to maintain, or enter, referral provisions to national enforcement and recovery laws into EC law and conventions during a predictable future.[24]

A method of step-by-step harmonization through EC law, which defines what objectives to be obtained and what goals to be achieved by the Member States in their national civil execution laws, in order to secure a more comparable equal level of the all-over content in such laws, stands out as the best approach to pursue for the establishment of any possible future EC law. Such harmonization meets the interests of a more developed mutuality and efficiency balanced against privacy and other relevant interests in the EC cross-border context, as needed in such laws. It has the advantage that the details of the national laws may still vary and be adapted to the relevant national circumstances in the different national laws of the Member States. It creates a balance between the autonomy of the Member States in terms of respect and understanding for their legal traditions and cultures[25] and the requirement of the Member States to meet the objectives and goals that are set in EC law.[26]

---

21. *See* 1.1.1.1 and 1.1.1.1.1.
22. *See* 2.10.5 about this suggestion, and 7.3 about the idea to start a work for the creation of a facultative Model Law on Enforcement Law by the United Nations Commission on International Trade Law (Uncitral).
23. *See* 1.4.1 about the impact on EC law by the European Convention on Human Rights.
24. The relationship between EC law, multilateral conventions, and national enforcement and recovery laws is treated in 6.2.
25. *See* Modéer, p. 81, where he states that when the law is harmonized an attempt is made to introduce rules, system of laws and legal phenomena to the extent they may be accepted within the framework of the legal culture of the country or region, and he further concludes that harmonization requires understanding and that such a process is primarily about an organic development.
26. Compare the method of harmonization recommended by de Leval, Civil Procedure in Europe 1, Une harmonisation des procédures d'exécution dans l'Union européenne est-elle concevable ?, p. 610, where he concludes 'L'harmonisation du droit de l'exécution ne peut donc s'entendre que comme un rapprochement progressif au niveau des principes essentiels entre les différents systèmes juridiques des États membres. Une telle solution se concilie parfaitement avec le

The method of step-by-step harmonization is best able to provide a higher quality of harmonization of national laws and responds more to, and it respects more, the needs in national laws than would a direct unification or harmonization through such European law of differing national enforcement laws. Even if the EC legislator would, for good reasons, at the application of such a step-by-step method introduce measures of harmonization into national laws,[27] an operation which may be time consuming, it has the advantage of providing the legislator with an opportunity of evaluating the success, or failure, of each such step of reforms in relation to national laws, and possibly, if needed, propose amendments related to previous steps of reforms, before advancing to other steps through new initiatives.

7.2 DIFFERENCES IN NATIONAL ENFORCEMENT PROCEDURES

The national European enforcement laws, which *i.a.* include the enforcement procedures of attachment of the earnings of the debtor, the seizure of intangible property and the executive real estate sale, show considerable variations.[28]

---

principe de la subsidiarité. En bref, il s'agit de dégager, par-delà la diversité, des principes communs permettant la même efficacité et la même humanité dans le recouvrement.' He also emphasizes that it is important to reduce the most significant national obstacles by promoting convergency of procedures towards the same goal by means of making better use of the resources offered by national legislations and international conventions, p. 626. *Also* compare Kennett, The Enforcement of Judgments in Europe, pp. 305-309, where she argues that any moves to harmonize the law in relation to aspects of civil procedure should build on the lessons learned in the context of private law and should take into account the national culture as a factor inhibiting harmonisation. *Also see* Schöberl, p. 80, where she agues that: 'Une plus forte harmonization peut être obtenue si le droit processuel européen vise à encourager les législateurs nationaux à adapter certaines dispositions, ou fait office de modèle.'

27. *See* Léger, p. 54, where he explains the reasons for the use of a step-by-step method as follows: 'La politique communautaire de coopération dans l'espace judiciare européen relève de cette politique des "petits pas" voulue par les pères fondateurs de l'Union européenne. L'Europe ne se fera pas d'un coup ni dans une construction d'ensemble: "elle se fera par des réalisations concrètes créant d'abord une solidarité de fait". Ces propos de Robert Schuman dans son célèbre discours du 9 mai 1950, réalistes et visionnaires à la fois, doivent être sans cesse rappelés. L'histoire de l'Europe au cours des cinquante dernières années montre bien que l'on ne revient pas sur les petits pas qui, ajoutés les uns aux autres, finissent par tracer chemins et routes que l'on parcourt de plus en plus rapidement.'

28. *See* the following works, which treat the law of civil execution: Bayo Delgado, Persons involved in the execution of court decisions (Spain), The execution of court decisions in civil cases, pp. 15-22, Civil Procedure in Europe 1, Seizure and Overindebtness, in the European Union in each of the national reports included regarding: Germany, Belgium, Denmark, Spain, France, Greece, Italy, Luxemburg, the Netherlands, Portugal, United Kingdom/England and Wales, Sweden and *i.b.*, pp. 3-46 (Summary), Cross Border Debt Recovery, section 13. Collection of debts, in each of the national reports included regarding: Austria, Belgium, Czech republic, Denmark, England and Wales, Estonia, Finland, France, Germany, Greece, Hungary, Ireland, Italy, Latvia, Lithuania, Northern Ireland, Norway, Russia, Spain, Sweden, Switzerland, the Netherlands and Ukraine, The execution of court decisions in civil cases, Synthesis on The

Consequently, they produce different, non-equal, results in the Member States of the EU. This becomes in particular evident to a creditor, who proceeds in parallel in several European States with the enforcement of his claim against a debtor based on EC law.[29] This result is a logical consequence of that the provisions in European community law in the cross-border context refer to the enforcement and recovery laws of Member States,[30] whose content of actual enforcement and recovery measures sometimes will differ.

Even if there also exist other possible issues of improvement concerning national civil execution laws for matters having cross-border implications for the better functioning of the Internal Common Market, there exist in particular three types of provisions, which in the first instance merit a future harmonization based on European community law and on other international principles and recommendations. These are the provisions for the attachment of the earnings of the debtor, the provisions of time-limits in enforcement procedures, and the provisions on access to information for enforcement purposes. The needs for improved access to national information for enforcement and recovery purposes in matters having cross-border implications is explained by its close relationship to the civil execution law area. These issues are here treated because of their importance, both based on the possible improved economic result they may produce for

execution of court decisions in civil cases, about the subject to proceedings, *i.a.* including attachable assets and domestic immunities from execution, and methods of execution in: Albania, Armenia, Austria, Azerbaijan, Belgium, Bulgaria, Croatia, Cyprus, Czech Republic, Denmark, Finland, France, Georgia, Germany, Greece, Hungary, Italy, Japan, Latvia, Lithuania, Luxemburg, Moldova, Norway, Poland, Portugal, Romania, Slovak Republic, Slovenia, Spain, Sweden, the former Yugoslav Republic of Macedonia, Ukraine and the United Kingdom, pp. 150-263, EC Study JAI/02/03/2002, A, I, 1, on the structural differences between the national enforcement procedures in Europe compared to C, the attachment of bank accounts, I, current state of the national laws, Jacobsson (Sweden), pp. 481-520, Kennett, The Enforcement of Judgments in Europe, pp. 251-265, about a comparison of garnishment in national laws, Kerameus, International encyclopedia of comparative law, volume XVI, Civil procedure, chapter 10, Enforcement proceedings, sections 82-138 (Monetary Enforcement) and sections 139-146 (Enforcement of Nonmoney Judgments and Orders) in some selected States, Koulo (Finland), pp. 537-571, Källström (France), pp. 696-711, de Leval, Subject of the proceedings, The execution of court decisions in civil cases, annexe 1, pp. 57-73, on what proportion of the debtors income (earnings) or benefits (unemployment, sickness, disability) cannot be garnished in each of some selected States, Morse (England and Wales), pp. 85-95, Rump Christensen (Denmark), pp. 521-536, Georges, La saisie de la monnaie scripturale, about the enforcement of money claims in Belgium, and Ds 2002:45 The Swedish Enforcement Code (2001: 337), official translation from Swedish to English. *Also see*, about national legislations for the enforcement of judgments, under headline Enforcement of judgments – General Information, website of the European Judicial Network in civil and commercial matters, <http://ec.europa.eu/civiljustice>, and about national legislations under the respective European associations of enforcement agents, which are members of the UIHJ, website of the UIHJ, <www.uihj.com>.

29. *See* 6.1.1 about the possibilities and the requirements of simultaneous and parallel procedures in the cross-border context in several other States regarding the enforcement of contractual claims and the recovery of tax claims.
30. The referral provisions of the Brussels I regulation and the Recovery directive are treated in the context of 6.2.1.1.1 (Brussels I regulation) and 6.2.2.1 (Recovery directive).

the benefit of the creditor, and the possibilities to obtain a more equal treatment for both the creditor and the debtor, in the international and national context.

7.2.1 Attachment of the Earnings of the Debtor

One of the most important enforcement procedures available to the enforcement organs is that of the attachment of the earnings of the debtor because of the economic result it produces for the benefit of the creditor. There exist a variety of different national, rather detailed and complex, provisions for the attachment of the earnings of the debtor and the thereto related provisions of the debtor's immunity against a too far-reaching attachment, expressed as a free amount or *beneficium*, often calculated in various ways as a proportion of the debtor's earnings or benefits.[31] This may partially, but not entirely, be explained by their close relationship to the different national living conditions of debtors. It may be argued that these differences, in comparison between the laws of the Member States of the EU, sometimes lead to an unequal treatment at the attachment of the earnings of the debtor for a claim in matters having cross-border implications in the EC for both a creditor and a debtor. It may also be argued that this constitutes an obstacle for a well functioning Internal Common Market.

The ECJ has emphasized an important aspect of equal treatment in the enforcement area in relation to the attachment of incomes of citizens in the

31. *See* de Leval, Subject of the proceedings, The execution of court decisions in civil cases, pp. 45-48, and annexe 1, pp. 57-73, on the governing parameters for the attachment of the debtor's earnings, such as if and to what extent earnings are attachable, number of dependents to be taken into account, priority for alimony creditors and what proportion of the debtor's income (earnings) or benefits (unemployment, sickness, disability) that represent his *beneficium* and cannot be garnished in each of some selected States, and The execution of court decisions in civil cases, about attachable assets and domestic immunities from execution in: Albania, Armenia, Austria, Azerbaijan, Belgium, Bulgaria, Croatia, Cyprus, Czech Republic, Denmark, Finland, France, Georgia, Germany, Greece, Hungary, Italy, Japan, Latvia, Lithuania, Luxemburg, Moldova, Norway, Poland, Portugal, Romania, Slovak Republic, Slovenia, Spain, Sweden, the former Yugoslav Republic of Macedonia, Ukraine, the United Kingdom, and Synthesis, pp. 150-263. *Also see* Civil Procedure in Europe 1, about immunities from the attachment of the earnings of the debtor (Germany, pp. 81-82, Belgium, pp. 143-145, Denmark, p. 198, Spain, p. 238, France, pp. 273-274, Greece, p. 344, the Netherlands, p. 481, and Sweden, p. 566), and EC Study JAI/02/03/2002, C, I, 2 and 4 on the procedure for obtaining a garnishment order respectively on the protection of the debtor and *i.b.*, C, I, 6, where it is stated that while the basic structures of garnishment are similar, the details are different in all Member States and even in similar national systems considerable divergence exists. *Also see* Kennett, The Enforcement of Judgments in Europe, pp. 258-259, on the debtor's immunities from execution, Kerameus, International encyclopedia of comparative law, volume XVI, Civil procedure, chapter 10, Enforcement proceedings, p. 73, on the garnishment of earnings and other monetary claims, Krings, Synthèse, Le droit des saisies dans les États membres de l'Union européenne, Civil Procedure in Europe 1, Seizure and Overindebtness in the European Union, pp.15-16, Théry, Droit de l'exécution: France, Actualités du droit, Revue de la Faculté de droit de l'Université de Liège, pp. 640-646, and about Swedish immunities, Utmätning, pp. 94-103.

community, who are debtors, irrespectively of where they are resident in the EU, as evident in its ruling in the case of *Pusa v. Osuuspankkien Keskinäinen Vakuutusyhtiö*.[32] The ECJ consequently decided that the free movement of citizens, in EC law, in principle precludes an enforcing Member State from not taking into account tax payments from a resident in another Member State at the computation of a free amount or *beneficium* at the attachment of a pension received in that first State.

It may also be argued that a harmonization of the provisions of attachment of the earnings of the debtor would create a more equal treatment in parallel procedures of attachments in more than one Member State within the EU, and also better correspond to the objective of the general State interest of a more efficient enforcement of claims in society. Any possible harmonization would also have to be based on a balanced equilibrium between the interest of efficiency of the creditor and the interests of humanity and dignity of the debtor in accordance with the European Convention on Human Rights.[33] This would not only mean that all earnings and incomes of the debtor and his spouse, or cohabitant, and other member of his family should be taken into account. It would also mean that the debtor would correspondingly be compensated for reasonable costs of living in order to be able to maintain a reasonably high level of living standard for himself, his spouse, or cohabitant, and other dependent members of his family, despite the payments of his debts.

---

32. The decision of the ECJ of 29 Apr. 2004 in *Pusa v. Osuuspankkien Keskinäinen Vakuutusyhtiö*, related to a question on the interpretation of Art. 18 of the EC Treaty concerning the right for every citizen of the EU to move and reside freely within the territory of the Member States raised in a procedure between Mr. Pusa and the Osuuspankkien Keskinäinen Vakuutusyhtiö (a mutual association of cooperative banks) as regards the calculation of the amount in which the latter is to be authorized to carry out an attachment on the pension, which Mr. Pusa received in Finland. Mr. Pusa was resident in Spain and his pension was attached in Finland based on a debt he owed to a bank in Finland. The double tax treaty between Finland and Spain stipulated that Mr. Pusa was liable to pay tax on his incomes in Spain. Therefore no tax at source was withheld in Finland and the attachable part of his pension was calculated on the gross amount of the pension without any deductions for the tax he had paid on his pension in Spain. The ECJ states, section 48, that: '. . . Community law in principle precludes legislation of a Member State under which the attachable part of a pension paid at regular intervals in that State to a debtor is calculated by deducting from that pension the income tax prepayment levied in that State, while the tax which the holder of such a pension must pay on it subsequently in the Member State where he resides is not taken into account at all for the purposes of calculating the attachable portion of that pension; on the other hand, Community law does not preclude such national legislation if it provides for tax to be taken into account, where taking the tax into account is made subject to the condition that the debtor prove that he has in fact paid or is required to pay within a given period a specified amount as income tax in the Member State where he resides. However, that is only the case to the extent that, first, the right of the debtor concerned to have tax taken into account is clear from that legislation; secondly, the detailed rules for taking tax into account are such as to guarantee to the interested party the right to obtain an annual adjustment of the attachable portion of his pension to the same extent as if such tax had been deducted at source in the Member State which enacted that legislation; and, thirdly, those detailed rules do not have the effect of making it impossible or excessively difficult to exercise that right.'
33. *See* 1.1.1.1.1.

The Storme report concluded, in its proposal on the harmonization in community law of seizure of assets, that all assets, which were able of being converted to money, should be subject to seizure and the result of their realization should be used for the payment of the obligation derived from the title of execution, with the exception for the humanitarian needs of the debtor. The exception for the humanitarian needs of the debtor mentioned in this report is as follows:[34]

(a) les provisions, sommes et pensions à caractère alimentaire,
(b) les biens nécessaires à la vie et au travail du débiteur,
(c) les biens indispensable aux personne handicapées ou destinés aux soins de personnes malades.

A possible harmonization in relation to matters having cross-border implications would lead to that both the creditors and the debtors would be treated more equally at the attachment of the earnings of the debtor, because the debtors would in such situations in all Member States be subject to a more nationally comparable level of equal treatment of incomes and costs of living. This would also be aimed to create a better functioning of the Internal Common Market.

A possible solution, also based on the Council of Europe's recommendation on enforcement, in order to achieve a harmonization through EC law in relation to matters having cross-border implications, except in relation to alimony creditors, would be to stipulate the following standard goals[35] for the laws of the Member States: A legally guaranteed minimum income, which cannot be garnished, but all other incomes of whatever nature exceeding this minimum income should be possible to garnish. The threshold above which all incomes can be garnished should be relatively high. The amount of incomes withheld should raise reasonably progressive. The incomes of spouses and cohabiting couples should be cumulated to calculate the garnish able portion of the incomes. The limits of non-garnish able incomes should be raised by the legislators by a reasonably fixed sum for each dependent, including spouse or cohabitant and other dependent members of the debtor's family and for special humanitarian needs of the debtor. Such special needs may *e.g.* be for medical care, costs of working tools and travelling to work. This free amount or *beneficium* should be adjusted once a year in accordance with the movement of the retail price index of Member States, as made available by Eurostat.[36] This is of importance as the cost of life differs to a great extent from one Member State to another.

The Proposal for a Council regulation on jurisdiction, applicable law, recognition and enforcement of decisions and cooperation in matters relating to maintenance obligations introduces several new possible solutions of indirect, or direct, importance in the area of the recovery of maintenance obligations aimed to ensure

34. *See* Rapprochement du Droit Judiciaire de l'Union européenne/Approximation of Judiciary Law in the European Union, pp. 153-154.
35. This idea is, on some aspects, similar to that of de Leval, *see* de Leval, Subject of the proceedings, The execution of court decisions in civil cases, annexe 1, pp. 76-77.
36. *See* website of Eurostat, <http://ec.europa.eu/eurostat>, under headline Consumer prices.

effectiveness and continuity of recovery in the cross-border context.[37] These solutions may also be of interest to further study in the context of any possible developments in the cross-border context for the attachment of the earnings of the debtor related to contractual claims and tax claims. Even if there may exist some different solutions, and several arguments in favour of the establishment of new EC law for the attachment of the earnings of the debtor in matters having cross-border implications in relation to contractual claims and tax claims, this, of course, has first to be subject to a more profound analysis and be further discussed between the Member States.

7.2.2 Time-Limits

Important subject-matters for harmonization are the time-limits, within which enforcement organs should, at the latest, after having received an application for the enforcement of a claim, enforced it, have reported back the results of the enforcement procedure, realized the assets of the debtor and transferred the payments to the creditor. Now, the national time-limits applied in enforcement procedures, after an application for the actual enforcement of a claim by the creditor at the enforcement organs in the Member States of the EU, vary substantially; if the seizure of the claim is unopposed, from one month up to a year, and if opposed, from a couple of months up to several years.[38] Provisions of time-limits of comparative interest in the enforcement area exist in EC law, *e.g.* in the Recovery directive,[39] in the Implementing recovery directive[40] and in the Late payment's directive.[41]

There are several examples of rulings of the ECHR, which *i.a.* deal with the enforcement of a title of execution, a judgment, or a notarial deed, within a 'reasonable time' in accordance to Article 6, 1 of the European Convention on Human Rights, and which illustrate the problem of excessive length of national enforcement procedures at the execution of such titles of execution, or the non-execution thereof.[42] The complaints about the enforcement procedures in the member States of the Council of Europe were in 2004, according to a report from the Council, mostly related to the excessive duration of the enforcement procedures.[43]

37. *See* 2.10.1.
38. *See* Enforcement of Foreign Judgments, chapter Europe, section 17 (Austria, Belgium, Cyprus, Czech Republic, Denmark, England and Wales, Finland, France, Germany, Greece, Hungary, Ireland, Italy, Luxemburg, the Netherlands, Poland, Portugal, Scotland, Spain and Sweden).
39. Article 11.
40. Articles 5-7.
41. *See* Art. 3 about interest in case of late payments and Art. 5 about recovery procedures for unchallenged claims.
42. *See* 4.3.1.
43. *See* Report on European judicial systems, pp. 143-144 and 176, which mentions the following main reasons for complaints against the enforcement procedures: no execution at all (16 countries or entities), lack of information (12 countries or entities), excessive length (34 countries or entities), unlawful practices (12 countries or entities), insufficient supervision (5 countries or entities), excessive cost (15 countries or entities) and other complaints (8 countries or entities).

The different time-limits in the enforcement procedures applied by the Member States of the EU, *e.g.* after the recognition of a judgment under the Brussels I regulation, is an issue, which produces an unequal treatment in relation to matters having cross-border implications, for both the creditor and the debtor. This also means that the efficiency and results of parallel enforcement procedures after such a recognition of a judgment in two or more Member States of the EU are correspondingly affected. It may be argued that a possible harmonization of the differing national provisions of time-limits in enforcement procedures would be motivated in order to promote a more equal and efficient treatment in matters having cross-border implications in the EC for both a creditor and a debtor. It may also be argued that this constitutes an obstacle for a well functioning Internal Common Market. A possible harmonization would correspond to the objective of efficiency in EC law and in the European Convention on Human Rights, as evident from some rulings of the ECHR.[44]

Consequently, efficiency means in the context of this convention a demand on the availability of all necessary means in order to realize the creditor's claim in the assets of the debtor in a reasonable time, and that the procedures for enforcement should be adequate and efficient.[45] A possible harmonization would also correspond to the objective of efficiency in the Council of Europe's recommendation on enforcement, and in the ALI-UNIDROIT Principles of Transnational Civil Procedure, and in the general State interest. Such a possible harmonization would correspond to the interest of efficiency of the creditor, which is, subject to that all legal conditions are fulfilled, of a greater weight than that of the debtor in relation to uncontested claims and consequently requires an efficient and expeditious treatment in enforcement procedures.

A possible idea for a harmonization through EC law of these provisions would be the establishment of goals for maximum time-limits in national enforcement procedures for matters having cross-border implications, within which enforcement organs should at the latest, after having received an application for the enforcement of a claim, have enforced the claim, reported back the results of the enforcement procedure, realized the assets of the debtor and transferred the payments to the creditor. These goals for maximum time-limits should be based on a combination of some decisive factors. Such factors may be the need of the creditor to get his claim enforced as soon as possible, within a reasonable time by the enforcement organs, and the need of protecting the debtor at the enforcement of opposed claims.

A possible solution, in order to achieve a harmonization through EC law in relation to matters having cross-border implications, should provide that their provisions of time-limits for the enforcement of both unopposed and opposed claims in enforcement procedures related to movable property should stipulate

---

44. *See* 4.3.1.
45. *Also see*, about the right of an efficient enforcement of a judgment, Danelius, pp. 259-260, Fricero, pp. 6-8, Isnard, p. 15, Yessiou Faltsi, pp. 234-236, and Verbeke, Execution Officers as a Balance Wheel in Insolvency Cases, pp. 7-9 and 11-12.

the following goal: A maximum time-limit of six months, counted from the date of the creditor's application for the enforcement of a claim at the enforcement organs, for all enforcement measures in enforcement procedures managed by the enforcement organs, including reports of the thereto related results. This should be supplemented by a maximum time-limit of one year, counted from the date of the creditor's application of enforcement of a claim at the enforcement organs, for the realization of the debtor's assets and payments to the creditor derived from the results of the realized assets of the enforcement measures taken by the enforcement organs. The posting of security by the creditor in enforcement procedures related to opposed claims should be possible, when needed, in the interest of a proportionate protection of the debtor, as determined by the national courts, based on some possible future established common European standards, that may departure from these provisions in national laws.[46] This amount for security should be fixed at a level, which is sufficient for the payment of any possible damages in compensation to the debtor, according to the legislation of the enforcing State.

At least two other solutions have been discussed, to balance off a too slow and inefficient enforcement procedure.[47] One is the introduction of a compensation to the creditor for losses through a permission of revaluation of debts until the payment to the creditor has been effected, the realization has been allocated, or the attached assets have been transferred, effected by a determined index of revaluation. Another is the sanction of astreinte, a penalty fee to be paid by the debtor to the creditor in case of missing cooperation.[48] Even if these two solutions would result in an increased pressure on the debtor to pay his debts to the creditor, they may just risk leading to an increase of non-enforceable debts, to the extent the debtor is not willing or actually is unable to pay.[49] They therefore represent

46. *See* EC Study JAI/02/03/2002, D, II, Provisional Enforceability, 1 b), where it is reported, in relation to the Member States of the EU, that: 'As a rule, the creditor must provide a security in case the judgment is set aside on appeal. In this circumstance, the judgment creditor is required to compensate all damages incurred by the debtor which result from enforcement of the judgment.' *Also see*, about the provisional enforceability of judgments, Kerameus, International encyclopedia of comparative law, volume XVI, Civil procedure, chapter 10, Enforcement proceedings, pp. 19-26. He states, p. 25, that: 'In all legal systems that provide for provisional enforceability of judgments the creditor is bound, upon reversal on appeal, to restitute what he has received by virtue (or because of the imminent danger) of enforcement, and, in addition, to pay full damages to the debtor.... The award of the amount of damages are ordinarily determined by the appellate judgment. Its enforcement, if the provisional execution has proceeded after posting of security by the creditor, will normally first address that asset before expanding to the creditor's other property.'
47. *See* Tarzia, Aussichten für eine Harmonisierung des Zwangsvollstreckungsrechts in der Europäischen Union, pp. 240-241.
48. *See*, for further information about astreinte, Kerameus, Enforcement in the International Context, Recueil des cours, collected courses of the Hague Academy of International Law, 1997, Tome 264 de la collection, pp. 321-324, Civil Procedure in Europe 1, de Leval and Partsch, Le droit belge des saisies, pp. 131-135 and *i.b.*, Théry, Le droit français de l'exécution, pp. 264-265.
49. *See* Tarzia, Aussichten für eine Harmonisierung des Zwangsvollstreckungsrechts in der Europäischen Union, pp. 236-237, who discusses the possibility to introduce some kind of obligation for the debtor to pay as a penalty to the creditor in the case of missing cooperation in an

solutions that are less attractive as compared to an introduction of a maximum time-limit. There exist some different possible solutions, and several arguments in favour of the establishment of new EC law for the establishment of maximum time-limits in matters having cross-border implications. This must, however, first be subject to a more profound analysis than can be undertaken in this work.

7.2.3 Access to Information for Enforcement Purposes in the National Context

7.2.3.1 Access to Information before a Title of Execution

Before the private creditor obtains an enforceable title of execution he can not normally seek the assistance of enforcement organs and therefore has to rely on information from public sources of information, such as public registers. Information about the address of the debtor, to the extent it is available to the creditor, may of course be found in commercial registers, EBR,[50] population registers, electoral rolls, motor-vehicle registers, land registers and telephone books.[51] Information from registers about the assets of the debtor, to the extent it is available to the creditor, may be found in the land registers, European Land Information Service (Eulis),[52] registers for aircrafts and ships, motor-vehicle registers and commercial registers.[53] It would be beneficial if the EU would continue to encourage initiatives by private and public institutions to provide public information from registers not only on paper, but also by means of accessibility over the Internet.[54] In addition, information is available for purchase to private creditors from private enquiry agencies and credit reference agencies.[55]

7.2.3.2 Access to Information after a Title of Execution

The legal situation of a creditor, who seeks information about the whereabouts of the assets of a debtor is considerably improved when he has obtained an enforceable title of execution and applied for enforcement measures at the enforcement organs. These organs may then based on the legal basis of this enforcement matter

enforcement procedure in a similar solution as in the French concept of the astreinte, but he concludes on the other hand that the benefit of such a concept may be rather dubious in actual cases, because the debtor may not reveal his assets and would consequently make an attempt of enforcement useless, with the result that such an attempt would just lead to an increase of non-enforceable debts.

50. *See* website of the EBR, <www.ebr.org>.
51. *See* EC Study JAI/02/03/2002, B, I.
52. *See* website of the European Land Information Service, <www.eulis.org>.
53. *See* EC Study JAI/02/03/2002, B, II.
54. *See*, about the same opinion, EC Study JAI/02/03/2002, B, V, 2.
55. Examples of such agencies are Schimmelpfennig, Dunn & Bradstreet or SCHUFA, EC Study JAI/02/03/2002, B, II. Another example is Intrum Justitia.

initiate a research for information as an integrated part of the enforcement proceeding. This search may relate to information in registers and from other sources, which are not open to the creditor, as an integrated part of the actual enforcement procedure. Such other sources of information may come from an investigation of assets in the living facilities of the debtor, or from an investigation in his commercial premises, or from a third-party declaration/garnishee declaration, or from a legal statement/declaration of the debtor. The services of these professionals are needed to guarantee a high quality in connection to that information, which often has to be understood, interpreted and completed with additional research in a national context and also requires knowledge of relevant national legislation and legal usage. Consequently, without a formal application for the enforcement of a title of execution, no such advanced and qualified research for information by the regulated enforcement agents for the benefit of the creditor will be possible.

The variety of direct accessibility to information for enforcement purposes to regulated enforcement agents, for the indirect benefit of the private creditor, is, however, in comparison between solutions in non-identical national laws evident in the civil law area, where we find the contractual claims.[56] Even if provisional

---

56. The variety and complexity in comparison between solutions in national law, providing more, or less, information directly or indirectly to a private creditor under different techniques, are evident. *See* EC Study JAI/02/03/2002, B, III and *i.b.* B, IV, 1, where it is concluded that it is no doubt that cross-border recovery of judgments is impaired by the differences between the national legal systems and that the creditors in Europe are not treated equally, but the similar underlying structures of the Member States' legal systems could be a basis for an approximation by community action. *Also see* The execution of court decisions in civil cases, about the possibilities to obtain information on the debtor's assets under the execution proceedings in: Albania, Armenia, Austria, Azerbaijan, Belgium, Bulgaria, Croatia, Cyprus, Czech Republic, Denmark, Finland, France, Georgia, Germany, Greece, Hungary, Italy, Japan, Latvia, Lithuania, Luxemburg, Moldova, Norway, Poland, Portugal, Romania, Slovak Republic, Slovenia, Spain, Sweden, the former Yugoslav Republic of Macedonia, Ukraine, the United Kingdom, and Synthesis, pp. 150-261, and Kennett, The Enforcement of Judgments in Europe, pp. 100-120 in a comparison between some States on information available at national level, Krings, Civil Procedure in Europe 1, pp. 18-20, where he makes a comparison between different solutions in some Member States of the EU, de Leval, Subject of the proceedings, The execution of court decisions in civil cases, pp. 49-51, in a comparison on the securing of information according to the legislation of some States of the EU and La Transparence patrimoniale, La localisation du débiteur: Belgium, pp. 27-30, Greece, pp. 30-31, France, pp. 31-33, United Kingdom, pp. 33-34, La localisation du patrimoine actifs par les tiers: Sweden, pp. 35-38, Greece, pp. 38-40, France, pp. 40-43, Italy, pp. 43-45, United Kingdom, pp. 45-47, La localisation du patrimoine actif par le débiteur: Germany, pp. 47-50, Belgium, pp. 51-53, Greece, pp. 53-54, Spain, pp. 54-56, the Netherlands, pp. 56-57, United Kingdom, pp. 57-58, La détermination du patrimoine passif: France, pp. 59-61, Sweden, pp. 61-62, Italy, pp. 62-64, Greece, pp. 64-66, United Kingdom, pp. 66-67, Le régime des créances spéciales, fiscales et alimentaires: France, pp. 67-69, Germany, pp. 69-71, Sweden, p. 71, Spain, pp. 71-74, Belgium, pp. 74-76. *Also see* about the differences of access to information for enforcement purposes in national laws in relation to third-party debtors Hesslén, Asset transparency – finding information – measures to make enforcement more effective, Globalisation of law in an area of universal justice/'Is the creation of a World Area of Justice a utopic vision?', pp. 29-30, where she concludes that the rules with regards to third-party debtors vary considerably, while in Denmark, Finland and Sweden the obligations

enforceable titles and provisional measures empower enforcement organs in several Member States in the EU to assist the private creditor in seeking information about the financial situation, some Member States do not allow any such seeking activity of an enforcement organ before the enforceable title becomes final.[57] The national differences are not only explained by different levels of access to information, but also by different kinds of principal techniques of access to information for enforcement purposes.

A proposal from the group of experts in the Storme report suggested a more efficient access to national information for enforcement purposes regarding the judgment debtor and reads as follows:[58]

> For the protection of a judgment creditor who establishes his inability to find sufficient assets in the hands of the judgment debtor for the satisfaction of the judgment, the law of Member States shall provide: 1. that the debtor shall disclose in their entirety the nature and location of his assets. Such disclosure shall be made to the creditor or the proper authority as provided by law: 2. that the proper authority may require third parties to disclose any information relating to the assets of the debtor which is in their possession. 'Third parties' includes any institution which holds an account in the name of the debtor. 3. sanctions whereby these obligations may be enforced.

This proposal has not been realized, and there exists no EC law in this area, which imposes direct rules for the harmonization of the differing national enforcement laws of the Member States of the EU on access to information for enforcement purposes.

7.2.3.3 Different Techniques of Access to Information

There exist at least two different kinds of principal techniques of access to information for enforcement purposes in the EU with different approaches about to

---

vis-à-vis the third-party debtors are particularly extensive, in England and in Hungary, on the other hand, third-party debtors are not obliged to provide such information on debtors. EC Study JAI/02/03/2002, B, III, 3, informs that in the context of garnishment procedures all Member States of the EU impose on the third debtor, *i.a.* banks, a duty to disclose information about the claim seized, the declaration is given in different procedures in different Member States, there are different obligations on the garnishee to disclose additional accounts of the debtor, including accounts situated in other branches of a bank or even in branches abroad, but a general European trend can be identified in that garnishees must reveal all accounts if the garnishment order embraces all assets of a debtor and concludes that although there remain considerable differences in the legal effects of the declaration and the sanctions which may apply these are mainly related to the different structures of the garnishment procedures.

57. France and Spain do not allow any activity of this kind of enforcement organs before the enforceable title becomes final, EC Study JAI/02/03/2002, B, III. Examples of States where a provisional title may give creditors access to information relating to the assets of the debtor are England, Germany and Luxemburg, *i.b.*, B, II.
58. *See* Art. 12.4 in the report Rapprochement du Droit Judiciaire de l'Union européenne, pp. 210-211.

whom the information for enforcement purposes primarily should be provided, to the private creditor in a court procedure, which may be used in a following actual enforcement procedure, or directly to the regulated enforcement agents to be used in an actual enforcement procedure. A declaration of the entire patrimony by the debtor in court, as a consequence of the initiative of the private creditor, provides information to the creditor according to a system which is applied in *e.g.* Germany.[59] The approach of the more individually related information research system based on registers on the initiative of regulated enforcement agents provides information to them, for the benefit of the private creditor, which they may use for the attachment of specific assets.

Some Member States, such as Denmark and England, deal with enforcement matters in court, subject to contradictory procedure, where the parties are obliged to contribute a disclosure on assets and other relevant information.[60] The more individually adopted system is applied in several States, however with big differences among them, in terms of access to registers and other sources of information and by means of support of powers of inquiry and examinations. One example of an individually adopted system, which also has a high degree of access to information based on registers and confers far-reaching powers of inquiry and examinations to regulated enforcement agents, is that of Sweden.[61] Some States also combine features from both these systems, even if one or

59. *See* Hess, La Transparence patrimoniale, pp. 47-50, about Germany. *Also see* Hesslén, Asset transparency – finding information – measures to make enforcement more effective, Globalisation of law in an area of universal justice/'Is the creation of a World Area of Justice a utopic vision?', p. 30, where she describes the German system in the following way '. . . Germany has chosen a system with particular features whereby the asset transparency is achieved through a declaration of the debtor who must draw up a complete inventory of his assets under oath. Any declaration of assets is registered in a public register. The obligation of the debtor to provide information presupposes that the seizure of movable property has failed and that the creditor does not dispose of sufficient information for enforcement. Under German law, its therefore the creditor who is responsible for tracking down the debtor's assets. If the debtor fails to present himself to the bailiff, he will be arrested and, in the event of a false or incomplete declaration, he may be punished by imprisonment of up to three years.' She also describes the system in Denmark, *i.b.*, p. 30, in the following way '. . . in Denmark there exists a system whereby the creditors are left to track down the debtor's assets with prison sentences for defaulting debtors, even in the case of private debt.' *Also see* Cuniberti, Les mesures conservatoires portant sur des biens situés à l'étranger, No. 160-162, on the use in England, in connection to a freezing order (previously referred to in literature as a Mareva injunction) of a disclosure order, when the debtor has to appear before the court in order to give a declaration of his assets, including assets abroad. Third parties could also be obliged to make such a declaration.
60. *See* 3.2.1 for further details on the organizational structures of European enforcement agents and similar professionals in court based systems.
61. *See* Berglund, La Transparence patrimoniale, pp. 61-62 and pp. 199-204. *Also* compare Verbeke, Execution Officers as a Balance Wheel in Insolvency Cases, p. 13. He there refers to Sweden as a notorious example where the patrimonial transparency is extremely large. *Also* compare Kennett, The Enforcement of Judgments in Europe, pp. 101-102, where she states that the Swedish system displays an unusual degree of openness and that the Dutch system has obtained a further advanced access to official records through computer support in recent years.

another national system could mainly be classified as falling under one of these systems.[62]

An argument in favour of an application of the technique of the more individually adopted system based on search in registers instead of the technique of the system of the debtor's declaration of his entire patrimony is that the first system compared to the latter normally is in a better way aimed to meet and satisfy the need of proportionality and protection of the debtor and of efficiency for the benefit of the creditors.[63] Consequently, no more information than necessary may be used from registers based on assets, *e.g.* related to salary or real estate, instead of making the debtor declare his entire patrimony. The need and to what extent searches in assets based registers normally are conducted are often determined by the size of the creditors' enforceable amounts. This means that a small amount may require less search work than a bigger amount to locate sufficient assets for enforcement. An argument in favour of an application of the technique of the system of the debtor's declaration of his entire patrimony is the right of a creditor to obtain all information in a Member State related to the debtors' assets in order to indicate a preference of choice between them.

The task to establish the justified balance between these conflicting interests of the debtor and the creditor, in the work of enforcing judgments, in the treatment and access to information for enforcement purposes in each Member State of the EU is, however, ultimately entrusted, not to the creditor, or the debtor, but instead to specific enforcement organs and the regulated enforcement agents.[64] Information should, when an application for enforcement from a creditor exists, based on a title of execution, be provided directly to the enforcement organs through provisions in national laws, which should meet a harmonized community minimum level in terms of an efficient disclosure of assets. This leads to the conclusion that any attempts of reform, at the community level, also must clearly departure

62. *See* Berglund, La Transparence patrimoniale, p. 202, on the possibilities for the Swedish enforcement authority to make the debtor declare his assets in a list under the threat of prescribed fines and under other sanctions.
63. *See* Verbeke, Execution Officers as a Balance Wheel in Insolvency Cases, pp. 16-18. *Also see* Tarzia, Aussichten für eine Harmonisierung des Zwangsvollstreckungsrechts in der Europäischen Union pp. 236-237, where he discusses the possibility to introduce a EC law that forces the debtor to cooperate and declare all his assets, as well known in German law, but concludes that a better solution would be to enable the official bodies for enforcement by execution to request all information from other administrative entities or other public corporations and in that case problems in relation to bank and professional secrecies have to be contemplated, and Tarzia, Vers un concept europèene du droit de l'exécution ?, Le droit processuel et le droit de l'exécution, p. 165, where he states that the European legislator has to make a choice between two systems, the German system of debtor's declaration of his entire patrimony, sanctioned in the worst case of disobedience of the debtor by his imprisonment, and the more individually related information research system for the attachment of specific assets as applied in France and in Spain, and concludes that the latter system seems to be more efficient. *Also* compare Hess, La Transparence patrimoniale, p. 50, where he argues in favour of replacing the system of debtor's declaration and instead introducing a system with proper investigation powers conferred to the enforcement organs.
64. *See* 3.2.1 about the professionals of such enforcement organs.

from and reflect the need of private creditors of an efficient disclosure of assets to such enforcement organs in their work of enforcing judgments in a balanced way, according to national laws in the interests of both the creditor and the debtor.

Consequently, for the reason of efficiency a clear preference should in this reform work be stipulated in favour of the more individually adopted system by research in registers as the main European model of disclosure. However, a more limited disclosure through a declaration which limits the obligation of the debtor to assets sufficient for the enforcement of the creditor's claim should also be possible when no other ways to obtain the needed information is available to the enforcement organs. The goal of the EC should be to improve and harmonize the level of efficient disclosure of assets and the right of enforcement organs to obtain such information from all sources of information available, *e.g.* from registers, debtor's declaration and disclosure of garnishees.

7.2.3.4 Public Law Sector

Access to national information for recovery purposes related to public claims is generally more developed than access to information in the civil law enforcement area, which at least to some extent may be explained by the interest of efficiency in order to secure the public financial interests of States. National tax administrations, where we find the tax claims, often have, in comparison to the civil law area, a more far-reaching right of access to information in terms of right of inquiry and examination.[65] Information obtained in the public law sector is, however, often not possible to exploit for other purposes than specific public purposes and consequently not possible to exploit by others outside of the public law sector, even if this, to some extent, may change after the Member States of the EU have implemented the directive 2003/98/EC of the European Parliament and of the Council on the re-use of public sector information.[66] The Council of Europe's recommendation on the interoperability of information systems in the justice sector and the Council of Europe's recommendation on archiving of electronic documents in the

65. *See*, about the revenue bodies' powers to gather information, their powers to obtain relevant information, their requests for information to third parties, and other investigating powers, Tax Administration in OECD and Selected Non-OECD Countries: Comparative Information Series (2006), the Forum on Tax Administration, Centre for tax policy and administration, pp. 83-84 compared to Table 18. *Also see* Verbeke, Execution Officers as a Balance Wheel in Insolvency Cases, p. 14, compared to Hesslén, Asset transparency – finding information – measures to make enforcement more effective, p. 30, where she concludes that, even though if in most countries foreign claims are treated in the same way as national claims in terms of access to information, public claims benefit from a more privileged position compared to private claims. *Also see*, about the sources of information that the Belgian tax authorities dispose over, Leroy, L'efficacité des procédures judiciaires au sein de l'union Européenne et les garanties des droits de la defense, Transparence patrimoniale, L'efficacité de la justice civile en Europe, pp. 323-328.
66. The directive encourages a minimum harmonization of the rules and practices in the Member States relating to the exploitation by re-use of public sector information, but does not contain any obligation to allow re-use of documents, Preambles (1, 6, 8 and 9) and Art. 1, ss 1, 3 and 4.

legal sector, which deals with the preservation of electronic documents, may possibly also in a longer perspective have an indirect impact in the enforcement area.

Consequently, access to information for the purpose of recovery of claims in national laws is better provided for in the public law sector than in the civil enforcement law area. There does not, however, exist any general principle that private and public debts must be equally enforced by means of access to information.[67] The present imbalance, which seems to be a more, or less, evident feature in most national laws in the EU, between the interests of efficiency and privacy in terms of access to information for the purpose of recovery and enforcement, is evident in comparison between the public law sector and the civil enforcement law area.

The balance seems to be more in favour of efficiency in the public law sector compared to the civil enforcement law area and more in favour of privacy in the civil law area compared to the public law sector. This means, at the present stage, that these two categories of legitimate claims are actually, even if legally correct under national laws, treated on a non-equal basis in terms of efficient access to information mainly for the same purpose, *i.e.* for the purposes of recovery and enforcement. However, a harmonization of access to information for enforcement purposes of contractual claims, as will be further developed in the following, would make the treatment of contractual claims and the recovery of tax claims more equal.

7.2.3.5 Improved Access to Information for Enforcement Purposes

The establishment of a minimum level of indirect harmonization of national laws for access to information for enforcement purposes and of a sufficiently efficient solution for access to information for enforcement purposes in the cross-border context in the civil enforcement law area is important. This is required to meet the objectives of the Council's draft programme of measures in seeking to make more efficient the enforcement, in the requested State, of judgments delivered in another Member State and to enable the precise identification of a debtors' assets in the territory of the Member States for implementing the principle of mutual recognition, based on the Tampere conclusions.[68]

---

67. *See* EC Study JAI/02/03/2002, B, IV, 4.
68. *See* Council draft programme C 12/01/2001/EC of measures for implementation of the principle of mutual recognition of decisions in civil and commercial matters, II, section B. Measures ancillary to mutual recognition, 2. Efficiency of measures providing for improved enforcement of decisions compared to III, section E. Ancillary measures. *Also see* 1.1.1.1 for further details about the following developments. *Also see* Green paper Effective enforcement of judgments in the European Union: Transparency of Debtors' assets, Commission of the ECs, Brussels, COM (2008) 128 final, which objective is to find possible measures at European level to improve the transparency of debtors' assets and the right of the creditors to obtain information, whilst respecting the principles of protection of the debtors' privacy which counter-balances the creditors' right to efficient recovery.

The establishment of such a more equal level of access to information provided to the enforcement organs would guarantee a better efficiency of justice and a more equal treatment of creditors and debtors in the European judicial area. Consequently, the national differences of access to information for enforcement purposes would be reduced and creditors, who are able to present a nationally enforceable foreign judgment, under *e.g.* the Brussels I regulation, at an application for its enforcement would then come into a more similar position to the creditors, who hold national judgments, on the disclosure of assets in all enforcing Member States.

An indirect harmonization of the national laws is also motivated and required in the interest of States to implement the Council of Europe's recommendation on enforcement and by such means respond to the legal objectives of this recommendation. Such a harmonization corresponds, in addition, to the objective of the general State interest of a more efficient enforcement of claims in society and to the interest of efficiency of the creditor. The Council of Europe has established the goals in its recommendation on enforcement. The debtors should provide up-to-date information about their income, assets and on other relevant matters. The search and seizure of the debtors' assets should be made as efficient as possible taking into account relevant human rights and data protection provisions in the Data protection Directive. Also, there should be a fast and efficient collection of necessary information on the debtors' assets achieved through access to relevant information in registers and other sources as well as the option for the debtor of making a declaration of his assets.[69] Consequently, the Council of Europe's recommendation on enforcement may, in a longer perspective, contribute to alter the variety in national laws of the Member States of the Council of Europe into more equal levels of access to information for enforcement purposes.

Several authors have also emphasized the importance, and confirmed the need, for access to information for enforcement purposes based on various aspects, particularly in the civil enforcement law area and including the twofold objectives to increase access to national information and to establish a multilateral cooperation system between States for the exchange of nationally available information.[70]

In order to obtain all these objectives of an improved access to information for enforcement purposes of judgments to enforcement organs in the civil enforcement law area, an indirect harmonization in EC law of national laws, under the option of any national system, should stipulate the goals of an efficient and up-to-date access to information to enforcement organs for enforcement purposes of judgments achieved preferably by 'electronic means', through access to relevant information in registers and other sources of information regarding the debtor.

The need of efficient access to information has of course to be balanced against the interests of the debtor of humanity, dignity and privacy, including data protection. Access to information regarding the assets of the debtor for enforcement and recovery purposes calls for a balanced equilibrium between the creditors' right to

---

69. *See* section III, 1, d, 1, g and 6 of the Council of Europe's recommendation on enforcement.
70. *See* 6.3.3.1.4.

efficient enforcement and recovery of his claim and the debtor's right to humanity and privacy in such situations. These rights can, as already often pointed at here, be derived from the European Convention on Human Rights. Arguments exist, *i.a.* based on the interpretation of Article 6, 1 of the European Convention on Human Rights, in favour of considering a demand of access to information for enforcement purposes an important requirement in order to make the execution of a judgment efficient.[71] It may be argued that efficiency in this context should also mean a demand on the availability of all necessary information for enforcement and recovery purposes, in order to safeguard the creditor's right of efficient recovery, and by such means to promote a realization of the creditor's claim, in the interest of his right of a peaceful enjoyment of his possessions according to Protocol No. 1, Article 1, of this European convention, in the assets of the debtor.

There exist strong arguments in favour of the principle to consider the availability of information for enforcement purposes related to the assets of the debtor at the enforcement and seizure of a creditor's claim, to constitute a fundamental right based on Article 6, 1 of the European Convention on Human Rights.[72] Efficient access to information regarding the assets of the debtor must, however, be balanced against the rights to a treatment of humanity and dignity for the debtor, and in case of a collision between these interests, in favour of the latter.[73] This access to

71. The ECHR has in its ruling *Hornsby v. Greece* of 19 Mar. 1997, and in some other rulings, *see* 4.3.1, confirmed that the execution of a judgment given by any court must be regarded as an integral part of the 'trial' for the purpose of Art. 6 of the European Convention on Human Rights.
72. *See* Verbeke, Execution Officers as a Balance Wheel in Insolvency Cases, pp. 8-9, where he argues that a demand on efficiency, *i.a.* implies the availability of all necessary information to realize such efficient recovery in due time and concludes that debtor patrimonial transparency and asset information constitute a fundamental right (under Art. 6, 1 of the convention) for each creditor. He also adds some arguments in support of his opinion 'One may add, in support of this argument, the first article of the First Additional Protocol of 20 Mar. 1952 to the European Rights Treaty, warranting each person the right to an undisturbed enjoyment of his property and ownership. Since a creditor's claim is a valuable patrimonial asset, the creditor has a fundamental right to an undisturbed enjoyment of this asset. This certainly implies the right to an efficient recovery of such claims. Some additional arguments may be put forward in furtherance of the creditor's basic right for an efficient recovery within a reasonable time, implying patrimonial transparency on the debtor's side. First of all, such right can be considered in a way to be an implied power of the creditor. Since it is a general and mostly explicit rule that a creditor may recover his claims from the entire estate of the debtor, it should be implied that he is equally entitled to information regarding that estate. How could he otherwise know where to recover ? Moreover, one may argue that a lack of patrimonial information, or any other inefficiency, leading to the impossibility to obtain execution of a court judgment, should be considered as "contempt of court". What respect does a society (or legislator) have for its own judicial system, if it makes it impossible for decisions of its judiciary to be executed?'.
73. *See* Verbeke, Execution Officers as a Balance Wheel in Insolvency Cases, p. 10, where he argues that: '. . . this (existential) value of humanity and dignity of a debtor cannot be in conflict with the creditor's right of recovery, since the former invariably is a superior right. Put that way, there will be no conflict, nor will there be any balancing needed. A person's insolvency can never be an excuse to injure his humanity and dignity. The latter is such an essential right that it can never be violated. Therefore, the basic right of human dignity constitutes the very minimum of protection for each debtor.'

information must also be balanced against the right of privacy for the debtor and be proportionate in relation to the need of information for enforcement and recovery purposes in order to avoid that the debtor is exposed to injuries as far as possible.[74]

Consequently, no more information should be obtainable, and used for the enforcement and recovery of a claim than corresponds to the necessary need, for the purpose of efficient enforcement or recovery of the creditor's specific claim. In this way only such a proportionate part of information should be made available, which would contribute to avoid an excessive abuse of information related to the assets of the debtor and subsequently minimize the risk to injure the debtor. Access to information should also be acceptable, and even beneficial, to the debtors under the conditions that it is used in a balanced way for enforcement and recovery purposes, not by the creditor in person or by obscure private recovery agencies, but under the control of an independent neutral third party, a regulated enforcement agent, who has the task of establishing this balanced equilibrium between the rights of the creditors and the debtors, under the rules of law and the supervision of State bodies, courts and authorities.[75]

Other important reasons, that motivate why an improved access to information for enforcement purposes should be provided directly to the enforcement agents, instead of to the private creditor, are that these agents, at an application for the enforcement of a claim by the creditor, would anyway have to review and evaluate received information about assets of the debtor from the creditor, as an integrated part of an actual enforcement procedure, in a justified balance between the interest of efficiency of the private creditor and the interest of privacy of the debtor, which may, or may not, result in the attachment of assets indicated by the private creditor.[76]

In an all-over evaluation of these reasons and conditions related to access to information for enforcement purposes, it becomes clear that the interest of

74. *See* Art. 8, 1 of the European Convention on Human Rights and Verbeke, Execution Officers as a Balance Wheel in Insolvency Cases, pp. 11 and 15.
75. *See* Verbeke, Execution Officers as a Balance Wheel in Insolvency Cases, pp. 11-18, where he argues that through the intervention of the execution officer 'as a balance wheel' the proportionality test can be met and secured because no information is given to the creditor in person, but to a neutral and objective party, the execution officer, who could not use it for any other purpose than the recovery of a specific claim. He also argues that the intervention of the execution officer has the advantages to answer to the need of a balanced and controlled patrimonial transparency in execution law not only required for the sake of the debtor, but equally in the interest of protecting the debtor, and it also constitutes an important contra measure against the establishment outside the control of law of private obscure recovery agencies with unacceptable recovery methods. In addition he also argues that the execution officer should be entrusted a similar neutral and objective role of profession as compared to a trustee in bankruptcy, or to a liquidator, *i.a.* in terms of access of information about the entire estate in order to realize as efficiently as possible the creditor's claims with as few injuries as possible for the debtor and his privacy. *Also see* the Preamble of the Council of Europe's recommendation on enforcement, which emphasizes ... 'that without an effective system of enforcement, other forms of "private justice" may flourish and have adverse consequences on the public's confidence in and credibility of the legal system'.
76. This is further treated in the context of 6.3.3.1.1.

efficiency is of a greater weight than that of the debtor's privacy, which, however, does not mean that this interest of the debtor may be ignored. There are good arguments favouring that national laws in the Member States of the EU should be more influenced by the interest of efficiency.

In order to achieve a harmonization through EC law, in relation to matters having cross-border implications, a detailed goal for the harmonization of national laws should be stipulated, under the option of any national system of regulated enforcement agents. National laws should meet the following goal for an efficient and up-to-date access of information to enforcement organs for enforcement purposes of judgments related to civil law claims. This goal should not be less precise than to secure access to information about the debtor's: address, or place of location, employer, or business, through corporate registers, or other sources of income, including private, or social, insurance institutions, incomes and other assets in his possession to the extent such information is available in the records of enforcement agents *e.g.* through debtor's registers kept by such officials, assets held in the possession by any third parties, including any financial institution, *e.g.* bank accounts, which hold an account, or a deposit, in the name of the debtor, declaration of his assets made to the enforcement agents, and status of indebtedness or insolvency, *i.e.* bankruptcy or other collective insolvency procedures.[77] This access to information should preferably be achieved by 'electronic means'.

7.3 UNCITRAL FACULTATIVE MODEL LAW ON ENFORCEMENT LAW

The idea of the creation of a World Code of Enforcement, which was raised at the Congress of the UIHJ in Washington in 2006,[78] merits, given the great importance in a global society of a well functioning enforcement of claims, *i.a.* in the context of international trade, to be further contemplated and discussed. However, a possible first step in this direction may be, only subject to being first proven to be politically acceptable, that the interested Member States of the United Nations take an initiative to suggest that a work is started by the United Nations Commission on International Trade Law (Uncitral).

The aim of such a work would be to create a facultative Model Law on Enforcement Law for the treatment of internal enforcement matters, *i.e.* not primarily for such matters having cross-border implications.[79] This is a global

77. This idea is to some extent more developed as compared to Art. 12.4 in the proposal from the group of European experts in the report Rapprochement du Droit Judiciaire de l'Union européenne/Approximation of Judiciary Law in the European Union, *see* 7.2.3.2, but they are both based on a similar idea of development.
78. *See* 2.10.5.
79. Compare 6.4.3 about the Uncitral Model Law on Cross-Border Insolvency, which instead aims to promote efficiency, on a facultative basis to Member States of the UN, in the cross-border context of general execution/insolvency.

political issue, which goes beyond the reach of the ALI-UNIDROIT Principles of Transnational Civil Procedure, the Council of Europe's recommendation on enforcement, and the established legal objectives of the EU. Such principles, recommendations and objectives may provide an inspiration, but more consistency is needed, such as might ensue from the proposed Model law.

Chapter 8
Bibliography

8.1 LEGAL HISTORICAL MATERIAL UNTIL 2001

References here follow the structure of the Contents.

8.1.1 Belgium

Treaty between Belgium, the Netherlands and Luxemburg on Jurisdiction, Bankruptcy, and the Validity and Enforcement of Judgments, Arbitration Awards and Authentic Instruments of 24 November 1961	2.4.2

8.1.2 Denmark

Agreement of 9 November 1972 between Sweden, Denmark, Finland, Iceland and Norway on administrative assistance in tax matters	2.6.3
City Codes, medieval	2.2.1
City Code of Ribe, medieval	2.2.1
Nordic convention on recognition and the enforcement of judgments in civil matters of 16 March 1932	2.4.2
Provincial Codes, medieval	2.2.1, 2.3.1
Retsplejeloven of 1917	3.1.5.1

8.1.3 Finland

Agreement of 9 November 1972 between Sweden, Denmark,	2.6.3

Finland, Iceland and Norway on administrative assistance in tax matters	
Enforcement Act of 1895	3.1.5.5
Nordic convention on recognition and the enforcement of judgments in civil matters of 16 March 1932	2.4.2
Statute concerning the attachment of levies and public fees of 1897	3.1.5.5

8.1.4 France

Code de Procédure Civile of 1806	2.3.1
Convention between the Swiss Confederation and France on jurisdiction and enforcement of judgments in civil matters, signed at Paris on 15 June 1869	2.7
Napoleonic cinq codes	2.3.1
Ordonance of 1285 related to the establishment of the institution of the Huissier de Justice	3.1.2

8.1.5 Germany

Allgemeines Landrecht für die Preußischen Staaten of 1792	2.3.1
Gerichtsverfassungsgesetz of 1877 related to the institution of the Gerichtsvollzieher	3.1.4

8.1.6 Iceland

Agreement of 9 November 1972 between Sweden, Denmark, Finland, Iceland and Norway on administrative assistance in tax matters	2.6.3
Nordic convention on recognition and the enforcement of judgments in civil matters of 16 March 1932	2.4.2

8.1.7 Italy and Roman law

Actio Pauliana	2.1.3, 2.2.4
Agreement between Verona and Venice of 1306 related to bankruptcy	2.2.4
Customary laws of the Italian merchant cities, medieval	2.2.3-4
Law of the Twelve Tables, about 451-450 B.C.	2.1.1
Lex Poetilia, about 330 B.C.	2.1.1
Loi Aebutia, peut-être vers 636	2.1.3
Statut de Pistoie de 1296 related to composition	2.2.3
Statut réformé de Padoue de 1420 related to composition	2.2.3

Treaty between Verona and Trent of 1204 related to bankruptcy — 2.2.4

8.1.8 Luxemburg

Treaty between Belgium, the Netherlands and Luxemburg on Jurisdiction, Bankruptcy, and the Validity and Enforcement of Judgments, Arbitration Awards and Authentic Instruments of 24 November 1961 — 2.4.2

8.1.9 Netherlands

Treaty between Belgium, the Netherlands and Luxemburg on Jurisdiction, Bankruptcy, and the Validity and Enforcement of Judgments, Arbitration Awards and Authentic Instruments of 24 November 1961 — 2.4.2

8.1.10 Norway

Agreement of 9 November 1972 between Sweden, Denmark, Finland, Iceland and Norway on administrative assistance in tax matters — 2.6.3

Decree for the Faeroe Islands, rettarbot for Færøyane, of 1273 — 3.1.5.3

Nordic convention on recognition and the enforcement of judgments in civil matters of 16 March 1932 — 2.4.2

8.1.11 Sweden

Agreement of 9 November 1972 between Sweden, Denmark, Finland, Iceland and Norway on administrative assistance in tax matters — 2.6.3

City Codes, medieval — 2.2.1, 3.1.5.4

Common Country law of king Magnus Eriksson of 1347 — 2.2.1, 3.1.5.4

Enforcement Law of 1877 — 2.3.1, 3.1.5.4

Execution Ordinance of 1669 — 2.3.1, 3.1.5.4

Gustavus II Adolphus' Court Proceedings of 1615 — 3.1.5.4

Nordic convention on recognition and the enforcement of judgments in civil matters of 16 March 1932 — 2.4.2

Provincial Codes, medieval — 2.2.1, 3.1.5.4

Sweriges rikes lag gillad och antagen på riksdagen åhr 1734 (The Law of the Swedish Realm accepted and approven — 2.3.1, 3.1.5.4

by the Parliament the year 1734), including an Utsökningsbalk (Enforcement Code)	
Royal Statutes, Resolutions and Ordinances concerning the Judicature of 1528	3.1.5.4

8.1.12 Switzerland

Convention between the Swiss Confederation and France on jurisdiction and enforcement of judgments in civil matters, signed at Paris on 15 June 1869	2.7

8.1.13 United Kingdom

Statute of 1340 related to the function of the Sheriff	3.1.3.1
Statute of 1510 related to the establishment of the institution of the Messengers-at-Arms (Scotland)	3.1.3.2

8.1.14 European Community Law

Directive 76/308/EEC on mutual assistance for the recovery of claims resulting from operations forming part of the system of financing the European Agricultural Guidance and Guarantee Fund, and of agricultural levies and customs duties and in respect of value added tax and certain excise duties	2.6, 2.6.1
Council Directive 79/1071/EEC of 6 December 1979 amending Directive 76/308/EEC on mutual assistance for the recovery of claims resulting from operations forming part of the system of financing the European Agricultural Guidance and Guarantee Fund, and of agricultural levies and customs duties	2.6, 2.6.1
Council Directive 92/108/EEC of 14 December 1992 amending Directive 12/92/EEC on the general arrangements for products subject to excise duty and on holding, movement and monitoring of such products and amending Directive 81/92/EEC	2.6, 2.6.1
Council Directive 2001/44/EC of 15 June 2001 amending Directive 76/308/EEC on mutual assistance for the recovery of claims resulting from operations forming part of the system of financing the European Agricultural Guidance and Guarantee Fund, and of agricultural levies and customs duties and in respect of value added tax and certain excise duties	2.6, 2.6.1

8.2 EUROPEAN COMMUNITY LAW AND CONVENTIONS

8.2.1 Contractual Claims

1923
Protocol on Arbitration Clauses, done at Geneva on 24 September 1923, LNTS No. 678, Vol. 27 (1924), p. 157

1927
Convention on the Execution of Foreign Arbitral Awards, done at Geneva on 26 September 1927, LNTS No. 2096, Vol. 92 (1929), p. 301

1958
Convention on the recognition and enforcement of foreign arbitral awards, done at New York on 10 June 1958, UNTS, No. 4739, Vol. 330 (1959), p. 3

1961
European Convention on International Commercial Arbitration, UNTS 1963-1964, Vol. VI, No. 7041, done at Geneva on 21 April 1961, completed by the Agreement relating to Application of the European Convention on International Commercial Arbitration, ETS 1962 No. 42, done at Paris on 17 December 1962

1968
Convention on jurisdiction and the enforcement of judgments in civil and commercial matters, done at Brussels on 27 September 1968, consolidated version of 26 January 1998, OJ 1998 C 27

1977
Convention between Sweden, Denmark, Finland, Iceland and Norway on recognition and the enforcement of judgments in civil matter, done at Copenhagen on 11 October 1977, UNTS, No. 16914, Vol. 1102 (1978)

1988
Convention on jurisdiction and the enforcement of judgments in civil and commercial matters, done at Lugano on 16 September 1988, UNTS No. 28551, Vol. 1659 (1992)

2001
Council regulation 44/2001/EC of 22 December 2000 on jurisdiction and the recognition and enforcement of judgments in civil and commercial matters, OJ 2001 L 12, as amended through the Act concerning the conditions of accession of the Czech Republic, the Republic of Estonia, the Republic of Cyprus, the Republic of Latvia, the Republic of Lithuania, the Republic of Hungary, the Republic of Malta, the Republic of Poland, the Republic of Slovenia and the Slovak Republic and the adjustments to the Treaties on which the European Union is founded – Annex II: List referred to in article 20 of the Act of Accession – 18. Cooperation in the fields of justice and home affaires – A. Judicial cooperation in civil and commercial matters, 3, OJ 2003 L 236

2004
Regulation 805/2004/EC of the European Parliament and of the Council of 21 April 2004 creating a European Enforcement Order for uncontested claims, OJ 2004 L 143

2005
Convention of 30 June 2005 on Choice of Court Agreements, Hague Conference on Private International Law. *Also see* website of the Hague Conference on Private International Law, www.hcch.net

Agreement between the European Community and the Kingdom of Denmark of 19 October 2005 on jurisdiction and the recognition and enforcement of judgments in civil and commercial matters, OJ 2005 L 299

2006
Regulation 1896/2006/EC of the European Parliament and of the Council of 12 December 2006 creating a European order for payment procedure, OJ 2006 L 399

2007
Regulation (EC) No. 861/2007 of the European Parliament and of the Council of 11 July establishing a European Small Claims Procedure, OJ 2007 L 199

Information concerning the date of entry into force of the Agreement between the European Community and the Kingdom of Denmark on jurisdiction and the recognition and enforcement of judgments in civil and commercial matters, OJ 2007 L 94

Convention on jurisdiction and the recognition and enforcement of judgments in civil and commercial matters, done at Lugano on 30 October 2007

8.2.2 Tax Claims

1952
Convention entre la Belgique, le Grand-Duché de Luxembourg et les Pays-Bas, relative à l'assistance réciproque en matière de recouvrement de créances fiscales, du 5 septembre 1952, publication dans Moniteur belge du 6 juillet 1956

1977
Council Directive 77/799/EEC of 19 December 1977 concerning mutual assistance by the competent authorities of the Member States in the field of direct taxation, OJ 1977 L 336, thereafter amended several times *i.a.* by the 1994 Act of accession followed by amendments through the Act concerning the conditions of accession of the Czech Republic, the Republic of Estonia, the Republic of Cyprus, the Republic of Latvia, the Republic of Lithuania, the Republic of Hungary, the Republic of Malta, the Republic of Poland, the Republic of Slovenia and the Slovak Republic and the adjustments to the Treaties on which the European Union is founded – Annex II: List referred to in article 20 of the Act of Accession – 9. Taxation, 4, OJ 2003 L 236

1983

Convention between Sweden and Japan for the avoidance of double taxation and the prevention of fiscal evasion with respect to taxes on income, done at Stockholm on 21 January 1983, as last amended on 19 February 1999

1988

Convention on mutual administrative assistance in tax matters, done at Strasbourg on 25 January 1988, Council of Europe and OECD, ETS No. 127 and UNTS No. 33610 (1997)

1989

Agreement between the Nordic countries for mutual adminstrative assistance in tax matters, done at Copenhagen on 7 December 1989, Sveriges internationella överenskommelser, No. 11, Avtal mellan de nordiska länderna om handräckning i skatteärenden, Köpenhamn den 7 december 1989 (Sweden's international agreements, No. 11, Agreement between the Nordic countries for mutual adminstrative assistance in tax matters, done at Copenhagen on 7 December 1989)

1992

Abkommen zwischen dem Köningreich Schweden und der Bundesrepublik Deutschland zur Vermeidung der Doppelbesteuerung bei den Steuern vom Einkommen und vom Vermögen sowie bei den Erbschaft- und Schenkungsteuern und zur Leistung gegenseitigen Beistand bei den Steuern/Avtal mellan Kungariket Sverige och Förbundsrepubliken Tyskland för att undvika dubbelbeskattning beträffande skatter på inkomst och förmögenhet och på arv och gåva samt för att lämna ömsesidig handräckning vid beskattning (Agreement between the Kingdom of Sweden and the Federal Republic of Germany for the avoidance of double taxation related to taxes on incomes and wealth and inheritance and gift and for the mutual assistance for taxation), done at Bonn on 14 July 1992

Council Directive 92/12/EEC of 25 February 1992 on the general arrangements for products subject to excise duty and on the holding, movement and monitoring of such products, OJ 1992 L 76

Council Directive 92/108/EEC of 14 December 1992 amending Directive 12/92/EEC on the general arrangements for products subject to excise duty and on holding, movement and monitoring of such products and amending Directive 81/92/EEC, OJ 1992 L 390

1993

Convention between the Kingdom of Sweden and the Republic of Estonia for the avoidance of double taxation and the prevention of fiscal evasion with respect to taxes on income and on capital, done at Stockholm 5 April 1993

Convention between the Kingdom of Sweden and the Republic of Latvia for the avoidance of double taxation and the prevention of fiscal evasion with respect to taxes on income and on capital, done at Stockholm 5 April 1993

Convention between the Kingdom of Sweden and the Republic of Lithuania for the avoidance of double taxation and the prevention of fiscal evasion with respect to taxes on income and on capital, done at Stockholm 27 September 1993

1994
Convention between the government of Sweden and the government of the United States of America for the avoidance of double taxation and the prevention of fiscal evasion with respect to taxes on income, done at Stockholm on 1 September 1994

1997
Convention between the government of the kingdom of Sweden and the government of the republic of India for the avoidance of double taxation and the prevention of fiscal evasion with respect to taxes on income and on capital, done at New Delhi on 24 June 1997

1998
Agreement entered into by the competent representatives of Denmark, the Faeroe Islands, Greenland, Finland, Iceland, Norway and Sweden according to article 20 of the agreement between the Nordic countries for mutual administrative assistance in tax matters of 7 December 1989, as amended on its entry into force on 1 January 1998, published in annex 1 to förordning (1997:1157) om handräckning i skatteärenden mellan de nordiska länderna (Swedish government decree on the administrative assistance in tax matters between the Nordic countries)

2001
Sixth Council Directive 77/388/EEC of 17 May 1977 on the harmonisation of the laws of the Member States relating to turnover taxes – Common system of value added tax: uniform basis of assessment, as amended by Council Directives 2000/65/EC of 17 October 2000 and 2001/115/EC of 20 December 2001

2002
Commission Directive 2002/94/EC of 9 December 2002 laying down detailed rules for implementing certain provisions of Council Directive 76/308/EEC on mutual assistance for the recovery of claims relating to certain levies, duties, taxes and other measures, OJ 2002 L 337

2003
Act concerning the conditions of accession of the Czech Republic, the Republic of Estonia, the Republic of Cyprus, the Republic of Latvia, the Republic of Lithuania, the Republic of Hungary, the Republic of Malta, the Republic of Poland, the Republic of Slovenia and the Slovak Republic and the adjustments to the Treaties on which the European Union is founded – Annex II: List referred to in article 20 of the Act of Accession – 9. Taxation, 2, OJ 2003 L 236

2004
Commission Directive 2004/79/EC of 4 March 2004 adapting Directive 2002/94/EC, in the field of taxation, by reason of the accession of the Czech Republic, Estonia, Cyprus, Latvia, Lithuania, Hungary, Malta, Poland, Slovenia and Slovakia, OJ 2004 L 168

2006
Commission Directive 2006/84/EC of 23 October 2006 adapting Directive 2002/94/EC laying down detailed rules for implementing certain provisions of Council Directive 76/308/EEC on mutual assistance for the recovery of claims relating to certain levies, duties, taxes and other measures, by reason of the accession of Bulgaria and Romania, OJ 2006 L 362

2008
Council Directive 2008/55/EC of 26 May 2008 on mutual assistance for the recovery of claims relating to certain levies, duties, taxes and other measures (Codified version), OJ 2008 L 150

8.2.3 Insolvency

1933
Convention between Denmark, Finland, Iceland, Norway and Sweden regarding bankruptcy of 7 November, LNTS No. 3574, vol. CLV (1935), p. 115, amended in 1977 and 1982, UNTS No. 16915, vol. 1102 (1978), p. 181 and No. 16915, vol. 1419 (1986)

1950
Convention relative à la faillite et à la liquidation judiciaire entre la France et la principauté de Monaco, signée à Paris le 13 Septembre 1950

1980
Council Directive (80/987/EEC) of 20 October 1980 on the approximation of the laws of the Member States relating to the protection of employees in the event of the insolvency of their employer, OJ 1980 L 283

1997
Uncitral Model Law on Cross-Border Insolvency of 30 May 1997, confirmed by the General Assembly of the United Nations on 15 December 1997 in resolution 52/158, (Uncitral). *Also see* website of Uncitral, www.uncitral.org

2000
Council regulation 1346/2000/EC of 29 May 2000 on insolvency proceedings, OJ 2000 L 160, as amended through the Act concerning the conditions of accession of the Czech Republic, the Republic of Estonia, the Republic of Cyprus, the Republic of Latvia, the Republic of Lithuania, the Republic of Hungary, the Republic of Malta, the Republic of Poland, the Republic of Slovenia and the Slovak Republic and the adjustments to the Treaties on which the European Union is founded – Annex II: List referred to in article 20 of the Act of Accession – 18. Cooperation in the fields of justice and home affaires – A. Judicial cooperation in civil and commercial matters, 1, OJ 2003 L 236

2001
Directive 2001/17/EC of the European Parliament and of the Council of 19 March 2001 on the reorganization and winding-up of insurance undertakings, OJ 2001 L 110

Directive 2001/24/EC of the European Parliament and of the Council of 4 April 2001 on the reorganization and winding-up of credit institutions, OJ 2001 L 125

2002
Directive 2002/74/EC of the European Parliament and of the Council of 23 September 2002 amending Council Directive 80/987/EEC on the approximation of the laws of the Member States relating to the protection of employees in the event of the insolvency of their employer, OJ 2002 L 270

8.2.4 Other European Community Law and Conventions

1929
Trattato fra la Santa Sede e L'Italia, Inter Sanctam Sedem et Italiae Regnum, Acta Apostolicae Sedis – Commentarium Officiale, N. 6, Annus XXI – Vol. XXI, 7 Iunii 1929

Convention pour l'Unification de certaines Règles relatives au Transport Aérien International, faite à Varsovie le 12 Octobre 1929

1945
Charter of the United Nations with the statute of the international court of justice annexed thereto, done at San Francisco on 26 June 1945

1950
Convention for the protection of human rights and fundamental freedoms, Council of Europe, done at Rome on 4 November 1950, as amended by protocol No. 11, ETS No. 45 and UNTS No. 2889, Vol. 213 (1955), and reservation from Monaco against article 1 of Protocol No. 4 to the convention deposited on 30 November 2005. *Also see* website of the Council of Europe, http://conventions.coe.int

1952
International convention relating to the arrest of seagoing ships, done at Brussels on 10 May 1952

1956
Convention on the Contract for the International Carriage of Goods by Road, done at Geneva on 19 May 1956, UNTS No. 5742, Vol. 399 (1961)

1957
Treaty establishing the European Economic Community, done at Rome on 25 March 1957

1960
Convention on Third Party Liability in the Field of Nuclear Energy, Paris 29 July 1960

1961
Vienna convention on diplomatic relations, done at Vienna on 18 April 1961, UNTS No. 7310, Vol. 500 (1964)

1962
Konvention med Danmark, Finland, Island och Norge angående indrivning av underhållsbidrag den 22 mars 1962 (Convention between Denmark, Finland, Iceland, Norway and Sweden regarding the enforcement of maintenance claims, done in Oslo on 22 March 1962), Sveriges överenskommelser med främmande stater (Sweden's agreements with foreign States), No. 14, 1963, UNTS No. 6793, as amended in Oslo on 25 February 2000 (Sweden's agreements with foreign States, No. 8, 2002)

Samarbetsöverenskommelse mellan Danmark, Finland, Island, Norge och Sverige, Helsingfors den 23 mars 1962 (Co-operation agreement between Denmark, Finland, Iceland Norway and Sweden, done in Helsinki on 23 March 1962), Sveriges överenskommelser med främmande stater (Sweden's agreements with foreign States), No. 14, 1962

Nordic agreement on the co-operation concerning the mutual assistance of enforcement of judgments or decisions on fines, confiscation or compensation for litigation costs of 1962, through similar enacted laws in the Nordic States, compare Kungl. Maj: ts proposition nr 203 år 1962 (Swedish travaux préparatoires to the Nordic agreement)

1963
Vienna convention on consular relations, done at Vienna on 24 April 1963, UNTS No. 8638, Vol. 596 (1967)

1965
Hague-convention on the service abroad of judicial and extrajudicial documents in civil or commercial matters of 15 November 1965, UNTS No. 9432, Vol. 658 (1969). *Also see* website of the Hague conference on private international law, www.hcch.net, on the text of the convention (No. 14), concise and full status reports on the convention and for details on the entry into force of the convention in relation to the States which are parties to the convention

1969
Convention on the law of treaties, done at Vienna on 23 may 1969, UNTS No. 18232, Vol. 1155 (1980)

1970
European Convention on the international validity of criminal judgments, done at Hague on 28 may 1970, ETS No. 70

1971
Council regulation 1408/71/EEC of 14 June 1971 on the application of social security schemes to employed persons and their families moving within the Community, OJ 1971 L 149

1972
European convention on State immunity, done at Basle on 16 may 1972, ETS No. 74 and UNTS No. 25699, Vol. 1495 (1988)

1977
Council Directive 77/249/EEC of 22 March 1977 to facilitate the effective exercise by lawyers of freedom to provide services, OJ 1977 L 78

1980
Convention on the law applicable to contractual obligations, opened for signature in Rome on 19 June 1980, OJ 1980 L 266

1981
Multilateral agreement related to route charges, done at Brussels on 12 February 1981

1988
United Nations Convention against illicit traffic in narcotic drugs and psychtropic substances, done at Vienna on 20 December 1988, UNTS No. 27627

1989
Council Directive 89/48/EEC of 21 December 1988 on a general system for the recognition of higher-education and training of at least three years' duration, OJ 1989 L 19

1990
Convention between the Member States of the European Communities on the simplification of procedures for the recovery of maintenance payments, done at Rome on 6 November 1990

Council of Europe's Convention on the laundering, search, seizure and confiscation of proceeds from crime, done at Strasbourg on 8 November 1990, ETS No. 141

1992
Council regulation 1765/92/EC establishing a support system for producers of certain arable crops, OJ 1992 L 181

1994
Act of accession of the Republic of Austria, the Kingdom of Sweden, the Republic of Finland and the Kingdom of Norway to the European Union, OJ 1994 C 241

1995
Directive 46/95/EC of the European Parliament and of the Council of 24 October 1995 on the protection of individuals with regard to the processing of personal data and on the free movement of such data, OJ 1995 L 281

1998
Directive 98/5/EC of the European Parliament and of the Council of 16 February 1998 to facilitate practice of the profession of lawyer on a permanent basis

in a Member State other than that in which the qualification was obtained, OJ 1998 L 77

Action plan of the Council and the Commission on how best to implement the provisions of the Treaty of Amsterdam on an area of freedom, security and justice of 3 December 1998, OJ 1999 C 19

1999
Presidency conclusions, Tampere, European council 15 and 16 October 1999. *Also see* website of the European Parliament, www.europarl.eu.int/summits/tam_en.htm

2000
Council regulation 1348/2000/EC of 29 May 2000 on the service in the Member States of judicial and extrajudicial documents in civil or commercial matters, OJ 2000 L 160

Directive 2000/35/EC of the European Parliament and of the Council of 29 June 2000 on combating late payment in commercial transactions, OJ 2000 L 200

2001
Council draft programme of measures for implementation of the principle of mutual recognition of decisions in civil and commercial matters of 15 January 2001, OJ 2001 C 12/01

Council programme of measures to implement the principle of mutual recognition of decisions in criminal matters of 15 January 2001, OJ 2001 C 12/02

Council regulation 1206/2001/EC of 28 May 2001 on cooperation between the courts of the Member States in the taking of evidence in civil or commercial matters, OJ 2001 L 174

Council decision 2001/470/EC of 28 May 2001 establishing a European Judicial Network in civil and commercial matters, OJ 2001 L 174/25. *Also see* the website of the European Judicial Network in civil and commercial matters, http://ec.europa.eu/civiljustice

Council regulation 2157/2001/EC of 8 October 2001 on the Statute for a European company (SE), OJ 2001 L 294

Resolution No. 3 of the 24th Conference of European Justice Ministers in Moscow in October 2001 on the 'General approach and the means of achieving effective enforcement of judicial decisions'

2002
Decision 2235/2002/EC of the European Parliament and of the Council of 3 December 2002 adopting a Community programme to improve the operation of taxation systems in the internal market (Fiscalis programme 2003-2007), OJ 2002 L 341

Treaty establishing the European community, consolidated version of 24 December 2002, OJ 2002, C 325/33, as amended through the Treaty of accession of the Czech Republic, Estonia, Cyprus, Latvia, Lithuania, Hungary, Malta, Poland, Slovenia and Slovakia and the Act concerning the conditions of accession of the Czech Republic, the Republic of Estonia, the Republic of Cyprus, the Republic of Latvia, the Republic of Lithuania, the Republic of Hungary, the Republic of Malta, the Republic of Poland, the Republic of Slovenia and the Slovak Republic and the adjustments to the Treaties on which the European Union is founded, OJ 2003 L 236

2003

Council Framework Decision 2003/577/JHA of 22 July 2003 on the execution in the European Union of orders freezing property or evidence, OJ 2003 L 196

Directive 2003/98/EC of the European Parliament and of the Council of 17 November 2003 on the re-use of public sector information, OJ 2003 L 345/90

Council of Europe's recommendation on the interoperability of information systems in the justice sector, Rec (2003) 14, of 9 September 2003

Council of Europe's recommendation on archiving of electronic documents in the legal sector, Rec (2003) 15, of 9 September 2003

Council of Europe's recommendation on the execution of administrative and judicial decisions in the field of administrative law, Rec (2003) 16, of 9 September 2003

Council of Europe's recommendation on enforcement, Rec (2003) 17, of 9 September 2003

2004

Regulation 883/2004/EC of the European Parliament and of the Council of 29 April 2004 on the coordination of social security systems, OJ 2004 L 200

2005

Council, the Hague Programme: strengthening freedom, security and justice in the European Union, OJ 2005 C 53/01

Council Framework Decision 2005/214/JHA of 24 February 2005 on the application of the principle of mutual recognition to financial penalties, OJ 2005 L 76

Treaty between the Kingdom of Belgium, the Czech Republic, the Kingdom of Denmark, the Federal Republic of Germany, the Republic of Estonia, the Hellenic Republic, the Kingdom of Spain, the French Republic, Ireland, the Italian Republic, the Republic of Cyprus, the Republic of Latvia, the Republic of Lithuania, the Grand Duchy of Luxembourg, the Republic of Hungary, the Republic of Malta, the Kingdom of the Netherlands, the Republic of Austria, the Republic of Poland, the Portuguese Republic, the Republic of Slovenia, the Slovak Republic, the Republic of Finland, the Kingdom of Sweden, the United Kingdom of

Great Britain and Northern Ireland (Member States of the European Union) and the Republic of Bulgaria and Romania, concerning the accession of the Republic of Bulgaria and Romania to the European Union of 21 June 2005, OJ 2005 L 157

Directive 2005/36/EC of the European Parliament and of the Council of 7 September 2005 on the recognition of professional qualifications, OJ 2005 L 255

Agreement between the European Community and the Kingdom of Denmark of 19 October 2005 on the service of judicial and extrajudicial documents in civil or commercial matters, OJ 2005 L 300

2006

Council Framework Decision 2006/783/JHA of 6 October 2006 on the application of the principle of mutual recognition to confiscation orders, OJ 2006 L 328

2007

Information concerning the date of entry into force of the Agreement between the European Community and the Kingdom of Denmark on the service of judicial and extrajudicial documents in civil or commercial matters, OJ 2007 L 94

Regulation (EC) No. 1393/2007 of the European Parliament and of the Council of 13 November 2007 on the service in the Member States of judicial and extrajudicial documents in civil or commercial matters (service of documents), and repealing Council Regulation (EC) No. 1348/2000, OJ 2007 L 324

Decision No. 1482/2007/EC of the European Parliament and of the Council of 11 December 2007 establishing a Community programme to improve the operation of taxation systems in the internal market (Fiscalis 2013) and repealing Decision No. 2235/2002/EC, OJ 2007 L 330

Treaty of Lisbon amending the Treaty on European Union and the Treaty establishing the European Community, signed at Lisbon, 13 December 2007, OJ 2007 C 306

2008

Council directive 2008/9/EC of 12 February 2008 laying down detailed rules for the refund of value added tax, provided for in Directive 2006/112/EC, to taxable persons not established in the Member State of refund but established in another Member State, OJ 2008 L 44

8.3 NATIONAL LAWS AND OTHER SOURCES

8.3.1 Belgium

1958

Exposé des motifs, Convention entre la Belgique, le Grand-Duché de Luxembourg et les Pays-Bas, relative a l'assistance réciproque en matière de recouvrement de créances fiscales, du 5 septembre 1952, Instructions relatives à l'exécution de la Convention: v. circulaire du 27 août 1958, No. 19 (annexe I)

8.3.2 DENMARK

1963
Bekendtgørelse nr. 269 af 28 juni 1963 om inddrivelse af underholdsbidrag i henhold til konvention af 23 marts 1962 mellem Danmark, Finland, Island, Norge og Sverige, som ændret ved bekendtgørelse nr. 156 af 19 marts 2002 (Decree for the Faeroe Islands about the application of the Nordic convention regarding the enforcement of maintenance claims)

1984
Bekendtgørelse af Lov om rettens pleje i Grønland nr. 99 af 21 marts 1984, som ændret ved Lov nr. 476 af 12 juni 1996 (Decree for Greenland about the application of the Nordic convention regarding the enforcement of maintenance claims)

1986
Lovbekendtgørelse 1986-09-15 nr. 635 om anerkendelse og fuldbyrdelse af nordiske afgørelser om privatretlige krav og om ændring af retsplejeloven, som ændret ved L 1995-03-29 nr. 209 og L 1995-06-14 nr. 389 (Act including the recognition and the enforcement of nordic judgments in civil matters) and Ad lbkg 1986 nr. 635 (Royal decree)

8.3.3 FINLAND

1961
Tax enforcement Act of 1961

1977
Lag om erkännande och verkställighet av nordiska domar angående privaträttsligt anspråk 21.7 1977/588 (Act on the recognition and the enforcement of Nordic judgments in civil matters)

1995
Regeringens proposition 106/1995 Lag om ändring av utsökningslagen

1999
Lagutskottets utlåtande 14/1999 till riksdagen angående statsrådets redogörelse om verkställighet av häradsreformen

2006
Regeringens proposition 83/2006 till riksdagen med förslag till utsökningsbalk och lag om verkställighet av skatter och avgifter samt vissa lagar som har samband med dem (Government Bill with a proposal on a new Enforcement Code, law about the enforcement of taxes and charges and certain laws which have a connection to them)

2007
Utsökningsbalk (Enforcement Code), Nr. 705 in Finlands författningssamling

8.3.4 Luxemburg

1989
Règlement grand-ducal du 24 mars 1989 précisant le secret bancaire en matière fiscale et délimitant le droit d'investigation des administrations fiscales, Mémorial (OJ) 1989, pp. 181-182

8.3.5 Norway

1977
Lov om anerkjennelse og fullbyrding av nordiska dommer på privatrettens område av den 10 juni 1977 (Act on the recognition and the enforcement of Nordic judgments in civil matters)

8.3.6 Sweden

8.3.6.1 Legislation and Decrees

1963
Lag (1963:193) om samarbete med Danmark, Finland, Island och Norge ang. verkställighet av straff, m.m. (Act on the co-operation with Denmark, Finland, Iceland and Norway concerning the enforcement of punishment)

1970
Förmånsrättslagen (1970:979), (Act on priority rights)

1977
Lag (1977:595) om erkännande och verkställighet av nordiska domar på privaträttens område (Act on the recognition and the enforcement of Nordic judgments in civil matters)

Förordning (1977:1005) om nordisk verkställighet på privaträttens område (Government decree on the Nordic enforcement in civil matters)

1979
Bötesverkställighetslagen (1979:189), (Law on the enforcement of fines)

1981
Utsökningsbalk (1981:774), (Enforcement Code)

1990
Lag (1990:746) om betalningsföreläggande och handräckning (Act on the injunction to pay and assistance)

1991
Förordning (1991:171) om avtal mellan de nordiska länderna om handräckning i skatteärenden (Government decree on an agreement between the Nordic countries on assistance in tax matters)

1997
Förordning (1997:1157) om handräckning i skatteärenden mellan de nordiska länderna (Government decree on the administrative assistance in tax matters between the Nordic countries)

2007
Lagen (2007:324) om Skatteverkets hantering av vissa borgenärsuppgifter

8.3.6.2 Travaux Préparatoires

1962
Kungl. Maj:ts proposition nr 203 år 1962 (Travaux préparatoires to the Nordic agreement on the co-operation concerning the mutual assistance of enforcement of judgments or decisions on fines, confiscation or compensation for litigation costs of 1962)

1989/90
Prop. 1989/90:14 om godkännande av Europaråds- och OECD-konventionen om ömsesidig handräckning i skatteärenden, m.m. (Travaux préparatoires to the Council of Europe and OECD convention on mutual administrative assistance in tax matters)

8.3.6.3 Others

1999
Statistics for the years 1996-1999 from the Swedish national tax board on the enforcement of private and public claims with a foreign connection relating to the activities of the enforcement authorities (Statistik med kommentarer över antalet offentligrättsliga och privaträttsliga indrivningsärenden med utlandsanknytning som berör kronofogdemyndigheterna), Riksskatteverkets diary numbers; 4126-97/96, 10847-98/713, 8056-99/830 and 2069-00/830

2005
Communications on 13, 15, and 18 April 2005, and 18 December 2007, from the Registry of the ECJ to Skatteverket, the Swedish Tax Agency, diary number 130213266/05, on article 256 (ex. article 192) of the EC treaty for the verification of the authenticity of decisions of the Council or of the Commission

2006
Belopp i allmänna mål avseende utlandsindrivningen, studie från Skatteverket (Study from the Swedish Tax Agency about the amount related to public claims recovered abroad), diary number 148686-06/121

Meddelanden för exekutionsväsendet, MEX 2006:9, notis 9, Ansökan om konkurs i annan EU-stat för svenska skattefordringar (Information to the Enforcement Service, MEX 2006:9, notice 9, Application for bankruptcy in another State of the EU based on Swedish tax claims)

8.3.7 United Kingdom

1933
Foreign Judgments Reciprocal Enforcement Act 1933

1993
Recognition of Foreign Judgments Act of 1993

2000
Insolvency Act of 2000

2006
Act of Sederunt (Sheriff Court Bankruptcy Rules 1996) Amendment (UNCITRAL Model Law on Cross-Border Insolvency) 2006, Scottish Statutory Instrument 2006, No. 197

Act of Sederunt (Rules of the Court of Session Amendment No. 2) (UNCITRAL Model Law on Cross-Border Insolvency) 2006, Scottish Statutory Instrument 2006, No. 199

Act of Sederunt (Sheriff Court Company Insolvency Rules 1986) Amendment (UNCITRAL Model Law on Cross-Border Insolvency) 2006, Scottish Statutory Instrument 2006, No. 200

The Cross-Border Insolvency Regulations 2006, Statutory Instrument 2006, No. 1030. *Also see* website of the UK government, www.insolvency.gov.uk

8.3.8 United States of America

1962
Uniform Foreign Money-Judgments Recognition Act, drafted by the national conference of commissioners on uniform State laws and by it approved and recommended for enactment in all the States at its annual conference meeting in its seventy-first year, Monterey, California, July 30-August 4, 1962, with prefatory note and comments. Approved by the American Bar Association February 4, 1963

8.4 LITERATURE

This part includes official documents, often from the European Union, or from other international organizations, and other literature. Literature has been quoted either by a reference to the title of the document or to the author's name, supplemented with additional information on the title of the work. When an author, who is listed here, has made a partial contribution in a work, he is first quoted by a reference to the title of his contribution or article and then in addition by a reference to the title of the work, including the indicated pages therein. Some titles of work, which include contributions from several authors, and which have been published as editorial works (ed.), have been quoted by the first part of, or complete, title, or in abbreviated form, as sometimes indicated by the use here in brackets. Literature from several languages is listed following the English alphabet. Literature, which includes the letters Å, Ä and Ö, are listed under A respectively O.

A

Akehurst's Modern introduction to international law (Akehurst), 7 th rev. ed., Malanczuk, P., Routledge, London and New York 1997

ALI-UNIDROIT Principles of Transnational Civil Procedure, Text of the Principles and the accompanying commentary adopted by the American Law Institute (ALI) in May 2004 and by the International Institute for the Unification of Private Law (UNIDROIT) in April 2004, Unif. L. Rev. 2004-4

Allmeida Cruz, M. de/Desantes Real, M./Jenard, P., Report on the Convention on the accession of the Kingdom of Spain and the Portuguese Republic to the convention on jurisdiction and the enforcement of judgments in civil and commercial matters and to the Protocol on its interpretation by the Court of Justice, OJ 1990 C 189 (Allmeida Cruz/Desantes Real/Jenard report)

Almquist, Jan Eric, Svensk rättshistoria, I. Processrättens historia, Tredje reviderad upplagan, Kompendier utgivna av Juridiska Föreningen vid Stockholms Universitet, Juridiska Föreningens Förlag, Stockholm 1976

Amissah, Austin, Mutual co-operation in the enforcement of tax liabilities and the collection of taxes, including exchange of information. Ad Hoc Group of Experts on International Co-operation in Tax Matters, Fourth meeting, Geneva, 30 November-11 December 1987. Geneva, UN – United Nations, 1987, pp. 1-27

Andrews, Neil, Provisional and Protective Measures: Towards an Uniform Protective Order in Civil Matters, Uniform Law Review/Revue de droit uniforme 2001-4, Harmonising Transnational Civil Procedure: The ALI/UNIDROIT Principles and Rules/Vers une procédure civile transnationale harmonisée: Les Principes et Règles ALI/UNIDROIT, pp. 931-949

Anners, Erik, Den europeiska rättens historia, Några huvudlinjer, del 1 och del 2, Norstedts Förlag, Stockholm 1974 and 1980

Ansvarsgenombrott, Brocker, Stefan och Grapatin, Jan, Skrifter utgivna av institutet för bolags- och värdepappersrätt 5, 1 uppl., Juristförlaget, Norstedts Juridik AB, Stockholm 1996

Arnt Nielsen, Peter,

- Forhandlingerne om en global domskonvention, Retsvidenskabeligt Tidsskrift 2002, pp. 66-73
- International privat- og procesret, 1 uppl., Jurist- og økonomforbundets Forlag 1997

Att klaga till Europadomstolen, Palm, Elisabeth and Ericsson, Margaretha, Jure Förlag AB, Stockholm 2005

B

Backman, J. H., Handbok uti Twiste-, Utsöknings- och Rättegångsmål, Örebro 1863

Badr, G.M., State immunity; an analytical and prognostic view, Martinus Nijhoff publishers, the Hague 1984

Baker, Philip, The transnational enforcement of tax liabilities, British Tax Review, No. 5, 1993, pp. 313-318.

Barron's Law Dictionary, second edition, Steven H. Gifis, Barrons's Educational Series, Inc. New York 1984

Bayo Delgado, Joaquin, Persons involved in the execution of court decisions, The execution of court decisions in civil cases, pp. 15-22

Van den Berg, Albert Jan, The New York Arbitration Convention of 1958, Towards a Uniform Judicial Interpretation, T. M. C. Asser Institute – The Hague, Kluwer Law and Taxation Publishers, Deventer and Boston 1981, 1994 reprint

Berglund, Mikael,

- Presentation 'The abolishment of exequatur proceedings in court and a more efficient cross border enforcement of court decisions of freezing orders related to the Brussels I regulation', La Chambre Nationale des Avoués près les Courts d'Appel, le 30ème anniveraire de l'entreé en vigueur en 1975 du Nouveau Code de Procédure Civile, Paris le 23 juin 2005
- 'Access to information for enforcement and recovery purposes and international co-operation' of 28 May 2003, annexed to the Swedish national report on European transparency of assets to European community Study JAI/02/03/2002
- Hur är kronofogdemyndighetens arbetsuppgifter organiserade i några EU-stater och i Norge ?, Ny juridik, No. 4: 2000, pp. 51-68
- Luganokonventionen i ett verkställighetsperspektiv, SvJT 1995, pp. 481-496
- Presentation 'Costs, repayment and priority rights' for the Fiscalis seminar 2003 for mutual assistance for recovery of tax claims in the area of direct taxation, Alicante, Spain, 10-12 December 2003
- Presentation 'The enforcement of the judgment, Innovative practices as regards the enforcement of judgments, the Swedish example' at the Conference jointly organised by the European Commission and the Council of

Europe 'Towards an ideal trial: A few examples of the most successful judicial proceedings in Europe', Brussels, 18-20 November 2004
- Presentation 'Mutual co-operation for the exchange of information for enforcement purposes related to private and public claims or is a euro-enforcement information assistance system for the exchange of the information needed ?' at the seminar in Helsinki on 17-18 March 1997 about 'Possibilities for European enforcement' held by the Finnish Ministry of Justice
- Presentation 'The recovery of a contested claim, costs and repayments and priority rights' for the Fiscalis seminar 2002 for the mutual assistance of recovery of tax claims in Viterbo, Italy, 29-31 May 2002
- Les recherches et l'accès aux informations des agents chargés de l'exécution, Le droit processuel et le droit de l'exécution, pp. 288-290
- Svensk internationell exekutions- och obeståndsrätt, published by the National (Swedish) Tax Board (Riksskatteverket) 1997, Riksskatteverket 942
- La Transparence patrimoniale, pp. 61-62, 199-204, and annex, pp. 217-237 of a draft proposal on an 'International legal instrument on the mutual co-operation between European enforcement authorities in the European Union for the exchange of information for enforcement purposes related to private and public claims' (a Euro- Information Assistance System for the exchange of information regarding the enforcement of claims)

Bernasconi, Christophe, The internationalization of law in a universal area of justice, International conference of the UIHJ in Tunis, 9 May 2003, The Hague Conference on Private International Law: a lengthy but ongoing task of harmonization, pp. 7-14

Bernitz, Ulf, Sverige och Europarätten, Norstedts 2002

Bertaux, Jacques, Les dérives de l'exécution forcée: vers un régime d'exécution privé, Le droit processuel et le droit de l'exécution, pp. 279 and 283

Bible, Revised Standard Version, Oxford University Press, 1965

Bluestone, Stephen, L., Recognition and Enforcement of Foreign Country Money-Judgments in the United States, The Harmonization of Enforcement Procedures in an Area of Justice with No Boundary, pp. 189-193

Bogdan, Michael,

- The Nordic Bankruptcy Convention, Current Developments in International and Comparative Corporate Insolvency Law, Clarendon Press, Oxford 1994, pp. 701-708
- Något om exekutionsväsendet i England, USA och Belgien, Festskrift till P.O. Bolding 1992, pp. 35-48
- Några spörsmål avseende indrivning utanför Norden av svenska skattefordringar, Svensk skattetidning 1993, pp. 408-432
- Svensk internationell privat- och processrätt, 5 uppl., Norstedts 1999
- Sveriges och EU:s internationella insolvensrätt, 1 uppl., Norstedts 1997

– Uteslutning av offentlig rätt från Bryssel I-förordningens tillämpningsområde, Festskrift till Hans-Heinrich Vogel, pp. 47-59, Juristförlaget i Lund 2008

Bryant, Arthur, The Story of England, Makers of the Realm, Collins, London 1963

C

Charter of the Intra-European Organisation of Tax Administrations, annex 4 to the Resolution of the 9th General Assembly of IOTA

Chevallier, R.M., Methods and reasoning of the European court in its interpretation of community law, Common Market Law Review 1964, pp. 21-35

Civil Procedure in Europe 1, Seizure and Overindebtness in the European Union, de Leval, G. (ed.), Kluwer Law International 1997

Civil Procedure in Europe 2, Recourse against Judgments in the European Union, Jolowicz, J.A. and van Rhee, C.H. (ed.), Kluwer Law International 1999

Civil Procedure in Europe 3, Recognition and Enforcement of Foreign Judgments Outside the Scope of the Brussels and Lugano Conventions, Walter, G. and Baumgartner, P. (ed.), Kluwer Law International 2000

Commission of the European communities' proposal for a Council regulation on jurisdiction, applicable law, recognition and enforcement of decisions and cooperation in matters relating to maintenance obligations, COM (2005) 649 final

Commission of the European communities' proposal for a regulation of the European Parliament and of the Council creating a European order for payment procedure, COM (2004) 173 final/3

Commission of the European communities' proposal for a regulation of the European Parliament and of the Council laying down the procedure for implementing Regulation (EC) No. 883/2004 on the coordination of social security systems, COM (2006) 16 final

Commission's communication to the Council and the European Parliament 'towards greater efficiency in obtaining and enforcing judgments in the European Union', OJ 1998 C 33/03

Commission's communication, COM (1999) 183 final, Amended proposal for a European Parliament and Council Directive amending Council Directive 76/308/EEC on mutual assistance for the recovery of claims resulting from operations forming part of the system of financing the European Agricultural Guidance and Guarantee Fund, and of agricultural levies and customs duties and in respect of value added tax and certain excise duties, OJ 1999 C 179/07

Committee on Fiscal Affairs, approval of the draft OECD Council of Europe multilateral convention on mutual administrative assistance in tax matters, 31st Session held at the Château de la Muette, Paris on 9th-10th July, 1986, document CFA/M(86)2

Communication from the Commission to the Council and the European Parliament on measures to be taken to combat terrorism and other forms of serious crime, in particular to improve exchanges of information, Proposal for a Council decision on the exchange of information and cooperation concerning terrorist offences, COM (2004) 221 final

La contribution des institutions dans l'aménagement de l'espace de liberté, de sécurité et de justice, Actes du colloque international de Reims des 3 et 4 novembre 2005 (UIHJ), Sous la direction de Natalie Fricero et Jacques Isnard, Éditions juridiques et techniques, Paris 2006

Council of Europe Parliamentary Assembly recommendation 833 (1978) on co-operation between Council of Europe member States against international tax avoidance and evasion of 24 April 1978

Cross Border Debt Recovery, Lawyers International Inkasso och Norstedts 1996

Cross-border Insolvency, A Commentary on the UNCITRAL Model Law, Chan Hoo, Look (ed.), Globe Law & Business, Globe Business Publishing Ltd., London 2006

Cross-Border Insolvency, A guide to Recognition and Enforcement, Ian F. Fletcher (ed.), website of Insol International, www.insol.org/pub.htm

Cross-Border Insolvency Law, International Instruments and Commentary, Bob Wessels (ed.), Kluwer Law International BV, The Netherlands 2007

Cuniberti, Gilles, Les mesures conservatoires portant sur des biens situés à l'étranger, Bibliothèque de droit privé, tome 341, Libraire Générale de Droit et de Jurisprudance, Paris 2000

D

Danelius, Hans, Mänskliga rättigheter i europeisk praxis, En kommentar till Europakonventionen om de mänskliga rättigheterna, 3 uppl., Norstedts Juridik 2007

David, R., Arbitration in international trade, Kluwer Law and Taxation Publishers, Deventer/Netherlands 1985

Debt Recovery in Europe, Richardson, J. (ed.), KPMG Peat Marwick and Blackstone Press Limited, London 1993

Declareuil, J., Rome et L'Organisation du Droit, La renaissance du livre, Paris 1924

Desch, Eberhard, La Commission européenne pour l'efficacité de la justice: un modèle de cooperation avec les professionnels et un laboratoire de recherches pour l'Union européenne, La contribution des institutions dans l'aménagement de l'espace de liberté, de sécurité et de justice, pp. 85-89

Le droit processuel et le droit de l'exécution, Nouveaux droits dans un nouvel espace européen de justice (Le droit processuel et le droit de l'execution), Chambre nationale des huissiers de justice (France) et Union Internationale des Huissiers de Justice et Officiers Judiciaires (UIHJ), Colloque international des 4 et 5 juillet 2001, sous la direction du Jacques Isnard, Président de la UIHJ, et Professeur Jacques Normand

Due, Ole, EF-domstolens fortolkningsmetoder og Wienerkonventionen om traktatretten, Festskrift till Ulf Bernitz, Europarättslig Tidskrift, pp. 71-80, Stockholm 2001

Duffy, Eamon, Saints and Sinners – A History of the Popes, Yale University Press in association with S4C (Wales) 1997

E

The EC Regulation on insolvency proceedings: A Commentary and Annotated Guide, Moss, Gabriel, Fletcher, Ian, F., and Isaacs, Stuart (ed.), Oxford University Press 2002

L'efficacité de la justice civile en Europe, Caupain, M.-T. and de Leval, G. (ed.), De Boeck & Larcier s.a., Bruxelles 2000

Eek, H., Internationell privaträtt, 2 uppl., Norstedts 1967

Enforcement of Foreign Judgments, Garb, L. and Lew, J. (ed.), Kluwer Law International 1995

Enforcement of Foreign Judgments Worldwide, second edition, Platto, C. and Horton, W. G. (ed.), Graham & Trotman and International Bar Association, London 1993

English Law Dictionary, engelsk-svensk-engelsk (English-Swedish-English), P.H. Collin och Esselte Ordbok AB 1989

Eichenhofer, Eberhard, Final report Cross-border recovery of social security contributions in the context of Regulation (EEC) No. 1408/71 to the European commission, Friedrich-Schiller University, Jena 1998

EU Banking and Insurance Insolvency, Moss, Gabriel and Wessels, Bob (ed.), Oxford University Press 2006

Europarättens grunder, Tredje upplagan, Bernitz, Ulf and Kjellgren, Anders, Norstedts 2007

European community Study JAI/02/03/2002, Study No. JAI/A3/2002/02 on making more efficient the enforcement of judicial decisions within the European Union: Transparency of a Debtors assets, Attachment of bank accounts, Provisional Enforcement and Protective Measures, general reporter Hess, Burkhard. *Also see* website of the Commission of the European Union, http://europa.eu.int/comm/justice_home/doc_centre/civil/studies/doc_civil_studies_en.htm

European community Study JLS/C4/2005/03, Report on the Application of Regulation Brussels I in the Member States, presented by Prof. Dr. Burkhard Hess, Prof. Dr. Thomas Pfeiffer, and Prof. Dr. Peter Schlosser, Final version September 2007

European Corporate Insolvency, a practical Guide, Rajak, H., Horrocks, P. and Bannister, J. (ed.) second edition, Wiley & Sons Ltd., United Kingdom 1995

The European Insolvency Regulation: Law and Practice, Virgós, Miguel, and Garcimartín, Francisco, Kluwer Law International 2004

European Tax Law, Terra, Ben J. M. and Wattel, Peter J., Fourth edition, Kluwer Law International, the Hague 2005

Evrigenis, D.I./Kerameus, K.D., Report on the accession of the Hellenic Republic to the Community Convention on jurisdiction and the enforcement of judgments in civil and commercial matters, OJ 1986 C 298, (Evrigenis/Kerameus report)

The execution of court decisions in civil cases, Multilateral seminar organised by the council of Europe in conjunction with the Japan foundation, Strasbourg, Palais de l'Europe 15-17 October 1997, Council of Europe publishing 1998

Explanatory report on the Convention on Laundering, Search, Seizure and Confiscation of Proceeds from Crime, Council of Europe, Strasbourg 1995

Explanatory report on the Convention on Mutual Administrative Assistance in Tax Matters, Council of Europe and OECD, Strasbourg 1989. The commentary in this report is also available on the website of the Council of Europe, http://conventions.coe.int

F

Ferrand, Frédérique, The internationalization of law in a universal area of justice, International conference of the UIHJ in Tunis, 9 May 2003, The model of civil global procedure: the ALI-UNIDROIT project of Principles and Rules of cross-border civil procedure, pp. 37-49

Fletcher, I., Theory and Principle in Cross-Border Insolvency, Insolvency in Private International Law, Oxford Monographs in Private International Law, 1999

Fliniaux, A., La faillite des Ammanati de Pistoie et le Saint-Siège (début du XIV:e siècle), Revue historique de droit français et étranger 1924, pp. 436-472

Focus on International association of judicial officers, booklet from the UIHJ

Forsman, Ernst, Utsökningslag för storfurstendömet Finland och öfriga dermed sammanhängande författningar, Weilin & Göös'aktiebolags förlag, Helsingfors 1895

Fricero, Natalie, Le droit européenne à l'exécution des judgments, Droit et Procedures (La Revue des Huissiers de Justice) 2001, pp. 6-8

Fridén, Hugo, Beneficium vid löneexekution, Uppsala 1992

Friman, Håkan, Modellag om gränsöverskridande insolvensförfaranden, SvJT 1997, pp. 736-755

G

Garcia Prats, Francisco Alfredo, Mutual Assistance in Collection of Tax Debts, International Tax Review (Intertax), Vol. 30, February 2002, Kluwer/Luchterhand, pp. 56-78

Georges, Frédéric

- (and de Leval, Georges, La saisie-arrêt bancaire dans l'union européenne, L'efficacité de la justice civile en Europe, pp. 185-204
- La saisie de la monnaie scripturale, De Boeck & Larcier, Bruxelles 2006

Gest, Guy, La convention et l'action des autorités fiscales, International Trade Law and Practice, Vol. 17, No. 4, 1991, pp. 546-562 (The European Convention on Human Rights and tax enforcement. Proceedings of a seminar)

Giuliano, M./Lagarde, P., Report on the Convention on the law applicable to contractual obligations, OJ 1980 C 282 (Giuliano/Lagarde report)

Glosband, Dan and Proctor, Goodwin, UNCITRAL Model Law on Cross Border Insolvency and Proposed Chapter 15 of United States Bankruptcy Code, pp. 1-30, Practitioner's Guide to Cross-Border Insolvencies

Göransson, Ulf, Återvinning utom konkurs, Svenskt och rättsjämförande kring Actio Pauliana, Anfechtung och fraudulent conveyances, Norstedts 1989, Institutet för rättsvetenskaplig forskning CXXXVI

Grau Ruiz, Maria Amparo, Mutual Assistance for the Recovery of Tax Claims, Kluwer Law International 2003

Green paper on a European order for payment procedure and on measures to simplify and speed up small claims litigation, Commission of the European communities, COM (2002) 746 final

Green paper on improving the efficiency of the enforcement of judgments in the European Union: the attachment of bank accounts, COM (2006) 618 final

Green paper Effective enforcement of judgments in the European Union: Transparency of Debtors' assets, Commission of the European communities, Brussels, 6 March 2008, COM (2008) 128 final

Guide to enactment of the Uncitral Model Law on Cross-Border Insolvency. *Also see* website of Uncitral, www.uncitral.org

Guinot, Thierry, L'Huissier de Justice: normes et valeures, Ethique, déontologie, discipline et normes professionnelles, Éditions juridiques et techniques, Paris, 2004

H

Hagerup, Francis, Den norske civilproces, Tredje del, tredje udgave, under medvirkning av P. I. Paulsen, forlagt af H. Aschehoug & Co. (W. Nygaard), Kristiania 1919

Hague Conference on Private International Law: draft convention on jurisdiction and foreign judgments in civil and commercial matters, Preliminary Document No. 8 of March 2003 (corrected) from the preliminary result of the work of the informal working group on the judgment project for the attention of the Special Commission of April 2003 on General Affairs and Policy of the Conference

Hallin, Anders, Bakgrunden till några exekutionsrättsliga institut i 1734 års lag, uppsats Nr. 26, Juridiska fakulteten, Stockholms universitet 1974, pp. 1-44

The Harmonization of Enforcement Procedures in an Area of Justice with No Boundary, Annals of the Washington International Congress 26-28 April 2006, 19th Congress of the UIHJ, Éditions Juridiques et techniques, Paris, 2007

Harris, D. J., Cases and materials on international law, fourth ed., Sweet & Maxwell, London 1991

Hassler, Å., Minnesskrift ägnad 1734 års lag av jurister i Sverige och Finland den 13 december 1934, 200-årsdagen av riksens ständers beslut, del I, Utsökningslagen, pp. 341-368, Stockholm 1934

Hazard, Geoffrey, C., Fundamentals of Civil Procedure, Uniform Law Review/ Revue de droit uniforme 2001-4, Harmonising Transnational Civil Procedure:

The ALI/UNIDROIT Principles and Rules/Vers une procédure civile transnationale harmonisée: Les Principes et Règles ALI/UNIDROIT, pp. 753-762

Hess, Burkhard,

- European community Study JAI/02/03/2002, general reporter
- La Transparence patrimoniale, pp. 47-50

Hesslén, Nicola,

- Asset transparency – finding information – measures to make enforcement more effective, Globalisation of law in an area of universal justice/'Is the creation of a World Area of Justice a utopic vision ?', publication/work of the congress committee from the XVIII Congres of the UIHJ in Tunis on the 6-9 May 2003, pp. 28-31 and 41
- Kan verkställighet ske i USA av svenska domar och beslut ?, SvJT 2006, pp. 770-773

Hostiarii, Chambre Nationale des Huissiers de Justice and l'Union internationale des huissiers de justice et officiers judiciaires (ed.), Edition révisée et augmentée à l'occasion du cinquantenaire de l'Union internationale des huissiers de justice, 2e édition – décembre 2002, Éditions Juridiques et techniques, Paris, 2002

I

Insolvenzen in Europa, recht und praxis, Economica Verlag GmbH, Bonn, 1994

International Civil Procedure, Shelby R. Grubbs (ed.), Kluwer Law International 2003

International Execution Against Judgment Debtors, Campbell, Dennis, (ed.), Oceana Publications, Inc., Dobbs Ferry, New York 1999, Binders 1-3

The internationalization of law in a universal area of justice, International conference of the UIHJ in Tunis, 9 May 2003, Éditions juridiques et techniques, Paris 2004

International mutual assistance through exchange of information, Cahiers de droit fiscal international, XLIV Congrès International de Droit Financier et Fiscal Stockholm 1990, volume LXXVb, deuxième sujet, International Fiscal Association (I.F.A.), Kluwer Law and Taxation Publishers

International Tax Glossary, International Bureau of Fiscal Documentation, Amsterdam 1988

Introduction to the Law of the European Communities, Gormley, L., W. (ed.) in cooperation with Kapteyn, P., J. G., VerLoren van Themaat, P., Geelhoed, L. A. and Timmermans, C. W. A., Kluwer Law International 1998, third ed.

Ismer, Roland, and Sailer, Norbert, Der neue Art. 27 OECD-MA: Amtshilfe bei der Betribung und Sicherung von Steueransprüchen, Zeitschrift für europäische und internationale Steuer- und Wirtschaftsberatung, No. 18, 2003, Organ der Deutschen Vereinigung für Internationales Steuerrecht, International Fiscal Association, pp. 622-632

Isnard, Jacques, Rapport introductif, La contribution des institutions à l'aménagement de l'espace de liberté, de sécurité et de justice, La contribution des institutions dans l'aménagement de l'espace de liberté, de sécurité et de justice, pp. 9-25

J

Jacobsson, Ulla, Enforcement proceedings in Sweden, Revue Hellénique de Droit International, 2/1997, L'Institut hellénique de droit international et étranger, RHDI 50 (1997), pp. 483-520

Jenard, P., Report on the Convention on jurisdiction and the enforcement of judgments in civil and commercial matters, OJ 1979 C 59 (Jenard report)

Jenard, P./Möller, G., Report on the Convention on jurisdiction and the enforcement of judgments in civil and commercial matters done at Lugano on 16 September 1988, OJ 1990 C 189 (Jenard/Möller report)

Jeuland, Emmanuel, Les garanties de la saisie européenne de créances bancaires, Le droit processuel et le droit de l'exécution, pp. 395-406

Jirousek, Heinz, Der neue Vollstreckungsamtshilfeartikel im OECD-Munsterabkommen 2002, Steuer und Wirtschaft International. – Wien. – Vol. 12 (2002), no. 5, pp. 215-224

K

Källström, Nicola, Den exekutiva verksamheten i Frankrike, SvJT 1979, pp. 696-711

Karlgren, H., Kortfattad lärobok i internationell privat- och processrätt, 5 uppl., LiberLäromedel, Lund 1974

Kaser, Max, Römische Rechtsgeschichte, Vandenhoeck & Ruprecht, Göttingen 1950

Kaser/Knütel, Römisches Privatrecht, 18. Auflage, Verlag C. H. Beck, München 2005

Kennett, Wendy,

- Aperçus comparatifs des différents modes d'exécution forcée des obligations pécuniaires dans l'Union Européenne, Le droit processuel et le droit de l'exécution, p. 264
- The Enforcement of Judgments in Europe, Oxford monographs in private international law, Oxford University Press 2000
- Enforcement of judgments, European Review of Private Law 2, 1997, Kluwer Law International 1998, pp. 321-427
- Regulation of enforcement agents in Europe: a comparative survey, vol. 1 Text, vol. 2 Legislation and annexes, report in the Grotius program 2001

Kerameus, D., Konstantinos,

- Enforcement Against the State and State Entities in a Comparative Perspective, Recht in Europa, Festschrift für Hilmar Fenge zum 65. Geburtstag

am 28.10.1996, pp. 75-84, herausgegeben von Pelayia Yessiou-Faltsi, Fritz Jost, Athanassios Kaissis and Charoula Apalagaki, Verlag Dr. Kovač
– Enforcement in the International Context, Recueil des cours, collected courses of the Hague Academy of International Law, 1997, Tome 264 de la collection, pp. 179-410
– International encyclopedia of comparative law, volume XVI, Civil procedure, chapter 10, Enforcement proceedings, under the auspices of the international association of legal science, J. C. B. Mohr (Paul Siebeck)/ Tübingen/ and Martinus Nijhoff publishers/ Dortrecht/ Boston/ Lancaster 2002

Kommentar zum EU-/EG-Vertrag, von der Groeben, Hans/Thiesing, Jochen/ Ehlermann, Claus-Dieter (Hrsg.), 5. Aufl. Band 5, pp. 443-474, Nomos Verlagsgesellschaft, Baden-Baden 1997

Kottmann, Hermann, Die rechtliche Stellung des Gerichtsvollziehers, Würzburg 1900

Koulo, Risto, Enforcement in Finland, Revue Hellénique de Droit International, 2/ 1997, L'Institut hellénique de droit international et étranger, RHDI 50 (1997), pp. 537-571

Krings, Ernest, Synthèse, Le droit des saisies dans les États members de l'Union européenne, Civil Procedure in Europe 1, Seizure and Overindebtness in the European Union, pp. 3-46

Kutscher, H., Méthodes d'interprétation vues par un juge à la Cour, Rencontre judiciaire et universitaire 27-28 septembre 1976 à Luxembourg, pp. 5-45

L

Langhammer, Walter, Die rechtliche und soziale Stellung der Magistratus municipales und der Decuriones in der Übergangsphase der Städte von sich selbstverwaltenden Gemeinden zu Vollzugsorganen des spätantiken Zwangsstaates (2.-4. Jahrhundert der römischen Kaiserzeit), Steiner, Wiesbaden 1973

Law and Institutions of the European Communities, Lasok, D., & Bridge, J.-W., fourth edition, Butterworths 1987

Law of the European Convention on Human Rights, Harris, D.J., O'Boyle, M. and Warbrick, C., Butterworths, London, Dublin, Edinburgh 1995

Leach, Philip, Taking a Case to the European Court of Human Rights, second edition, Blackstone's Human Rights series, Oxford University Press 2005

Léger, Philippe, La Cour de justice des communautés européennes, pilier de la construction de l'espace de liberté, de sécurité et de justice ?, La contribution des institutions dans l'aménagement de l'espace de liberté, de sécurité et de justice, pp. 45-54

Lenzing, Katja, Les prochaines étapes dans l'aménagement de l'espace de liberté, de sécurité et de justice, La contribution des institutions dans l'aménagement de l'espace de liberté, de sécurité et de justice, pp. 193-200

Lemann Kristiansen, Bettina, Pantefogderne og deres retsanvendelse i retssociologisk belysning, Jurist- og økonomforbundets Forlag, København 2001

Leroy, Étienne,

- L'efficacité des procédures judiciaires au sein de l'union Européenne et les garanties des droits de la défense. Transparence patrimoniale, L'efficacité de la justice civile en Europe, pp. 273-402
- La Transparence patrimoniale, pp. 144-145

Lesage, Xavier, L'Huissier, L'Histoire de la fonction d'Huissier de Justice, Uitgeverij Pelckmans, Kappelen 1993

de Leval, Georges,

- (and Partsch, Philippe-Emmanuel) Civil Procedure in Europe 1, Le droit belge des saisies, pp. 131-187
- Civil Procedure in Europe 1, Une harmonisation des procédures d'exécution dans l'Union européenne est-elle concevable ?, pp. 595-626
- (and Georges, Frédéric) La saisie-arrêt bancaire dans l'union européenne, L'efficacité de la justice civile en Europe, pp. 185-204
- Subject of the proceedings, The execution of court decisions in civil cases, pp. 45-56

Lewis, C., State and diplomatic immunity, 3 ed., Lloyd's of London Press Ltd, Bodmin, Cornwall, 1990

Lindblom, Per-Henrik, Rättssfärernas harmoni, Om arbetet på en enhetlig europeisk processrätt, SvJT 1996, pp. 793-834

Lintott, Andrew, The Constitution of the Roman Republic, Clarendon Press, Oxford 1999

Lortie, Philippe, La Conférence de la Haye et l'Union européenne. Quels points communs ?, La contribution des institutions dans l'aménagement de l'espace de liberté, de sécurité et de justice, pp. 183-190

Lysén, G., State Responsibility and International Liability of States for Lawful Acts, Iustus förlag, Uppsala 1997

M

Macpherson, Roderick,

- La pratique des mesures conservatoires et provisoires en Angleterre, Pays de Galles et Ecosse, Le droit processuel et le droit de l'exécution, pp. 419-429
- Scotland: A shrinking espace de justice for the huissier, Globalisation of law in an area of universal justice/'Is the creation of a World Area of Justice a utopic vision ?', publication/work of the congress committee from the XVIII Congres of the UIHJ in Tunis on the 6-9 May 2003, pp. 76-145

Manual for the collection of a sum of money abroad, Briers, M. and Soulard, R., (ed.) international association of sheriff officers and judicial officers, Convention of Monacco, 25-27 May 1988, E. Story-Scientia, Bruxelles 1988

Mellqvist, Mikael,

- EU:s insolvensförordning, m.m., En kommentar, Norstedts Juridik AB, Stockholm 2002

– Gränsöverskridande konkurshantering – EU:s konvention om insolvensförfaranden, Ny Juridik 4/96, pp. 7-44

Menut, Bernard, For a World Code of Enforcement, The Harmonization of Enforcement Procedures in an Area of Justice with No Boundary, pp. 19-75 and 217-233 (Summary Report), Éditions juridiques et techniques, Paris 2007

Modéer, Kjell, Å., Optimala rättsliga kulturer ?, Om modernitet och kontinuitet i nationella och globala rättsliga kulturer, Juridisk Tidskrift Nr. 1 1999-2000, pp. 71-87

Model Convention on double taxation between developed and developing countries, United Nations, 1979, second version 2001

Model Tax Convention on Income and on Capital, OECD Committee on Fiscal Affaires, condensed version of January 2003

Montesquieu, Charles de Secondat de La Brède et de Montesquieu, De L'Esprit des Lois, Tome premier et Tome second, texte établi avec une introduction des notes et des variantes par Gonzague Truc, l'imprimerie André Tardy, numéro d'édition 496, Bourges 25 décembre 1956

Morse, Melissa, Enforcement methods available in England and Wales, The execution of court decisions in civil cases, pp. 85-95

Moss, Gabriel, The Impact of the EU Regulation on UK Insolvency Proceedings, INSOL International Insolvency Review, pp. 139-152, John Wiley & Sons, Ltd. 2002

Les moyens modernes de transmission des actes judiciares et extrajudiciares en Europe, Colloque international de Paris les 21 et 22 octobre 1999, Chambre nationale des huissiers de justice (France), avec le soutien de la Commission européenne au titre du programme Grotius

Munch-Petersen, Erwin, Konkurssurrogater, En retssammenlignende undersøgelse, Nyt Nordisk Forlag København 1932

Munch-Petersen, H., Den danske Retspleje, Tredje del, Den borgerlige retspleje, andet hovedafsnit: Tvangsfuldbyrdelse og foreløbige retsmidler, G. E. C. Gads Forlag, København 1924

N

Nehrman-Ehrenstråle, David, Inledning til then Swenska Processum Civilem, efter Sweriges Rikes Äldre och Nyare Stadgar, tryck hos Ludwig Decreaux, Kongl. Carolinska Academiens Boktryckare, Lund 1732

Nerep, Erik, Extraterritorial Control of Competition under International Law, With Special Regard to United States Antitrust Law, Norstedts 1983

Nordiskt samarbete om indrivningsfrågor (Nordic co-operation in recovery matters), report to the Nordic Council of Ministers of July 2002, TemaNord 2002:549

Nordstoga, Olav, Lensmenn i 800 år, Jubileumsbok Norges Lensmannslag 1893-1993, Utgitt av Norges Lensmannslag i samarbeid med Justisdepartementet, Leseselskapet AS, Oslo 1992

Norstedts dansk-svenska ordbok, tredje upplagan, 1980
Norstedts latinsk-svenska ordbok, andra upplagan, Stockholm 2001
Norstedts norsk-svenska ordbok, första upplagan, Stockholm and Oslo 1992
Norstedts uppslagsbok, illustrerad encylopedi i ett band, P.A. Norstedt & Söners Förlag/Stockholm 1942
Nouveau Petit Larousse illustré, Dictionnaire encyclopédique, publié sous la direction de Claude Augé et Paul Augé, Librairie Larousse, Paris 1948
Nuβbaum, Arthur, Die Zwangsverfteigerung und Zwangsverwaltung, Tübingen 1916

O

OECD Manual on the Implementation of Assistance in Tax collection, Article 27 and Commentary of the OECD Model Tax Convention on Income and on Capital, approved by the OECD Committee on Fiscal Affairs on 26 January 2007-09-06, unclassified, Centre for Tax Policy and Administration, Organisation for Economic Co-operation and Development
Oppenheim's international law (Oppenheim), 9 th ed., Jennings, R. and Watts, A., (ed.), Vol. I, introduction and part 1 and part 2 to 4, Longman Group UK Limited 1992
Ordbok över svenska språket, åttonde bandet, utgiven av svenska akademien, A.-B. P.H. Lindstedts univ.- bokhandel, Lund 1925
Ordlista för exekutionsväsendet på engelska, franska och tyska, Svensk-Engelsk, Engelsk-Svensk, Svensk-Fransk, Fransk-Svensk, Svensk-Tysk, Tysk-Svensk, (Wordlist for the Enforcement Service in English, French and German, Swedish-English, English-Swedish, Swedish-French, French-Swedish, Swedish-German, German-Swedish) Berglund, M., Hesslén, N., Häggman, B., published by the National (Swedish) Tax Board (Riksskatteverket) 1994, Riksskatteverket 903
Oxford Latin Dictionary, Oxford at the Clarendon Press 1968

P

Pålsson, Lennart,

- Brysselkonventionen, Luganokonventionen och Bryssel I-förordningen, Norstedts 2002
- Interim Relief under the Brussels and Lugano Conventions, Liber Amicorum Kurt Siehr, Private Law in the International Arena, From National Conflict Rules Towards Harmonization and Unification, Basedow, J., Meier, I., Schnyder, A., Einhorn, T., Girsberger, D. (ed.), Asser Press, the Netherlands 2000, pp. 621-638
- Romkonventionen – tillämplig lag för avtalsförpliktelser, Norstedts 1998

Partsch, Philippe-Emmanuel, (and de Leval, Georges), Civil Procedure in Europe 1, Le droit belge des saisies, pp. 131-187
Personligt ansvar vid likvidationsplikt, olovlig vinstutdelning, företrädaransvar, m.m., Löfgren, Kent och Kornfeld, Martin, Norstedts 1998

Practical Handbook on the Operation of the Hague Service Convention, Permanent Bureau of the Hague Conference on Private International Law, Wilson & Lafleur Ltée, Montreal 2006

Practitioner's Guide to Cross-Border Insolvencies, Arnason, Jon Yard and Fletcher, Ian M. (ed.), Oceana Publications, Inc., Dobbs Terry, NY 2003

Presidency note, document 5910/00 of the Council of the European Union of 3 February 2000 on the subject of Mutual assistance for the recovery of claims

Prevention of organised crime: The registration of legal persons and their directors and the international exchange of information, a comparative legal study in the EU Member States on the possibilities for the improvement of the international exchange of information on legal persons with the purpose of (transnational) organised crime prevention, Final Report of the Follow-Up Study, T.M.C Asser Instituut Commissioned by the Netherlands Ministry of Justice, December 2006

Principles of European Insolvency law, Law of Business and Finance, Volume 4, W.W. McBryde, A. Flessner and S.C.J.J. Kortmann (ed.), Kluwer Legal Publishers, the Netherlands 2003

R

Rapport om näringsförbudens efterlevnad, Rapport 2004:2, Ekobrottsmyndigheten (Swedish National Economic Crimes Bureau)

Rapprochement du Droit Judiciaire de l'Union européenne/Approximation of Judiciary Law in the European Union, Storme, Marcel (ed.), published by Seminarie voor Privaatrechtelijk Procesrecht at the University of Ghent, Kluwer/ Martinus Nijhoff Publishers 1994

Report from the Commission to the Council and the European Parliament on the use of the provisions on mutual assistance for the recovery of claims relating to certain levies, duties, taxes and other measures, COM (2006) 43 final

Report on European judicial systems – Edition 2006 (2004 data), European Commission for the Efficiency of Justice, Council of Europe, 15 September 2006. *Also see* website of the European Commission for the Efficiency of Justice (CEPEJ), www.coe.int/cepej

Report on the Convention on Insolvency proceedings, Virgós, Miguel and Schmit, Etienne, (Virgós-Schmit Report on the Convention on Insolvency proceedings), *see* www.iiiglobal.org/country/european_union/virgos_schmidt.pdf

Rump Christensen, Gerda, Is the system of civil enforcement up-to date ? Trends of developments and review in Danmark, Revue Hellénique de Droit International, 2/1997, L'Institut hellénique de droit international et étranger, RHDI 50 (1997), pp. 521-536

S

Schlosser, Peter,

- Recent Developments in Transit-border Insolvency, Saggi, Conferenze e Seminari 35, Centro di studi e ricerche di diritto comparato e straniero, Roma 1999

– Report on the Convention on the Association of the Kingdom of Denmark, Ireland and the United Kingdom of Great Britain and Northern Ireland to the Convention on jurisdiction and the enforcement of judgments in civil and commercial matters and to the Protocol on its interpretation by the Court of Justice, OJ 1979 C 59 (Schlosser report)

Schöberl, Elisabeth, L'espace de liberté, de sécurité et de justice, facteur d'harmonisation du droit processuel interne (droit processuel et droit de l'execution en matière civile), La contribution des institutions dans l'aménagement de l'espace de liberté, de sécurité et de justice, pp. 73-82

Schrevelius, Fredrik, Lärobok i Sveriges allmänna nu gällande Civil-Process, Berlings Förlag, Lund 1853

Schwebel, S. M., May Preparatory Work be Used to Correct Rather than Confirm the 'Clear' Meaning of a Treaty Provision ?, SvJT 1997, pp. 797-804

Sevastik, P., The binding force of treaties under international law, Iustus förlag, Uppsala 1997

'Si L'Union m'était contée...', Ouvrage édité à l'occasion du Cinquantième anniversaire de L'Union Internationale des Huissiers de Justice et Officiers Judiciaires (1952-2002), Paris décembre 2002, booklet from the UIHJ

Sinclair, Ian, The Vienna Convention on the Law of Treaties, second edition, Manchester University Press 1984

Sjögren, Wilhelm, Bidrag till Den svenska exekutivprocessens historia, Tidsskrift for Retsvidenskab 1901, pp. 1-43

Sjöholm, Sten, Några glimtar ur exekutionsväsendets historia, published in Riksskatteverkets Info 6/85 and Riksskatteverket 909, utg. 1. *Also see* website of the Kronofogdemyndigheten (Swedish Enforcement authority), www.kronofogden.se, under headline Historik, Några glimtar ur exekutionsväsendets historia

SKUNORD, Nordiskt arbetsseminarium i skuldsaneringsfrågor (Nordic working seminar concerning debt relief), report to the Nordic Council of Ministers of 2 March 2000, TemaNord 2000:529

Spann, Michael, Der Haftungszugriff auf den Schuldner zwischen Personal- und Vermögensvollstreckungen, Eine exemplarische Untersuchung der geschichtlichen Rechtsquellen ausgehend vom Römischen Recht bis in das 21. Jahrhundert unter besonderer Berücksichtigung bayerischer Quellen, Augsburger Schriften zur Rechtsgeschichte, Band 1, Herausgegeben von Dr. Christoph Becker, Universitätsprofessor in Augsburg, Münster 2004

Spinelli, Jean-Paul, Les différent conventions internationales et la signification des actes à l'étranger, Les guides de l'Huissier de Justice 001, Paris 1999

Statutes of the international union of judicial officers (UIHJ), as amended in May 2003

Statut et fonctions de l'Huissier de Justice en droit compare, Union Internationale des Huissiers de Justice et Officiers Judiciaires, XIVème Congrès International des 15-17 Mai 1991 à Bruxelles, sous la direction du Luc Claes, Huissier de Justice à Bruxelles et Jean-Pierre Faget, Huissier de Justice à Paris

Stemann, Chr. L. E., Den danske Retshistorie indtil Christian V.'s Lov, Forlagt af den Gyldendalske Bokhandel, København 1871

Stora Focus, Band 5-8 and 10, Esselte Focus uppslagsböcker AB, Stockholm 1988

Storme, Marcel,

- Procedural Law and the Reform of Justice: from Regional to Universal Harmonisation, Uniform Law Review/Revue de droit uniforme 2001-4, Harmonising Transnational Civil Procedure: The ALI/UNIDROIT Principles and Rules/Vers une procédure civile transnationale harmonisée: Les Principes et Règles ALI/UNIDROIT, pp. 763-777
- Rapprochement du Droit Judiciaire de l'Union européenne/Approximation of Judiciary Law in the European Union, the general introductory report

Strahl, Ivar, Makt och rätt, Rättsidéns gång genom historien, Från Babylonien till FN, En överblick, 8 uppl., Bonniers – Aldusserien, Stockholm 1979

Strömholm, Stig,

- Användning av utländskt material i juridiska monografier. Några anteckningar och förslag, SvJT 1971, pp. 251-263
- Inledning och urval: Om lagarnas anda eller det förhållande som bör råda mellan lagarna och respektive styrelses författning, seder, klimat, religion, handel, etc: vartill författaren fogat nya forskningar över de romerska successionslagarna, de franska lagarna och feodallagarna, andra upplagan, City University Press, Ratio klassiker, Stockholm 1998

Sucharitkul, S., State immunities and trading activities in international law, Stevens & sons limited, London 1959

Suetonius, Kejsarbibliografier, översättning från latinet (*De vita Caesarum*, translation from Latin to Swedish), med inledande kommentarer av Ingemar Lagerström, Wallin & Dalholm Boktryckeri AB, Lund 2001

Swedish Bankruptcy Act (1987:672), official translation to English, Ds 1998:41

Swedish Enforcement Code (2001: 337), official translation to English, Ds 2002:45

Svensk ordbok 1, A-M, utarbetad vid Språkdata Göteborgs universitet 1990, Språkdata och Esselte Ordbok AB

T

Tamm, Ditlev, Romersk rätt och europeisk rättsutveckling, andra upplagan, Nerenius & Santérius Förlag, Stockholm 1996, translation from the Danish original title Romersk ret og europeisk retsudvikling to Swedish by Claes Peterson

Tarzia, Giuseppe,

- Aussichten für eine Harmonisierung des Zwangsvollstreckungsrechts in der Europäischen Union, Zeitschrift für Europeisches Privatrecht, Vol. 4, pp. 231-242, München 1996

- Vers un concept européene du droit de l'exécution ?, Le droit processuel et le droit de l'exécution, p. 165

Tax Administration in OECD and Selected Non-OECD Countries: Comparative Information Series (2006), the Forum on Tax Administration, Centre for tax policy and administration, October 2006

Tax Treaties concluded by European Countries, International Bureau of Fiscal Documentation, Amsterdam 1963-1998

Théry, Philippe,

- Civil Procedure in Europe 1, Le droit français de l'execution, pp. 264-265
- Droit de l'exécution: France, Actualités du droit, Revue de la Faculté de droit de l'Université de Liège 1995, pp. 627-687

Thomashausen, André, Legal cooperation among unequal associates: cross-border law enforcement in the countries of the SADC, The internationalization of law in a universal area of justice, pp. 97-119

Traité théorique et pratique de Procédure civile et commerciale en justice de paix et devant les conseils de prud'hommes, par E. Garsonnet et Ch. Cézar-Bru, Tome IV, troisième partie, Voies D'Exécution, Volume I, Saisies mobilières – Saisie immobilière, Paris 1913, et Tome V, troisième partie, Voies D'Exécution, Volume II, Saisie immobilière Ordre et Contribution, Paris 1914

La Transparence patrimoniale, Condition nécessaire et insuffisante du titre conservatoire européen ?, Union Internationale des Huissiers de Justice et Officiers Judiciaires (UIHJ), Séminaire d'experts des 14 et 15 octobre 1999, sous la direction du Professeur Alain Verbeke et de Maitre Marie-Thérèse Caupain avec le soutien de la Commission européenne au titre du programme Grotius

U

UIHJ Europe, booklet from the UIHJ, Mars 2008

Uniform Law Review/Revue de droit uniforme 2001-4, Harmonising Transnational Civil Procedure: The ALI/UNIDROIT Principles and Rules/Vers une procédure civile transnationale harmonisée: Les Principes et Règles ALI/UNIDROIT, NS – Vol. VI, UNIDROIT, Kluwer Law International

Un titre exécutoire européen, Les Dossiers du Journal des tribunaux 53, van Drooghenbroeck, Jean- François, and Brijs, Stan, Larcier, Bruxelles 2006

Utmätning, Kronofogden, KFM 901 utgåva 5, Stockholm 2008

V

Verbeke, Alain,

- Execution Officers as a Balance Wheel in Insolvency Cases, Tilburg Foreign Law Review 2001, volume 9 Nr. 1, pp. 8-18
- Quel Huissier de Justice pour l'Europe ?, Le droit processuel et le droit de l'exécution, pp. 309-313

Vertragstreue und Erfüllungszwang in der mittelalterlichen Rechtswissenschaft, Rechts- und Staatswissenschaftliche Veröffentlichungen der Görres-Gesellschaft. Neue Folge, Band 73, Tilman Repgen, Herausgegeben von Alexander Hollerbach, Hans Maier, Paul Mikat, Ferdinand Schöningh, Paderborn 1994

Vogenauer, Stefan and Weatherill, Stephan, The European Community's competence for a comprehensive harmonisation of contract law – an empirical analysis, European Law Review, December 2005, pp. 821-837

W

Wahl, Nils, The Lugano Convention and Legal Integration, Juridiska fakulteten i Stockholm, skriftserien nr 29, Juristförlaget 1990

Walker, David, Le Statut de L'Huissier de Justice (Sheriff officer) en Écosse, L'efficacité de la justice civile en Europe, pp. 263-264

Walter, Gerhard and Baumgartner, Samuel P., General Report: The Recognition and Enforcement of Foreign Judgments Outside the Scope of the Brussels and Lugano Conventions, Civil Procedure in Europe 3, Recognition and Enforcement of Foreign Judgments Outside the Scope of the Brussels and Lugano Conventions, pp. 1-45

Welamson, Lars, Konkursrätt, Norstedt & Söner, Stockholm 1961

Wessén, Elias, Våra ord, deras uttal och ursprung, kortfattad etymologisk ordbok, Nämnden för svensk språkvård, andra, tillökade upplagan, Läromedelsförlagen, språkförlaget, Stockholm 1973

Westbrook, J. L., Global Insolvencies in a World of Nation States, Current Issues in Insolvency Law, Stevens & Sons, London 1991

Wingren, Claes, PM (memorandum) 1990-11-09 ang. det norska exekutionsväsendet, Riksskatteverkets diarie nr 5096-99/1112

Wood, P., Principles of International Insolvency, Law and Practice of International Finance, Sweet & Maxwell, London 1995

Wrede, R. A., Finlands gällande civilprocessrätt, tredje bandet, Utsökningsväsendet, andra upplagan, Söderström & C:o Förlagsaktiebolag, Helsingfors 1936

Y

Yessiou Faltsi, Pelayia, Le droit de l'exécution selon la cour Européenne des droits de l'homme: analyse et prospective, Le droit processuel et le droit de l'exécution, pp. 195-237

Z

Das Zivil-Prozessrecht der Kulturstaaten, Band III, Der Zivilprozess Oesterreichs, von Franz Klein mit Ergänzungen von Friedrich Engel, J. Bensheimer Verlag, Mannheim/Berlin/Leipzig 1927

8.5 TABLE OF COURT CASES

The following listed rulings of the ECHR and the ECJ are here only briefly described as reported upon in this work. Readers, who would like to have complementary information concerning a ruling, may consult the here indicated references, which follow the structure of the Contents.

8.5.1 EUROPEAN COURT OF HUMAN RIGHTS (ECHR)

1993

Funke v. France of 25 February — 1.1.1.7, 4.3.1

(Article 6, 1 was violated in a matter of a suspected violation of currency regulations, where the authorities attempted to compel the applicant himself to provide documents about his assets abroad to be used as evidence of the offences he had allegedly committed. This could not justify such an infringement of the right of anyone 'charged with a criminal offence', to remain silent and not to contribute to incriminating himself)

1994

Bendenoun v. France of 26 January — 4.3.2

(Article 6, 1 was in principle applicable in a matter relating to French tax penalties, but that there had been no violation of it because there were no infringement of the rights of the defense or the principle of equality of arms)

Silva Pontes v. Portugal of 23 March — 4.3.1

(Article 6, 1 was applicable in relation to damages, which the plaintiffs suffered after an accident and that was determined in an enforcement proceeding. The total of proceedings lasted for more than 11 years)

1995

Scollo v. Italy of 28 September — 4.3.1

(Article 1 of Protocol No. 1 and article 6, 1 were violated in a matter, which related to a procedure for the eviction of a tenant from an apartment and lasted over 11 years before it was settled)

1996

Di Pede v. Italy of 26 September — 4.3.1

(Article 6, 1 was violated in a matter, which related to the enforcement proceedings initiated in court on the basis of a judgment about the demolish of a building erected in violation of the statutory provisions on minimum distances from the boundaries of adjacent properties, the remove of four trees for the same reasons, the restoration of the site to its previous state, and the payment of damages, and lasted more than 18 years)

Zappia v. Italy of 26 September 4.3.1
(Article 6, 1 was violated in a matter, which related to the enforcement proceedings initiated for damages for breach of a contract of sale of a flat under construction, and lasted more than 23 years)

1997

Hornsby v. Greece of 19 March 4.3.1, 7.2.3.5
(Article 6, 1 was applicable and was violated in a matter, which related to the refraining of the enforcing of a judgment for more than five years. The execution of a judgment given by any court must be regarded as an integral part of the 'trial' and the refraining for more than five years from taking the necessary measures to comply with a final, enforceable judicial decision deprived this article of all useful effect)

A.P., M.P. and T.P. v. Switzerland of 29 August 4.3.2
(Article 6, 2 was applicable and had been violated due to the imposition of Swiss criminal sanction on heirs for tax evasion by a deceased person because it was contrary to the presumption of innocence to impose criminal sanctions on the living in respect of acts committed by a deceased person.)

1998

J.J. v. Netherlands of 27 March 4.3.2
(Article 6, 1 was applicable and had been violated in a matter relating to an appeal against Dutch tax penalties, which was declared inadmissible on sole ground that court registration fee not had been paid, because the plaintiff in taxation proceedings in Supreme Court was unable to reply to advisory opinion of advocate-general)

Estima Jorge v. Portugal of 21 April 4.3.1
(Article 6,1 was applicable and had been infringed in an enforcement proceeding, which lasted 13 years, and related to a notarial deed providing security for a specific debt)

2001

Platakou v. Greece of 11 January 4.3.1
(Article 6,1 was violated in a matter concerning proceedings following the expropriation of property in relation to an error in the service of court documents by court bailiffs)

Pellegrini v. Italy of 20 July — 4.3
(Article 6,1 was violated in a matter concerning of a divorce judgment, where the Italian courts breached their duty of satisfying themselves, before authorising enforcement of the Roman Rota's judgment, that the applicant had had a fair trial in the proceedings under Canon law)

2002

Burdov v. Russia of 7 May — 1.1.1.5, 4.3.1
(Article 6,1 and article 1 of the Protocol No. 1 were violated in a matter of the enforcement of an awarded penalty in compensation to the applicant following the Chernobyl nuclear plant disaster. A claim can constitute a possession if it is sufficiently established to be enforceable)

Vasiliopoulou v. Greece of 21 June — 1.1.1.5, 4.3.1
(Article 6, 1 and article 1 of Protocol No. 1 of the Convention were violated in a matter related to the refusal of the State to fulfil its obligation to pay the additional pension as specified in a judgment)

Göktan v. France of 2 July — 4.3
(Article 1 of Protocol No. 4 to the convention was found not to be applicable on imprisonment for failing to pay French customs fines on the basis that it prohibits imprisonment for debt solely when the debt arises under a contractual obligation)

Janosevic v. Sweden of 23 July — 4.3.1-2
(Article 6, 1 was applicable and had been violated in a matter relating to a request for a stay of execution for the enforcement of Swedish taxes and tax penalties because the tax authority failed to act with the urgency required by the circumstances of the case and thereby unduly delayed a court determination of the main issues concerning the imposition of additional taxes and tax surcharges in a situation when the enforcement measures taken against the applicant called for a prompt examination of his appeal, and as a consequence the applicant, in respect of the length of the proceedings, did not have effective access to the courts)

Västberga Taxi Aktiebolag and Vulic v. Sweden of 23 July — 4.3.1
(Compare the principally similar case of *Janosevic v. Sweden*)

2003

Timofeyev v. Russia of 23 October (Article 6, 1 and article 1 of the Protocol No. 1 were violated in a matter of the enforcement of compensation to the applicant from the Russian State for confiscation of property. The judgment of compensation remained unenforced for almost three years) 1.1.1.5, 4.3.1

2004

Silvester's Horeca Service v. Belgium of 4 March 4.3.2
(Article 6, 1 was applicable and had been violated in a matter relating to an appeal against Belgium tax penalties, because the applicant did not have access to a tribunal in the sense of this article of the convention)

Wasserman v. Russia of 18 November
(Article 6,1, and article 1 of Protocol No. 1 were violated concerning the non-enforcement of a judgment debt in the favour of the creditor. Also compare the second judgment in the case of *Wasserman v. Russia* of 10 April 2008) 4.3.1

2005

Matheus v. France of 31 March 4.3.1
(Article 6, 1 was violated because of the non-execution of a judgment, rendered in 1988, for the eviction of a tenant in French Guadeloupe. In addition, the protection of property in article 1 of the Protocol No. 1 to the convention was violated)

2006

Apostol v. Georgia of 28 November 4.3.1
(Article 6, 1 was violated in a matter, which related to the non-enforcement of a judgment after that the applicant had applied to the Ministry of Justice requesting the initiation of enforcement proceedings, based on his judgment against the debtor, and after having been informed by this Ministry that he was to bear the 'preliminary expenses associated with enforcement measures', without specifying which measures were foreseen and what their costs were)

2007

Viktor Konovalov v. Russia of 24 May 4.3.1
(Article 1 of Protocol No. 1 was violated because it did not meet the requirement of 'lawfulness'. The bailiff had disregarded the legal requirements applicable to the procedure for enforcement of the custom's decision and

sale of the applicant's property through the failure to inform the applicant about the opening of the proceedings affecting his possessions and to ensure his effective participation)

Wagner et J.M.W.L. v. Luxembourg of 28 June 4.3
(Articles 6, 8 and 14 were violated in relation to an adoption judgment from Peru)

2008

Wasserman v. Russia of 10 April 4.3.1
(Articles 6,1, 13, and article 1 of Protocol No. 1 were violated in a matter of the continued non-enforcement of the same national judgment as was subject to the ruling of the ECHR in its first case of *Wasserman v. Russia* of 18 November 2004)

Sukhorukov v. Russia of 31 July 4.3.1
(Articles 6, 1, 13, and article 1 of Protocol No. 1 were violated where the non-enforcement of a judgment against a local welfare authority for a delayed payment of social benefits has lasted for over nine years. Where a judgment is against the State, even if most of the delay was attributed by the Government to the applicant's failure to follow the changing procedure of enforcement, a person may not be expected to bring separate enforcement procedures)

8.5.2 European Court of Justice (ECJ)

1976

Jozef de Wolf v. Harry Cox BV. of 30 November 6.1.1.1.1
(Article 31 of the Brussels convention. The provisions of the convention prevent a party who has obtained a judgment in his favour in a Contracting State, being a judgment for which an order for enforcement under the convention may be issued in another Contracting State, from making an application to a court in that other State for a judgment against the other party in the same terms as the judgment delivered in the first State)

LTU Lufttransportunternehmen GmbH & Co. KG v. Eurocontrol of 14 October 5.2.1.1.1
(Article 1 of the Brussels convention. The decisive factor for the determination of if a claim should be included,

or excluded, under the scope of application of claims covered by the convention is not its formal origin from whatever court or tribunal, but the underlying nature of the original claim)

1977

Bavaria Fluggesellschaft Schwabe & Co. Kg and Germanair Bedarfsluftfahrt GmbH & Co. Kg v. Eurocontrol of 14 July 5.3.1.1.1

(Article 56 of the Brussels convention. The Brussels convention does not prevent a bilateral agreement, such as the German-Belgian convention, from continuing to have effect in relation to judgments which do not fall under the second paragraph of article 1 of the Brussels convention, but to which nevertheless that convention does not apply)

Industrial Diamond Supplies v. Luigi Riva of 22 November 6.1.1.3.1

(Articles 30 and 38 of the Brussels convention. The expression 'ordinary appeal' shall be determined by an autonomous interpretation of the convention. Any appeal which may result in the annulment or the amendment of the judgment which is the subject matter of the procedure for recognition and enforcement under the convention and the lodging of which is bound, in the State in which the judgment was given, to a period which is laid down by the law and starts to run by virtue of the same judgment constitutes an 'ordinary appeal' which has been lodged, or may be lodged against a foreign judgment)

1978

Somafer SA v. Saar-Ferngas AG. of 22 November 1.4.1

(Article 5, 5 of the Brussels convention. An autonomous interpretation of the ECJ of the words 'Branch' and 'Agency' within the meaning of this article of the Convention because of the need to ensure legal certainty and equality of rights and obligations for the parties as regards the power to derogate from the general jurisdiction of article 2, which requires an independent interpretation, common to all Contracting States, of the concepts in this article of the Convention)

1979

Henri Gourdain v. Franz Nadler of 22 February 5.2.1.1.1

(Article 1 of the Brussels convention. A decision such as that of a French civil court ordering the de facto manager of a legal person to pay a certain sum into the assets of a company must be considered as given in the context of bankruptcy, proceedings relating to the winding-up of insolvent companies, or other legal persons, or analogous proceedings, and is therefore excluded from the scope of the convention)

1980

Louise de Cavel v. Jacques de Cavel of 6 March 6.1.1.1.1.1
(Articles 1 and 24 of the Brussels convention. The convention is applicable, on the one hand, to the enforcement of an interlocutory order made by a French court in divorce proceedings whereby one of the parties to the proceedings is awarded a monthly maintenance allowance and, on the other hand, to an interim compensation payment, payable monthly, awarded to one of the parties by a French divorce judgment)

Bernard Denilauler v. SNC Couchet Frères of 21 May 6.1.1.1.1.1
Title III of the Brussels convention. Orders made by a court in proceedings *ex parte* on provisional and protective measures are not recognized under the convention)

1981

Peter Klomps v. Karl Michel of 16 June 6.1.1.1.1.1
(Article 27, 2 of the Brussels convention. Service in sufficient time of the document, which instituted the proceedings)

1984

Calzaturificio Brennero sas v. Wendel GmbH Schuhproduktion International of 27 November 6.1.1.3.1
(Article 38 of the Brussels convention. A court with which an appeal has been lodged against a decision authorizing enforcement may make enforcement conditional on the provision of security only when it gives judgment on the appeal)

1985

Leon Emile Gaston Carlos Debaecker and Berthe Plouvier v. Cornelis Gerrit Bouwman of 11 June 6.1.1.1.1.1
(Article 27, 2 of the Brussels convention. In examining whether service was effected in sufficient time, the court in which enforcement is sought may take account of exceptional circumstances which arose

after service was duly effected. The fact that the plaintiff was apprised of the defendant's new address, after service was effected, and the fact that the defendant was responsible for the failure of the duly served document to reach him are matters which the court in which enforcement is sought may take into account in assessing whether service was effected in sufficient time)

Deutsche Genossenschaftsbank v. S A Brasserie du Pêcheur of 2 July 5.2.1.1.1
(Article 50 of the Brussels convention. Confirmation of the enforceability under the convention of an instrument attested by a German notary)

P. Cappelloni et F. Aquilini v. J. C. J. Pelkmans of 3 October 1985 6.1.1.1.1.1
(Article 39 of the Brussels convention. A party, who has applied for and obtained authorization for enforcement may, within the period mentioned in article 39, proceed directly with protective measures against the property of the party against whom enforcement is sought and is under no obligation to obtain specific authorization until the expiry of the period prescribed in article 36 for lodging an appeal and, if such an appeal is lodged, until a decision is given thereon. A party, who has proceeded with the protective measures referred to in article 39 is under no obligation to obtain, in respect of those measures, any confirmation required by the national law of the court in question)

1988

Horst Ludwig Martin Hoffmann v. Adelheid Krieg of 4 February 6.1
(Article 26 of the Brussels convention. A foreign judgment, which has been recognized by virtue of the Brussels convention, as the convention 'seeks to facilitate as far as possible the free movement of judgments, and should be interpreted in this spirit', must in principle have the same effects in the State in which enforcement is sought as it does in the State in which judgment was given)

1990

Mario P. A. Reichert and others v. Dresdner Bank of 10 January 6.2.1.1

(Article 16, 1 of the Brussels convention. A donation of immovable property was challanged by a creditor in a French court on the basis of French law, under which creditors may challange in their own name transactions entered into by debtors in fraud of their rights by a procedure known as an action paulienne. Such an action does not come within the scope of the Brussels convention)

Isabelle Lancray SA v. Peters und Sickert KG of 3 July 6.1.1.1.1.1
(Article 27, 2 of the Brussels convention. A judgment given in default of appearance may not be recognized where the document instituting the proceedings was not served on the defendant in due form, even though it was served in sufficient time to enable him to arrange for his defence, and the curing of defective service are governed by the law of the State in which judgment was given, including any relevant international agreement)

1991

Marc Rich & Co. AG v. Società Italiana Impianti PA. of 25 July 5.2.1.1.1
(Article 1, 4 of the Brussels convention. The exclusion in the Brussels convention of arbitration also extends to litigation proceedings before a national court concerning the appointment of an arbitrator, even if the existence or validity of an arbitration agreement is a preliminary issue in that litigation)

Andrea Francovich and Danila Bonifaci and others v. Italian Republic of 19 November 7.1
(Italian State failed to implement the Council Directive (80/987/EEC) of 20 October 1980 on the approximation of the laws of the Member States relating to the protection of employees in the event of the insolvency of their employer, and was required to make good loss and damages caused to individuals by failure to transpose this directive)

1992

Mario Reichert, Hans-Heinz Reichert and Ingeborg Kockler v. Dresdner Bank AG. of 26 March 6.1.1.1.1.1, 6.2.1.1
(Articles 5, 3, 16, 5, and 24 of the Brussels convention. An action provided for by national law, such as the action paulienne in French law, whereby a creditor seeks to

obtain the revocation in regard to him of a transfer of rights in rem in immovable property by his debtor in a way which the creditor regards as being in fraud of his rights does not come within the scope of the convention)

1993

Volker Sonntag v. Hans Weidmann, Elisabeth Weidmann and Stefan Weidmann of 21 April 5.2.1.1.1

(Article 1 of the Brussels convention. The decisive factor for the determination of if a claim should be included, or excluded, under the scope of application of claims covered by the convention is not its formal origin from whatever court or tribunal, but the underlying nature of the original claim)

1994

Mund & Fester v. Hatrex Internationaal Transport of 10 February 1.1.1.1.2, 6.1

(Article 7 of the EC Treaty, read in conjunction with article 220 of the Brussels convention, precludes a national provision of civil procedure which, in the case of a judgment to be enforced within the national territory, authorizes seizure only on the ground that it is probable that enforcement will otherwise be made impossible, or substantially more difficult, but, in the case of a judgment to be enforced in another Member State, authorizes seizure simply on the ground that enforcement is to take place abroad)

Halliburton Services BV v. Staatssecretaris van Financiën of 12 April 5.2.2.1

(Taxes on real estate transfers were considered to fall within the scope of Council Directive 77/799, to which reference is made to by the Recovery directive)

Solo Kleinmotoren GmbH v. Emilio Boch of 2 June 5.2.1.1.1

(Article 27 of the Brussels convention. The convention precludes treating a court settlement as a judgment given by a court, or tribunal, because in order to be a 'judgment' for the purposes of the Convention the decision must emanate from a judicial body of a Contracting State deciding on its own authority on the issues between the parties. This condition is not fulfilled in the case of a settlement, even if it was reached in a court of a Contracting State and brings legal proceedings to an end, and settlements in court are essentially contractual in that their terms depend first and foremost on the parties' intention)

1995

Société d'Informatique Service Réalisation Organisation v. Ampersand Software BV. of 11 August 6.1.1.3.1
(Articles 37, 2 and 38, first paragraph, of the Brussels convention. A decision of a court in the enforcing Member State for the authorization to enforce an enforceable judgment of another Member State under the convention can not be contested by an appeal, which is limited to the examination of points of law, and this court does not have jurisdiction to impose a stay of the proceedings)

1998

Lease Plan Luxembourg SA v. Belgian State of 7 May 1.1.1.1.2, 5.2.2.1
(Article 9, 1 and 2 e of the Sixth VAT Directive. The application of more advantageous conditions for the calculation of interest in internal situations, compared to cross border situations, constitutes discrimination)

Bent Jensen and Korn- og Foderstofkompagniet A/S v. Landbrugsministeriet of 19 May 6.2.2.1.1.3
(Conditions for set-off of amounts paid under community law, related to Council regulation 1765/92 establishing a support system for producers of certain arable crops, against debts payable to a Member State)

Van Uden Maritime BV, trading as Van Uden Africa Line v. Kommanditgesellschaft in Firma Deco-Line and Another of 17 November 6.1.1.1.1.1
(Articles 5, 1 and 24 of the Brussels convention concerning an application for interim relief relating to the payment of debts arising under a contract containing an arbitration clause. Even if arbitration is excluded under the scope of application of the Brussels convention, provisional measures are possible, under the conditions that a measure ordering interim payment of a contractual consideration does not measure unless, first, repayment to the defendant of the sum awarded is guaranteed if the plaintiff is unsuccessful as regards the substance of his claim and, second, the measure sought relates only to specific assets of the defendant located, or to be located, within the confines of the territorial jurisdiction of the court to which application is made)

1999

Hans-Hermann Mietz v. Intership Yachting Sneek BV. of 27 April 6.1.1.1.1.1

(Article 24 of the Brussels convention, related to proceedings before a German court with a view to securing an order in Germany for the enforcement of a judgment delivered in the Netherlands following adversarial interim proceedings. Provisional measures are possible, under the conditions that a measure ordering interim payment of a contractual consideration does not measure unless, first, repayment to the defendant of the sum awarded is guaranteed if the plaintiff is unsuccessful as regards the substance of his claim and, second, the measure sought relates only to specific assets of the defendant located, or to be located, within the confines of the territorial jurisdiction of the court to which application is made)

Eric Coursier v. Fortis Bank and Martine Coursier, née Bellami, of 29 April 6.1

(Article 31 of the Brussels Convention. The term 'enforceable' in its first paragraph is to be interpreted as referring solely to the enforceability, in formal terms, of foreign decisions and not to the circumstances in which such decisions may be executed in the State of origin. The Brussels Convention is intended to facilitate the free movement of judgments by establishing a simple and rapid procedure in the Contracting State, where enforcement of a foreign decision is applied for, and that the enforcement procedure constitutes an autonomous and complete system. It is the court of the State in which enforcement is sought, in appeal proceedings brought under article 36 of the Brussels Convention, to determine, in accordance with its domestic law, including the rules of private international law, the legal effects of a decision given in the State of origin in relation to a court-supervised liquidation)

Unibank A/S v. Flemming G. Christensen of 17 June 5.2.1.1.1

(Article 50 of the Brussels convention. An acknowledgment of indebtedness enforceable under the law of the State of origin, whose authenticity has not been established by a public authority, or other authority empowered for that purpose, does not constitute an authentic instrument within the meaning of the Brussels convention. Since instruments drawn up between private parties are not inherently authentic, the involvement of a public authority, or any other authority empowered for that purpose by the State of origin, is needed in order to endow them with the character of authentic instruments)

2000

Dieter Krombach v. André Bamberski of 28 March — 1.4.1, 6.1.1.1.1.1
(Article 27, 1 of the Brussels convention. Recourse to the public-policy clause must be regarded as being possible in exceptional cases where the guarantees laid down in the legislation of the State of origin and in the Convention itself have been insufficient to protect the defendant from a manifest breach of his right to defend himself before the court of origin, the right to a fair hearing, as recognized by the European Convention on Human Rights)

Régie nationale des usines Renault SA v. Maxicar SpA and Orazio Formento of 11 May — 6.1.1.1.1.1
(Article 27, 1 of the Brussels convention. A judgment of a Contracting State recognising the existence of an intellectual property right in body parts for cars, and conferring on the holder of that right protection by enabling him to prevent third parties trading in another Contracting State from manufacturing, selling, transporting, importing or exporting in that Contracting State such body parts, can not be considered to be contrary to public policy)

2001

Commission v. France of 15 February — 5.2.2.1
(Claims of a taxation nature do not fall under the Council regulation 1408/71/EEC on the application of social security schemes to employed persons and their families moving within the Community)

2002

Italian Leather SpA v. WECO Polstermöbel GmbH & Co. of 6 June — 6.1.1.1.1.1
(Article 27, 3 of the Brussels convention. A foreign decision on interim measures ordering an obligor not to carry out certain acts is irreconcilable with a

decision on interim measures refusing to grant such an order in a dispute between the same parties in the State where recognition is sought. The court of the State in which recognition is sought is then required to refuse to recognise the foreign judgment)

Roquette Frères SA v. Directeur général de la concurrence, de la consommation et de la repression des frauds of 22 October — 1.4.1
(Article 14 of Regulation No. 17 of the Council of 6 February 1962, related to competition law). An example of when the ECJ has paid attention to the European Convention on Human Rights)

Gemeente Steenbergen v. Luc Baten of 14 November 2002 — 5.2.1.1.1
(Article 1 of the Brussels convention. An action under a right of recourse under national legislation providing for payment of allowances by way of social assistance should be included under the Brussels convention to the extent it is governed by ordinary law in regard to maintenance obligations and not by law, which confers on the public body a prerogative of its own)

2003

Préservatrice foncière TIARD SA v. Staat der Nederlanden of 15 May — 5.2.1.1.1, 5.4.2.1
(Article 1 of the Brussels convention. An action based on a guarantee contract, entered into in order to satisfy a condition imposed by the State on associations of carriers, as principal debtors, for the payment of customs duties, between the State and an insurance company, falls under the scope of application of the convention)

2004

Freistaat Bayern v. Jan Blijdenstein of 15 January — 5.2.1.1.1
(An action for the recovery brought by a public body subrogated to the rights of the maintenance creditor should be excluded under the Brussels convention)

Heikki Antero Pusa v. Osuuspankkien Keskinäinen Vakuutusyhtiö of 29 April — 7.2.1
(Article 18 of the EC Treaty means that the right of free movement of citizens in principle precludes an enforcing member State from not taking into account tax payments from a resident in another member State

at the computation of a free amount, or beneficium, at the attachment of a pension received in that first State)

Commission v. Council of 29 April 2.6.1
(Articles 93 and 94 of EC Treaty constitute a correct legal basis for the adoption of Council Directive 2001/44/EC of 15 June 2001 amending Directive 76/308/EEC on mutual assistance for the recovery of claims resulting from operations forming part of the system of financing the European Agricultural Guidance and Guarantee Fund, and of agricultural levies and customs duties and in respect of value added tax and certain excise duties)

Greece v. Nikolaos Tsapalos and Konstantinos Diamantakos of 1 July 1.1.1, 5.3.2.1
(Recovery directive constitutes procedural law and takes retrospective effect)

2006

Susanne Staubitz-Schreiber of 17 January 6.4.1
(Article 3, 1 of the Insolvency regulation must be interpreted as meaning that the court of the Member State within the territory of which the centre of the debtor's main interest is situated at the time when the debtor lodges the request to open insolvency proceedings retains jurisdiction to open those proceedings if the debtor moves the centre of his main interests to the territory of another Member State after lodging the request but before the proceedings are opened)

Plumex v. Young Sports NV of 9 February 6.1.1.1.1.1
(Articles 4-11 and 14 of the Old service of legal documents' regulation does not establish any hierarchy between the method of transmission and service and, consequently, it is possible to serve a document by one or both of those methods. In order to determine vis-à-vis the person on whom service is effected, the point from which time starts to run for the purposes of a procedural time-limit linked to effective service, reference must be made to the date of the first service validly effected)

Eurofood IFSC Ltd. of 2 May (Articles 3, 1 and 16, 1, and 26 of the Insolvency regulation. Matters of competent jurisdiction, based on the interpretation of the Insolvency regulation, in some particular circumstances, for the bankruptcy of a subsidiary company situated on Ireland, while the parent company was found in Italy)	6.4.1
Commissioners of Customs & Excise and Attorney General v. Federation of Technological Industries and Others of 11 May (Article 21, 3 of the Sixth VAT-directive. A taxable person, to whom a supply of goods or services has been made and who knew, or had reasonable grounds to suspect, that some or all of the value added tax payable in respect of that supply, or of any previous or subsequent supply, would go unpaid, may be made jointly and severally liable, with the person who is liable, for payment of that tax)	5.4.2.2.2
Banca popolare di Cremona Soc. coop. arl v. Agenzia Entrate Ufficio Cremona of 3 October (Article 33, 1 of the Sixth VAT-directive. The levy of an Italian regional tax on productive activities was not subject to the prohibition in the directive for Member States to impose other turnover taxes than VAT based on the four essential features of VAT)	5.2.2.1
ASML Netherlands BV v. Semiconductor Industry Services GmbH of 14 December (Article 34, 2 of the Brussels I regulation about the service of a judgment, and an example of when the ECJ has paid attention to the European Convention on Human Rights)	1.4.1, 6.1.1.1.1.1
2008	
Ingenieurbüro Michael Weiss und Partner GbR v. Industri- und Handelskammer Berlin and Nicholas Grimshaw & Partners Ltd of 8 May (Article 8, 1 of the Old service of legal documents' regulation about the refusal to accept a document. The consequences when the annexes to the documents served are not translated)	6.1.1.1.1.1

8.6 WEBSITES

- La Confédération suisse, Federal Office of Justice, http://www.bj.admin.ch/bj/en/home.html
- Council of Europe, www.coe.int and http://conventions.coe.int
- European Business Register, www.ebr.org
- European Commission for the Efficiency of Justice (CEPEJ), www.coe.int/cepej
- European Court of Human Rights, www.echr.coe.int
- European Judicial Atlas in Civil Matters, http://ec.europa.eu/civiljustice
- European Judicial Network in civil and commercial matters, http://ec.europa.eu/civiljustice
- European Land Information Service, www.eulis.org
- European Parliament, www.europarl.eu.int
- Eurostat, http://ec.europa.eu/eurostat
- Eurolex, http://eur-lex.europa.eu
- Hague Conference on Private International Law, www.hcch.net
- Intra-European Organisation of Tax Administrations, www.iota-tax.org
- Kronofogdemyndigheten, www.kronofogden.se
- Nordic Council of Ministers, www.norden.org
- Notaires de France, www.notaires.fr
- Society of Messengers-at Arms and Sheriff Officers, www.smaso.org
- UK government, www.insolvency.gov.uk
- UNIDROIT, www.unidroit.org
- Unión Internacional del Notariado Latino, www.uinl.org
- Union Internationale des Huissiers de Justice et Officiers Judiciaires, http://www.uihj.com
- United Nations Commission on International Trade Law, www.uncitral.org

Annexes

ANNEX 1

Overview of some subjects in the Recovery directive and in the Implementing recovery directive

Recovery directive	*Implementing recovery directive*
Preamble Objectives of the directive **Art 1** Appellation of the directive **Art 2** Scope of claims **Art 3** Definitions of certain claims **Art 4** Requests for information **Art 5** Requests for service of documents **Art 6** Application of national law to recovery **Art 7** Prerequisites for an application of recovery **Art 8** Recognition and enforcement **Art 9** Currency, extension of time for payment and authorization of payment by installment **Art 10** Priority rights **Art 11** Requested authority's duty to inform the applicant authority **Art 12** Recovery of a contested claim **Art 13** Precautionary measures **Art 14** Reasons of refusal of recovery in the requested State	**Preamble** Reasons for implementation **Art 1** Stipulation of detailed rules for the implementation **Art 2** Definitions of transmission 'by electronic means' and the 'CCN/CSI' network **Art 3-8** Requests for information **Art 9-11** Requests for service of documents **Art 12-20** Requests for recovery or for precautionary measures **Art 21-24** Transmission of communications **Art 25-26** Eligibility and refusal of requests for assistance **Art 27-28** Reimbursement arrangements **Art 29-34** Final provisions

Recovery directive	*Implementing recovery directive*
Art 15 Periods of limitation **Art 16** Restrictions on the requested authority to further communicate information **Art 17** Translation **Art 18** Costs resulting from mutual assistance **Art 19** List of authorities authorized to make or receive requests for assistance **Art 20-21** Recovery Committee **Art 22** Procedure of adoption of implementing certain detailed rules **Art 23** Relationship to international agreements **Art 24-26** Final provisions, entry into force, national implementation, addressees (Member States), duties to report statistics and results	

ANNEX 2

Details on the entry into force and on certain reservations in relation to the States which are parties to the Convention on the recognition and enforcement of foreign arbitral awards of 10 June 1958

The New York convention has entered into force in relation to the following States indicated bellow. The moment of entry into force and certain reservations made are indicated after each State. The mutual reservation is indicated below as (1) and the commercial reservation as (2). If none of those reservations have been made it is indicated below as (-). The readers are for further detailed information on declarations and reservations referred to consult the depositary of the convention, the United Nations.

Afghanistan 2005-02-28 (1-2), Albania 2001-09-25 (-), Algeria 1989-05-08 (1-2), Antigua and Barbuda 1989-05-03 (1-2), Argentina 1989-06-12 (1-2), Armenia 1998-03-29 (1-2), Australia 1975-06-24 (-), Austria 1961-07-31 (-), Azerbaijan 2000-05-29 (-), Bahamas 2007-03-20 (-), Bahrain 1988-07-05 (1-2), Bangladesh 1992-08-04 (-), Barbados 1993-06-14 (1-2), Belarus 1961-02-13 (1), Belgium 1975-11-16 (1), Benin 1974-08-14 (-), Bolivia 1995-07-27 (-), Bosnia and

Herzegovina 1992-03-06 (1-2), Botswana 1972-03-19 (1-2), Brazil 2002-09-05 (-), Brunei Darussalam 1996-10-23 (1), Bulgaria 1962-01-08 (1), Burkina Faso 1987-06-21 (-), Cambodia 1960-04-04 (-), Cameroon 1988-05-19 (-), Canada 1986-08-10, Central African Republic 1963-01-13 (1-2), Chile 1975-12-03 (-), China 1987-04-22 (1-2), Colombia 1979-12-24 (-), Costa Rica 1988-01-24 (-), Côte d'Ivoire 1991-05-02 (-), Croatia 1991-10-08 (-), Cuba 1975-03-30 (1-2), Cyprus 1981-03-29 (1-2), Czech Republic 1993-01-01 (-), Denmark 1973-03-22 (1-2), Djibouti 1977-06-27 (1-2), Dominica 1989-01-26 (-), Dominican Republic 2002-07-10 (-), Ecuador 1962-04-03 (1-2), Egypt 1959-06-07 (1), El Salvador 1998-03-27 (-), Estonia 1993-11-28 (-), Finland 1962-04-19 (-), France 1959-09-24 (1), Gabon 2007-03-15 (-), Georgia 1994-08-31 (-), Germany 1961-09-28 (1), Ghana 1968-07-08 (-), Greece 1962-10-14 (1-2), Guatemala 1984-06-19 (1-2), Guinea 1991-04-23 (-), Haiti 1984-03-04 (-), Holy See 1975-08-12 (1-2), Honduras 2001-01-01 (-), Hungary 1962-06-03 (1-2), Iceland 2002-04-24 (-), India 1960-10-11 (1-2), Indonesia 1982-01-05 (1-2), Iran 2002-01-13 (1-2), Ireland 1981-08-10 (1), Israel 1959-06-07 (-), Italy 1969-05-01 (-), Jamaica 2002-10-08 (1-2), Japan 1961-09-18 (1), Jordan 1980-02-13 (-), Kazakhstan 1996-02-18 (-), Kenya 1989-05-11 (1), Korea, republic of 1973-05-09 (1-2), Kuwait 1978-07-27 (1), Kyrgyzstan 1997-03-18 (-), Laos 1998-09-15 (-), Latvia 1992-07-13 (-), Lebanon 1998-11-09 (1), Lesotho 1989-09-11 (-), Liberia 2005-12-15 (-), Lithuania 1995-06-12, Luxemburg 1983-12-08 (1), Macedonia 1992-11-20 (-), Madagascar 1962-10-14 (1-2), Malaysia 1986-02-03 (1-2), Mali 1994-12-07, Malta 2000-09-20 (1), Marshall Islands 2007-03-21 (-), Mauritania 1997-04-30 (-), Mauritius 1996-09-17 (1-2), Mexico 1971-07-13 (-), Moldova 1998-12-17 (1), Monaco 1982-08-31 (1-2), Mongolia 1995-01-22 (1-2), Montenegro 2006-06-03 (1-2), Morocco 1959-06-07 (1), Mozambique 1998-09-09 (1), Nepal 1998-06-02 (1-2), the Netherlands 1964-07-23 (1), New Zealand 1983-04-06 (1), Nicaragua 2003-12-23 (-), Niger 1965-01-12 (-), Nigeria 1970-06-15 (1-2), Norway 1961-06-12 (1), Oman 1999-05-26 (-), Panama 1985-01-08 (-), Paraguay 1998-01-06 (-), Peru 1988-10-05 (-), Philippines 1967-10-04 (1-2), Poland 1962-01-01 (1-2), Portugal 1995-01-16 (1), Qatar 2003-03-30 (-), Romania 1961-12-12 (1-2), Russian Federation 1960-11-22 (1), Saint Vincent and the Grenadines 2000-12-11 (1-2), San Marino 1979-08-15 (-), Saudi Arabia 1994-07-18 (1), Senegal 1995-01-15 (-), Serbia 1992-04-27 (1-2), Singapore 1986-11-19 (1), Slovakia 1993-01-01 (-), Slovenia 1992-06-25 (-), South Africa 1976-08-01 (-), Spain 1977-08-10 (-), Sri Lanka 1962-07-08 (-), Sweden 1972-04-27 (-), Switzerland 1965-08-30 (-), Syrian Arab Republic 1959-06-07 (-), Tanzania 1965-01-11 (1), Thailand 1960-03-20 (-), Trinidad and Tobago 1966-05-15 (1-2), Tunisia 1967-10-15 (1-2), Turkey 1992-07-02 (1-2), Uganda 1992-05-12 (1), Ukraine 1961-01-08 (1), United Arab Emirates 2006-11-19 (-), United Kingdom of Great Britain and Northern Ireland 1975-12-23 (1), United States of America 1970-12-29 (1-2), Uruguay 1983-06-28 (-), Uzbekistan 1996-05-07 (-), Venezuela 1995-05-09 (-), Viet Nam 1995-12-11 (1-2), Zambia 2002-06-12 (-), Yugoslavia 1982-05-27 (1-2) and Zimbabwe 1994-12-28 (-).

ANNEX 3

Agreement between the Nordic countries on mutual administrative assistance in tax matters of 7 December 1989, translation[1]

Agreement between the Nordic countries on mutual administrative assistance in tax matters

The Government of Denmark together with the governing bodies of the Faeroe Islands and Greenland, as well as the Governments of Finland, Iceland, Norway and Sweden, which desire to enter into an agreement for mutual administrative assistance in tax matters, which confirm that matters comprised by this agreement concerning the Faeroe Islands and Greenland and their relationship to foreign countries are matters in the area of the autonomy of the Faeroe Islands and Greenland, have agreed as follows:

General provisions

Article 1

The Contracting States undertake to provide assistance to each other in tax matters in accordance with this Agreement with respect to:

a) the service of documents,
b) the investigation in tax matters, such as the procurement of tax returns, or other information and the exchange of information without special request, or upon a request in a specific matter,
c) the procurement of tax return forms, or other tax forms,
d) the measures to avoid the imposition of preliminary tax withheld in more than one Contracting State,
e) the collection of tax,
f) the transfer of tax, and
g) the recovery of tax and the securing of payment of tax claims.

Article 2

1. The present taxes on which this Agreement shall be applicable are:

a) in Denmark

1) the national income tax (inkomstskatten till staten),
2) the municipal income tax (den kommunala inkomsskatten),

---

1. Non-official translation by Mikael Berglund from Swedish of the Agreement between the Nordic countries for mutual administrative assistance in tax matters, annexed to lag (1990:226) om handräckning i skatteärenden mellan de nordiska länderna (Act on the administrative assistance in tax matters between the Nordic countries).

3) the county income tax (den amtskommunala inkomstskatten),
4) the special income tax (den särskilda inkomsskatten),
5) the church tax (kyrkoskatten),
6) the tax on dividends (utdelningsskatten),
7) the interest tax (ränteskatten),
8) the tax on royalties (royaltyskatten),
9) the tax imposed under the Hydrocarbon Tax Act (skatterna enligt kolväteskattelagen),
10) the national wealth tax (förmögenhetsskatten till staten), and
11) the seamen's tax (sjömansskatten)

b) on the Faeroe Islands

1) the tax to the regional treasury (skatten till landskassan),
2) the municipal tax (skatten till kommunerna),
3) the church tax (kyrkoskatten),
4) the tax on dividends (utdelningsskatten), and
5) the tax on royalties (royaltyskatten)

c) in Greenland

1) the regional tax (landsskatten),
2) the special regional tax (den särskilda landsskatten),
3) the municipal tax (kommunskatten),
4) the tax on dividends (utdelningsskatten),
5) the common municipal tax (den gemensamma kommunala skatten), and
6) the tax imposed under the Hydrocarbon Tax Act (skatterna enligt kolväteskattelagen)

d) in Finland

1) the national income and wealth tax (den statliga inkomst- och förmögenhetsskatten),
2) the municipal tax (kommunalskatten),
3) the church tax (kyrkoskatten), and
4) the tax at source (källskatten)

e) on Iceland

1) the national income tax (den statliga inkomstskatten),
2) the municipal tax (den kommunala inkomstskatten), and
3) the national wealth tax (den statliga förmögenhetsskatten)

f) in Norway

1) the national income and wealth tax (inkomst- och förmögenhetsskatten till staten),
2) the municipal income and wealth tax (inkomst- och förmögenhetsskatten till kommunerna),
3) the shire income tax (inkomstskatten till fylkena),

4) the common tax to the tax distribution fund (den gemensamma skatten till skattefördelningsfonden),
5) the tax imposed under the Petroleum Tax Act (skatterna enligt petroleumskattelagen)
6) the duty to the State on honoraria to foreign artists (avgiften till staten på ersättningar till utländska artister), and
7) the seaman's tax (sjömansskatten)

g) in Sweden

1) the national income tax, including seaman's tax and withholding tax on dividends (den statliga inkomstskatten, däri inbegripet sjömansskatten och kupongskatten),
2) the licensing fee on certain public performances (bevillningsavgiften för vissa offentliga föreställningar),
3) the compensation tax (ersättningsskatten),
4) the distribution tax (utskiftningsskatten),
5) the profit-sharing tax (vinstdelningsskatten),
6) the municipal income tax (den kommunala inkomstskatten), and
7) the national wealth tax (den statliga förmögenhetsskatten)

h) in all Contracting States

1) the inheritance and gift taxes,
2) the motor vehicle taxes, to the extent indicated in the Agreement in accordance with Article 20,
3) the value added tax and other general turnover taxes, to the extent indicated in the Agreement in accordance with Article 20, and
4) the excise duties, to the extent indicated in the Agreement in accordance with Article 20, and
5) the social insurance duties and other public fees, to the extent indicated in the Agreement in accordance with Article 20.

2. Payments in advance of such tax, and duty as included under subsections a)-g) of paragraph 1, are to be equaled to taxes.
3. The Agreement shall also apply to any identical substantially similar taxes which are imposed after the date of the signing of the Agreement, in addition to, or in place of the present existing taxes.

Article 3

Unless the context otherwise requires, the following terms of this Agreement shall at their application have these meanings:

a) the term 'Contracting State' shall mean Denmark, Finland, Iceland, Norway and Sweden, and the term also covers the autonomous regions of Greenland and the Faeroe Islands within the Kingdom of Denmark.

b) the term 'competent authority' means:
   1) in Denmark, the Ministry of taxes,
   2) on the Faeroe Islands, the Faeroe's Council of Taxation,
   3) in Greenland, the Directorate of Taxation,
   4) in Finland, the Ministry of Finance,
   5) on Iceland, the Ministry of Finance,
   6) in Norway, the Ministry of Finance and Customs,
   7) in Sweden, the Ministry of Finance,
   or the authority in each of these Contracting States to which any of the above named
   authorities has empowered in their place to handle issues concerning this Agreement,
c) 'Nordic Double Taxation Agreement' means the Agreement on 12 September 1989 between the Nordic countries for the avoidance of double taxation with respect to taxes on income and capital and the Agreement of 12 September 1989 between Denmark, Finland, Iceland, Norway and Sweden for the avoidance of double taxation with respect to taxes on inheritance and gift taxes, as well as the corresponding Agreements between the Nordic countries which, after the signing of this Agreement are entered into, in addition to, or in place of, these Agreements.

Article 4

1. A Contracting State is, according to Article 1, obliged to provide administrative assistance in all tax matters and with consideration to all tax claims, which arise in another Contracting State concerning taxes and duties covered under Article 2.
2. Assistance may include measures not only with respect to taxpayers, but also with respect to others, who, according to the legislation of the Contracting State receiving the request, are obligated to assist the tax authorities.
3. Assistance may only be requested if the requested measure not could be taken in the own State without significant difficulties, and if the Contracting State presenting the request according to its own legislation could render similar assistance to the State to which the request was directed.
4. A request for assistance and written correspondence between Contracting States in accordance with this Agreement shall be undertaken by the competent authorities in these States.

Article 5

1. Requests and other documents in matters of assistance shall be written in Danish, Norwegian, or Swedish, or shall be accompanied by a translation in any of these languages. Regarding matters of service of documents this applies, however, only to the request of service.
2. A request for assistance shall contain the authority which in the first place made the demand for assistance and the name, profession, or title, address,

date of birth and permanent residence, and if possible place of employment and place of physical presence concerning the person of the subject matter. Further, the request ought to contain information about other circumstances that may contribute to the identification of this person.

Article 6

1. A request for administrative assistance may be refused, if the Contracting State from which the assistance is requested, considers this to be in conflict with its own public interests.
2. Where a question concerning the application of a provision in any of the Nordic double taxation Agreements is pending before the competent authority of the Contracting State from which the assistance is requested, this Contracting State may, after consultations with the requesting State, declare the request for assistance for the recovery of tax resting.

Article 7

1. If a request for assistance is not complied with, the Contracting State, which has requested the assistance, shall, without delay, be informed of the decision and the reasons thereof.
2. If the assistance is enforced, the Contracting State from which the assistance is requested, shall, as soon as possible, inform the other Contracting State of the results of the assistance.
3. Information according to this article shall also include such circumstances as may be significant for further measures in the tax matter.

Article 8

Documents which have been issued or certified by a court, or an administrative authority, in a Contracting State do not need to be legalized to be used in tax matters within the territory of another Contracting State. The same applies with respect to documents, which have been signed by an official of the court or the authority, if such a signature is sufficient according to the legislation of the Contracting State of that court, or authority.

Service of documents

Article 9

1. Service of documents according to this Agreement shall be effected in the manner prescribed for similar service according to the legislation, or the administrative practise, of the Contracting State from which the service of documents shall be requested. The request for service of a document shall contain a brief statement regarding the contents of the document.

2. If the Contracting State requesting service of documents so desires, the service may be effected subject to special formalities, provided that the demanded procedure is in accordance with the legislation of the Contracting State in which the service is to be effected.
3. The service of documents shall be evidenced by either a dated admission of the service by the person receiving the document, or by a certificate from the authority of the Contracting State in which the service is requested, which shows the form and the time of service.

Procurement of information, etc.

Article 10

1. Information shall be procured in accordance with the legislation of the Contracting State to which the request has been directed.
2. A request for the procurement of information may be refused if business, industry or professional secrets would become disclosed if the request would be honoured.

Article 11

1. The competent authority in a Contracting State shall, in so far as based on available information of control, or corresponding information, as soon as possible after the end of each calendar year, and without special request, forward to the competent authorities in each of the Contracting States information, based on available forms, concerning resident natural persons, or there belonging legal entities, in each of the other Contracting States, regarding:
   a) dividends from limited liability companies and similar legal entities,
   b) interest on bonds and similar securities,
   c) credit balances in banks, savings banks, and similar institutions and interest on such credit balances,
   d) ownership of immovable property,
   e) royalties and other periodic charges for the use of copyrights, patents, designs, trade marks, or other such right or property,
   f) salaries, remunerations, pensions or annuities,
   g) damages, insurance and other such compensation, received in connection with business activity, and
   h) other incomes, or assets, to the extent an agreement has been concluded about that according to Article 20.
2. The competent authorities of a Contracting State is committed to forward information which has been revealed in an investigation in this State in a tax matter and which could be assumed to be of interest for another Contracting State, as soon as possible, by transmitting it to the competent authority of this other Contracting State.

3. If the Contracting State, which has received information, ascertains that the information does not conform to the actual circumstances, the competent authority of this Contracting State must in a suitable way inform the competent authority of the Contracting State, which has provided the information of this circumstance.
4. When a person domiciled in one Contracting State is deceased and leaves immovable property in another Contracting State or assets invested in a business there, the competent authority of the first named State shall inform the competent authority of the other Contracting State as soon as this circumstance is known.

Article 12

1. At the request of one Contracting State shall two, or more, Contracting States consult with each other in order to determine the object and the procedure of simultaneous tax investigations. Each Contracting State determines itself if it wishes to participate in a certain simultaneous tax investigation.
2. A 'simultaneous tax investigation' as referred to in paragraph 1 means an agreement between two, or more, Contracting States under which each of them in its territory makes arrangements for simultaneous investigations of tax related circumstances regarding a person of common or complementary interest with the purpose of exchanging obtained information of importance.

Article 13

1. In a tax matter of significant interest to a Contracting State, a representative of that Contracting State, may upon request from the competent authority of the same State, be allowed to be present during the investigation in such a tax matter in another Contracting State. A request is decided upon by the competent authority of the other Contracting State, which, as soon as possibly, should inform the competent authority of the first named State of its decision. If the request is granted, the communication thereof should include the time and place of the investigation, and such other information as presumed necessary for the requesting competent authority.
2. The representatives as referred to in paragraph 1 may not decide upon issues regarding the investigation, but may make suggestions on such issues to the authority, or to the official who has undertaken to perform the investigation. Decisions regarding such suggestions are made by the authority, or the official.
3. Information which has been obtained in an investigation as referred to in paragraph 1 shall be treated as confidential, and may not be disclosed to other individuals, or authorities, including officials of the courts and other judicial authorities, than these who handle the assessment, or the collection,

or the recovery of taxes to which this Agreement applies, or who decide on appeals, or on issues of prosecution in connection thereto.

4. Where a request as referred to in paragraph 1 is refused, the provisions in Article 7, paragraph 1, shall apply correspondingly.

Recovery of tax

Article 14

1. A decision in a tax matter, which according to the legislation in a Contracting State is enforceable in this State, shall be recognized as enforceable in another Contracting State.
2. Issues concerning time limits after which a tax claim can not be enforced shall be determined according to the legislation of the applicant State.
3. Recovery measures carried out by the requested State after a request for assistance, which according to the legislation in this State, cancel, or interrupt, time limits as referred to in paragraph 2, shall also have these effects at the application of the legislation in the applicant State. The requested State shall inform the applicant State when such measures are taken.
4. The authority which first requests assistance for recovery, shall certify in its request that the decision is enforceable, and state the date on which all, or part, of the claim becomes time-barred due to periods of limitation. The competence of this authority shall be certified by an authority as referred to in Article 3.

Article 15

When a tax liable person, or anybody else, as referred to in Article 4, section 2, is deceased, the amount recovered may not exceed the value of the assets in the decedents estate. If the estate has been distributed, recovery against an heir, or other person, who have acquired assets owing to the decease of the owner may not exceed an amount, which corresponds to the equal value of assets received at the time of the acquisition.

Article 16

1. Taxes which are to be recovered according to this agreement in the Contracting State which has been requested for assistance do not benefit from such special priority right which there may be applicable to its own taxes.
2. In matters of recovery of taxes according to this Agreement, may no litigation proceedings in any court other than an administrative court be commenced, nor any bankruptcy proceedings be initiated in the Contracting State in which recovery has been requested, unless the competent authority in this State, upon a request from the competent authority in the Contracting State, which forwarded the request, expressly consents to such measures.

Article 17

1. Ceases, before the recovery of tax has been completed, in accordance with this Agreement, the right to levy tax, in full, or in part, according to the legislation of the Contracting State which has requested assistance, due to payment, reduction, or cancellation, of assessment, cut-downs, or other reasons, shall the competent authority of that State, as soon as possible, report the occurrence to the competent authority of the other Contracting State.
2. The provisions in paragraph 1 shall apply correspondingly to matters when a deferment of tax payments has been granted.

Article 18

When recovery has taken place in one Contracting State in accordance with this Agreement, and the recovered amount has been received by an authority of recovery in this State, this State is responsible for the recovered amount to the Contracting State, which requested the recovery.

Securing of the payment of tax claims

Article 19

1. The securing of the payment of tax claims according to this Agreement shall be effected according to the legislation or the administrative practice of the Contracting State by which the security has been demanded. Such a securing may also be effected even if the claim has not been fixed.
2. If the tax claim has been reduced, in full, or in part, after measures of security have been taken according to this Agreement, shall the competent authority of the requesting Contracting State, as soon as possible, inform the competent authority of the other Contracting State of this event.
3. The provisions of Articles 14-18 shall in appropriate parts also apply to the securing of payment of tax claims in accordance with this Agreement.

Special provisions

Article 20

1. The competent authorities in the Contracting States may conclude an agreement to carry out the provisions of this Agreement. They may specially agree to exchange information according to Article 11, paragraph 1h), on minimum amounts for requests for recovery, on administrative assistance concerning taxes and duties according to Article 2, paragraph 1h) 2-5, on measures to avoid that preliminary taxes are withheld by more than one Contracting State, on the collection of tax and the transfer of tax, as well as for interest, litigation costs, fines and other similar amounts, which are imposed in connection to taxation or recovery, on fixing the currency

exchange rate for amounts which are to be recovered, and for the accounts of the amounts, which have been recovered.

2. If difficulties, or doubts, arise between two, or more, of the Contracting States on the interpretation or the application of this Agreement, the competent authorities of these States shall make consultations in order to try to resolve the issue by a special agreement. The results of such consultations shall be reported to the competent authorities of the other Contracting States as soon as possible.
3. Should the competent authority of one Contracting State consider that consultations on an issue according to paragraph 2 should come about between the competent authorities in all Contracting States, such consultations shall take place at the request of that State.
4. If a request for assistance for the recovery of a tax claim concerns income which has been taxed in another Contracting State than the one requesting the assistance, and such double taxation is not regulated in an agreement to avoid double taxation, may the competent authority of the requested State consult on this matter with the competent authority of the requesting State with the purpose to reach a mutual agreement in order to try to avoid that the income is double taxed. Pending such an agreement, the recovery of a tax claim may be postponed.

Article 21

With respect to inquiries, information, statements, and other communications, which are received by a Contracting State, in accordance with this Agreement, the secrecy provisions of the legislation of that Contracting State shall apply.

Article 22

The Contracting State, which has requested the assistance, in accordance with this Agreement, is obliged to reimburse costs for such litigation proceedings in another court than in an administrative court, or in bankruptcy proceedings, in the other Contracting State, which have been caused by the matter of assistance.

Article 23

This Agreement shall not apply to Svalbard and Jan Mayen and the Norwegian dependencies outside Europe.

Article 24

1. This Agreement shall enter into force on the thirtieth day after the date by which all of the Contracting States have informed the Danish Ministry of Foreign Affairs that the Agreement has been approved. The Danish Ministry of Foreign Affairs shall inform the other Contracting States of the receipt of these notifications, and of the date of the entry into force of the Agreement.

2. After the entry into force of this Agreement, its provisions apply to matters which, subsequent to the entry into force of the Agreement, have been submitted to the competent authority of the Contracting State to which a request has been directed.
3. The Agreement of 9 November 1972 between Sweden, Denmark, Finland, Iceland and Norway on administrative assistance in tax matters, as amended, shall cease to exist and should for the last time apply regarding matters, which were submitted by a directed request to the competent authority of a Contracting State prior to the entry into force of this Agreement.
4. This Agreement neither limits, nor is limited by the Agreement of 18 October 1979 between the Danish government and the regional Council of Greenland to avoid double taxation, etc. and the Agreement according to paragraph 20 in the appendix to the latter mentioned Agreement.
5. This Agreement neither limits, nor is limited by, the provisions of administrative assistance in the Agreement of 12 August 1986 between the Danish government and the regional Council of the Faeroe Islands to avoid double taxation, etc.

Article 25

A Contracting State may give written notice of termination of the Agreement no later than 30 June of a calendar year, to the Danish Ministry of Foreign Affairs, which will notify the other Contracting States of the receipt of such notice and its contents. When notice of termination has been properly given, the Agreement shall cease to apply between the State, which has submitted the notice of termination, and the other Contracting States, as of the end of that calendar year.

The original copy of this Agreement should be deposited with the Danish Ministry of Foreign Affairs, which will transmit certified copies thereof to the other Contracting States.

In confirmation of this, the duly undersigned plenipotentiaries, have signed this Agreement.

Done in Copenhagen, on 7 December 1989, in copies in Danish, Faeroese, Greenlandic, Finnish, Icelandic, Norwegian and Swedish languages, with two Swedish language texts, one for Finland and one for Sweden, all texts being equally authentic.

ANNEX 4

Details on the entry into force in relation to the States which are parties to the Convention on jurisdiction and the enforcement of judgments in civil and commercial matters of 27 September 1968

The Brussels convention has entered into force in relation to the following States on the below indicated moments: Austria (1998-12-01), Denmark (1998-12-01), Finland (1999-04-01), France (2000-08-01), Germany (1999-01-01), Greece (1999-10-01), Ireland (1999-12-01), Italy (1999-06-01), Luxemburg (2000-05-01), the Netherlands (1998-12-01), Portugal (1999-10-01), Spain (1999-04-01), Sweden (1999-01-01) and the United Kingdom (2001-01-01).

ANNEX 5

Details on the entry into force in relation to the States which are parties to the Convention on jurisdiction and the enforcement of judgments in civil and commercial matters of 16 September 1988

The Lugano convention has entered into force in relation to the following States on the below indicated moments: Austria (1996-09-01), Belgium (1997-10-01), Denmark (1996-03-01), Finland (1993-07-01), France (1992-01-01), Germany (1995-03-01), Great Britain and Northern Ireland (1992-05-01), Greece (1997-09-01), Iceland (1995-12-01), Ireland (1993-12-01), Italy (1992-12-01), Luxemburg (1992- 02-01), the Netherlands (1992-01-01), Norway (1993-05-01), Poland (2000-02-01), Portugal (1992-07-01), Spain (1994-11-01), Sweden (1993-01-01) and Switzerland (1992-01-01).

ANNEX 6

Details on the entry into force and on certain reservations in relation to the States which are parties to the Convention on mutual administrative assistance in tax matters of 25 January 1988

The convention has entered into force in relation to the following States on the below indicated moments: Azerbaijan (2004-10-01), Belgium (2000- 12-01), Denmark, including Greenland (1995-04-01), Finland (1995-04-01), France (2005-09-01), Iceland (1996-11-01), Italy (2006-05-01), the Netherlands (1997-02-01), Norway (1995-04-01), Poland (1997-10-01), Sweden (1995-04-01), the United Kingdom (2008-05-01) and the United States of America (1995-04-01). States which have made reservations against the recovery provisions of the convention are: Italy, the Netherlands, Poland and the United States of America.

See for the latest developments and for further details on signature, ratification, entry into force, reservations, declarations, authorities, territorial application, communication and objection, website of the Council of Europe, <http://conventions.coe.int>.

ANNEX 7

Convention between Denmark, Finland, Iceland, Norway and Sweden regarding bankruptcy of 7 November 1933, as amended in 1977 and 1982, translated extracts[2]

---

2. Translation by the League of Nations, except regarding Art. 7, para. 3, which is a non-official translation by Mikael Berglund.

Article 1, paragraph 2 which *i.a.* reads:

> 'Unless otherwise provided, the law of the country in which bankruptcy takes place shall determine the effects of such bankruptcy in the matter of . . . the rights of creditors in respect of the payment of their claims. . . . '

Article 7, paragraph 1

> 'The rules applicable to preferential claims against particular assets and the question of priority as between such preferential claims, mortgages, pledges, or other rights *in rem,* attaching to the said assets shall be determined by the law of that country in which such property is situated when bankruptcy takes place. The specific preferential rights aforementioned shall have priority over all general preferential rights.'

Article 7, paragraph 2

> 'The extent to which preferential treatment shall be due to taxes and other public dues levied by a State other than that in which bankruptcy has been declared shall be governed by the law of the State to which such taxes and dues are payable. The extent to which preferential treatment shall be due to a lessor, the owner of premises in the territory of one of the other States, shall be determined by the law of the State in which the said premises are situated. Such preferential rights shall only apply to the property of the bankrupt in the State by which the aforesaid taxes and dues are levied, or in whose territory are situated the premises in question. As between such preferential rights, priority shall be determined, when they are of a specific character, in accordance with the first paragraph of the present Article: when they are of a general character, they shall have priority over all other general preferential rights. The provisions of the first paragraph notwithstanding, priority as between general preferential rights of a fiscal character and the specific preferential rights referred to in the said paragraph shall be determined by the law of the State by which the taxes, or dues, are levied. It shall, however, be understood that the present Convention shall not affect the question of how far claims in respect of public taxes and dues levied by a State other than that in which bankruptcy is declared can be charged against the bankrupt estate.'

Article 7, paragraph 3, as amended in 1982, which *i.a.* reads:

> 'If a tax claim enjoys a general preferential right under the law of the country by which it is imposed, it shall be paid with such priority from the assets situated in that country, but only after a portion of other claims against the bankruptcy estate enjoying other general preferences than applicable to taxes and fees has been deducted from these assets. The portion to be deducted is determined in such a way that it corresponds to the relation between the property in the country where the tax is imposed and the total of assets included in the bankruptcy estate.'

ANNEX 8

Draft of a Nordic agreement on the exchange of information in recovery matters, translation[3]

The Governments of Denmark, Finland, Iceland, Norway and Sweden, desiring to enter into an agreement on the exchange of information in recovery matters, have agreed as follows

Definitions

Article 1

In this agreement the following words have been given this meaning

Competent authority, the or those national authorities, which a Contracting State has appointed, to forward, or respectively receive, a request on assistance according to Article 2,

Applicant authority, the national competent authority in a Contracting State, which forwards a request of assistance according to Article 2,

Requested authority, the national competent authority in a Contracting State, which receives a request of assistance according to Article 2,

Authority of recovery, a national legally regulated organ, which has been conferred the legal powers to exercise public authority at the national enforcement of claims, or which represent the States in their capacity of creditors at the recovery of public claims according to national legislation,

Debtor, a personal, or legal person, who is liable for the payment of a claim according to national legislation of the Contracting State, where the applicant authority is situated.

Area of application

Article 2

1. The Contracting States shall, if no other provisions in this agreement stipulate otherwise, through their legally applying authorities, in order to promote an efficient national and international recovery, assist each other through the transfer of information to authorities of recovery in matters, which are handled there, including matters of interim measures, such as provisional measures, regarding the following claims
   a) private and public law claims, which are subject to national enforcement,

3. Non-official translation by Mikael Berglund from Swedish of the draft of a Nordic agreement on the exchange of information in recovery matters, pp. 25-30 in the report Nordiskt samarbete om indrivningsfrågor (Nordic co-operation in recovery matters) to the Nordic Council of Ministers.

b) public claims, which by public organs in their capacity of creditors, could be made valid through an application of recovery in other States according to provisions in community law, or in present, or future, bilateral, or multilateral, agreements between the States.

2. The Contracting States ought to, when needed, inform each other on how the work of enforcement is carried out and organized nationally, and on the content in national law, which is of importance in the enforcement in the other State.

Article 3

Each Contracting State can reserve the right not to transfer information

- which, shall be used in the applicant State for the enforcement of a private claim,
- which, has been obtained in, or could have been obtained in, the work of national enforcement of a private claim, if the request relates to a matter of recovery of a public claim, or vice versa,
- which, exists at a court in the requested State.

Article 4

The Contracting States shall transfer information, regardless of where the debtor, the private, or legal, person concerned, has his domicile, or is a citizen.

Request on information

Article 5

1. A request for information may relate to the debtor's assets and debts, etc. If there is more than one person, who besides the main debtor is responsible for the payment of the debt according to valid provisions in the State where the applicant authority is situated, a request may also relate to the assets and debts, etc. of that or those persons.
2. If the applicant authority is aware of assets being in the possession of a third party, which belong to the person mentioned in the foregoing paragraph, the request of the authority may also relate to this third party.
3. A request for information may be forwarded, if it could be assumed that information exists in the or those requested States, which could be of importance in the matter.

Article 6

1. When information is requested by the applicant authority, the requested authority shall, if no exceptions are made according to the provisions of Article 13, or the applicant authority has limited its request to only certain

kind of information, transmit all information, which is considered to be of importance in the matter and, which is available at a national authority of recovery, independent of if it is public, or protected by secrecy. The requested authority shall also transmit information, which this authority, or a national authority of recovery, without difficulties could obtain from databases, or in similar ways.

2. The requested authority may in addition, on its own initiative, or due to wishes forwarded by the applicant authority, transmit other information, which it considers to be of importance for the recovery.

Article 7

1. A request for information shall include the name, address and other relevant information, which is needed in order to identify the subject of the request, *e.g.* personal number of identification, or other such number of registration, which has been attributed to this subject in the applicant State, and if possible the corresponding number, which has been attributed in the requested State, and a specification of the claim.
2. A request shall, according to paragraph 1, be made in writing, according to the model in annex x to this agreement. The request should bear the official stamp or other official mark and be signed by an official of the authority, which is competent to make such a request. The requested authority may, if it is possible according to the legislation of the Contracting State, where it is situated, grant an exception from what has been said and instead accept that the demand is made by electronic means.

Article 8

1. The requested authority shall in writing, if possible by electronic means, confirm the reception of a request of information as soon as possible and at the latest within seven days after the reception.
2. The requested authority shall, as soon as it has obtained access to the requested information, transmit it to the applicant authority, with an indication of both such number of registration, which is related to in Article 7.1 and which has been attributed to the subject of the request by the applicant State and the corresponding number, which has been attributed to the subject in the requested State.
3. If all or some parts of the requested information in a specific matter can not be obtained within a month, the requested authority shall inform the applicant authority thereof and the reasons therefore.

Article 9

The applicant authority shall, without delay, withdraw the request if there no longer exists any reasons for a request, according to Article 5. A withdrawal shall be transmitted in writing, and if possible by electronic means.

Article 10

A request for assistance and applicable documents shall be accompanied by a translation to the official language, or one of the official languages, in the Contracting State, where the requested authority is situated. This authority has the right to renounce from a translation.

Article 11

The competent authorities in two, or more, Contracting States may reach an agreement on the right for the national authorities of recovery to communicate directly with each other, after a request has been made by the competent authority according to Article 5.

Protection of persons, limitations of obligations to grant assistance and secrecy

Article 12

1. This agreement does not effect the rights, or the protection, which are attributed to persons according to the legislation and administrative usage of the requested State.
2. The requested authority shall not be obliged to provide information
   a) which, it would not have been able to obtain for the recovery of similar claims in a national matter of recovery,
   b) which, would reveal business, industrial, or professional secrecies, or
   c) which, if they were to be revealed, would be of damage to the national security in this State.
3. The requested authority shall inform the applying authority of the reasons for refusal if it does not comply with the request for the information. This notification should be delivered by the requested authority as soon as the decision has been made and at the latest within a month after the day of the confirmed reception of the request.

Article 13

Requests for information, communicated facts and other messages, which are transmitted to a Contracting State according to this agreement, should be governed by the secrecy provisions, which are valid according to the legislation of this State.

Final provisions

Article 14

1. States shall refrain from all claims on each other for costs incurred in mutual assistance given to each other according to this agreement.

Article 15

Provisions in this agreement should not prevent a greater measure of mutual assistance being afforded by a Contracting State in accordance with present, or future, agreements, or arrangements.

Article 16

1. If difficulties, or uncertainties, arise between two, or more, of the Contracting States on the interpretation, or the application, of this agreement, the competent authorities of these States shall by consulting one and other try to resolve the issue in a special agreement. The results of such consultations shall be reported to the competent authorities of the other Contracting States as soon as possible.
2. Should the competent authority in one Contracting State consider that the consultations on an issue according to paragraph 1 should involve the competent authorities in all Contracting States, such consultations shall take place at the request of that State.

Article 17

This agreement shall not apply to Svalbard and Jan Mayen and the Norwegian dependencies outside Europe.

Article 18

This agreement shall enter into force on the thirtieth day after the date by which all of the Contracting States have notified the . . . foreign ministry that the agreement has been approved. The . . . foreign ministry should inform the other Contracting States of the receipt of these notifications, and of the date on which the agreement enters into force.

Article 19

1. If one Contracting State wishes to change the content as concerning that State in any of the annexes to this agreement this change shall be notified to the . . . foreign ministry. The change shall enter into force thirty days after the day when the . . . foreign ministry has notified the other Contracting States about the change.
2. A Contracting State may give written notice of termination of the agreement no later than 30 June of a calendar year, to the . . . foreign ministry, which will notify the other Contracting States of the receipt of such notice and its contents. Where notice of termination has been properly given, the agreement shall cease to apply between the State, which has submitted the notice of termination, and the other Contracting States, as of the end of that calendar year.

ANNEX 9

Details on the entry into force in relation to the States which are parties to the European convention on State immunity of 16 May 1972

The European State immunity convention has entered into force in relation to the following States. The moment of the entry into force are indicated after each State.

Austria 1976-06-11, Belgium 1976-06-11, Cyprus 1976-06-11, Germany 1990-08-16, Luxemburg 1987-03-12, the Netherlands 1985-05-22, Switzerland 1982-10-07 and the United Kingdom 1979-10-04.

Further detailed information on declarations could be provided by the depositary of the convention, the Council of Europe, *see* website of the Council of Europe, <http://conventions.coe.int>.

ANNEX 10

National authorities designated by the Member States of the European Union in accordance to Article 256 of the EC Treaty for the verification of the authenticity of decisions of the Council or of the Commission[4]

Austria: Bezirksgericht, Belgium: Minister of Foreign Affairs verifies authenticity: enforcement order appended by the Registrar of the Court of Appeals in Brussels through intermediary of the Ministry of Justice, Bulgaria: State Receivables Collection Agency (SRCA) within the Ministry of Finance, Denmark: Ministry of Justice, Germany: Minister of Justice, Greece: Minister of Foreign Affairs verifies authenticity: enforcement order appended by the Judge in charge of the Court of First Instance in Athens, Spain: Minister of Justice, with possibilities of delegation, Finland: Ministry of Justice, France: Minister of Justice, with possibilities of delegation, Ireland: Minister for Justice verifies authenticity: enforcement order appended by the Master of the High Court, Italy: Minister of Foreign Affairs, Luxemburg: Minister of Foreign Affairs verifies authenticity: enforcement order appended by the Minister of Justice, the Netherlands: Minister of Justice, who transmits to the Registrar of the Hoge Raad for verification of authenticity and appending of the enforcement order, Portugal: Ministry of Foreign Affairs verifies authenticity: enforcement order (through intermediary of the Ministry of Justice) appended by the Court of Appeal of which the person concerned depends, United Kingdom: Secretary of State verifies authenticity: enforcement order appended by the High Court (England and Wales), High Court (Northern Ireland) and the Court of Session (Scotland), Sweden: national court administration, Czech Republic: Ministry of Justice, Estonia: Ministry of Justice, Slovak Republic: Ministry of Justice, Poland: the district court, having jurisdiction in respect of the debtor according to the general rules, and Romania: Ministry of Justice.

4. *See* Communications on 13, 15, and 18 Apr. 2005, and 18 Dec. 2007, from the Registry of the ECJ to Skatteverket, the Swedish Tax Agency, diary number 130213266/05, on Art. 256 (ex. Art. 192) of the EC Treaty for the verification of the authenticity of decisions of the Council or of the Commission.

Index

The choice of words has been determined by the desire to here reflect the most important items in the text. Words from several languages are listed here following the English alphabet. Words, which include the letters Å, Ä and Ö, are listed under A respectively O. References to words here follow the structure of the Contents.

A

Acta gestionnis 4.1.1
Acta jure imperii 4.1.1, 5.2.1.1.2
Acte authentique 5.2.1.1.1
Actes notariés 5.2.1.1.1
Action plan of the Council and the Commission (19/99/EEC) on how best to implement the provisions of the Treaty of Amsterdam on an area of freedom, security and justice of 3 December 1998 1.1.1.1
Actio Pauliana/Action paulienne 2.1.3, 2.1.4, 6.1.1.1.1.1, 6.2.1.1.1
Agreement according to article 20 of the agreement between the Nordic countries for mutual administrative assistance in tax matters of 7 December 1989, as amended on 1 January 1998 2.6.3, 5.2.2.2, 5.3.1.2.1
Agreement between the European Community and the Kingdom of Denmark of 19 October 2005 on jurisdiction and the recognition and enforcement of judgments in civil and commercial matters 2.5.1
Agreement between the European Community and the Kingdom of Denmark of 19 October 2005 on the service of judicial and extrajudicial documents in civil or commercial matters 5.3.1.3
Agreement between the Nordic countries for mutual administrative assistance in tax matters on 7 December 1989 and in order of provisions 2.6, 2.6.3, 5.1.3, 5.3.1.2.2, 5.4.2.2.1-2
– Preamble 5.1.3, 5.3.1.2.1
– 1 a 6.1.3.3.1
– 1 b 5.3.1.2.1, 6.3.2.2
– 1 g 5.4.2.2.1
– 2 2.6.2, 5.2.2.2
– 3 3.3.2
– 4, 1 5.3.1.2.1, 5.4.2.2.1, 6.3.2.2
– 4, 3 6.1.2.2.1
– 6, 1 6.1.2.2.1
– 10 5.3.1.2.1, 6.1.2.2.1, 6.3.2.2
– 13, 1 6.3.2.2
– 13, 3 5.3.1.2.1, 6.3.2.2
– 14, 1 5.3.1.2.1, 6.1.2.4, 6.2.2.2
– 14, 2-3 6.1.2.2.1, 6.1.2.3
– 15 5.4.2.2.2
– 16, 1 5.3.2.1, 6.2.2.3

- 16, 2 5.3.1.2.1, 6.1.2.5, 6.2.2.2
- 19 6.1.2.2.2, 6.2.2.2
- 20 2.6.3
- 20, 1 2.6.2, 5.2.2.2
- 22 6.1.2.5, 6.2.2.2
- 23 5.1.3
- 24, 1 2.6.3
- 24, 2 5.3.1.2.1

Agricultural levies 2.6, 5.2.2.1
American Law Institute 1.1.1.1, 2.10.4
Appeals 6.1.1.3.1-2, 6.1.2.4.1-2, 6.1.3.5
Approximation, Community method of 7.1
Astreinte 7.1, 7.2.2
Attachment of bank accounts, cross-border 2.10.1, 6.1.3.2
Attachment of the earnings of the debtor 7.2.1
Authentic enforceable instrument 5.2.1.1.1
Automatic recognition of judgments and decisions 6.1

B

Bank accounts, cross-border attachment of 2.10.1, 6.1.3.2
Bank secrecy 6.3.2.1
Bankruptcy
- Art. 6 of the Recovery directive, by use of 6.2.2.1.1.1
- Convention between France and Monaco 2.7, 5.1.4, 6.4.2
- Convention between France and Switzerland, related to 2.7
- Directive 2001/24/EC of the European Parliament and of the Council of 4 April 2001 on the reorganization and winding-up of credit institutions 6.4.1
- Directive 2001/17/EC of the European Parliament and of the Council of 19 March 2001 on the reorganization and winding-up of insurance undertakings 6.4.1
- History of 2.1.3, 2.2.4
- Insolvency regulation 1.1.1.1.5, 2.7, 5.1.1, 6.4.1
- Nordic bankruptcy convention 2.7, 5.1.4, 6.4.1-2
- Priority rights 6.4.1-2
- Transnational judicial co-operation in insolvency management 6.4.3
- Uncitral Model Law on Cross-Border Insolvency 6.4.3

Beneficium 2.1.1, 7.2.1
Betalningsföreläggande 5.2.1.2.1
British territories 5.1.1, 6.4.3

C

Capital, tax on 2.6.1, 5.2.2.1
Co-debtor 5.4.2-3, 5.4.2.2, 5.4.2.2.2
Collection 1.6
Co-liability 5.4.2-3, 5.4.2.2, 5.4.2.2.2
Commissaire à l'exécution 3.2.1
Commission Directive (2002/94/EC) of 9 December 2002 laying down detailed rules for implementing certain provisions of Council Directive 76/308/EEC on mutual assistance for the recovery of claims relating to certain levies, duties, taxes and other measures and in order of provisions 2.6.1
- Preamble 2.6.1
- 1 2.6.1
- 3 5.3.1.2.1
- 4 5.3.1.2.1
- 4, 1 5.4.2.2.1
- 4, 2 5.2.1.1.1, 5.3.1.2.1, 5.4.2.2.2
- 4, 3 5.4.2.2.2
- 5-7 5.3.1.2.1, 7.2.2
- 8 5.1.3.2.1
- 13 5.2.1.1.1, 5.3.1.2.1, 5.4.2.2.1-2
- 14, 2 6.1.2.5
- 25 6.1.2.1
- 25, 2 5.3.1.2.1, 6.1.2.1
- 26 6.1.2.1
- 27 6.1.2.5
- 28, 1 6.1.2.5
- 30 2.6.1
- 31 3.3.2
- 32 2.6.1

Comity of nations, principle of 4.2.1
Competent authorities 1.6, 3.2.2, 3.3.2
Composition 1.6, 2.2.3
Contested claims 6.1.1.3.1-2, 6.1.2.4.1-2
Contractual claims 1.6, 5.2.1

Contradictory principle 2.1, 4.3.1
Contrainte par corps 1.1.1.4, 2.3
Convention between Denmark, Finland, Iceland, Norway and Sweden regarding bankruptcy of 7 November 1933, as amended in 1977 and 1982 and in order of articles 2.7, 2.4.2, 2.10.3, 6.4.1-2
– 1 5.1.4, 5.3.1, 6.2.2.1.1.1
– 1, § 2 6.4.2
– 7, § 1-3 6.4.2
– 10 5.3.1
Convention between Denmark, Finland, Iceland, Norway and Sweden regarding the enforcement of maintenance claims of 22 March 1962 and in order of articles 2.4.2
– 1, § 1 6.1
– 2, § 2 6.1.3.1.1
– 3, § 1 6.1
Convention between Sweden, Denmark, Finland, Iceland and Norway on recognition and the enforcement of judgments in civil matters on 11 October 1977 and in order of articles 2.4.2, 2.5, 2.5.5, 3.2.2, 5.1.2, 5.2.1.2.1, 5.3.1.1.1-2, 6.1.1.2.1, 6.1.1.3.2, 6.2.1.2.1
– 1 2.5.5, 5.2.1.2.1, 5.3.1.1.2, 6.1.1.1.2.1, 6.2.1.2.1
– 2 6.1.1.1.2.1, 6.1.1.3.2
– 2, 2 2.5.5, 5.2.1.2.1, 5.3.1.1.2
Convention between the Member States of the European Communities on the simplification of procedures for the recovery of maintenance payments and in order of articles 6.1.3.1.1, 6.3.1
Convention entre la Belgique, le Grand-Duché de Luxembourg et les Pays-Bas, relative à l'assistance réciproque en matière de recouvrement de créances fiscales du 5 September 1952 and in order of articles 2.4.2, 2.6
– 1 5.3.1.2.2
– 2 5.2.2.2
– 2, § 1 5.2.2.2
– 3 5.4.2, 6.1.2.2.2
– 3, § 3 6.1.2.2.1
– 4, § 1 6.1.2.2.2, 6.2.2.2
– 5 6.2.2.3
– 6 6.3.2
– 7 6.1.2.5
Convention for the protection of human rights and fundamental freedoms, Council of Europe on 4 November 1950, as amended by protocol No. 11 1.1.1.1, 1.1.1.1.1-3, 4.3
– Access to information for enforcement purposes 4.3.1
– Access to justice 4.3.1
– Appeal, right to 4.3.1-2
– Dynamic interpretation 1.4.1
– Effective remedy before a national authority 4.3.1
– Efficency 1.1.1.1.1, 4.3
– Execution of a national court judgment within a reasonable time 4.3.1
– Execution of the judgments of the ECHR 6.2
– Non-discrimination 1.1.1.1.2, 4.3
– Peaceful enjoyment of possessions 1.1.1.1.1, 4.3, 4.3.1
– Privacy 1.1.1.1.1, 4.3
– Prohibition of imprisonment for debt 1.1.1.4, 4.3
– Proportionality 1.1.1.1, 1.1.1.1.3, 4.3
– Right not to incriminate oneself 4.3.1
– Right to remain silent in a criminal proceeding 4.3.1
– Tax penalties 4.3.2
– Territorial scope of application 5.1
Convention for the protection of human rights and fundamental freedoms, as amended by protocol No. 11, in order of articles
– 6, 1 1.1.1.1.1, 4.3.1-2, 7.2.3.5
– 6, 2 4.3.1-2
– 8, 1 1.1.1.1.1, 7.2.3.5
– 13 4.3.1
– 14 1.1.1.1.2
– 46, 1-2 6.2
– 56 1.1.1.5
– Protocol No. 1 to the convention, article 1 1.1.1.1.1, 1.1.1.1.3, 4.3.1, 7.2.3.5
– Protocol No. 4 to the convention, article 1 1.1.1.4, 4.3

Convention on Choice of Court Agreements of 30 June 2005 2.10.2, 6.2
Convention on jurisdiction and the enforcement of judgments in civil and commercial matters on 27 September 1968 1.1.1.1, 2.5, 2.5.1, 5.1.2, 5.3.1.1.1
Convention on jurisdiction and the enforcement of judgments in civil and commercial matters on 16 September 1988 2.5, 2.5.1, 2.7, 5.1.2, 5.2.1.2, 5.3.1.1.1-2
Convention on jurisdiction and the recognition and enforcement of judgments in civil and commercial matters on 30 October 2007 2.5
Convention on mutual administrative assistance in tax matters on 25 January 1988 and in order of articles 2.6, 2.6.2, 5.1.3
- Preamble 1.1.1.1.1
- 1, 3 5.3.1.2.2, 5.4.2.2.1-2
- 2 2.6.2, 5.2.2.2
- 3, 1 3.3.2, 5.4.2.2.1
- 4-5 5.3.1.2.1, 6.3.2.2
- 10 5.3.1.2.1
- 11, 1 6.2.2.2
- 11, 2 6.1.2.4.2
- 11, 3 5.4.2.2.2
- 12 6.1.2.2.2, 6.1.3.2.1, 6.2.2.2
- 14 6.1.2.2.1, 6.1.2.3
- 15 5.3.1.2.1, 6.2.2.3
- 17 6.1.3.3.1
- 18 5.3.1.2.1, 6.1.2.2.1, 6.3.2.2
- 19 6.1.2.2.1
- 20, 2 6.3.2.2
- 20, 3 5.3.1.2.1
- 21 5.3.1.2.1, 6.1.2.2.1, 6.3.2.2
- 22 5.3.1.2.1, 6.3.2.2
- 26 6.1.2.5
- 27 5.3.1.2.2
- 28, 1 2.6.2
- 30, 1 c 5.3.1.2.1
Convention on the Execution of Foreign Arbitral Awards on 26 September 1927 2.5.6, 5.3.1.1.2
Convention on the Contract for the International Carriage of Goods by Road on 19 May 1956 6.2
Convention on the law applicable to contractual obligations on 19 June 1980 6.1.1.2
Convention on the law of treaties on 23 May 1969 1.1.1.1.4, 1.4.1
Convention on the recognition and enforcement of foreign arbitral awards on 10 June 1958 and in order of articles 2.5, 2.5.6
- I 5.3.1.2
- I, 1-2 5.2.1.2
- I, 3 2.5.6
- III 6.1.1.1.2.2, 6.2.1.2
- IV 6.1.1.2.2
- V 6.1.1.1.2.2, 6.1.1.3
- V, 2 3.2.2
- VII 5.3.1.1.2
- X 5.1.2
- XIV 5.3.1.1.2
Convention on Third Party Liability in the Field of Nuclear Energy on 29 July 1960 6.2
Convention pour l'Unification de certaines Règles relatives au Transport Aérien International le 12 Octobre 1929 6.2
Convention relative à la faillite et à la liquidation judiciaire entre la France et la principauté de Monaco le 13 Septembre 1950 2.7, 5.1.4, 6.4.2
Co-operation in European community law, differing features of 2.9
Costs 6.1.1.4, 6.1.2.5
Council decision (2001/470/EC) of 28 May 2001 establishing a European Judicial Network in civil and commercial matters 3.2.3.3, 6.3.3.1.4
Council Directive 2008/55/EC of 26 May 2008 on mutual assistance for the recovery of claims relating to certain levies, duties, taxes and other measures (Codified version) and in order of provisions 1.1.1.1.1, 2.6.1, 5.1.1
- Preamble 1.1.1.1.1, 1.1.1.1.6, 2.6.1, 5.3.1.2.1
- 1 2.6.1
- 2 2.6, 2.6.1, 5.2.2.1-2, 5.3.1.2.2, 5.4.2.2.2
- 3 5.2.2.1-2, 5.3.1.2.1

– 4 2.6.1, 5.3.1.2.1, 6.1.2.1.1, 6.3.2.1, 6.3.3.2
– 5 2.6.1, 6.1.3.3.1
– 6 2.6.1, 6.1.2.1.1, 6.1.3.2.1, 6.1.3.4, 6.2.2.1.1-2, 6.3.3.2.2
– 7, 2 b 6.1.2.1.1, 6.1.3.3.2
– 8 1.1.1.1.6, 6.1.2.1.2, 6.1.3.2.1, 6.2.3, 7.1
– 9 2.9.2, 5.2.2.1, 6.1.2.5, 6.2.2.1.1
– 10 5.3.1.2.1, 6.2.2.3
– 11 7.2.2
– 12, 2 b 5.3.1.2.1, 6.1.2.4.1, 6.1.2.5, 6.1.3.2.1
– 13 6.1.2.1.2, 6.1.2.4.1, 6.1.3.2.1, 6.2.2.1.2
– 14 6.1.2.1.1, 6.1.2.3, 6.1.2.4.1
– 15 5.3.1.2.1, 6.1.3.4
– 18 6.1.2.4.1, 6.1.2.5, 6.1.3.4, 6.2.2.1.1.1
– 19 3.3.2
– 20-21 3.3.3
– 23 2.4.2, 5.1.3, 5.2.2.2, 5.3.1.2.1
Council Directive 77/249/EEC of 22 March 1977 to facilitate the effective exercise by lawyers of freedom to provide services 3.2.3.2
Council Directive (80/987/EEC) of 20 October 1980 on the approximation of the laws of the Member States relating to the protection of employees in the event of the insolvency of their employer, as amended through Directive 2002/74/EC of the European Parliament and of the Council of 23 September 2002 1.1.1.6, 7.1
Council Directive 89/48/EEC of 21 December 1988 on a general system for the recognition of higher-education and training of at least three years duration 3.2.3.1-2
Council directive 2008/9/EC of 12 February 2008 laying down detailed rules for the refund of value added tax, provided for in Directive 2006/112/EC, to taxable persons not established in the Member State of refund but established in another Member State 6.3.3.2.4
Council draft programme (2001/C 12/01) of measures for implementation of the principle of mutual recognition of decisions in civil and commercial matters 1.1.1.1, 6.3.3.1, 7.2.3.5
Council Framework Decision (2003/577/JHA) of 22 July 2003 on the execution in the European Union of orders freezing property or evidence 5.1.1
Council Framework Decision (2005/214/JHA) of 24 February 2005 on the application of the principle of mutual recognition to financial penalties 1.1.1.1.6, 1.1.1.4, 5.4.2.2.2, 6.1.2.5, 6.2
Council Framework Decision (2006/783/JHA) of 6 October 2006 on the application of the principle of mutual recognition to confiscation orders 1.1.1.1.6, 5.4.2.2.2, 6.1.2.5, 6.2
Council of Europe 2.5
Council of Europe's Convention on the laundering, search, seizure and confiscation of proceeds from crime of 8 November 1990 5.3.2.2, 6.1.2.5, 6.2
Council of Europe's recommendation on archiving of electronic documents in the legal sector of 9 September 2003 7.2.3.4
Council of Europe's recommendation on enforcement of 9 September 2003 1.1.1.1, 1.1.1.1.1, 1.1.1.1.3-4, 1.6, 2.4.2, 3.2.1, 3.2.3, 3.2.3.1-2, 6.1.3.6, 7.1, 7.2.1-2, 7.2.3.5
Council of Europe's recommendation on the interoperability of information systems in the justice sector of 9 September 2003 7.2.3.4
Council regulation (1765/92/EC) of 30 June 1992 establishing a support system for producers of certain arable crops 6.2.2.1.1.3
Council regulation 1348/2000/EC of 29 May 2000 on the service in the Member States of judicial and extrajudicial documents in civil or commercial matters 5.3.1, 6.1.1.1.1.1
Council regulation 2157/2001/EC of 8 October 2001 on the Statute for a European company (SE) 1.1.1.8.1
Council regulation (EC)/No 1346/2000 of 29 May 2000 on insolvency proceedings, and in order of provisions 1.1.1.1.5, 2.4.2, 2.7, 5.1.1, 5.2.1.1.1, 6.4.1

– Preamble 1.1.1.1.3, 1.1.1.1.5, 6.2.2.1.1.1, 6.4.1
– 1 5.3.1, 6.3.3.2.2, 6.4.1
– 2 a-b 5.3.1, 6.3.3.2.2, 6.4.1
– 3 6.1, 6.4.1
– 4 6.2.2.1.1.1, 6.4.1
– 5-15 6.4.1
– 16 6.1, 6.2.2.1.1.1
– 17 6.1, 6.2.2.1.1.1, 6.4.1
– 18, 3 6.2, 6.4.1
– 21 6.2.2.1.1.1
– 25 5.3.1, 6.2.2.1.1.1
– 39 6.2.2.1.1.1, 6.4.1
– 40 6.2.2.1.1.1
– 41 6.2.2.1.1.1, 6.4.1
– 43 6.4.1
– 44 2.4.2, 2.7, 6.2.2.1.1.1, 6.4.1
– 47 6.4.1

Council regulation (44/2001/EC) on jurisdiction and the recognition and enforcement of judgments in civil and commercial matters and in order of provisions 1.1.1.1.1, 2.5, 2.5.1, 5.3.1.1.1
– Preamble 1.1.1.1.1, 5.3.1.1.1
– 1 5.2.1.1, 5.3.1, 5.3.1.1.2
– 22 6.2.1.1.1
– 31 6.1.1.1.1.1, 6.2.1.1.1
– 32 5.2.1.1, 6.1.1.1.1.1
– 33 6.1.1.1.1.1, 6.1.3.1.1
– 34-35 6.1.1.1.1.1
– 39, 1 3.2.2
– 43 6.1.1.3.1, 6.1.3.5
– 44 6.1.3.5
– 46 6.1.1.3.1, 6.2.1.1.1
– 47 6.1.1.1.1.1, 6.2.1.1.1
– 49 6.2.1.1.1
– 57-58 5.2.1.1
– 66-67 5.3.1.1.1
– 68, 1 2.5, 5.3.1
– 69 2.5, 5.3.1.1.1
– 70-71 5.3.1.1.1

Council regulation (1408/71/EEC) on the application of social security schemes to employed persons and their families moving within the Community 5.2.1.1, 5.2.2.1, 6.2, 6.3.2

Court cases, table of the
– ECHR 8.5.1
– ECJ 8.5.2

Court of Justice of the EC 1.1, 1.1.1.1, 1.4.1

Creditor 1.6, 5.4.1

D

Data protection Directive (46/95/EC) 1.1.1.7, 7.2.3.5

Debtor 1.6, 5.4.2-4,

Debt relief 2.10.3, 3.1.5.4

Debt thresholds 5.3.1.2.1, 6.1.2.2

Decedent's estate 5.4.2.2.2

Development trends, present 2.10

Differing features of co-operation in European community law 2.9

Directive 98/5/EC of the European Parliament and of the Council of 16 February 1998 to facilitate practice of the profession of lawyer on a permanent basis in a Member State other than that in which the qualification was obtained 3.2.3.2

Directive 2000/35/EC of the European Parliament and of the Council of 29 June 2000 on combating late payment in commercial transactions 6.1, 6.2, 7.2.2

Directive 2005/36/EC of the European Parliament and of the Council of 7 September 2005 on the recognition of professional qualifications 3.2.3.2

Disqualification orders against an individual for carrying on a non-serious, or illegal, business activity 5.4.3

Double tax treaties, including recovery provisions 2.6, 5.2.2.2, 6.1.3.5

E

Efficiency, interest of 1.1.1.1.1

Enforcement 1.6
– Agents, modern 1.6, 3.2.1
– Agents, history of 3.1
– Outside the scope of conventions 4.2

Euroex, a European co-operation body between States in the civil execution law area 3.2.3.3, 6.3.3.1.4

European Assets Declaration 2.10.1, 6.3.3.1.1
European associations of enforcement agents 2.10.5
European Business Register 7.2.3.1
European Commission for the Efficiency of Justice 2.5
European common educational and training standards for the right to exercise the profession of an enforcement agent 3.2.3.1-2
European company 1.1.1.8.1, 5.4.2
European community law, principles of
– Efficiency 1.1.1.1.1
– Increased legal integration in the Internal Common Market 1.1.1.1.7
– Mutuality 1.1.1.1.6
– Non-discrimination 1.1.1.1.2
– Privacy 1.1.1.1.1
– Proportionality 1.1.1.1.3
– Territoriality 1.1.1.1.4
– Universality 1.1.1.1.5
European convention on State immunity on 16 May 1972 4.1.1
European Convention on the international validity of criminal judgments of 28 May 1970 5.3.1.2.2, 6.1.2.5, 6.2
European Court of Human Rights 1.1, 1.4.1, 4.3.1-2, 5.2.2.1, 6.2, 7.2.2
European Court of Justice 1.1, 1.1.1.1, 1.4.1
European enforcements agents 3.2.1
European Garnishee's Declaration 6.3.3.1.2
European Garnishment Order for Bank Accounts 6.1.3.2, 6.3.1
European Land Information Service 7.2.3.1
European Union 2.4.2, 2.10.1
Exchange of information 6.3
Excise duties 2.6, 5.2.2.1
Exequatur proceedings 1.6, 6.1

F

Fiscalis programme 1.1.1.3
Foreign State's immunity against civil execution 4.1
French overseas departments and territories 5.1.1, 5.1.4

H

Harmonization of civil execution laws 7
Hague Conference on Private International Law 2.5, 2.10.2
Hague convention on the service abroad of judicial and extra judicial documents in civil or commercial matters of 15 November 1965 5.3.1.3
Hague Programme of the European Council on 5 November 2004 1.1.1.1, 1.1.1.1.6
History
– Enforcement and recovery agents 3.1
– Middle Ages 2.2
– Period of 1500-1806 2.3
– Period of 1807 to our age 2.4
– Roman law 2.1
– Universities, European 2.2-3

I

Immunity against civil execution
– Consuls 4.1.2
– Diplomats 4.1.2
– Foreign State's 4.1
Imprisonment for debt
– European convention on Human Rights 1.1.1.4, 4.3
– Period of 1500-1806 2.3
– Roman law 2.1.1
Income tax 5.2.2
Injonction de payer 2.5.3
Instalment plan 1.6, 2.9.2, 6.2.2.1.1
Insolvency proceedings 1.1.1.1.5, 1.6, 6.4
Insurance premiums, tax on 5.2.2
Interim measures 2.1.1, 6.1.1.1.1.1, 6.1.2.1.2, 6.1.2.2
Internal Common Market 1.1.1.1, 1.1.1.1.7
International convention relating to the arrest of seagoing ships on 10 May 1952 5.3.1.1.1, 6.2
International Court of Justice and Statute of 1.4.1
International Institute for the Unification of Private Law 1.1.1.1, 2.10.4
Interpretation, method of interpretation

– European community law 1.4.1
– European Convention on Human Rights 1.4.1
– Public international law 1.4.1
Intra-European Organisation of Tax Administrations 2.10.7
Inversion du contentieux 2.5.3

J

Joint responsibility 5.4.2.1, 5.4.2.2.2

L

Lateran Treaty between the Holy See and Italy of 1929 1.1.1.1.4
Limitation, periods of 1.6, 6.1.1.2, 6.1.2.3

M

Mahnverfahren 2.5.3
Multilateral agreement related to route charges of 12 February 1981 6.2

N

Nordic Council of Ministers 2.10.3
Nordic agreement on the cooperation concerning the mutual assistance of enforcement of judgments or decisions on fines, confiscation or compensation for litigation costs 2.4.2, 5.3.1.2.2, 6.1.2.5, 6.2
Norwegian dependencies outside of Europe 5.1.3

O

OECD Model Tax Convention, article 27 5.2.2.2, 6.1.3.2, 6.3.2

P

Personalities
– Augustus, Roman emperor 2.1.1, 2.1.3
– Alexander III, pope 2.2
– Dinus, Glossarist 2.2
– Edward III, English king 2.2
– Frederick II, German emperor and king of Sicily 2.2
– Frederik I, Danish king 2.3.1
– Gratian, Bolognese monk 2.2
– Gustavus II Adolphus, Swedish king 2.3.1, 3.1.5.4
– Håkon Magnusson, Norwegian feudal lord 3.1.5.3
– Huber, Dutch author 4.2.1
– Justinianus, East Roman emperor 2.1.1
– Magnus Lagabøtar, Norwegian king 3.1.5.3
– Margareta, Nordic queen 3.1.5
– Matthew, tax collector, Apostle and Saint 3.1.1
– Montesquieu, Constitutional doctrines of 1.1.1.4, 2.3, 3.2.3
– Philippe-le-Bel, French king 3.1.2
– Solon, Greek statesman and Arkont in Athens 2.1.1
– de Somoza, Salgado, Spanish author 2.1.3
– Soulard, Jean, initiator of the creation of l'Union Internationale des Huissiers de Justice et Officiers Judiciaires 2.10.5
– Urban II, pope 2.2
– William the Conqueror, English king 2.2.2
Precautionary measures 6.1.2.1.2, 6.1.2.2, 6.1.2.4.1-2, 6.1.2.5, 6.2.2.1.2, 6.2.2.2
Presidency conclusions of the European council 15 and 16 October 1999 in Tampere 1.1.1.1
Principles of Transnational Civil Procedure adopted by the American Law Institute and by the International Institute for the Unification of Private Law 1.1.1.1, 1.1.1.1.1, 1.1.1.1.3, 2.4.2, 2.5, 2.10.4
Priority rights
– Contractual claims 6.2.1.3
– Tax claims 6.2.2.3
– Insolvency 6.4.1-2
– Systems of distribution (attachment): "first in time first in right" principle and the "group" principle 6.2.1.3
Privacy, interest of 1.1.1.1.1
Procedural autonomy of States 6.1.1, 7.1
Proportionality, principle of 1.1.1.1.3

Protocol on Arbitration Clauses on 24 September 1923 2.5.6, 5.3.1.1.2, 5.4.1
Public international law, principles of
- Foreign State's immunity against civil execution 4.1
- Sovereignty 1.1.1.1.4
- Territoriality 1.1.1.1.4

R

Reciprocity 2.4.2, 2.5, 4.2.1
Recognition of the profession of an enforcement agent in other European States 3.2.3.2
Recovery
- Agents, modern 1.6, 3.3.1
- Agents, history of 3.1
- Committee 3.3.3
- Outside the scope of convention 4.2
Refusal, grounds of 6.1.1.1.1.2-4, 6.1.2.1.1, 6.1.2.2.1, 6.1.3.3, 6.2.1.1.2, 6.3.2.1-2
Regulation (805/2004/EC) of the European Parliament and of the Council of 21 April 2004 creating a European Enforcement Order for uncontested claims and in order of articles 1.1.1.1.6, 2.5, 2.5.2, 5.1.1, 6.1.1.1.1.2
- Preamble 2.5.2
- 1 2.5.2
- 2 5.2.1.1.2
- 2, 1 5.2.1.1.2
- 2, 2 a 5.2.1.1.2
- 2, 3 2.5.2
- 3 5.2.2.1, 6.1.1.1.1.2
- 4, 7 5.2.1.1.2
- 5 6.1, 6.1.1.1.1.2
- 6 5.2.2.1, 6.1.1.1.1.2
- 7 5.2.1.1.2
- 20, 1 6.2.1.1.2
- 20, 2 6.1.1.1.1.2
- 21 6.1.1.1.1.2
- 22, 3 6.1.1.1.1.2
- 27-28 5.3.1
- 33 2.5.2
Regulation (883/2004/EC) of the European Parliament and of the Council of 29 April 2004 on the coordination of social security systems 5.2.1.1.2, 5.2.2.1, 6.1, 6.2, 6.3.2
Regulation (EC) No 861/2007 of the European Parliament and of the Council of 11 July establishing a European Small Claims Procedure and in order of articles 1.1.1.1.6, 2.5.4, 5.1.1, 6.1.1.1.1.4
- Preamble 2.5.4
- 1 2.5.4, 5.3.1
- 2 2.5.4, 5.2.1.1.2, 6.1.1.1.1.4
- 3 5.3.1, 6.1.1.1.1.4
- 13, 2 5.3.1
- 15 6.1.1.1.1.4
- 20 6.1, 6.1.1.1.1.4
- 21, 1 6.2.1.1.2
- 22-23 6.1.1.1.1.4
- 29 2.5.4
Regulation (1896/2006/EC) of the European Parliament and of the Council of 12 December 2006 creating a European order for payment procedure and in order of articles 1.1.1.1.6, 2.5.3, 5.1.1, 6.1.1.1.1.3
- Preamble 2.5.3
- 1 2.5.3
- 2 5.2.1.1.2, 6.1.1.1.1.3
- 2, 1 5.2.1.1.2
- 2, 2 a 5.2.1.1.2
- 2, 3 2.5.3
- 3 5.3.1, 6.1.1.1.1.3
- 6 5.3.1
- 18 6.1.1.1.1.3
- 19 6.1, 6.1.1.1.1.3
- 21, 1 6.2.1.1.2
- 21, 3 6.1.1.1.1.3
- 22-23 6.1.1.1.1.3
- 27 5.3.1
- 33 2.5.3
Regulation (EC) No 1393/2007 of the European Parliament and of the Council of 13 November 2007 on the service in the Member States of judicial and extrajudicial documents in civil or commercial matters 5.3.1, 5.3.1.3, 6.1
Relationship between European community law and conventions 5.3
Reorganization and winding-up of
- Credit institutions, directive 6.4.1
- Insurance undertakings, directive 6.4.1
Repayment 6.1.1.4, 6.1.2.5

Representatives of legal entities
- Co-liability 5.4.2.1, 5.4.2.2.2
- Joint responsibility 5.4.2.1, 5.4.2.2.2

Resolution No. 3 of the 24th Conference of European Justice Ministers in Moscow in October 2001 on the "General approach and the means of achieving effective enforcement of judicial decisions" 1.1.1.1, 1.1.1.1.3

Retention of a tax credit 6.2.2.1.1.2

Retrospective effect 5.3.1.1.1, 5.3.1.2.1

S

Scope of claims in European community law and conventions 5.2
- Contractual claims 5.2.1
- Tax claims 5.2.2

Sequestration 2.1.1, 2.3.1, 6.1.1.1.1.1

Set-off of a tax claim 6.2.2.1.1.3

Simultaneous enforcement proceedings in several States 6.1.1

Sixth VAT directive 1.1.1.1.2, 5.1.1, 5.4.2.2.2

Societas Europaea 1.1.1.8.1, 5.4.2

Sovereignty, principle of 1.1.1.1.4

Statistics 1.2

Stay of execution 1.1.1.6, 4.3.1, 6.1.1.1.1.3-4, 6.1.1.3.1, 6.2.1.1.1

Summary procedures 2.5.3, 5.2.1.1.1-2

T

Tax claims 1.6, 5.2.2

Territoriality, principle of 1.1.1.1.4

Territorial scope of application
- Bankruptcy, conventions 5.1.4
- Contractual claims, conventions 5.1.2
- European community law 5.1.1
- Public international law 1.1.1.1.4
- Tax claims, conventions 5.1.3

Time limits in enforcement procedures 7.2.2

Titre Exécutoire Européen 2.5, 2.10.5

Transnational judicial co-operation for the enforcement of a foreign civil law judgment 2.5

Transnational judicial co-operation in insolvency management 6.4.3

Treaty establishing the European community in order of provisions
- 12 1.1.1.1.2
- 45 3.2.3.2
- 56 6.1.3.2
- 61 c 2.5.2-4
- 65 1.1.1.1.7, 2.5.1, 7.1
- 65 c 2.5.3-4
- 67, 5 2.5.2
- 93-94 2.6.1
- 95 1.1.1.1.7, 7.1
- 244 6.1, 6.2
- 256 6.1, 6.2
- 299 5.1.1, 5.3.1.1.1

Treaty of Lisbon amending the Treaty on European Union and the Treaty establishing the European Community and in order of provisions 1.1.1.1
- article 6, 1-3 1.1.1.1
- article 16 d 1.1.1.1.2
- article 49 c 5.1.1
- article 61, 3 1.1.1.1.6
- 65 1.1.1.1
- Final provisions, article 6, 2 1.1.1.1

U

Uncitral facultative Model Law on Enforcement Law 7.3

Uncitral Model Law on Cross-Border Insolvency 6.4.3

United Nations 2.10.6

United Nations Commission on International Trade Law 6.4.3

United Nations Convention against illicit traffic in narcotic drugs and psychtropic substances of 20 December 1988 6.1.2.5, 6.2

United Nations Model Convention on double taxation between developed and developing countries 2.10.6

Unión Internacional del Notariado Latino 5.2.1.1

Union Internationale des Huissiers de Justice et Officiers Judiciaires 2.10.5

V

Value added tax 5.2.2.1
Verification of the authenticity of decisions of the Council or of the Commission 6.1
Vienna convention on consular relations on 24 April 1963 4.1.2
Vienna convention on diplomatic relations on 18 April 1961 4.1.2

W

Works in progress and present development trends 2.10
World Code of Enforcement 2.10.5, 7.3

EUROPEAN MONOGRAPH SERIES

1. Lamm Betten (ed.), *The Future of European Social Policy* (1991), ISBN 9065445854, ISBN-13 9789065445858.
2. Annemarie Loman, Kamiel Mortelmans, Harry H.G. Post, Stewart Watson, *Culture and Common Law: Before and After Maastricht* (1992), ISBN 9065446389, ISBN-13 9789065446381.
3. John A.E. Vervaele, *Fraud against the Community: The Need for European Fraud Legislation* (1994), ISBN 9065446346, ISBN-13 9789065446343.
4. Philip Raworth, *The Legislative Process in the European Community* (1993), ISBN 9065446907, ISBN-13 9789065446909.
5. Jules Stuyck, *Financial and Monetary Integration in the European Economic Community* (1993), ISBN 9065447180.
6. Jules Stuyck, A.J. Vossestein (eds), *State Entrepreneurship, National Monopolies and European Community Law* (1993), ISBN 9065447733, ISBN-13 9789065447739.
7. Jules Stuyck, A. Looijestijn-Clearie (eds), *The European Economic Area EC-EFTA* (1994), ISBN 9065448152.
8. Rosita B. Bouterse, *Competition and Integration: What Goals Count?* (1995), ISBN 9065448160, ISBN-13 9789065448163.
9. René Barents, *The Agricultural Law of the EC: An Inquiry into the Administrative Law* (1994), ISBN 9065448675, ISBN-13 9789065448675.
10. Nicholas Emiliou, *Principles of Proportionality in European Law: A Comparative Study* (1996), ISBN 9041108661, ISBN-13 9789041108661.
11. Eivind Smith, *National Parliaments as Cornerstones of European Integration* (1996), ISBN 904110898X, ISBN-13 9789041108982.
12. Jan H. Jans, *European Environmental Law* (1996), ISBN 9041108777, ISBN-13 9789041108777.
13. Síofra O'Leary, *The Evolving Concept of Community Citizenship: From the Free Movement of Persons to Union Citizenship* (1997), ISBN 9041108785, ISBN-13 9789041108784.
14. Laurence W. Gormley (ed.), *Current and Future Perspectives on EC Competition Law* (1983), ISBN 904110691X, ISBN-13 9789041106919.
15. Simone White, *Protection of the Financial Interests of the European Communities: The Fight against Fraud and Corruption* (1998), ISBN 9041196471, ISBN-13 9789041196477.
16. Morten P. Broberg, *The European Commission's Jurisdiction to Scrutinize Mergers*, 3rd Edition (2006), ISBN 9041124748, ISBN-13 9789041124746.
17. Doris Hildebrand, *The Role of Economic Analysis in the EC Competition Rules: The European School*, 2nd Edition (2002), ISBN 9041117067, ISBN-13 9789041117069.
18. Christof R.A. Swaak, *European Community Law and the Automobile Industry* (1999), ISBN 9041111409, ISBN-13 9789041111401.

19. Dorthe Dahlgaard Dingel, *Public Procurement: A Harmonization of the National Judicial Review of the Application of European Community Law* (1999), ISBN 9041111611, ISBN-13 9789041111616.
20. John A.E. Vervaele (ed.), *Compliance and Enforcement of European Community Law* (1999), ISBN 9041111514, ISBN-13 9789041111517.
21. Martin Trybus, *European Defence Procurement Law: International and National Procurement Systems as Models for a Liberalized Defence Procurement Market in Europe* (1999), ISBN 9041111670, ISBN-13 9789041111678.
22. Helen Staples, *The Legal Status of Third Country Nationals Resident in the European Union* (1999), ISBN 9041112774, ISBN-13 9789041112774.
23. Damien Geradin (ed.), *The Liberalization of State Monopolies in the European Union and Beyond* (1999), ISBN 9041112642, ISBN-13 9789041112644.
24. Katja Heede, *European Ombudsman: Redress and Control at Union Level* (2000), ISBN 9041114130, ISBN-13 9789041114136.
25. Ulf Bernitz, Joakim Nergelius (eds), *General Principles of European Community Law* (2000), ISBN 9041114025, ISBN-13 9789041114020.
26. Michaela Drahos, *Convergence of Competition Laws and Policies in the European Community* (2002), ISBN 9041115625, ISBN-13 9789041115621.
27. Damien Geradin (ed.), *The Liberalization of Electricity and Natural Gas in the European Union* (2001), ISBN 9041115609, ISBN-13 9789041115607.
28. Gisella Gori, *Towards an EU Right to Education* (2001), ISBN 9041116702, ISBN-13 9789041116703.
29. Brendan P.G. Smith, *Constitution Building in the European Union* (2001), ISBN 9041116958, ISBN-13 9789041116956.
30. Friedl Weiss, Frank Wooldridge, *Free Movement of Persons within the European Community*, 2nd Edition (2007), ISBN 9041125450, ISBN-13 9789041125453.
31. Ingrid Boccardi, *Europe and Refugees: Towards an EU Asylum Policy* (2002), ISBN 9041117091, ISBN-13 9789041117090.
32. John A.E. Vervaele, André Klip (eds), *European Cooperation Between Tax, Customs and Judicial Authorities* (2001), ISBN 9041117474, ISBN-13 9789041117472.
33. Wouter P.J. Wils, *The Optimal Enforcement of EC Antitrust Law: Essays in Law and Economics* (2002), ISBN 9041117571, ISBN-13 9789041117571.
34. Damien Geradin (ed.), *The Liberalization of Postal Services in the European Union* (2002), ISBN 9041117806, ISBN-13 9789041117809.
35. Nick Bernard, *Multilevel Governance in the European Union* (2002), ISBN 9041118128, ISBN-13 9789041118127.
36. Jill Wakefield, *Judicial Protection through the Use of Article 288(2) EC* (2002), ISBN 9041118233, ISBN-13 9789041118233.

37. Sebastiaan Princen, *EU Regulation and Transatlantic Trade* (2002), ISBN 9041118713, ISBN-13 9789041118714.
38. Amaryllis Verhoeven, *The European Union in Search of a Democratic and Constitutional Theory* (2002), ISBN 9041118721.
39. Paul L.C. Torremans, *Cross Border Insolvencies in EU, English and Belgian Law* (2002), ISBN 9041118888, ISBN-13 9789041118882.
40. Malcolm Anderson, Joanna Apap (eds), *Police and Justice Cooperation and the New European Borders* (2002), ISBN 9041118934, ISBN-13 9789041118936.
41. Christin M. Forstinger, *Takeover Law in EU and USA: A Comparative Analysis* (2002), ISBN 9041119191, ISBN-13 9789041119193.
42. Antonio Bavasso, *Communications in EU Antitrust Law: Market Power and Public Interest* (2003), ISBN 9041119744, ISBN-13 9789041119742.
43. Fiona G. Wishlade, *Regional State Aid and Competition Policy in the European Union* (2003), ISBN 9041119752, ISBN-13 9789041119759.
44. Gareth Davies, *Nationality Discrimination in the European Internal Market* (2003), ISBN 9041119981, ISBN-13 9789041119988.
45. René Barents, *The Autonomy of Community Law* (2003), ISBN 9041122516, ISBN-13 9789041122513.
46. Gerhard Dannecker, Oswald Jansen (eds), *Competition Law Sanctioning in the European Union* (2004), ISBN 9041121005, ISBN-13 9789041121004.
47. Nauta Dutilh (ed.), *Dealing with Dominance: The Experience of National Competition Authorities* (2004), ISBN 9041122117, ISBN-13 9789041122117.
48. Stefaan van den Bogaert, *Practical Regulation of the Mobility of Sportsmen in the EU Post Bosman* (2005), ISBN 904112327X, ISBN-13 9789041123275.
49. Katalin Judit Cseres, *Competition Law and Consumer Protection* (2005), ISBN 9041123806, ISBN-13 9789041123800.
50. Philipp Kiiver, *The National Parliaments in the European Union: A Critical View on EU Constitution Building* (2006), ISBN 9041124527, ISBN-13 9789041124524.
51. Alexander Turk, *The Concept of Legislation in European Community Law* (2006), ISBN 9041124721, ISBN-13 9789041124722.
52. Dimitrios Sinaniotis, *The Interim Protection of Individuals before the European and National Courts* (2006), ISBN 9041124985, ISBN-13 9789041124982.
53. M. Holoubek, D. Damjanovic, M. Traimer (eds), *Regulating Content: The European Regulatory Framework for the Media and Related Creative Sectors* (2006), ISBN 9041125973, ISBN-13 9789041125972.
54. Anneli Albi, Jacques Ziller (eds), *The European Constitution and National Constitutions: Ratification and Beyond* (2006), ISBN 9041125248, ISBN-13 9789041125248.
55. Gustavo E. Luengo, *Regulation of Subsidies and State Aids in WTO and EC Law: Conflicts in International Trade Law* (2007), ISBN 9041125477, ISBN-13 9789041125477.

56. Eniko Horvath, *Mandating Identity: Citizenship, Kinship Laws and Plural Nationality in the European Union* (2007), ISBN 9041126627, ISBN-13 9789041126627.
57. Rass Holdgaard, *External Relations Law of the European Community: Legal Reasoning and Legal Discourses* (2007), ISBN 904112604X, ISBN-13 9789041126047.
58. Jill Wakefield, *The Right to Good Administration* (2007), ISBN 904112697X, ISBN-13 9789041126979.
59. Dimitry Kochenov, *EU Enlargement and the Failure of Conditionality: Pre-accession Conditionality in the Fields of Democracy and the Rule of Law* (2008), ISBN 9041126961, ISBN-13 9789041126962.
60. Despina Mavromati, *The Law of Payment Services in the EU: The EC Directive on Payment Services in the Internal Market* (2008), ISBN 9041127003, ISBN-13 9789041127006.
61. Anne Meuwese, *Impact Assessment in EU Lawmaking* (2008), ISBN-13 9789041127204.
62. Ulf Bernitz, Joakim Nergelius and Cecilia Cardner (eds.), *General Principles of EC Law in a Process of Development* (2008), ISBN-13 9789041127051.
63. Johan van de Gronden (ed.), *The EU and WTO Law on Services* (2008), ISBN-13 9789041128096.
64. Alina Tryfonidou, *Reverse Discrimination in EC Law* (2009), ISBN-13 9789041127518.
65. Mikael Berglund, *Cross-Border Enforcement of Claims in the EU: History, Present Time and Future* (2009), ISBN-13 9789041128614.